David C. Cook Bible Lesson Commentary

The Essential Study Companion *for* Every Disciple

David C. Cook Bible Lesson Commentary

KJV

transforming lives together

DAVID C. COOK KJV BIBLE LESSON COMMENTARY 2014–2015
Published by David C Cook
4050 Lee Vance View
Colorado Springs, CO 80918 U.S.A.

David C Cook Distribution Canada
55 Woodslee Avenue, Paris, Ontario, Canada N3L 3E5

David C Cook U.K., Kingsway Communications
Eastbourne, East Sussex BN23 6NT, England

David C Cook and the graphic circle C logo
are registered trademarks of Cook Communications Ministries.

All rights reserved. Except for brief excerpts for review purposes,
no part of this book may be reproduced or used in any form
without written permission from the publisher.

Unless otherwise noted, Scripture quotations are taken from the King James Version
(Public Domain); or the New Revised Standard Version Bible, copyright 1989, Division
of Christian Education of the National Council of the Churches of Christ in the
United States of America. Used by permission. All rights reserved.

Lessons based on *International Sunday School Lessons: The International Bible Lessons for Christian Teaching*, © 2010 by the Committee on the Uniform Series.

ISBN 978-0-7814-0915-5

© 2014 David C Cook

Written and edited by Dan Lioy, PhD
The Team: John Blase, Doug Schmidt, Amy Kiechlin, Tonya Osterhouse, and Karen Athen
Cover Design: Amy Kiechlin
Cover Photo: iStockphoto

Printed in the United States of America
First Edition 2014

1 2 3 4 5 6 7 8 9 10

022514

Contents

A Word to the Teacher 7
Using the *David C. Cook KJV Bible Lesson Commentary* with Material from Other Publishers ... 8

September, October, November 2014
Remaining Steadfast in Hope

Unit I: A Brighter Day

1	September 7	A Vision of the Future	9
2	September 14	A Promise of Restoration	17
3	September 21	A Fresh Start	25
4	September 28	An Incredible Pledge	33

Unit II: A Time of Difficulty

5	October 5	Choosing to Rejoice	41
6	October 12	Awaiting Vindication	49
7	October 19	Longing for Justice	57
8	October 26	Receiving God's Blessing	65

Unit III: A Vision of God's Grandeur

9	November 2	God's Glory Returns	73
10	November 9	God Accepts His People	81
11	November 16	God Revives His People	89
12	November 23	God Transforms His People	97
13	November 30	God Frees His People	105

December 2014, January, February 2015
Offering Genuine Worship

Unit I: Revering the Lord

1	December 7	Worship the Messiah	113
2	December 14	Shout for Joy	121
3	December 21	Offer God Praise (Christmas)	129
4	December 28	Affirm the Savior's Power	137

Unit II: Praying to the Lord

5	January 4	A Model Prayer	145
6	January 11	Jesus Prays for Us	153
7	January 18	Jesus Intercedes for Us	161
8	January 25	Pray for One Another	169

Unit III: Serving the Lord

9	February 1	Fasting while Serving	177
10	February 8	Serving God and Others	185
11	February 15	Serving the Least	193
12	February 22	Serving in God's Strength	201

Contents

March, April, May 2015
Operating in the Spirit's Power

Unit I: Experiencing God's Presence

1	March 1	The Lamb of God	209
2	March 8	The Promised Advocate	217
3	March 15	The Spirit of Truth	225
4	March 22	The Spirit's Presence	233
5	March 29	The Savior's Arrival (Palm Sunday)	241

Unit II: Serving God's People

6	April 5	Affirming Jesus' Resurrection (Easter)	249
7	April 12	Loving One Another	257
8	April 19	Recognizing God's Love	265
9	April 26	Remaining Vigilant	273
10	May 3	Promoting the Truth	281

Unit III: Abiding in Unity

11	May 10	The Gifts of the Spirit	289
12	May 17	The Unity of the Body	297
13	May 24	The Gift of Languages	305
14	May 31	The Great Gift of Love	313

June, July, August 2015
Upholding Justice

Unit I: Denouncing Injustice

1	June 7	Pronouncing God's Judgment	321
2	June 14	Doing What Is Right	329
3	June 21	Ending Complacency	337
4	June 28	Answering to God	345

Unit II: Demanding Justice

5	July 5	Censuring False Prophets	353
6	July 12	Rebuking Corrupt Leaders	361
7	July 19	Fostering Godly Virtues	369
8	July 26	Experiencing God's Pardon	377

Unit III: Promoting Justice

9	August 2	The Redeemer's Presence	385
10	August 9	A Call to Reform	393
11	August 16	A Call to Obey	401
12	August 23	Administer True Justice	409
13	August 30	Fidelity to the Lord	417

A Word to the Teacher

In 1521, Martin Luther appeared before the Diet of Worms. Holy Roman Emperor Charles V presided over the imperial assembly held at Worms, Germany. Luther's life was clearly in danger. While under oath, he acknowledged that he wrote the books the religious and civil authorities declared to be heretical. But he refused to renounce his teachings unless convinced that he had strayed from the Scriptures.

One tradition has held that Luther's concluding words in his heroic display of faith were as follows: "Here I stand. I cannot do otherwise." This solitary religious leader, filled with courage from his fresh reading of Scripture, dared to challenge the might of the church and state in his day. Through his writings and teachings, he (along with many others) helped to set in motion the Protestant Reformation.

Like the believers alive during the time of Luther, it is your privilege as a Sunday school teacher to present the whole counsel of God's Word. Sometimes you will discuss a positive subject, such as the promises the Lord made to His people. On other occasions, you will present a less pleasant topic, such as God's judgment. Both of these themes are emphasized in this year's *David C. Cook KJV Bible Lesson Commentary*.

Regardless of the subject matter the Spirit empowers you to present to your students, your job as a Sunday school teacher is eternally relevant. After all, you are not just giving the students important biblical information (even though this is true). The Spirit is also giving you the courage to be an agent of change in the students' lives. This is an awesome responsibility, and one I know you take seriously.

As you purpose to teach God's Word to your students, take a few moments to think about what the Spirit has done and is doing through you. Also, pray that your students will discover that the Scriptures are as relevant today as they were in the time of Luther and the other Protestant reformers. Then, watch in fascination as your students discover that the Lord is both just and merciful.

May God richly bless you as you share the riches of His truth and grace with your students!

Your fellow learner at the feet of the Master Teacher,
Dan Lioy

USING THE *DAVID C. COOK KJV BIBLE LESSON COMMENTARY* WITH MATERIAL FROM OTHER PUBLISHERS

Sunday school materials from the following denominations and publishers follow the International Sunday School Lesson outlines (sometimes known as the Uniform Series). Because the *David C. Cook KJV Bible Lesson Commentary* (formerly *Tarbell's*) follows the same ISSL outlines, you can use the *Commentary* as an excellent teacher resource to supplement the materials from these publishing houses.

Nondenominational:
  Standard Publishing—*Adult*
  Urban Ministries—*All ages*

Denominational:
  Advent Christian General Conference—*Adult*
  American Baptist (Judson Press)—*Adult*
  Church of God in Christ (Church of God in Christ Publishing House)—*Adult*
  Church of Christ Holiness—*Adult*
  Church of God (Warner Press)—*Adult*
  Church of God by Faith—*Adult*
  National Baptist Convention of America (Boyd)—*All ages*
  National Primitive Baptist Convention—*Adult*
  Presbyterian Church (U.S.A.) (Bible Discovery Series—Presbyterian Publishing House or P.R.E.M.)—*Adult*
  Progressive National Baptist Convention—*Adult*
  Union Gospel Press—*All ages*
  United Holy Church of America—*Adult*
  United Methodist Church (Cokesbury)—*All ages*

LESSON 1 — SEPTEMBER 7

A Vision of the Future

Background Scripture: Jeremiah 30
Devotional Reading: Jeremiah 29:10-14

Key Verse: The days come, saith the Lord, that I will bring again the captivity of my people Israel and Judah, saith the Lord: and I will cause them to return to the land that I gave to their fathers, and they shall possess it. Jeremiah 30:3.

KING JAMES VERSION

JEREMIAH 30:1 1The word that came to Jeremiah from the Lord, saying, 2 Thus speaketh the Lord God of Israel, saying, Write thee all the words that I have spoken unto thee in a book. 3 For, lo, the days come, saith the Lord, that I will bring again the captivity of my people Israel and Judah, saith the Lord: and I will cause them to return to the land that I gave to their fathers, and they shall possess it. . . .

18 Thus saith the Lord; Behold, I will bring again the captivity of Jacob's tents, and have mercy on his dwellingplaces; and the city shall be builded upon her own heap, and the palace shall remain after the manner thereof. 19 And out of them shall proceed thanksgiving and the voice of them that make merry: and I will multiply them, and they shall not be few; I will also glorify them, and they shall not be small. 20 Their children also shall be as aforetime, and their congregation shall be established before me, and I will punish all that oppress them. 21 And their nobles shall be of themselves, and their governor shall proceed from the midst of them; and I will cause him to draw near, and he shall approach unto me: for who is this that engaged his heart to approach unto me? saith the Lord. 22 And ye shall be my people, and I will be your God.

NEW REVISED STANDARD VERSION

JEREMIAH 30:1 The word that came to Jeremiah from the Lord: 2 Thus says the Lord, the God of Israel: Write in a book all the words that I have spoken to you. 3 For the days are surely coming, says the Lord, when I will restore the fortunes of my people, Israel and Judah, says the Lord, and I will bring them back to the land that I gave to their ancestors and they shall take possession of it. . . .

18 Thus says the Lord:
I am going to restore the fortunes of the tents of Jacob,
  and have compassion on his dwellings;
the city shall be rebuilt upon its mound,
  and the citadel set on its rightful site.
19 Out of them shall come thanksgiving,
  and the sound of merrymakers.
I will make them many, and they shall not be few;
  I will make them honored, and they shall not be disdained.
20 Their children shall be as of old,
  their congregation shall be established before me;
  and I will punish all who oppress them.
21 Their prince shall be one of their own,
  their ruler shall come from their midst;
I will bring him near, and he shall approach me,
  for who would otherwise dare to approach me?
    says the Lord.
22 And you shall be my people,
  and I will be your God.

Home Bible Readings

Monday, September 1	Jeremiah 22:1-9	*Act with Justice and Righteousness*
Tuesday, September 2	Jeremiah 11:1-10	*Hear the Words of This Covenant*
Wednesday, September 3	Isaiah 2:10-19	*Only the Lord Will Be Exalted*
Thursday, September 4	Jeremiah 18:1-10	*Turn from Your Evil Way*
Friday, September 5	Jeremiah 29:10-14	*A Future with Hope*
Saturday, September 6	Jeremiah 12:14-17	*Hope for Israel's Neighbors*
Sunday, September 7	Jeremiah 30:1-3, 18-22	*The Days Are Surely Coming*

Background

The regathering and reunification of Israel and Judah foretold in Jeremiah 30:3 is in keeping with what Moses declared in Deuteronomy. For instance, in chapter 28, the lawgiver described how the Lord would bless the Israelites if they remained faithful to Him in the Promised Land or curse them if they were unfaithful. Repeatedly, Moses implored God's chosen people to obey His decrees. But the Israelite leader must have realized that at some future point, the nation might turn away from God and disregard His ordinances. And when it happened, God would allow foreign powers, such as the Egyptians, Assyrians, and Babylonians, to overrun Israel and Judah, remove many of the inhabitants, and disperse them around the known world.

Sometime after that period of deep distress had occurred, the Israelites would come to their senses and realize that their dispersion had taken place because of their disobedience. Moses revealed that at that time, the people would recall God's commands. The lawgiver also declared that if the Israelites returned to the Lord in obedience, He would bless them. Even though they would be scattered among the surrounding nations, God would regather them, forgive them, and again grant them prosperity in the promised land. Jeremiah 29:10-14 discloses that at the end of Babylon's 70 years of rule, the Lord would fulfill His pledge to restore His people. In particular, as they reflected on His promise of a future filled with hope, they would pray to God. Then, He would listen and respond by bringing "Israel and Judah" (30:3) back from "captivity" and reestablish them in the "land" He previously gave to their ancestors.

Notes on the Printed Text

Jeremiah 30 through 32 have been called the Book of Consolation or Comfort because the message of future hope contrasts with the dominant note of judgment throughout the rest of the book. In chapter 30, the Lord summoned Jeremiah to record a divinely inspire message (vs. 1). These oracles of hope, which appear in chapters 30 and 31, came directly from the Lord and were to be placed in a scroll (that is, thin strips of leather or papyrus joined together in long rolls; 30:2). Jeremiah's prophecies would be a permanent record of God's pledge to redeem His chosen people from their lengthy time of deep distress in Babylon (vs. 3).

In verses 4-11, God promised to deliver His people from a period characterized by anguish and terror. The latter would be a time of panic, not peace, in which even those who were physically strong would grab their stomachs in pain like a pregnant woman giving birth. In that terrible circumstance, the all-powerful Lord pledged to free His people from their bonds of servitude to Babylon. This dramatic turn of events would enable them to serve Him under a restored Davidic ruler. The New Testament reveals this king to be the Lord Jesus, Israel's Messiah.

In light of these fantastic promises, God urged the exiles in Babylon not to be paralyzed with fear. After all, He was supremely powerful to deliver them from their captivity in faraway lands and establish them once again safely and securely in Judah. The Lord acknowledged that He would overturn such oppressors as Babylon to end the displacement of His chosen people. God also affirmed that He would chastise them in an equitable manner for their centuries of unfaithfulness. Yet He would not utterly wipe them out.

Verses 12-17 recount God's promise to heal the wounds He inflicted on His people for their insubordination. When the Lord allowed foreigners to overrun Israel and Judah and exile many of their inhabitants, the result seemed like an incurable injury. Their situation appeared to be utterly hopeless, especially in the absence of anyone to uphold their cause and bind up their wounds. In that terrifying circumstance, all the people's former political and religious allies (including Egypt, Edom, Moab, Ammon, Phoenicia, and Assyria) had forsaken them. God explained that His severe chastening of His people through the hands of their enemies was due to the extreme extent of the nation's iniquity and numerous transgressions.

The Lord was genuinely aware of the plight of His people. He knew about the distress and shame they felt over the indignities they suffered. God reminded the exiles that the injustices they endured were the consequence of them having sinned greatly and incurring an enormous amount of guilt. Nonetheless, the Lord declared that their time of trouble would eventually come to an end. Those who forced God's people into captivity would experience exile. Likewise, those who had plundered the Israelites would be pillaged. In contrast, the Lord pledged to heal the nation's wounds and restore it to health. The people of Jerusalem would no longer be considered as outcasts whom others glibly abandoned.

In verse 18, God promised He would completely reverse the circumstance of the exiles. They would return to Judah and be empowered to rebuild their "tents" or dwelling places. Even their bygone homes would become the object of the Lord's "mercy." The latter term renders a Hebrew verb that denotes the presence of God's tender affection and compassion. Moreover, He would enable the returnees to rebuild Jerusalem and the cities of Judah on their former ruins. Similarly, Jerusalem's palace, as well as the nation's fortified enclaves, would be reestablished where they once stood.

It's not difficult to imagine the intense joy the former exiles would feel once they resettled their families in Judah. Whereas before there was grief and mourning over being in captivity in Babylon, verse 19 anticipated a future time in which the returnees expressed "thanksgiving" and rejoicing through songs. Previously, foreign invaders had moved scores of God's people from the promised land. Yet in a future day of restoration, the Lord would cause the population of Judah to increase.

In the preceding decades, the enemies of the exiles held them in utter contempt. But God promised that a time was coming when He would replace such disdain with honor for His people. Then their "children" (vs. 20) would prosper as in earlier times (for example, when David and Solomon reigned). Moreover, the Lord would reestablish the former political and religious institutions of the covenant "congregation." Judah would be so secure that God would visit with punishment any foe who tried to mistreat His people.

According to verse 21, a prince would arise from among the returnees to Judah and oversee them. Also, in God's grace, He would grant this "governor" permission to approach Him, perhaps on special occasions to pray and obtain guidance. Ezra 1 reveals that in 537 B.C., the Lord worked through Cyrus, Persia's king, to authorize a Jewish official named Sheshbazzar to lead a group of exiles from Babylon to Judah. Then, 3:8 discloses that in 536 B.C., God raised up another leader named Zerubbabel, along with Jeshua the high priest, to lead the people in their temple rebuilding efforts.

Some scholars have speculated that Zerubbabel and Sheshbazzar were the same person, but this is highly improbable. Zerubbabel was likely born during Judah's exile in Babylon. He was a grandson of Jehoiachin, one of the last Davidic kings, who had died in Babylon (see 1 Chron. 3:16-19). Jehoiachin had been honored in exile (see 2 Kings 25:27-30), and it was natural that his descendant would be highly respected in the Jewish community.

Through the Old Testament prophet, Haggai, the Lord declared that He was appointing Zerubbabel for a special mission of high honor (Hag. 2:23). While Zerubbabel did have a claim to the throne of Israel, the Persian domination of Judah during that time prevented him from assuming the monarchy. In all likelihood, Haggai was looking forward to the Messiah, who would come through Zerubbabel (see Matt. 1:12). Jesus is the "Son of the Highest" (Luke 1:32) whom Gabriel revealed to Mary would sit on David's "throne."

This interpretation is further supported by the Lord's designation of Zerubbabel as "my servant" (Hag. 2:23). In Isaiah, the Lord repeatedly referred to the Messiah by that title (see Isa. 41:8; 52:13; 53:11). The Lord also said He would make Zerubbabel His "signet" (Hag. 2:23) ring. The latter contained an official seal that served as a signature carrying the full authority of the owner of the signet ring. For instance, when Pharaoh appointed Joseph the governor of the land, he gave his signet ring to him as a symbol of his new office (see Gen. 41:42). The royal signet ring gave the bearer the full authority of the ruler.

This act was symbolic of God's reestablishing the messianic line after the exile in Babylon. In contrast to earthly rulers, the Messiah came for the eternal benefit of the lost. His divinely appointed mission was to serve others and to lay down His life so that the lost could receive His promise of salvation (see Matt. 20:28; Mark 10:45). Jesus, the King of kings and Lord of lords (see Rev. 17:14; 19:16), humbled Himself by becoming the penalty for our sins so that we might inherit eternal life.

During the Israelites' time of captivity in Babylon, it was understandable that they might have doubted whether God still loved them and considered them His chosen people. Hosea 2:23 declares that the Lord, in faithfulness to His ancient covenant, would have mercy and show compassion on the wayward Israelites. Furthermore, in their day of restoration, they would realize once again that the Lord was their God and they were His people (Jer. 30:22). In short, the Lord promised to abide with, watch over, and provide for the returnees from exile. Their joyous and heartfelt response would be to remain loyal to God and obedient to His will. As Christians, it is also important for us to acknowledge God in all that we do and remain steadfast in our devotion to Him.

SUGGESTIONS TO TEACHERS

Life demands making choices. Encourage the members of your class to relate some of the toughest decisions they have faced in their lives and to explain why these were so hard to make. In light of this week's lesson, help them to consider how God calls His people to make big decisions in the context of the largest choice of all, namely, to put the Lord first by trusting and obeying Him.

1. DOING EVIL THINGS. In the centuries and decades leading up to the exile, God's chosen people had profaned His name by doing all the evil things the surrounding nations did. Indeed, there was virtually no distinction between the Israelites' practices and their neighbors' deeds.

2. EXPERIENCING GOD'S GRACE. Even though God's people had been unfaithful to Him, He would keep His covenant promises to restore the nation. In His grace, the Lord pledged to bring the scattered tribes of Israel and Judah back together to again form a nation. He alone was sufficiently powerful and wise to place them back in their homeland.

3. RECALLING GOD'S MIGHTY ACTS. This week's lesson reminds us what God had done in the past for the Israelites and what He pledged to do for them in the future. A good point in making the right choices in life is for us to recall the Lord's mighty acts in the past, both those recorded in Scripture and those remembered in one's personal life. Our doing so can encourage us to remain faithful to God and confident that one day He will fulfill the promises He has made to us in the Bible.

4. FORSAKING ALL FORMS OF IDOLATRY. Our decision to experience spiritual renewal in loving relationship with God means forsaking all the idols prevalent today in society. List the following items on a whiteboard, overhead, or chartpaper:

knowledge, success, popularity, money, pleasure, power, physical attractiveness, and consumerism. Then explain that these are just some of the many "idols" that people in our society typically worship. Discuss with the class how difficult it is to replace these things with exclusive devotion to the Lord.

For Adults

■ **Topic:** A Promise Assured

■ **Questions:** 1. When Jeremiah prophesied, what was the plight being experienced by God's people? 2. How would God bring about the restoration of His people? 3. Why was it important for the former exiles to know that the Lord was their God? 4. How can believers demonstrate that they are totally committed to serving God? 5. In what ways does God bless believers? How might they use His blessings to help others?

■ **Illustrations:**

Becoming God's People. In Jeremiah 30:22, the Lord promised to the exiles living in Babylon, "ye shall be my people, and I will be your God." Today, when we trust in the Lord Jesus, we become members of His body, the global church.

The preceding statement isn't just a truth we affirm. More importantly, by God's grace we are to live it out on a daily basis. Becoming God's people—both individually and collectively—takes a lot of work. We need to say *no* to our sinful desires and *yes* to God's will for us. We also devote as much time and attention to the interests of others as to what excites us.

Living in this way means God's priorities take precedence over ours. It also means we care so much about the community of faith that we do all we can to meet people where they are in the midst of their human brokenness.

Restored by Grace. It was by God's grace that the once rebellious Israelites would repent of their sins and be restored to the promised land. Jeremiah 30 revealed that God alone had the power to set them free from their captivity and enable them to rebuild Judah and Jerusalem.

Five years ago, Amelia (not her real name) felt that her world had officially come to an end. The Internal Revenue Service ruling had just arrived, and the news was the worst that it could be. Not only did she owe over $400,000, but she was probably going to jail for embezzlement, tax evasion, and securities fraud.

Three years later, Amelia was trying to get back on her feet again. She had spent the last 20 months in jail and had lost her home and assets, and still had over $100,000 dollars due for back taxes. But there was also some good news. A year earlier, the Spirit used a representative of Prison Fellowship Ministries to lead Amelia to faith in Christ.

Today, the Savior, in His grace, is helping Amelia to rebuild her life. Amelia married a wonderful Christian man a year after she was released on parole. And now the couple has a beautiful young daughter. Amelia also has part-time employment working for a non-profit organization that trusts her and respects her talents.

Whenever Amelia shares here testimony, it gives listeners an opportunity to experience spiritual renewal. It turns out that Amelia's world did not come to an end after all, just the mixed-up life that she had previously known.

Life Choices. Jeremiah 30 reveals that prior to the exile, God's chosen people had made very poor choices. It was only after nearly 70 years of captivity in Babylon that they were ready as a people to abandon their sinful ways and choose to be faithful to the Lord.

Consider the following. If God gave you 70 years of life, you would spend 24 years sleeping; 14 years working; 8 years in amusement; 6 years at the dinner table; 5 years in transportation; 4 years in conversation; 3 years in education; and 3 years reading.

If you went to church every Sunday and prayed five minutes every morning and night, you would be giving God five months of your life. That's only five months out of 70 years!

For Youth

■ **Topic:** A Connection Is Made

■ **Questions:** 1. Why did God allow foreigners to remove His people from the Promised Land? 2. What turn of events would prompt God's people to sing hymns of thanksgiving to Him? 3. In a future day of restoration, what did God declare He would do to those who tried to oppress His people? 4. How can God's compassion for believers help them be more kind and sensitive in their relationships with others? 5. What specific things can believers do to remain devoted to the Lord?

■ **Illustrations:**

We Belong. Every four years the Olympic torch is passed hand-to-hand by runners from all over the world. People thrill when the last runner arrives at the stadium and ignites the Olympic torch to open the games.

Young people are on the receiving end of something far more precious than the Olympic torch. When they accept the Christian faith from their parents, they join themselves to the community of believers from every part of the globe and down through history. This is in keeping with Jeremiah 30:22, which declares, "ye shall be my people, and I will be your God."

As members of the community of faith, it is the duty of saved young people to pick up the torch of the Lord Jesus and carry it, until they in turn pass it on to their children. For a parent, the most satisfying thing in life is to see one's children preparing to take up the torch of Christian faith!

Choosing Life. The Lord used Jeremiah to prophesy the restoration of Israel and Judah to their homeland. By choosing to worship and serve the Lord, they would be affirming the life He wanted them to enjoy as His chosen people.

We learn from Scripture that mere association with Christians does not make a person a believer. Even the most "spiritual" people we know must have a personal conversion in which they make a decision for the Lord Jesus.

A musician and church leader named John Wimber learned this truth while at seminary (a divinity school), when he realized a fellow student had not had such a conversion to Jesus. Immediately, Wimber began to pray for his peer. Soon after, the Spirit gave Wimber an opportunity to privately witness to the student. In response, the student gave a 30-minute oration outlining why he couldn't live the Christian life. As Wimber groped for words, the Spirit provided a much-needed, simple insight.

"Do you know what a breech baby is?" Wimber broke in. "Yes," the surprised student answered. "Well, that's what you are . . . and Jesus has sent me to see that you get delivered," Wimber explained. The student began to sob. Within minutes, he acknowledged his sin and asked Jesus to be his Savior.

Afterward, the student asked Wimber how he knew the analogy of a breech baby would speak to the student's heart. The truth is, Wimber didn't know—but the Lord did. Before seminary, the student had been an army nurse who had helped deliver many breech babies!

Competing Loyalties. For centuries, God's people had disobeyed Him. It was only after decades of being in exile that they recognized the value of remaining loyal to God as His "people" (Jer. 30:22) and affirming Him as their "God."

Nine-year-old John Rosemond's bike broke. Because it could not be repaired, he asked his stepfather to buy him a new one. Several days later, at the bike shop, John looked over the rows of shiny new bikes and made his selection. When he showed it to his stepfather, he was told that he was in the wrong section and that he did not need a new bike. A used one would be fine.

When John protested, his stepfather took him outside and showed him the family car, which was purchased a few months earlier. "Do you know what year's model this is?" the stepfather asked. John learned that even though his parents could have bought a new car, they chose not to so that some of their income could be used in charitable ways. Their loyalty was in helping others, not in merely gratifying their own desires. John's stepfather was trying to teach him the same lesson about the choices he made.

Like John and his family, you need to decide where you want your loyalties to be. Will they reside with you, or will you offer your love and loyalty to God and His people? If you choose the first option, this will lead to an inflated sense of your own importance, intolerance of others, and a lack of charity.

LESSON 2 — SEPTEMBER 14

A Promise of Restoration

Background Scripture: Jeremiah 31
Devotional Reading: Hebrews 8:1-7, 13

Key Verse: Behold, the days come, saith the LORD, that I will make a new covenant with the house of Israel, and with the house of Judah. Jeremiah 31:31.

KING JAMES VERSION

JEREMIAH 31:31 Behold, the days come, saith the LORD, that I will make a new covenant with the house of Israel, and with the house of Judah: 32 Not according to the covenant that I made with their fathers in the day that I took them by the hand to bring them out of the land of Egypt; which my covenant they brake, although I was an husband unto them, saith the LORD: 33 But this shall be the covenant that I will make with the house of Israel; After those days, saith the LORD, I will put my law in their inward parts, and write it in their hearts; and will be their God, and they shall be my people.
34 And they shall teach no more every man his neighbour, and every man his brother, saying, Know the LORD: for they shall all know me, from the least of them unto the greatest of them, saith the LORD: for I will forgive their iniquity, and I will remember their sin no more.
35 Thus saith the LORD, which giveth the sun for a light by day, and the ordinances of the moon and of the stars for a light by night, which divideth the sea when the waves thereof roar; The LORD of hosts is his name:
36 If those ordinances depart from before me, saith the LORD, then the seed of Israel also shall cease from being a nation before me for ever. 37 Thus saith the LORD; If heaven above can be measured, and the foundations of the earth searched out beneath, I will also cast off all the seed of Israel for all that they have done, saith the LORD.

NEW REVISED STANDARD VERSION

JEREMIAH 31:31 The days are surely coming, says the LORD, when I will make a new covenant with the house of Israel and the house of Judah. 32 It will not be like the covenant that I made with their ancestors when I took them by the hand to bring them out of the land of Egypt—a covenant that they broke, though I was their husband, says the LORD. 33 But this is the covenant that I will make with the house of Israel after those days, says the LORD: I will put my law within them, and I will write it on their hearts; and I will be their God, and they shall be my people. 34 No longer shall they teach one another, or say to each other, "Know the LORD," for they shall all know me, from the least of them to the greatest, says the LORD; for I will forgive their iniquity, and remember their sin no more.
35 Thus says the LORD,
who gives the sun for light by day
　and the fixed order of the moon and the stars for light
　　by night,
who stirs up the sea so that its waves roar—
　the LORD of hosts is his name:
36 If this fixed order were ever to cease
　from my presence, says the LORD,
then also the offspring of Israel would cease
　to be a nation before me forever.
37 Thus says the LORD:
If the heavens above can be measured,
　and the foundations of the earth below can be
　　explored,
then I will reject all the offspring of Israel
　because of all they have done,
　　says the LORD.

Home Bible Readings

Monday, September 8	Hebrews 8:1-7, 13	*A Better Covenant*
Tuesday, September 9	Hebrews 9:11-15	*Mediator of a New Covenant*
Wednesday, September 10	2 Corinthians 3:4-11	*Ministers of a New Covenant*
Thursday, September 11	Jeremiah 31:7-11	*I Will Gather Them*
Friday, September 12	Jeremiah 31:12-17	*Hope for Your Future*
Saturday, September 13	Jeremiah 31:18-25	*Set Up Road Markers*
Sunday, September 14	Jeremiah 31:31-37	*I Will Make a New Covenant*

Background

In the Book of Jeremiah, "covenant" is a critical term. In chapter 11, the term appears five times, where the prophet reminded the people that the coming judgment was simply the consequence (or curse) of breaking their mutual agreement with God. In chapters 31—34, the word "covenant" appears 15 times, contrasting the blessings of the new covenant with the curses of the old.

The primary way people in the ancient Near East understood interpersonal relationships was by a legally binding obligation. Although the term "covenant" included the concept of a modern day contract or treaty, it was a much broader idea. To people in Bible times, a covenant extended to any relationship that involved responsibility: marriage, parenthood, and even friendship. That is why the entire Mosaic law could be summed up as love—love for God with all one's being, and love for one's neighbor as for oneself (see Matt. 22:37-40).

Notes on the Printed Text

Jeremiah 31:31-34 represents the apex of the prophet's ministry. By declaring, "the days come" (vs. 31), Jeremiah indicated that the new (or renewed) covenant would be part of a future age of blessing. More than a century before (722 B.C.), the Assyrians had defeated and removed the residents of Israel (see 2 Kings 17:5-6). Even though Israel no longer existed as an independent nation, it would be included along with Judah in the new covenant. This indicated that the new covenant would be for all God's people. The problem with the old covenant that God made with Israel at Mount Sinai was that God's chosen people continually broke it. This remained the case, even though the Lord had miraculously delivered them from Egypt and remained faithful to them (Jer. 31:32). The new covenant would have to address the problem inherent in the old one and compensate for the inability of the people to perform up to God's standards.

Whereas before God's people disobeyed Him, under the new covenant they would obey Him. It was as if He were inscribing the moral code on their hearts and minds (vs. 33). The close relationship between God and His people would be undergirded by the people's intimate understanding and application of the Mosaic law to the emotional, intellectual, and ethical aspects of their lives. Jeremiah is the only Old Testament prophet who spoke specifically about the new covenant that Jesus inaugurated (see Matt. 26:28).

Perhaps one of the most precious truths contained in the new covenant is the promise that the Lord "will be their God, and they shall be [His] people" (Jer. 31:33). This pledge is reiterated in Revelation 21:3-4. In John's vision of the new Jerusalem, he learned that, in the eternal state, God will permanently dwell, or tabernacle, among the redeemed of all ages. The various scourges of human existence will not occur in the eternal state. In fact, all unhappiness must, of necessity, be gone from life when God dwells with His people. The new order of things—which will be undergirded by the new covenant—will permit no sadness. It is no wonder we read in 22:20, "Amen. Even so, come, Lord Jesus."

Some, in their zeal to stress the importance of the new covenant, have tried to disparage the old covenant. Nonetheless, a careful reading of Scripture indicates that there was nothing wrong with the Mosaic covenant that the Lord had graciously given to Israel. It was never God's intent that the law of Moses be used as a means to obtain salvation. Instead, forgiveness of sins has always been the Lord's gracious gift to those who have humbled themselves before Him in faith (see Gen. 15:6; Rom. 4:3). The law was God's way of pointing out the moral pathway that believers should walk (see Rom. 7:7-8; Gal. 3:19, 24).

Thus, the problem with the covenant ratified at Mount Sinai was not in God's provision, but rather in Israel's response. The people had continually violated their legally binding obligation. Time and again through the priests and prophets God had called the Israelites to repent, but any change of heart they underwent was soon abandoned (see 2 Kings 17:7-23). For example, in the days of Jeremiah, King Josiah destroyed the idols that were in the land (see 23:4-20). But soon after this godly ruler died, the people turned back to worshiping the idols of the neighboring countries (see vss. 31-32, 36-37). Tragically, the calloused hearts of the people remained unchanged. Only God Himself could radically transform the hearts and minds of His people.

Consequently, a new covenant was needed. The Lord described the essential difference between the covenants by saying that the new one would be internal, while the old one was external. The new covenant represented a sacred relationship, while the old one was more of a legal document. The old one was written on tablets of stone, while the new one would be written on human hearts (see 2 Cor. 3:3). Once the law of God could be implanted within the inmost being of people, their relationship with God could be permanent. The Lord showed Jeremiah a time when all His people, regardless of class distinctions, would directly know Him (Jer. 31:34). This verse signifies more than a mere intellectual awareness of theological truths about God. Implicit is the notion of being wholeheartedly committed to the Lord and steadfastly obedient to His will. When that day finally arrived, the role of prophets such as Jeremiah would become obsolete. The people would no longer need someone to exhort them to love and serve the Lord.

A critical aspect of this new relationship between God and His people hinged on the forgiveness of sins. God's law could not be written on hearts stained by iniquity. The people's hearts required cleansing as a result of God's grace so they could be changed. Once the Lord had forgiven them, He would deliberately forget their sins. Consequently, interpersonal relationships would be transformed by the reality of God's forgiveness. His refusal to recall the sins committed by His people would enable them to relate to one another with forgiveness, patience, and love. Sin remains the insurmountable human problem. No matter how hard people try, they can do nothing to defeat sin. Hope rests entirely on God's love and forgiveness. Thankfully, the Father sent His Son to die for our sins (and rise again) so that we might be forgiven and enjoy the benefits of the new covenant. On the basis of the Son's atoning sacrifice, the Father declares to us, "Your sins are forgiven." That is the wonderful news of the Gospel!

In Jeremiah 31:35, the Lord vowed that Israel would continue to exist as a nation. "LORD of hosts" is more literally rendered "Yahweh of armies" and depicts Him as a divine warrior who maintains absolute control over everything and everyone in creation. As the Creator of the universe, God had the ability to fulfill His promise to His chosen people. For instance, the all-powerful Lord established the sun to light the day and ordained that the moon and stars would brighten the night. He is the same sovereign King who sets the sea in motion so that its waves clap like thunder as they roll across the ocean's billowing surface.

According to 51:15, God used His awesome power to establish the earth. He also utilized His unfathomable wisdom to set the world firmly in its place. Moreover, by means of His infinite understanding, the Lord spread out the heavens. Verse 16 reveals that when God's voice thunders, rains pour down from the sky. He also effortlessly causes the clouds to arise from distant horizons. Furthermore, as it rains, the Lord makes bolts of lightning flash, and He unleashes the wind from His storehouses. This naturally occurring phenomenon signified God's ability to guarantee a future for Israel and Judah as one people ruled by their Creator. Just as God would never undermine the fixed ordering of the cosmos, so too He would never allow Israel to cease to exist as a nation in His sight (31:36).

Advances in modern science had enabled people to learn much about the world in which we live. For all that, there are a seemingly infinite number of unanswered questions scientists have about how the cosmos operates. Indeed, the quest for increased knowledge and understanding appears endless. In keeping with this sobering reality, the Lord implied in verse 37 that it was impossible for people to measure every aspect of the universe or explore all possible aspects of the planet on which they lived. God used the poetic expressions appearing in this verse to stress His strong commitment to His people. Rhetorically speaking, if the infinite could be measured or the unfathomable could be investigated, only then would there be any possibility that God would reject His people.

In verse 38, Jeremiah prophesied about the coming kingdom age and the rebuilding of Jerusalem. The phrase "the days come" suggests a rebuilding in the messianic age and not just the rebuilding that came after the exile in Babylon. Jeremiah described the renovation in concrete terms. He named sites along the wall, listing them from the Tower of Hananel near the northeast corner of Jerusalem and proceeding counterclockwise around the city (vss. 38-40). The prophet declared that this rebuilt Jerusalem would never again be uprooted or overthrown. Since the Romans destroyed Jerusalem in A.D. 70, it is likely that this was Jeremiah's glimpse of the new Jerusalem, God's eternal dwelling with His people.

SUGGESTIONS TO TEACHERS

God's people could not escape His judgment for their national lifestyle of rebelliousness that had persisted for centuries. Even as the Babylonian armies starved Jerusalem into surrender, God sent a promise through Jeremiah that He would restore His people in the future. From this we see that sin brings discipline, but God does not abandon His people. He corrects them so that they can know Him more intimately and thereby flourish spiritually.

1. HOPE FOR A NEW START. The Lord assured His people in the face of judgment that they had a future. They would survive because they belonged to Him. Even Israel, though no longer a nation, would be restored in the end. The chastening of the Lord is never pleasant, but in time it can lead to a new beginning, one that is free from the burden of sin that brings God's discipline.

2. HOPE FOR A NEW BLESSING. Israel and Judah's new beginning would be more than a shoestring survival in hard times. God would abundantly bless His people. When God is done chastening any of His children in response to a persistent sin, He doesn't treat them as second-class citizens in His kingdom. He blesses them with eternal riches and joy.

3. HOPE FOR A NEW ATTITUDE. In Jeremiah's day, the people of Judah felt destined to judgment because of the sins of their ancestors. They had distorted the idea that sin has generational consequences. God's people need to accept personal responsibility for their sins. This attitude of responsibility carries with it the glad expectation that when those sins are forgiven, God welcomes His people back into His favor.

4. HOPE FOR A NEW HEART. Through Jeremiah, the Lord revealed that a whole new arrangement was needed between Him and His people to deal with their inability to keep the terms of the Mosaic law. God promised a new covenant that would give His people new hearts capable of keeping their commitment to Him. Jesus initiated the new covenant through His sacrificial death for sins.

For Adults

■ **Topic:** Hope for Tomorrow
■ **Questions:** 1. Why did God determine it was important to make a new covenant with His chosen people? 2. Why did Israel repeatedly violate the Mosaic covenant? 3. In what ways had Israel sinned against the Lord? 4. How might believers draw comfort from knowing that God is all-powerful? 5. How does the new covenant change the way believers relate to God and to one another?

■ **Illustrations:**

Hope to the Weary. Life is filled with ups and downs, joys and disappointments. We tend to become weary when there are more losses than gains, and more failures than successes. In that situation, we can begin to feel as if life is hopeless.

It's possible that for the upright living during the time of Jeremiah, things looked pretty bleak. Sin was rampant, idolatry seemed in vogue, and the disadvantaged were being exploited. Worst of all, people ignored and disobeyed God.

Jeremiah 31:31 reveals that in the future, the Lord would establish a "new covenant" with His people. Verse 33 pictures God inscribing His moral code on their hearts. The close relationship between God and His people would be undergirded by the people's intimate understanding and application of the law.

Even today, under the new covenant the Son inaugurated, everyone who trusts in Him can know the Father intimately. Indeed, God's pardon creates the possibility of transforming all interpersonal relationships within a congregation with forgiveness, patience, and hope.

A Memorable Day. Some people are startled to learn that God wants His spiritual children to know Him personally. It's difficult for these individuals to imagine God's "law" (Jer. 31:33) being embedded on their "inward parts" and written on their "hearts." Yet this is what the Lord promised in the "new covenant" (vs. 31) He pledged to make with His people.

James Boswell, the famous eighteenth century biographer of Samuel Johnson, liked to tell a story about going fishing when he was a boy with his father. The day was fixed in his adult mind like a digital recording he could play over and over. He remembered several pointers about fishing that his father had given him that day.

Years later, a friend decided it would be interesting to find out what Boswell's father had thought about that day. The father's journals had become available for research, so the scholar in question found the pertinent journal ledger for Boswell's red letter fishing trip. The scholar read the following entry, written in the father's firm handwriting: "Gone fishing with my son today; a day wasted."

No new covenant children of God need ever worry that their heavenly Father will consider time with them "a day wasted." The new covenant is one based on forgiveness and intimacy. It is the basis for us spiritually flourishing in His heavenly family.

Hope for a New Heart. It was Stewardship Sunday at church and the richest man in town had volunteered to "share" his thoughts with the congregation about giving to the Lord. He announced, "I'm a millionaire, and I credit all my wealth to the rich blessing of God. It all started with a moment of faith. I had just earned my first dollar, and I went to church that evening with that dollar folded in my pocket. The speaker was a missionary who told about his work."

The boastful man declared, "I only had that dollar. I had to give it all to God's work or give nothing at all. So at that moment I decided to give my all my money to God. I believe God blessed that choice to give Him all I had, and that's why I'm a wealthy man today!"

There was an awed silence in the church as the millionaire swaggered to his seat. As he settled in, an elderly woman in the same pew leaned over to him and whispered loudly, "I dare you to do it all again!" That challenge was a good test of the millionaire's disposition. If he had a "new covenant" (Jer. 31:31) heart, and God (not the elderly woman) wanted him to give all his money to Christian work, would he do it again? How would we respond?

FOR YOUTH

■ **TOPIC:** Begin with a Fresh Start

■ **QUESTIONS:** 1. In what ways was the old covenant between God and Israel deficient? 2. How had God demonstrated His love and faithfulness to His chosen people? 3. What did Jeremiah mean when he talked about knowing the Lord? 4. How can our detailed study of God's Word help us to know the Lord better? 5. Why is it important for believers to affirm God's unwavering commitment to them?

■ **ILLUSTRATIONS:**

A New Opportunity. Teenagers learning to drive a car achieve the goal of obtaining a driver's license because they have more than one opportunity to pass the driving test. If we flunked everyone who rear-ended another car or ripped off the side molding of the garage door, very few individuals would be licensed drivers.

God made it clear to Jeremiah that, even though His people would be judged for their sins, in the future He would usher in a new society in which people would spiritually flourish because they loved and obeyed Him. Since we know that this is God's wise and loving plan, how much better for us if we get in step with it now!

The world might scoff at this idea of a fresh start. Yet believers know from God's Word that it is true. Remember, God's promises are sure to happen. Of this we can be certain!

Heart to Heart. God wanted a heart-to-heart relationship with His people. And His promise to "make a new covenant" (Jer. 31:31) with them would ensure they grew in their intimate knowledge of Him.

"What does God want from me, anyway?" Sharon voiced in frustration. The question came out of nowhere after the youth group's music rehearsal at church. She loved the Lord and was using music as a vehicle to communicate the gospel.

But now Sharon was showing a part of herself that her best friend, Carmela, had never seen and found unsettling. After all, she thought, if Sharon didn't have it as "together" as Carmela imagined, maybe the other teens in the youth group didn't quite have it together, either. It turned out that Sharon was doing God's work without His direction. Sharon wasn't sure about her own relationship with God and the adolescent needed a steady hand to help her.

Odd as it might appear, some people are very good at practicing the Christian life without ever having met the Lord Jesus personally. Usually, their veneer wears away at some point. When it does, a loving Christian friend or acquaintance can point them to the very real Savior, who has desired a one-on-one relationship with them all along.

Making the Connection. Jeremiah 31:31-37 reveals that God wanted more than a superficial relationship with His people. This prophecy discloses that God would use the new covenant to make it possible for His people to know Him personally and flourish spiritually.

Brian grew up in a minister's home. Though his parents loved him and had thoroughly grounded him in the essentials of the Christian faith, Brian found himself looking for answers in his sophomore year of college. His answers came through a lovely girl named Anna.

Brian had met Anna in one of his English classes at the university. True, she was bright and attractive. But what interested Brian most was Anna's spirituality. Brian had never seen a peer with such a vibrant relationship with God.

Brian knew that though he had heard and learned about God as a child, he never had come close to experiencing the kind of relationship with the Lord that Brian could see at work in Anna's life. The more Brian saw of this, the more he wished that he, too, could experience that kind of spiritual intimacy with God.

When Brian turned 20, after the surprise birthday party that his college friends threw for him, he was invited to an even bigger party. This time the festivities took place in heaven, as the angels of God rejoiced in the heartfelt prayer Brian uttered. It was then that he asked the Savior to begin a lifelong relationship with him.

LESSON 3 — SEPTEMBER 21

A Fresh Start

Background Scripture: Jeremiah 32
Devotional Reading: Isaiah 12

Key Verse: Thus saith the Lord of hosts, the God of Israel; Houses and fields and vineyards shall be possessed again in this land. Jeremiah 32:15.

KING JAMES VERSION

JEREMIAH 32:2 For then the king of Babylon's army besieged Jerusalem: and Jeremiah the prophet was shut up in the court of the prison, which was in the king of Judah's house. 3 For Zedekiah king of Judah had shut him up, saying, Wherefore dost thou prophesy, and say, Thus saith the Lord, Behold, I will give this city into the hand of the king of Babylon, and he shall take it; 4 And Zedekiah king of Judah shall not escape out of the hand of the Chaldeans, but shall surely be delivered into the hand of the king of Babylon, and shall speak with him mouth to mouth, and his eyes shall behold his eyes; 5 And he shall lead Zedekiah to Babylon, and there shall he be until I visit him, saith the Lord: though ye fight with the Chaldeans, ye shall not prosper. 6 And Jeremiah said, The word of the Lord came unto me, saying, 7 Behold, Hanameel the son of Shallum thine uncle shall come unto thee, saying, Buy thee my field that is in Anathoth: for the right of redemption is thine to buy it. 8 So Hanameel mine uncle's son came to me in the court of the prison according to the word of the Lord, and said unto me, Buy my field, I pray thee, that is in Anathoth, which is in the country of Benjamin: for the right of inheritance is thine, and the redemption is thine; buy it for thyself. Then I knew that this was the word of the Lord. 9 And I bought the field of Hanameel my uncle's son, that was in Anathoth, and weighed him the money, even seventeen shekels of silver. . . . 14 Thus saith the Lord of hosts, the God of Israel; Take these evidences, this evidence of the purchase, both which is sealed, and this evidence which is open; and put them in an earthen vessel, that they may continue many days. 15 For thus saith the Lord of hosts, the God of Israel; Houses and fields and vineyards shall be possessed again in this land.

NEW REVISED STANDARD VERSION

JEREMIAH 32:2 At that time the army of the king of Babylon was besieging Jerusalem, and the prophet Jeremiah was confined in the court of the guard that was in the palace of the king of Judah, 3 where King Zedekiah of Judah had confined him. Zedekiah had said, "Why do you prophesy and say: Thus says the Lord: I am going to give this city into the hand of the king of Babylon, and he shall take it; 4 King Zedekiah of Judah shall not escape out of the hands of the Chaldeans, but shall surely be given into the hands of the king of Babylon, and shall speak with him face to face and see him eye to eye; 5 and he shall take Zedekiah to Babylon, and there he shall remain until I attend to him, says the Lord; though you fight against the Chaldeans, you shall not succeed?"

6 Jeremiah said, The word of the Lord came to me: 7 Hanamel son of your uncle Shallum is going to come to you and say, "Buy my field that is at Anathoth, for the right of redemption by purchase is yours." 8 Then my cousin Hanamel came to me in the court of the guard, in accordance with the word of the Lord, and said to me, "Buy my field that is at Anathoth in the land of Benjamin, for the right of possession and redemption is yours; buy it for yourself." Then I knew that this was the word of the Lord.

9 And I bought the field at Anathoth from my cousin Hanamel, and weighed out the money to him, seventeen shekels of silver. . . . 14 Thus says the Lord of hosts, the God of Israel: Take these deeds, both this sealed deed of purchase and this open deed, and put them in an earthenware jar, in order that they may last for a long time. 15 For thus says the Lord of hosts, the God of Israel: Houses and fields and vineyards shall again be bought in this land.

HOME BIBLE READINGS

Monday, September 15	Jeremiah 32:16-23	*The Steadfast Love of God*
Tuesday, September 16	Jeremiah 32:26-35	*Provoking God*
Wednesday, September 17	Isaiah 10:20-25	*Very Soon My Anger Will End*
Thursday, September 18	Jeremiah 32:36-44	*I Will Surely Gather Them*
Friday, September 19	Isaiah 11:1-12	*The Wolf and Lamb Live Together*
Saturday, September 20	Isaiah 12	*Surely God Is My Salvation*
Sunday, September 21	Jeremiah 32:2-9, 14-15	*Hope for a Distant Future*

BACKGROUND

Zedekiah (Jer. 32:3) was 21 years old, just three years older than his deposed nephew, Jehoiachin, when he became king (2 Kings 24:18). He reigned for 11 years, from 597 to 586 B.C. His mother, Hamutal from Libnah, had also been King Jehoahaz's mother (see 23:31). Like his predecessors, Zedekiah did evil in the eyes of the Lord. The quality of his kingdom only validated God's intention to remove the people of Judah from His presence in the Promised Land (see 24:19-20).

Zedekiah figures prominently in the Book of Jeremiah. The monarch consulted with the prophet (see 21:1-2) and even begged for Jeremiah's help (see 37:3), but Zedekiah never had the courage to do what he knew was right. While the king seemed to want Jeremiah, the man of God, on his side, Zedekiah had lost his independence and much of his power to aristocrats around him. In fact, these ungodly counselors in the royal court always got their way (see 38:1-5). One contingent of those advisors convinced Zedekiah that he could rebel against the Babylonians, who had put him in power (see 2 Kings 24:20).

Zedekiah shuttled ambassadors between Jerusalem and the capitals of Edom, Moab, Ammon, Tyre, and Sidon to discuss allegiance to Babylon (see Jer. 27:3). In 595 B.C., Nebuchadnezzar faced a rebellion in Babylon. It may have been at that time that Zedekiah and the other small nations around him decided they could break from Babylonian control. In 589 B.C., Pharaoh Hophra ascended the throne in Egypt and declared his independence from Babylon. The Lachish letters, 21 pottery fragments with military messages on them, reveal that Hophra was in communication with the commander of Zedekiah's forces in southern Judah. Jeremiah consistently bore witness to Zedekiah that the Lord wanted Judah to submit to Babylon (see Jer. 27:12-14).

When the Babylonians temporarily lifted the siege of Jerusalem to deal with Pharaoh Hophra's approaching Egyptian army (see Jer. 37:5; Ezek. 17:15), Zedekiah asked Jeremiah to pray that the siege would be over for good (Jer. 37:3). Instead, the prophet declared that the Babylonians would soon be back (vss. 6-8). When Jeremiah tried to leave Jerusalem to attend to some property in his hometown of Anathoth (see 1:1), he was arrested as a deserter to the Babylonians (37:11-13). Next, he was beaten and put in a dungeon, where Zedekiah visited the prophet, hoping to hear a favorable message from the Lord (vss. 14-17). As before, Jeremiah repeated his oracle of judgment and protested the injustice of his imprisonment (vss. 18-20). In response, the king transferred Jeremiah to a better cell in the courtyard of the guardhouse and ordered that he be fed as long as rations held out (vs. 21).

NOTES ON THE PRINTED TEXT

Jeremiah 32 and 33 were written during the horrible 18-month siege of Jerusalem by Nebuchadnezzar (587–586 B.C.). At this time, Zedekiah was in his tenth year on the throne of Judah (32:1). As the Babylonian army tightened its grip on the city, Zedekiah imprisoned Jeremiah in the "court" (vs. 2) adjacent to the guardhouse that was attached to the king's royal palace. Evidently, Jeremiah was a political prisoner who was permitted to receive visitors and conduct business.

During Jeremiah's confinement, Zedekiah censured his political prisoner for his dire, prophetic warnings (vs. 3). Yet Jeremiah remained unrelenting in his assertion that the Lord would deliver Jerusalem into hand of Nebuchadnezzar and permit him to overrun it. Moreover, Jeremiah had the courage to declare that Judah's king would be unsuccessful in his attempt to flee from the Babylonian army. Rather, God would allow Zedekiah to be delivered to Nebuchadnezzar's control. The Hebrew phrase rendered "speak with him mouth to mouth" (vs. 4) denotes a scene of harsh interrogation in which Zedekiah would be forced to answer personally to his captor for his insurrection. Jeremiah prophesied that Zedekiah then would be carried off to Babylon (vs. 5; see 52:11).

At the time of Jeremiah's call in 626 B.C., God challenged Jeremiah to prepare himself for the resistance he would encounter when he began to prophesy a message of judgment. He would have to stand against the tide of public opinion and resist every tendency to be afraid (1:17). The Lord promised to make Jeremiah like an impregnable fortress in the face of attacks by Judah's kings, government leaders, priests, and ordinary people (vs. 18). God promised the prophet that no matter how frequently or viciously his opponents attacked him (for example, Zedekiah), they would not overcome Jeremiah. The Lord would always be with the prophet to deliver him (vs. 19).

When the Lord wanted to proclaim judgment and doom on His people, He took Jeremiah from his mother's womb and shaped him into an instrument He could use (vs. 9). What kind of man was Jeremiah? Was he as tough as nails, impervious to criticism, and eager to blast away at sin? No. He had none of the credentials we might associate with a prophet foretelling imminent destruction. Instead, Jeremiah possessed a sensitive soul. He anguished—just as God did—over the devastation coming to his people. All the same, Jeremiah stood firm—just as the Lord did—for the truth.

While Jeremiah remained imprisoned, he received an oracle from the Lord (32:6). The prophet had a cousin named Hanamel, who was the son of Shallum, Jeremiah's uncle (vs. 7). Hanamel owned a field in Anathoth, which was located about three miles northeast of Jerusalem. Anathoth was one of the 45 cities previously allotted to the Levites from the territory belonging to the tribe of Benjamin (see Josh. 21:18). While the Babylonians laid siege to Jerusalem, Hanamel asked Jeremiah, as Hanamel's cousin (Jer. 32:7), to exercise his "right" and fulfill his responsibility as a guardian of the family interests (or kinsmen-redeemer) to purchase the property.

Leviticus 25:25-55 provides the scriptural backdrop for Hanamel's request (see Ruth 4:3-4). The Mosaic law stipulated that if the owner of a tract became so destitute that he had to sell his land, the nearest male relative had the "right of redemption" (Jer. 32:7) to purchase it. This transaction was intended to keep the property within the possession of the extended family. In the year of Jubilee, the original owner regained control of the land (see Lev. 25:13-17). The implication is that Jeremiah would only be obtaining permission to use the property, not permanently own it.

As God had revealed, Hanamel visited Jeremiah while he was imprisoned and asked that he fulfill his obligation as the family guardian. This incident confirmed to the prophet that he truly had received an oracle from the Lord (Jer. 32:8). From a financial standpoint, the transaction seemed absurd. Yet, despite this, the "LORD God" (vs. 25) directed His spokesperson to purchase the field with "money" and the acquisition be confirmed by witnesses. In obedience to God, Jeremiah paid his cousin 17 "shekels" (or about seven ounces; vs. 9) of "silver" for the property. In the ancient Near East, the shekel was the basic weight used for financial transactions. Nonetheless, archaeological evidence indicates that there was no uniform standard established for the shekel's size, weight, and value.

In the presence of witnesses, Jeremiah "subscribed the evidence" (Jer. 32:10) of purchase. Also, scales (that is, a beam balance) were used to weigh out the money. Two copies of the "evidence of the purchase" (vs. 11) were drafted. The first sheet of papyrus was sealed with wax and the second was left unsealed (to be used for future reference, if required). On the first copy were recorded the terms and conditions of the transaction. Next, Jeremiah gave both copies to his trustworthy friend and personal scribe, "Baruch" (vs. 12), the son of a man named "Neriah" (see 32:16). Looking on were Hanamel, along with the "witnesses" (32:12) who had put their names on the sealed document and the "Jews" (or Judeans) sitting in the courtyard of the guardhouse. Then, Jeremiah relayed the Lord's instructions to Baruch (vs. 13). Specifically, he was to place both the sealed and unsealed copies of the deed in an "eathern vessel" (vs. 14) so that the documents would be preserved for "many days" (that is, until the return of the exiles to Judah from captivity in Babylon).

The reason for the divine directive is that the sovereign Lord, who declared Himself to be the "God of Israel" (vs. 15), promised to bring about the restoration of His chosen people from captivity. Jeremiah's purchase symbolized the Lord's pledge that in a future day, a righteous remnant would once again buy "houses and fields and vineyards" in their ancestral homeland. Jeremiah was so moved by the implication of the transaction that he spent some time in prayer (vs. 16). He affirmed his belief that almighty God created "the heaven and the earth" (vs. 17) by His mighty "power" and infinite strength. In light of this truth, it was not "too hard" for Him one day to return the exiles to the Promised Land.

SUGGESTIONS TO TEACHERS

As the armies of Babylon laid siege to Jerusalem, the Lord directed Jeremiah to purchase a field owned by Hanamel. This became a symbolic act of the hope connected with God's promise to one day restore His people to Judah. Similarly, even when our life circumstance seems bleak, God does not give up on us.

1. TURNING AWAY FROM SIN. In His righteous anger, God brought calamity on His wayward people by permitting Nebuchadnezzar to overrun Jerusalem and Judah. When we give ourselves to sin, we replace the joy of the Lord with the agony of disobedience. It is only when we abandon our sin that God's light and life can be fully appropriated.

2. REMAINING FAITHFUL TO GOD. How many of us would be able to faithfully declare God's message while confined as a political prisoner? This is exactly what Jeremiah did as he endured confinement in the palace courtyard. Despite being pressured by King Zedekiah to recant his dire pronouncements, Jeremiah never wavered. Because we know that God is faithful to us, we also can remain just as faithful to Him.

3. DEVELOPING A SENSE OF ENDURANCE. Undoubtedly, Jeremiah struggled with being jailed for proclaiming the truth. Through it all, though, he developed a sense of endurance. During his trying situation, he continued to trust in God. In the end, because of Jeremiah's patience and persistence, God brought great blessings out of the prophet's challenging situation. As we face tough circumstances, may we strive to develop a sense of endurance.

4. DISCERNING GOD'S LARGER PURPOSE. At first, Jeremiah seemed unsure about God's larger purpose in directing the prophet to buy his cousin's property. It was only through a process of time and discernment that the Lord's intent became clear. Even today, we cannot always know how God's purpose is taking shape in our lives. Certainly, we will not realize the full importance and impact of our lives until we look back from the perspective of eternity.

■ **TOPIC:** Property for Sale

■ **QUESTIONS:** 1. What kind of king was Zedekiah? 2. Why was the army of Babylon besieging Jerusalem? 3. Why did God direct Jeremiah to purchase property owned by his cousin, Hanamel? 4. In what ways have you seen God use vexing events in your life to shape your character? 5. What negative influences from your past must you resist in order to grow spiritually?

■ **ILLUSTRATIONS:**
Doing God's Work. The situation for the people of Jerusalem was bleak as Nebuchadnezzar surrounded the city with his army. Even as Jeremiah was a political prisoner in the palace courtyard, he was willing to sacrifice his personal desires and ambitions for the good of others.

Florence Nightingale (1820–1910) also exemplified this mindset. At age 17, she felt God calling her to serve Him. She found her place of service in nursing, which in the early 1800's was done mostly by untrained volunteers. During the Crimean War (1853–1856), Nightingale and 38 nurses whom she trained organized hospitals for 5,000 wounded British soldiers. She established the first real nurses' training, fought for sanitary hospitals in Britain, and helped make nursing the respectable profession it is today.

But Nightingale felt uncomfortable when Queen Victoria and Parliament honored her. She explained that she was doing God's work. "Christ is the author of our profession," Nightingale said about nursing. She later refused a national funeral and burial in Westminster Abbey when it was promised as a reward for her work. She only wanted to be buried with her family in a rural churchyard with a simple service.

Never Alone. Jeremiah had to endure confinement as a political prisoner. Yet even as he journeyed through that bleak circumstance, he knew that God remained with him.

In *Forgotten God*, author and pastor Francis Chan recounts the harrowing experience 23 missionaries endured in July 2007 as the Taliban held them hostage in Afghanistan. One of the missionaries described the "horrors of being locked up in a cell" and sensing that "martyrdom was a strong possibility." Despite this, each of the captives "surrendered their lives to God" and "told Him they were willing to die for His glory."

Chan learned that one of the missionaries had a "small Bible" that the hostages "secretly ripped" into 23 "pieces so each could glance at Scripture when no one was watching." Several of the missionaries recalled experiencing a "deep kind of intimacy with God in the prison." Moreover, all of them were convinced that the "Word of God and the Spirit of God" enabled them to endure the 40 days of imprisonment.

Chan explains that the presence of God experienced by these missionaries is the "precious gift of intimacy the Holy Spirit offers us." The author describes the latter as a "security that is priceless." Indeed, it is "worth any loss of safety and comfort, even imprisonment by the Taliban."

Recast as Jesus' Follower. As Jerusalem withered under the relentless siege of the Babylonians, the future for God's people looked bleak. After all, this dire circumstance was the end result of their unrelenting disobedience. But the Lord had not given up on His people. He used Jeremiah's act of purchasing his cousin's field to point to a future day of forgiveness and restoration for a beleaguered remnant. Only the Lord, who is the Commander of heaven's armies, had the power to bring about this amazing reversal.

In *The Persecutor*, Sergei Kourdakov recounts his 150 raids on Christians who lived behind the Iron Curtain. Believers were unsafe wherever they assembled. Prayer meetings, church services, and outdoor baptisms were all fair game to execute Kourdakov's well-orchestrated attacks. He handsomely paid judo champions, boxers, and athletes to carry out his brutality. Knives and rubber-covered steel clubs were weapons of choice.

We might wonder how Kourdakov could enlist people to actually perform such barbaric acts on believers. Consider the words of a local Communist party chairman: "The believers are like murderers. They kill the spirits of our children. They cripple with their poisonous beliefs. We must rid our country of these people."

That kind of rhetoric had spurred on Kourdakov, who was a product of a nation sold out to atheism. Amazingly, God's grace liquefied the cold steel of Kourdakov's unbelief. He began to notice the conviction and courage of the Christians whom he tried to silence. Eventually, through the sovereign working of the Spirit, Kourdakov was recast as one of Jesus' followers!

■ **Topic:** A Risk for a New Future

■ **Questions:** 1. Why had Zedekiah imprisoned Jeremiah? 2. Why did Jeremiah prophesy that God would let the Babylonians conquer Jerusalem? 3. How did Jeremiah know that God wanted him to purchase property owned by Hanamel? 4. What fears might you have that sometimes keep you from serving God? 5. How can you use times of crisis to grow spiritually?

■ **Illustrations:**

Refusing to Quit. Homeless, hungry refugees often fill our television screens. We watch them clamor and fight for food and clothing being thrown from trucks. Thousands of years ago, an even worse circumstance had settled over Jerusalem as the Babylonian army laid siege to the city.

At this time, Jeremiah was jailed in the guardhouse that was attached to the king's royal "house" (Jer. 32:2). What kept the prophet going? It was his faith in God and the prophet's courage to remain devoted to God's people. Jeremiah had no earthly prospects for a brighter future. Yet he refused to quit, for he knew that trusting and obeying the Lord was his highest goal.

Many adolescents experience times of crisis in their lives—losing a loved one, moving to a strange place, struggling to make ends meet, and so on. Saved teens also know that peers who do not share their faith in the Lord Jesus sometimes treat them like outcasts. They should be encouraged to remain loyal to their Christian faith and heritage. They can do so knowing that the Lord will be with them every step of the way.

Amazing Grace. God directed Jeremiah to buy a field owned by his cousin in their hometown of Anathoth. Through this symbolic act, God proclaimed to His people that He had not given up on them. Even though they had sinned against Him, their Redeemer had a brighter future in store for them.

Not too many people have committed worse sins than John Newton, and yet he wrote one of America's favorite hymns, "Amazing Grace." Newton lived in the 18th century, and he was a slave trader. In fact, he was a captain of an English slave ship, which transported many Africans during trips across the Atlantic. During such voyages, these men, women, and children were chained side by side in the crowded decks below, and if any got sick, they were thrown overboard. Those who lived were sold for sugar and molasses in the New World and lived as slaves for the rest of their lives.

Although Newton claimed that he was a Christian even before he became the captain of a slave ship, his inhumane treatment of the Africans finally compelled him to quit the sea and enter the ministry. Not only did he write some of the most beloved Christian hymns, but he also worked tirelessly for the abolition of the slave trade. What Newton did as a sea captain haunted him all his life. Yet at 82, he said, "My memory is nearly gone, but I remember two things, that I am a great sinner, and that Christ is a great Savior."

Never Beyond God's Reach. Initially, we might conclude that once God punished His people for their sins, He was done with them. Yet, we learn from Jeremiah's symbolic act of purchasing his cousin's field that God would both forgive His people and restore a remnant to their homeland. Clearly, none of them were beyond God's reach.

These days, there are many popular musicians and music groups who live and sing about the dark side of life. That was also true when I was a teenager. I remember some musicians who decorated their album covers with overtly anti-Jesus slogans. A few even boasted about making personal pacts with the devil in exchange for the success they most desired.

I remember how rattled I was when one of the rankest of the rock music stars of my era declared one day he had been gloriously saved by Jesus. It was especially shocking since I knew that this person was one of those who had made an overt resolution to serve the kingdom of darkness. I knew that if there was an "unpardonable" sin, he was an example of someone who had committed it.

Yet, while I was busy condemning him, he was turning his life over to Jesus. As I watched this person's lifestyle and heard his sincere testimony of experiencing Jesus' abiding, restorative presence, I found myself rejoicing. Admittedly, I also wondered whether anyone could be beyond the reach of God's salvation, especially if this music star could commit his life to the Savior. Then I remembered what 2 Peter 3:9 says about God's mercy: "[He] is longsuffering to us-ward, not willing that any should perish, but that all should come to repentance."

LESSON 4 — SEPTEMBER 28

AN INCREDIBLE PLEDGE

BACKGROUND SCRIPTURE: Jeremiah 33
DEVOTIONAL READING: Jeremiah 9:17-24

Key Verse: I will cause to return the captivity of the land, as at the first, saith the LORD. Jeremiah 33:11.

KING JAMES VERSION

JEREMIAH 33:2 Thus saith the LORD the maker thereof, the LORD that formed it, to establish it; the LORD is his name; 3 Call unto me, and I will answer thee, and shew thee great and mighty things, which thou knowest not. 4 For thus saith the LORD, the God of Israel, concerning the houses of this city, and concerning the houses of the kings of Judah, which are thrown down by the mounts, and by the sword; 5 They come to fight with the Chaldeans, but it is to fill them with the dead bodies of men, whom I have slain in mine anger and in my fury, and for all whose wickedness I have hid my face from this city. 6 Behold, I will bring it health and cure, and I will cure them, and will reveal unto them the abundance of peace and truth. 7 And I will cause the captivity of Judah and the captivity of Israel to return, and will build them, as at the first. 8 And I will cleanse them from all their iniquity, whereby they have sinned against me; and I will pardon all their iniquities, whereby they have sinned, and whereby they have transgressed against me. 9 And it shall be to me a name of joy, a praise and an honour before all the nations of the earth, which shall hear all the good that I do unto them: and they shall fear and tremble for all the goodness and for all the prosperity that I procure unto it.

10 Thus saith the LORD; Again there shall be heard in this place, which ye say shall be desolate without man and without beast, even in the cities of Judah, and in the streets of Jerusalem, that are desolate, without man, and without inhabitant, and without beast, 11 The voice of joy, and the voice of gladness, the voice of the bridegroom, and the voice of the bride, the voice of them that shall say, Praise the LORD of hosts: for the LORD is good; for his mercy endureth for ever: and of them that shall bring the sacrifice of praise into the house of the LORD. For I will cause to return the captivity of the land, as at the first, saith the LORD.

NEW REVISED STANDARD VERSION

JEREMIAH 33:2 Thus says the LORD who made the earth, the LORD who formed it to establish it—the LORD is his name: 3 Call to me and I will answer you, and will tell you great and hidden things that you have not known. 4 For thus says the LORD, the God of Israel, concerning the houses of this city and the houses of the kings of Judah that were torn down to make a defense against the siege ramps and before the sword: 5 The Chaldeans are coming in to fight and to fill them with the dead bodies of those whom I shall strike down in my anger and my wrath, for I have hidden my face from this city because of all their wickedness. 6 I am going to bring it recovery and healing; I will heal them and reveal to them abundance of prosperity and security.
7 I will restore the fortunes of Judah and the fortunes of Israel, and rebuild them as they were at first. 8 I will cleanse them from all the guilt of their sin against me, and I will forgive all the guilt of their sin and rebellion against me. 9 And this city shall be to me a name of joy, a praise and a glory before all the nations of the earth who shall hear of all the good that I do for them; they shall fear and tremble because of all the good and all the prosperity I provide for it.

10 Thus says the LORD: In this place of which you say, "It is a waste without human beings or animals," in the towns of Judah and the streets of Jerusalem that are desolate, without inhabitants, human or animal, there shall once more be heard 11 the voice of mirth and the voice of gladness, the voice of the bridegroom and the voice of the bride, the voices of those who sing, as they bring thank offerings to the house of the LORD:

"Give thanks to the LORD of hosts,
 for the LORD is good,
 for his steadfast love endures forever!"

For I will restore the fortunes of the land as at first, says the LORD.

HOME BIBLE READINGS

Monday, September 22	Isaiah 30:9-17	*In Returning You Shall Be Saved*
Tuesday, September 23	Jeremiah 2:26-32	*Where Are Your Gods?*
Wednesday, September 24	Jeremiah 3:11-15	*I Will Bring You to Zion*
Thursday, September 25	Jeremiah 3:19-23	*I Will Heal Your Faithlessness*
Friday, September 26	Jeremiah 17:12-17	*The Hope of Israel*
Saturday, September 27	Jeremiah 9:17-24	*The Lord Acts with Steadfast Love*
Sunday, September 28	Jeremiah 33:2-11	*Voices of Mirth and Gladness*

BACKGROUND

In ancient conflicts, siege warfare played a major role. City walls kept invaders out, but they could also isolate the inhabitants within. By laying siege to a city, an attacking army could cut off the defenders' food, supplies, and—if possible—water. A siege could be a long and tedious means to weaken a city, but certain tactics helped the process along. Iron-tipped battering rams were swung from ropes or rolled forward on wheels to break through the city gates. Soldiers dug trenches beneath city walls to weaken their foundations. When they burned the support beams, the walls would collapse. Fires were also set against the base of the wall to weaken the sandstone or limestone blocks.

A favorite Babylonian tactic was to build up a ramp of soil and debris against the weakest point of a city's wall. It could take months, but eventually the attackers could rush up the ramp and over the city's walls. Meanwhile, they denuded the surrounding countryside of trees to acquire material for building the ramp. Another result was that the process demoralized the defenders. With towers rolled into place, attackers could shoot arrows at defenders from the same height as the top of the wall. While archers cleared defenders away from the wall, soldiers climbed numerous ladders in an attempt to overrun the top.

NOTES ON THE PRINTED TEXT

In last week's lesson, we learned that Jeremiah was confined as a political prisoner in the palace courtyard. At this time, the Babylonians had laid siege to Jerusalem (see Jer. 32:2). We also found out that while imprisoned, Jeremiah received an oracle from the Lord (see vs. 6). According to 33:1, as the prophet remained incarcerated, he received a second oracle from God. Jeremiah introduced this divine message with the statement, "thus saith the LORD" (vs. 2). An examination of how the phrase is used in Scripture indicates that it is the hallmark of a prophet's message from God (for example, see Isa. 7:7; Jer. 2:5; Ezek. 5:5).

The Book of Jeremiah gives repeated emphasis to God as the Creator (see 10:11-13; 51:15-16). He is the Lord who made the earth (33:2), as well as shaped the planet and firmly established it. These truths are also found throughout the Psalms. For instance,

Psalm 104 (along with Job 38 and Psalms 8 and 29) produces a magnificent poetic and musical commentary on the creation. Even the structure of Psalm 104 draws praise in that it is modeled quite closely on the day-by-day creation events recorded in Genesis. Indeed, as the psalmist described in grandiose detail the daily acts of creation, he seemed to preach in glowing terms that what God created on each day is reason enough to praise Him. It is clear that the poet used the various stages of creation as his starting points for praise. But as he developed each creation-day theme, there is a constant anticipation for more, especially for the later days of the creation.

Jeremiah 33:3 directs our attention to the prayers uttered by God's people. When virtuous individuals such as Jeremiah petitioned the Lord for justice and righteousness to prevail, He promised to answer their requests. Elsewhere, the Hebrew participle rendered "great and mighty things" is used to refer to a nation's fortified cities and walls (see Num. 13:28; Deut. 1:28; 9:1; Josh. 14:12). But in Jeremiah 33:3, the emphasis is metaphorical and denotes the Lord's inscrutable, mysterious ways (see Isa. 48:6). The latter includes God's revelation to Jeremiah that He was going to allow Jerusalem to be razed (Jer. 33:4-5) and His people later restored to the promised land (vss. 6-26). These are breathtaking truths that the Lord first had to disclose to Jeremiah before he could declare them to God's people.

Previously, late in 609 or early in 608 B.C., the Lord instructed Jeremiah to deliver a warning to the worshipers at the Jerusalem temple. Following God's directions, the prophet positioned himself at the temple gate (perhaps the New Gate; see 26:10), where he could address the people who came to worship there (7:2). Though they attended temple activities, their religion was nothing but insincere ritual. Jeremiah challenged them to live in ways that were consistent with their apparent worship (vs. 3). The prophet also warned his peers that trusting in the temple would not keep them safe and that those who said it would were false prophets (vs. 4). Simply chanting the phrase "the temple of the LORD" was believed to ward off destruction. The pious were convinced that God would never allow His own temple and city to be destroyed.

Jeremiah 33:4-5 discredits all false hopes of safety. Already, as the siege of Jerusalem dragged on, the desperate inhabitants had dismantled their "houses" (including those built into or right next to the city's walls) and royal palaces. In turn, they used these building materials to create a thicker, sturdier structure in a final attempt to strengthen Jerusalem's defenses (see Isa. 22:10). Ultimately, the frantic efforts made by Jerusalem's defenders would prove futile against a relentless foe. God, in His "anger and . . . fury"(Jer. 33:5), would use the Babylonians to slaughter Jerusalem's warriors. The Lord would abandon His people because of all the evil deeds they and their predecessors had committed in His sight.

The dreary circumstance detailed in verses 2-5 stands in sharp contrast to the blessed future foretold in verses 6-11. The Hebrew term rendered "behold" (vs. 6) can also be translated "gaze upon" to emphasize God's unwavering commitment to one day restore the exiles in Babylon to their homeland. The reference in verse 7 to "Judah and . . . Israel" indicates that the Lord would bring back from "captivity" His previously divided people and enable all of them to rebuild their towns (see 3:18). This amazing turn of events remained true, even though the Lord permitted Nebuchadnezzar's army to destroy Jerusalem and its temple (see 30:8, 16; 32:36-37). When the time came for the remnant to return to Judah, God pledged to "bring . . . health" (33:6) to Jerusalem and wellness to its people. Indeed, their lives would be overflowing with "peace and truth." A comparison with 30:17 suggests that the Lord had in view both the spiritual and political well being of the returnees. This signifies a dramatic reversal of the divine judgment God brought on the promised land (see 8:21-22).

God's promises of restoration were not intended to ignore the harsh reality of what brought about the exile of His people to Babylon. Specifically, generations of them were guilty of sinning against the Lord, and He had to spiritually purify them from their iniquity. God also declared His intent to pardon the exiles for all their transgressions against Him (33:8). We find a similar emphasis in 1 John 1. Verse 8 discloses that those who declare themselves to be free of "sin" were self-deceived and not abiding in God's "truth." Oppositely, if they acknowledged their sins to God, He remained "faithful and just" (vs. 9) to pardon the guilt of their sin and "cleanse" them from their "unrighteousness."

God declared that once the exiles in Babylon were restored to Judah, all the surrounding "nations" (Jer. 33:9) would learn about the remarkable outcome. In turn, all the "good" the Lord did for the upright remnant would bring Him fame, glory, and honor. Moreover, as His renown spread to the Gentiles, they would "tremble" with "fear," especially at the sight of the "goodness and . . . prosperity" God poured out on the returnees. Hosea 3:5 reveals that they too would begin to earnestly "seek the LORD," submit in reverence to Him, and experience the fullness of His blessings.

As the Babylonian siege continued, the holdouts in Jerusalem realized that the enemy would eventually succeed in breaking through the city's defenses. After all, the invaders had laid waste to the "cities of Judah" (Jer. 33:10) so that they lacked any inhabitants, whether people or animals. The desolation of the nation was a harbinger of the destruction Nebuchadnezzar would bring to Jerusalem. That outcome notwithstanding, the Lord revealed that a future day was coming when Judah's cities and Jerusalem's streets would no longer be empty. Instead, they would be filled with people and animals.

Furthermore, the activity of the inhabitants within these population centers would produce an assortment of sounds, including the following: "joy" (vs. 11) and "gladness," marriage celebrations, and the jubilant songs of worshipers as they brought their "sacrifice of praise" to the rebuilt Jerusalem temple. The latter group would invite all who heard them to express their gratitude to the Lord of heaven's armies. Their motivation for doing so was the goodness of God and His eternal, steadfast "mercy" (see Pss. 106:1; 118:1; 136:1). His unfailing compassion was demonstrated in restoring the prosperity of Judah as it was before the exile of God's people. It would also signify a reversal of His judgment on the promised land and its inhabitants (see 7:34; 16:9; 25:10).

SUGGESTIONS TO TEACHERS

In the second oracle Jeremiah received from Lord, the prophet was told about a remarkable development God would undertake. He pledged that one day He would reverse the devastation resulting from the Babylonian invasion. At that time, His people would experience His cleansing and forgiveness. Believers today can also trust God to make their lives whole, regardless of the challenges they face.

1. LIVE FOR GOD TODAY. As God's people endured the present and anticipated the future, they knew they faced a burdensome situation. Yet, their challenging circumstance did not have to prevent them from living for the Lord. That is an important principle in spiritual life. We cannot wait until everything is perfect before taking steps in our walk with God. So let's begin today.

2. LIVE IN FAITH, NOT FEAR. God's people were surrounded by a powerful foe. Understandably, Jerusalem's residents lived in dread of their assailants. We can sometimes feel overwhelmed by those who are opposed to God and His Word. They may seem more powerful, wealthy, and influential. That does not matter. Let us learn to live out of our faith, not out of our fear.

3. GIVE GOD PRAISE. A day was coming when God's people would express joyful praise to Him. That gives us a clear lesson about the importance of offering praise to God. It is not an act that can be taken lightly. Let us learn to praise God here and now, no matter what is happening in our lives.

4. WORSHIP THE LORD OF PRESENT, NOT JUST THE PAST. God's people were aware of the desolation occurring in Judah and Jerusalem from the Babylonian invasion. Undoubtedly, the survivors struggled with feelings of dejection. In our moments of despair, Hebrews 13:8 reminds us that the Lord is the God of yesterday, today, and tomorrow. Let us not get stuck in the past, imagining that it was better than today or tomorrow. The Lord is still God. Not everything new is necessarily bad.

FOR ADULTS

■ **TOPIC:** Laughter Will Return

■ **QUESTIONS:** 1. Why did the Lord stress that He is the creator of the earth? 2. What unfathomable truths was God revealing to Jeremiah? 3. Why would it be necessary for the Lord to spiritually cleanse and forgive His people? 4. When you compare the good times with the difficult times you have experienced, how do you choose to deal with these realities? 5. Why is focusing on the positive aspects disclosed in God's Word so critical to having a perspective that pleases God?

■ **ILLUSTRATIONS:**

Joy in the Lord. In Jeremiah 33:9, the Lord declared that one day Jerusalem and its inhabitants would bring Him "praise and . . . honour." Then, all the surrounding nations would witness the marvelous things God had done for His people.

During their town's annual autumn parade, two or three churches made magnificent floats—so good that often one of them took home first prize. It was their way of informing the public that the joyful worship of God was still a viable option for many people.

Then, as time went on, the floats these congregations made gradually disappeared. Why? It's because they required too much work to build and there were not enough people who volunteered to make them.

Making floats, of course, is just one way we can share with others the joy we have in the Lord Jesus. Sometimes we can celebrate with music that has a Christian emphasis. On other occasions, we can give praise to the Lord through acts of service. Regardless of what we do, our focus should remain on God and not ourselves.

The Sound of Laughter. As the Babylonians laid siege to Jerusalem, life for its residents grew increasingly dismal. The Lord provided His people with hope by promising that a day was coming when He would reverse the tragedies of the present. Desolation and death would give way to life and abundance.

When Lorna celebrated her fifth anniversary as a breast cancer survivor, she looked better than ever. At one point, she had thought she would never reach this milestone.

Previously, Lorna and Felix had been career missionaries in Asia. Raising five kids in a foreign country is not easy, but it seemed delightful compared to the 18 months following Lorna's dreaded talk with the oncologist.

Stage four is not the best time for a woman to learn that she has breast cancer, but that was the prognosis of Lorna's physician when they sat together one brisk autumn day. At that time, the possibility of survival seemed small. So Lorna immediately began the course of treatment that was presented to her. Chemotherapy and other procedures were just part of the plan, to be augmented with radical surgeries.

As Lorna walked in the beautiful flower gardens of her parents' south Florida home, she remembered the days that brought her so close to death's door. However, today she was alive! And she thanked God for the sound of laughter coming down the garden path. It was coming from Lorna's grown children—and she was there to listen.

Dealing with Radical Change. The reality facing Jerusalem's residents looked grim. It was only a matter of time before they were defeated and exiled by their enemies. God helped His people deal with such radical change by promising to one day restore a remnant to Judah and enable them to rebuild their city and its temple.

Sheila's grandmother, Eunice, is 82, and Sheila occasionally shakes her head in disbelief when she realizes how Eunice has adapted to a new church tradition. Sheila grew up in the same church Eunice raised Sheila's mother in: a traditional, evangelical congregation.

Yet today, Eunice attends a church Sheila might call "radical," especially if she didn't understand its vision. It's to communicate the Gospel in a new way to nonbelievers in the community. This body of believers uses nontraditional methods to convey the teachings of Scripture. The message is not compromised, but the approaches are far from what Eunice experienced earlier in life.

Nevertheless, Eunice joyfully puts aside her preferences because she is excited about what the Spirit is doing as this church brings new people to trust in the Savior. Eunice sits through dramas she can't always hear and contemporary music she can't often appreciate. She does so because she gets to witness the Spirit working in the lives of many people. And Eunice keeps attending, praying in the background for the gospel to be clearly presented.

FOR YOUTH

■ **TOPIC:** Return to the Original

■ **QUESTIONS:** 1. How do you think Jeremiah felt when the Lord declared Himself to be the one who formed and established the earth? 2. Why had Jerusalem's inhabitants torn down their houses and royal residences? 3. In what way did God promise to one day heal His people and their homeland? 4. How can focusing on God's promises help believers to handle difficult circumstances? 5. How is it possible for believers to praise God even when life seems overwhelming?

■ **ILLUSTRATIONS:**

A Chance for a New Beginning. "It's too late! I can't make it!" Young people often say such things after they have wasted their academic opportunities. For example, they might wish they had made better grades in high school so they could get into the college of their choice.

When it comes to the things of eternity, it's never too late to start over. Every day is a fresh opportunity to break from our sinful past and renew our commitment to God. He is always willing to extend His love and forgiveness to us.

The second oracle Jeremiah received from God emphasizes this truth. Jeremiah's peers had sinned greatly, but one day God would restore an upright remnant to the promised land. Then God would pardon them and enable them to start over. The gospel likewise tells us that our Lord is the God of new beginnings. When we turn to Jesus in faith, He opens the door to abundant, satisfying, and eternal life.

Fully Trusting Our Master. The cartoon book, *Proverbs According to Ruggles*, by Cindy Bunch and Doug Hall, gives readers a "dog's eye view" of maxims by which we have come to live. For instance, "Ask and it will be given to you" features the portly, spotted Ruggles wagging its tail while presenting its dinner dish to its master—who is asleep on the couch. The next page reads, "Be persistent." Beneath that admonition, we see Ruggles atop its master's belly, dish in mouth—and the master, wide awake!

On a more serious page, the happy pooch loses its doghouse to a large, fallen tree. Its secure shelter lies in ruins. On the next page, we see a shocked, scared Ruggles clinging to its master's sweater and pants. Above, we read, "Know where to find security."

This is the sort of maxim the beleaguered residents of Jerusalem needed to embrace, especially as they experienced the hardship of the Babylonians laying siege to their city. Even today, we are wise when we affirm that the Lord is the source of our security. If a "tree" were to fall on our "doghouse" today, would we trust our Master to provide for us? And would we be thankful for it?

Being Grateful. Jeremiah 33:9 reveals that in the day of Jerusalem's restoration, its inhabitants would fill the city with joy and praise. In turn, the gratitude of the returnees would bring God renown.

Greg Anderson is the author of *Living Life on Purpose*. In it, he tells a story about a man whose wife had left him. This rejection left the man feeling depressed and unhappy.

One rainy morning, this man went to a small neighborhood diner for breakfast. Even though several patrons were at the diner, everyone ate in silence. Likewise, this recently divorced man hunched silently over the counter while stirring his coffee with a spoon.

In one of the small booths along a window were a young mother and her little girl. They had just been served their food when the little girl broke the sad silence by almost shouting, "Momma, why don't we say our prayers here?"

The waitress, who had just served the two their breakfast, turned around and said, "Sure, honey, we pray here. Will you say the prayer for us?" And she turned and looked at the rest of the people in the restaurant and said, "Please bow your heads."

Surprisingly, one by one, the heads went down. Then, the little girl bowed her head, folded her hands, and said, "God is great. God is good. And we thank Him for our food. Amen." That prayer changed the entire atmosphere in the diner. People began to talk with one another. The waitress said, "We should do that every morning."

"All of a sudden," said the divorced man, "my whole frame of mind started to improve. From that little girl's example, I started to thank God for all that I did have and stop majoring in all that I didn't have. I started to be grateful."

Imagine how being grateful can change our attitude about things. It can transform how we feel about ourselves. And being appreciative can change the nature of our relationships with others. Most of all, when we express thanks to God for His blessings in our lives, it helps us to be more appreciative of our relationship with Him.

LESSON 5 — OCTOBER 5

CHOOSING TO REJOICE

BACKGROUND SCRIPTURE: Job 1; Psalm 56; Habakkuk 1–3
DEVOTIONAL READING: Psalm 56:8-13

Key Verse: Yet I will rejoice in the LORD, I will joy in the God of my salvation. Habakkuk 3:18.

KING JAMES VERSION

HABAKKUK 2:1 I will stand upon my watch, and set me upon the tower, and will watch to see what he will say unto me, and what I shall answer when I am reproved. 2 And the LORD answered me, and said, Write the vision, and make it plain upon tables, that he may run that readeth it. 3 For the vision is yet for an appointed time, but at the end it shall speak, and not lie: though it tarry, wait for it; because it will surely come, it will not tarry. 4 Behold, his soul which is lifted up is not upright in him: but the just shall live by his faith.

5 Yea also, because he transgresseth by wine, he is a proud man, neither keepeth at home, who enlargeth his desire as hell, and is as death, and cannot be satisfied, but gathereth unto him all nations, and heapeth unto him all people. . . .

3:17 Although the fig tree shall not blossom, neither shall fruit be in the vines; the labour of the olive shall fail, and the fields shall yield no meat; the flock shall be cut off from the fold, and there shall be no herd in the stalls: 18 Yet I will rejoice in the LORD, I will joy in the God of my salvation. 19 The LORD God is my strength, and he will make my feet like hinds' feet, and he will make me to walk upon mine high places. To the chief singer on my stringed instruments.

NEW REVISED STANDARD VERSION

HABAKKUK 2:1 I will stand at my watchpost,
  and station myself on the rampart;
I will keep watch to see what he will say to me,
  and what he will answer concerning my complaint.
2 Then the LORD answered me and said:
Write the vision;
  make it plain on tablets,
  so that a runner may read it.
3 For there is still a vision for the appointed time;
  it speaks of the end, and does not lie.
If it seems to tarry, wait for it;
  it will surely come, it will not delay.
4 Look at the proud!
  Their spirit is not right in them,
  but the righteous live by their faith.
5 Moreover, wealth is treacherous;
  the arrogant do not endure.
They open their throats wide as Sheol;
  like Death they never have enough.
They gather all nations for themselves,
  and collect all peoples as their own. . . .
3:17 Though the fig tree does not blossom,
  and no fruit is on the vines;
though the produce of the olive fails
  and the fields yield no food;
though the flock is cut off from the fold
  and there is no herd in the stalls,
18 yet I will rejoice in the LORD;
  I will exult in the God of my salvation.
19 GOD, the Lord, is my strength;
  he makes my feet like the feet of a deer,
  and makes me tread upon the heights.
To the leader: with stringed instruments.

Home Bible Readings

Monday, September 29	Habakkuk 1:1-5	*How Long Shall I Cry Out?*
Tuesday, September 30	Habakkuk 1:12-17	*Why Are You Silent?*
Wednesday, October 1	Ruth 1:12-21	*The Lord Has Turned against Me*
Thursday, October 2	Job 1:13-21	*Blessed Be the Name*
Friday, October 3	Psalm 56:1-7	*Be Gracious to Me, O God*
Saturday, October 4	Psalm 56:8-13	*In God I Trust*
Sunday, October 5	Habakkuk 2:1-5; 3:17-19	*Yet I Will Rejoice*

Background

As hard as it might have been for Habakkuk to accept, sometimes the Lord allowed the innocent to suffer as He punished evildoers for their transgressions. Whether one is considering wicked attitudes, actions, or aims, this evil results from the absence of the moral perfection that God originally intended to exist in the world.

Ultimately, only God knows why He has allowed evil to exist in the world. It nevertheless remains true that the Lord might use evil to bring home to us the distressing fact of our mortality, to warn us of greater evils, to bring about a greater good, or to help defeat wickedness (to name a few options). The last two reasons are especially evident in the cross of Christ. Despite the tragedy of the Messiah's suffering on the cross, His atoning sacrifice resulted in a greater good (namely, the salvation of the lost) and the defeat of evil (for instance, sin and death).

Notes on the Printed Text

Though the Lord had shown Habakkuk a powerful army that ruthlessly devoured nations in its path, God had not yet revealed their destiny. After Habakkuk stated his case before the Lord, the prophet stood "watch" (Hab. 2:1), waiting for an answer to his questions. The image here is one of a guard standing on the walls of Jerusalem, keeping an eye out for a possible military response to a political challenge. The prophet had presented his complaint in faith, not skepticism, and fully expected God to respond.

God not only gave Habakkuk an answer, but also commanded him to engrave the "vision" (vs. 2) legibly on "tables" (possibly made of stone, wood, clay, or metal). Doing this would enable heralds to read the oracle of judgment correctly and quickly proclaim it to others. The Lord would punish Babylon for its sins and bring deliverance for His people. Because God's message awaited a future and certain fulfillment (vs. 3), it was especially important that it be transmitted through a permanent record. Though the judgment of Babylon and the deliverance of God's people would not come immediately, the Lord asked the upright remnant to wait for it. God promised that it would assuredly take place. From a human standpoint, it would seem like an unreasonable delay, but from God's perspective the fulfillment would arrive on time. Despite the prolonged wait, the outcome was certain.

Nebuchadnezzar was possibly the most illustrious of ancient Babylon's rulers. The son of Nabopolassar and the king of the Babylonian Empire from 605 to 562 B.C., Nebuchadnezzar was a powerful monarch who would stop at nothing to bring neighboring countries into submission. His forces were known for their military drive and their savage treatment of conquered peoples. From the outset of Nebuchadnezzar's reign, the Lord used the pagan king to discipline His wayward people. While the arrogant ignored God's message of judgment for the wicked and deliverance for His people, the righteous lived by faith (vs. 4). For a period of time, circumstances would appear contrary to what one would expect from a holy God. But those who waited and remained faithful to the Lord would not be disappointed in the final results. They would eventually see God's promised salvation (see Rom. 1:17; Gal. 3:11; Heb. 10:38-39).

God began His sentence of judgment on the Babylonians by saying, "Yea also, because he transgresseth by wine" (vs. 5). Ancient writers confirm that the Babylonians were addicted to strong drink. In fact, Babylon was overthrown in precisely the state of drunkenness and bravado described in this passage (see Dan. 5). Moreover, God revealed to Habakkuk that the Babylonians were egotistical and restless. Their greed was large as the grave's appetite for cadavers. Also, just like "death" (vs. 5), the aggressors' craving for dead bodies seemed insatiable. It appeared as if no one could determine the number of battlefields filled with the corpses of warriors from surrounding nations whom the Babylonians had slaughtered.

Even though Habakkuk 3 is called a "prayer" (vs. 1), in its form and language this passage is closely related to the Psalms. For instance, Habakkuk echoes the terminology and imagery of hymns expressing lament, such as Psalms 18 and 77. Even some phrases used from Psalms are used in Habakkuk 3. "Upon Shigionoth" (vs. 1) is an obscure literary or musical term about which little is known. Some think it indicates a highly emotional poetic form. The title of Psalm 7 is the only other time the term appears in the Old Testament (in the singular form).

"Selah" (Hab. 3:3, 9, 13) is often used in the Psalms. The term possibly indicates the spot for a brief musical interlude or a short liturgical response by the congregation (for example, Ps. 3:2). "To the chief singer" (Hab. 3:19) is a liturgical note that appears in the headings of 55 psalms. It might have designated that the piece was to be used in the temple worship or recited by the leader of the choir. "On my stringed instruments" (Hab. 3:19) is a liturgical note appearing in the heading of several psalms (for instance, Pss. 61; 67). The term comes from a Hebrew verb that means "to strike a chord," and might indicate the manner in which a stringed instrument (such as a harp or lyre) was used to perform the musical piece.

Habakkuk 3:2 is the prophet's formal petition. Verses 3-15 recall the Lord's past dealings with His people, and verses 16-19 express trust and confidence in God's preservation of the upright. Habakkuk knew the testimonies of God's mighty acts as celebrated in song, as well as in feasts and festivals of Israel. These displays of divine power included the exodus from Egypt, the miracles of the Red Sea, and the conquest of the Promised Land. In verse 2, Habakkuk asked the Lord to once again help His people in their time of great need. In the midst of God's punishment of Judah at the hand of the Babylonians, Habakkuk begged the Lord to "remember mercy." Expressed differently, the prophet wanted God to turn from His anger, be gracious to His people, and rescue them from their plight.

As Habakkuk meditated on God's work in human affairs, he was overcome with an awe-inspiring sense of the greatness of the Lord. Accordingly, in verse 3, the prophet used figures from God's past intervention on His people's behalf to paint a picture of their future redemption. Habakkuk took these images from the deliverance of God's people from Egypt and the conquest of Canaan. Habakkuk declared that the Lord was the same holy God who came from Teman and Paran to help His people from slavery in Egypt. Teman was a district in Edom, but the name was sometimes used for the entire country. Paran was in the hill country along the western border of the Gulf of Aqaba. In Judges 5:4, the Lord is said to have marched from Edom to help His people, and in Deuteronomy 33:2, Paran is mentioned in connection with the Lord's appearance at Sinai.

The glory of God, which protected and led Israel from Egypt through the wilderness (see Exod. 40:34-38), was another physical display of the divine presence. The prophet declared that the brightness of God's glory covered the heavens, and His praises were heard throughout the earth (Hab. 3:3). The prophet noted that the brilliant light of God's glory was more intense than the sun, and also that light flashed from His hands and hid His mighty power (vs. 4).

Verse 17 reveals the desolation the Babylonians would bring on Judah. Fig trees would be so damaged they would not blossom. Likewise, grape plants would fail to produce fruit on their withered vines. Olive groves and grainfields would become barren. Flocks of sheep and herds of cattle would be decimated by the Babylonian onslaught. Despite the hardships that awaited the people of Judah, Habakkuk determined that it was best to trust God's sovereign handling of the circumstances.

The prophet declared he would find his joy in the Lord (vs. 18). This reveals the depth of his faith in God. Habakkuk also asserted he would exult in the God of his salvation. Rather than look to earthly powers and idols for relief from foreign oppression, the prophet would focus his confidence and joy on his Redeemer and Lord. All earthly rulers and governments are subject to failure and defeat. Consequently, if the people of Judah had looked to powerful kings and armies for deliverance, they would have been deeply disappointed. Only God had the ability to rescue them from danger and watch over them in times of trouble. Unlike trusting in earthly powers, God's people would never be disappointed for placing their confidence in Him.

The prophet announced in verse 19 that the Lord and God of Israel was his source of strength. As long as Habakkuk depended on the all-powerful Ruler of the universe, God's spokesperson would not stumble, but remain sure-footed as a deer (see 2 Sam. 22:34; Ps. 18:33). Even if he were to walk on dangerous mountain slopes (metaphorically speaking), God would watch over him.

SUGGESTIONS TO TEACHERS

Habakkuk addressed some classical spiritual problems. How can God be just if He lets the unrighteous get away with their sins? How can God be loving if He lets the bullies of the world beat up on the little people? Habakkuk thought he could win an argument with God, only to find out that he had no idea how all-encompassing God's plan was for His people and the world.

1. STARK CONTRASTS. The sobering message of this week's lesson reminds us that the lifestyle and priorities of believers should contrast with that of unbelievers. Jesus taught His followers to be lights in the darkness and beacons of hope in a night of despair. There is evidence that our Lord's desire for His people is being realized. Here and there, believers are making a significant impact in race relations, in the political arena, and in ministering to the world's downtrodden.

2. TRAGIC COMPROMISES. Regrettably, there are also indications that believers are yielding to the world's pressures to conform. The values around us are seldom adopted all at once. The first stage may be reluctance to speak out against a practice believers know to be wrong. In time, though, the activity is treated as insignificant, and eventually believers may embrace it without reservation.

3. IMPORTANT CHOICES. By pressuring us to take the shape of the world around us, unbelievers keep us from being the positive moral influence Jesus intended. The Lord, however, calls us to live faithfully according to His values. We need to place our lifestyles and priorities under the focus of His Word and see what is reflected before the Lord and the world. If we are true to the teachings of Scripture, we will please our Lord and draw others to Him. But if we live in a way that contradicts the Word of God, then we need to change our lifestyles. Ultimately, those who rebel against the Lord will experience His judgment.

4. SOBERING CONCLUSIONS. Point out that even though Habakkuk's message was primarily directed to people in a specific category—the wicked Babylonians—he expected God's faithful remnant to heed the warnings. Indeed, messages of God's judgment still apply to us today. All of us must come to grips with any behavior that might offend the Lord.

FOR ADULTS

■ **TOPIC:** The Rewards of Patience

■ **QUESTIONS:** 1. What was the nature of the complaint Habakkuk voiced to God? 2. In what ways did the Babylonians demonstrate extreme arrogance? 3. How did Habakkuk describe the harsh judgment awaiting Judah? 4. What does it mean for believers to walk by faith in devastating circumstances? 5. How is it possible to rejoice in the Lord when life is filled with anguish?

■ ILLUSTRATIONS:

Faith Overrides Despair. Don and Joyce's teenage son had already been through two surgeries to relieve pressure on his brain caused by a tumor. He faced a third operation. While on a business trip, they met a woman whose brain tumor had disappeared just before she was scheduled for surgery. She told them, "If you and your son had faith, he would be healed too."

Don and Joyce and their son and two daughters struggled to understand God's ways, just like Habakkuk did when God told him that the pagan Babylonians were going to invade and destroy God's people. In Habakkuk's case, God revealed that he would judge the Babylonians and that the prophet should patiently live by faith. Therefore, Habakkuk rejoiced and found strength in the Lord.

But what about Don and Joyce and many other Christians who try to understand why God has brought suffering into their lives? They get no clear words from the Lord. They get a variety of messages from other people.

In the end, such people decide to patiently live by faith. Habakkuk believed the word of God. The prophet's country was not spared, but he found new resources of joy and strength in the Lord. That has been the experience of Christians who work through their difficulties in light of what they know to be true about the Lord.

Kidnapped, but Still Blessed. In their invasion of Judah and Jerusalem, the Babylonians would devastate every crop and destroy every animal. Rather than look to earthly powers for rescue, Habakkuk trusted God's handling of the circumstances.

In May 1984, while Benjamin Weir was a missionary in Beirut, Lebanon, Shiite Moslems kidnapped him. For 16 months, Weir was blindfolded most of the time and his hands were manacled. This is his report on one of the early days of captivity:

"I lifted my blindfold and began examining the room. What was here that could bring me close to the sustaining presence of God? I let my imagination have total freedom.

"Looking up, I examined an electric wire hanging from the ceiling. The bulb and socket had been removed so that it ended in an arc with three wires exposed. To me, those wires seemed like three fingers. I could see a hand and an arm reaching downward—like the Sistine Chapel in Rome, Michelangelo's fresco of God reaching out His hand and finger toward Adam. Here God was reaching toward me, reminding me, saying, 'You are alive. You are mine. I have made you and called you into being for a divine purpose.'"

By the end of the day, Weir was humming the hymn, "Count Your Blessings." Among other things, he counted his health, life, food, mattress, pillow, blanket, wife, family, hope, prayer, and the love of the Father, Son, and Spirit—33 items in all. As a result of reviewing these blessings, Weir found that his feelings of fear and helplessness had melted away.

Surefooted Confidence. In this week's lesson, we get an up close and personal look at a prophet named Habakkuk, who struggled to see how his nation would overcome its problems. Instead of endlessly questioning God, Habakkuk put his complete faith in the Lord—trust so full that the prophet felt he could climb any mountain with surefooted confidence (Hab. 3:19).

Experts say that the number-one cause of marital distress and division is money problems. For Huan and Takeko, that could have been the case—but it wasn't. Instead of letting their financial woes overtake an otherwise wonderful life together, the couple learned to commit their struggles to the Lord. Takeko had great faith in the promise found in James 5:16, "Confess your faults one to another, and pray one for another, that ye may be healed."

So, even though Huan and Takeko seemed to barely squeak by year after year, the couple not only stayed together, but they also grew closer to one another and to God each year. Financial pressures seemed to be a part of their life's burden. Yet, through regular prayer, lack of money was a burden that could be endured. While they were lower-income by human standards, they felt rich by God's standards. Today, Huan and Takeko have raised five godly children and are mentors and trusted confidants to an ever-growing circle of friends.

FOR YOUTH

■ **TOPIC:** Choice: To Trust or Not to Trust
■ **QUESTIONS:** 1. What about God's plan to judge His people specifically troubled Habakkuk? 2. What was the nature of the revelation God wanted Habakkuk to record? 3. What verbal imageries did Habakkuk use to describe God's care for him? 4. What is the biggest problem you ever faced and how did God bring you through it? 5. What are some specific ways you can encourage your saved peers to let God be the center of their joy?

■ **ILLUSTRATIONS:**
Keep on Believing. How many times do we feel torn and troubled like Habakkuk over the prevalence of evil in the world? When our faith is under fire, we would rather run than stand and fight.

Habakkuk's quarrel with God instructs us to continue believing, even when we feel weak and unqualified for the life of faith. No Christian ever feels up to the task. But that should not deter us in our quest to remain faithful to the Lord.

God does not expect us to get A's in all of life's courses. (Jesus, for example, worked with people who stumbled miserably but never quit.) God wants us to be honest with Him about our fears. He can give us the courage to move ahead, despite the obstacles and disappointments we may face along the way.

Start Listening. Several generations ago, Jed Harris was a successful producer of plays. He may be best known for staging the original production of Thornton Wilder's *Our Town*. In the midst of a season of endless days filled with the pressure of countless details, Harris started losing his hearing. He couldn't hear people standing next to him, and he was missing vital information.

Harris went to a noted hearing specialist who listened patiently to the producer's sad tale of diminished hearing. At the end of this narration, the audiologist pulled a fine gold pocket watch from his vest and held it to Harris's ear. "Can you hear the ticking of this watch?" the specialist asked. "Of course," Harris replied.

The audiologist walked to the door of his office and held up his watch. Harris concentrated and said, "Yes, I hear it quite plainly." The specialist stepped into the adjacent room and called out, "Can you hear anything now?" Jed Harris was astounded. "Yes, I still hear it!" The audiologist came back into the room and pocketed his watch. "I see this occasionally with busy, successful people. There's nothing wrong with your hearing, Mr. Harris. You've simply quit listening."

Sometimes in the hustle and bustle of life, we lose touch with God. He's still there, but our spiritual "hearing" and "vision" switch off. It's then that we, like Habakkuk, need to have a fresh, awe-inspiring encounter with Him that leads us to appeal to Him to act in our lives as He acted in biblical days.

Faith Knows God Has the Answers. A *Time* magazine reporter asked Russian-born novelist, Ayn Rand, "Ms. Rand, in a sentence, what's wrong with the modern world?"

The novelist replied, "Never before has the world been clamoring so desperately for answers to crucial problems, and never before has the world been so fanatically committed to the belief that no answers are possible. To paraphrase the Bible, the modern attitude is 'Father, forgive us for we know not what we are doing and please don't tell us.'"

Rand didn't get it in one sentence, but she did capture an important concept. When things fall apart, as they were doing in Habakkuk's day, we need to look to God for explanation, for refuge, and for strength. If we don't, we will be full of despair.

LESSON 6 — OCTOBER 12

AWAITING VINDICATION

BACKGROUND SCRIPTURE: Job 19; Psalm 57
DEVOTIONAL READING: 1 Chronicles 16:28-34

Key Verse: I know that my redeemer liveth, and that he shall stand at the latter day upon the earth. Job 19:25.

KING JAMES VERSION

JOB 19:1 Then Job answered and said, 2 How long will ye vex my soul, and break me in pieces with words? 3 These ten times have ye reproached me: ye are not ashamed that ye make yourselves strange to me. 4 And be it indeed that I have erred, mine error remaineth with myself. 5 If indeed ye will magnify yourselves against me, and plead against me my reproach: 6 Know now that God hath overthrown me, and hath compassed me with his net. 7 Behold, I cry out of wrong, but I am not heard: I cry aloud, but there is no judgment. . . .

23 Oh that my words were now written! oh that they were printed in a book! 24 That they were graven with an iron pen and lead in the rock for ever! 25 For I know that my redeemer liveth, and that he shall stand at the latter day upon the earth: 26 And though after my skin worms destroy this body, yet in my flesh shall I see God: 27 Whom I shall see for myself, and mine eyes shall behold, and not another; though my reins be consumed within me. 28 But ye should say, Why persecute we him, seeing the root of the matter is found in me? 29 Be ye afraid of the sword: for wrath bringeth the punishments of the sword, that ye may know there is a judgment.

NEW REVISED STANDARD VERSION

JOB 19:1 Then Job answered:
2 "How long will you torment me,
   and break me in pieces with words?
3 These ten times you have cast reproach upon me;
   are you not ashamed to wrong me?
4 And even if it is true that I have erred,
   my error remains with me.
5 If indeed you magnify yourselves against me,
   and make my humiliation an argument against me,
6 know then that God has put me in the wrong,
   and closed his net around me.
7 Even when I cry out, 'Violence!' I am not answered;
   I call aloud, but there is no justice. . . .

23 "O that my words were written down!
   O that they were inscribed in a book!
24 O that with an iron pen and with lead
   they were engraved on a rock forever!
25 For I know that my Redeemer lives,
   and that at the last he will stand upon the earth;
26 and after my skin has been thus destroyed,
   then in my flesh I shall see God,
27 whom I shall see on my side,
   and my eyes shall behold, and not another.
   My heart faints within me!
28 If you say, 'How we will persecute him!'
   and, 'The root of the matter is found in him';
29 be afraid of the sword,
   for wrath brings the punishment of the sword,
   so that you may know there is a judgment."

Home Bible Readings

Monday, October 6	Job 19:13-21	*Forsaken by Family and Friends*
Tuesday, October 7	Psalm 10:1-11	*Why Do You Stand Far Off?*
Wednesday, October 8	Isaiah 44:1-8	*Do Not Fear*
Thursday, October 9	Psalm 57:1-6	*God's Purpose for Me*
Friday, October 10	Psalm 57:7-11	*My Heart Is Steadfast*
Saturday, October 11	1 Chronicles 16:28-34	*Love That Endures Forever*
Sunday, October 12	Job 19:1-7, 23-29	*My Redeemer Lives!*

Background

We learn from Scripture that Job was a spiritually mature person (Job 1:1, 8; 2:3). He was also the father of many children (1:2; 42:13) and the owner of many herds (1:3; 42:12). Scripture portrays Job as a wealthy and influential man (1:3), a priest to his family (vs. 5), and a loving, wise husband (2:9). He was both a person of prominence in community affairs (29:7-11) and someone known for his benevolence (29:12-17; 31:32). In addition, Job was a wise leader (29:21-24) and a farmer (31:38-40).

Concerning when Job was written, there is no conclusive evidence that has been found. Some have suggested an early date because of the fact that the book makes no mention of the patriarchs, the 12 tribes of Israel, or Moses. This leads some to think that the book originated in the time before Moses (about 1566–1446 B.C.). If so, then Job is the oldest book of the Bible. As such, it offers us insight into people's conceptions of God before they possessed written revelation. Some Bible scholars propose much later dates for the writing of Job. Some say it was penned during the reign of Solomon (970–930 B.C.), while others are far more general, saying it was composed sometime between the lives of Moses and Ezra. While the numerous details in Job indicate that the events occurred during the patriarchal era, the literary evidence suggests that the book was produced sometime later during an era when wisdom flourished.

After the prologue to Job (chaps. 1—2), chapter 3 records Job's complaints about his anguishing circumstance. This is followed by a series of dialogues he had with his friends, which are recorded in chapters 4 through 27. Job's three counselors were likely princes and sages in each of their own areas. Eliphaz's name was derived from an Arabic word meaning "God is the victor." He was from Teman, an Edomite city south of Canaan that was known to be a center for philosophical discussions. Teman is the only hometown of the three comforters that can be definitively located today. The name Bildad came from a Hebrew phrase meaning "Baal is Lord." Bildad may have been a descendant of Shuah, Abraham's youngest son by his wife Keturah. His tribe of Shuhites probably made their home somewhere east of Canaan, but the precise location of their settlement is unknown (Gen. 25:2, 6). Zophar is translated as "little bird." His tribe was from Naamah, perhaps a small town in Arabia.

NOTES ON THE PRINTED TEXT

Chapter 19 features Job's reply to Bildad's second speech (vs. 1). Prior to this point in Job's conversations with his friends, he was able to scoff at or show some indifference toward their admonitions. But after Bildad's cruel speech, Job had apparently reached his limit. In anguish, Job asked how long he had to endure being tortured by Bildad's reproach and pulverized by his condemnation (vs. 2).

Job claimed that his counselors had "reproached" (Job 19:3) him "ten times" with no cause. The Hebrew verb translated "reproached" implies that Job felt insulted and humiliated by the shameless verbal attacks he received from his advisers. By saying "ten times," Job probably was not referring to the actual number of incidents in which his friends had rebuked him. More likely, he was indicating his feeling that they had turned against him completely (see Gen. 31:7, 41; Num. 14:22; 1 Sam. 1:8). While desiring some sort of pity from his peers, Job had received, instead, their unrelenting harassment and condemnation.

What we see portrayed throughout Job is how damaging words can be in a counseling context. This is especially true in regard to people who are suffering. Contrary to Satan when he brought the devastation recorded in chapters 1 and 2, Job's advisers did not lift a finger against him. But their words caused him great pain—perhaps greater mental and emotional anguish than that produced by all else that had happened to Job. All along, he maintained his innocence, despite the fact that his friends alleged he had morally strayed from the path of virtue and integrity (19:4). Even if he had erred in some minor way, Job maintained that the guilt of any unintentional missteps rested with him. In short, he was telling his counselors to mind their own business.

Job accused his advisers of exalting themselves at his expense. In verse 5, the Hebrew verb rendered "magnify" indicates that the three friends clung to an insolent and lofty attitude. Even worse, they seized on the disgrace caused by Job's physical and emotional suffering to insist that he was guilty of blatantly sinning against God. Job countered that God, by allowing Job to be afflicted without a cause, had mistreated him. Job referred to part of a hunter's equipment when he claimed that God had encircled and ensnared Job like an animal in a "net" (vs. 6).

As Job continued his response to Bildad, Job expressed his feelings in two ways. First, he felt abandoned by God (vs. 7). Second, Job felt as though God was opposed to him and attacking him with an army (vss. 8-12). The Hebrew noun translated "wrong" (vs. 7) indicates that an extreme violation of justice had occurred. Even though Job might shout for help, he received no answer from God. Of course, Job's feeling of isolation is understandable. He knew he had lived in a virtuous manner, and yet he had been struck down. Previously, God had been Job's friend and his source of security. But now God seemed to be Job's enemy, for God exposed Job to all sorts of danger. Even though he had boldly cried out for relief from his suffering, God remained silent.

Perhaps in desperation Job pleaded with his counselors to take "pity" (vs. 21) on him. He hoped that his description of being unjustly persecuted by God would finally soften the calloused hearts of the three advisers. Of course, this was not the first time Job had pleaded for them to be merciful. He had appealed for their devotion in an earlier speech (see 6:14). What Job wanted was their friendship and compassion. What he was getting instead was their disapproval and condemnation. So Job complained that they were harassing him even as God was (vs. 22). In Job's mind, his counselors were trying to take on the role of God as judge. This can especially be seen in Eliphaz's earlier assumption that he was speaking for the Lord: "Are the consolations of God [referring to the words of Job's advisers] small with thee? is there any secret thing with thee?" (15:11).

Despite their sincere intentions, the admonishment offered by Job's peers failed miserably. Rather than consoling Job or prompting him to seek God's mercy, their words were annoying and destructive. In a metaphorical sense, the derisive comments voiced by Job's advisers were devouring his soul. So Job asked whether they would ever be satiated with his "flesh" (19:22). He was using a Semitic expression in which consuming someone's flesh referred to slander. With death an apparent certainty, Job cried out for the means to make a permanent record of his claim to be innocent. As he yearned for an enduring way to defend his integrity, Job expressed his desire to write his words in a "book" (vs. 23), chisel them in "lead" (vs. 24), or engrave them in rock. That way, those who came after Job would know and concur with his case, and perhaps he would be vindicated, even if it was long after he was gone.

After many sorrowful expressions of despair, Job uttered perhaps the greatest words of hope recorded in his book. In his deepest anguish, when all his loved ones had deserted him, Job expressed faith in one last hope—an even greater one than having his claim of innocence chiseled on a rock. He placed his confident expectation in a "redeemer" (vs. 25), in which the underlying Hebrew verb refers to a protector and vindicator. (For background information, see Lev. 25:25-55 and the comments in lesson 3 on the kinsman-redeemer.) Throughout the Hebrew Scriptures, God is often seen as the Defender of the oppressed and the Savior of the exploited (see Ps. 103:2-4; Prov. 23:10-11). Job was convinced that even though he faced eventual death, his divine Advocate would take His stand on the earth, like a witness in a courtroom, to acquit Job of guilt, affirm his integrity, and restore his honor.

Moreover, Job asserted that even after his lifeless body had decayed in the grave, he somehow would be raised from the dead and meet God (Job 19:26; see 14:10-14). Indeed, Job would personally see his Defender with his own "eyes" (19:27). Bible scholars think that the idea of an advocate—namely, someone to champion one's case before God—was prevalent in Job's day. Despite his present anguish, he was overcome with the thought of God vindicating him in the afterlife. Even though Job did not spell out any details of his longed-for resurrection, he clearly believed it would happen because of God's intervention.

At times, the Hebrew verb translated "redeemer" (vs. 25) referred to a "blood avenger," that is, a member of a victim's family who had the responsibility to obtain justice from the person who killed his relative. The objective of the vindicator, as it would have been in Job's case, was to obtain justice, not retribution. Job clearly saw himself as the target of unwarranted accusations. Figuratively speaking, he had been verbally murdered, and he was calling for an advocate to represent him in the court of justice. Later, Job would learn that it was God who was his Redeemer, Friend, and Provider. At this point in Job's life, having God reveal Himself as Job's vindicator was his heart's intense desire.

At the end of Job's response to Bildad, Job directed his comments to his advisers. He realized that even after his declaration of eventually being vindicated by a Redeemer, Job's peers were still mired in their erroneous views. So he admonished them not to pursue him in a misguided attempt to convince him of presumed sin. After all, they were mistaken to conclude that his sufferings were due to transgression in his life (vs. 28). He also warned his three friends that since they had misjudged him, God would punish them more severely for their iniquity (for example, by the edge of the "sword"; vs. 29). Here we see Job resolutely maintaining that he was innocent of any wrongdoing. His desire for his counselors to be punished shows that he still had a glimmer of hope that there could be some measure of justice in the world.

SUGGESTIONS TO TEACHERS

In some respects the Book of Job is a long answer to a pointed question: if God is the sovereign Lord of the universe, why does He allow suffering to come to the godly and good fortune to the wicked? For Job, thinking about this question moved him to consider the nature of God. In the face of Job's multiple calamities, he was forced to examine the foundations of his faith and to scrutinize his concept of the Lord.

1. KNOWING GOD. Job remained loyal to God in blessings as well as in turmoil. Job's faithfulness is an example for all ages. But what made Job's faith so great? The answer: its object. Job knew God. Job had invested himself in a relationship with God. And Job's faith rested squarely on who God had revealed Himself to be.

2. REMAINING RESOLUTE. Pain could rock Job's world, but it could not destroy his faith. So convinced was Job that God was worthy of His servant's trust that Job would not change his mind. Job remained resolute in his devotion to God even when his body was covered with disgusting, festering boils; even when his wife had lost her own faith; even when Job's friends accused him of sin; and even though God was silent.

3. CHOOSING THE RIGHT OPTION. Our suffering brings each of us to a unique crossroads in our faith. At these crucial times, we have two clear, distinct options. We can choose to remain steadfast in our commitment to God and believe what Scripture says, or we can decide to modify or abandon our trust in God, according to our circumstances and the feelings we have at that moment. This week's lesson encourages us to be loyal to God.

4. STANDING FIRM. As Jesus' followers, we must encourage our hearts by remembering that our suffering is never in vain. The Creator will redeem every tear and every sigh. For now, though, we are to be doing what He has given us to do: to stand firm in our faith, even as we suffer, and to minister with compassion to those who need comfort in their time of sorrow.

For Adults

■ **Topic:** Confident of Redemption
■ **Questions:** 1. Why did Job feel tormented by his three friends? 2. Why did Job believe he was innocent of any wrongdoing? 3. Why did Job conclude that God had abandoned him? 4. What promises from Scripture reassure you of God's unfailing love for you? 5. How can knowing that God is your Redeemer encourage you in your daily life?

■ **Illustrations:**

Holding Firm in Suffering. Anna was blind from birth. Everything she knew and accomplished in life she owed to her parents' sacrifice and dedication. When her mother fell ill, Anna was distraught. She had never seen her mother. She knew only her voice and touch.

For months Anna sat with her mother in a nursing home, holding her hands and talking to her. But her mother had lost her speech and could not respond. Nevertheless, Anna held on firmly every day, speaking words of comfort and hope.

In times of suffering, we hold on to each other and especially to God. Even when God does not seem to reply to our cries, we follow the example of Job by continuing to trust in our Redeemer. Faith drives us to prayer and worship every day. In the darkness, we keep pursuing the light by faith. We claim our Savior's promise that nothing can separate us from His love (see Rom. 8:31-39).

A Distinctive Opportunity. A few years ago, Drew had a unique spiritual insight while meditating upon the Scriptures that tell about Job's suffering. Though Drew's own life was not in any particular upheaval or tumult, he found himself unusually empathizing with Job's desire not to curse God in the course of the misfortune.

The insight surrounded the nature of our existence in this life and the existence that a believer will enjoy in the life to come. As result of his Bible study and prayer, Drew came to see the unique opportunity we have in this life of our mortal flesh. In the life to come, we know that there will be no more suffering, sickness, sorrow, and death. No bad memories will plague us, nor will any temptations succeed against us. Life will be bliss in our offering of praise to God.

However, this present life is another matter. Drew realized that we have a distinctive opportunity to give sacrifices of thanks and obedience to God in this life that we will never again have the chance to give in the life to come. It is only in this life we can choose to love and worship God in the midst of our sufferings and temptations. It is only now that we can offer our Creator the supreme sacrifice of adoration by saying "Yes" when He asks, "Do you truly love me more than these?" (John 21:15).

Waiting Patiently. On a sunny autumn day, Mia remembers saying to her husband, Cyrus, "I'm so glad this school year won't begin with you out of work again. Those six months of unemployment were hard ones." But after the words rolled off Mia's tongue, her conscience was pricked. She thought, *It could happen again, you know.*

Two months later an episode of unemployment reoccurred. Once again, the couple started the school year a bit off kilter. But this period of unemployment lasted longer. The "reserves" economists had recommended families set aside for job loss would have been exhausted, that is, if Cyrus and Mia hadn't listened to the Spirit's promptings to better prepare themselves in "times of plenty" for "times of loss."

Even now, life has not been as comfortable for this couple as it used to be. But the two are making it, day by day. Cyrus' second, "statistically improbable" job loss has taught them once more to wait patiently. While they do so, they thank their Redeemer for His many blessings, and also for the "trouble" of unemployment.

As the couple looks back, they can see the Lord's provision during Cyrus' first job loss. And as they look forward, they know God will continue to take care of them, just as He did Job in his time of anguish. Waiting is not always easy, but trusting in God is always right.

FOR YOUTH

■ **TOPIC:** Hope Faces Misery
■ **QUESTIONS:** 1. On what basis did Job's three friends censure him? 2. How had the words of Job's advisers left him feeling crushed? 3. Why did Job want to plead his case before God? 4. How does God respond to His children when they turn to Him for help? 5. When your family members and friends are suffering, how can you encourage them in their faith in God?

■ **ILLUSTRATIONS:**

Holding Fast in Tough Times. One of the basic therapies for strengthening hand, wrist, and arm muscles is squeezing a rubber ball tightly several times a day. This exercise is prescribed after injuries or surgeries—incidents and events we would prefer to avoid. In cases like these, holding fast to a rubber ball is a discipline that produces results. At first we feel the tension and pain, but gradually our muscles respond and we are able to function normally.

God sometimes takes us through tough times to strengthen our spiritual muscles (so to speak). He knows how flabby we get when we neglect our worship and obedience to His good and perfect will. But when He gets our attention, we respond with therapies that give us new love and zeal for Him.

Job's account tells us that it is possible to be faithful to God, even when hard times come. We surmount our difficulties by the Spirit's indwelling power and presence.

Serving God with One Hand. Cassandra was a high school senior and had won many music awards as a pianist. A major university had offered her a full scholarship to study piano in its school of music. During the summer following her graduation from high school, Cassandra was involved in an automobile accident. One of her hands was so badly mangled that it had to be removed.

Cassandra's Sunday school teacher dreaded visiting her in the hospital. How would Cassandra respond to this tragedy? Would she be bitter? To the teacher's surprise, Cassandra met her with a smile. Cassandra's eyes sparkled as she told her Sunday school teacher that God knew her future, and apparently it was not His plan for her to perform. But Cassandra could teach. She would train other young people to play the piano. Just as Job did not sin with his lips because of his great loss, so Cassandra determined to glorify God with her life regardless of what had happened to her.

The Gold Ring. Cory was a college freshman. Through his high school years, he was deeply involved in the youth group in his church. His last two summers before college, he had worked in Christian camps for young children. Because of his outgoing personality, he made friends quickly in college.

One night, following a football game, three fellow students asked Cory to go with them for a late-night snack. When they stopped at a roadside café, one of the boys retrieved a carton of beer from the trunk of the car. When Cory refused to accept a can, the other boys began to pressure him. "Just one drink! What will it hurt? So you've never tried it—you need to know what it's like!"

Cory wanted very much to be accepted. He was about to weaken when he felt the plain gold ring on the little finger of his right hand. His mother had given it to him the day he left home. His mother said, "Cory, when you are tempted to do something wrong, feel this ring. It will remind you that I am praying for you daily." Cory's resolve was strengthened and he was able to resist the temptation. Because of Job's strong faith in God, he too was able to resist the "easy way out" (as the saying goes) of his terrible dilemma.

LESSON 7 — OCTOBER 19

LONGING FOR JUSTICE

BACKGROUND SCRIPTURE: Job 5; 24; Psalm 55:12-23
DEVOTIONAL READING: Jeremiah 14:14-22

Key Verse: As for me, I will call upon God;
and the LORD shall save me. Psalm 55:16.

KING JAMES VERSION

JOB 24:1 Why, seeing times are not hidden from the Almighty, do they that know him not see his days? . . . 9 They pluck the fatherless from the breast, and take a pledge of the poor. 10 They cause him to go naked without clothing, and they take away the sheaf from the hungry; 11 Which make oil within their walls, and tread their winepresses, and suffer thirst. 12 Men groan from out of the city, and the soul of the wounded crieth out: yet God layeth not folly to them. . . .

19 Drought and heat consume the snow waters: so doth the grave those which have sinned. 20 The womb shall forget him; the worm shall feed sweetly on him; he shall be no more remembered; and wickedness shall be broken as a tree. 21 He evil entreateth the barren that beareth not: and doeth not good to the widow. 22 He draweth also the mighty with his power: he riseth up, and no man is sure of life. 23 Though it be given him to be in safety, whereon he resteth; yet his eyes are upon their ways. 24 They are exalted for a little while, but are gone and brought low; they are taken out of the way as all other, and cut off as the tops of the ears of corn.
25 And if it be not so now, who will make me a liar, and make my speech nothing worth?

NEW REVISED STANDARD VERSION

JOB 24:1 "Why are times not kept by the Almighty,
and why do those who know him never see his days? . . .
9 "There are those who snatch the orphan child from the breast,
and take as a pledge the infant of the poor.
10 They go about naked, without clothing;
though hungry, they carry the sheaves;
11 between their terraces they press out oil;
they tread the wine presses, but suffer thirst.
12 From the city the dying groan,
and the throat of the wounded cries for help;
yet God pays no attention to their prayer. . . .
19 Drought and heat snatch away the snow waters;
so does Sheol those who have sinned.
20 The womb forgets them;
the worm finds them sweet;
they are no longer remembered;
so wickedness is broken like a tree.
21 "They harm the childless woman,
and do no good to the widow.
22 Yet God prolongs the life of the mighty by his power;
they rise up when they despair of life.
23 He gives them security, and they are supported;
his eyes are upon their ways.
24 They are exalted a little while, and then are gone;
they wither and fade like the mallow;
they are cut off like the heads of grain.
25 If it is not so, who will prove me a liar,
and show that there is nothing in what I say?"

Home Bible Readings

Monday, October 13	Job 14:7-13	*Set a Time to Remember Me*
Tuesday, October 14	Job 14:14-22	*You Destroy the Hope of Mortals*
Wednesday, October 15	Jeremiah 15:10-18	*Why Is My Pain Unending?*
Thursday, October 16	Jeremiah 14:14-22	*Our Hope Is in God*
Friday, October 17	Psalm 55:1-8	*Shelter from the Storm*
Saturday, October 18	Psalm 55:12-23	*I Call upon God*
Sunday, October 19	Job 24:1, 9-12, 19-25	*The Poor and the Mighty*

Background

The question of Job's authorship has been debated for centuries, and no one has come up with evidence for his or her view that satisfies everyone. The main reason for this uncertainty is that the book neglects to identify its author. In fact, the complexity of the language makes it difficult even to determine a specific period of time within which the discourse was written. Bible critics tend to view Job as a work of fiction. Some conjecture an Israelite took a foreign epic and made it stylistically palatable for a Hebrew audience. Others suggest the book was stitched together by a number of people over an extended period of time.

In contrast to such critical theories, one long-held view maintains that Job was indeed a historical person and that he wrote the book himself sometime after his ordeal. If this is the case, the account of an encounter between God and Satan in the prologue of the book could have come to Job only by divine revelation. Another traditional view holds that, while Job was a historical person, someone else wrote his account. Some think the writer personally knew Job and made keen observations and carefully recorded the poetic speeches. Others suggest the writer lived some years after Job and put his account together in poetic form based on what he knew about the historical person. Whatever view is taken, it is evident that the author was both divinely inspired and possessed literary genius.

Notes on the Printed Text

As was noted in lesson 6, a series of three speeches are recorded between Job and his three counselors. The first round occurs in chapters 4 through 14; the second round takes place in chapters 15 through 21; and the third round is found in chapters 22 through 27. In the final cycle of speeches, Eliphaz and Bildad spoke, with Job responding to each of them. Zophar did not speak in this last round, and no explanation is given for why he remained silent. By now in the book, Eliphaz seems to have lost his patience with Job, and he blamed Job's woes on his great and endless wickedness (as Eliphaz saw it). Yet Eliphaz also said that all Job had to do to regain peace and prosperity was to submit to God's will (chap. 22).

Job responded by saying he wanted to talk to God directly, even though it seemed to Job that God was nowhere to be found. Job felt both confident and terrified, trusting that he could withstand God's judgment, and yet knowing God could do as He pleased (chap. 23). Next, Job probed more deeply God's providence over earthly matters. The burning issue for Job was God's presumed indifference in the prevalence of misdeeds and injustices in the world. Job openly asked why it appeared as if the "Almighty" (24:1) did not appoint a time of judgment for the wicked, and why the godly had to wait in vain for a day of reckoning to occur. "Almighty" renders the Hebrew term *Shaddai*, which appears 31 times in the book. While scholars debate the exact origin and precise meaning of the word, its use in Scripture reminds us that God is supremely powerful. His invincibility encourages believers to serve Him faithfully and with integrity (see Gen. 17:1).

Job 24:2-12 records a series of injustices that occurred in Bible times. For instance, verse 2 notes how the evildoers "remove the landmarks," which were used to indicate the precincts of an owner's property. God regarded those who illegally changed these longstanding boundary stones as thieves who stole acreage and livestock from their neighbors to enlarge their own estate (see Deut. 19:14; 27:17; Prov. 22:28; 23:10). Job 24:3 highlights a circumstance in which the wicked ruthlessly exploited orphans and widows by seizing what little they had (for example, a donkey or an ox) until they paid their debts. In the ancient Near East, orphans and widows were at an extreme disadvantage, for they had no extended family members to care for them. Also, many in society viewed widowhood with reproach.

Tragically, a widow without legal protection was often vulnerable to neglect or exploitation. Moreover, it was far too common for greedy and unscrupulous agents to defraud a destitute widow and her children of whatever property they owned. There were three primary ways a widow could provide for the financial needs of herself and her children. First, she could return to her parents' house; second, she could remarry, especially if she was young or wealthy; and third, she could remain unmarried and obtain some kind of employment. The last prospect was rather bleak, for it was difficult in the patriarchal era for a widow to find suitable work that would meet the economic needs of herself and her family.

Verse 4 reveals that the impoverished were forced to hide themselves to escape further oppression. These displaced groups of people were like "wild" (vs. 5) donkeys who roamed through a barren "desert" in search of "food" to feed their starving "children." At times, the vulnerable of society were driven to eke out a living by gleaning through the fields and vineyards of the wicked rich (vs. 6). Because the poor were also homeless, they spent their nights without clothing to provide them with warmth and protection from the "cold" (vs. 7). "Showers of the mountains" (vs. 8) soaked the dispossessed of society, and they huddled in the cracks of rocks as makeshift shelters.

Evildoers brazenly confiscated nursing babies from their penniless mothers. In turn, these infants were sold to liquidate the mothers' debt (vs. 9). The wicked rich coerced society's outcasts to wander "naked" (vs. 10), and wealthy landowners seized the bundles of grain their day laborers harvested, leaving them to starve. Even though the homeless pressed out olive oil among the terraced grove of trees, they did not benefit from their hard labor. Others endured "thirst" (vs. 11) while expending lots of energy to crush out the juice from grapes in wine vats. In the cities, the pleas of the dying and the cries of the "wounded" (vs. 12) for help could be heard. Yet, despite their affliction, it seemed as if God ignored the petitions of the downtrodden and did not charge anyone with abusing them.

In Ecclesiastes 4:1-3, Solomon provided a somber assessment of the various kinds of oppression that repeatedly occurred on earth. Included were acts of tyranny and injustice committed throughout human history. The victims of such cruelty lamented over their plight, but there seemed to be no one to comfort them. Because their oppressors wielded tremendous power, potential deliverers were unable or unwilling to rescue the victims of maltreatment (vs. 1). It was distressing enough that life could seem vexing. But even more tragic was the circumstance when one group of individuals abused another group.

Solomon considered people who had died long ago, noting that they seemed better off than those who were still alive. In this way of thinking, the deceased escaped the misfortune of being oppressed. To Solomon, it was ironic that the dead experienced a greater degree of happiness than the living (vs. 2). Yet an even greater paradox was the perceived advantage of never having been born (see 6:3). The reason is that they had not witnessed and experienced the "evil" (4:3) that people committed on earth. "Evil" renders a Hebrew adjective denoting actions that are vicious, injurious, or malignant in character.

Job 24:13-17 provides a more personalized description of the evildoers who preyed on the vulnerable in ancient times. For example, they openly defied the light-filled truth of God's Word. They neither understood its teaching nor followed the direction it instructed the upright to heed (vs. 13). At the crack of dawn, murderers awoke to kill the indigent, and they used the cover of darkness to steal from the impoverished (vs. 14). Similarly, adulterers waited for twilight to arrive to commit sexual sin without being seen (vs. 15). Likewise, thieves avoided the light of day, instead choosing the camouflage of the night to vandalize "houses" (vs. 16). Indeed, they were more at home in the darkness than in the light of day (vs. 17).

Some think that Job could not have spoken what appears in verses 18-24, since the monologue so closely agrees with what his advisers previously declared. Nonetheless, it is legitimate to regard this portion of chapter 24 as part of Job's petition for God to vindicate the righteous and judge the wicked. For instance, Job observed that evildoers were as insignificant as scum carried away by river currents. Their "vineyards" (vs. 18) were under God's curse so that neither they nor others would dare enter their property.

Those who transgressed God and incurred His wrath were as transient as melted snow waters" (vs. 19) dissolved by "drought and heat." *Sheol* is the Hebrew noun rendered "grave" and refers to the abode of the dead. In Job's day, it was believed to be a dismal place where the deceased were cut off from God and people alive on earth. Verse 20 declares that the wombs of the mothers who bore the unrighteous abandoned all memory of them. Even worse, maggots devoured their rotting corpses, and their wrongdoing was destroyed like a "tree" overturned by a windstorm.

Verse 21 provides the justification for the miserable end awaiting the wicked (as poetically described in verses 18-20). These evildoers targeted women who were barren and childless and abused widows (vs. 21). As noted earlier, both groups were among the most defenseless members of society. Verse 22 declares that God would make the wicked pay for their crimes. Like a mighty warrior, He would sweep them away. Even though they might rise up for a season, their days were numbered. Admittedly, God might permit some wealthy criminals to enjoy a false sense of security for a while (vs. 23), but He constantly scrutinized whatever they did. Though the unrighteous might prosper, suddenly they would be disgraced. They would waste away like discarded weeds and be cut down like "ears of corn" (vs. 24). Job ended his monologue by asking his friends whether they could deny the validity of his assertions and demonstrate that what he declared was worthless (vs. 25). The presumption is that he spoke the truth.

SUGGESTIONS TO TEACHERS

Job could not understand why disasters had come into his life (see Job 24:1). He had acknowledged God in his daily circumstance and worshiped Him in sincerity and truth. Job had also been faithful in prayer and modeled a righteous life before his family and those in his community. Now, the strong spiritual foundation Job always had taken for granted was crumbling.

1. LONGING FOR ANSWERS. The God who had been so real to Job seemed to be far away and indifferent to human suffering (see vss. 2-17). The words of Job's friends were inadequate, and Job's own reasoning gave him no answers. He then determined to search for God, whom he believed could help him unravel the mystery of what was happening in his life.

2. TALKING OPENLY WITH GOD. Job's relationship with God enables us to see how responsive God is to our heartfelt concerns. In Job's affliction, he had questions, he was confused, and he felt ignored by God. We, too, can dialogue honestly with God. He's not ambivalent; He's not shocked at our emotions; and He's not waiting to punish us. Instead, He wants us to tell Him what's on our hearts and minds.

3. BEING HONEST WITH GOD. Many Christians have been trained to "be nice" in relationships, especially in their relationship with God. That means saying "nice" prayers as well. But the account of Job, including his candid statements about the presence of injustice in the world (see vss. 2-17), indicates that God likely prefers honesty to etiquette. Therefore, in prayer, we might need to become willing to lay down our dainty spoons of nice prayer and pick up a dirty shovel of gut-level honesty. Perhaps the only thing we have to lose is our dignity. However, living authentically with God is more than worth a bit of humiliation.

4. AFFIRMING GOD'S JUSTICE. Through all of the darkness and confusion of his despair, Job affirmed that one day God would judge the wicked and vindicate the righteous (see vss. 18-24). This is a wonderful truth that enables believers to weather life's worst storms and even face death. Our Lord remains with us during the most devastating crises we face in life and enables us to affirm our commitment to Him.

For Adults

■ **Topic:** Defiant Faithfulness

■ **Questions:** 1. Why did Job at first assume that God was indifferent to the crimes of the wicked? 2. Why were the poor without food or clothing? 3. What was the basis for Job's belief that God would one day bring an end to the wicked? 4. How can believers affirm that only God has answers to the complex questions of life? 5. How can believers be certain that they are walking in God's ways?

■ **Illustrations:**

Seeking God in Times of Trial. An elderly man—not a believer—suffered a heart attack after a personal disaster. His Christian daughter appealed to him to repent. Could he not see God's hand in what had happened? Absolutely not, the man said. It was just bad luck.

Some people reach the point in their lives where God no longer figures in their thinking. How important it is for Christians to show by example that God is the only one who really counts. When we seek Him in times of trial, we set a powerful example for others to follow.

Admittedly, some of us may be hampered by the fear of God becoming angry with us for telling Him about negative emotions or thoughts we harbor. In Job's time of trial, he felt free to tell God what was on his heart (see Job 24:1). We can also communicate openly with God in our distress, yet at the same time show respect for Him.

God Is Not Surprised. Rebekah had a burden she needed to share. Because of her prominence in the Christian community, she didn't feel comfortable telling her story to a believer she knew well. Unaware of this, Molly accepted Rebekah's invitation to tea.

While Molly sat in Rebekah's living room, Molly sensed something was wrong. She thought perhaps it was her own awkwardness, so she dismissed it. She had just picked up her teacup when Rebekah abruptly stated, "I invited you here because I thought you might be able to listen—and not judge me." Down went the teacup and up went Molly's ears.

Quite unexpectedly, Rebekah unloaded the grief she had been carrying. Molly reminded Rebekah that God, whom Molly had told so many people would forgive them, would also forgive Rebekah. Molly assured Rebekah that God still loved her, mistakes and all.

Rebekah let out a sigh and a little laugh. She admitted that because she couldn't forgive herself, she thought God couldn't do so either. Soon after, Rebekah prayed in a candid way, asking for forgiveness—both of her initial sin and of her pride of covering it up. Afterward, the visit between Molly and Rebekah took on a lighter tone, as they enjoyed cookies and laughter.

As Job 24:1 reveals, almighty God is not put off by our struggles and candid admissions to Him. Our questions, cares, frustrations, and mistakes—as well as our joys—have a place in prayer. The Lord understands it all, and has redeemed us anyway. Nothing surprises Him.

Justice Will Prevail. Perhaps the most famous statement made that relates to humankind's first visit to the moon came from the mouth of Astronaut Neil Armstrong. After stepping from his lunar module to stand on the surface of the moon, his first words were: "One small step for man; one giant leap for mankind."

Extended periods of trouble and crisis are extremely oppressive. The darkness of despair seems to close in, and the steps we take are extremely small. Often it seems that we take one step forward and three backwards.

Job was having this kind of experience until, gradually, God allowed him to see beyond and above his present dilemma. We can imagine Job shouting, "Justice will prevail!" A new day dawns for us when, in the midst of our darkness, God breaks through with His eternal truth.

FOR YOUTH

■ **TOPIC:** Will Justice Reign?
■ **QUESTIONS:** 1. Why did Job long for God to bring the wicked to justice? 2. How did evildoers treat orphans and infants? 3. What future did Job declare awaited the unrighteous? 4. How might God use difficult experiences in the lives of believers to clarify their understanding of His will for them? 5. How does Job's experience demonstrate that God is receptive to the heartfelt prayers of believers?

■ **ILLUSTRATIONS:**
Stand by Me. Community tragedies, especially when they involve children and youth, invariably draw people closer together. Outpourings of love and support for the suffering play a major role in personal and community recovery. Schools and businesses employ grief counselors.

When tragedies happen, we are forced to reflect on our faith, just as Job did (see Job 24:1). The big question always seems to be "Why?" We must avoid glib answers and admit limited knowledge. At the same time, we can confess our faith and hope in the Savior. As we live for Him, others might be drawn to us.

Like Job, we must also develop strong disciplines of obedience to God and love for His Word. We can only be an effective witness for Jesus in times of tragedy if we have a treasure of Scripture in our hearts (see Ps. 119:11).

Speaking Freely and Respectfully. At one point in Job's life, it seemed as if he had lost everything. He felt free to pray to God candidly. Yet Job also showed respect to the Lord by referring to Him as the "Almighty" (Job 24:1).

When Owen was a young boy, his father, Logan, was an intimidating man of few words. Owen knew better than to ever challenge or talk back to his father, as the sting of his father's backhand seemed to still linger in Owen's memory.

Now that Owen and his wife, Zoe, had boys of their own, it would be a different situation for their boys than what Owen had known growing up. He had decided that a child is stunted in his or her development if he or she is not allowed to speak freely—at least at certain times.

In Owen's college courses, he had learned the importance of communication and critical-thinking skills. He knew that unless people are allowed to freely analyze and make assessments about life, they might never have confidence in their own ability to make decisions. Owen was determined to raise his sons with the ability to be critical thinkers, but also to be respectful, disciplined young men.

When Owen's sons were young adults, both of them thanked their father for his willingness to be open with them. They were grateful that on many occasions he had given them the freedom to talk with him without the fear of intimidation or punishment.

Complaining to God. Along with Job, David in his psalms is another wonderful example in Scripture of someone speaking freely with God. Here are some examples: "Why standest thou afar off, O LORD? why hidest thou thyself in times of trouble?" (Ps. 10:1). "How long wilt thou forget me, O LORD? for ever? . . . How long shall I take counsel in my soul, having sorrow in my heart daily?" (13:1-2). "Hear my voice, O God, in my prayer" (64:1).

David's love relationship with God gave Israel's ruler confidence to approach the Lord with his concerns. We, too, can approach God with our questions, concerns, frustrations, and fears. The Father welcomes His spiritual children before His "throne of grace" (Heb. 4:16), that they might find "mercy" and "grace to help" in their "time of need."

LESSON 8 — OCTOBER 26

RECEIVING GOD'S BLESSING

BACKGROUND SCRIPTURE: Job 42; Psalm 86
DEVOTIONAL READING: Ephesians 1:11-19

Key Verse: I know that thou canst do every thing, and that no thought can be withholden from thee. Job 42:2.

KING JAMES VERSION

JOB 42:1 Then Job answered the LORD, and said, 2 I know that thou canst do every thing, and that no thought can be withholden from thee. 3 Who is he that hideth counsel without knowledge? therefore have I uttered that I understood not; things too wonderful for me, which I knew not. 4 Hear, I beseech thee, and I will speak: I will demand of thee, and declare thou unto me. 5 I have heard of thee by the hearing of the ear: but now mine eye seeth thee. 6 Wherefore I abhor myself, and repent in dust and ashes.

7 And it was so, that after the LORD had spoken these words unto Job, the LORD said to Eliphaz the Temanite, My wrath is kindled against thee, and against thy two friends: for ye have not spoken of me the thing that is right, as my servant Job hath. 8 Therefore take unto you now seven bullocks and seven rams, and go to my servant Job, and offer up for yourselves a burnt offering; and my servant Job shall pray for you: for him will I accept: lest I deal with you after your folly, in that ye have not spoken of me the thing which is right, like my servant Job. 9 So Eliphaz the Temanite and Bildad the Shuhite and Zophar the Naamathite went, and did according as the LORD commanded them: the LORD also accepted Job.

10 And the LORD turned the captivity of Job, when he prayed for his friends: also the LORD gave Job twice as much as he had before.

NEW REVISED STANDARD VERSION

JOB 42:1 Then Job answered the LORD:
2 "I know that you can do all things,
 and that no purpose of yours can be thwarted.
3 'Who is this that hides counsel without knowledge?'
Therefore I have uttered what I did not understand,
 things too wonderful for me, which I did not know.
4 'Hear, and I will speak;
 I will question you, and you declare to me.'
5 I had heard of you by the hearing of the ear,
 but now my eye sees you;
6 therefore I despise myself,
 and repent in dust and ashes."

7 After the LORD had spoken these words to Job, the LORD said to Eliphaz the Temanite: "My wrath is kindled against you and against your two friends; for you have not spoken of me what is right, as my servant Job has. 8 Now therefore take seven bulls and seven rams, and go to my servant Job, and offer up for yourselves a burnt offering; and my servant Job shall pray for you, for I will accept his prayer not to deal with you according to your folly; for you have not spoken of me what is right, as my servant Job has done." 9 So Eliphaz the Temanite and Bildad the Shuhite and Zophar the Naamathite went and did what the LORD had told them; and the LORD accepted Job's prayer.

10 And the LORD restored the fortunes of Job when he had prayed for his friends; and the LORD gave Job twice as much as he had before.

Home Bible Readings

Monday, October 20	Psalm 38:9-15	*I Wait for You, O Lord*
Tuesday, October 21	Psalm 86:1-10	*You Alone Are God*
Wednesday, October 22	Psalm 86:11-17	*Give Strength to Your Servant*
Thursday, October 23	Ephesians 1:11-19	*God Has Called You to Hope*
Friday, October 24	Psalm 62:1-8	*My Hope Is from God*
Saturday, October 25	Psalm 65:1-5	*You Are the Hope of All*
Sunday, October 26	Job 42:1-10	*Wonderful Things I Did Not Know*

Background

In God's first major speech (Job 38:2—39:30), He had exposed Job to His power over the natural universe. In the Lord's second speech (40:7—41:34), He presented to Job His lordship over the moral universe. God's intent was to encourage Job to rely upon and rest in the Creator's omnipotence. Job's two replies are recorded in 40:3-5 and 42:1-6. We learn that he laid aside his rage as well as his stance of stubbornly challenging the Lord.

At several points during his suffering, Job had dared to question God's justice by suggesting that the Lord was not running the universe in the way Job thought it should be run. But now, obviously chastened by what God had told Job, he replied humbly and with reverence (40:3). Job acknowledged that he was insignificant when compared to God's overall scheme of creation (vs. 4). In light of all God had told Job, he felt ashamed that he had ever raised his voice. To register his regret for saying too much, Job went on to promise that he would place his hand over his mouth in order to say no more. Indeed, he had nothing to add to what he had already stated (vs. 5).

Notes on the Printed Text

After hearing the voice of God, Job seems to have lost his desire to vindicate himself. He knew God is all-powerful and that nothing can hinder His plans (Job 42:2). In God's mighty hands, all things—even justice for the suffering—would be worked out eventually.

Job went on to apologize for his earlier attitude and behavior. He referred specifically to statements God had made in His speeches. For instance, Job quoted God's reprimand at the beginning of His first speech. God had asked on what basis Job dared to question the Creator's wisdom, especially knowing how oblivious Job was concerning the vast universe (vs. 3; see 38:2). Now Job admitted his ignorance. His answer was simple and contrite. He was guilty of prattling on about marvels too mysterious for him to comprehend (42:3). In the end, all Job's understanding, reasoning, and doubting had to give way to faith.

In 42:4, Job referred to a statement God had made at the beginning of both major speeches. God had ordered Job to listen because He was going to ask questions (see

38:3; 40:7). Before God's interrogation of him, Job said, he had only known about God. For example, Job had known the Lord through what His servant had learned from tradition and from what others had told him. Perhaps Job was referring specifically to the words about God he had heard from his counselors. But all such words conveyed only indirect knowledge about the Lord. Through God's interrogation, Job experienced the Lord and His holy nature firsthand. Job learned about God's power and righteousness by being allowed to enter the Lord's sacred presence and listen to His voice. Even though Job didn't actually see God, he felt as though he had met the Lord face-to-face (Job 42:5; see Job 19:25-27; Pss. 25:14-15; 123:1-2; 141:8).

Most likely, the only reaction Job could have had to this experience was to loathe himself, that is, to see his own knowledge, self-assessment, and arguments for the nonsense they were (Job 42:6). His words "I abhor myself" could also be translated "I reject what I said." In this case, Job might have intended to take back all the spiritually rebellious statements he had made in his speeches to Eliphaz, Bildad, and Zophar. Job also reproached himself "in dust and ashes," which drew attention to his humiliation and insignificance (see Gen. 18:27; Job 2:8, 12). But his sorrow should not be taken to be regret for the host of sins his counselors had accused him of committing. Job was correct in his opinion that his miserable condition was not a result of personal transgressions. In addition, he had learned from God that life and suffering are far more complex and mysterious than he or his friends had ever imagined.

Job's repentance, therefore, was for boldly questioning God's wisdom, justice, and ability to manage human affairs (see Job 40:2, 8-9). Job wanted the Lord to know that His servant had experienced a dramatic change in his attitude. In this context, the Hebrew verb translated "repent" (42:6) denotes more than confessing one's sins. It also means to "console oneself" or to "be comforted." In essence, Job discarded all his previous, false notions about and bitter accusations against God. Moreover, Job was placing his assurance in the truth that God was not his enemy but his Friend and Redeemer.

The concluding portion of Job (42:7-17) was written in narrative form like the introduction (chaps. 1—2). In the epilogue, God scolded Job's friends and ordered them to make a sufficient and satisfactory offering as a sign of their repentance and to atone for their errant counsel. The conclusion also includes the account of how God restored Job's prosperity—in fact, giving him more than he had previously possessed. Before Job's restoration took place, God voiced His anger with Job's three counselors—Eliphaz, Bildad, and Zophar. Curiously missing from the group is Elihu.

Sometime after the Lord taught Job about His dominion over the universe, God spoke to Eliphaz, who may have been the community leader and eldest among the friends of Job. God not only announced His anger with Job's three friends, but the Lord also stated the cause of His anger. He told Eliphaz that he and his peers had declared falsehoods, not truths, about the Creator (vs. 7). How surprised these three advisers must have been! They likely assumed that they had been speaking on God's behalf. Now they learned that they were facing the brunt of His anger because of their erroneous words.

God told Eliphaz that Job had escaped condemnation because he had spoken what was "right." But how could God say this when He had just accused Job of obscuring His counsel (see vs. 3)? After all, Job had ranted and raved, as well as questioned God's justice. In short, Job had spoken in ignorance. The Hebrew verb translated "right" denotes what is firm, fixed, or established. One option is that God commended Job for taking the risk of being honest in voicing his feelings openly to the Lord. A second possibility is that God was praising Job for his sincerity. A third alternative is that God was simply saying Job was correct about his alleged sins not being the cause of his suffering. In retrospect, it seems that both Job and his counselors were partly correct and partly incorrect. Job was right about the fact that he was not suffering as a punishment for his sins, but he was wrong in questioning God's justice. Job's counselors were right about God's control over the universe, but they were wrong to assume Job's suffering was linked to some hidden trespass. Certainly, both Job and his advisers had a limited view of God and His plan for the world.

Eliphaz, Bildad, and Zophar must have been stunned when they learned that it was they, not Job, whom God required to offer a sacrifice as a sign of their repentance. The Lord told them to go to Job, taking with them "seven bullocks and seven rams" (vs. 8; in which "seven" denotes a complete number). In Job's presence—so that God's "servant" could look on—the three "friends" (vs. 7) were to sacrifice these animals. This was a large "burnt offering" (vs. 8) to make, perhaps indicating how seriously God took their error. As part of the ceremony, Job would "pray" for them so that God would not deal harshly with them for their "folly." At this point God repeated His judgment that the three counselors had not spoken the truth, in contrast to Job, who had done so.

Job's three discredited friends obeyed what the Lord had commanded them. Job prayed for their forgiveness, and God answered His servant's prayer (vs. 9). Presumably, it was soon after this ritual was completed that the Hebrew text literally says God "returned the captivity of Job" (vs. 10). This clause means that the Lord restored the prosperity Job previously lost. Indeed, God doubled His servant's former wealth. The Lord did so, not coincidentally, but only after Job prayed for his friends. In his newfound wisdom and humility, Job obeyed his Creator, and He graciously and abundantly bestowed on Job both inner and outer healing.

The final verses of Job show in dramatic fashion just how magnificent was his restoration. Not only was his prosperity doubled, but also his relatives, who had remained distant throughout his ordeal, returned to his side to comfort him. Moreover, as they returned, each bore expensive gifts for Job—"a piece of money" (vs. 11) and an "earring of gold"—and joined him in a meal of celebration. Verse 12 states that "the LORD blessed the latter end of Job more than his beginning." Some of those blessings are then listed, beginning with Job's flocks. Those flocks included 14,000 sheep, 6,000 camels, 2,000 oxen, and 1,000 donkeys. In all, Job's livestock were replenished so that he owned at least 23,000 animals!

In retrospect, the message of the Book of Job is that God is sovereign, regardless of what happens to the wicked or the righteous. Job had endured his test. He had shown his uprightness and unselfishness. In the end, God chose to bless His servant. He did so not necessarily to teach Job or anyone else a lesson, but simply because it was His pleasure. As far as Satan's original challenge to God is concerned (see 1:9-11; 2:4-5), Job not only withstood Satan's onslaught, but Job also won the contest the accuser had proposed. Job demonstrated that a person can love the Lord simply because He is God, and not because that person expects a reward for all his or her efforts.

SUGGESTIONS TO TEACHERS

Although Job had resisted the lectures of his friends because they were incorrect, he quickly understood what God had said to him. Job freely acknowledged God's supremacy in the universe, thereby admitting that Job was wrong to doubt God's ways.

1. GOD'S PIERCING QUESTIONS. Instead of dwelling on Job's questions, suddenly the ending of the book is an outpouring of God's questions to Job! Consider a few: *Can a human know the Eternal One's thoughts? Can a creature challenge the supremacy of the Lord? Can a mortal human remember when the Eternal One made possible the beginning of the universe? Can a finite human know the Eternal One's thoughts?* Invite your students to discuss each of these for a few minutes.

2. JOB'S HUMBLE RESPONSE. Focus on the way Job responded to the Lord, as recorded in Job 42. Here are some important points: the power of God is supreme; the purposes of God will prevail; the humility of a human is essential; and the presence of God is recognized.

3. GOD'S ABIDING PRESENCE. When we suffer, we ask *why*. We want explanations. We think that answers will help us handle our afflictions. We might even demand that God give an account of Himself. The Book of Job, among other things, makes it clear that answers aren't always forthcoming and that God does not need to give an account of Himself. The conclusion of the drama does not contain a list of answers to our questions. Rather, Job became aware that the Lord was still God. And the Creator was still with His servant.

4. GOD'S TRANSFORMATIVE WORK. God revealed to Job the reasons behind the painful tests and trials he endured. Because of them, the dross would be burned away from Job's life. He would come forth eventually like gold that had been subjected to the fires of the furnace. As we hold to the everlasting truths in God's Word and daily look to Him for strength to remain faithful, we, too, one day will stand before Him as pure gold.

For Adults

■ **Topic:** Who's in Control?

■ **Questions:** 1. How did Job come to the realization that God is all-powerful? 2. Why did Job presume to speak about matters that he did not understand? 3. How did Job come to terms with the ignorant assertions he had made? 4. Why is human pride such a hindrance to receiving spiritual insight from God? 5. What is necessary to live a holy life despite not knowing all the answers?

■ **Illustrations:**

Taking a Fresh Look. How much time do we spend crying out to God for answers, and how much time do we spend listening to God? Unfortunately, we are much better at demanding than at listening.

The outcome of Job's experience forces us to listen. Under the probing searchlight of God's questions, we must take a fresh look at ourselves and our pride. Too often we listen only when God has laid us aside and caught our attention. How much better it is for us to sharpen our spiritual eyes and ears by faithful prayer, worship, and study of God's Word.

Job repented when he heard from God (see Job 42:6). Job's response enables us to see that we need to abandon our pride. Furthermore, we have to learn to repent of wrong attitudes, of exalted views of ourselves, and of trying to bring God down to our level. Job points us in the right direction toward a healthy regard for our awesome God and toward an appropriately humble view of ourselves.

Our Great God. The astronomers have shown us a universe so immense that we feel lost in it. And so we think God must be lost, too. Then there is the mighty torrent of history sweeping human beings and civilizations along. In addition, all the vast upheavals of our time leave our faith shaken. The reason for this is, quite simply, we have believed in a God too much like ourselves, that is, a pint-sized and puny deity.

We feel overwhelmed and we imagine God must be, too. But this only means that we have confused the great Creator revealed in the Book of Job with frail and mortal people. And when we stop believing in a supreme Lord, we try to play God. In our efforts to make ourselves masters, we become fanatics who are intolerant and ruthless.

Herman F. Reissig, in *The Greatness and Nearness of God*, poignantly remarked, "Oh man, remember! You are a creature, not the Creator; a servant, not the Master. Our times are in His hand."

Led by the Kindly Light. A brilliant young Oxford graduate was traveling in Italy. Despite outstanding grades and a superior intellect, this gifted writer and speaker was restless and uncertain. He was a Christian, but life seemed bleak at the time.

While in Sicily, this believer became seriously ill and took weeks to recover. On the way home, his travel plans were disrupted and changed. He was confused about his future. Feeling deeply depressed, he was also intensely homesick and lonely. But out of that period of darkness, this young man, John Henry Newman, wrote a poem that was later set to music. Many know the poem as the words of a beautiful hymn:

Lead kindly light,
Amid the encircling gloom.
Lead thou me on.
The night is dark and I am far from home,
Lead thou me on.

The more we learn about the Creator who revealed His awesome presence and power to Job, the more we discover how good and gracious He is to us. The Father, through His Son, can bring us spiritual light in the midst of our darkest gloom.

FOR YOUTH

■ **TOPIC:** Good Results in Due Time

■ **QUESTIONS:** 1. Why was it important for Job to understand that no one could thwart God's purposes? 2. In what way had Job spoken in ignorance about the Creator? 3. What brought Job to the place where he decided to repent? 4. Under what circumstances are believers likely to demand answers from God? 5. How might Job's account help believers comfort one another in times of suffering?

■ **ILLUSTRATIONS:**

Admitting Our Limits. Youth today grow up in a culture that says we can control our destinies, we can fix anything, and, given time and technology, we can explain everything. Our culture teaches the superiority of human intellect and technical prowess, so the idea of God is irrelevant.

How hard it is then for teenagers to confess, as Job did, that there are some things beyond human understanding, that some things are "too wonderful . . . [to] know" (Job 42:3). Pride says we comprehend it all and we can do anything. Christian humility says God is greater than we are, and we will one day have to answer to Him for our thoughts and deeds.

At the same time, God has given us ample evidence for faith and humility, as opposed to pride and self-sufficiency. We must encourage teens to look for the Lord's good and gracious hand in the created world about them. They must look at the universe through the spiritual eyes of faith. Then focus their attention on the demonstration of the Father's love and power in the death and resurrection of His Son for our sins.

No One Likes Me! Charles Shultz, the creator of the comic strip *Peanuts*, often produced familiar scenes of human situations. On one occasion, Charlie Brown, the hero of the comic strip, visited Lucy's outdoor psychiatrist stand because he was convinced that no one liked him.

Lucy told her "client" to look on the bright side of things. "Cheer up, Charlie Brown. You have lots of friends." Charlie's face brightened, and he said to Lucy, "I do? I do?" As Charlie walked away saying to himself, "I do! I have lots of friends!" Lucy taunted him in her typical, sarcastic way. "Name one," she said.

Human reason often is our worst enemy. Job was convinced that no one seemed to care for him. And he struggled desperately to find a reason why terrible things had happened to him and left him feeling so isolated. But then out of the whirlwind, God spoke to Job. He learned that the all-powerful Creator of the universe loved and cared for him.

Despite the passage of time, God still responds to our concerns on the most personal level. Have you spoken today with the Lord, your Creator?

Sincere, Pointed Questions. On Friday, December 14, 2012, a reclusive 20-year-old named Adam Lanza shot dead his mother in their home in Newtown, Connecticut. Then, in one of the worst mass killings in U.S. history, Lanza entered Sandy Hook Elementary School and gunned down 20 children and 6 adults before taking his own life.

In the aftermath of this horrible tragedy, everyone was full of questions. Perhaps the most pointed of all was captured in a news report written by correspondent John Burnett of *NPR*: "Would a Good God Allow Such Evil?" Admittedly, there were no easy answers. Some even argued that it was wrong to question, believing that no one should have doubts about God's will.

Perhaps you are uneasy about questioning. Yet it is fine to ask God sincere, pointed questions. It is all right to wonder, even to doubt, as we seek the truth. Jesus never censured the questions or doubtings of the honest seeker (though He condemned stubborn unbelief in the face of truth).

Job questioned and sought answers. While he did not receive all the answers he wanted, he discovered that God was with him. Likewise, while no answers were available to those touched by the senseless loss of life in Newtown, God shared His presence there, too. He did so through the acts of heroism and kindness performed by countless unnamed individuals from across America and around the world.

LESSON 9 — NOVEMBER 2

GOD'S GLORY RETURNS

BACKGROUND SCRIPTURE: Ezekiel 40:1—43:12
DEVOTIONAL READING: Psalm 138

Key Verse: The glory of the LORD came into the house by the way of the gate whose prospect is toward the east. So the spirit took me up, and brought me into the inner court; and, behold, the glory of the LORD filled the house. Ezekiel 43:4-5.

KING JAMES VERSION

EZEKIEL 43:1 Afterward he brought me to the gate, even the gate that looketh toward the east: 2 And, behold, the glory of the God of Israel came from the way of the east: and his voice was like a noise of many waters: and the earth shined with his glory. 3 And it was according to the appearance of the vision which I saw, even according to the vision that I saw when I came to destroy the city: and the visions were like the vision that I saw by the river Chebar; and I fell upon my face. 4 And the glory of the LORD came into the house by the way of the gate whose prospect is toward the east. 5 So the spirit took me up, and brought me into the inner court; and, behold, the glory of the LORD filled the house. 6 And I heard him speaking unto me out of the house; and the man stood by me.

7 And he said unto me, Son of man, the place of my throne, and the place of the soles of my feet, where I will dwell in the midst of the children of Israel for ever, and my holy name, shall the house of Israel no more defile, neither they, nor their kings, by their whoredom, nor by the carcases of their kings in their high places. 8 In their setting of their threshold by my thresholds, and their post by my posts, and the wall between me and them, they have even defiled my holy name by their abominations that they have committed: wherefore I have consumed them in mine anger. 9 Now let them put away their whoredom, and the carcases of their kings, far from me, and I will dwell in the midst of them for ever. 10 Thou son of man, shew the house to the house of Israel, that they may be ashamed of their iniquities: and let them measure the pattern. 11 And if they be ashamed of all that they have done, shew them the form of the house, and the fashion thereof, and the goings out thereof, and the comings in thereof, and all the forms thereof, and all the ordinances thereof, and all the forms thereof, and all the laws thereof: and write it in their sight, that they may keep the whole form thereof, and all the ordinances thereof, and do them. 12 This is the law of the house; Upon the top of the mountain the whole limit thereof round about shall be most holy. Behold, this is the law of the house.

NEW REVISED STANDARD VERSION

EZEKIEL 43:1 Then he brought me to the gate, the gate facing east. 2 And there, the glory of the God of Israel was coming from the east; the sound was like the sound of mighty waters; and the earth shone with his glory. 3 The vision I saw was like the vision that I had seen when he came to destroy the city, andlike the vision that I had seen by the river Chebar; and I fell upon my face. 4 As the glory of the LORD entered the temple by the gate facing east, 5 the spirit lifted me up, and brought me into the inner court; and the glory of the LORD filled the temple.

6 While the man was standing beside me, I heard someone speaking to me out of the temple. 7 He said to me: Mortal, this is the place of my throne and the place for the soles of my feet, where I will reside among the people of Israel forever. The house of Israel shall no more defile my holy name, neither they nor their kings, by their whoring, and by the corpses of their kings at their death. 8 When they placed their threshold by my threshold and their doorposts beside my doorposts, with only a wall between me and them, they were defiling my holy name by their abominations that they committed; therefore I have consumed them in my anger. 9 Now let them put away their idolatry and the corpses of their kings far from me, and I will reside among them forever.

10 As for you, mortal, describe the temple to the house of Israel, and let them measure the pattern; and let them be ashamed of their iniquities. 11 When they are ashamed of all that they have done, make known to them the plan of the temple, its arrangement, its exits and its entrances, and its whole form—all its ordinances and its entire plan and all its laws; and write it down in their sight, so that they may observe and follow the entire plan and all its ordinances. 12 This is the law of the temple: the whole territory on the top of the mountain all around shall be most holy. This is the law of the temple.

Home Bible Readings

Monday, October 27	Deuteronomy 5:23-29	God's Glory and Greatness
Tuesday, October 28	Psalm 138	God's Exalted Name
Wednesday, October 29	Exodus 3:1-6	Standing on Holy Ground
Thursday, October 30	Psalm 24	God's Holy Place
Friday, October 31	Psalm 5	Worshiping in Awe
Saturday, November 1	Psalm 11	God Examines Humankind
Sunday, November 2	Ezekiel 43:1-12	God's Glory Returns to the Temple

Background

Sometime in 573 B.C., on the twenty-fifth anniversary of his exile to Babylon, Ezekiel was supernaturally transported to Jerusalem (see Ezek. 40:1). There the prophet received a remarkable and detailed vision of a future temple to be built in Israel's restored land. Chapters 40–42 report that Ezekiel saw the sanctuary measured with a reed that was ten feet, four inches long. An angel sent by the Lord guided the prophet through the temple. During the tour, Ezekiel was given detailed measurements and descriptions of the entire sanctuary complex, including the temple proper and the chambers in the inner court.

The prophet's vision has been interpreted in four main ways: (1) This was supposed to be the temple built by Zerubbabel in 520–515 B.C., after the return from the Babylonian exile, but it fell short of Ezekiel's blueprint; (2) The temple is symbolic of the Christian church's earthly glory, blessing, and true worship of God in the present age; (3) The temple is a symbolic description of the final form of God's kingdom when His presence and blessing fill the whole earth; and (4) Ezekiel's temple is a literal, future sanctuary that will be built in Israel during the 1,000-year reign of the Messiah on earth.

Notes on the Printed Text

Ezekiel not only described to the exiles the newly constructed temple, but also presented the sanctuary as an important sign that God would indeed dwell among His people once again, just as He promised He would. Ezekiel explained how a newly established service of worship would provide the means of access to God. Finally, the prophet unveiled the grand divisions and blessings of the new land awaiting the people of Israel.

About 18 and a half years earlier, Ezekiel had witnessed in a vision the departure of God's glory through the gateway Solomon built into the retaining wall directly east of where his temple stood (also called the "king's gate" in 1 Chron. 9:18). Then the divine glory continued to move eastward across the Kidron Valley to the Mount of Olives (see Ezek. 10:18-19; 11:22-23). Led by the same angelic emissary who had taken him through the temple, the prophet saw the return and reentry of the Lord into the new temple through the "gate that looketh toward the east" (43:1). What joy Ezekiel must have felt to see God's presence in the midst of His people once again. The prophet surely longed, as most believers do, for the time when the glorified Lord will return to live among His people forever.

In Ezekiel's vision, he saw the glory of Israel's God appearing from the east (vs. 2). Most likely, the gateway located on the eastern side of Solomon's temple was the main entrance to the court of the sanctuary (see Exod. 27:13). The sound of the Lord's presence was comparable in intensity to waves crashing against the shore. Moreover, the entire landscape radiated God's "glory" (Ezek. 43:2). This apparently signified His power and majesty. The prophet mentioned that this vision was like others he had seen previously (vs. 3). The vision regarding the destruction of the city is recorded in chapters 8—11, while those by the Kebar River may be found in chapters 1 and 10.

In Ezekiel's first vision, he saw an awesome, ice-blue "firmament" (1:22) that glistened like crystal. The prophet also heard a voice coming from the dome-shaped platform (vs. 25). Above the vault was a blue, sapphire-shaped royal seat (vs. 26; see 10:1). Furthermore, on this chariot-throne was a figure who resembled a human being (1:26). The torso and head of the figure Ezekiel saw had the appearance of glowing, yellow amber in the middle of a fire. Also, from the waist down, the Lord looked like a burning flame, while all around Him was a brilliant light (vs. 27). His dazzling "appearance" (vs. 28) was as bright-hued as a rainbow that appears after a storm (see Gen. 9:12-16). When the prophet realized he was gazing on the "glory of the LORD" (Ezek. 1:28), he fell face downward on the ground in submission and worship (see 3:23; 9:8; 11:13; 43:3; 44:4). For the rest of Ezekiel's life, he would carry the memory of his surreal encounter with the Creator-King.

We can only imagine the wonder and excitement Ezekiel must have felt as he witnessed the glorious presence of the Lord enter through the eastern gateway of the temple (43:4). This episode signified that God's approval and blessing rested on the sanctuary. Next, the prophet felt his body being lifted up by the Spirit and placed within the inside courtyard of the temple. Then, as the prophet looked on, the Lord's glory completely engulfed the sanctuary (vs. 5).

Prior to the Babylonian captivity, the Jerusalem temple was the central religious institution in Israel. For instance, the sanctuary was the locale where the Lord manifested His holy presence in Israel. It was also the place where sacrifices were made in response to God's gracious choice of Israel as His people. In the temple, they could spend time in prayer. Moreover, its design, furniture, and customs were object lessons that prepared them for the Messiah.

Additionally, the sanctuary had important political and economic roles to play in Israelite society. It was the institution that held together the entire covenant community— the past as well as the present and the future. Moreover, the sanctuary gave political identity to the people. Access to its courts identified who was properly a citizen and who was excluded. From an economic perspective, rooms in the temple functioned as a treasury—in effect, the society's bank. Because of the temple's demands for tithes and offerings, a large portion of the nation's economy passed through the sanctuary personnel and storehouses. In brief, without the temple, God's people had little opportunity to pull together as a coherent society to face the challenges of the future and experience the fullness of God's kingdom blessings.

As the Lord's glory returned to the rebuilt temple, His emissary stood beside Ezekiel. Next, he heard someone else speak to him from within the sanctuary (most likely God, whose sacred name, out of reverence, is left undisclosed; vs. 6). The prophet is addressed as "Son of man" (vs. 7) more than 90 times in this book. This title was used quite frequently of Jesus to call attention to His true humanity. In Ezekiel's case, it was a reminder that he was a mere mortal who served the all-powerful Lord of the universe. The prophet learned that God was accepting the new temple as His throne and dwelling place among the Israelites (see 1 Sam. 4:4; 2 Sam. 6:2; 2 Kings 19:15; 1 Chron. 13:6; Pss. 80:1; 99:1; 132:13-14; Isa. 37:16). Ezekiel also discovered that since the sanctuary was to be God's permanent place of residence among His people (Ezek. 43:7, 9), no defilement of any kind would be allowed there.

Before the exile, the rulers and people of Israel had desecrated God's "holy name" (vs. 7) by revering pagan deities in the Jerusalem temple (see 8:1-18). The meaning of the Hebrew noun rendered "their whoredom" (43:7, 9) is unclear. Certain forms of idol worship involved shrine prostitutes. Some have suggested that is the meaning here. Others, however, understand the term in a figurative sense as signifying the "spiritual adultery" of God's people. The nation is often portrayed in Scripture as an unfaithful spouse enticed away from the Lord by pagan deities.

The Israelites also profaned the Lord by offering sacrifices at funeral pillars set up to venerate their deceased monarchs. The phrase, "the carcases of their kings" (vss. 7, 9), probably refers to the practice of placing the tombs of Israelite rulers on the same hill as the temple. In earlier times, the monarch's palace and the temple were connected, but separated by a wall (vs. 8). Thus, Ezekiel was told that the shameful tradition of placing the kings' memorial graves (as well as their living quarters) near the sacred precincts, where vile deeds often occurred, would no longer be tolerated.

God directed Ezekiel to describe to the exiled Israelites the divine design of the reconstructed temple and the nature of the religious observances to be practiced there (vss. 10-11). The plans upon which Israel's earlier sanctuaries were built also originated with God. By disclosing a clear picture of God's ideal blueprint for the people, Ezekiel would prompt them to recall the glory of Solomon's temple. Also, by writing it all down in their sight, the prophet would remind them of their iniquities, which brought the Lord's judgment upon them. Moreover, the people would be motivated to return to God in obedience with a desire to follow all of the decrees and statutes instituted in the new temple (see chaps. 40–42).

Ezekiel described the new temple, God's future dwelling place, in terms and depictions the people could easily understand. God wanted His people to see what was in store for those who lived in faithful obedience to Him. The hard road of sin ultimately leads to judgment, as Israel learned all too well. But the pathway of obedience to the Lord leads to blessing, joy, and a peace that only God can give.

God emphasized that maintaining the holiness of the future temple was supremely important. Indeed, the entire region on the mountaintop where the sanctuary was placed would be "most holy" (vs. 12). Holiness was the basic "law" of the Lord's new temple, because He is absolutely holy. Even His name is holy. Just as God is holy, He expects those who follow Him to live in a way that is characterized by holiness (see Lev. 19:1-2; 1 Pet. 1:15-16). This requires a complete devotion to the Lord and a constant rejection of sin. Even today, growth toward Christian maturity is vitally linked to the practice of holy living.

SUGGESTIONS TO TEACHERS

Ezekiel's vision of the new temple was intended to compel the Babylonian captives to live a life of holiness. God still calls believers to be holy people. His summons to holiness is accompanied by His guiding commands—directives that speak to our lifestyles as well as to our hearts.

1. AFFIRMING THE VALUE OF A HOLY LIFESTYLE. God used Ezekiel to stress to the Babylonian captives that a holy lifestyle was worth pursuing. The Lord also calls believers today to holiness and gives them clear guidelines for carrying out what He wants them to do. Be sure to emphasize that through the empowering presence of the Spirit, Jesus' followers can remain faithful to Him.

2. REFLECTING GOD'S HOLINESS TO OTHERS. God desired that His people would reveal His grace and mercy to the nations. As a covenant-keeping community, they would reflect His holy character to the Gentiles, who would be drawn to God by what they saw. Similarly, today Jesus' followers are to be an example of His saving grace by the holy way in which they live.

3. BEARING WITNESS THROUGH A HOLY LIFESTYLE. God's will for His chosen people was very specific. They were to be holy in every aspect of their lives. It is quite different from our modern way of approaching life. Ours is a pick-and-choose society. Supposedly, we can decide which of God's commands we want to keep and forget the rest. Because so much of society is at risk, and so many people's lives are messed up, believers must bear witness to the Savior by choosing to be holy.

FOR ADULTS
■ **TOPIC:** Seeking a Place of Peace
■ **QUESTIONS:** 1. Why had God's glory previously departed from the Jerusalem temple? 2. In what way was the vision Ezekiel saw like the

previous ones he had experienced? 3. Why did God emphasize that His people must never again profane His "holy name" (Ezek. 43:8)? 4. What does it mean to live in holy manner? 5. How can believers use God's Word to help them live holy lives?

■ ILLUSTRATIONS:

Teaching Holiness. Many believers have sung the hymn "Holy, Holy, Holy" at one time or another. That hymn of praise, which is based on Revelation 4:8, rightly portrays God as the only one who is absolutely holy—"only Thou art holy, there is none beside Thee." We are reminded that we will always fall short of God's holy standard, which is "perfect in power, in love and purity."

But the preceding truth doesn't mean we think of holiness as some heavenly concept with no earthly application. On the contrary, Ezekiel 43:1-12 urges God's people to be holy. Admittedly, this emphasis on holiness is not popular, even in the church, but it is necessary. After all, if we don't teach God's standards and exhort that they be followed, the sins of the world might become the sins of the church. Then, instead of being a sanctuary characterized by peace, our congregations will soon become filled with turmoil and dissention.

Remembering God's Summons. A young man had received his doctoral degree and then applied for teaching positions around the United States. After an exhausting search, he was offered a position in a university in Canada. He, his wife, and their two children discovered what it meant to be summoned to a new life. It was a stressful challenge for them, but because they understood this offer to be God's call, they accepted it.

The message God wanted Ezekiel to deliver to the exiles in Babylon was something like that. This included reminding them about God's summons to holiness. They could live in a morally-pure manner as they rested in the assurance of what the Lord had in store for them. The promise of a new temple would energize them to move out in hope, obedience, and faith.

Our call to holiness comes not once but many times in our lives. When we are assailed by doubts, troubles, fears, and depression, we must remember our summons and trust the living God.

Choosing the Path of Holiness. A man observed a woman in the grocery store with a three-year-old girl in her cart. As they passed the cookie section, the little girl asked for cookies, and her mother refused. The child immediately began to whine and fuss, and the mother said quietly, "Now Monica, we just have half of the aisles left to go through. Don't be upset. It won't be long."

Soon they came to the candy aisle, and the little girl began to shout for candy. And when the girl was told she couldn't have any, she began to cry. The mother said, "There, there, Monica, don't cry. Only two more aisles to go, and then we'll be checking out."

When the two got to the checkout stand, the little girl immediately began to clamor for gum and burst into a terrible tantrum upon discovering there'd be no gum purchased. The mother patiently said, "Monica, we'll be through this checkout stand in five minutes and then you can go home and have a nice nap."

The man followed the mother and child out to the parking lot and stopped the woman to compliment her. "I couldn't help noticing how patient you were with little Monica," he began. Whereupon the mother said, "I'm Monica. My little girl's name is Samantha!"

Sometimes, like Ezekiel's exiled peers, we need to keep reminding ourselves of the glorious future the Lord has in store for us. Just as the prophet exhorted God's people in captivity to be resolute in choosing the path of holiness, so too the Lord summons us to do the same. The goal is to live as God wants us to in the face of the pressures and temptations of the world.

For Youth

■ **Topic:** Glorious Light and Clear Sacred Places

■ **Questions:** 1. How do you think Ezekiel felt as he saw God's glory approaching? 2. Why would the vision of the Lord's glory filling the new temple be significant to His chosen people? 3. Why did God direct Ezekiel to describe the specifications of the temple to the exiles (see Ezek. 43:11)? 4. Why is it important for believers to live a life of holiness? 5. What are some ways believers can cultivate holiness in their lives?

■ **Illustrations:**

How to Stay Pure. Is it really possible for saved adolescents to live in a way that is characterized by holiness, especially around their unbelieving peers? The following story can give regenerate teens the insight they need to be successful in doing so.

A minister who was visiting a coal mine noticed a pure white flower growing at one of the tunnel entrances. When he asked the miner with him how the flower stayed white, the miner said, "Throw some coal dust on it." When the minister did, the dust slid right off of the flower's smooth surface, so it remained white. That's how the youth in our congregations should be in the world, namely, individuals who remain holy in an unholy place.

A Divine Summons. What's the biggest thing we could be called to? President? Not many of us want that. Football or basketball star? Possibly. Movie, music, or television stardom? Perhaps. A good job and happy family? Yes. To be people characterized by holiness? What's that?

We have to dig deeply to understand Ezekiel's emphasis on God calling His people in Babylonian captivity to be holy. Now, as then, God does not summon us to a vocation. He calls us to Himself, to be His faithful, trusting, hopeful, and holy children. Because He redeemed us with the Son's blood, He wants us to confess Him as Lord and testify about Him to others. That's a tough calling. It's a divine summons to be part of something really big, something that involves holy living.

The Best Is Yet to Come. As Ezekiel and his peers languished in exile in Babylon, it might have been difficult for them to imagine that one day God in His glory would return to a new temple. The Lord, though, would be faithful to His promise. In turn, this amazing future would give His people the motivation they needed to obey Him.

Martha was one of the dearest folks in Pastor Jim's church, and she was dying. Pastor Jim faced Martha across her small living room wondering what words of comfort he could share with her. Martha read his concerned look and said, "Don't look so glum. I have lived a long life. The Lord has been good. I'm ready to go. Don't you know that?" "Yes, but I still wish it wasn't so," Pastor Jim said.

Martha ignored that and plowed ahead with what was on her mind. "I do want to talk about my funeral. I been thinking about it, and this is what I want." Martha had her hymns and Scripture passages picked out. She had some stories she wanted told about heeding the Lord's will and remaining unwavering in her devotion to Him.

When it seemed that the two had covered just about everything, Martha paused, looked at her pastor with a twinkle in her eye, and added, "One more thing, preacher. When they bury me, I want my old Bible in one hand and a fork in the other." "A fork?" Pastor Jim was sure he had heard everything, but this caught him by surprise. "Why do you want to be buried with a fork?"

"I must have gone to a thousand pot-luck church suppers through the years," Martha explained. "At every one of those dinners, when it was time to clear the dishes, somebody would say, 'Be sure and save your fork.' I knew dessert was coming! Not a cup of gelatin or pudding or even a dish of ice cream. You don't need a fork for that. It meant the good stuff, like chocolate cake or cherry pie! When they told me I could keep my fork, I knew the best was yet to come!"

"You tell them that at my funeral. Oh, they can talk about all the good times we had together. That would be nice. But when they walk by my casket and look at my pretty blue dress, I want them to turn to one another and say, 'Why the fork?'" "That's when you say, 'Martha wants you to know the best is yet to come. She just got hers.'" Our full inheritance may be future, but it inspires hope for holy living right now!

LESSON 10 — NOVEMBER 9

GOD ACCEPTS HIS PEOPLE

BACKGROUND SCRIPTURE: Ezekiel 43:10—46:24
DEVOTIONAL READING: Psalms 130:1—131:3

Key Verse: When these days are expired, it shall be, that upon the eighth day, and so forward, the priests shall make your burnt offerings upon the altar, and your peace offerings; and I will accept you, saith the Lord GOD. Ezekiel 43:27.

KING JAMES VERSION

EZEKIEL 43:13 And these are the measures of the altar after the cubits: The cubit is a cubit and an hand breadth; even the bottom shall be a cubit, and the breadth a cubit, and the border thereof by the edge thereof round about shall be a span: and this shall be the higher place of the altar. 14 And from the bottom upon the ground even to the lower settle shall be two cubits, and the breadth one cubit; and from the lesser settle even to the greater settle shall be four cubits, and the breadth one cubit. 15 So the altar shall be four cubits; and from the altar and upward shall be four horns.
16 And the altar shall be twelve cubits long, twelve broad, square in the four squares thereof. 17 And the settle shall be fourteen cubits long and fourteen broad in the four squares thereof; and the border about it shall be half a cubit; and the bottom thereof shall be a cubit about; and his stairs shall look toward the east. 18 And he said unto me, Son of man, thus saith the Lord GOD; These are the ordinances of the altar in the day when they shall make it, to offer burnt offerings thereon, and to sprinkle blood thereon. 19 And thou shalt give to the priests the Levites that be of the seed of Zadok, which approach unto me, to minister unto me, saith the Lord GOD, a young bullock for a sin offering. 20 And thou shalt take of the blood thereof, and put it on the four horns of it, and on the four corners of the settle, and upon the border round about: thus shalt thou cleanse and purge it. 21 Thou shalt take the bullock also of the sin offering, and he shall burn it in the appointed place of the house, without the sanctuary.

NEW REVISED STANDARD VERSION

EZEKIEL 43:13 These are the dimensions of the altar by cubits (the cubit being one cubit and a handbreadth): its base shall be one cubit high, and one cubit wide, with a rim of one span around its edge. This shall be the height of the altar: 14 From the base on the ground to the lower ledge, two cubits, with a width of one cubit; and from the smaller ledge to the larger ledge, four cubits, with a width of one cubit; 15 and the altar hearth, four cubits; and from the altar hearth projecting upward, four horns. 16 The altar hearth shall be square, twelve cubits long by twelve wide. 17 The ledge also shall be square, fourteen cubits long by fourteen wide, with a rim around it half a cubit wide, and its surrounding base, one cubit. Its steps shall face east.
18 Then he said to me: Mortal, thus says the Lord GOD: These are the ordinances for the altar: On the day when it is erected for offering burnt offerings upon it and for dashing blood against it, 19 you shall give to the levitical priests of the family of Zadok, who draw near to me to minister to me, says the Lord GOD, a bull for a sin offering. 20 And you shall take some of its blood, and put it on the four horns of the altar, and on the four corners of the ledge, and upon the rim all around; thus you shall purify it and make atonement for it. 21 You shall also take the bull of the sin offering, and it shall be burnt in the appointed place belonging to the temple, outside the sacred area.

Home Bible Readings

Monday, November 3	Joshua 22:21-34	Quest for a True Altar
Tuesday, November 4	Judges 6:24-32	Pulling Down False Altars
Wednesday, November 5	2 Samuel 24:17-25	A Costly Altar and Sacrifice
Thursday, November 6	Psalm 71:1-8	You, O Lord, Are My Hope
Friday, November 7	Psalms 130:1—131:3	Hope in the Lord Forevermore
Saturday, November 8	Ezekiel 43:22-27	I Will Accept You
Sunday, November 9	Ezekiel 43:13-21	The Ordinances for the Altar

Background

In Ezekiel, at least two major structural features are evident. The first of these are the chronological presentation of significant events, visions, and oracles. This chronological arrangement is paralleled by a presentation of the material based on content. The central theme of chapters 1–24 is the judgment of Judah, while that of chapters 33–48 is Judah's future restoration. Between these two major focal points, in chapters 25–32, Ezekiel pronounced God's judgment upon pagan kingdoms. The content of Ezekiel's prophecies was delivered through a variety of literary means. These included symbolic actions, allegories or parables, and most importantly, visions. In broad outline, the first vision focused on the presence of God's glory in Babylon (1–3), the second on the judgment of Jerusalem (8–11), and the third (37) and fourth visions (40–48) on the future restoration of Judah.

Strange visions like spinning wheels and a valley of dry bones that come to life have caused many readers of Ezekiel's prophecy more than a little puzzlement. Also, not surprisingly, these visions have generated wildly different interpretations of many passages. The problem of understanding Ezekiel's prophecies has a long history. At least as early as the late fourth and early fifth centuries, the great Bible scholar, Jerome, offered numerous apologies in his commentaries for an inability to better explain difficult passages. But for the reader who is willing to dig a little deeper into Ezekiel's prophecies, there is a wealth of spiritual insight into God's patient involvement and dealings with His people during this dark period of Israel's history.

Notes on the Printed Text

In last week's excursion through 43:1–12, we learned about Ezekiel's vision of a new temple whose design originated with God. This was also the special place where the glory of God returned. He revealed to His spokesperson that because the reconstructed sanctuary would serve as the divine throne and dwelling place, the Lord would not permit any kind of defilement within its precincts. As a result of Ezekiel disclosing this information to the exiles in Babylon, they would be compelled to abandon their sinful ways and return to God in obedience. This included heeding all the "ordinances" (vs. 11) and "laws" pertaining to the new temple.

With the completion of the rebuilt sanctuary and the divine glory filling it, worship services would begin. To set the stage for this, Ezekiel detailed the dimensions of the future altar (vss. 13-17; see 40:47). Next, he presented the regulations for offering sacrifices on the altar (see 43:18-27 and the Bible lesson commentary that appears below). The measurements for the altar, like those for the temple itself, were given to Ezekiel in great detail. To avoid any confusion, the prophet was even informed that the dimensions were in long "cubits" (vs. 13).

A long or royal "cubit" was approximately 21 inches in length, while a short cubit measured about 18 inches. A "hand breadth" was about three inches long and a "span" was approximately nine inches in length. The altar, which was probably made of dressed stones, consisted of four stages or platforms, including the base or gutter section on the very "bottom." This design resembled a Mesopotamian ziggurat, which was a type of symmetrical step-pyramid. The altar's lowest base level was 21 inches high and extended 21 inches out from the next higher platform on all sides. It had a nine-inch rim or molding all around it.

The next level up from the base of the altar was a stone platform three and a half feet high. It also extended 21 inches out from the next higher platform on all sides. The third level, just beneath the horned altar itself, was seven feet high with a surrounding ledge, in a base design like the base, 21 inches wide (vs. 14). This third level was 24 and a half feet long on each side with a rim or molding 10 and a half inches high (vs. 17). The topmost level of the altar complex, the "altar" (vs. 15) hearth or altar proper, was also seven feet high like the platform below. But it was distinguished by a 21-inch horn or stone projection at each of its four corners. The top level measured 21 feet on each side (vs. 16). The entire altar complex had "steps" (vs. 17) on the east side that led up to the top of the altar. This was actually forbidden by the Mosaic law (see Exod. 20:26). But at a height of 19 feet—nearly two stories—the altar would be impossible to reach without them.

Ezekiel 43:18 introduces the statutes Israel's all-powerful Lord wanted His people to follow when they offered sacrifices on the altar in the reconstructed temple. These sacrifices included "burnt offerings," as well as splashing "blood" against the altar. In a sense, Ezekiel's vision here was looking backward and forward at the same time. It looked backward to the time of Moses when the imperfect sacrificial system was first instituted. It also looked forward to the Messiah's perfect sacrifice, which fulfilled the potential and promise of the imperfect animal sacrifices. The Israelites could approach God and receive forgiveness for their sins only because of Calvary. Today, it is still the only means by which we can gain acceptance by God and experience complete pardon from sin (see Rom. 3:25-26).

Since the dawn of human history, people offered sacrifices to God. For instance, at the end of the growing season, Cain (the first son of Adam and Eve) brought some of his harvest as an offering to the Lord (Gen. 4:3). Likewise, Abel (Cain's brother) offered to the Lord "fat" (v. 4) portions taken from some of the "firstlings" of the sheep of his herd. Later, after the great flood, Noah presented "burnt offerings" (8:20) to God to express his gratitude for the Lord's deliverance of him and his family. Be that as it may, it was not until the Israelites had camped in the Sinai desert that the Lord instituted formal sacrifices among His people.

Moses instructed the Israelites to make five different types of sacrifices: burnt, grain, fellowship, sin, and guilt offerings (see Lev. 1:1–7:21). Sacrificial animals were laid out on the altar hearth. The blood of the animal was smeared on the altar horns (see Exod. 29:12; Lev. 4:7, 18). The horns of the altar were also regarded as places of refuge (see 1 Kings 1:49-53). If an individual were in mortal danger because of some wrong done to another, grasping the horns of the altar was supposed to prompt mercy from the person seeking revenge. This act was presumably symbolic of God's gracious acceptance of Israelite sacrifices offered in atonement for the people's sins.

In Ezekiel's vision, it was revealed that a seven-day ritual administered by the priests, from the family of "Zadok" (Ezek. 43:19), who were members of the tribe of Levi, would be required to consecrate the altar of the new temple to God (see vs. 26). The Zadokite priesthood originated when Solomon set aside the priestly line of Eli by deposing Abiathar and putting Zadok in his place (see 1 Kings 2:26-27). God had already condemned the priesthood of the house of Eli because of Eli's two worthless sons, Hophni and Phinehas (see 1 Sam. 2:30-36).

The Lord indicated that the altar would be truly purified after "blood" (Ezek. 43:20) from the sin offering was applied to the "four horns" of the altar, the "four corners" of the platform below the altar hearth, and on the rim of the base. After the blood of a young, domesticated "bullock" (vs. 21) was used for this sacrificial purpose, the carcass of the animal was supposed to be burned in a specific place outside the "sanctuary." Everything in temple worship had a precise purpose, place, and order. God required that it all be done exactly as He instructed.

Many interpreters of Scripture object to the idea of the reinstatement of sacrifices in the new temple and thus view Ezekiel's description of future sacrifices as symbolic rather than literal. They argue that to reinstate animal sacrifices in the last days implies that the Messiah's death was somehow deficient. They point out that according to Scripture, Jesus' atoning sacrifice was the permanent remedy for sin, making all further animal offerings unnecessary (see Rom. 6:10; Heb. 9:12; 10:10, 18). Other Bible scholars think the problem is solved when the function of Ezekiel's sacrifices are properly understood. For instance, they explain that animal sacrifices could not take away sin. These interpreters assert that the only way to be saved in any age is by grace through faith in the shed blood of the Son (see Heb. 10:1-4, 10).

Proponents of the latter view note that even after the church began at Pentecost, Jewish Christians still offered sacrifices in Herod's temple, perhaps as memorials to the Savior's death (see Acts 2:46; 21:26). In the new temple, say these interpreters, animal sacrifices also serve as memorials honoring the ultimate, efficacious sacrifice of the Son. The conclusion of the matter is essentially the same as the controversy surrounding the building of the new temple. Whether understood symbolically or literally, the Israelites no doubt simply took Ezekiel's message at face value. The message was clear. The worship and fellowship with God that His chosen people had lost because of divine judgment for sin, would one day be restored.

SUGGESTIONS TO TEACHERS

In Ezekiel's vision, he not only learned about a new temple, but also about the altar to be placed within it. Details about the latter included its dimensions and the regulations for offering sacrifices on it. In this way, the Lord disclosed to the exiles in Babylon the wonderful future He had in store for them.

1. AN OPPORTUNITY TO THRIVE SPIRITUALLY. God worked through His spokesperson, Ezekiel, to disclose to the remnant in Babylon that the Lord had not forgotten them. The details about the new temple, its altar, and its sacrifices signaled to the captives that God wanted them to thrive spiritually as His chosen people.

2. AN OCCASION TO HEED GOD'S WILL. The Lord's commitment to the spiritual wellness of the exiles did not mean they could do whatever they wanted. Instead, God's will for them was to follow His sacred laws, to serve His divine purposes, and to be a reflection of His holy character to the people around them. These truths explain why God was so specific about the size of the altar to be built and the nature of the sacrifices to be offered on it.

3. A VICTORIOUS PRIESTHOOD. During the Old Testament era, all the priests offered their sacrifices in the Jerusalem temple. They then returned home, only to go back to the sanctuary on other days to offer still more sacrifices. In contrast, Jesus offered one eternally perfect sacrifice. After His resurrection, He "passed into the heavens" (Heb. 4:14), returning to His eternal home. The other priests' sacrifices may have had some effect, but any benefit was temporary. In offering His atoning sacrifice, Jesus defeated Satan, sin, and death once and for all.

4. AN EFFECTIVE PRIESTHOOD. Jesus alone achieved the goal of redemption. By offering Himself as a sacrifice in the manner the Father wished, the Son became the "author of eternal salvation unto all them that obey him" (5:9). His submissive expression of love and obedience has enabled innumerable lost people down through the centuries to find new life in Him. We are wise to devote every aspect of our lives in adoration and service to the Savior.

FOR ADULTS
■ **TOPIC:** A Sign of Hope
■ **QUESTIONS:** 1. What function would the altar serve in the new temple? 2. What was the theological purpose of the sacrifices offered

on the altar? 3. In what sense did Ezekiel's vision of the altar look backward and forward in time? 4. Why are the Old Testament sacrifices no longer necessary? 5. What did Jesus accomplish by His once-for-all-time sacrifice?

■ **ILLUSTRATIONS:**

The Promise of Restoration. Restoration follows cleansing. That principle works when we take a bath, when we confess our sins, and when we forgive each other and give up our grudges. How pleasant it is to put on clean clothes. How much more delightful it is to be restored to God and one another.

Before we apply soap to our bodies, we have to be convinced that we need a shower. The spiritual counterpart of this is that we must admit that we really have offended God and other people by our behaviors. That's the hard part.

Many people are unconvinced that they need to be spiritually renewed. They refuse to admit the consequences of their sins. They fail to see the necessity of the cleansing that Jesus offers them through His atoning sacrifice at Calvary.

Through Ezekiel's prophecy about the new temple, its altar, and the sacrifices to be offered on it, the prophet declared that God provides forgiveness and complete restoration to those who come to Him in humility and faith. Even today, the Lord is our only hope for a future in which we can be pardoned and reconciled to Him.

Seeing Beyond Our Limitations. For the captives in Babylon, life could not feel more disheartening. They were exiled from their homeland and living among strangers in a foreign place. Yet, in the midst of that seemingly dismal circumstance, God unveiled to His people a vision of a new temple and altar. In doing so, the Lord wanted them, in faith, to see beyond the limitations of their present situation.

Now let's consider Mary. About 12 hours earlier, she had fallen. Since she was unable to get up, she stayed down until help arrived. A whirlwind of events followed: an extended hospital stay, a temporary transfer to a nursing facility, and finally, admission to a skilled nursing home.

Then it really hit: *I won't be returning to my house. I've delegated control of my assets and my medical decisions. Help! I feel so powerless!* In addition, Mary was forced to confront limitations in her own personality, such as her distrust of people and her fear of opening up to them in a meaningful way.

As a result, Mary complained every day and to everyone. Finally, a wise but fed-up resident asked, "Mary, were you hit by a train today?" "Heavens, no!" came her retort. "Then it seems to me you have something to be thankful for," the man said with a smile.

God tries to tell us the same sort of thing: Stop complaining! It is so easy to focus on the limitations before us. Yet the Father asks us to look beyond, to faithfully focus on what He has done and will do for us as a result of His Son's atoning sacrifice at Calvary.

Living in the Present. As God's people languished in exile, they needed their hope in the future renewed. Ezekiel's vision of a new temple, along with an altar and animal sacrifices, provided his peers with the encouragement they needed to live in the present.

In 1943, a young soldier was experiencing World War II combat for the first time in a bloody battle in the Italian mountains. He dived into a foxhole just ahead of some bullets and began deepening the shallow pit. As he frantically scraped with his helmet, he unearthed something shiny. It was a metal cross, lost by a former foxhole occupant.

A second man hurtled in beside the frightened soldier as another round of artillery screamed overhead. After the explosions, the soldier noticed his companion was a chaplain. Holding out the cross, the soldier gasped, "Am I glad to see you! How do you work this thing?"

When circumstances are going bad, help from God can look pretty attractive. If a person doesn't have a relationship with the Father through faith in the crucified and risen Son, figuring out how to connect with the Lord can seem puzzling. It's best to come to faith in Jesus and walk with Him in obedience all along so there's no need to try to figure out how to get in touch with Him when life feels overwhelming.

For Youth

■ **Topic:** An Opportunity to Meet God

■ **Questions:** 1. What kinds of sacrifices would be offered on the altar in the new temple? 2. Why did the altar complex require the provision of steps? 3. In what way did Ezekiel's peers understand his message about the altar and its sacrifices? 4. What is the basis of believers being made right with God? 5. How is it possible for God to never again remember our sins?

■ **Illustrations:**

God's Amazing Plan. As the years and decades passed by for the exiles in Babylon, life must have seemed bleak. Then they heard Ezekiel declare to them God's amazing plan for a new temple and altar. Many of the specific instructions the Lord conveyed through Ezekiel were reminders of God's commitment to meet His people's deepest spiritual needs.

For New Testament believers, Jesus is the One who satisfies their longing to be restored to fellowship with God. When they trust in Jesus, they experience new life. Their rebelliousness and unbelief are supplanted by obedience and dependence, and their hatred is exchanged for unconditional love.

The world might scoff at the idea of receiving new life in the Son. However, believers know from God's Word that this is a reality. Remember, lasting inner renewal cannot be purchased with money or earned by doing good deeds. The lost must put their faith in Jesus, who atoned for their sins at Calvary.

Rising to the Challenge. Riley was born blind. Being sightless, he depends upon his ears and other senses as well as friends for help. More than anything, though, this high school junior wanted to be like his father, who lettered all four years at the same academic institution and won a college football scholarship. Many youth would see the disability as an impossibility to overcome. Few would ever try to play football, let alone dream of succeeding at the sport.

Riley started playing football on the junior varsity team. He worked out on the weight machines. He also went through the training, the drills, and the practice sessions, all for a few occasional plays. Riley never felt overwhelmed by the problem of being blind. And he never gave up his dream. Despite the enormity of the obstacle facing him, he rose to the challenge and strove to succeed.

Thousands of years ago, there were many among the exiles who wanted to give up in the midst of the challenge before them. It was then that God unveiled to Ezekiel a vision of a future that included a new temple and altar. God did so to convince the remnant that they could survive and thrive as His chosen people. Even today, because of what the Father has done for us through His Son's atoning sacrifice on the cross, we can step out in faith and overcome our challenges.

Whom Do You Trust? At the west end of Constitution Avenue in Washington, D.C., screened from the street by a grove of elm and holly trees, sits a bronze statue of Albert Einstein. The theoretical physicist's figure is 21 feet tall. He's seated on a three-step base of white granite. The intellectual genius is depicted in a baggy sweater, wrinkled corduroy trousers, and sandals. His shock of hair is in familiar disarray.

At Einstein's feet is a map of the universe—a 28-foot square slab of granite in which 2,700 small metal studs are embedded. Each stud represents the location in the sky of a planet, major star, or familiar celestial body at noon on April 22, 1979 —the time the memorial was dedicated.

The expression on the face of Einstein's statue is a mixture of wisdom, peace, and wonder. The face reflects the serenity of a man who believed a divine mind had conceived the universe he spent his life trying to understand. He would tell his colleagues who believed in a random universe, "God does not play dice."

Einstein was not a Christian. He put his confidence in an impersonal deity. Thousands of years earlier, Ezekiel used his vision of an altar and sacrifices to be offered on it in a new temple to exhort his peers to trust in the personal God of the Bible. Likewise, we can go beyond Einstein by trusting in the Lord Jesus. Because of His sacrificial death and subsequent resurrection, we have the assurance that He will bring us safely through any difficulty in our lives.

LESSON 11 — NOVEMBER 16

God Revives His People

Background Scripture: Ezekiel 47:1, 3-12
Devotional Reading: Psalm 1

Key Verse: Every thing that liveth, which moveth, whithersoever the rivers shall come, shall live: and there shall be a very great multitude of fish, because these waters shall come thither: for they shall be healed; and every thing shall live whither the river cometh. Ezekiel 47:9.

KING JAMES VERSION

EZEKIEL 47:1 Afterward he brought me again unto the door of the house; and, behold, waters issued out from under the threshold of the house eastward: for the forefront of the house stood toward the east, and the waters came down from under from the right side of the house, at the south side of the altar. . . . 3 And when the man that had the line in his hand went forth eastward, he measured a thousand cubits, and he brought me through the waters; the waters were to the ankles.
4 Again he measured a thousand, and brought me through the waters; the waters were to the knees. Again he measured a thousand, and brought me through; the waters were to the loins. 5 Afterward he measured a thousand; and it was a river that I could not pass over: for the waters were risen, waters to swim in, a river that could not be passed over. 6 And he said unto me, Son of man, hast thou seen this? Then he brought me, and caused me to return to the brink of the river. 7 Now when I had returned, behold, at the bank of the river were very many trees on the one side and on the other. 8 Then said he unto me, These waters issue out toward the east country, and go down into the desert, and go into the sea: which being brought forth into the sea, the waters shall be healed. 9 And it shall come to pass, that every thing that liveth, which moveth, whithersoever the rivers shall come, shall live: and there shall be a very great multitude of fish, because these waters shall come thither: for they shall be healed; and every thing shall live whither the river cometh. 10 And it shall come to pass, that the fishers shall stand upon it from Engedi even unto Eneglaim; they shall be a place to spread forth nets; their fish shall be according to their kinds, as the fish of the great sea, exceeding many. 11 But the miry places thereof and the marishes thereof shall not be healed; they shall be given to salt. 12 And by the river upon the bank thereof, on this side and on that side, shall grow all trees for meat, whose leaf shall not fade, neither shall the fruit thereof be consumed: it shall bring forth new fruit according to his months, because their waters they issued out of the sanctuary: and the fruit thereof shall be for meat, and the leaf thereof for medicine.

NEW REVISED STANDARD VERSION

EZEKIEL 47:1 Then he brought me back to the entrance of the temple; there, water was flowing from below the threshold of the temple toward the east (for the temple faced east); and the water was flowing down from below the south end of the threshold of the temple, south of the altar. . . .

3 Going on eastward with a cord in his hand, the man measured one thousand cubits, and then led me through the water; and it was ankle-deep. 4 Again he measured one thousand, and led me through the water; and it was knee-deep. Again he measured one thousand, and led me through the water; and it was up to the waist.
5 Again he measured one thousand, and it was a river that I could not cross, for the water had risen; it was deep enough to swim in, a river that could not be crossed. 6 He said to me, "Mortal, have you seen this?"
Then he led me back along the bank of the river.
7 As I came back, I saw on the bank of the river a great many trees on the one side and on the other. 8 He said to me, "This water flows toward the eastern region and goes down into the Arabah; and when it enters the sea, the sea of stagnant waters, the water will become fresh. 9 Wherever the river goes, every living creature that swarms will live, and there will be very many fish, once these waters reach there. It will become fresh; and everything will live where the river goes. 10 People will stand fishing beside the sea from En-gedi to En-eglaim; it will be a place for the spreading of nets; its fish will be of a great many kinds, like the fish of the Great Sea. 11 But its swamps and marshes will not become fresh; they are to be left for salt. 12 On the banks, on both sides of the river, there will grow all kinds of trees for food. Their leaves will not wither nor their fruit fail, but they will bear fresh fruit every month, because the water for them flows from the sanctuary. Their fruit will be for food, and their leaves for healing."

Home Bible Readings

Monday, November 10	Jeremiah 2:5-13	*Forsaking the Living Water*
Tuesday, November 11	Zechariah 14:1-8	*Living Water Flows from Jerusalem*
Wednesday, November 12	John 7:37-44	*Let the Thirsty Come to Me*
Thursday, November 13	Revelation 7:13-17	*Guided to the Water of Life*
Friday, November 14	John 4:7-15	*Give Me This Water*
Saturday, November 15	Psalm 1	*Planted by Streams of Water*
Sunday, November 16	Ezekiel 47:1, 3-12	*Water Flowing from the Sanctuary*

Background

We previously learned that in 573 B.C., on the twenty-fifth anniversary of Ezekiel's exile to Babylon, he was supernaturally transported to Jerusalem. There the prophet received a vision of a new temple to be built in Israel's restored land (Ezek. 40:1-4). Chapters 40–43 contain a thorough description of the reconstructed sanctuary. The new service of worship in the temple is detailed in chapters 44–46. This is followed in chapters 47–48 by a picture of the new land of Israel, with its life-giving river, its boundaries, and its divisions. Taken all together, the revelation is a dazzling portrait of a bright future ahead for God's people.

In Ezekiel 44, God revealed to His spokesperson the routine operation of the future temple. The Lord's angelic guide discussed the duties of its appointed ministers, the priests and Levites, and the means of their support. Chapter 45 delineates the allotments of the new land reserved for the priests, Levites, the whole house of Israel, and the prince. The identity of the "prince" (vs. 7) is impossible to determine with certainty. Some think he is the Messiah, but this cannot be since this prince needs a sin offering (see vs. 22) and he has sons (see 46:16). Others conjecture the prince is King David, or some other human representative of the Messiah in the government of the kingdom age to come (see 34:23-24; 37:24).

In any case, chapter 46 gives God's directions to the Israelite princes for proper conduct toward the people of the nation. There are also instructions on the required preparation and procedure for presenting offerings and celebrating holy days. Ezekiel's tour of the future temple ended with the angelic guide bringing the prophet back to the entrance of the sanctuary (47:1). As he stood in the temple's inner courtyard, he saw a life-giving river flowing from it.

Notes on the Printed Text

In Ezekiel's vision of the future temple, the sacred enclosure faced "east" (Ezek. 47:1). The prophet noticed that water also flowed east from beneath the threshold, or entrance, of the temple. The stream passed to the right of the altar of sacrifice on its south side, continued east through the courtyard, and then exited from the sanctuary complex. The angelic guide escorted God's spokesperson outside the temple through the north gateway. From there, the two went around the wall of the compound to the gate that faces east. A small stream of water could be seen trickling out from the south side of the gate (vs. 2).

The presence of water flowing from the future temple brings to mind the river that flowed from Eden to water its orchard and suggests that the end-time sanctuary will be the center of God's new creation (see Gen. 2:10). The perennial streams of the garden were a source of life-sustaining refreshment. The lushness of this Edenic paradise forms the backdrop of Psalm 46:4. A figurative "river" and its "streams" are depicted as bringing joy to the "city of God." The latter is none other than the special, holy dwelling place of the "most High."

A corresponding depiction is found in Joel 3:18. The Lord promised the remnant that in the time of restoration, the mountains of Zion would drip with sweet "wine," the hills would "flow with milk," and Judah's ravines would run with water. A spring would flow out from the temple of the Lord and water the parched "valley" of acacia trees (possibly located in the plains of Moab, northeast of the Dead Sea). The language used here is an embellished way of describing the overflowing blessing that God would shower on His people in the kingdom age.

Accompanying God's abundant provision is forgiveness of sin. In the future, He who is the spring of life-giving water (see Jer. 2:13; 17:13) not only declared that bountiful streams would "go out from Jerusalem" (Zech. 14:8), but also that a fountain would be opened up to "the house of David and the inhabitants of Jerusalem" (13:1) to cleanse them from "sin" and impurity. Ultimately, through Jesus and the Holy Spirit, believers find this abundance of pardon (see John 7:37-39). The eternal life Jesus offers amply satisfies the spiritual thirst of people forever (see 10:10). Indeed, God's gift of salvation is comparable to a fountain of water that vigorously wells up in believers in an inner, unending, and overflowing supply (see 4:14).

As the angelic guide led God's spokesperson in an eastward direction, the escort used a measuring "line" (Ezek. 47:3) he held in his hand to mark off a "thousand cubits" (or 1,750 feet) downstream. Then the guide led Ezekiel through the water, which was up to his ankles. Next, the escort measured off another "thousand" (vs. 4) cubits downstream. As the two waded through at this point, the water came up to the prophet's knees. After another thousand cubits, the water came up to his waist. Just one thousand cubits downstream from there, the current had become an impassable river. The water was deep enough to swim in, but too deep to walk through (vs. 5). The series of measurements appearing in these verses contribute to a larger, complex scenario that symbolically depicts God's abundant provision. The latter includes the promise of forgiveness, new life, and fruitful service in His kingdom.

In a corresponding way, Isaiah 55 reassured the captives in Babylon of God's abundant provision. In this case, the Lord called out to the remnant as if He were a street vendor selling food and water. Life for the exiles may not always have been good, but it was at least secure and familiar. A return to Judah would involve unknown hardships and hazards. Thus, God promised spiritual benefits if the exiles would take the risk of returning. God had many blessings to offer His people, including water, wine, and milk. He urged His people to obtain His goods, but to do so without spending any money (vs. 1). The idea is that they were to take freely from Him what they normally would have had to pay for. This is a marvelous picture of God's unmerited favor, which is otherwise known as grace.

The angelic guide asked whether Ezekiel had been paying attention to the unfolding vision (Ezek. 47:6). The answer is that the prophet had carefully noted everything he saw. When the escort led Ezekiel back to the riverbank, he was surprised by the sight of a large number of "trees" (vs. 7) growing on both sides of the river. Such abundance is reminiscent of the Garden of Eden, where God caused all kinds of beautiful, fruitful trees to grow. In the middle of this pristine orchard stood the tree that gives life (see Gen. 2:9). In Ezekiel's vision of the new temple, the river and its orchard indicated the Lord's intent to transform Jerusalem and its environs into a paradise-like garden.

The angelic guide explained to Ezekiel that the water flowed eastward through the desert to the Jordan River valley and emptied into the stagnant, filthy Dead Sea (which is approximately 25 percent saline). In so doing, the salty water became fresh and pure (Ezek. 47:8). The Hebrew text of this verse literally reads "the waters become healed," which is figuratively expressive of the power of God to bring about restoration and renewal. Just as in the original creation the earth teemed with life (see Gen. 1:20-25), so too swarms of living creatures would one day flourish wherever the river from the temple flowed.

Unlike today, the Dead Sea would become the habitat for a "very great multitude of fish" (Ezek. 47:9). Also, as hard as it is to currently imagine, people would fish on the shore of the sea from En Gedi (located about midway along the western shore of the Dead Sea) to En Eglaim (possibly near the northwestern corner of the Dead Sea; vs. 10). Moreover, they would spread out their nets on the coast to dry. Indeed, there would be as many different kinds of fish swarming in the Dead Sea as the aquatic life populating the Mediterranean Sea. The only exception would be the swamps and "marshes" (vs. 11) along the shore. These waters would remain briny, so that people could extract salt from it, perhaps for use in temple sacrifices (see 43:24).

The angelic guide revealed that all kinds of fruit "trees" (47:12) would flourish on both sides of the river's banks. Amazingly, the leaves of these trees would never wither, and they would always bear fresh fruit on their branches. Every month a new crop would be ready for God's people to enjoy. This was made possible by the water from the temple, which streamed continuously to the orchard. People would harvest the luscious fruit to eat and use the leaves for healing. This depiction of agricultural abundance signifies the extent to which God intended to restore His people to their homeland after the exile.

Revelation 22:1-5 draws upon similar imagery to describe the eternal state. John, while exiled on the island of Patmos (see 1:9), saw a "pure river" (22:1) containing the "water of life." The river was crystal clear, and it flowed from God's throne down the middle of the city's main thoroughfare. The river and its water are a symbol of the fullness of eternal life that proceeds from the presence of God. To those living in the hot and dry climate of Palestine this scene would be a vivid image of God's ability to satisfy their spiritual thirst (see John 4:7-14; Rev. 22:17).

John noted that a "tree of life" (Rev. 22:2) grew on "either side of the river." Some think the Greek noun rendered "tree" (vs. 2) should be taken in a collective sense to refer to an orchard lining both sides of the riverbank. In either case, the tree bears 12 different kinds of "fruit," with a new crop appearing each "month" of the year. The fruit gives life, and the "leaves" are used as medicine to heal the "nations." The presence of health-giving leaves does not mean there is illness in heaven. Rather, the leaves symbolize the health and vigor that believers enjoy in eternity.

In the new creation, the Father and the Son are seated on their thrones, and the redeemed worship and serve them continually (vs. 3). God establishes unbroken communion with His people, and He claims them as His own (vs. 4). The end of history is better than the beginning, for a radiant city replaces the Garden of Eden, and the light of God's glory drives out all darkness. There is neither idleness nor boredom in the eternal state, for God gives His people ruling responsibilities (vs. 5). Revelation, as the final book in Scripture, assures us of God's enduring purposes and should also increase our longing for communion with the Lord.

SUGGESTIONS TO TEACHERS

For believers, trust is acquired one experience at a time. They often place their faith in people and confidence in circumstances, only to be let down or disappointed. In contrast, God will never fail His people. As the "Alpha and the Omega" (Rev. 21:6), He has the ability to do what He says. Also, as "the beginning and the end," He has the power to fulfill all His promises—including those associated with Ezekiel's vision of the new temple.

1. DECIDING TO TRUST. Three kinds of evidence prove that we can trust our all-powerful God. First, we have the witness of Scripture. Second, we have the testimony of others concerning what God has done for us. Third, we learn to trust God through personal experience. Each time we experience His strength, love, and goodness, our trust has an opportunity to grow like a flourishing tree planted next to the life-giving waters of a deep river (see Ezek. 47:6-7).

2. RECALLING THE PAST. God repeatedly told His people to remember what He had done for them (see, for example, Deut. 6:12). Also, Jeremiah said that God's mercies "are new every morning" (Lam. 3:23). Moreover, Israel failed morally because the nation had a limited spiritual memory bank (see Isa. 17:10). These truths stress how important it is for us as believers to strengthen our trust in God.

3. RESOLVING TO TRUST. Through prayer and Bible study, we can plant our feet daily on Jesus, our Rock. We can also strengthen our trust in God by testifying to His work in our lives. Doing this brings to our conscious level of awareness just how involved the Lord is in our daily matters.

For Adults

■ **Topic:** Life Needs Water
■ **Questions:** 1. What did Ezekiel see at the entrance to the temple? 2. Why do you think the angelic guide progressively measured off the riverbank? 3. What was the significance of the orchard growing on both sides of the river? 4. What kind of spiritual life does the Father make available to us through faith in His Son? 5. In what ways is the Lord able to bring about spiritual wellness in our lives?

■ **Illustrations:**

Spiritual Fruitfulness and Healing. The television series, *Extreme Makeover*, showcases everyday people who undergo a series of cosmetic procedures and supposedly have their lives changed forever. One season included two sisters who struggled with cleft palates and underwent nearly 40 surgeries; a colorful bull rider who had his teeth knocked out and wanted to be transformed into an urban cowboy; and a female rock musician who spent her days hiding behind her shocking stage appearance. These and other participants recuperated at the "Makeover Mansion," a luxurious residence tucked away in the Hollywood Hills, complete with stunning views, a swimming pool, fully equipped home gym, and plasma televisions.

This primetime version of a new start on life is a far cry from what we find revealed in Ezekiel 47:1-12. God doesn't promise to remodel our dying physical bodies. And we aren't going to be given a lavish estate that will eventually decay and fall apart. What the Lord has in store for us—spiritual fruitfulness and healing—is far better and will be everlasting.

Home Where I Belong. Earl and Christine were settled into their lives in western Kansas. They thought they had found their "hometown." They had lots of friends and ministry opportunities that made them feel wanted and loved.

However, both Earl and Christine felt God calling them into full-time ministry. For them that meant they had to move away to a large city in another state to attend seminary (a divinity school). They left their nice home to live in a small two-bedroom apartment on the seminary campus. They left friends who knew all of their strengths and weaknesses to be with people they initially did not know. They left good-paying jobs with lots of benefits to work five part-time jobs between them with no benefits.

Even with all of the losses, Earl and Christine found a wonderful new home. God blessed them with new friends, caring professors, and exciting challenges. As Earl and Christine look back on those years of change and sacrifice, they realized that God always provided for their needs—even if it was at the last minute! God also helped the couple grow spiritually in ways they never had imagined. They both felt they had finally come home to a place they had always needed to be.

For Earl and Christine, their experience was just a small taste of what their new home will be like in God's eternal presence. As Ezekiel 47:1-12 reveals, everything will be pristine and full of life, and believers will feel like they have come home to the place where they belong.

Let's Go to Your House. Tom was elderly, and for many years he had enjoyed taking long walks with the Lord each evening. On these walks, Tom and the Lord would talk about all kinds of things, especially about many of the important times in Tom's life, such as when he met his wife, the birth of his children, and special Christmases.

One day, while Tom was out walking with the Lord for an especially long time, Tom sensed the Lord conveying to him, "We are closer to My house than we are to yours. Why don't you just come home with Me?" Tom was glad to go and experience the abundance of God's healing "waters" (Ezek. 47:8).

I think that is the way God would like for all of us to view being in His eternal presence. In Revelation 21:7, the Lord said He would be our God and we would be His children. Going to heaven is coming home to be part of the everlasting family of God.

For Youth

■ **Topic:** More than Enough

■ **Questions:** 1. From where did the water originate that Ezekiel saw? 2. What did Ezekiel notice as he waded farther downstream? 3. What did Ezekiel see growing on each side of the river? 4. How is it possible for the Lord to enable us to thrive spiritually? 5. What spiritual resources has God made available so that we can grow stronger in our faith?

■ **Illustrations:**

Water Power! In 1990, the comedy *Home Alone* appeared in movie theaters. The film is about eight-year-old Kevin McAllister, who is accidentally left behind when his family takes off for a vacation in France over the holiday season. Once he realizes they've left him home by himself, Kevin learns to fend for himself. He eventually has to protect his house against bumbling burglars, Harry and Marv, who are planning to rob every house in Kevin's suburban Chicago neighborhood.

In the eternal state, God does not leave the redeemed all alone in their celestial home to fend for themselves. As we learn from Ezekiel 47:1-12 (the focus of this week's lesson), He makes His dwelling place among them and graces them with His overflowing, glorious presence. He removes every trace of vice, permitting only what is virtuous to remain. Best of all, His people reign with Him forever. Now that is good news worth sharing!

Leaving the Old Behind. During Alexa's childhood, her family often moved because of her dad's job. By the time Alexa graduated from high school, she had attended six different schools.

While going to new schools was often scary for Alexa, her mother tried to help her look for the good things that could come from new challenges. Alexa's mom said it was a golden opportunity for Alexa to change her attitude and grow more confident. No one would know how scared Alexa felt. It was a chance for her to make new friends and set new goals.

Alexa especially remembers her family's move during her middle school years. She came from a school with about 300 students to one with over 900 students. Alexa decided she was going to be more outgoing and not as shy in this new school. It was fun to create a "new world" for herself. She was still true to herself—with the same likes, dislikes, and morals, for example—but she was "allowed" to talk more freely in class and to be more adventurous. She even tried out for the school play and joined several clubs!

Thousands of years ago, God used Ezekiel to show the Israelites a sacred new place known for its abundance of life and fresh opportunities to thrive. Even today, as we look ahead to the new world God creates for believers in heaven, we can be excited to know that all old things pass away. No one will care about the past mistakes and failures in our lives if our name is written in the Lamb's book of life.

A Happy Ending. Sasha was given a chance to choose a dog for her birthday present. At the pet store, she was shown a number of puppies. From them she picked the one whose tail was wagging furiously. When asked why she chose that particular dog, Sasha exclaimed, "I wanted the one with the happy ending!"

Everyone will share in the ultimate "happy ending," if they make the choice now to follow the living Savior. In Ezekiel's day, the Lord promised the exiles in Babylon that a new opportunity awaited them in which they would enjoy the abundance of His life-giving presence (see 47:1-12). The Bible also promises us that a new world is coming for all believers, and what a happy "beginning" it will be!

LESSON 12 — NOVEMBER 23

GOD TRANSFORMS HIS PEOPLE

BACKGROUND SCRIPTURE: Ezekiel 47:13-23; Acts 2:37-47
DEVOTIONAL READING: Psalm 51:1-13

Key Verse: Peter said unto them, Repent, and be baptized every one of you in the name of Jesus Christ for the remission of sins, and ye shall receive the gift of the Holy Ghost. Acts 2:38.

KING JAMES VERSION
EZEKIEL 47:13 Thus saith the Lord GOD; This shall be the border, whereby ye shall inherit the land according to the twelve tribes of Israel: Joseph shall have two portions. 14 And ye shall inherit it, one as well as another: concerning the which I lifted up mine hand to give it unto your fathers: and this land shall fall unto you for inheritance. 15 And this shall be the border of the land toward the north side, from the great sea, the way of Hethlon, as men go to Zedad; 16 Hamath, Berothah, Sibraim, which is between the border of Damascus and the border of Hamath; Hazarhatticon, which is by the coast of Hauran. 17 And the border from the sea shall be Hazarenan, the border of Damascus, and the north northward, and the border of Hamath. And this is the north side. 18 And the east side ye shall measure from Hauran, and from Damascus, and from Gilead, and from the land of Israel by Jordan, from the border unto the east sea. And this is the east side. 19 And the south side southward, from Tamar even to the waters of strife in Kadesh, the river to the great sea. And this is the south side southward. 20 The west side also shall be the great sea from the border, till a man come over against Hamath. This is the west side. 21 So shall ye divide this land unto you according to the tribes of Israel. 22 And it shall come to pass, that ye shall divide it by lot for an inheritance unto you, and to the strangers that sojourn among you, which shall beget children among you: and they shall be unto you as born in the country among the children of Israel; they shall have inheritance with you among the tribes of Israel. 23 And it shall come to pass, that in what tribe the stranger sojourneth, there shall ye give him his inheritance, saith the Lord GOD.

NEW REVISED STANDARD VERSION
EZEKIEL 47:13 Thus says the Lord GOD: These are the boundaries by which you shall divide the land for inheritance among the twelve tribes of Israel. Joseph shall have two portions. 14 You shall divide it equally; I swore to give it to your ancestors, and this land shall fall to you as your inheritance.
15 This shall be the boundary of the land: On the north side, from the Great Sea by way of Hethlon to Lebo-hamath, and on to Zedad, 16 Berothah, Sibraim (which lies between the border of Damascus and the border of Hamath), as far as Hazer-hatticon, which is on the border of Hauran. 17 So the boundary shall run from the sea to Hazar-enon, which is north of the border of Damascus, with the border of Hamath to the north. This shall be the north side.
18 On the east side, between Hauran and Damascus; along the Jordan between Gilead and the land of Israel; to the eastern sea and as far as Tamar. This shall be the east side.
19 On the south side, it shall run from Tamar as far as the waters of Meribath-kadesh, from there along the Wadi of Egypt to the Great Sea. This shall be the south side.
20 On the west side, the Great Sea shall be the boundary to a point opposite Lebo-hamath. This shall be the west side.
21 So you shall divide this land among you according to the tribes of Israel. 22 You shall allot it as an inheritance for yourselves and for the aliens who reside among you and have begotten children among you. They shall be to you as citizens of Israel; with you they shall be allotted an inheritance among the tribes of Israel. 23 In whatever tribe aliens reside, there you shall assign them their inheritance, says the Lord GOD.

Home Bible Readings

Monday, November 17	Isaiah 42:5-9	*God Declares New Things*
Tuesday, November 18	Isaiah 42:10-16	*A New Song, a New Way*
Wednesday, November 19	Psalm 51:1-13	*A New and Right Spirit*
Thursday, November 20	Lamentations 3:19-26	*New Mercies Every Morning*
Friday, November 21	1 Peter 1:1-7	*A New Birth, a Living Hope*
Saturday, November 22	Acts 2:37-47	*All Who Believed Were Together*
Sunday, November 23	Ezekiel 47:13-23	*Inheritance for the Immigrants*

Background

The division of the Promised Land into equal portions among Israel's 12 tribes was in accordance with God's promise to the patriarchs that their descendants would inherit the entire region (Ezek. 47:14). For instance, Genesis 12:7 records God's appearance to Abraham (Abram) when he was 75 and the Lord's pledge to give Canaan to the patriarch's offspring. Ten years later, when he was 85, God again appeared to Abraham. On this occasion, the Lord made a covenant with the patriarch and defined the extent of the land his descendants would receive. The territory lay between the river of Egypt (probably one of the seasonal rivers in the Negev) in the south to the Euphrates River in the north. At that time, this land was occupied by ten people groups (see 15:18-21).

Thirty-one years after that, when Abraham was 116, God once more reiterated His promise to the patriarch (see 22:17). The Lord declared that He would give Abraham innumerable descendants, that they would be victorious over their foes, and that through the patriarch's offspring all nations on earth would experience God's blessing. One hundred twenty-one years later, when Jacob was 77 years old, his father, Isaac (the son of Abraham), pronounced a blessing on his son, Jacob. He learned that he would receive the divine blessings originally given to Abraham. This included the promise of many descendants, who would one day occupy Canaan (see 28:3-4).

Notes on the Printed Text

In last week's lesson, we learned about Ezekiel's vision of a life-giving river that flowed from the new temple (see Ezek. 47:1-12). This week we turn our attention to the boundaries of the Promised Land (vss. 13-20) and its distribution to the 12 tribes of Israel. God's spokesperson discovered that the land would be fully restored to the order and oversight that God decreed. Also, the land would be divided equally among the nation's "tribes" (vs. 13). The tribe of Levi was the one exception, since its members lived on a designated portion of the sacrifices offered in the rebuilt temple (see 44:28-31; 45:1-8; 48:8-14). So, in order to keep the number of Israelite tribes at 12, Joseph's tribe was divided into two. This meant that one portion of Joseph's allocation would go to Ephraim and the other to Manasseh.

During the reigns of David and Solomon, God brought to pass what He previously pledged to the patriarchs concerning their descendants' inheritance of the promised land. For instance, at the dedication of the Jerusalem temple Solomon had built, those who attended the ceremony came from Lebo Hamath to the brook of Egypt (1 Kings 8:65), that is, a domain extending from the Euphrates River to the border of Egypt (see Num. 34:1-12; 2 Sam. 8:3; 1 Kings 4:21; 1 Chron. 13:5; 2 Chron. 9:26). These boundaries roughly correspond to the borders recorded in Ezekiel 47:15-20. On the eastern section of the promised land, the boundary started at the source of the Jordan River south of Damascus and extended south to the shore of the Dead Sea. Toward the west, the Mediterranean Sea formed the border. The northern boundary began near Tyre and extended east to a spot north of the Sea of Galilee. In the south, the border proceeded from an area below the Dead Sea to the Wadi of Egypt (that is, the Wadi el-Arish, about 50 miles southwest of Gaza) on the coast of the Mediterranean Sea.

In 1406 B.C., the Lord used Joshua to lead the Israelites in the conquest of Canaan. During this extended military operation, which is recorded in Joshua 1–12, God demonstrated to the inhabitants exactly who He was. In particular, His miraculous display of power over nature put to shame the pagan deities of the Canaanites. Next, the division of the promised land is summarized in Joshua 13–21. By enabling His chosen people to settle Canaan, God fulfilled His promise to Abraham. In Ezekiel's vision of the new temple and restored land, the Lord revealed to the remnant that one day they would have the opportunity to divide the territory among Israel's 12 tribes (Ezek. 47:21).

In verse 22, the mention of resident foreigners reveals that in a future day, the faith community would include both Jews and Gentiles. Furthermore, God disclosed to Ezekiel that the foreigners living among the remnant would be considered as citizens of "Israel" (see Lev. 19:34; 24:22; Num. 15:29; Isa. 56:3-8). This amazing display of welcoming outsiders as equals included them receiving an "inheritance" (Ezek. 47:22) allotment along with God's chosen people. Verse 23 states that the foreigners were to be given some land within the "tribe" in which they took up residence. This directive was not optional, either, for it came directly from the "Lord GOD."

A foretaste of this inclusiveness occurred in A.D. 30 on the day of Pentecost (see Acts 2). The name *Pentecost* comes from a Greek word meaning "fiftieth." The festival fell on the fiftieth day after the Passover Sabbath. Along with the festivals of unleavened bread and tabernacles, Pentecost was one of the three great Jewish religious holy days. The population of Jerusalem swelled during each of these festivals as pilgrims streamed into the city from all over the Roman Empire. The risen Lord had commanded His disciples not to immediately leave Jerusalem but to wait for the arrival of the Spirit (see Luke 24:49; Acts 1:4). In obedience to Jesus, His followers were all together "in one place" (Acts 2:1).

Ten days after Jesus ascended into heaven, the Holy Spirit came upon Jesus' disciples as they assembled in one location. Some think His followers were at that moment in one of the courts of the Jerusalem temple (see Luke 24:52-53), while others maintain that the disciples were in the upper room of a house (see Acts 1:13). Observable evidences of the Spirit's arrival included the sound of wind, the appearance of what looked like tongues of flame resting on each disciple, and supernatural empowerment to speak in tongues. Because the Spirit enabled the disciples to converse in other languages, God's message of salvation reached people from many nations that day. These foreign Jews, along with Gentile converts, were amazed to hear locals fluently speaking in dialects from around the empire.

When the Spirit spoke to the multitude through Peter in a powerful sermon, many people became deeply convicted of their sin and asked the apostle what they should do. He instructed them to turn away from sin, be baptized in Jesus' name, and receive His forgiveness. About 3,000 people accepted the message that day and were baptized. The Father would use them to take the good news of salvation in the Son back with them to their homelands. Even the people who did not respond to Peter's message were filled with wonder at what they heard and saw. Miraculous signs were evidence of God's power and presence with the believers.

Moreover, the believers were devoted to the issues that made them one: hearing the teaching of truth, fellowship and the Lord's Supper, corporate worship in the Jerusalem temple, and prayer. It did not matter whether Jesus' followers were native-born Jews or foreigners. In harmony with the directives recorded in Ezekiel 47:22-23, as the faith community focused on their common devotion to the Savior, they freely shared their material goods with the needy in their midst. Because both love and unity characterized the lives of these believers, each day more and more people put their trust in the Messiah and were saved.

SUGGESTIONS TO TEACHERS

In this week's lesson, we encounter Ezekiel's vision of a future inheritance in which the boundaries and distribution of the promised land are detailed. It serves as a picture of new beginnings for the redeemed, a preview of which occurred on the day of Pentecost. As Acts 2 reveals, with the coming of the Holy Spirit, believers had every important thing in common.

1. A MARVELOUS REMINDER. On one level, Ezekiel's vision of the borders and allotment of the promised land specifically concerned the 12 tribes of Israel. Yet, on another level, as Ezekiel 47:22 discloses, even foreigners living among the 12 tribes would receive an allotment. Indeed, these resident outsiders would be considered as citizens of Israel. This is a marvelous reminder of God's gracious inclusion of anyone who comes to Him in faith, regardless of their gender, ethnicity, or race.

2. A NEW SPIRITUAL BEGINNING. The day of Pentecost was an episode characterized by inclusiveness. After all, as Acts 2 states, people from all over the Roman

Empire heard Jesus' followers proclaim the risen Lord and the coming of the Holy Spirit. Jews and Gentiles alike had an opportunity to embrace this new spiritual beginning and share with others this gift from God.

3. A CONCERN FOR OTHERS. Some today whimper that God seems absent or that He has deserted them. But this isn't true of those who have been touched by the Spirit. Those rejoicing in the Spirit know they're never alone. When we're saved, the Spirit abides in us and helps us live for Jesus. When we yield control of our lives to the Spirit, He helps us overcome our selfish impulses. And when God's Spirit is in control of our lives, we consider other people's needs above our own wants and desires.

4. A COMMITMENT TO ONE ANOTHER. Those early Spirit-filled Christians were confident that they were empowered to carry on the ministry Jesus had entrusted to them. They were also committed to one another. There were no isolationist tendencies among these believers, and neither should there be among us.

FOR ADULTS

■ **TOPIC:** A New Beginning

■ **QUESTIONS:** 1. Why did God stress to Ezekiel that it was the sovereign "Lord" (Ezek. 47:13, 23) who was speaking to the prophet? 2. In specifying the boundaries for the land, how was God being faithful to the promise He made to the patriarchs? 3. Why would God decree that foreigners living among the Israelites were to receive an allotment of the promised land? 4. Why is it important for believers to share what they have with one another? 5. How can believers show that the good news about the Lord is meant for all people to receive by faith?

■ **ILLUSTRATIONS:**

Making a New Start. What do Andrew Carnegie, Henry Ford, Luther Burbank, and Charlie Chaplin have in common? Each rose from an impoverished background and became a superachiever in his field.

Carnegie came to America as an immigrant and rose to become one of the wealthiest businesspersons in America. Ford's interest in machinery while living on a Michigan farm started a revolution to the motorcar industry.

Burbank's lack of a formal education did not prevent him from becoming a world-class breeder of plants. Last, Chaplin overcame his impoverished childhood to become a famous star of silent movies. All these persons, at one point, felt they had little to contribute to the world.

Ezekiel 47:22-23 reminds us that regardless of our backgrounds, God can work in our lives to do good for His glory. His grace is that inclusive. As we submit to His will, we have an opportunity not only to make a new start, but also to share with others how God can enable them to do so too.

Common Ground at Sea. Ezekiel experienced a vision of a future in which there would be no distinction between regenerate Israelites and non-Israelites (see Ezek. 47:22). The day of Pentecost offered Jesus' followers a glimpse of what this would be like when different races of people from across the Roman Empire heard the Gospel and turned to the Savior in faith (see Acts 2).

From the time he heard the Gospel from a missionary in the jungles of his native Ivory Coast, to the last months of his life as a student at Taylor University, Samuel "Sammy" Morris (1872–1893) drew everyone he met to a unique oneness in Christ. When Morris decided to sail to America from Africa to learn more about the Gospel, the crew of the ship he was on mutinied. Amazingly, through prayer, Morris was able to calm that situation. His strong faith had a dramatic impact on the captain and crew. A biography of his life, *The March of Faith*, describes what happened next:

"The crew as a whole were without ideals, and had no common ground or affinity, being recruited from all parts of the world. Each lip proclaimed a different tongue. Each heart recalled a different home. But now [after several weeks of Sammy's influence], all prayed and sang with Samuel Morris. Differences of race, country, language, and creed were forgotten. Sammy's God became their God. The Light that had brought him to them shone through him so radiantly that all could see it, and seeing it found a new bond of brotherhood."

A Beautiful Unity. Perhaps Ezekiel marveled when he learned that God's vision for the future included Israelites and non-Israelites commonly experiencing the Lord's blessings (see Ezek. 47:22-23). Similarly, Jesus' followers must have been filled with awe when thousands of foreigners from diverse regions of the Roman Empire joined the Christian faith on the day of Pentecost (see Acts 2:41).

Marissa was a young woman who worked in a manufacturing company. In her first few months at the company, she had run into several Christians from different church denominations. One afternoon at lunch, Marissa was talking with Fran—a Christian coworker—who had an idea.

Fran said, "Let's start a Bible study and prayer group during our lunch hour once a week and invite anyone who'd like to attend." Marissa was skeptical. "I've had conversations with some of the Christians around here, and a few of them are pretty dogmatic about their specific beliefs. A Bible study could get messy," she intoned. "Well then," Fran replied, undaunted, "let's just get together and pray for each other and for the people here at work."

Marissa had to laugh. Fran was never one to give up easily, and her faith was always shining through everything she did. She was a great encouragement to Marissa and to everyone Fran met. "OK," Marissa agreed. "When do we start?" "How about next Thursday?" Fran suggested.

The following Thursday, a handful of Christians began meeting together to pray.

Marissa knew that some of them could be tenacious about defending their belief traditions. But in the prayer meeting, no one was at odds. Everyone had the same purpose—to bring their needs and praise before their common Lord and Savior. In those meetings, differences fell away, and a beautiful unity prevailed. Marissa couldn't help but come away each time feeling as if she'd tasted a bit of heaven.

FOR YOUTH

■ **TOPIC:** God's Gift of New Starts

■ **QUESTIONS:** 1. Why did God decree that the promised land was to be divided equally among Israel's tribes? 2. Why would the tribe of Joseph be allotted a double portion? 3. In what way were foreigners living among God's people to be considered citizens of Israel? 4. How does God's Spirit help us become more sensitive to the needs of others? 5. What are some ways we can share God's gift of a new spiritual beginning with others?

■ **ILLUSTRATIONS:**

Reaching Others with God's Message. Ezekiel's vision of the new temple also included details about the land where it was located. The Lord disclosed to His spokesperson what the boundaries of that land would be and how it would be distributed. Amazingly, both native-born Israelites and resident foreigners would be allotted an "inheritance" (Ezek. 47:22).

At times, we might think God's gift of a new start applies to others, not us. Our circumstantial limitations—whether physical, mental, emotional, or financial—can feel disqualifying, and we might conclude that God has disregarded us. Or perhaps a personal failure leads us to believe that God has written us out of His plan and purpose.

This week's lesson is a reminder that God uses His unlimited power in many ways: to create, to disclose the future, to save, to fulfill His Word, and to use whomever He wishes for His purposes. He can even bring about a new beginning in our lives. He also can use us in extraordinary ways to reach others with His message of love and grace. None of our limitations limit God. He delights to demonstrate His power through us.

God's Grace Freely Offered. Ezekiel's vision of God's chosen people restored to the promised land included foreigners being considered as citizens of Israel (Ezek. 47:22). Thousands of years ago, on the day of Pentecost, Jesus' followers caught a glimpse of this inclusive vision when thousands of people from all over the Roman Empire became followers of Jesus (see Acts 2:41). Even today, God's grace reaches out to the unsaved in remarkable ways.

According to Ethan Fowler, a correspondent for *Reporter News*, in October 2012, tough-looking bikers held a "bike blessing and service" as the "final event" of the "White Buffalo Bikefest." It took place at the Coliseum at Western Texas College in Snyder, Texas. The men and women who participated were part of the Christian Motorcyclists Association (CMA), which has about 125,000 members worldwide.

Many Christian bikers are ex-motorcycle gang members who were once mixed up in drugs, drinking, and crime and had given their lives to the Savior. Others are former business people who hit rock bottom, sometimes because of drugs and partying. Members reach out to non-Christian bikers by establishing a presence at motorcycle rallies, shows, and gang funerals, where they freely offer to counsel anyone who wants help.

The Christian bikers are low-key. Sometimes motorcycle toughs sneer them at. But usually the bikers get along with CMA members because of their common appearance—denim jackets, aviator sunglasses, tattoos, long hair, and studded leather—and love for motorcycles.

We Belong Together. God revealed to the captives in Babylon that a time was coming when Israelites and non-Israelites would jointly experience His blessings (see Ezek. 47:22-23). Centuries later, on the day of Pentecost, the Lord brought together thousands of people from different regions of the Roman Empire and showered them with His saving grace (see Acts 2:41).

During World War II, after the Nazis had forced the surrender of the French troops, the enemy compelled many captured soldiers to work in Nazi factories. One group of prisoners quickly discovered that they were being made to help produce bombs in a munitions plant. That's when they remembered who they were and what their priorities should be.

Though reduced to the status of slave laborers, these prisoners tried to serve France in whatever ways they could. They worked on the production line, and saw the bombs they had helped make sent off to be dropped on their fellow citizens and their allies. But these brave workers had carefully and deliberately fixed the detonating mechanism on each bomb in such a way that it would not set off an explosion.

For some time, the Nazi Luftwaffe dropped these deadly looking bombs before they discovered what these workers had done. Investigators found small slips of paper in the dummy bombs that said, "We're doing the best we can with what we've got, where we are, and in every opportunity we get."

Perhaps a similar message to us as Jesus' followers would be this: "We belong together through faith in the Lord. So be faithful to Him by doing the best you can for others with what you have, where you are, and in every opportunity you get!"

LESSON 13 — NOVEMBER 30

GOD FREES HIS PEOPLE

BACKGROUND SCRIPTURE: Psalm 33; Isaiah 52:1-2, 7-12
DEVOTIONAL READING: Psalm 42:5-11

Key Verse: How beautiful upon the mountains are the feet of him that bringeth good tidings, that publisheth peace; that bringeth good tidings of good, that publisheth salvation; that saith unto Zion, Thy God reigneth! Isaiah 52:7.

KING JAMES VERSION

ISAIAH 52:1 Awake, awake; put on thy strength, O Zion; put on thy beautiful garments, O Jerusalem, the holy city: for henceforth there shall no more come into thee the uncircumcised and the unclean. 2 Shake thyself from the dust; arise, and sit down, O Jerusalem: loose thyself from the bands of thy neck, O captive daughter of Zion. . . .

7 How beautiful upon the mountains are the feet of him that bringeth good tidings, that publisheth peace; that bringeth good tidings of good, that publisheth salvation; that saith unto Zion, Thy God reigneth! 8 Thy watchmen shall lift up the voice; with the voice together shall they sing: for they shall see eye to eye, when the LORD shall bring again Zion. 9 Break forth into joy, sing together, ye waste places of Jerusalem: for the LORD hath comforted his people, he hath redeemed Jerusalem. 10 The LORD hath made bare his holy arm in the eyes of all the nations; and all the ends of the earth shall see the salvation of our God. 11 Depart ye, depart ye, go ye out from thence, touch no unclean thing; go ye out of the midst of her; be ye clean, that bear the vessels of the LORD. 12 For ye shall not go out with haste, nor go by flight: for the LORD will go before you; and the God of Israel will be your rereward.

NEW REVISED STANDARD VERSION

ISAIAH 52:1 Awake, awake,
   put on your strength, O Zion!
Put on your beautiful garments,
   O Jerusalem, the holy city;
for the uncircumcised and the unclean
   shall enter you no more.
2 Shake yourself from the dust, rise up,
   O captive Jerusalem;
loose the bonds from your neck,
   O captive daughter Zion! . . .
7 How beautiful upon the mountains
   are the feet of the messenger who announces peace,
who brings good news,
   who announces salvation,
who says to Zion, "Your God reigns."
8 Listen! Your sentinels lift up their voices,
   together they sing for joy;
for in plain sight they see
   the return of the LORD to Zion.
9 Break forth together into singing,
   you ruins of Jerusalem;
for the LORD has comforted his people,
   he has redeemed Jerusalem.
10 The LORD has bared his holy arm
   before the eyes of all the nations;
and all the ends of the earth shall see
   the salvation of our God.
11 Depart, depart, go out from there!
   Touch no unclean thing;
go out from the midst of it, purify yourselves,
   you who carry the vessels of the LORD.
12 For you shall not go out in haste,
   and you shall not go in flight;
for the LORD will go before you,
   and the God of Israel will be your rear guard.

Home Bible Readings

Monday, November 24	Psalm 42:5-11	Hope in God!
Tuesday, November 25	Psalm 33:1-9	Fear, Awe, and Praise
Wednesday, November 26	Psalm 33:10-22	O Lord, We Hope in You
Thursday, November 27	1 Timothy 4:4-11	Hope Set on the Living God
Friday, November 28	Psalm 85:1-7	The God of Our Salvation
Saturday, November 29	Genesis 15:1-6	God Is Our Shield
Sunday, November 30	Isaiah 52:1-2, 7-12	God before Us, God behind Us

Background

In Isaiah 51:1—52:12, we read how God, through Isaiah, spoke to the Jews in exile long after the prophet's day. The Lord reminded the remnant of His faithfulness by utilizing the metaphor of rocks being drawn from the same quarry. God's chosen people were all descended from Abraham through Isaac and Jacob (51:1-2). As God had called Abraham while he was living in Ur, and out of one person had produced many descendants, God would call the exiles out of Babylon and multiply them.

Isaiah enthusiastically called upon God to rise to action and demonstrate His power as He had done in the past with Egypt, which was symbolized by the mythological monster, Rahab (vs. 9). The Lord is twice called to "awake" (vs. 9) and use His strength on behalf of the remnant. In verse 17, this summons is turned back upon Jerusalem, but this time in anticipation of the royal city's deliverance. Conquered Jerusalem is represented as a drunken woman who is staggering about, unaided by her children. Now, under Babylonian captivity, she had by choice drained the cup of God's wrath and become drunk with His judgment. Certainly, none of Jerusalem's children could come to her aid (vs. 18), for they too had drunk from the cup of God's wrath and were as immobile (or completely helpless) as an antelope caught in a net (vs. 20).

The exiles could not even help themselves. Indeed, they all had experienced two disasters (vs. 19). This means God's judgment on His people had been thoroughly sated. Because Jerusalem had endured "desolation, and destruction, and the famine, and the sword," the city was consequently inconsolable. God, in response to this pathetic state, offered encouragement and a promise. He had always defended His people (vss. 21-22), and He pledged He would remove the cup of wrath from Jerusalem. The day would come when the exiles would never again drink from God's judgment. In fact, He would pass it to the tormentors, who mocked and mistreated God's people, and made them drink fully of His wrath (vs. 23).

Notes on the Printed Text

Once more, in Isaiah 52:1, God's wake-up-call rejoinder is proclaimed to the remnant. "Zion" is exhorted to arise and dress herself in "strength." Likewise, "Jerusalem" is directed to robe herself with beautiful garments, that is, priestly attire characterized by splendor. Doing so was in keeping with the "holy" status of the city, where the temple was located. The latter truths suggest that when God rescued the exiles from captivity, He would fortify and purify them. The "uncircumcised and the unclean" is a reference to Jews' pagan oppressors. The Lord pledged that a day was coming when tyrants would no longer bother the remnant.

Next, Isaiah told the Jewish exiles to throw off the dirt covering them. In the ancient Near East, sitting in "dust" (vs. 2) was a sign of mourning. The prophet's command was that the remnant was to cease their lamenting over their captivity, tragic as it was, for it would end. Isaiah also commanded the exiles to get up, sit upon a throne, and remove the chains of their captivity. They could do so, for they knew that God would deliver and honor them.

In verse 3, the Lord declared to the Jewish captives that when He "sold" them into exile, He received no payment. So, He would redeem the remnant without being compensated. Expressed differently, Babylon offered no "money" for acquiring the chosen people, and they would now be released from Babylon for nothing. Moreover, God would claim the exiles as belonging exclusively to Him. Isaiah illustrated God's meaning by briefly reviewing the history of Israel's past oppressions. The Hebrews had been slaves in Egypt, and more recently the Assyrians had invaded Judah (vs. 4). In both instances, the Lord had gloriously delivered His people. This brief history lesson showed that no oppressor of the Jewish remnant had any legitimate claim on them.

Now the captives were enslaved by the Babylonians, who made a habit of ridiculing and slandering God's name (vs. 5; see Rom. 2:24). Just as the Lord had delivered His people from the Egyptians and the Assyrians, so now He would rescue the Jews from the Babylonians. When that deliverance came, the chosen people would realize that the Lord had foretold this remarkable event and had accomplished it. In that day, the remnant would "know" (Isa. 52:6) God's name. Put another way, they would recognize the Lord's identity as their Deliverer and Redeemer (see 49:26). They would also come to see that He alone had brought about their amazing deliverance from captivity in Babylon.

Isaiah 52:7-12 foretells the glorious return of the exiles to their homeland. In Bible times, a messenger would survey the horizon and then rush from the location of a major battle and report the "good tidings" (vs. 7) of the conflict's aftermath to an anxious ruler and his court officials (see 2 Sam. 18:26). In Isaiah 52:7, the herald does not announce the outcome of a military clash, but of the release of God's people from captivity in Babylon to return to Jerusalem. Isaiah observed how delightful it was for the messenger's "feet" to travel over the "mountains" in order to declare "peace" and "salvation." With the ending of oppression for the remnant and the commencement of their rescue, they would experience firsthand that God, as a triumphant warrior, had established His sovereign reign over Zion (see Ps. 93:1; Isa. 40:9; 41:27; Rev. 19:6).

Because of the joyous event described in Isaiah 52:7-8, the "waste places of

Jerusalem" (vs. 9) were exhorted to shout and rejoice together. There was good reason to sing, for the Lord would deliver, protect, and console His beleaguered people (see 44:23; 49:13; 55:12). Also, all the surrounding "nations" (52:10) would recognize this amazing redemption as a demonstration of the Lord's royal power. Even the remotest regions of the planet would become aware of God's strong and "holy arm" (see Exod. 6:6; Isa. 40:4; 45:22).

In view of the divine promises of deliverance and restoration, the exiles in Babylon would have a choice to make. Given the freedom to leave, they would have to decide whether they wanted to stay in Babylon or risk taking the long journey back to Judah and participating in the difficult rebuilding period. Life in Babylon had become comfortable for the exiles. But of course their spiritual health depended upon their fleeing from the defiling atmosphere of Babylon and setting themselves toward the blessings promised by God.

One can almost hear Isaiah calling joyously across time to the exiles, exhorting them to "depart" (Isa. 52:11) from the land of their captivity. The "unclean thing" spoken of here probably refers to pagan religious objects in Babylon. Those who carried the "vessels of the LORD" were likely the priests and Levites, who reclaimed the articles of the temple that had formerly been seized by Nebuchadnezzar (see Num. 3:6-8; 2 Kings 25:14-15; 2 Chron. 5:4-7; Ezra 1:7-11; 5:14-15). In a way, God also calls believers today to separate themselves from the spiritual impurities of the world (see Jam. 4:4-6; 1 John 2:15-17). After all, the Lord desires Jesus' followers to be holy and distinct from the world (see 1 Pet. 1:13-25). Even in the midst of such a clear victory by God, the reminder to remain pure must be remembered. The Lord wants His people to be holy and distinct from the world.

For the preceding reasons, Paul quoted Isaiah 52:11 to urge the believers in Corinth to separate themselves from the wickedness around them. In return for the believers' purity, God promised that He would receive them. The Christian life is not a barren list of regulations. Instead, it is a relationship. God calls us away from the evil practices around us so He can enjoy fellowship with us and we can enjoy communion with Him and His people. The Lord is not seeking to diminish our joy. Rather, He wants to make it greater through the blessing of our walk with Him.

Isaiah 52:12 reveals that the remnant leaving Babylon and heading for Judah would not be forced to leave quickly or depart in a panic. In contrast to the Israelites' departure from Egypt (see Exod. 12:33, 39), the exiles did not have to fear pursuit and recapture, because the Lord would be with them. Indeed, just as God had been their rear guard in the exodus with the pillar of cloud and fire (Isa. 52:12; see Exod. 13:21-22; 14:19-20), so too He would protect them as they returned to their homeland (see Isa. 42:16; 48:20; 49:10; 58:8). There are some notable comparisons between our passage and the Exodus account. In both cases, God's people were enslaved by powerful nations (Exod. 3:7-10; Isa. 40—66); God's mighty power was displayed in delivering His people from bondage (Exod. 7:5; Isa. 52:10); the offending nations were judged by the hand of God (Exod. 6:28—7:25; Isa. 51:23); God acted as His people's rear guard in the journey home (Exod. 14:19, 20; Isa. 52:12); and there was joyful singing upon deliverance (Exod. 15:1-21; Isa. 52:9).

SUGGESTIONS TO TEACHERS

Regardless of our current circumstances, regardless of our stressful situations, and regardless of our times of trial and testing, God watches over and guides us (see Isa. 52:12). And when we commit to trust and obey Him, He promises us that His peace and consolation remain with us (see 7).

1. THE RELIABILITY OF GOD'S PROMISES. The promises God made in Isaiah 52:1-12 are dependable, and they continue to have relevance for us. For instance, the Lord promises to walk with us through the darkest valleys of life (see Ps. 23:4). He also pledges to give us His incomprehensible peace (see Phil. 4:6-7). He even vows to never forsake us in our time of need (see Heb. 13:5).

2. THE CRIPPLING POWER OF FEAR. Often, when we need to trust in God's promises, we focus on our fears. Everyone knows about the crippling power of fear. Sometimes this knowledge comes from a firsthand encounter. At other times, it is based on the reports of others. Whatever the source, the result is the same. Fear restrains progress, quenches the adventuresome spirit, and steers people away from interesting challenges that are high-risk.

3. THE DECISION TO BELIEVE GOD'S PROMISES. Fear undoubtedly was present in the Jewish community in Babylon, especially when they learned they had been granted permission to leave their place of captivity and return home to Jerusalem. The people, few of whom had ever seen their homeland, must have felt a surge of faith and hope, particularly when they realized that God would do for them what He had done for the patriarchs centuries earlier. Likewise, Christians share the encouragement of their Old Testament predecessors when they believe in the promises of God.

4. THE WAY TO FIND ENCOURAGEMENT. In those moments when fear rears its ugly head, we find encouragement in the many promises of God's Word. We can examine the ones that relate to our anxieties and problems, and trust in those promises. When we focus on the "good tidings" (Isa. 52:7) of God's Word (rather than our fears), we will be filled with hope, peace, strength, and understanding to get us through the toughest moments in our lives.

FOR ADULTS
■ **TOPIC:** Seeking Words of Hope
■ **QUESTIONS:** 1. Why did God exhort His people to clothe themselves with strength? 2. In what dramatic way would the Lord make His name known to the exiles? 3. Why was the ruined city of Jerusalem urged to burst forth in a

joyful shout? 4. What are some ways believers can renew their confidence in the Lord? 5. How do God's words of consolation offer believers hope when they go through hard times?

■ ILLUSTRATIONS:

A Provision of Hope. One of the unfortunate characteristics of adults is our tendency to forget. We record in our mobile devices phone numbers, bank account information, tasks to do, and birthdays so we won't forget. Some of us are better at remembering than others, but everyone slips now and then.

Another regrettable inclination is that we tend to dwell on the negatives that happen to us or are verbalized to us. If someone tells us we're stupid, that remark sticks much longer than if someone praises us for providing the correct answer. Psychologists suggest that it takes seven positive statements to make up for one negative statement. In light of this ratio, we are certainly in need of hearing and delivering some encouraging statements.

Isaiah 52:1-12 provides us with hope by offering us reminders of God's faithfulness. Here we also encounter words of encouragement that we can share with others. The latter includes the "good tidings" (vs. 7) of the Father's "peace" and "salvation," which He graciously offers and which can be freely received through faith in the Son.

Hope for the Raging. Two shoppers in a supermarket got into a fistfight over who should be first in a newly opened checkout lane. An airline flight returned to a major American city after a passenger was accused of throwing a can of beer at a flight attendant and biting a pilot. One father in an eastern state beat another father to death in an argument over rough play at their sons' hockey practice. *USA Today* reported all these events over the span of a few months.

"Bad tempers are on display everywhere," wrote reporter Karen S. Peterson. The media is constantly reporting incidents of road rage, airplane rage, biker rage, surfer rage, grocery store rage, and rage at youth sporting events. This has led scientists to say the United States is in the middle of an anger epidemic.

Experts searching for causes blame an increasing sense of self-importance, the widespread feeling that things should happen "my" way. Other factors, they say, include too little time, overcrowding, intrusive technology, and too many demands for change in a society that is slowly recovering from the effects of a global economic downturn. In the midst of our rage, we are desperately in need of hope—and of the God who provides it, as He has revealed Himself in Isaiah 52:1-12.

God for the Pressured. Lloyd J. Ogilvie, in his book *Life without Limits*, tells the story of a pastor who, in the space of one week, heard the following comments from various people:

A husband said, "My wife is never satisfied. Whatever I do, however much I make, it's never enough. Life with her is like living in a pressure cooker with the lid fastened down and the heat on high."

A middle-aged wife said, "My husband thinks my faith is silly. When I feel his resistance to Christ, I wonder if I'm wrong and confused. As a result, I've developed two lives; one with him and one when I'm with my Christian friends."

An elderly woman said, "My sister thinks she has all the answers about the faith and tries to convince me of her point of view. I feel pressured to become her brand of Christian, but I keep thinking if it means being like her, I don't want it at all. When she calls, I just put the phone on my shoulder and let her rant on while I do other things. A half-hour later, she's still on the line blasting away, but I still feel pressure."

Each of these individuals have one thing in common. Other people are pressuring them and they are in need of hope. As Isaiah 52:1-12 makes clear, it is the Lord who consoles the frazzled, speaks tenderly to the downcast, and gives strength to the weary.

For Youth

■ **Topic:** From Hopeless to Hopeful

■ **Questions:** 1. In what way would the exiles in Babylon be set free? 2. How had the Babylonians slandered God's name? 3. What is the nature of the good news referred to in Isaiah 52:7? 4. This week, to whom can you bring the good news of God's salvation? 5. What are some ways you can encourage your saved peers to look to God for strength in their times of difficulty?

■ **Illustrations:**

Making a Fresh Start. What do you do with a broken-down car that needs repairs and paint? You see beyond the wreck and envision a sparkling new paint job and a motor that purrs sweetly down the road. You give that car all the sweat you can muster because you have high hopes for it and yourself.

Perhaps if we were writing Isaiah's sermons today, rather than comparing God to an attentive parent, we would compare Him to a sensitive, careful, hardworking, and loving mechanic. That's because we bestow the same kind of love on our cars that parents do on their children.

The main point is that God can bring about restoration and healing in the lives of youth, especially if they submit to His will. He has wonderful plans for them that they can't even imagine. Metaphorically speaking, God can take their dings and dents, and all the misfirings of their cylinders, and make a beautiful automobile out of their lives. Through faith in His Son they can make a fresh start down the road to hope!

The Basis of Hope. If you visit Yosemite National Park in California, you will find beautiful and immense sequoia trees. Imagine a tour guide showing you a cross section of one these giants. You would notice various rings of the tree that provide a graphic record of its development history.

For instance, one group of rings might reveal the presence of severe drought, while another group of rings might bear silent witness to a time when there was too much rain. You might see one ring toward the center of the tree indicating a season when a forest fire almost destroyed it. You might also notice another ring near the outer edge pointing to a time when the tree was struck by lightning.

Beneath the protective layers of our lives is a history of all the pains and hurts we have experienced. Where can we find the consolation we need to cope with our hurts? Isaiah 52:1-12 reminds us that God's faithfulness and promises are the basis for our hope. In fact, His sovereign, abiding presence gave the exiles in Babylon the courage and determination they needed to make the perilous journey back to Judah.

The Best Good News. Until recently, I had never taken great consolation in the advice to cheer up because things could get worse. Sometimes just the hint that a bad situation could deteriorate used to crush all hope of a brighter day. Doubt would pervade my thinking and rob me of the joy I knew God wanted me to have.

Recently, however, I have been seeing strong rays of God's bright love and grace pierce some ominously dark clouds. For example, I was encouraged to hear "good news" (Isa. 52:7, NRSV) about Matt, a 14-year-old hockey player. He has emerged from a long bout with serious illness and is sharing his personal testimony with others.

Last summer, Matt felt desperately ill during a hockey training camp and was hospitalized for an emergency appendectomy. While awaiting surgery, Matt received disturbing news. An *E. coli* virus was raging through his body, and he had a collapsed lung and pneumonia. Next, medical specialists informed Matt that cancer had invaded his lymphatic system, and he required nine months of chemotherapy.

In the nine months that followed that terrible news, Matt's body was racked with pain. He lost his hair, his strength, his immunity, but not his faith. Admittedly, at times he doubted God's fairness. But more often, Matt just wondered whether he would ever play hockey again.

Finally, light appeared at the end of the long ordeal. Matt received an encouraging report that he would survive and grow strong again. Next, he discovered that his hair was beginning to grow back. Then, he was filled with hope when he strapped on skates, picked up a hockey stick, and won the admiration of his fellow players and coach.

Still, Matt would be quick to admit that the very best "glad tidings" (KJV) he ever heard had nothing to do with being restored to health and hockey. Rather, it is the assurance that the Father forgives and gives eternal life to all who trust in His Son as Savior. That is the best "good news" we are privileged to pass along to others!

LESSON 1 — DECEMBER 7

WORSHIP THE MESSIAH

BACKGROUND SCRIPTURE: Hebrews 1:1-9
DEVOTIONAL READING: 1 Timothy 1:12-17

Key Verse: Who being the brightness of his glory, and the express image of his person, and upholding all things by the word of his power. Hebrews 1:3.

KING JAMES VERSION

HEBREWS 1:1 God, who at sundry times and in divers manners spake in time past unto the fathers by the prophets, 2 Hath in these last days spoken unto us by his Son, whom he hath appointed heir of all things, by whom also he made the worlds; 3 Who being the brightness of his glory, and the express image of his person, and upholding all things by the word of his power, when he had by himself purged our sins, sat down on the right hand of the Majesty on high;

4 Being made so much better than the angels, as he hath by inheritance obtained a more excellent name than they. 5 For unto which of the angels said he at any time, Thou art my Son, this day have I begotten thee? And again, I will be to him a Father, and he shall be to me a Son? 6 And again, when he bringeth in the firstbegotten into the world, he saith, And let all the angels of God worship him. 7 And of the angels he saith, Who maketh his angels spirits, and his ministers a flame of fire. 8 But unto the Son he saith, Thy throne, O God, is for ever and ever: a sceptre of righteousness is the sceptre of thy kingdom. 9 Thou hast loved righteousness, and hated iniquity; therefore God, even thy God, hath anointed thee with the oil of gladness above thy fellows.

NEW REVISED STANDARD VERSION

HEBREWS 1:1 Long ago God spoke to our ancestors in many and various ways by the prophets, 2 but in these last days he has spoken to us by a Son, whom he appointed heir of all things, through whom he also created the worlds. 3 He is the reflection of God's glory and the exact imprint of God's very being, and he sustains all things by his powerful word. When he had made purification for sins, he sat down at the right hand of the Majesty on high, 4 having become as much superior to angels as the name he has inherited is more excellent than theirs.

5 For to which of the angels did God ever say,
"You are my Son;
  today I have begotten you"?
Or again,
"I will be his Father,
  and he will be my Son"?
6 And again, when he brings the firstborn into the world, he says,
"Let all God's angels worship him."
7 Of the angels he says,
"He makes his angels winds,
  and his servants flames of fire."
8 But of the Son he says,
"Your throne, O God, is forever and ever,
  and the righteous scepter is the scepter of your
    kingdom.
9 You have loved righteousness and hated wickedness;
therefore God, your God, has anointed you
  with the oil of gladness beyond your companions."

Home Bible Readings

Monday, December 1	Daniel 9:3-10	*Great and Awesome God*
Tuesday, December 2	Daniel 9:11-19	*O Lord, Hear and Forgive*
Wednesday, December 3	Revelation 19:1-8	*God the Almighty Reigns*
Thursday, December 4	Revelation 22:8-14	*First and Last, Beginning and End*
Friday, December 5	Matthew 3:13-17	*My Son, the Beloved*
Saturday, December 6	1 Timothy 1:12-17	*Honor and Glory Forever*
Sunday, December 7	Hebrews 1:1-9	*The Son Reflects God's Glory*

Background

While it is virtually certain that the Letter to the Hebrews was written to Jewish Christians in the first century A.D., it is impossible to tell with certitude just where those believers lived. Alexandria, Egypt, is one place that some experts have suggested. The identity of the author is also shrouded in mystery. At one time or another, scholars have suggested all the following people as the writer of this letter: Barnabas (by Tertullian), Paul, Luke (by John Calvin), Apollos (by Martin Luther), Priscilla, and Clement of Rome (one of the church's early theologians).

Whoever penned the letter had a keen command of Greek and a razor-sharp intellect. The author of Hebrews set his course in chapter 1 by testifying to Jesus' supremacy over all things. The letter reminds readers of God's ways under the old covenant and affirms the Father's new and better way in the Son. Themes common throughout the letter are incarnation, redemption, perseverance, faith, and mutual love among believers.

Some professing Jewish Christians, who were recipients of this letter, may have been on the brink of relinquishing their commitment to the Lord Jesus. They had begun to consider leaving the church and reintegrating fully into the Jewish synagogue worship of the day. In response to their circumstances, the writer of Hebrews encouraged them to remain firm in their faith in the Messiah.

In particular, the author of Hebrews said the full and final revelation of God had come in the form of His incarnate Son. The phrase "in these last days" (vs. 2) would carry a special significance for the Hebrew readers, who probably interpreted the phrase as meaning that Jesus, as the Redeemer, had ushered in the messianic age. Jesus is not merely the end of a long line of Old Testament prophets. He is the one for whom the Hebrews had waited for centuries (see Mark 15:43; Luke 1:25, 38; 23:50-51). He is the complete and superlative revelation of God's being.

The author of Hebrews did not intend to diminish the value of God's revelation through the Hebrew prophets. The fact that the writer considered them the transmitters of God's revelation is evidence of just how much respect he held for these faithful servants of the Lord. For all that, the same God who had revealed Himself in a limited way during the Old Testament era, now had disclosed Himself completely and absolutely in the Messiah.

Notes on the Printed Text

In Hebrews 1:1, the author compared the incompleteness of God's revelation through the Old Testament prophets with the completeness of His revelation through His Son. Various prepositional phrases indicate some of the characteristics of God's communication: the timing was long ago; the target was our spiritual ancestors; the medium was through the prophets; and the methods were diverse and varied.

Regardless of the manner in which the Lord communicated, He conveyed His message to people of faith, and those spokespersons for God passed on His inspired declarations to others. Though acknowledging these ancient revelations for what they taught people about God, the author implied that they were fragmentary and transitional. At most they pointed to a time when the Father would reveal Himself fully and finally in His Son.

To show Jesus' superiority, the writer made a number of statements describing the Son. First, the Father appointed His Son as "heir of all things" (vs. 2). In Hebrew culture, the firstborn son was the highest ranked of all children. Therefore, he was also the family heir. Jesus is the heir, owner, and Lord of the whole created order. Second, it is through the Son that the Father "made the worlds." The Greek noun rendered "worlds" not only refers to the heavens and the earth, but also to the temporal ages (see 11:3).

Third, the Son is the "brightness" (1:3) of the triune God's glory. Because the Messiah is God Himself, He is the source of God's splendor. Fourth, the Son is the "express image" of the triune God's being. The Greek noun in this verse was used in pagan literature to refer to objects (such as coins or seals) that exactly reproduced the imprint and contours of the die from which they were cast. Regarding Jesus, who He is corresponds exactly to that of the Godhead. Fifth, not only did the Son create the cosmos, but He also holds it together by His powerful command (see Col. 1:17). The Son has a continued interest in the world and loves it. For that reason, He is carrying it toward the fulfillment of His divine plan.

At the heart of God's plan was to make redemption freely available to the lost. The Son died on the cross to wash away the stain of our sins from us (see Rom. 4:25; 2 Cor. 5:21; 1 Pet. 1:18-19). The Greek noun rendered "purged" (Heb. 1:3) denotes a thorough cleansing that brings about spiritual renewal. The idea is that through Jesus' atoning sacrifice at Calvary, He removed the defiling presence of sin from the very core of our innermost being (see 9:14; 10:22).

The writer expressed his thoughts in the past tense to emphasize that the Messiah's redemptive work on our behalf has already been accomplished. Because He completed the task for which He was sent (see John 3:16; 17:4), He was granted the place of highest honor—at God's "right hand" (Heb. 1:3). Jesus did once and for all what the Hebrew priests were required to do on a regular basis (see 9:26-28). Now, as our great High Priest, the Son continually applies to us the purification for "sins" He obtained at the cross. This enables us to worship in God's presence (see 4:14-16).

Because the Son has come to earth and sacrificed His own life for the sins of the world (see 1 John 2:2), He is to be considered superior to all things. This includes the angels (Heb. 1:4). The Hebrew people had long held angels in high esteem because these heavenly beings were instrumental in giving the law at Mount Sinai (Heb. 2:2; see Acts 7:38, 53). The author told the Hebrews that God's Son is absolutely higher in rank than all angels (Heb. 1:4). To emphasize his point, the writer said Jesus' name is superior to that of the angels (see Phil. 2:9-11). To Jews, a name summed up all that a person was—his or her character and even profession. For this reason, the author explained that Jesus' essence and work were far superior even to those of the heavenly beings.

Next, the author of Hebrews quoted various Old Testament Scripture passages to show how and why Jesus is superior to the angels. The writer apparently intended to imply that Jesus, as the Messiah, is to be seen throughout the Hebrew Scriptures (see Luke 24:27, 44). The writer began this series of quotations with a question: "For to which of the angels did God ever say" (Heb. 1:5).

Quoting first a messianic psalm (Ps. 2:7) and then 2 Samuel 7:14, the author indicated that the Father had never singled out an angel and applied to that being the exalted status He had accorded His Son (Heb. 1:5). In the first quotation, the writer made a clear distinction: the angels are created heavenly beings, but Jesus is the only Son of God, the long-awaited Messiah who gives salvation to those who trust in Him. Even though the second quotation originally referred to Solomon, the author of Hebrews applied it to the Messiah. Jesus enjoys a unique, one-of-a-kind relationship with the Father (see John 1:14, 18), something the angels cannot claim.

The writer of Hebrews referred to Jesus as God's "firstbegotten into the world" (1:6). Here the idea is not of the Messiah being first in order of birth, but highest in rank. The Son's unique relationship as an heir to God the Father is depicted in this verse. As God's firstborn heir, Jesus is the source of both righteousness and eternal life for all those who will come after Him—in essence, for all those who place their faith in His atoning work.

Bible scholars dispute the source of the quotation in verse 6. Some say it was taken from Deuteronomy 32:43 of the Septuagint (a pre-Christian Greek version of the Hebrew Scriptures) and was not included in other ancient texts of the Bible. Others say it was taken from Psalm 97:7, and still others say the author of Hebrews combined the Deuteronomy and Psalm passages. Whatever the case, the writer's purpose in using the quotation was to indicate that the Son is worthy of the angels' worship in the same way that the Father and the Spirit deserve the angels' veneration. The quotation also affirms the Son's essential deity. This worship of the Son was no small matter. Indeed, all of God's angels would participate in venerating Jesus.

The author then cited a quotation—the Septuagint version of Psalm 104:4—describing the character of the angels (Heb. 1:7). In the original Hebrew version, that

Psalm's verse appears to describe the wind and lightning of a storm as God's servants. The Septuagint version, however, identifies angels as God's servants, and that's the point the author of Hebrews wanted to make. They are much lower in existence than the royal Son of David, who is enthroned in the heavens as the eternal Creator and King (see vss. 10-12).

While the angels are God's servants, Jesus is God's Son and the divine King. This truth is stressed in verses 8-9, which contain a quotation from Psalm 45:6-7. Here we find one of the Bible's strongest affirmations of Jesus' deity. In Hebrews 1:8-9, the Son is addressed as God. Also, His royal status is alluded to in the words "throne," "sceptre," and "kingdom." As the Father's representative and co-regent, the Son rules over all creation forever. His scepter symbolizes His regal authority, which is characterized by justice and equity. Because these virtues are the basis of His unending rule, He enjoys an infinitely exalted status as the true and everlasting King (see Rev. 19:16).

The latter emphasis can be found in the phrase "oil of joy" (Heb. 1:9). The allusion is to an ancient Israelite practice of anointing the head of a king with olive oil at his coronation. The event was a time of great celebration and renewed hope. The ultimate focus, of course, is Jesus Christ, who reigns as King over the cosmos. Like the Father, the Son loves righteousness and hates wickedness. Because of these characteristics, the Father set His Son above all other people and beings, and anointed Him to carry out the most sacred function of all time—to bring people to salvation.

Suggestions to Teachers

As the writer to the Hebrews opened his letter, he must have been thinking that the most alluring temptations his readers faced did not involve obvious evils such as murder or adultery. Instead, they were tempted to overvalue the good (such as the Old Testament and angels) by elevating them to the level of the perfect (namely, God's Son). Christians today face similar temptations. Encourage your students to see the truth of the following statements.

1. ALL GOD'S GIFTS ARE VALUABLE. Just as the writer to the Hebrews valued the divine gifts of the Old Testament and the angels, so God's people today can appropriately enjoy all the good gifts God has given us. When God looked down on the world He had just made, He called it all very good.

2. YET GOD'S GREATEST GIFT IS HIMSELF. God has given His people gifts such as natural beauty, the Scriptures, family, friends, and churches. Yet, none of them can compare with His greatest gift—God Himself coming to earth in the form of His Son, Jesus Christ.

3. ALONG WITH HIS GIFTS, GOD GIVES A WARNING. God instructs His people to worship Him, the Giver. They become guilty of idolatry when any of God's gifts take first priority in their lives.

4. WE CAN ENJOY GOD AND HIS GIFTS. The writer of Hebrews wanted his readers to avoid worshiping the Old Testament and the angels. So he instructed them to obey the teaching of the Old Testament and follow the example of the angels in worshiping the one true God (namely, the Father, the Son, and the Holy Spirit), the giver of all good gifts. The writer knew that, when God's people worship Him alone, they can best enjoy both God and all His many gifts.

For Adults

■ **Topic:** Better than Angels

■ **Questions:** 1. In what sense is the Son the complete and final revelation of the Father? 2. What did the writer of Hebrews mean when he declared Jesus to be the reflection of God's glory? 3. In what ways is the Son's superior status to angels emphasized? 4. Why does Jesus deserve our unwavering commitment? 5. What are some ways we can worship the Son, both individually and corporately?

■ **Illustrations:**

Learning about God. Until his retirement in 1981, Robert Jastrow was the director of NASA's Goddard Institute for Space Studies. In his book entitled, *God and the Astronomers*, Jastrow took note of the "scientist who has lived by his faith in the power of reason," only for "the story" to end "like a bad dream." The scientist has "scaled the mountains of ignorance, he is about to conquer the highest peak; as he pulls himself over the final rock, he is greeted by a band of theologians who have been sitting there for centuries!"

Where do we learn about God, the one who created and sustains all things? The writer of Hebrews does not point us to angels or any other created being. Instead, the author points us to Jesus Christ, who is "the brightness of his glory, and the express image of his person" (Heb. 1:3). As your students get to know the Son better, they will come to know the Father too (see John 14:9).

Twins. We have since moved across the country, but when we resided in the Midwest, we lived near Jack and Mary. They had three young children: Hannah, Helen, and Mark.

I could easily distinguish Mark, for he was a boy and a bit smaller than his sisters. But the two girls were identical twins. Maybe I should have tried harder, but I never could tell the two of them apart. I miss this family, but we recently heard news that would have made living next to them even more confusing. Mary is expecting another set of twins!

You may have had similar problems with distinguishing twins you know. Even if you are not a twin, you may look similar enough to one of your siblings that other people confuse the two of you.

The first readers of Hebrews were forgetting who Jesus was. Some of them somehow thought angels more impressive than Jesus Himself. But when the writer of this letter called Jesus the "express image of [God's] person" (1:3), the writer helped his readers see that the Father and the Son are even more alike than identical twins could be.

Unusual Gifts Used for God. The opening paragraph of Hebrews offered its readers a wonderful example of using the Greek language with great stylistic effect. We are not sure who wrote this letter, but we do know that he must have been a highly educated person.

When the writer became a Christian, God did not ask him to leave his education and talents behind. Instead, God called him to use his thinking and writing abilities for the glory of God and the growth of the church. Perhaps you know people who offer their skills and experience to God for His use.

Joy piloted a casino boat in Baton Rouge, Louisiana, before she heard God's call on her life. Today she gives her time ministering to riverboat captains and crews. Joy knows what it's like to spend entire months away on the river. From her experience, she can minister empathetically to others who face that situation.

Barb is an Internet genius. She now gives half her time to building and maintaining a Christian website. Her site offers all kinds of information enabling Christians to minister better to nearby people of other ethnic groups.

FOR YOUTH

■ **TOPIC:** Who's in Charge?

■ **QUESTIONS:** 1. Why did God choose to reveal Himself in progressive stages? 2. Why is the Father's message through His Son clearer than His message was in Old Testament times? 3. Why did the writer of Hebrews emphasize Jesus' superiority over angels? 4. How can knowing about Jesus' superiority as the Son of God strengthen our faith? 5. What do you think is the most compelling reason to worship Jesus?

■ **ILLUSTRATIONS:**

Jesus: The Reflection of God. "She's the spitting image of her mother!" "He's a virtual clone of his father!" And on it goes, as well-intentioned friends and family members congratulate a couple on the birth of their newborn daughter or son. While such statements might be slight exaggerations, they remind us that we resemble our parents in many ways.

The writer of Hebrews went beyond such sentiments when he talked about the Son. We learn in 1:3 that the Lord Jesus reflects God's glory. Indeed, everything about the Son exactly represents the Father. Moreover, Jesus sustains the entire universe. As the saved adolescents in your class become more and more like Jesus in their thoughts and actions, in turn they will reflect the glory of God in their lives.

God with Skin On. The little girl's voice echoed across the hallway to the master bedroom. "Daddy, I'm scared!" The father tried his best to focus his thoughts. "Honey, don't be afraid. Daddy's right across the hall."

After a brief pause the girl said, "I'm still scared." Theologically astute, the father replied, "You don't need to be afraid. God is with you. God loves you." After a longer pause, the girl said in a quivering voice, "Daddy, I want someone with skin on." Jesus, the Son, "put skin" on the glory and the character of God the Father so that the Son might reveal the Father to us.

Getting to Know You. For several decades, Don Kroodsma has studied the songs of birds. In fact, he is considered an expert on the biology of bird vocal behavior. It's no wonder, then, that in 2005 he wrote a book about the art and science of birdsong: *The Singing Life of Birds*.

Kroodsma is no ordinary researcher, either. To learn as much as possible about his subject, he toured the North American continent on his bicycle. In 2003, he pedaled completely across the U.S. Also, in 2004, he biked his way from the Atlantic shore to the Mississippi. In each case, he lugged his recording equipment with him.

Such dedication reflects the sort of attitude believers should have about their relationship with God. As the author of Hebrews explained, they learn about the Father by getting to know the Son. Indeed, becoming more knowledgeable of Jesus should be their lifelong desire.

LESSON 2 — DECEMBER 14

SHOUT FOR JOY

BACKGROUND SCRIPTURE: Psalm 95:1-7a
DEVOTIONAL READING: 1 Timothy 1:12-17

Key Verse: O come, let us sing unto the LORD: let us make a joyful noise to the rock of our salvation. Psalm 95:1.

KING JAMES VERSION

PSALM 95:1 O come, let us sing unto the LORD: let us make a joyful noise to the rock of our salvation.
2 Let us come before his presence with thanksgiving, and make a joyful noise unto him with psalms. 3 For the LORD is a great God, and a great King above all gods. 4 In his hand are the deep places of the earth: the strength of the hills is his also. 5 The sea is his, and he made it: and his hands formed the dry land. 6 O come, let us worship and bow down: let us kneel before the LORD our maker.
7 For he is our God; and we are the people of his pasture, and the sheep of his hand.

NEW REVISED STANDARD VERSION

PSALM 95:1 O come, let us sing to the LORD;
  let us make a joyful noise to the rock of our
  salvation!
2 Let us come into his presence with thanksgiving;
  let us make a joyful noise to him with songs of
  praise!
3 For the LORD is a great God,
  and a great King above all gods.
4 In his hand are the depths of the earth;
  the heights of the mountains are his also.
5 The sea is his, for he made it,
  and the dry land, which his hands have formed.
6 O come, let us worship and bow down,
  let us kneel before the LORD, our Maker!
7 For he is our God,
  and we are the people of his pasture,
  and the sheep of his hand.

Home Bible Readings

Monday, December 8	Deuteronomy 13:1-8	*Hold Fast to God*
Tuesday, December 9	1 Kings 8:54-62	*Devote Yourselves to the Lord*
Wednesday, December 10	Hebrews 12:22-29	*Worship with Reverence and Awe*
Thursday, December 11	1 Chronicles 16:7-15	*Sing Praises to God*
Friday, December 12	Deuteronomy 32:1-7	*Ascribe Greatness to Our God*
Saturday, December 13	Hebrews 13:6-15	*A Sacrifice of Praise to God*
Sunday, December 14	Psalm 95:1-7	*Let Us Worship and Bow Down*

Background

What is worship? It is ascribing worth, respect, or praise to the Lord. In ancient times, the Israelites worshiped God in a variety of ways. Their expressions of praise were formal and informal, structured and unstructured, solemn and joyous. They would glorify God through song, prayer, and the study of Scripture. There are incidents mentioned in the Old Testament where God was worshiped on an individual basis (see Gen. 24:26). However, corporate worship seems to have been more common (see Exod. 33:10; 1 Chron. 29:20).

Both instrumental music and singing were integral parts of worship (see 2 Chron. 5:11-13). The Israelites also praised God through dancing (see Exod. 15:20; 2 Sam. 6:14) and the clapping of hands (see Ps. 47:1). Such emotions as gladness (see Ps. 42:4) and rejoicing (see Lev. 23:40; Deut. 16:11) were present when God's people worshiped Him. These expressions of joy were accompanied by an attitude of reverence (see Ps. 95:6).

There are a variety of Hebrew terms used in the Old Testament for worship. *Saha* (sha-CHAH; the term rendered "worship" in verse 6) means to prostrate oneself. *Hallel* (ha-LAL) means to acclaim, boast of, or glory in, and is used in passages where homage is given to God for His wonderful acts and qualities. *Yada* (yah-DAH) means to praise or give thanks and is used in passages where God's works or character are being acknowledged. *Zamar* (zah-MARE) means to sing praise or to make music and is used in passages where God is being revered for who He is and what He has done. Finally, *sabah* (shah-BACK) means to praise or commend and is used in passages where God is worshiped for His mighty acts and abundant goodness.

Notes on the Printed Text

The Psalms are songs and prayers that give deep expression to Israel's faith. Perhaps more than any other part of Scripture, the Psalms tell us what it feels like to walk in the way of the Lord. The traditional Hebrew title of the Psalms is *Sepher Tehillim*, meaning "Book of Praises." But the title "Psalms" had become attached to the book by the first century A.D. The Greek words translated "Psalm" and

"Psalter" once referred to stringed instruments. In time, though, the terms came to mean songs accompanied by those instruments.

The outpourings of many poets, living over a period of hundreds of years, flow together to make up the Psalms. Probably groups of these psalms were collected at different times. By the third century B.C., the book had received its final form, presumably through the efforts of temple musicians. The best-known author of psalms was David. More psalms—nearly half the book—are attributed to him than to any other author. Furthermore, historians recorded that David was the "sweet psalmist of Israel" (2 Sam. 23:1) and that he organized the sanctuary's music program (see 1 Chron. 15:3-28). In addition to David, several other people are claimed to be authors by the psalm titles. These are Moses, Solomon, Asaph (a Levite choir director), the Sons of Korah (a group of Levite musicians), Heman the Ezrahite (founder of the Sons of Korah), and Ethan the Ezrahite (probably also called Jeduthun). Of the several authors, only David is represented in each of the book's major divisions.

Old Testament scholars have noted the similarity of forms and themes among many of the psalms. In turn, they have tried to classify the poems according to their literary type. For instance, due to the fact that Psalm 95 places specific emphasis on extolling the Lord (vs. 1), some specialists consider it a praise or worship psalm. Yet, because the writer acknowledges God as the supreme King (vs. 3), others categorize the piece as a royal or enthronement psalm. Still others label the composition as a prophetic hymn, since it reiterates themes found in the Old Testament prophets. Moreover, the incidents the psalm revisits from Israel's past (namely, the episode that occurred at Meribah and Massah; vs. 8) lead some to designate the song as an historical psalm.

In all likelihood, the original context for the psalm would have been a gathering of Israelites at the Jerusalem temple. The worship leader would have been a priest or a Levite. He summoned the faith community to revere the Lord (vss. 1-3), to heed His will (vss. 6-7), and to remain unwavering in their commitment to Him (vss. 8-11). Like other Hebrew poems, this one exhibits a distinguishing characteristic called parallelism. This term simply means that two (or sometimes three) lines of the poetry are, in one way or another, parallel in meaning.

For instance, verse 1 reflects equivalent parallelism, in which the second line repeats the thought of the first. More specifically, the summons for congregants to sing joyfully to the Lord is synonymous with the call to shout out praises to God. The second stanza refers to the Lord as the "rock" of Israel's "salvation." The depiction is that of a rocky summit that provides protection. For God's people, He was comparable to a lofty fortress where they could find refuge from temporal threats (see Pss. 18:2; 31:2; 62:2, 6; 89:26; 92:15; 94:22). In 95:2, the second stanza not only repeats the thought in the first, but also advances it. The worship leader invites the assembled Israelites to enter God's presence with an attitude of "thanksgiving." Additionally, they are directed to shout out praises to Him with a "joyful noise." The idea is that both gratitude and celebration mark the sacred gathering.

Verses 3 through 5 explain why the Israelites who had assembled at the Jerusalem temple were to offer praise to the Lord. Verse 3 declares Him to be the "great God," and adds that He is the "great King" who is superior to all the false "gods" venerated by Israel's pagan neighbors (see Exod. 15:11; Pss. 5:2; 82:1; 97:9). In 1 Corinthians 8, Paul noted that idols are nothing more than humanly-made objects and that they represented no real existence or power (vs. 4). Nonetheless, many people believed that they existed. The apostle stated that people worshiped all sorts of "gods" and "lords" (vs. 5), some of which they venerated as objects they could see and some of which they believed to exist in heaven. That said, Paul revealed there is only one God and one Lord (vs. 6; see Deut. 6:4).

The apostle further described God as the Father, who was the source of all Creation, and the Lord as Jesus Christ, through whom all creation came into existence. In addition, the apostle noted that the believer lives for God alone and gets his or her power to serve the Father from the Son. Psalm 95:4-5 declares similar truths. Believers learn that even the "deep places of the earth" are under the Creator's authority and control. Likewise, He reigns supreme over every aspect of the mountains, including their peaks. Similarly, because Israel's God made the "sea" and the "dry land," all of it belongs to Him (see 24:1-2; 96:4-5). This biblical view of reality sharply contrasted with the mindset that prevailed throughout the ancient Near East. Supposedly, a different god or goddess controlled a particular region of the heavens or the earth. Even various aspects of life (including a person's birth, death, livelihood, and so on) belonged to a different patron deity.

In Psalm 95:7, the worship leader declared to the assembled Israelites that the Lord was their God. In a metaphorical sense, He was their Shepherd and they were the "people of his pasture," as well as the "sheep of his hand." David stated similar truths in Psalm 23. He was himself a shepherd in Israel, and his familiarity with the shepherd's life permeates this poem. He compared himself to a sheep on the mountains of Israel, tenderly cared for and kept by his Shepherd (vs. 1). In David's opening confession, he acknowledged that the God of the universe can be known in a warm, personal relationship. In ancient times, shepherds were responsible for the total care of their sheep. That theme emerges in this hymn. Because David knew God as his Shepherd, he had everything he needed to be an effective servant for the Lord.

The implications of David's shepherding imagery are profound, for sheep in Bible days typically were at the mercy of the elements and wild beasts. The safety of sheep had to be maintained on a day by day and moment by moment basis. Like a sheep exposed to the perils of life, David had tasted danger when various enemies threatened his life. Despite these difficult circumstances, David knew that his Shepherd, the King of Israel, would provide everything he needed. David had complete confidence in God's protection, guidance, and provision. While we may not have experienced the same kind of outdoor life that David did, his imagery still moves us to reflect on our own relationship with God. We feel the intensity of David's emotions toward the Lord. David's poem, along with Psalm 95:6, invites believers from all walks of life to examine how they relate to God.

David described with vivid poetic imagery what it was like to be fed and watered by his Shepherd. The Lord allowed David to rest in green, fertile pastures, having grazed to his fill. Israel's God led David to quiet pools of fresh water so that his thirst could be satisfied (23:2). The image is one of total satisfaction, contentment, and peace. When we allow God, our Shepherd, to guide us, we have contentment. This is because He knows the "green pastures" and "still waters" that will restore us. We can reach these places only by following Him obediently. Otherwise, if we rebel against the leading of our Shepherd (an issue dealt with in Ps. 95:7-11 and Heb. 3:7—4:13), we will bring frustration, dissatisfaction, and sadness into our lives.

Suggestions to Teachers

While we might not be tempted to worship pagan deities (though literal idolatry is becoming more common in the West), we do struggle with priorities when we put the concerns of this world before the Lord. Just as with the Israelites, we need to be brought back to reality by acknowledging that God rules in our hearts, rather than other things that compete for our attention.

1. PRAISING GOD WITH HEARTFELT WORDS. Psalm 95:1 summons us to praise God with our words. And verse 2 invites us to worship Him with songs. In these verses, we learn that worship is not just a set of ideas or attitudes that we keep to ourselves. It must be felt as well as expressed. When we voice our adoration for the Lord in hymns, He is honored and our spirits are uplifted.

2. REVERING GOD FOR HIS GREATNESS. Verses 3-5 remind believers of God's surpassing greatness. No other being can be compared to Him. Because the Lord is the one and only true God, He is to be revered above anyone or anything in the universe. Ultimately, God is worthy of our praise and obedience because no entity in the entire cosmos can match His magnificence and splendor.

3. BEING PROACTIVE IN OFFERING PRAISE. One athletic company uses the slogan "Just Do It" to promote its products. In many ways, that is also true of offering praise to God. It is often just a matter of taking the time to "make a joyful noise" (vs. 2) to Him with other believers or even by ourselves.

4. EXTOLLING GOD ON ALL OCCASIONS. While formal worship of God with other Christians is a necessary part of our spiritual walk, we are also encouraged to rejoice in our faith at all times (see Phil. 4:4). It doesn't just have to be while we are having devotions or are in church. We can praise God while driving in our car, at work, at home, or any time we are reminded of His caring presence (see Ps. 95:7).

FOR ADULTS

■ **TOPIC:** Sing a Song of Praise

■ **QUESTIONS:** 1. What feelings do you experience when you worship the Lord? 2. How can believers cultivate an attitude of thanksgiving as they sing praises to God? 3. Why is it important for Christians to affirm that the Lord reigns supreme over all the so-called "gods" (Ps. 95:3) of the world? 4. In what sense is the Lord our Shepherd, and we are the "sheep of his hand" (vs. 7)? 5. What obvious ways have you seen God care for you—protect you, provide for you, and so on—in the past?

■ **ILLUSTRATIONS:**

Extol the Lord. The men's boarding house had a weekly meeting convened by the owner. The residents were expected to attend. More than that, they were invited to tell about something that God had done in their lives.

Of course, a few attendees were not too keen about this idea. But something always happened after those meetings. The stories about fresh encounters with God were like blood transfusions. The accounts injected spiritual vitality into those who were just going through the same old religious routines.

Every gathering of believers can benefit from testimonies of how God has been powerfully at work among His people. That's why Psalm 95 (the focus of this week's lesson)—which is a hymn of worship and praise—is so invigorating and life-changing. We all need to contemplate specific ways we can extol the Lord, for doing so helps to keep our love for Jesus from growing cold.

The Rock of Our Salvation. The two-inch letters in front of the mailing I received from my bank proclaimed, "Change is good!" To emphasize the point, the flyer used characters dressed in 1960s clothes, replete with peace signs, bandannas, and round "shades."

But the true message could not be hidden. In my case, change was bad. A careful examination of the text of the mailing indicated that the benefits I would gain would be dwarfed by the benefits I would lose.

Packaging can be deceptive. That goes for spiritual matters, too. Consider these attractively packaged religious ideas: (1) "Good works can get you to heaven." (2) "Do the best you can and leave the rest to God." (3) "God loves all people. It doesn't matter what religion they are." And (4) "Don't be so rigid. We're all going to the same place anyway."

Thankfully, there is a spiritual package we can trust. Psalm 95:1 declares the Lord to be the "rock of our salvation." Indeed, the way of salvation, provided over two thousand years ago in the person of Jesus Christ, has not changed. On this truth we can rest assured!

To Want or Not to Want. Along with Psalm 95:7, we learn in 23:1 that the Lord is our "shepherd." Many children who hear the last part of this verse—"I shall not want"—suffer a bit of confusion. To their ears, the phrase sounds as if the speaker does not want the Lord as a Shepherd.

Ironically, the children's misunderstanding of this passage is not far from what is often the experience of adult believers. As grown-ups, we know that the Shepherd is good. Our intellect grasps His ability to protect and provide for us in a way that no one else can (see 95:1). However, as verses 8 through 11 reveal, there are times when we state by our actions—by our stubborn self-sufficiency or by our overdependence on other people or things—that we don't want God's shepherding.

Here is one way we can monitor this problem. Whenever neediness surfaces in our lives, we can ask ourselves the following: *To want, or not to want, the Lord as my Shepherd?* That is the question to which even a child knows the best answer!

For Youth

■ **Topic:** Sing His Praises

■ **Questions:** 1. In what sense is God the "rock" (Ps. 95:1) of the believers' "salvation"? 2. What are some ways you and your peers at church offer praise to God? 3. How can knowing that God remains in control of the universe give believers comfort in times of sorrow? 4. Why is it important for Christians to maintain a humble and obedient attitude when they gather together for worship? 5. How does verse 7 prompt you to trust God implicitly in all circumstances?

■ **Illustrations:**

A Joyful Song. "Declare his glory among the nations" has been the theme of student missionary conventions. Thousands of students have responded to the command. They have given their lives to serve Christ where His name is not known, loved, and obeyed. These dedicated young people have changed countless communities and brought hope to innumerable people.

When we sing a joyful song of praise to God for what He has done for us (see Ps. 95:1-2, 7), we should also think about people locally and around the world who have no reason to sing. Some have never heard the good news of Jesus, while others have rejected it. In either case, we should continue filling our hearts with the truth that Jesus is the "rock of our salvation" (vs. 2), as well as our "maker" (vs. 6) and Shepherd (vs. 7). Doing so will keep us from hardening our hearts to the needs of the lost around us.

God, Our Shepherd. James Harriet was a Yorkshire veterinarian and author until his death in 1995. He tells the story of a lamb named Smudge. The episode began one spring morning when twin lambs were born at the Cobb family farm.

Young Harry had decided to get up early to help his dad. As a special reward, the shepherd agreed to let Harry have the two lambs as his own. Harry said he would watch the lambs every day. He named them Smudge (after the white mark on one lamb's nose) and Smartie.

While Smartie was content to stay within the borders of the fold, Smudge's gaze took it beyond. Eventually, its feet followed. The lamb wriggled through the fence and toddled along the road outside the barrier. Though the animal adored its mother and sister, it was a wanderer.

About an hour into exploring, Smudge glanced back to discover Smartie having a meal. But Smudge couldn't get back through the fence. The lamb cried loudly and its mother responded. Just then, a big dog came and Smudge ran. The animal kept running.

Eventually, a snowstorm slowed down the weary, hungry lamb, and he collapsed. The little girl who found Smudge revived it with a hair dryer and warm milk. The next day, the animal was reunited with Harry, its young shepherd.

Psalm 95:7 reminds us that God is our Shepherd and we are the "sheep of his hand." We can rest assured that He will always watch over us and never fail to take care of us. This remains true, regardless of the difficult circumstances we encounter in life as the "people of his pasture."

God's Abiding Presence. In Psalm 95:1, the poet declared that God is the "rock of our salvation." Later, in verse 7, we learn that we are the "people of his pasture," whom He lovingly guides and protects with His abiding presence.

In an *Upper Room* devotional, Ellen Bergh writes how Amtrak's Coast Starlight train was filled with excited passengers, craning their necks to enjoy the Oregon scenery as the train rolled through green forests. A shining lake gleamed through the trees, and cheerful conversation filled the air.

Suddenly, the light, airy feeling was gone, like a candle blown out in a draft, as the train entered a tunnel. Expecting the sun to reappear quickly, Ellen was uncomfortable as it became even darker.

The happy sounds were a thing of the past. Everyone sat in awe of the inky blackness. The longer they traveled in the tunnel, the harder it was to remain calm without any visual cues to reassure them. Even the movement of the train seemed to fall away into pitch darkness. When they came out of the tunnel, laughter and relief filled the compartment.

"My life in Christ is like that unforgettable train ride," Ellen reflects. "Events may plunge me into darkness where I have no clues to sense the Lord's presence. Yet I can trust God is with me even when I can't see what lies ahead."

LESSON 3 — DECEMBER 21

Offer God Praise

Background Scripture: Luke 2:1-20
Devotional Reading: Psalm 19

Key Verse: The shepherds returned, glorifying and praising God for all the things that they had heard and seen, as it was told unto them. Luke 2:20.

KING JAMES VERSION

LUKE 2:8 And there were in the same country shepherds abiding in the field, keeping watch over their flock by night. 9 And, lo, the angel of the Lord came upon them, and the glory of the Lord shone round about them: and they were sore afraid. 10 And the angel said unto them, Fear not: for, behold, I bring you good tidings of great joy, which shall be to all people. 11 For unto you is born this day in the city of David a Saviour, which is Christ the Lord. 12 And this shall be a sign unto you; Ye shall find the babe wrapped in swaddling clothes, lying in a manger. 13 And suddenly there was with the angel a multitude of the heavenly host praising God, and saying, 14 Glory to God in the highest, and on earth peace, good will toward men. 15 And it came to pass, as the angels were gone away from them into heaven, the shepherds said one to another, Let us now go even unto Bethlehem, and see this thing which is come to pass, which the Lord hath made known unto us. 16 And they came with haste, and found Mary, and Joseph, and the babe lying in a manger. 17 And when they had seen it, they made known abroad the saying which was told them concerning this child. 18 And all they that heard it wondered at those things which were told them by the shepherds. 19 But Mary kept all these things, and pondered them in her heart. 20 And the shepherds returned, glorifying and praising God for all the things that they had heard and seen, as it was told unto them.

NEW REVISED STANDARD VERSION

LUKE 2:8 In that region there were shepherds living in the fields, keeping watch over their flock by night. 9 Then an angel of the Lord stood before them, and the glory of the Lord shone around them, and they were terrified. 10 But the angel said to them, "Do not be afraid; for see—I am bringing you good news of great joy for all the people: 11 to you is born this day in the city of David a Savior, who is the Messiah, the Lord. 12 This will be a sign for you: you will find a child wrapped in bands of cloth and lying in a manger." 13 And suddenly there was with the angel a multitude of the heavenly host, praising God and saying,

14 "Glory to God in the highest heaven,
   and on earth peace among those whom he favors!"

15 When the angels had left them and gone into heaven, the shepherds said to one another, "Let us go now to Bethlehem and see this thing that has taken place, which the Lord has made known to us." 16 So they went with haste and found Mary and Joseph, and the child lying in the manger. 17 When they saw this, they made known what had been told them about this child; 18 and all who heard it were amazed at what the shepherds told them. 19 But Mary treasured all these words and pondered them in her heart. 20 The shepherds returned, glorifying and praising God for all they had heard and seen, as it had been told them.

Home Bible Readings

Monday, December 15	1 Chronicles 16:35-41	Give Thanks to God's Holy Name
Tuesday, December 16	2 Chronicles 5:2-14	Praising and Thanking God
Wednesday, December 17	Psalm 19	Proclaiming God's Handiwork
Thursday, December 18	Psalm 108:1-6	God's Glory over All the Earth
Friday, December 19	Romans 5:1-5	Our Hope of Sharing God's Glory
Saturday, December 20	Luke 2:1-7	Expecting a Child
Sunday, December 21	Luke 2:8-20	A Savior Born This Day

Background

Luke 2:1-4 reveals that even such a seemingly unimportant individual as Joseph was affected by the mandatory census occuring throughout the Roman Empire. At the time, Joseph was living in Nazareth, a town situated in lower Galilee. To comply with the census, Joseph had to travel about 90 miles—at least a three-day journey—from Nazareth to Bethlehem, the town of his ancestors (and possibly those of Mary; vs. 5). Bethlehem was the ancestral home of David, and it was there that Samuel the prophet anointed David as Saul's successor (see 1 Sam. 16:1, 13; 17:12).

At the time Joseph made the journey, he was betrothed to Mary (Luke 2:5). In Jewish culture, betrothal was as legally binding as marriage itself. Evidently, Mary was living with Joseph as his wife, though they had not yet consummated their relationship (see Matt. 1:24-25). Because Mary was almost ready to give birth to Jesus, the trip from Nazareth to Bethlehem was not the best time for her. But there was no way Joseph could delay the journey. So, they decided Mary should go with him.

While Joseph and Mary were in Bethlehem, Mary prepared to deliver her child (Luke 2:6). Suitable accommodations were difficult to find because the town was overflowing with travelers who sought to register in the census. The "inn" (vs. 7) could have been a guest room in a private home or a space at a public outdoor shelter, but it was probably not a large building with several individual rooms.

Like many peasant children, Mary's son would have been washed in a mixture of water and olive oil, rubbed with salt, and then wrapped in strips of linen. These would be placed around the arms and legs of the infant to keep the limbs protected. Mary then laid her child in a trough used for feeding animals. We discover that the world's Messiah would not mobilize the militant Zealots to throw off the Roman yoke. Instead, the Christ child came to serve (see Matt. 20:28; Mark 10:45), as well as to seek and to save the lost (see Luke 19:10).

Notes on the Printed Text

An angel announced the Messiah's birth to ordinary shepherds, not the powerful rulers or religious leaders (Luke 2:8). According to verse 9, an angel of the Lord suddenly appeared near or in front of the shepherds, and the radiance of

God's glory surrounded them. The sight of the angel terrified the shepherds. But the heavenly emissary reassured them with good news of a joyous event (vs. 10), namely, the birth of Israel's "Saviour," Messiah, and "Lord" (vs. 11). The one who eternally existed in regal splendor had been born that night in Bethlehem. Indeed, He who is sovereign and all-powerful would make redemption available to humanity, including the weak and oppressed—even society's outcasts. Military and political leaders during those times were frequently called "lord" and "savior." But Jesus was unique, being the Anointed One of God.

The Gospel is always "good tidings of great joy" (vs. 10) for everyone who receives it by faith. The wonderful news is that God loves us despite our sinful thoughts, words, and deeds (see John 3:16-21; Eph. 2:1-10; 1 John 4:10). Jesus was born to die on the cross for our sins, but He would not stay dead (see 1 Cor. 15:3-4). It is His victory over death through His resurrection that gives us life (see vss. 56-57). "Great joy" (Luke 2:10) is experienced when we trust in the Son, who reconciled us to the Father (see 2 Cor. 5:17-21). He bestows on us eternal life (see John 3:36), His Spirit (see Eph. 1:13-14), unrestricted access to His throne of grace (see Heb. 4:14-16), a promise that the Son is always with us (see Matt. 28:20), and the assurance that the Father will complete the work He begins within us in union with His Son (see Phil. 1:6).

The angel encouraged the shepherds to find the Christ child lying in a manger, wrapped snugly in strips of cloth (Luke 2:12). In fact, this would be a sign from the Father validating the birth of His Son, the Messiah. It's worth mentioning that *Christ* is a word borrowed from Greek. It means "Anointed One," signifying divine commissioning for a specific task. In Old Testament times, kings and priests were anointed with oil as a sign of their divine appointment. The Hebrew word for the Anointed One is translated *Messiah*. It was used of the promised one who would deliver Israel from oppression. Most Jews thought He would be a political leader. They did not consider that His mission might be to free them from sin.

Stories about the shepherds make them out to be profane on the one hand or deeply faithful on the other. Though it's hard to know for sure, we can at least assume they were familiar with God's messianic promises. (The angel's announcement would have otherwise meant nothing to them.) We can also marvel at God's wisdom, love, and grace in choosing these rugged individuals (rather than the religious elite in Jerusalem) as the ones who first heard the good news of Jesus' birth.

We can imagine the shepherds staring in amazement, trying to grasp the significance of the angel's announcement. Suddenly the night sky exploded with the sounds of "the heavenly host" (vs. 13). This was a large group of angels who offered a hymn of praise to God. And what a joyful carol it has become! We can only imagine the glory and praise that must have filled the nighttime sky. The news was simple. The angels gave glory to God and said His peace remained on those with whom He was pleased.

The idea of verse 14 is not so much a general feeling of goodwill toward all people as it is of God's favor resting on those who experience inner peace through faith in Christ (see Rom. 5:1). The reference to God's favor in Luke 2:14 reminds us of His grace made available to all humankind through the Savior (see Eph. 2:8-9). To some the idea of being at peace with God seems far-fetched, especially in a world continually plagued by war. But the absence of peace can be traced to humanity's stubborn refusal to accept God's Son as their Savior. The potential for harmony is there, and God's offer of peace still stands. In fact, His grace extends to all who repent of their sin and trust in the Messiah for salvation.

The shepherds' initial response to the unusual sights and sounds was fear. But following the words about the birth of the baby, and after the praise of the angelic host, the shepherds moved from fear to curiosity (Luke 2:15). The angel had told the shepherds the specific location and situation of the holy birth. Now they decided to travel to Bethlehem and see for themselves what the Lord had told them about it. It's not easy to convey in English the urgency of the shepherds' words. We might paraphrase it by saying, "Come on, let's hurry and see Him, before it's too late!"

So, the shepherds hurried off and successfully found Mary and Joseph (vs. 16). The shepherds also saw the baby lying on the bed of hay. These most common of all people had the privilege of being the first on record to see the holy child. We can only guess as to what the shepherds said to Joseph and Mary. Obviously, they told the couple about the angels. Perhaps the excitement of the shepherds filled Joseph and Mary with wonder and prompted them to rehearse the ancient messianic prophecies, especially that the Savior was to be born in Bethlehem (Mic. 5:2).

At the time of Jesus' birth, there was a heavy messianic expectation among the Jews. Many believed the Anointed One was coming. Old Testament prophecy inspired this hope among them, and Roman domination made them long for the Messiah as well. With respect to the former point, Micah had foretold that a ruler of Israel would come out of Bethlehem. The prophet had also declared that this king would bring lasting security to Israel and would extend His influence to the ends of the earth. The birth of Jesus in Bethlehem fulfilled this prophecy. Also, God chose Bethlehem to indicate Jesus' royal status.

Today, as soon as babies are born, their parents get on the phone to call relatives and friends. They might also share the information by using email or text messages. But in ancient Bethlehem, the good news could only be spread by word of mouth. In the case of the shepherds, after they had seen Jesus, they became instant evangelists. Being in His presence must have convinced them that what the angel had said to them was true. Indeed, the shepherds felt compelled to tell every person they met that they had seen the Messiah (Luke 2:17).

We can imagine the shepherds saying, "Angels told us the Messiah has been born in Bethlehem, and we went to see for ourselves. We found Him lying in a bed of hay and wrapped in strips of cloth." Regardless of what they actually said, their key point would have been that they had found the Savior. It's no wonder all who heard them were amazed (vs. 18). The shepherds could have responded differently to the wonderful things they had seen and heard. They could have been so paralyzed by fear that they told no one about the wonders. The shepherds could have remained quiet. Thankfully, they spread the good news about the Messiah's birth.

Those who heard the news were astonished. The Greek verb translated "wondered" (vs. 18) conveys the idea that when the people heard the testimony of the shepherds, chills ran down their spines. As with most listeners, some believed, while others probably dismissed the message as nonsense. The latter may have occurred because the information came from lowly shepherds, not from religious leaders and experts. Perhaps from the day of Jesus' birth, the announcement of His advent was an enigma to many. We can imagine skeptics wondering whether the news sounded too good to be true. For people of faith, the answer is clear. The Father had sent His Son into the world so that the lost might be saved.

SUGGESTIONS TO TEACHERS

Between a humble birth and a debasing (but ultimately victorious) death, Jesus lived simply, spoke vividly, and was often in the company of people whom polite society either rejected or ignored. Therefore, it is not surprising that the Redeemer was born in a stable, and lowly shepherds were the first to see Him.

1. THE HUMILITY. Few occasions seem as humbling as not receiving the respect that one deserves. On that premise, the most disrespected person to ever live was Jesus. At the start, His life was humbly cradled in a wooden manger. Then, at the end, His life humbly crumpled on a wooden cross. Jesus was the model of patience and silent endurance. What an example for us to follow!

2. THE IRONY. At first glance, the shepherds were an unlikely group to hear first about the Messiah's arrival. They were rough, rugged men living independently from the bustle of Jewish society, performing an undesirable job, garnering little respect. The truth, however, is that the rich and noble were not the first to be informed of Jesus' advent. Practical, honest, hardworking people were. The Lord deserves our praise for grafting all believers—both Jews and Gentiles—into the Vine of Life.

3. THE GLORY. From great humility to great glory can look like a lengthy road, but it was one that Jesus traveled. The bystanders at the stable saw the beginning, but the shepherds had a glimpse of the end. They heard the tremendous affirmation and respect that was accorded to Jesus from the heavenly host. It's important to remember that God does not evaluate us from the same standard that we are prone to use in our assessment of others and ourselves. Rejection at the inn, or being overlooked by the masses—none of this was of concern to God. Glory comes from God alone, and He graciously bestows it to the humble.

4. THE MEDITATION. Mary's contemplation probably involved the thought that of all the women of Israel, she—a poor and seemingly insignificant peasant woman—had been favored by God to give birth to the Messiah. It is also probable that Mary told the details of this event to Luke, the writer of the third Gospel. After all, Luke was familiar with many of the key people in the life of Christ.

FOR ADULTS

■ **TOPIC:** Spontaneous Joy!

■ **QUESTIONS:** 1. What were the shepherds doing when an angel of the Lord appeared to them? 2. What was the joyous good news the angel announced to the shepherds? 3. What sign did the angel give to the shepherds concerning the Christ child? 4. How should we respond to the account of the shepherds' encounter with the Christ child? 5. Why is it important for us to glorify the Father for the gift of His Son?

■ **ILLUSTRATIONS:**

The Gift of Kept Promises. Charles Schultz's *Peanuts* characters frequently give insight into human nature. As a bewildered Charlie Brown thinks about Christmas, Lucy comments, "Who else but you, Charlie Brown, could turn a wonderful season like Christmas into a problem?"

For many, Christmas is a problem to be endured rather than a holiday to be celebrated. Exhaustion from too much activity exaggerates family tensions. Parents are tired and children are anxious. A demoralizing Christmas might also result from feelings of loss or incompleteness. Living with memories of happier holidays past, an elderly person might long for those who have died or are far away. The single person might feel miserably alone at Christmas, when everyone else seems to have someone. Even dreary weather can contribute to the Christmas blues.

Although your students may not put their feelings into words, they will bring some of these thoughts to your class. Use this lesson to focus on the good news of Jesus' wondrous birth as the gift of God's kept promise. Giving Jesus the central focus can turn a gloomy holiday into a joy-filled occasion.

Good News of Salvation. Did you know that people of other religions also esteem Jesus? Muslims, for example, recognize Jesus as a great prophet and revere Him as Isa ibn Maryam—Jesus, the son of Mary, the only woman mentioned by name in the Quran (or Koran). At a time when many Christians deny Jesus' birth to a virgin, Muslims find the account in their holy book and affirm it as true.

"Many Westerners also do not believe Jesus ascended into heaven, but Muslims do," says Seyyed Hossein Nasar, professor of Islamic studies at George Washington University. *Newsweek* magazine says that, according to one recent estimate, alleged visions of Jesus or Mary have occurred some 70 times in Muslim countries since 1985.

It is the Cross, however, that separates Christianity from Islam and all other religions and spiritual traditions. Other religions may celebrate Jesus as a great prophet, but the holy child born in a manger became the holy servant hanging from a tree. This same Redeemer, who was raised from the dead as the holy Son, brings eternal life to all who believe. Here we find the ultimate message of salvation that is Good News to everyone.

Poet's Longing. Thomas Hardy's poem, "The Oxen," describes an old English folk legend in which the oxen are said to kneel in their stalls every Christmas Eve at the stroke of midnight, in memory of Jesus' birth in Bethlehem. At the end of the poem, Hardy imagines someone telling him that in a remote farm, the animals were kneeling that night. If he were invited to see this, the agnostic Hardy said he would "go with the person in the . . . hope that it might be so."

Perhaps you, like the poet Hardy, have wished that there might be some cause for hoping, some reason for worshiping, and some evidence for rejoicing in the truth of the Messiah's birth. Consider again Luke 2:11, "For unto you is born this day in the city of David a Saviour, which is Christ the Lord."

The Father has come to us in the person of His Son, Jesus. And at the manger, God has reached out to us in love. All of us are residents of this planet where Jesus made His home! This is the reason for hoping, worshiping, and rejoicing.

FOR YOUTH

■ **Topic:** Go Tell It on the Mountain!

■ **Questions:** 1. Why do you think the angel appeared to shepherds? 2. Why were the shepherds eager to see Jesus after hearing the angelic announcement and praises? 3. Why did God choose Bethlehem to be the birthplace of the Savior? 4. What aspects of Jesus' birth have universal appeal? 5. How might telling the account of Jesus' birth interest a non-Christian in knowing more about the Savior?

■ **Illustrations:**

Good News of the Ultimate Shepherd. In our culture of plenty, we find it hard to find a Christmas gift that an adolescent really needs. But if we plan ahead, we can find something that is surprisingly desirable. When that happens, the giver is as happy as the receiver.

Perhaps that's how the angels felt when they delivered good news to the shepherds. At least we know the shepherds were surprised. We also know they valued the news because they rushed off to Bethlehem to worship the Christ child.

The Christmas account is, after all, God's monumental surprise. His people had waited centuries for some word from their prophets, but there was none. Then suddenly, seemingly out of nowhere, the good news of the ultimate Shepherd came not from a prophet but from humble shepherds.

Never count God out of the picture. He will surprise you and do far more than you can ask, think, or even dream about (Eph. 3:20).

Doing Something with the Good News. After the shepherds heard about the birth of the Christ child, they told others the good news. When we discover something that is of great value to us, don't you think that it should be shared with others, especially if, by our sharing, our own portion is enhanced, rather than reduced?

The story is told of a missionary physician working in the interior regions of mainland China. One day, he cured a patient by a performing a simple cataract procedure. The man was overjoyed, for he had been unable to see for years. He left the compound, and the physician continued with his daily routines, only to be astonished weeks later by a visitor.

The man who had been healed of his cataracts returned to the physician's compound. But this time he was not alone. He was carrying a long rope, and holding on to this rope were more than 50 men, women, and children. Yes, they were all blind! Some had come from as far as 250 miles away, journeying through the wilderness, holding onto the rope for their guidance.

Don't ever forget that our world is filled with spiritually blind people. Perhaps as you offer them the rope of the gospel, they will follow the light of Christ.

The First Creche. Legend has it that in December of 1223, Francis of Assisi was on his way to preach in the village of Greccio, Italy. As he walked, he pondered how he could bring home to the impoverished, illiterate peasants the true meaning of Christmas. He wanted the account of the Savior's birth to live in their hearts.

Suddenly, Francis had an idea. He would recreate the manger scene for his audience. First, he went to a friend in the village, and between them they fashioned the first creche, or nativity scene. Then, when the peasants came to the church on Christmas Eve, they stopped in amazement and fell on their knees in adoration. There they saw a live donkey and ox. They also noticed real people playing the parts of Joseph, Mary, and the shepherds. Moreover, in a crude manger lay a representation of the infant Jesus.

Francis proceeded to tell the onlookers the joyous account of the birth of the Messiah. This enabled the peasants to feel as if they were actually in ancient Bethlehem. This experience also helped them never to forget the message of hope and gladness they heard that night.

LESSON 4 — DECEMBER 28

AFFIRM THE SAVIOR'S POWER

BACKGROUND SCRIPTURE: Matthew 14:22-36
DEVOTIONAL READING: Mark 9:15-24

Key Verse: When they were come into the ship, the wind ceased. Then they that were in the ship came and worshipped him, saying, Of a truth thou art the Son of God. Matthew 14:32-33.

KING JAMES VERSION

MATTHEW 14:22 And straightway Jesus constrained his disciples to get into a ship, and to go before him unto the other side, while he sent the multitudes away. 23 And when he had sent the multitudes away, he went up into a mountain apart to pray: and when the evening was come, he was there alone. 24 But the ship was now in the midst of the sea, tossed with waves: for the wind was contrary. 25 And in the fourth watch of the night Jesus went unto them, walking on the sea. 26 And when the disciples saw him walking on the sea, they were troubled, saying, It is a spirit; and they cried out for fear. 27 But straightway Jesus spake unto them, saying, Be of good cheer; it is I; be not afraid. 28 And Peter answered him and said, Lord, if it be thou, bid me come unto thee on the water. 29 And he said, Come. And when Peter was come down out of the ship, he walked on the water, to go to Jesus. 30 But when he saw the wind boisterous, he was afraid; and beginning to sink, he cried, saying, Lord, save me. 31 And immediately Jesus stretched forth his hand, and caught him, and said unto him, O thou of little faith, wherefore didst thou doubt? 32 And when they were come into the ship, the wind ceased. 33 Then they that were in the ship came and worshipped him, saying, Of a truth thou art the Son of God.

34 And when they were gone over, they came into the land of Gennesaret. 35 And when the men of that place had knowledge of him, they sent out into all that country round about, and brought unto him all that were diseased; 36 And besought him that they might only touch the hem of his garment: and as many as touched were made perfectly whole.

NEW REVISED STANDARD VERSION

MATTHEW 14:22 Immediately he made the disciples get into the boat and go on ahead to the other side, while he dismissed the crowds. 23 And after he had dismissed the crowds, he went up the mountain by himself to pray. When evening came, he was there alone, 24 but by this time the boat, battered by the waves, was far from the land, for the wind was against them.
25 And early in the morning he came walking toward them on the sea. 26 But when the disciples saw him walking on the sea, they were terrified, saying, "It is a ghost!" And they cried out in fear. 27 But immediately Jesus spoke to them and said, "Take heart, it is I; do not be afraid."
28 Peter answered him, "Lord, if it is you, command me to come to you on the water." 29 He said, "Come." So Peter got out of the boat, started walking on the water, and came toward Jesus. 30 But when he noticed the strong wind, he became frightened, and beginning to sink, he cried out, "Lord, save me!" 31 Jesus immediately reached out his hand and caught him, saying to him, "You of little faith, why did you doubt?" 32 When they got into the boat, the wind ceased. 33 And those in the boat worshiped him, saying, "Truly you are the Son of God."
34 When they had crossed over, they came to land at Gennesaret. 35 After the people of that place recognized him, they sent word throughout the region and brought all who were sick to him, 36 and begged him that they might touch even the fringe of his cloak; and all who touched it were healed.

Home Bible Readings

Monday, December 22	Hebrews 11:1-6	*By Faith We Please God*
Tuesday, December 23	Luke 8:19-25	*Where Is Your Faith?*
Wednesday, December 24	Mark 9:15-24	*I Believe; Help My Unbelief*
Thursday, December 25	John 1:1-9	*The Light Overpowers Darkness*
Friday, December 26	Matthew 17:14-20	*A Mustard-Seed-Sized Faith*
Saturday, December 27	Matthew 15:21-31	*Great Is Your Faith*
Sunday, December 28	Matthew 14:22-36	*Oh You of Little Faith*

Background

The incident recorded in Matthew 14:22-33 took place on the Sea of Galilee. This is not really a sea in the same sense as the Mediterranean Sea and other large bodies of water are called "seas." Instead, the Sea of Galilee is actually a pear-shaped lake lying below sea level, being 6 miles wide, 15 miles long, and approximately 150 feet deep.

During the Old Testament era, this body of water was known as the Lake (or Sea) of Kinnereth. Later, it became know as Lake Gennesaret, the Sea of Tiberias, and the Sea of Galilee. In the time of Jesus, the steep hills that surround most of the lake's shoreline were prime locations for villages. Despite its relatively small size and unpredictable, often violent weather, the lake was vital to the economy of the local villages. Even today, fish from the Sea of Galilee are as important to modern Israelis as they were to the people living in the area when Jesus ministered.

Notes on the Printed Text

The episode in which Jesus walked on the water is preceded by Him feeding over 5,000 people in a remote area near Bethsaida (see Luke 9:10, 12). The latter was a town on the northeast shore of the Sea of Galilee. Both events occurred in the spring of A.D. 29, which was the third year of Jesus' earthly ministry. It was a time in which the civil and religious authorities increasingly opposed Jesus. For instance, Matthew 14:1-12 states that Jesus' forerunner, John the Baptizer, was beheaded by Herod Antipas a few months earlier. Antipas ruled over Galilee and Perea from 4 B.C. to A.D. 39. Based on reports he received about Jesus' preaching and miracles, Antipas incorrectly surmised that Jesus was the Baptizer "risen from the dead" (vs. 2).

The increasingly precarious situation prompted Jesus to leave the area by boat (vs. 13). He felt a need to get away and spend some time by Himself in prayer (perhaps to reflect on John's beheading; vs. 23). That said, Jesus was unable to remain alone for long, even in a relatively unpopulated region. Large crowds of people had heard of His whereabouts and followed Him on foot from the nearby towns of Galilee (vs. 13). Indeed, when Jesus arrived at the shore of the lake and began to disembark, He spotted many people already there waiting for Him (vs. 14). This incident indicates that

Jesus was tremendously popular among the people and that they looked to Him to fill a spiritual void in their lives.

After Jesus miraculously fed a large number of people (vss. 15-21), and with the day drawing to a close, Jesus directed the Twelve to get into a boat without Him and cross over to the other side of the Sea of Galilee. This would have been the northwest shore of the lake, near the Plain of Gennesaret. Meanwhile, the Savior dispersed the crowds (vs. 22). The Greek verb rendered "sent" means to compel someone to act in a certain manner and hints at the presence of a crisis. We learn from John 6:14 that the miraculous supply of food prompted many to wonder whether Jesus was the prophet that Moses referred to in Deuteronomy 18:15 and 18. In their desperation, the people wanted to force Jesus to be their king (John 6:15). But the kind of ruler they wanted, a brigand who would overthrow Israel's oppressors, was not in God's plan (see John 18:36–37; Acts 1:6; Rom 14:7).

After Jesus dispersed the crowds, He ventured up the side of a mountain to spend the night in prayer (Matt. 14:23). As the sun set over the horizon, Jesus was finally alone with the Father. We don't know what Jesus prayed about. Jesus might have talked to the Father about the needs of the people, the direction of the Son's earthly ministry in the face of growing opposition, and His upcoming crucifixion. Certainly, the Savior recognized the importance of spending private time with His Father in prayer.

While Jesus was beginning to pray, His disciples had already gone far out on the lake. As the Twelve made their way, a gale-force wind sent huge waves crashing against the sides of the boat (Matt 14:24; John 6:18). At times, the sudden appearance of violent storm episodes occurred on the Sea of Galilee. Evidently, the disciples spent most of the night fighting the elements as they tried to cross. Despite their efforts, they only went about three miles, which placed them near the middle of the lake (Mark 6:47; John 6:19).

It was the "fourth watch of the night" (Matt. 14:25) when Jesus saw the trouble embroiling His disciples. In ancient times, the night was divided into "watches," that is, time periods used by watchmen to regulate their shifts. The Jews divided the night into three watches: (1) sunset to about 10:00 P.M.; (2) about 10:00 P.M. to about 2:00 A.M.; and (3) about 2:00 A.M. to sunrise (see Exod. 14:24; Judg. 7:19; Lam. 2:19). In contrast, the Romans had four watches: (1) sunset to about 9:00 P.M.; (2) about 9:00 P.M. to about midnight; (3) about midnight to about 3:00 A.M.; and (4) about 3:00 A.M. to sunrise. Our verse reflects the Roman practice.

In the hours immediately preceding dawn, Jesus came to rescue His friends. He didn't take a boat, though, for He didn't need one. He came to the Twelve by walking on the lake (Matt 14:25; Mark 6:48). Not even the wind, waves, and gravity could stop the one who is the Lord of all creation (see Job 38:8-11; Pss. 29:3-4, 10-11; 65:5-7; 77:19; 89:9; 107:23-32; Isa. 43:2, 16). While God used Moses to part the waters of the Red Sea, not even the famed leader, liberator, and lawgiver of Israel could claim authority and control over the elements the way the Savior did.

Jesus' form appeared mysteriously out of the darkness like a ghost, and He seemed as if He intended to pass on ahead of the fishing boat (Mark 6:48). The disciples' minds must have turned to the old Jewish superstition that a spirit seen at night brings disaster. In this case, they mistook Jesus for an apparition (Matt 14:26; Mark 6:49-50). It seems that whenever the Savior was absent, the Twelve fell into distress through lack of faith. Jesus quickly calmed their fears. Undoubtedly, the familiar sound of His voice identifying Himself reassured His disciples that they would not be harmed (Matt 14:27; John 6:20). Jesus' declaration, "It is I" (Matt. 14:27), is more literally rendered "I am" (Matt. 14:27). This might be an intentional allusion to Exodus 3:14, where God made Himself known to Moses as "I AM THAT I AM" (see Isa. 43:10; 51:12).

Peter took Jesus at His word by boldly asking the Savior to allow His disciple to venture out on the water toward Him (Matt. 14:28). When Jesus gave Peter permission to do so, he initially exercised great faith by leaving the boat (vs. 29). For a moment, he could actually walk on the water (vs. 29). Perhaps at first Peter felt exhilarated. But when he shifted his attention from Jesus to the tempestuous wind, Peter became terrified, began to sink into the water, and shrieked, "Lord, save me" (vs. 30).

Despite Peter's alarm, Jesus remained in full control of the situation. He quickly extended His hand and took hold of Peter. The Savior wasted no time in focusing on Peter's real problem. He had allowed doubt to squash his faith (vs. 31). If Peter had remained unwavering in his trust, he would have experienced no difficulties. From this incident, Peter (and the rest of the Twelve) learned that any task done for Jesus must be accompanied by faith in Him from start to finish (see John 15:5). The episode also reminds us of our need for faith throughout our spiritual lives. Faith is not only necessary for conversion. Living day by day with Jesus requires us to trust Him to take care of us. Admittedly, this is difficult when we see the risks that are involved. Yet we can persevere if we remain focused on our all-powerful Savior.

The moment Jesus and Peter returned to the fishing boat, the turbulent wind ceased (Matt. 14:32). The Twelve, now completely dumbfounded over what had taken place (see Mark 6:52-53), fell prostrate in worship before the feet of the Messiah. As they did so, they exclaimed, "Of a truth thou art the Son of God" (Matt. 14:33). This messianic title emphasizes the special and intimate relationship between Jesus and the Father (see 3:17; 16:16; 27:54). The title also spotlights Jesus' unwavering commitment and obedience to the Father's will. As the second Person of the Trinity, Jesus is equal with the Father (and the Spirit), exercises divine prerogatives, and is worthy of our trust, obedience, and adoration.

After the crisis had passed, the fishing boat landed and moored at Gennesaret (14:34). This was a fertile plain located on the northwest bank of the Sea of Galilee. According to local belief, the numerous mineral springs in the area could heal the infirm and crippled who flocked to them. When the people of the region recognized who Jesus was, they told others who lived there that He had come (vs. 35). Consequently, a large crowd hurriedly carried all who were sick to Him to be healed. The crowds were so desperate and needy that they begged to simply touch the edge of Jesus' cloak (or loose outer garment) in the hope that they might be cured (vs. 36). He granted the people's requests and healed all who touched Him.

Jesus performed many miracles during His earthly ministry, some of which are not recorded in the Gospels. His miracles were extraordinary expressions of God's power. When Jesus performed a miracle, God directly altered, superseded, or counteracted some established pattern in the natural order. The miracles of Jesus served several purposes. First, they confirmed His claim to be the Messiah. Second, they validated His assertion that He was sent by God and represented Him. Third, they substantiated the credibility of the truths He declared to the people of Israel. Fourth, they encouraged the doubtful to put their trust in Him. Fifth, they demonstrated that the One who is love was willing to reach out to people with compassion and grace.

SUGGESTIONS TO TEACHERS

Through Jesus' calming the storm and feeding over 5,000 people, He revealed His mastery over nature (Matt. 14:13-33). Indeed, as the "Son of God," Jesus makes magnificent use of natural things in supernatural ways. And His eternal power, care, and concern make Him the most qualified person to be the Master of our lives.

1. JESUS' CONTROL OF THE STORM. Physical, mental, emotional, and spiritual "storms" often barge into our lives, and, like the disciples, a sudden burst of fear can chase away our faith (see vs. 26). Of all times, this is when we must call on Jesus to renew our faith (see vs. 30). Through faith we come to understand who God really is. We also begin to realize that He who brings calm to the storms of nature can also bring calm to the storms of our hearts.

2. JESUS' COMPASSION. Certainly Jesus performed miracles for different reasons. Some were done to teach important truths, and some were performed as signs of His messianic identity. But we recognize that Jesus healed people because he had compassion for them (see vss. 14, 35-36). Jesus was a loving, caring, and concerned person. Of course, He still is. He knows and understands our suffering and our hurts. And when the time is right, His compassion will bring about the restoration we need.

3. JESUS' CONCERN FOR OUR WELL-BEING. As in Jesus' day, one of our most basic life needs is for physical wellness. Even when our circumstance seems bleak, we can entrust our physical well-being to Jesus. We can also depend on Him to meet our deepest spiritual needs, both now and for all eternity.

4. JESUS' INTEGRITY. Any other person might have been tempted to exploit the needs of the crowds who sought help from Jesus. Imagine the applause Jesus could have received wherever He went. He could have become a media star, perhaps across the entire region. Thankfully, Jesus resisted that temptation, moving to areas where He was less known. Even then He tried to escape notice. Jesus steadfastly pursued the best plan, the Father's will. As we encounter Jesus' integrity, can we not trust Him?

FOR ADULTS

■ **TOPIC:** Believing in the Savior

■ **QUESTIONS:** 1. After feeding over 5,000 people, why did Jesus compel His disciples to get into a fishing boat? 2. How important was it for Jesus to spend time in prayer? 3. After Peter left the boat and began walking on the water to Jesus, what prompted Peter to doubt? 4. Why is it important for believers to give Jesus their heartfelt devotion? 5. How can the divine authority of Jesus give us confidence in life's most difficult circumstances?

■ **ILLUSTRATIONS:**

Filling Our Needs. Life is filled with hardships, many of which are unexpected and unavoidable. It's in these tough, overwhelming circumstances that Christian faith swings into action. We find that Jesus is loving, wise, powerful, and trustworthy. How exciting it is to discover that, even in life's darkest moments, the Lord is there to watch over and provide for us.

Christians sometimes say, "Oh, that wouldn't matter to Jesus." Or, "It's too trivial to pray about." But we soon learn that nothing is inconsequential to the Lord. He invites us to experience the great privilege of praying to Him about everything, not just major crises. In fact, we grow the most spiritually when we place all of our needs in His hands.

This week's study of Jesus walking on the water and healing scores of people brings us fresh insight concerning the ability He has to meet our needs. We learn that nothing is impossible for Him to do for us (see Luke 18:27).

No Substitutes. A monarch butterfly is as beautiful as a viceroy butterfly. A bird, looking for a light lunch, might snatch either, expecting a pleasurable meal. God designed both with beautiful orange and black wings. In fact, the only major differences are the viceroy's slightly smaller size and a black stripe along its hind wings.

The viceroy would be a feathered diner's delight, but a monarch would not. Poison ingested from the milkweed plant while the monarch was a caterpillar makes the butterfly taste bitter. Once a bird eats a monarch, it won't repeat the mistake.

All around us, there are subtle counterfeits. The most dangerous are religious frauds (see 2 Cor. 11:14). When the Twelve declared Jesus to be the "Son of God" (Matt. 14:33), they recognized Him as the true Savior of the world. They discovered on the Sea of Galilee that only He had the power and authority to calm a fierce storm, as well as meet the deepest spiritual needs of His followers.

Count on the Storms. Before former journalist and news anchor John Chancellor succumbed to cancer in 1996, he observed in an interview: "If you want to make God laugh, tell Him your plans." One of the things believers can count on in this life is storms. As it was with Jesus' disciples traveling in a fishing boat on the Sea of Galilee, we just can't plan when turbulence in our lives will occur.

Physical storms will assault our bodies and make us weak. Mental storms will assault our brain and make us unsure about our decisions. Emotional storms will assault our heart and make us wonder whether our feelings have slipped into chaos.

Even spiritual storms will assault our soul and make us question our long-held faith. But we should always remember that Jesus has a purpose in the storms that come our way. It may be to increase our trust in Him; it may be to show us His power; or it may be to remind us that He, alone, is in control.

FOR YOUTH

■ **TOPIC:** Surprised by Power

■ **QUESTIONS:** 1. Why do you think Jesus was so prompt in dismissing the crowds after miraculously feeding them? 2. What sorts of issues do you think Jesus prayed about to the Father? 3. Why were the Twelve initially terrified at the sight of Jesus walking to them on the water? 4. What negative impact does doubt have on our relationship with Jesus? 5. In what ways has Jesus recently demonstrated His power in your life?

■ **ILLUSTRATIONS:**

Depending on Jesus More. The teenager and his father returned to the car after fishing a couple of hours, only to discover that the car keys were nowhere to be found. They searched everywhere and finally the father said, "Let's pray and ask Jesus to help us find those keys." So the two did just that, and in a matter of minutes the keys turned up.

Was this a minor miracle? Regardless of our response, the lesson is clear. Our faith in Jesus covers all areas of our lives. Faith is not confined to the church building, the Sunday worship services, or the youth meeting. Rather, Jesus wants us to trust Him in every circumstance of life.

The Savior encountered people at the point of their greatest needs. He used incidents such as His walking on the water to teach His disciples to trust Him more (see Matt. 14:22-33). There were also opportunities for the crowds to receive His healing touch (see vss. 34-36). By studying the way Jesus ministered to others, we are encouraged to depend on Him more in our trying situations.

Nothing to Fear. In a scene from the movie *Star Wars Episode I: The Phantom Menace*, the Jedi Council is interviewing young Anakin Skywalker to determine whether this boy with special abilities should be trained to become a Jedi knight. At one point,

Master Jedi Yoda expresses to Anakin that "I sense much fear in you," and clarifies his feeling by adding, "Fear losing your mother, do you?"

Anakin responds by asking, "What's that got to do with anything?" Yoda answers Anakin's question with one of the favorite lines from the movie: "Everything! Fear leads to anger; anger leads to hate; hate leads to suffering."

When Jesus' disciples were faced with a dangerous storm on the Sea of Galilee, their immediate fear caused their faith to virtually disappear. It's also possible that their lack of faith allowed their fear to overcome them. But whatever the case, faith cannot survive in a climate of fear, nor can fear survive in a climate of faith—especially when it remains focused on Jesus, our all-powerful Lord.

Trust Jesus. From 1993 to 2002, The *X-Files* was a popular American science fiction television drama. The catch phrase of the show declared, "Trust no one; fear everything." Even today, bumper stickers scream the opposing messages, "No Fear" and "Fear This!" In reality, it is hard to imagine a life lived in which no one is trusted and everything is feared. And yet, trust is hard to come by, and fear seems to be on the increase.

Some parents don't trust their kids, and some kids don't trust their parents. Politicians in one party don't trust those in another party, and vice versa. The elderly don't trust the young, and the young don't trust the elderly. Regardless of age, everyone seems afraid of being left out or found out, of running out of money or prestige or status, of being expected to accomplish the impossible, or of being ostracized as a failure.

In the ongoing battle between trust and fear, fear sometimes seems to be winning out. Yet in the midst of this strife, Jesus calls out a question to us: "O thou of little faith, wherefore didst thou doubt?" (Matt. 14:31). Put your faith in the one who calms storms and hearts and feeds stomachs and minds. Trust Jesus, and fear little else.

LESSON 5 — JANUARY 4

A Model Prayer

Background Scripture: Luke 11:1-13
Devotional Reading: Psalm 103:1-13

Key Verse: [Jesus] said unto them, When ye pray, say, Our Father which art in heaven, Hallowed be thy name. Thy kingdom come. Thy will be done, as in heaven, so in earth. Luke 11:2.

KING JAMES VERSION

LUKE 11:1 And it came to pass, that, as he was praying in a certain place, when he ceased, one of his disciples said unto him, Lord, teach us to pray, as John also taught his disciples. 2 And he said unto them, When ye pray, say, Our Father which art in heaven, Hallowed be thy name. Thy kingdom come. Thy will be done, as in heaven, so in earth. 3 Give us day by day our daily bread. 4 And forgive us our sins; for we also forgive every one that is indebted to us. And lead us not into temptation; but deliver us from evil. 5 And he said unto them, Which of you shall have a friend, and shall go unto him at midnight, and say unto him, Friend, lend me three loaves; 6 For a friend of mine in his journey is come to me, and I have nothing to set before him? 7 And he from within shall answer and say, Trouble me not: the door is now shut, and my children are with me in bed; I cannot rise and give thee. 8 I say unto you, Though he will not rise and give him, because he is his friend, yet because of his importunity he will rise and give him as many as he needeth. 9 And I say unto you, Ask, and it shall be given you; seek, and ye shall find; knock, and it shall be opened unto you. 10 For every one that asketh receiveth; and he that seeketh findeth; and to him that knocketh it shall be opened. 11 If a son shall ask bread of any of you that is a father, will he give him a stone? or if he ask a fish, will he for a fish give him a serpent? 12 Or if he shall ask an egg, will he offer him a scorpion? 13 If ye then, being evil, know how to give good gifts unto your children: how much more shall your heavenly Father give the Holy Spirit to them that ask him?

NEW REVISED STANDARD VERSION

LUKE 11:1 He was praying in a certain place, and after he had finished, one of his disciples said to him, "Lord, teach us to pray, as John taught his disciples."
2 He said to them, "When you pray, say:
  Father, hallowed be your name.
   Your kingdom come.
3 Give us each day our daily bread.
4 And forgive us our sins,
    for we ourselves forgive everyone indebted to us.
   And do not bring us to the time of trial."
5 And he said to them, "Suppose one of you has a friend, and you go to him at midnight and say to him, 'Friend, lend me three loaves of bread; 6 for a friend of mine has arrived, and I have nothing to set before him.' 7 And he answers from within, 'Do not bother me; the door has already been locked, and my children are with me in bed; I cannot get up and give you anything.' 8 I tell you, even though he will not get up and give him anything because he is his friend, at least because of his persistence he will get up and give him whatever he needs.
9 "So I say to you, Ask, and it will be given you; search, and you will find; knock, and the door will be opened for you. 10 For everyone who asks receives, and everyone who searches finds, and for everyone who knocks, the door will be opened. 11 Is there anyone among you who, if your child asks for a fish, will give a snake instead of a fish? 12 Or if the child asks for an egg, will give a scorpion? 13 If you then, who are evil, know how to give good gifts to your children, how much more will the heavenly Father give the Holy Spirit to those who ask him!"

Home Bible Readings

Monday, December 29	Matthew 6:1-8	*Whenever You Pray*
Tuesday, December 30	Leviticus 22:26-33	*You Shall Not Profane My Name*
Wednesday, December 31	Psalm 103:1-13	*Bless God's Holy Name*
Thursday, January 1	Luke 10:1-11	*God's Kingdom Has Come Near*
Friday, January 2	Matthew 6:25-34	*Do Not Worry about Your Life*
Saturday, January 3	Psalm 37:27-34	*The Lord Will Not Abandon You*
Sunday, January 4	Luke 11:1-13	*Lord, Teach Us to Pray*

Background

Evidently, the model prayer Jesus offered in Luke 11:2-4 prompted some of His disciples to wonder how confident they should be in bringing small, personal matters to God. Also, if it is permissible for God's spiritual children to make specific requests to Him, then why doesn't He appear to answer all their petitions? These are some of the concerns Jesus addressed in His parable on being bold in prayer (vss. 5-8). From this story, they learned that if they prayed, God would answer.

It would be incorrect to infer from Jesus' story that God will eventually answer our prayers if we keep pestering Him. He is not like a sleepy man who does not want to be troubled and has to be shamed into responding. In reality, our heavenly Father is completely opposite the friend in the house. Jesus' point is that if this man was willing to respond to the pleas of his friend, how much more willing is God to give us the things we really need. He is not reluctant to give us what we ask, but instead is eager to do so (vss. 9-13).

Notes on the Printed Text

In Luke 11:1, we learn that one day Jesus' disciples were with Him as He spent time in prayer with His heavenly Father. When Jesus finished, one of the Twelve asked Him to teach them how to pray, just as John the Baptizer had done for his followers. In response, Jesus outlined a model prayer (vss. 2-4). This is traditionally known as the Lord's Prayer (see also the longer version in Matt. 6:9-13).

A fuller understanding of what Jesus taught can be obtained by considering both Luke's and Matthew's versions of the Lord's Prayer. We discover that God wants us to address Him in a way that reflects our close, personal relationship with Him (see Rom. 8:14-17; Gal. 4:4-7). Like a father, God has authority over us, and yet at the same time He loves us and wants to give us what we need to be effective in our service for Him. Because He lives in heaven, He is transcendent (namely, going beyond our earthly existence) and has the ability to grant our requests.

The Greek phrase rendered "hallowed be thy name" (Luke 11:2) emphasizes how important it is for us to honor and revere the Lord, as represented by His holy name. So, the initial focus of prayer is not on our personal needs, but on God's glory. The one who prays also desires that God's rule over His creatures would extend to its fullest bounds and that people on earth would come to obey the Lord as perfectly as do the angels in heaven.

Verses 3-4 indicate that we are to look to God for our needs (not our greeds)—no matter how basic—on a day-to-day basis. Accordingly, while our foremost priority should be giving God the honor that is due Him, there's nothing wrong with asking Him to give us the things we think we need, whether they are material or spiritual in nature. Three personal requests are delineated in the Lord's Prayer.

The first petition is for bread, which was a staple of the Jewish diet in Jesus' day. Bread stands for all the basic needs people have. The second personal request is for forgiveness. The Father is the one who can cancel our spiritual debts because the Son paid them in full on the cross. But as Jesus stated, before we ask God to pardon our sins, we should first forgive the wrongs others have done to us. The third request is for protection from temptation and Satan. This reminds us that we should ask for God's help in preserving our spiritual health.

Jesus' parable recorded in verses 5-8 differs from other stories He told in that He made His point by means of contrasts, rather than similarities. In particular, God is not like the friend or the father in these stories, but rather different from them. The parable about the unexpected guest spotlights a typical, though embarrassing, situation in the time of Jesus.

It's late at night when a hungry traveler arrives at the home of a friend and requests some food to eat. The friend, however, does not have anything to feed his friend. And since showing hospitality was important in that culture, the friend would feel ashamed if he could not satisfy his guest's request for a meal. This prompts the host to go to a neighbor around midnight to pester him for a loan of three loaves of bread (vss. 5-6). In a simple Galilean village such as this, in which women baked bread in common courtyards, all the residents would know who had a fresh supply of bread.

In Jesus' parable, the head of the household told his neighbor not to bother him. The former explained that the wooden door was already bolted shut, and he and his children were in bed. Moreover, the homeowner declared that he was unable to get up and give his neighbor anything to eat (vs. 7).

This scene can be better understood with some background information about the typical sleeping arrangements of a home in Jesus' day. The dwelling was probably a peasant's cottage made up of one large room that served the entire family's needs. The bedding was kept in a recessed part of a wall and taken out at night and spread on reed mats on the floor. The parents would sleep in the center of the room, with the male children positioned on the father's right-hand side and the female children on the mother's left-hand side. Even with a modest-sized family, the father's getting up would have disturbed the whole household, especially any children sleeping closest to him.

In that day, it was a matter of cultural honor for a neighbor to be a good host to visitors. Thus, the host in Jesus' parable continued to nag his friend for food to give to the hungry traveler. The Savior noted that the inconvenienced fellow would not comply with the request out of friendship. Instead, he caved in to the demand because of the neighbor's "importunity" (vs. 8). Indeed, the worn-down head of the household gave his neighbor not just three loaves of bread, but whatever he requested.

The Greek noun rendered "importunity" is used only here in the New Testament. It denotes a lack of sensitivity to what others would consider proper. Such ideas as "shamelessness," "impertinence," and "boldness" are wrapped up in the KJV translation. Other possible renderings include "sheer persistence" and "shameless audacity." The idea is that the neighbor gave his friend as much bread as he needed because the man kept harassing him. In addition, the head of the household possibly wanted to avoid the shame that would come from a breach of hospitality (see Prov. 3:27-28).

Jesus stated that when they asked the Father for something, it would be given to them. This meant He delighted to hear and answer their requests. It also meant the disciples were totally dependent on the Lord. The more they looked to God to meet their needs, the less inclined they would be to covet what others had. Whatever Christians sought from God would be found, and whatever door of ministry opportunity they accessed in His will would be opened to them (Luke 11:9). The idea of knocking suggests that a sense of urgency should accompany the disciples' praying. The Greek verb tenses used in this verse (present imperatives) indicate continuous action—keep on asking, keep on seeking, and keep on knocking.

Jesus explained that His followers need not fear being rejected, for the Father would answer their petitions (vs. 10). Moreover, Jesus' comments implied that His followers were to persist until the answer came. Perseverance in prayer would produce tangible results, for no prayer went unheard or unanswered by God (see 18:1). The Lord would neither disregard the petitions of His children nor treat them as insignificant. In fact, their prayers were important and would get His personal attention. It would be mistaken to assume from what the Son said that the Father would fulfill unbiblical requests. In that regard, verses 9 and 10 (see also Matt. 7:7-8) are not a blank check that God issues to people for them to fill in as they please. Before the Lord answers a believer's request, she or he should be seeking to live and pray in His will (see 1 John 5:14-15).

Jesus ultimately intended His comments to encourage, not discourage, His followers to pray. The Savior illustrated His Father's eagerness to fulfill the requests of His children by referring to the sensible practices of all parents. Normally when a child asked for a fish, a reasonable parent would not hand her a water snake, for that would be cruel and insensitive (Luke 11:11). Moreover, if a child asked for an egg, he would not get something as inappropriate and harmful as a scorpion (vs. 12; see Matt. 7:9-10). Similarly, God is not cruel and insensitive toward His children. Rather, He is kind and reasonable in handling their requests.

Human beings, who are fallen and inclined to do evil, understand how to give beneficial and appropriate things to their children. This being true, believers were to consider how much more their heavenly Father would do for them when they brought their requests to Him. He would always give them what was sensible and appropriate to meet their needs for that moment. This includes virtues such as righteousness, purity, and wisdom (see Matt. 7:11; Jas. 1:5). Luke 11:13 specifies that the Holy Spirit is the ultimate good gift we can receive from God. From the Spirit believers receive wisdom and guidance to live in a godly manner in a fallen world (see 1 Cor. 2:10-16).

SUGGESTIONS TO TEACHERS

God longs to give us any and every desire that is in line with His will for our lives. Sometimes, though, we have to wait for these things. Our faith is challenged when the Lord doesn't seem to answer in the way we hoped or in the timeframe we expected. But as Luke 11:1-13 reveals, our job is to remain faithful, to continue praying, and to keep trusting God no matter what the circumstances look like.

1. PRAYING IN A HUMBLE MANNER. In the Lord's Prayer, Jesus provided His followers a model of humble praying. We learn that God is both exaltedly holy above His creatures and intimately concerned with us. He is sovereign and we are totally dependent on Him. We need Him for daily sustenance of life, for forgiveness of our sin, and for rescue from both temptation and the tempter.

2. PRAYING IN A CANDID MANNER. What are your students' "material needs" today? Encourage them to be sincere in asking God for what they need to be more effective in their service for Him. Remind them to avoid making up spiritual-sounding reasons for asking for their daily necessities. Also, the class members need not hesitate to tell God about their fears and anxieties concerning every dimension of their lives. Let them know that it's important to their spiritual growth and integrity to be willing to tell God everything.

3. PRAYING IN AN OBEDIENT MANNER. Jesus taught His disciples to pray to the Father that they might do His will. That shouldn't be surprising, since the whole purpose of Jesus' life was to do His Father's will. Ask the students if they have ever wondered how they can expect their prayers to be in accordance with the will of God? The Scripture passage for this week's lesson can help them answer that concern.

FOR ADULTS

■ **TOPIC:** Finding the Right Words

■ **QUESTIONS:** 1. What are the key aspects of Jesus' model prayer? 2. In Jesus' parable, what prompted one friend to go to another friend and request some food? 3. In what way is the Father in heaven unlike the reluctant neighbor? 4. What time of the day is best for you to pray? 5. What are some of your recent prayers that God has answered?

ILLUSTRATIONS:

Practicing Genuine Piety. People learn new skills all the time. For instance, they like to talk about how they learned to use different types of electronic equipment, including laptops, smart phones, and tablet devices. We laugh about the mistakes we made and how we inadvertently wiped out some important information. We keep taking refresher courses to upgrade our computer skills.

Learning to pray is like that, because praying is a new skill. It's not something you fall into. Prayer is a developed discipline that expresses our sincere piety. Prayer takes the same kind of training and discipline. While we pray, we learn more about it and find new pleasure in it, but it requires time and concentration.

Prayer is not like technology, however, because anyone can pray. That's because prayer is having a conversation with the Father (see Luke 11:2). But in order for it to be satisfying, we have to think about what we say and how we say it. We have to use our best thoughts and skills, conditioned by a proper attitude (see vss. 3-4).

Advanced Answer to Prayer. This week's Scripture passage reminds us how important it is for us to worship God in prayer and to bring our petitions to Him. Indeed, Jesus encourages us to be bold and persistent in prayer, all the while assured of God's concern for our needs.

Until 1981, Oliver Mitchell Sr. was the president of the John E. Mitchell Manufacturing Company in Dallas, Texas. He relates a unique personal account of how God answered a prayer. Oliver was awakened one night in a cold sweat. He had just had a terrible dream in which he was the driver of a car that had run over a small child. The dream was so real to him that he immediately got out of bed and went to his knees, asking God not to allow such a tragedy to happen to him. He remembers the great peace that he received almost immediately and how he went right back to sleep and didn't think about the dream again.

The next day, Oliver was driving his car with four companions to a luncheon across town. Driving at 25 miles per hour, he immediately felt impressed to slam on the brakes. His companions lurched forward, but as they recovered, they looked up just in time to see a diaper-clad toddler run out from between two parked cars. Oliver said his reactions were in direct response to God's prodding.

The Hard Work of Prayer. Luke 11:1 reveals that even though Jesus' disciples recognized the importance of prayer, they desired teaching from Him about how to pray and what to expect as a result of doing so. In turn, Jesus emphasized the importance of praying to God in humility, trust, and boldness (vss. 2-13).

In *My Utmost for His Highest*, Oswald Chambers makes the following admonishment: "Prayer is a battle; it is a matter of indifference where you are. Whichever way God engineers circumstances, the duty is to pray. Never allow the thought, 'I am no use where I am'; because you certainly can be of no use where you are not. Wherever God has dumped you down in circumstances, pray."

But what if we don't see results? Perhaps we too easily fall into the same trap as the disciple Thomas: "Seeing is believing." We want to know the results of our prayers immediately. According to Chambers, "We won't pray unless we get thrills; that is the intensest form of spiritual selfishness." The author goes on to note that there is "nothing thrilling about a laboring man's work, but it is the laboring man who makes the conceptions of the genius possible; and it is the laboring saint who makes the conceptions of his Master possible."

For Youth

■ **Topic:** Talk to Your Father

■ **Questions:** 1. What is the connection between our forgiving others and God forgiving us? 2. In Jesus' parable, why was the neighbor initially unwilling to give his neighbor bread? 3. What eventually persuaded the neighbor to give in to his friend's request? 4. What do you like most about praying to God? 5. Who is someone you could pray for today?

■ **Illustrations:**

Practicing My Faith. The concept of prayer as conversation with the Father has tremendous appeal (see Luke 11:2). We have to take prayer out of the realm of stuffy, pious jargon. We have to show saved teens that prayer is not limited to the people who do the praying in public services. Rather, prayer pleases God because it shows that we love Him and His fellowship.

Many times Christian adolescents pray for the first time on retreats or in small campus and church groups. They touch levels of intimacy in prayer because they are vulnerable to each other, more so than many adults. Therefore, our concern is not with the right words and tone of voice, but in practicing our faith with honesty and integrity. That's what Jesus talked about.

Our goals for youth are to cultivate strong daily prayer habits, as well as quality prayer in fellowship groups. Then as they pray, they can develop the needed spiritual muscles for standing up in spiritual battles (see vss. 3-4).

A Problem with the Radio. Luke 11:3-4 instructs believers about praying to God for their needs. In fact, the petition, "Give us day by day our daily bread," advocates a daily trust in the Father's provisions for life.

Years ago, as my extended family gathered around my cousin Tim's shortwave radio to listen, six sets of ears were met with blaring static. After months of work, the 14-year-old's project was a disappointment. Even worse, he had to replace the useless filter with one we ordered through the mail.

Less than a week remained until the science fair. Tim said in frustration, "I just don't see how this thing can work out!" His father countered, "Maybe there will be time—just enough time. But in case there isn't, are you willing to let this go?" Tim agreed to pray with his father. Tim asked the Lord for His help. But Tim also prayed that God would give him the grace and courage to accept that he might not get his project done.

A postal worker delivered the replacement filter the day before the science fair. Within a few hours, Tim tracked down an old yet essential component—a radio frequency generator. After buying it, he worked late into the night tuning the radio, until he heard French over the airwaves. Tim then told his father that if the radio hadn't worked, it would have been OK, too. Tim realized God knew best. As if to be reminded of his comment, right after the fair, the new filter went bad. We concluded that our loving Father in heaven meets our every need—and also has a sense of humor!

Prayers for a Hostage. The request in the Lord's Prayer concerning forgiveness (see Luke 11:4) is not only about personal salvation, but also about forgiving those who have wronged us. Jesus asked His followers to admit that they could not truly (or logically) repent of their offenses against God while at the same time refusing to forgive those who had offended them (see Matt. 6:14-15).

For seven long years (1985–1991), friends, colleagues, and loved ones brought their petitions to God to deliver Terry Anderson from his captors. Anderson, an *Associated Press* employee, was one of several Americans that Muslims kidnapped in Lebanon and held hostage.

In his book, *Den of Lions*, Anderson says that despite the beatings and deprivation he suffered, his faith in the Lord Jesus remained strong. When Anderson was finally released and asked about his feelings toward his abductors, he said, "I am a Christian. I am required to forgive." After God had answered the petitions of those who prayed for Anderson, as well as Anderson's own prayers for release, the former hostage praised the Lord in churches, on television, and in print.

LESSON 6 — JANUARY 11

JESUS PRAYS FOR US

BACKGROUND SCRIPTURE: John 17:1-26
DEVOTIONAL READING: John 15:1-11

Key Verse: That they all may be one; as thou, Father, art in me, and I in thee, that they also may be one in us: that the world may believe that thou hast sent me. John 17:21.

KING JAMES VERSION

JOHN 17:6 I have manifested thy name unto the men which thou gavest me out of the world: thine they were, and thou gavest them me; and they have kept thy word. 7 Now they have known that all things whatsoever thou hast given me are of thee. 8 For I have given unto them the words which thou gavest me; and they have received them, and have known surely that I came out from thee, and they have believed that thou didst send me. 9 I pray for them: I pray not for the world, but for them which thou hast given me; for they are thine. 10 And all mine are thine, and thine are mine; and I am glorified in them.

11 And now I am no more in the world, but these are in the world, and I come to thee. Holy Father, keep through thine own name those whom thou hast given me, that they may be one, as we are. 12 While I was with them in the world, I kept them in thy name: those that thou gavest me I have kept, and none of them is lost, but the son of perdition; that the scripture might be fulfilled. 13 And now come I to thee; and these things I speak in the world, that they might have my joy fulfilled in themselves. 14 I have given them thy word; and the world hath hated them, because they are not of the world, even as I am not of the world. 15 I pray not that thou shouldest take them out of the world, but that thou shouldest keep them from the evil. 16 They are not of the world, even as I am not of the world.

17 Sanctify them through thy truth: thy word is truth. 18 As thou hast sent me into the world, even so have I also sent them into the world. 19 And for their sakes I sanctify myself, that they also might be sanctified through the truth.

20 Neither pray I for these alone, but for them also which shall believe on me through their word; 21 That they all may be one; as thou, Father, art in me, and I in thee, that they also may be one in us: that the world may believe that thou hast sent me.

NEW REVISED STANDARD VERSION

JOHN 17:6 "I have made your name known to those whom you gave me from the world. They were yours, and you gave them to me, and they have kept your word. 7 Now they know that everything you have given me is from you; 8 for the words that you gave to me I have given to them, and they have received them and know in truth that I came from you; and they have believed that you sent me. 9 I am asking on their behalf; I am not asking on behalf of the world, but on behalf of those whom you gave me, because they are yours. 10 All mine are yours, and yours are mine; and I have been glorified in them. 11 And now I am no longer in the world, but they are in the world, and I am coming to you. Holy Father, protect them in your name that you have given me, so that they may be one, as we are one. 12 While I was with them, I protected them in your name that you have given me. I guarded them, and not one of them was lost except the one destined to be lost, so that the scripture might be fulfilled. 13 But now I am coming to you, and I speak these things in the world so that they may have my joy made complete in themselves. 14 I have given them your word, and the world has hated them because they do not belong to the world, just as I do not belong to the world. 15 I am not asking you to take them out of the world, but I ask you to protect them from the evil one. 16 They do not belong to the world, just as I do not belong to the world. 17 Sanctify them in the truth; your word is truth. 18 As you have sent me into the world, so I have sent them into the world. 19 And for their sakes I sanctify myself, so that they also may be sanctified in truth.

20 "I ask not only on behalf of these, but also on behalf of those who will believe in me through their word, 21 that they may all be one. As you, Father, are in me and I am in you, may they also be in us, so that the world may believe that you have sent me.

Home Bible Readings

Monday, January 5	Exodus 4:27-31	*Revealing the Words of the Lord*
Tuesday, January 6	Psalm 119:9-16	*Treasuring God's Word*
Wednesday, January 7	Jeremiah 35:12-17	*Obey the Words of the Lord*
Thursday, January 8	John 15:1-11	*Abide in My Love*
Friday, January 9	John 17:1-5	*This Is Eternal Life*
Saturday, January 10	John 17:22-26	*Making Known the Lord's Name*
Sunday, January 11	John 17:6-21	*Sanctified in the Truth*

Background

John 17 contains Jesus' longest recorded entreaty. In it He prayed for Himself (17:1-5), the disciples who were with Him (vss. 6-19), and everyone who would later come to believe in Him (vss. 20-26). Indeed, Jesus prayed for all of us as He was about to take our place on the cross. In Jesus' prayer, He referred to Judas Iscariot as the "son of perdition" (John 17:12). Early in the evening before much of Jesus' farewell discourse, Judas Iscariot had left the upper room (see 13:21-30). Now Jesus described Judas as the disciple who had been lost (17:12).

Evidently, the remaining eleven could not figure out whom Jesus meant. Yet He knew that at that very moment Judas was betraying Him for 30 silver coins (see Matt. 26:14-16; Mark 14:10-11; Luke 22:3-6). As a consequence of this wicked act, which Scripture had foretold, Judas was headed for eternal ruin. While Jesus did not state the Old Testament passages He had in mind, Psalm 41:9 is a likely candidate (see John 13:18). The fulfillment of biblical prophecy does not mean that the Father forced Judas to betray the Son, especially since Judas decided to do this evil deed on his own. That said, God used Judas' treachery to accomplish His greater redemptive plan.

Notes on the Printed Text

Jesus knew that His death and the disciples' temporary abandonment of Him would rock their fragile faith. So the Son devoted the major portion of His prayer to entrust His followers into the hands of His Father. Even before Jesus had "manifested" (vs. 6), or disclosed, the Father's holy character to the disciples, they belonged to God. In fact, God had taken them from the "world" and given them to His Son (see 6:37, 44-45; 15:16, 27). Jesus commended them for having kept God's Word. Despite their brief lapse in faith (see Matt. 26:56; Mark 14:50), they would be obedient to the truth about the Father, which the Son unveiled through His teachings and miracles.

Not only Jesus' disciples, but also everything that belonged to the Son came from the Father (John 17:7). In contrast to the religious elite, the Eleven had finally understood that all they knew about the Son had the Father as its source. The disciples' comprehension was based on their receiving and believing the message that Jesus had imparted to them (see 1:12). Though their understanding was not yet complete, they were convinced that the Father had sent the Son to earth to proclaim eternal truths. Jesus understood that the Eleven had much more to learn and that their faith needed to be strengthened. Yet, Jesus also knew that He could count on their devotion. After all, His Father had given them to the Son, and they truly believed in Him (17:8).

Jesus made it clear that He was praying for the Eleven and not for the rest of the "world" (vs. 9), which was opposed to God. This did not imply a lack of concern for other people. Jesus wanted the Eleven to know His specific concern for them, they who would glorify Him by being the first to take the gospel to the lost. These disciples belonged to the Father, and He had given them to the Son. As the Father had released them into His Son's care, now He was giving them back into His Father's care.

Jesus stated that the Father owned whatever belonged to the Son. Likewise, the Son owned everything that belonged to the Father. Jesus' statement included the Eleven (vs. 10). A mere mortal could not legitimately make such a claim, so the Son was clearly declaring here His equality with the Father (and the Spirit). Furthermore, the disciples heard Jesus express His confidence in them by stating that glory had come to Him as a result of them following Him. Perhaps at times over the past three years they felt doubtful about what they had accomplished for the Savior. They might have even thought that Jesus was annoyed with their inability to grasp His teachings. Now, however, they knew that the Messiah was pleased with them, for they had brought and would bring honor to Him.

Jesus indicated that He was not going to be with His disciples much longer, but that He was returning to His Father in heaven. For a brief period, the Eleven would be left alone in the world. Without the Son they would need protection from people and circumstances that could cause unbelief and disunity among them. They would also need protection from human and supernatural enemies who would oppose their efforts to declare the Good News to the lost. So Jesus petitioned His Father to guard His disciples by the power of His "name" (vs. 11).

Jesus' reference to God as the "Holy Father" is striking because a similar statement is not recorded anywhere else in the Gospels (though see 1 Pet. 1:15-16; Rev. 4:8; 6:10). Evidently, Jesus was focused on God's righteousness when He asked His Father to use His supreme power and authority to protect the disciples (see John 17:25). Indeed, no form of evil could stand in the presence of God's upright character, as denoted by His sacred name. Jesus, however, was not implying that God's name is a magic formula that people can use to wield supernatural power. Rather, God's name reveals His awesome splendor, which is epitomized by righteousness, truth, and love. The Father shared all these attributes with the Son (as well as the Spirit).

Just as the three Persons of the Trinity were united in thought and purpose, so too Jesus prayed that His disciples would be characterized by such unity (vs. 11). Indeed, the primary purpose of God's protection of Jesus' disciples was the preservation of their unity, which they had as regenerate members of Christ's spiritual body (see John

15:4-5; 1 Cor. 12:12-13). While Jesus was with His disciples, He preserved them as a unified group and guarded them from outside threats (see John 10:28-29). The supernatural power behind the name the Father had given the Son enabled Him to keep His disciples from denying Him (17:12). Only one of them was lost, Judas Iscariot.

Jesus continued to pray aloud in the presence of the Eleven so that they might be completely filled with His "joy" (vs. 13). In the brief time left before the Son returned to the Father, He wanted to encourage the Eleven with His final words, which would always be a source of delight for them. It was important for Jesus to give His disciples His joy because they would bear the brunt of the world's displeasure.

Since Jesus had given His followers God's Word—that is, His full revelatory message—the "world" (vs. 14) hated them (see 15:18-25). Though Jesus' disciples did not belong to the world, the Son did not ask the Father to deliver the Eleven "out of the world" (17:15). They had a mission to fulfill, and they could not accomplish it if they were removed from the earth. Nevertheless, Jesus did pray for the protection of His disciples from the one who is "evil." Jesus did not pray that the Eleven be freed from hardship and persecution, but that they would not fall under the corrupting influence of Satan's control. Once more, Jesus emphasized in His parting prayer that He and His disciples did not belong to the "world" (vs. 16). While the Eleven listened, they could not miss the implication of Jesus' statement. They had come to learn that unsaved humanity neither owned nor controlled the Savior. Likewise, the pagan world system had no legitimate claim on His followers.

Previously, in verse 11, Jesus referred to God as the "Holy Father." Now in verse 17, the Son asked the Father to "sanctify" the disciples through the "truth," which Jesus equated with divine revelation, including His own teachings. The Greek verb rendered "sanctify" means to "dedicate" or "set apart." In brief, Jesus asked His Father to use the truth of His Word to separate the disciples from evil and consecrate them for a life of service. Just as the Father had appointed the Son to perform His earthly ministry (see 3:17; 10:36), so too Jesus commissioned His disciples to proclaim His message of redemption throughout the earth. To ensure their success, Jesus consecrated Himself by dying on the cross (17:19; see 1:29, 36; 10:17-18; 11:49-52; 18:11; 19:30). Jesus did not mean He had to make Himself more pure. Instead, He was affirming His commitment to finish the Father's plan of redemption so that believers could be pardoned, justified, and made holy (see Rom. 4:25; 1 Cor. 1:2).

The scope of Jesus' farewell prayer broadened as He focused on those who would come to saving faith as a result of the Good News the Eleven proclaimed (John 17:20). Previously, Jesus had spoken about the message He had taught His disciples, but now He referred to the truth they would herald to the lost (see Matt. 28:18-20; Mark 16:15-16; Luke 24:45-47; Acts 1:8). So, Jesus' petitions in John 17:20-26 were for all future believers, including those who follow Jesus now.

Jesus' prayer for believers today is that we be unified in our faith. He prayed that our unity be like the oneness that He has with the Father and the Spirit (vs. 21). Jesus was not calling for all believers to be the same in every way, just as the three Persons of the Trinity are not identical. Instead, Jesus was praying that all believers would bond together in mutual love while preserving our distinctiveness. Furthermore, Jesus prayed that as the world sees believers dependent upon God, many would come to believe that the Father did in fact send the Son to earth to die for their sins. They would recognize that God loves them just as much as He loves His Son (see 3:16).

SUGGESTIONS TO TEACHERS

An American traveling in India noticed that the Indian in the seat beside him was studying a copy of the New Testament. "I see that you're a Christian," the visitor commented. The man from India looked up and replied, "I'm a Canadian Primitive Baptist." The denominational labels seem to have spread everywhere, and sectarian divisions are evident in India as well as in North America. Our lesson's Scripture passage compels us to mourn our divisiveness, especially as we look at Jesus' final great prayer for us.

1. EXPERIENCING GOD'S PROTECTION. Jesus prayed that His followers would be given God's protection. The disciples were frightened. All of us also have fears. Have the class mention some of the fears troubling them and their peers. Fears can cripple a person. Fears can seriously inhibit us from serving as Jesus' followers. Point out that John 17:11 includes a petition for us to be protected in order to be productive members of God's family.

2. WITHSTANDING THE EVIL ONE. Jesus' prayer was not to have God take us out of the world and safely removed from all strife and problems. Instead, the Son prayed that the Father would keep us safe from the evil one (see vs. 15). Sometimes, believers mistakenly try to escape the world's trials and terrors. Jesus assures us that He continues to pray that we might withstand the onslaughts of Satan. Best of all, we can be confident that Jesus' prayers strengthen us in that spiritual battle.

3. CHOOSING TO SERVE OTHERS. Verse 18 emphasizes Jesus' prayer that we might be aware of our mission to serve, just as the Father sent His Son into the world to serve. What are some forms of ministry your congregation is doing? What are additional ways your church could serve the people in your neighborhood?

4. REMAINING UNITED AS CHRISTIANS. Allow plenty of time for the key part of Jesus' prayer, as shown in verses 11 and 21. In the face of the divisions often seen in the Christian community, Jesus prayed that we might be one even as the Father, the Son, and the Spirit are one. Complete unity among believers shows the world that the Father actually sent the Son and that the Father loves the lost just as much as He loves the Son. Without compromising convictions or violating consciences, what are some practical steps that your congregation could take in your community to witness to the unity that all believers have in Jesus?

FOR ADULTS

■ **TOPIC:** A Friend in High Places

■ **QUESTIONS:** 1. In what ways did Jesus make the Father known to the disciples? 2. Why did Jesus pray that the Father would protect the disciples? 3. What role does God's Word have in sanctifying believers? 4. Why is it important to emphasize that God's Word is truth? 5. Why did Jesus stress the importance of believers being unified?

■ **ILLUSTRATIONS:**

Jesus' Personal Concern. A certain efficiency expert finally met the woman of his dreams. Because the specialist was a busy person, he decided to use his management and administrative skills to help him in his courtship.

The professional quickly sat down at his computer and prepared a note saying, "I love you." Then he had 365 copies made, each addressed to his newfound love. He then instructed his office staff to send one note each day for the coming year. At the end of the 365 days, he planned to propose to the woman. The notes went out as the expert had instructed. A year later, he called the woman and was surprised to learn that she planned to marry the postman!

Jesus never treats us in an impersonal way. As we discover in John 17 (the focus of this week's lesson), He is always at hand. Jesus has no perfunctory consideration of our needs, but constantly intercedes for us.

Experience of a Lifetime? For Karen Gale of Pacific School of Religion in Berkeley California, it was supposed to be the experience of a lifetime: Easter worship at the Church of the Holy Sepulchre. According to tradition, the latter is the site of Jesus' tomb. Gale, however, didn't count on competition among seven Christian groups who claim the right to worship at the historic site. The mood for worship was set by a procession of Franciscan monks chanting the Easter liturgy. "It was beautiful and the Spirit moved," Gale remembered, "for about 20 seconds."

The singing was suddenly drowned out by a great crashing and clanging of bells as a group of Armenian Christians entered. In response, the Franciscans began playing the organ. Immediately after that, the Greek Christians led a Palm Sunday procession, surrounded by an honor guard whose members pounded miters on the floor in rhythm to their steps. "This was Easter, our most holy day, and we could not worship amidst this competition for holy space," Gale said, appalled.

Jesus' prayer, which is recorded in John 17, was that all His followers might be one in Him, even as He and the Father (along with the Spirit) are one. Jesus continues to pray that we live as one family, showing the loving unity He originally intended.

A United Community. Many surveys show that those who are not saved remain ambivalent about trusting in Christ. It's because they see congregations filled with stubbornly independent people who refuse to unite around a common goal. The solution to this problem starts with the pastoral leadership of a church.

Consider Matthew, a fatigued, frustrated, and burned-out minister. He had pastored a country church with less than a hundred members for six years—ever since his first week out of seminary. Wanting to do a good job in the eyes of God, as well as in the eyes of the congregation, he had initially set himself to his task at full speed.

Within six months, the pastor was preaching three times a week, leading an adult Bible study and three small groups, counseling five or six people a week, visiting the hospitalized and sick, and calling on prospective members. He also performed a host of administrative duties—such as printing the weekly bulletin, mailing out correspondence, meeting with the church's various committees, and leading a much-needed building campaign. One day, Pastor Matthew decided to bare his soul to an older, neighboring minister. After listening intently and patiently to Pastor Matthew's troubles, his friend asked him, "What have you done to encourage your church members to get involved?"

As Pastor Matthew pondered his answer, he realized that he had assumed numerous tasks that had once been carried out by his members. It was as if every time a role came open in the church, he took it on without asking other gifted members to shoulder the task themselves. Rather than fulfill his pastoral role of equipping the saints, he had assumed too many duties himself. God never intended the church to be a "one-man show." He provides numerous spiritual gifts throughout every congregation so that individual members of the church serve together as a united community of believers (see John 17:11, 21).

For Youth

■ **Topic:** Together as One

■ **Questions:** 1. How did Jesus' disciples know with certainty that the Father had sent the Son? 2. Why did Jesus want His disciples to have the full measure of His joy within them? 3. What do you think it means to be sanctified by the truth of God's Word? 4. Why was the ongoing unity of believers so important? 5. How can we and other believers remain united in purpose, yet diverse in our expression and practices?

■ **Illustrations:**

Talking and Listening. In the film *Oh God!*, George Burns starred as "God," who supposedly came in human form and appeared to a young man played by John Denver. As the appearances and miracles increased, the man's commitment deepened, causing him to be ostracized by his friends.

"God" finally decreed that He would not put in any more appearances. This decision prompted the young man to lament that he would never be able to talk with "God" anymore. In turn, "God" pointedly responded, "You talk, I'll listen."

John 17 records Jesus' farewell prayer. He asked that His all-powerful and glorious Father in heaven would listen to His children. And unlike the character played by George Burns, God not only listens, but also protects His children. Moreover, He enables them to be united and with one voice bring His message of truth and love to a lost and dying world.

All for One. Michael Jordan is often considered the best basketball player ever. Yet when he first joined the NBA's Chicago Bulls out of the University of North Carolina, the Bulls failed to have a winning season for years.

Jordan told the management that to win championships, the Bulls would have to build a strong and solid team. He could not win championships on his own. Only when the management listened to Jordan's advice and brought in other multitalented players like Scottie Pippen and Horace Grant did the Bulls begin winning back-to-back championships.

Jesus, too, is interested in building a strong and solid team called the church. To do so, He grants a perfect mix of talents, skills, and gifts. Yes, some players on His team might have more talents than others. Yet, as John 17:11 and 21 reveal, it's when the players work together—as a team—that championships are won.

One in the Lord. To launch their summer youth program, a Baptist church decided to host an outdoor event in the parking lot of the local shopping center, with live Christian music, evangelistic movies on a large screen, and drama. The Baptist youth pastor knew they would not be able to do this alone, so he invited other churches in town to join them. Only one congregation agreed to participate: the First Assembly of God.

The Baptist youth pastor chuckled to himself. The two churches seemed perfect opposites. For instance, the Assembly of God congregation stressed a living, charismatic relationship with the Holy Spirit. Meanwhile, the Baptist church emphasized focused preaching from the Word. At the latter congregation, drums and guitars were allowed only at one youth service each month. But at the Assembly of God church, the pastor himself was the Sunday morning drummer.

The night of the event, the Baptist youth pastor was impressed with the way the adolescents from the two congregations interacted. They seemed to form a single entity determined to reach out as one to the community. The minister wondered, *Why didn't we get together sooner?* and, *When can we do this again?*

Although denominations and other Christian groups exist in many varieties for good reasons, the preceding experience helped remind two churches that they truly were united in the Savior. And while their distinctions remained, they tasted the reality of Jesus' prayer in John 17:11 that God's people might be one, even as the Father, the Son, and the Holy Spirit are one.

LESSON 7 — JANUARY 18

JESUS INTERCEDES FOR US

BACKGROUND SCRIPTURE: Hebrews 4:14—5:10
DEVOTIONAL READING: Psalm 107:1-15

Key Verse: We have not an high priest which cannot be touched with the feeling of our infirmities; but was in all points tempted like as we are, yet without sin. Hebrews 4:15.

KING JAMES VERSION

HEBREWS 4:14 Seeing then that we have a great high priest, that is passed into the heavens, Jesus the Son of God, let us hold fast our profession. 15 For we have not an high priest which cannot be touched with the feeling of our infirmities; but was in all points tempted like as we are, yet without sin. 16 Let us therefore come boldly unto the throne of grace, that we may obtain mercy, and find grace to help in time of need.

5:1 For every high priest taken from among men is ordained for men in things pertaining to God, that he may offer both gifts and sacrifices for sins: 2 Who can have compassion on the ignorant, and on them that are out of the way; for that he himself also is compassed with infirmity. 3 And by reason hereof he ought, as for the people, so also for himself, to offer for sins. 4 And no man taketh this honour unto himself, but he that is called of God, as was Aaron. 5 So also Christ glorified not himself to be made an high priest; but he that said unto him, Thou art my Son, to day have I begotten thee. 6 As he saith also in another place, Thou art a priest for ever after the order of Melchisedec. 7 Who in the days of his flesh, when he had offered up prayers and supplications with strong crying and tears unto him that was able to save him from death, and was heard in that he feared; 8 Though he were a Son, yet learned he obedience by the things which he suffered; 9 And being made perfect, he became the author of eternal salvation unto all them that obey him;

10 Called of God an high priest after the order of Melchisedec.

NEW REVISED STANDARD VERSION

HEBREWS 4:14 Since, then, we have a great high priest who has passed through the heavens, Jesus, the Son of God, let us hold fast to our confession. 15 For we do not have a high priest who is unable to sympathize with our weaknesses, but we have one who in every respect has been tested as we are, yet without sin. 16 Let us therefore approach the throne of grace with boldness, so that we may receive mercy and find grace to help in time of need.

5:1 Every high priest chosen from among mortals is put in charge of things pertaining to God on their behalf, to offer gifts and sacrifices for sins. 2 He is able to deal gently with the ignorant and wayward, since he himself is subject to weakness; 3 and because of this he must offer sacrifice for his own sins as well as for those of the people. 4 And one does not presume to take this honor, but takes it only when called by God, just as Aaron was.

5 So also Christ did not glorify himself in becoming a high priest, but was appointed by the one who said to him,
"You are my Son,
 today I have begotten you";
6 as he says also in another place,
"You are a priest forever,
 according to the order of Melchizedek."
7 In the days of his flesh, Jesus offered up prayers and supplications, with loud cries and tears, to the one who was able to save him from death, and he was heard because of his reverent submission. 8 Although he was a Son, he learned obedience through what he suffered; 9 and having been made perfect, he became the source of eternal salvation for all who obey him, 10 having been designated by God a high priest according to the order of Melchizedek.

HOME BIBLE READINGS

Monday, January 12	Titus 2:11-15	*The Grace of God Has Appeared*
Tuesday, January 13	1 John 2:1-6	*An Advocate with God*
Wednesday, January 14	Hebrews 3:1-6	*Our Faithful High Priest*
Thursday, January 15	Luke 22:39-46	*Jesus Prayed in Anguish*
Friday, January 16	Psalm 107:1-15	*Gratitude for God's Steadfast Love*
Saturday, January 17	Ephesians 3:7-13	*Confidence through Faith*
Sunday, January 18	Hebrews 4:14—5:10	*A Great High Priest*

BACKGROUND

Aside from Psalm 110:4, Genesis 14:17–20 is the most extensive passage in the Old Testament concerning Melchizedek. The writer of Hebrews summarized the biblical data by noting that Melchizedek was the monarch who ruled over the city-state of Salem (later Jerusalem). In addition, he ministered as a "priest of the most high God" (7:1). The key factor is that Melchizedek was both a king and priest. Here was an individual outside the boundaries of God's revelation to Israel and yet he worshiped the Lord.

The author recounted how Melchizedek met with Abraham (probably before 2000 B.C.) when the patriarch was returning from his victory over the kings of Elam, Goiim, Shinar, and Ellasar. During their meeting, Mechizedek blessed Abraham. The patriarch, from whom God promised to build the nation of Israel, responded by presenting Melchizedek with a tenth of the spoils he had taken in his victory over the four kings (vs. 2). In ancient times, the person who collected the tithe was considered to be greater than the one who presented it. Also, the person who blessed was thought to be greater than the one who received the blessings (vss. 4-7). The implication is that Melchizedek was higher in rank than Abraham, along with all his descendants, including Levi and the priesthood originating from him (vss. 8-10).

The recipient of Abraham's gift was both a "King of righteousness" (vs. 2) and "peace." As it stands, there is no record in Scripture of Melchizedek's parents and ancestors. It is almost as if the life and priesthood of this person had no beginning or ending. In these ways, he prefigured the "Son of God" (vs. 3). Based on the Greek phrase rendered "without father, without mother," there is the possibility of incorrectly concluding that Melchizedek was a preincarnate appearance of the Messiah. But this supposition misunderstands the actual intent of the author of Hebrews. He was making a sophisticated, nuanced comparison between Melchizedek and the Lord Jesus. For instance, like Melchizedek, there was no record of the Messiah's priesthood beginning or ending. Yet, unlike Melchizedek, it was because there really is no beginning or ending to Jesus' high priestly ministry. The implication is that the Messiah, the King-Priest according to the royal "order" (vs. 17) of Melchizedek, was superior to all Levitical priests.

NOTES ON THE PRINTED TEXT

In Hebrews, Jesus is presented as the believers' great High Priest. Perhaps 4:14 might be regarded as the thesis statement of the epistle. Indeed, there is no other strong and straightforward declaration about Jesus' priesthood in the rest of Scripture. The author had touched on Jesus as our High Priest in 2:17 and 3:1, but at this point in the letter, the topic becomes a controlling concept. By calling Jesus a "great high priest" (4:14), the writer implied Jesus' superiority to all the generations of Jewish high priests.

Though the high priests were the only ones permitted to pass beyond the final curtain of the tabernacle or temple into the most holy place, Jesus has passed through the heavenly regions and taken His lawful place at the right hand of the Father. Many think this is a reference to Jesus' ascension into heaven. The Hebrews were beginning to lack spiritual steadfastness. The writer thus urged them to unyieldingly embrace their faith in "the Son of God." As was noted in lesson 4, this significant biblical title for Jesus highlights the special and intimate relationship that exists between the first and second persons of the Trinity (see Matt. 16:16; Luke 1:35). "Son of God" indicates that Jesus is to be identified with the Father and considered fully and absolutely equal to Him (and the Spirit; see John 5:18; 10:30, 36).

A key reason we, as believers, can put our trust in Jesus is that He can sympathize with our "infirmities" (Heb. 4:15). He became one of us and experienced life just as we do. In fact, Jesus faced all the sorts of temptations we do. But unlike us, our High Priest remained "without sin" (see John 7:18; 8:46; 1 Pet. 1:19; 2:22; 1 John 3:5). Some might think that because Jesus never sinned, He cannot really empathize with our weaknesses. But only a person who has never sinned has experienced and resisted the full force of temptation. Unlike the rest of sinful humanity, Jesus never yielded to the enticements He experienced.

As one who lived through trials and tribulations on this earth, Jesus is able to understand what believers endure. The innocent one, rather than turning haughtily away from transgressors, invites such people to His Father's "throne of grace" (Heb. 4:16). They can do so with confidence, not as a result of what they have achieved, but in what the Lord Jesus has accomplished for them. His ability to understand us, His proximity to the Father, and Jesus' reconciling act on the cross embolden believers to draw near in their time of need to "obtain mercy, and find grace to help."

The writer's exhortation to persevere in the pilgrimage of faith is grounded in his argument. He maintained that the Old Testament itself testified to the imperfection of the covenant at Sinai and its sacrificial system. This, in turn, pointed ahead to a new High Priest—Jesus Christ. The Messiah is better than the mediators, sanctuary, and sacrifices of the old order. In association with Jesus, there is greater grace and glory. Also, He is the guarantee of this better covenant bond, for He links believers inseparably with the Lord of grace.

Having stressed Jesus' ability to serve as our Redeemer and Advocate, the writer of Hebrews next discussed the nature of the high-priestly office in ancient Israel. He noted that the nation's religious leaders chose a high priest from a pool of qualified men (namely, the descendants of Aaron) and appointed him to that office (5:1). This means that no person could lobby to be a priest. The eligibility for priestly service was already settled by God's choosing (vs. 4). The high priest represented his fellow Israelites in matters pertaining to God. Specifically, he offered "gifts" (vs. 1; which were voluntary) and "sacrifices" (which were required) for their sins.

The author of Hebrews noted that the priests had weaknesses of their own. For this reason, they could understand the frailty of the ones they were representing, offer kindly direction to the ignorant, and gently admonish the wayward (vs. 2). Furthermore, a priest's sinful nature required him to offer sacrifices to atone for his own misdeeds as well as for those of the people he represented (vs. 3). Verse 4 stresses that the high-priestly office was a sacred duty, and it was an honor to serve in this role. Consequently, to seize control of this office would be a sign of disrespect for God, who had graciously instituted it. The Bible records several instances in which disaster occurred when someone tried to perform high priestly duties without authorization.

The author of Hebrews noted that in addition to being descended from Aaron, the high priests were to be free of physical defects. As we noted earlier, God established the priesthood in Israel as a way of giving His people access to Him. The Lord used the institution of the priesthood to teach His people that they needed a mediator between themselves and Him. This prepared God's people for Jesus, who would reconcile them to the Lord (see Rom. 5:10-11; 1 Tim. 2:5).

The writer of Hebrews explained that Jesus did not take it upon Himself to assume the high priesthood, but rather was called to the office by God (5:5). To illustrate this point, the author of the epistle first quoted Psalm 2:7. The idea is that the Father declared Jesus to be His Son when He raised Him from the dead (see Acts 13:30; Rom. 1:4). Consequently, only the Son has a right to minister as High Priest in heaven. The writer of Hebrews then quoted from Psalm 110:4 to emphasize that the Father appointed His Son to a unique high-priestly office. Jesus' priesthood was not in the Aaronic line. He is a High Priest forever in the "order" (Heb. 5:6) of Melchizedek. This person foreshadows the Messiah.

In verse 7, the writer directed his readers' attention to the time in the Garden of Gethesemane when Jesus anguished over the prospect of having to die on the cross (see Matt. 26:36-44; Mark 14:32-40; Luke 22:39-44). With loud cries and tears, Jesus appealed to the one who could deliver Him from the clutches of death. Because Jesus honored and obeyed the Lord, God the Father answered the Son's request by raising Him from the dead (see Rom. 1:4).

The author, in Hebrews 5:8, may have been alluding to Jesus' temptation in the desert as well as to the crucifixion when he wrote about Jesus' afflictions. In the process of His suffering, Jesus "learned . . . obedience." This does not mean Jesus turned from disobedience to obedience. Instead, it means that He obeyed God in a way that He had never done before, that is, as a human being. Verse 9 says that Jesus was "made perfect." This does not mean that Jesus was ever morally imperfect. The writer was stressing that Jesus' human experience entered a new realm of fullness and completion as a result of overcoming temptations and dying on the cross.

Whereas Aaron and his successors offered many sacrifices that could never really atone for sin, Jesus offered one perfect sacrifice—Himself—to expiate transgressions forever. Also, whereas the Aaronic priests served for a limited time, Jesus' priesthood abides forever (see 7:23-28). Though the Jewish religion with its Aaronic priesthood might have looked appealing to the initial recipients of the author's epistle, the former paled in comparison to Jesus and His eternal, heavenly priesthood. Jesus' life of learned obedience and His victory over sin offset the disobedience of Adam (see Rom. 5:19). That is why Jesus could become the source of "eternal salvation" (Heb. 5:9) for all who "obey him." Stated another way, Jesus lives forever to intercede as the believer's "high priest" (vs. 10).

SUGGESTIONS TO TEACHERS

In his commentary on Hebrews, entitled *Christ above All*, Raymond Brown uses four adjectives to describe the portrayal of Jesus' high priesthood. You can profitably use this material to take your students through this week's lesson text.

1. JESUS' PRIESTHOOD WAS VICTORIOUS. All other high priests offered their sacrifices in the Jerusalem temple. They then returned home, only to go back to the sanctuary on other days to offer still more sacrifices. In contrast, Jesus offered one eternally perfect sacrifice. After His resurrection, He "passed into the heavens" (4:14), returning to His eternal home. The other priests' sacrifices may have had some effect, but any benefit was temporary. In offering His sacrifice, Jesus defeated Satan, sin, and death once and for all.

2. JESUS' PRIESTHOOD WAS COMPASSIONATE. Perhaps God could have designed a world where a mere snap of His fingers offered forgiveness and salvation to people. Also, He who had created the world through His Word possibly could have redeemed it merely by speaking. But God willingly chose the costlier method that more fully revealed Himself, particularly His love for humanity. Verse 15 especially portrays how the God-man, Jesus Christ, made Himself vulnerable to demonstrate His compassion for the lost.

3. JESUS' PRIESTHOOD WAS SUBMISSIVE. Verses 7-8 describe how Jesus willingly accepted and fulfilled the Father's plan of redemption. The Son humbled Himself by taking on the role of a unpretentious servant who learned obedience through the things He suffered. As a human being, He petitioned His Father for some relief from the trauma He faced. But when there was no other way to offer salvation, Jesus fully submitted to the Father's will.

4. JESUS' PRIESTHOOD WAS EFFECTIVE. Jesus achieved the goal of redemption. By offering Himself as a sacrifice in the manner the Father wished, Jesus became the "author of eternal salvation unto all them that obey him" (5:9). His submissive expression of love and obedience enabled a host of lost people down through the centuries to find new life in Him. We are wise to devote every aspect of our lives in adoration and service to Him.

For Adults

■ **Topic:** Someone's on My Side

■ **Questions:** 1. How does Jesus demonstrate that He is our great High Priest? 2. How is it possible for Jesus to identify with our struggles when He never succumbed to temptation? 3. Why did God establish the priesthood in Israel? 4. How did God's mercy and grace help you in your relationships this past week? 5. What is the best way to respond when you recognize your need for God's mercy and grace?

■ **Illustrations:**

Approach in Boldness. To approach God boldly is not to approach Him flippantly. Some people are so casual with God that they take His name in vain. In contrast, some people are so unfamiliar with God that they find it hard to pray to Him.

Christians enjoy confidence before the Father because they know the Son has opened the door to fellowship with Him (see Heb. 4:16). God is holy, yet He gave His Son to save us from judgment and death. The only way we can approach the Father without fear is through His Son. In fact, no one comes to the Father except through His Son (see John 14:6).

We can pray and worship with boldness because Jesus sits at the Father's right hand. Jesus intercedes for us as our merciful and faithful High Priest. Because He is our heavenly representative, we are freed to worship God with joy.

Our Need for God's Mercy and Grace. In life, everyone needs mercy and grace. For instance, we need God's saving grace, which rescues us from sin and reconciles us to Him. We also continually need God's lovingkindness to keep our attitudes, actions, and relationships on track.

Consider Bill and Nancy. They have two children, a fourth and a seventh grader, and Nancy's mother lives with them. Bill works long hours, and Nancy is busy with major home-improvement projects. The situation can at times be filled with tension, with everyone's schedules, needs, and desires heading in different directions.

Bill and Nancy recognize at least two ways they need God's mercy and grace in their lives. First, when tensions build, they know they need to ask God to give them the ability to respond to each other in a loving and constructive way.

Second, Bill and Nancy find they need God's grace after one of them has done or said something inappropriate. During these times, the person who committed the offense needs God's help to admit personal failure to the family members he or she has wronged. And the ones who have been offended need God's help to extend forgiveness.

Our Need for an Intermediary. When I was younger, professional athletes negotiated their own contracts with team owners. Today that practice is quite rare. Most of the players feel they will end up with a better deal if an agent represents them.

Andruw Rudolf Jones, after enjoying his first few years with the Atlanta Braves, wanted to stay with this team. He was even willing to sacrifice larger salaries he might have received from other teams to stay where he was. Because he knew the Braves would offer what he considered a fair amount of money, he did not employ an agent to work with him in his contract renewal.

Only after signing a new contract did Jones realize that the new agreement omitted one crucial factor. It did not include a no-trade clause. Jones had sacrificed money out of loyalty to his team, but his team had made no similar agreement of strong loyalty to him. In this case, Jones would have been much better off had he worked through an intermediary.

Hebrews 4:14-16 reveals that Jesus cares about the people He represents. He understands the struggles we face. As our great High Priest, the Son appeals to the Father on our behalf when we sin. Jesus also offers guidance on how we can live uprightly.

FOR YOUTH

■ **TOPIC:** Jesus Cares about Me

■ **QUESTIONS:** 1. How could Jesus, who is God, be truly tempted? 2. What makes Jesus' priesthood superior to that of Aaron? 3. Why did the writer of Hebrews emphasize the superiority of Jesus' priesthood? 4. How can the truth that Jesus is your great High Priest give you comfort in times of need? 5. What might you say to other believers to encourage them to find strength in Jesus when faced with difficult problems?

■ **ILLUSTRATIONS:**

Who Cares for Me? Brian's case was fairly typical. His parents divorced, and he lived with his father, who had a hard time building a good relationship with him. Brian got into trouble at school. He developed emotional problems and was hospitalized. To put it simply, Brian could not fill the vacuum in his life caused by a broken family.

Many adolescents rightly ask, "Who cares for me?" They lack strong family ties. They don't have any good friends. They wander fruitlessly from one activity to another and often get into deep trouble.

Without sounding sanctimonious, we should try to introduce teens like Brian to

Jesus. In order to do so, we must enjoy a vibrant faith ourselves. We must be able to explain how Jesus makes a difference as our "great high priest" (Heb. 4:14), even when no one else seems to care.

Our Greatest Source of Strength. Perhaps you have seen or read Charles Dickens's *Oliver Twist*. Early in the story, Oliver's single mother had died. He ended up as an inmate of a barely livable Victorian orphanage. The children there received little love. Each child was allotted adequate food to survive, but never enough to fill his or her stomach.

After one meal of nothing more than oatmeal porridge, Oliver did what no child in memory had done before him. He bravely approached the master of the dining hall. As Oliver did so, he held his empty bowl before him, and asked, "Please, sir, I want some more." The rest of the boys watched in utter amazement. Oliver's master reacted with rage, blatantly rejecting Oliver's wish.

In contrast, the writer to the Hebrews encouraged us to approach our heavenly Father boldly, knowing that He loves us and will give us what is best (see Heb. 4:16). There's nothing wrong with turning to the pastor or our friends when we have problems. But we need to understand that Jesus is our greatest source of strength.

True, we cannot see Jesus. Yet like the anchor on the ocean floor, Jesus is still doing His high priestly work on our behalf. He alone provides us the stability we need to face the issues of life.

Someone Who Can Relate to Us. Gallaudet University in Washington, D.C., has had a distinguished history of serving students with hearing impairments. In the late 1980s, the university was in turmoil because the president had no hearing difficulties. The student body grew increasingly unhappy with her lack of empathy and understanding, and the unrest threatened to bring campus programs to a standstill. Finally, the trustees asked the president to resign.

I. King Jordan was appointed to the presidency (1988–2006), and he immediately took steps to bring healing after the controversy over his predecessor's leadership. Jordan met with the president of the student body and the chairman of the university's board of trustees to discuss the future of Gallaudet. As they walked out of the meeting, the head of the student association turned to Jordan, and then, with great emotion, stated, "There was no interpreter!"

The reason is that Jordan was also deaf. The young president of the student body realized that their new leader was a person like themselves who had experienced all their struggles with hearing impairment. Similarly, Jesus can relate to us. In Him we have a great High Priest who has shared the trials and tribulations of our humanity, yet without sinning (see Heb. 4:15).

LESSON 8 — JANUARY 25

PRAY FOR ONE ANOTHER

BACKGROUND SCRIPTURE: James 5
DEVOTIONAL READING: Lamentations 3:52-58

Key Verse: Confess your faults one to another, and pray one for another, that ye may be healed. The effectual fervent prayer of a righteous man availeth much. James 5:16.

KING JAMES VERSION

JAMES 5:13 Is any among you afflicted? let him pray. Is any merry? let him sing psalms. 14 Is any sick among you? let him call for the elders of the church; and let them pray over him, anointing him with oil in the name of the Lord: 15 And the prayer of faith shall save the sick, and the Lord shall raise him up; and if he have committed sins, they shall be forgiven him.
16 Confess your faults one to another, and pray one for another, that ye may be healed. The effectual fervent prayer of a righteous man availeth much. 17 Elias was a man subject to like passions as we are, and he prayed earnestly that it might not rain: and it rained not on the earth by the space of three years and six months. 18 And he prayed again, and the heaven gave rain, and the earth brought forth her fruit. 19 Brethren, if any of you do err from the truth, and one convert him; 20 Let him know, that he which converteth the sinner from the error of his way shall save a soul from death, and shall hide a multitude of sins.

NEW REVISED STANDARD VERSION

JAMES 5: 13 Are any among you suffering? They should pray. Are any cheerful? They should sing songs of praise. 14 Are any among you sick? They should call for the elders of the church and have them pray over them, anointing them with oil in the name of the Lord. 15 The prayer of faith will save the sick, and the Lord will raise them up; and anyone who has committed sins will be forgiven. 16 Therefore confess your sins to one another, and pray for one another, so that you may be healed. The prayer of the righteous is powerful and effective. 17 Elijah was a human being like us, and he prayed fervently that it might not rain, and for three years and six months it did not rain on the earth. 18 Then he prayed again, and the heaven gave rain and the earth yielded its harvest.
19 My brothers and sisters, if anyone among you wanders from the truth and is brought back by another, 20 you should know that whoever brings back a sinner from wandering will save the sinner's soul from death and will cover a multitude of sins.

Home Bible Readings

Monday, January 19	Zechariah 8:18-23	*Let Us Seek God's Favor Together*
Tuesday, January 20	Jeremiah 42:1-6	*Pray to the Lord for Us*
Wednesday, January 21	2 Thessalonians 1:5-12	*We Pray to God for You*
Thursday, January 22	Lamentations 3:52-58	*You Heard My Plea*
Friday, January 23	1 Samuel 12:19-25	*Never Ceasing to Pray for You*
Saturday, January 24	James 5:1-12	*Suffering and Patience*
Sunday, January 25	James 5:13-18	*The Prayer of Faith*

Background

James 5 opens with a volley of accusations aimed at wealthy people who were morally bankrupt. Though successful in their economic pursuits, they were indicted for their disregard for God's righteous principles. In the end, rather than enjoying their riches, the affluent would be condemned by their wealth. In the same way James addressed the boasting merchants in 4:13-16, the author called on the self-indulgent rich to listen attentively (5:1).

While the prosperous were usually envied for their abundant assets, James had only contempt for their status and condemnation for their failure to be good stewards of what God had entrusted to them. James declared that they would be judged for their ill-gotten gain. The author's comments resemble the Old Testament prophets' condemnation of the immorally rich (see Isa. 23; Ezek. 27). Unlike eternal treasures, which can be stored in heaven, earthly wealth is transient (see 1 Tim. 6:17). For instance, hoarded possessions rot and fancy clothes make fine meals for moths (Jas. 5:2; see Matt. 6:19-21). Gold and silver are regarded throughout the world as standards of real, tangible wealth. Technically speaking, these metals cannot rust or even corrode. Perhaps James 5:3 uses the image of corroding gold and silver as a metaphor to emphasize the eternal worthlessness of temporal opulence.

In their quest for riches, the wealthy often took the poor to court on trumped-up charges in order to rob them of what little they had (see 2:6). With no influence or connections, the poor were unable to resist. James charged the rich oppressors with living in ease at the expense of others. By doing this in excess, the wicked were unknowingly preparing themselves like fattened animals for the slaughter (5:5). The author's initial Jewish readers would have known very well the fate of fattened animals—the altar of sacrifice. This was a fitting end for people who brought unjust condemnation and sometimes death on those too powerless to defend themselves (vs. 6).

Notes on the Printed Text

James concluded his letter with an emphasis on prayer. Prayer is the most potent action a believer can take in time of trouble. Prayer ought to be a Christian's reflexive response to all of life's problems—accompanied with praise to God for His bountiful gifts. The English word *prayer* comes from the Latin word *precarious*, which means to be in a vulnerable position. In prayer, we are acknowledging our vulnerability and deepest needs before an all-powerful and holy God. The author employed a series of questions as springboards for conveying some important principles of prayer to his readers. The Greek verb rendered "afflicted" (5:13) in the first question refers to physical pain, hardship, or distress that comes from any source. The author used the same word in verse 10 when describing the trials of the prophets. The matter of offering songs of praise (a type of prayer) in response to happiness is easy to understand. The difficulty, however, comes in times of sickness.

If a Christian is ill, God should be the first healer to whom he or she turns. It is also a faith action to turn to other members of the church body. The elders should be available for counsel and comfort and willing to help the afflicted in any way possible (vs. 14). Elders were leaders in the early church. They are first mentioned in Acts 11:30 as the recognized leaders of local congregations (see 1 Tim. 3:1-7; 5:17; Titus 1:6-9). Once called, the elders were to pray over the sick and anoint them with oil in the Lord's name. The oil symbolized the presence of God (see Ps. 23:5). But in Bible times, it was also thought to contain some medicinal properties (see Luke 10:34).

Since olive trees, which grew even in rocky places, produced much oil, olive oil came to be regarded as a special gift from God. This oil was also associated with the outpouring of God's Spirit. Anointing with oil customarily accompanied the consecration of individuals to God's service. It was used to dedicate prophets (1 Kings 19:16), priests (Lev. 8:12), and kings (1 Sam. 16:13; 1 Kings 1:34). The use of oil for healing is seen in Jesus' parable of the good Samaritan. As we will learn in lesson 10, the Samaritan first bound the wounds of the man who had been mugged and then poured in oil and wine (Luke 10:34). Apparently, it was for the same purpose that the 12 disciples took oil for healing when Jesus sent them out two by two on a ministry mission (see Mark 6:13).

James 5:15 says that if the elders had faith when they prayed for the sick, they would get well. In fact, the Lord would restore the afflicted to health. "Faith" primarily refers to a person's belief or trust in God. The term is also used in the New Testament to refer to the body of truths held by followers of Christ. This second use became increasingly prevalent as church leaders and scholars defended the truths of the faith against the attacks of false teachers. Faith can be understood as having four recognizable elements. First is cognition, an awareness of the facts; second is comprehension, an understanding of the facts; third is conviction, an acceptance of the facts; and fourth is commitment, trust in a reliable object. As James made clear in his epistle, genuine faith is evidenced by more than mere words. It leads to a transformed life in which the believer reaches out with the Savior's love to others in need.

Some have understood 5:15 to teach that complete physical health is always assured through prayer. Whenever illness strikes, the Christian should pray in faith as a guarantee for healing. If illness persists (in this view), then the prayer must not have been offered in genuine faith. Others see the verse as teaching cooperation between prayer and medicine (the anointing with oil), between God and a physician. According to this view, just prayer or just medicine alone is less than a full prescription for renewed health. Together they are a powerful remedy for serious illness.

An important question concerns what is meant by the Greek verb rendered "sick." In verse 14, the term denotes a state of incapacity or weakness, and is used in the New Testament for physical illness as well as for weakness of faith or conscience (see Acts 20:35; Rom. 6:19; 14:1; 1 Cor. 8:9-12). So, James could have meant either sicknesses of the body or the spirit. This reminds us that there are times when physical illness might have a spiritual cause, namely, sin. The remark in James 5:15 about forgiveness of sin might be a reference to an illness brought on by personal sin in the believer's life. In this case, the writer assured the sick that the prayer of faith would result in forgiveness and spiritual restoration. Of course, the use of the word "if" implies that sometimes illness is not the result of personal sin. Irrespective of the details, God is not limited as to the methods He might employ in restoring health to ill believers. Also, with regard to prayer, God answers only according to His will. Sometimes God's will does not include physical healing (see 2 Cor. 12:7-9).

All of us need some kind of healing, whether physical, spiritual, or emotional, and we should be able to turn to other believers for help. This includes confessing our sins to each other, as well as praying for each other (Jas. 5:16). The acknowledgment of sins among believers helps to promote wellness and wholeness of individuals and relationships. In particular, believers draw their fellow Christians toward a deeper, more mature walk with the Savior. Members of the community of faith also deepen their commitment to one another in the bonds of Christian love. This verse does not signify a call for indiscriminate airing of a believer's every shortcoming. The Holy Spirit should always be given complete charge over the matter of conviction and confession of sin. He will lead the believer in the knowledge of which sins to confess in private prayer and which to confess in the company of other believers.

In any case, whether public or private, one truth is clear, namely, that prayer is an effective means of accomplishing the will of God. The Lord especially uses the earnest prayer of righteous believers (those who are characterized by virtue and integrity) to produce wonderful results in the lives of believers. As was his practice, James offered an illustration to support his point. This time it was Elijah, an Old Testament prophet with the same human frailties that we have. This person, who was just like us, prayed earnestly that no rain would fall, and none fell for three and a half years (vs. 17; see Luke 4:25). Then, when he prayed again, rain fell from the skies and made the crops grow (Jas. 5:18; see 1 Kings 17:1; 18:41-46). Because prayer is our most powerful tool, it should be our first option in responding to a crisis, not a last resort. It only makes sense to rely on God's power, which is infinitely greater than our own.

The author's final appeal to his readers concerned individuals who had wandered from the way of truth. Some think James 5:19 refers to those who claimed to be Christians but whose faith was spurious (see Heb. 6:4-6; 2 Pet. 2:20-22). Others think James 5:19 is dealing with genuine believers who have strayed into sinful patterns. In either case, when anyone belonging to a congregation wanders from the path of moral rectitude, it is the duty of God's people to seek out the wayward and bring them back into the fellowship—through prayer, counseling, friendship, or whatever it takes. When sinners are turned back from their error-prone ways, it means they have been rescued from the path of destruction.

For some, the "death" (vs. 20) being averted is interpreted as eternal separation from God (see Rev. 21:8). For others, James 5:20 denotes avoiding the experience of premature physical death (see 1 Cor. 11:29-32; 1 John 5:16). When the wayward are spiritually restored, it signifies the forgiveness of many sins (Jas. 5:20). Often, the process includes godly sorrow that leads to repentance and salvation (see 2 Cor. 7:10). Most likely, there will also be the confession of sin, which brings about divine pardon and cleansing from all unrighteousness (see 1 John 1:9). James provided his readers with the valuable instruction necessary for progress on the road to spiritual restoration and growth. Whether the issue was taming the tongue or persevering in persecution, all that a believer needed to grow in holiness was found in the One who answered the prayers of the faithful.

SUGGESTIONS TO TEACHERS

We sometimes forget the truth revealed in James 5:16-18, namely, that God hears and understands our prayers. Jesus' earliest disciples offered prayers that God answered—some right away, and others further down the road. They learned that prayers based on God's Word and will are petitions that particularly please the Lord.

1. GOD KNOWS US. We may wonder how God is able to understand our prayers when we feel so confused. But when we read the teachings of Scripture, we will discover that God knows our prayers better than we do ourselves. Even when we're not sure what the right prayers should be or the best method of prayer to use, God actively searches our hearts (see Rom. 8:27), and He is able to see the motive of our prayers and respond in kind.

2. GOD IS HERE TO HELP. We know that the Bible says Jesus Christ is the "same yesterday, and to day, and for ever" (Heb. 13:8). But do we really believe that? The same God who was available thousands of years ago to help the readers of the Letter of James (see 5:13-15) is the one that will help us today.

3. GOD WILL RESPOND TO OUR REQUESTS. From the Letter of James we learn that the most important attribute we can cultivate is a view of an awesome God who works on behalf of anyone who is willing to trust and obey Him. It seems like the prayers God delights most in answering are the ones that begin with an acknowledgement of who He is, are filled with humble cries for help, and end with an affirmation of trust that God will always do what is right. Ultimately, the issue is not whether God will hear and respond to our requests, but whether we are willing to trust Him to do so and pray accordingly.

For Adults

■ **Topic:** Powerful and Effective Living

■ **Questions:** 1. Why is prayer appropriate in times of trouble? 2. Why are ill believers encouraged to summon the elders of the church? 3. What is the purpose of anointing an ailing believer with oil in the name of the Lord? 4. In what way is Elijah an example of someone who prayed humbly and earnestly? 5. How can concerned believers restore the wayward to the truth?

■ **Illustrations:**

In Need of God's Grace through Prayer. During Haddon Robinson's tenure as president of Denver Seminary, lawsuits were brought against the school. Because he was named in one of the suits, Robinson had to give a deposition. For two days, prosecutors relentlessly grilled him as they questioned his motives and tried to cast everything he said in a negative light.

Robinson not only faced legal problems, but he also had to deal with attacks against his reputation. For example, a disgruntled former employee of the seminary spread false statements about Robinson throughout the community. Robinson and his wife responded to the devastating emotional pain they experienced by bathing their circumstance in prayer (something enjoined in James 5:13).

Looking back on this trying ordeal, Robinson wrote, "If anything good for me came out of this painful time, it was the overwhelming sense of my need of God. I felt completely vulnerable. Although I was not guilty of any legal negligence or failure, I felt more in need of grace than ever."

Just in Time. A Christian woman, Joan (not her real name), married an unbelieving husband, Brian. He was a salesman who often traveled during the week, so Joan had lots of time to pray for her husband's salvation. Joan had great joy in her heart knowing that God was hearing her pleas as she lifted Brian in continuous prayer (see Jas. 5:16). But Joan was devastated the day she received news that Brian had been instantly killed in a highway accident. Joan's faith was deeply shaken, that is, until nearly five years later, when she received a surprise visit from a young man who came looking for Brian.

As it turned out, this young man, Josh, was the last person to see Joan's husband alive. Brian had picked him up as Josh was hitchhiking on a country highway. When Brian dropped off Josh, Brian gave him his address and said if he was ever in Indianapolis to look him up. Josh was shocked to hear Joan report that Brian had been killed only five miles beyond the place that Josh had last seen Brian. But that tragic news felt less dreadful when Josh informed Joan that 10 minutes before the fatal crash, he had prayed with Brian, and that Brian had repented of his sins and asked God to give him a personal relationship through faith in Jesus Christ (see vss. 19-20).

Down, But Not Out. When Rick and Sandy married 25 years ago, Rick was energetic and healthy. But for the last four years, he has struggled with chronic fatigue syndrome. Extreme tiredness, forgetfulness, difficulty concentrating, and irritability are symptoms to which Rick and his family have had to adjust.

Rick's role as the pastor of a busy church seemed to compound the problem. For health reasons, he considered leaving the pastorate. *Should I give up ministry altogether?* he wondered. *Can God use someone so spent? Perhaps a different kind of job—or even disability—is what God wants.* Then the Lord seemed to confirm He could still use Rick in ministry. His denominational superintendent met with him to say, "Rick, we value your gifts and abilities. We will find another church for you to serve."

As Rick and Sandy started out on this new road, Sandy wrote, "We can either rail against circumstances, questioning God's wisdom, or we can pour ourselves into Bible study and prayer and faithfully allow the all-powerful Lord to work in us." This mindset reflects the truth recorded in James 5:16, "The effectual fervent prayer of a righteous man availeth much."

For Youth

■ **Topic:** Help, I'm in Trouble!

■ **Questions:** 1. Why is prayer appropriate in times of joy? 2. What are the elders of a church instructed to do for ailing believers? 3. Why and when should believers confess their sins to each other? 4. How did Elijah demonstrate his earnestness in prayer? 5. What incentive is there for believers to restore the wayward to the truth?

■ **Illustrations:**

Knee Theology Works! Oswald Chambers (1874–1917) was a Scottish minister whose teachings on the life of faith have endured to this day. He observed that prayer is hard work. "There is nothing thrilling about a laboring man's work but it is the laboring man who makes the conceptions of the genius possible; and it is the laboring saint who makes the conceptions of the Master possible. You labor at prayer and results happen all the time from His standpoint. What an astonishment it will be to find, when the veil is lifted, the souls that have been reaped by you, simply because you had been in the habit of taking your orders from Jesus Christ."

As God did with Chambers, He also upholds us during joyful and sad times in our life (see Jas. 5:13). As we invest energy and effort on our knees in prayer, the Lord gives us the strength to remain faithful to the work He has called us to do (see vs. 16).

Under the Gallows. Back in 1738, London's main detention center was Newgate prison. Charles Wesley (later a great Christian hymn writer) frequently went there, preaching to the prisoners who were sentenced to death. On one occasion, Charles was locked in overnight in order to comfort and pray with the prisoners. He drew his inspiration for doing so from James 5:19-20.

In his *Journal*, Wesley wrote about a poor man who was condemned to die. Wesley told him about "one who came down from heaven to save the lost and him in particular." Wesley led this man to faith in Christ. After Wesley served this man communion, he accompanied the man to the gallows. The assurance of salvation was etched on the new convert's face. Because of his new friend's faith, Wesley penned, "That hour under the gallows was the most blessed hour of my life."

Devoted to Prayer. How much difference in the world could a humble dishwasher make—especially one who worked far from the bustle of daily life? Brother Lawrence of the Resurrection (1605–1691) left a mark on the lives of Christians everywhere—a contribution for eternity.

This humble Carmelite monk and mystic worked in a monastery among other men of his order. His daily tasks included the routine work of kitchen help. During these countless hours laboring over the kitchen sinks—hours alone with God—Brother Lawrence began to develop his habit of communing with God in prayer.

In his later years, Brother Lawrence penned out the pathways to the discipline that had made his hours of menial labor seem so sweet. In a book entitled, *The Practice of the Presence of God*, Lawrence tells how to keep God uppermost in the conscious and subconscious of our intellect and imagination.

This small treatise on how to incorporate prayer into every function of life has made a deep impact on the lives of many Christians. The meditations of Brother Lawrence can be a continual encouragement for you to always be mindful of an ever-present God in your daily routines, regardless of whether the circumstances you face are filled with joy or sorrow (see Jas. 5:13).

LESSON 9 — FEBRUARY 1

Fasting while Serving

Background Scripture: Daniel 1:5, 8-17; Matthew 6:16-18; 9:9-17
Devotional Reading: 2 Chronicles 7:11-18

Key Verse: When thou fastest, anoint thine head, and wash thy face; that thou appear not unto men to fast, but unto thy Father which is in secret: and thy Father, which seeth in secret, shall reward thee openly. Matthew 6:17-18.

KING JAMES VERSION
DANIEL 1:5 And the king appointed them a daily provision of the king's meat, and of the wine which he drank: so nourishing them three years, that at the end thereof they might stand before the king. . . .

8 But Daniel purposed in his heart that he would not defile himself with the portion of the king's meat, nor with the wine which he drank: therefore he requested of the prince of the eunuchs that he might not defile himself. 9 Now God had brought Daniel into favour and tender love with the prince of the eunuchs. 10 And the prince of the eunuchs said unto Daniel, I fear my lord the king, who hath appointed your meat and your drink: for why should he see your faces worse liking than the children which are of your sort? then shall ye make me endanger my head to the king. 11 Then said Daniel to Melzar, whom the prince of the eunuchs had set over Daniel, Hananiah, Mishael, and Azariah, 12 Prove thy servants, I beseech thee, ten days; and let them give us pulse to eat, and water to drink. 13 Then let our countenances be looked upon before thee, and the countenance of the children that eat of the portion of the king's meat: and as thou seest, deal with thy servants. 14 So he consented to them in this matter, and proved them ten days. 15 And at the end of ten days their countenances appeared fairer and fatter in flesh than all the children which did eat the portion of the king's meat. 16 Thus Melzar took away the portion of their meat, and the wine that they should drink; and gave them pulse.

17 As for these four children, God gave them knowledge and skill in all learning and wisdom: and Daniel had understanding in all visions and dreams. . . .

MATTHEW 6:16 Moreover when ye fast, be not, as the hypocrites, of a sad countenance: for they disfigure their faces, that they may appear unto men to fast. Verily I say unto you, They have their reward. 17 But thou, when thou fastest, anoint thine head, and wash thy face; 18 That thou appear not unto men to fast, but unto thy Father which is in secret: and thy Father, which seeth in secret, shall reward thee openly.

NEW REVISED STANDARD VERSION
DANIEL 1:5 The king assigned them a daily portion of the royal rations of food and wine. They were to be educated for three years, so that at the end of that time they could be stationed in the king's court. . . .

8 But Daniel resolved that he would not defile himself with the royal rations of food and wine; so he asked the palace master to allow him not to defile himself. 9 Now God allowed Daniel to receive favor and compassion from the palace master. 10 The palace master said to Daniel, "I am afraid of my lord the king; he has appointed your food and your drink. If he should see you in poorer condition than the other young men of your own age, you would endanger my head with the king." 11 Then Daniel asked the guard whom the palace master had appointed over Daniel, Hananiah, Mishael, and Azariah: 12 "Please test your servants for ten days. Let us be given vegetables to eat and water to drink. 13 You can then compare our appearance with the appearance of the young men who eat the royal rations, and deal with your servants according to what you observe." 14 So he agreed to this proposal and tested them for ten days. 15 At the end of ten days it was observed that they appeared better and fatter than all the young men who had been eating the royal rations. 16 So the guard continued to withdraw their royal rations and the wine they were to drink, and gave them vegetables. 17 To these four young men God gave knowledge and skill in every aspect of literature and wisdom; Daniel also had insight into all visions and dreams. . . .

MATTHEW 6:16 "And whenever you fast, do not look dismal, like the hypocrites, for they disfigure their faces so as to show others that they are fasting. Truly I tell you, they have received their reward. 17 But when you fast, put oil on your head and wash your face, 18 so that your fasting may be seen not by others but by your Father who is in secret; and your Father who sees in secret will reward you."

Home Bible Readings

Monday, January 26	Psalm 69:5-18	*Draw Near to Me, O Lord*
Tuesday, January 27	Psalm 109:21-27	*Help Me, O Lord My God*
Wednesday, January 28	Luke 18:9-14	*Humility before God*
Thursday, January 29	2 Chronicles 7:11-18	*If My People Humble Themselves*
Friday, January 30	2 Chronicles 34:24-33	*Humble Yourselves Before God*
Saturday, January 31	Matthew 9:9-17	*An Appropriate Time for Fasting*
Sunday, February 1	Daniel 1:5,8-17; Matthew 6:16-18	*To Honor God*

Background

When Judah fell and Josiah was killed in a battle with Egypt in 609 B.C., Josiah's eldest son, Jehoiakim, was made king of Judah by Pharaoh Neco. For four years, Judah was an Egyptian vassal nation until Nebuchadnezzar defeated Egypt at Carchemish in 605 B.C. That same year, the Babylonian king swept into Judah and captured Jerusalem (Dan. 1:1). He had Jehoiakim, who was in the third year of his reign, carried off to Babylon. Nebuchadnezzar also ordered treasures from the Jerusalem temple sent back home and placed in the shrine of his pagan deity (vs. 2).

Nebuchadnezzar had the best educated, most attractive, most capable and talented among Judah's citizens sent back to Babylon. In essence, only the poorer, uneducated people were left behind to populate conquered lands (see 2 Kings 24:14). Included among those deported from Judah to Babylon were Daniel, Hananiah, Mishael, and Azariah (Dan. 1:3, 6). Most likely, they would have been about 14 or 15 years of age at this time. Nebuchadnezzar commanded Ashpenaz, who was in charge of the king's court officials, to bring in some of the Israelites. The king specifically wanted to see members of Judah's royal family and others who came from the ranks of nobility (vs. 3). Nebuchadnezzar was obviously looking for the captives with the highest aptitudes and abilities. He wanted young men of such physical and mental superiority that they would be qualified for service to him (vs. 4).

Notes on the Printed Text

Ashpenaz was charged with teaching the young men the Babylonian language (Akkadian) and literature. The latter was written in cuneiform (a complex, syllabic writing system made up of wedge-shaped characters) and mainly engraved on clay tablets. The intent was to assimilate the captives into their new culture. Additionally, they were to undergo an intensive, three-year study program to prepare them for royal service. The course of study most likely included mathematics, history, astronomy, astrology, agriculture, architecture, law, and magic.

During this time, the young men would receive a daily ration of delicacies from the royal kitchen (Dan. 1:5). But because Daniel was certain the provisions would bring ritual uncleanness, he decided not to partake of them. Daniel's concern undoubtedly centered on the realization that the king's food was not prepared in compliance with the law of Moses. Even the simple fact that it was prepared by Gentiles rendered it unclean. The king's diet included pork and horseflesh, which were forbidden by the Mosaic law (see Lev. 11; Deut. 14). Furthermore, the Gentile monarch's food and wine would have been offered to Babylonian idols before they reached his table. Consuming anything offered to pagan deities was strictly forbidden in Exodus 34:15.

Daniel made up his mind not to defile himself by breaking the Mosaic law. "Purposed" (Dan. 1:8) translates a Hebrew phrase that literally means "placed on his heart" and refers to a determined, committed stand. When Daniel took this position, it was simply the natural result of a lifelong pledge to be obedient to God's will in every situation. With boldness and courage, Daniel asked Ashpenaz for permission not to eat the king's delicacies or drink his wine. Evidently, Daniel's three companions shared his resoluteness and made the same commitment as well.

According to verse 9, God caused the overseer to be sympathetic to Daniel. Despite the respect, kindness, and compassion of Ashpenaz, he was afraid of violating the edict of the king. We previously learned from verse 5 that Nebuchadnezzar had assigned the trainees a regular amount of food and wine that his servants prepared for him. Ashpenaz realized the monarch would hold him responsible if Daniel and his three Israelite peers looked malnourished in comparison to the other young men their age. The chief official also knew he would be decapitated for neglecting his duties (vs. 10).

Since Daniel got nowhere with Ashpenaz, the young Israelite captive turned his attention to the guardian or warden placed over him by the chief official (vs. 11). The petition was for the guardian to put Daniel and his friends on a 10-day trial diet. In the Old Testament, the number 10 was sometimes used as an ideal figure to denote completeness. Daniel proposed that the four be given nothing but vegetables to eat and water to drink (vs. 12). The Hebrew noun for "pulse" meant "that which grows from sown seed." Thus, grains, bread made from grain, and even fruit would also have been included. Since no plants were designated unclean by the law of Moses, there was no danger of ceremonial defilement with this diet.

At the end of 10 days, the warden could compare the appearance of the test subjects with that of the young men who were eating the royal delicacies. Based on what the guardian saw, he would decide what to do with Daniel and his friends (vs. 13). The warden agreed to Daniel's proposal (vs. 14). Perhaps the guardian was reassured by Daniel's confidence that the Jews would fare better on the vegetarian diet than those who ate the king's food. In any case, the warden probably reasoned that 10 days was not enough time for the health of the four youths to suffer any permanent damage.

At first, Ashpenaz worried that Daniel and his friends would become pale and thin compared to the other youths their age (vs. 10). But at the end of the 10 days, the four looked healthier in appearance and their bodies looked better nourished than the rest of the young men who had been eating the royal delicacies (vs. 15). So after that, the warden removed the rich foods and wines from their diet and instead gave them only vegetables to eat (vs. 16).

While Daniel and his three friends were being groomed for service in the royal court, God was preparing them for service to Him and to His people. The Lord gave the four Israelites "knowledge and skill" (vs. 17). They had a special ability to reason clearly and logically, and to approach any subject with insight and discernment. Under royal tutelage and with divine assistance, the four youths excelled in a wide range of subjects in the arts and sciences. Daniel, however, surpassed all the other students in a special field. God gave him "understanding" into all kinds of "dreams and visions."

Centuries later, before Jesus delivered the Sermon on the Mount (Matt. 5–7), He traveled throughout Galilee and proclaimed the Good News of the Kingdom. He taught in the synagogues and healed large numbers of people. During this time, His popularity grew considerably, with many people following Him from all over Palestine and its surrounding regions (see Matt. 4:23-25 and similar observations made in lesson 4). In chapter 6, Jesus targeted a variety of pious acts the religious leaders performed in a hypocritical manner. This included charitable giving (vss. 1-4), praying (vss. 5-15), and fasting (vss. 16-18). Whereas Jerusalem's elite participated in various rituals to gain attention from other people, Jesus emphasized the importance of worshiping God discreetly and serving others without fanfare.

In verse 16, the reference to fasting referred to abstaining from eating for a limited period of time. Throughout the Scripture, we can see that God's people fasted for a variety of reasons: to express grief over the death of a loved one or a leader (1 Sam. 31:13), to petition God for a matter of great urgency (2 Sam. 12:15-23), to humble oneself before God (1 Kings 21:27-29), to seek God's help (2 Chron. 20:1-4), to confess sins (Neh. 9:1-2), and to prepare oneself spiritually (Matt. 4:1-2). Fasting was difficult, requiring self-discipline and sacrifice. It gave God's people the opportunity to devote more time to spiritual pursuits. It said to God, in effect, that the matter they were bringing before Him was more important than anything else, even eating.

The Greek noun rendered "hypocrites" (6:16) originally referred to an actor on a stage. It eventually came to denote individuals who pretended to be something they were not. In the moral realm, they were religious leaders characterized by duplicity and pretense. For instance, whenever the hypocritical religious leaders of Jesus' day fasted, they would look dreary and gloomy. They deliberately disfigured their faces by heaping ashes on their heads and disheveling their hair and beards. The intent was to let everyone know they were doing something pious. Yet any admiration they received would be their only reward.

In New Testament times, people would perfume their heads with olive oil and splash their faces with water to help rejuvenate and invigorate them. Jesus instructed His followers to put oil on their heads and wash their faces when they fasted (vs. 17). They were to look refreshed and joyful, not sullen and unkempt, so that others might not realize they were fasting. In other words, they were supposed to hide their fasting. But their unseen heavenly Father would know, and He would reward whatever they did in private (vs. 18).

SUGGESTIONS TO TEACHERS

Although the king's servant commanded Daniel to eat food forbidden under the Mosaic law, he found a way to remain obedient to God. As Christians, we often find ourselves in complex situations that make it difficult for us to know how to be faithful to God (for example, the circumstance concerning fasting recorded in Matt. 6:16-18). Yet we must obey Him, especially if we wish to please Him and live virtuously.

1. THE VALUE OF DISCERNMENT. The four Israelite youths knew exactly what was wrong with eating the king's food. Most likely, they learned this from pious parents (Deut. 6:4-9). Resisting temptation is easier and more effective if our principles are established ahead of time. The very moment at which temptation presents itself is a poor time to take a crash course in ethics.

2. THE COURAGE OF CONVICTION. Daniel and his friends were not afraid to speak up when their principles were challenged. But it was more than just talk. Their refusal to eat the king's food could have cost them their lives. The same courage of conviction was revealed later in a fiery furnace and a den of lions.

3. THE POWER OF PERSEVERANCE. Daniel and his companions were determined to overcome any obstacle in order to follow God. With respect and humility, Daniel presented his request to Ashpenaz that he not be required to defile himself with the king's food. But when Ashpenaz refused, Daniel, in quiet persistence, went to the guard and proposed a test that was both reasonable and feasible.

4. THE NEED FOR DIVINE WISDOM. Some Christians seem to believe that God has called them to be either apologetic doormats or loud, obnoxious, "in your face" witnesses for Christ. Neither approach is effective. God wants us to hold to our convictions with courage, and to witness for Him with love, humility, and a healthy dose of common sense. The lives of Daniel and his friends proved that divine wisdom is the best possible guide. Daniel demonstrated what wisdom, coupled with quiet confidence and gentle persuasion, can accomplish.

FOR ADULTS

■ **TOPIC:** The Cuisine of Resistance

■ **QUESTIONS:** 1. Why did Daniel resolve not to defile himself by eating food and wine provided by Nebuchadnezzar? 2. Why would Daniel take the risk of approaching the guardian with the proposal of a vegetarian diet? 3. What was the basis for the superior intellectual abilities of Daniel and his three friends? 4. What is the connection between being humble and serving others in Jesus' name? 5. Why can we never impress God with our righteous acts, such as fasting?

■ ILLUSTRATIONS:

Lures. To aid you as you speak this illustration, you could ask an appropriate member of your class to bring in a variety of fishing lures. Holding several where the class can see them, remind the students that most lures don't look at all like food a fish would enjoy. They merely offer shiny or colorful surfaces that catch a fish's attention. Attracted by the novelty, the fish swims over to investigate. The fisherman knows there's nothing for the fish in his lures but danger and potential death. But the fish is not smart enough to figure that out.

Satan's temptations are like fishing lures. They catch our attention. But we end up getting hurt, sometimes seriously. In many situations we face, determining to follow the right course can be difficult, but like Daniel, we must be obedient to God in all things. And we have the assurance of Scripture that He will not allow us to be tempted beyond what we can withstand. In fact, when we are enticed to sin, the Lord will show us a way out so that we can endure (see 1 Cor. 10:13).

Go Along to Get Along? These days, being a working adult is like entering a foreign land where new rules for survival must be learned. Believers discover that their faith and their culture often offer competing rules for that survival. Also, they come to see that supervisors and peers have an influence on their lives that might at times encourage priorities that are at odds with their Christian faith. In fact, many believers feel great pressure to go along to get along with their colleagues and friends.

Consider Cheryl. She wants to live out her faith at work. However, new rules at her office prohibit anyone from verbally sharing his or her own religious beliefs with coworkers. Her boss has even frowned at a small poster with a Scripture verse Cheryl has hanging in her cubicle.

In the break room last week, Cheryl talked briefly with Jan, who told Cheryl about the difficulties in her life. Cheryl would like to invite Jan to her Bible study group, where Jan could find help and support. But how can Cheryl do that without causing problems for herself and Jan?

Being a Christian in a non-Christian society can create situations in which it is difficult to serve God. This week we study how Daniel obeyed the Lord despite the possible negative consequences of his actions. God calls us to display the same kind of obedience in difficult circumstances.

Call for Public and Private Morality. This week's lesson text shows Daniel in a challenging situation. The Babylonian king had commanded that Daniel eat food forbidden by the laws of Moses. The Lord helped Daniel discover a way to remain obedient to Scripture, yet avoid confrontation with his Babylonian masters.

In contrast to the immoral lives of many of our modern leaders, John Adams stands apart as a person who was convinced that public and private morality are interconnected. He speaks to self-indulgent Westerners who prefer to use pundits and polls as their moral guides and divorce their actions from the traditional biblical moral codes. Adams was convinced that a corrupt nation could not long remain free. An immoral person, he insisted, could not be free, but was instead a slave to unreasoning passion.

This great leader, who was a force behind the American Revolution and the establishment of our nation, demanded strict discipline, excellence, and integrity as the characteristics required in all persons, and especially in leaders. To attract and keep virtuous, disciplined people, Adams stated that society as a whole must foster virtue and discipline in its citizens.

"The best republics," Adams wrote, "will be virtuous and have been so." He noted that to remain virtuous, one must adhere to the rule of law and keep private passions in check. "A passion continually indulged feeds upon itself, eventually warping the owner's inherent capacity to judge right from wrong. People entrusted with unlimited power thrive upon their passions. The passion that is long indulged and continually gratified becomes mad; it is a species of delirium; it should not be called guilt, but insanity."

For Youth

■ **Topic:** Refusing the Royal Treatment

■ **Questions:** 1. What caused Ashpenaz to be sympathetic toward Daniel? 2. Why was Ashpenaz afraid? 3. What proposal did Daniel make to the guardian? 4. What does it mean to be a spiritual show-off? 5. Why does Jesus want us to be sincere, rather than hypocritical, in our righteous acts?

■ **Illustrations:**

Resisting Temptation. Every temptation promises saved teens relief from some form of "hunger" inside them. In their weakest moments, what allures them most might involve eating, spending, or lusting (to name a few possibilities).

One way for believing adolescents to get through sinful enticements is this: look steadily at what is being offered and ask whether the activity is really what they want. If they let that question sink in, they can discover, as Daniel did, a deeper need beneath their pressing desire of the moment: their hunger for unconditional love and fulfillment. As Daniel learned while in captivity in Babylon, it's a need only God can meet.

Overcoming Obstacles. King Nebuchadnezzar decreed that selected youths from the Jewish nobility be brought to Babylon and trained to serve in his court. The training of this handpicked group required them to adapt, in some degree, to the Babylonian culture. Although Daniel was a member of the cohort, he did not defile himself by partaking of Babylonian food and wine. Also, while Daniel did not persuade Ashpenaz, the chief official, to exempt him and his three friends from eating royal food and wine, Daniel's guard granted his request.

In 1921, an attack of infantile paralysis left Franklin D. Roosevelt crippled from the waist down. Experts at the time thought this would end his promising political career. Roosevelt, however, would not permit illness to hinder him from pursuing his political goals. With determination, he learned how to walk with artificial supports and a cane. By 1928, Roosevelt had made a successful comeback, becoming governor of New York. And in 1932, he was elected president of the United States, an office that he held until his death in 1945.

We encounter many obstacles that can deter us from living victoriously for Jesus. However, with the Lord's help, we can overcome these problems and be triumphant in our efforts to behave in an upright manner.

The Devil Is Ambidextrous. During court training in Babylon, Daniel was to be given a daily portion of food from the king's table. For the young Hebrew captive and his three friends, this favor clashed with strict Jewish dietary laws. So, by eating the king's food, the Israelite captives would have violated God's law.

Daniel's resistance to breaking God's law began in Daniel's heart. But the success of his resistance depended on his initial commitment and strategy. He did not wait until the situation was upon him before he decided what to do.

George Brushaber, an advisory editor for the magazine *Christianity Today*, tells a story of a rainy day at summer camp when the program director was scrambling to keep the campers occupied. The director invited a local law enforcement officer to come. The officer wowed the audience with demonstrations of nightsticks and handcuffs. Finally, the officer called a camper up to help him demonstrate how to deal with a mugger.

The boy eagerly followed his stage directions. He slipped up behind the officer and jabbed his plastic water pistol into the officer's back. The bold hero lunged to his left, swung his right elbow fiercely, and was "shot" squarely in the back by the junior gunman. The huge water spot between the officer's shoulder blades was clear evidence of the failure of his supposedly safe maneuver. Red-faced and fumbling for words, the lawman scolded the junior gunman, "You're supposed to hold the gun in your right hand!" The left-handed robber, however, was not impressed.

Brushaber concludes, "I can, for example, deal successfully with temptations from the usual and expected sources—from the right side; but it is when I become too confident that I get gunned down from the left—any blind side, really—by the sins and failures I least expect. To make matters worse, Satan is ambidextrous, always ready to attack from either side; and so the price of moral growth is perpetual vigilance."

LESSON 10 — FEBRUARY 8

SERVING GOD AND OTHERS

BACKGROUND SCRIPTURE: Luke 10:25-34
DEVOTIONAL READING: Matthew 22:34-40

Key Verse: Which now of these three, thinkest thou, was neighbour unto him that fell among the thieves? And he said, He that shewed mercy on him. Then said Jesus unto him, Go, and do thou likewise. Luke 10:36-37

KING JAMES VERSION

LUKE 10:25 And, behold, a certain lawyer stood up, and tempted him, saying, Master, what shall I do to inherit eternal life? 26 He said unto him, What is written in the law? how readest thou? 27 And he answering said, Thou shalt love the Lord thy God with all thy heart, and with all thy soul, and with all thy strength, and with all thy mind; and thy neighbour as thyself. 28 And he said unto him, Thou hast answered right: this do, and thou shalt live. 29 But he, willing to justify himself, said unto Jesus, And who is my neighbour? 30 And Jesus answering said, A certain man went down from Jerusalem to Jericho, and fell among thieves, which stripped him of his raiment, and wounded him, and departed, leaving him half dead. 31 And by chance there came down a certain priest that way: and when he saw him, he passed by on the other side. 32 And likewise a Levite, when he was at the place, came and looked on him, and passed by on the other side. 33 But a certain Samaritan, as he journeyed, came where he was: and when he saw him, he had compassion on him, 34 And went to him, and bound up his wounds, pouring in oil and wine, and set him on his own beast, and brought him to an inn, and took care of him.

NEW REVISED STANDARD VERSION

LUKE 10:25 Just then a lawyer stood up to test Jesus. "Teacher," he said, "what must I do to inherit eternal life?" 26 He said to him, "What is written in the law? What do you read there?" 27 He answered, "You shall love the Lord your God with all your heart, and with all your soul, and with all your strength, and with all your mind; and your neighbor as yourself." 28 And he said to him, "You have given the right answer; do this, and you will live."

29 But wanting to justify himself, he asked Jesus, "And who is my neighbor?" 30 Jesus replied, "A man was going down from Jerusalem to Jericho, and fell into the hands of robbers, who stripped him, beat him, and went away, leaving him half dead. 31 Now by chance a priest was going down that road; and when he saw him, he passed by on the other side. 32 So likewise a Levite, when he came to the place and saw him, passed by on the other side. 33 But a Samaritan while traveling came near him; and when he saw him, he was moved with pity. 34 He went to him and bandaged his wounds, having poured oil and wine on them. Then he put him on his own animal, brought him to an inn, and took care of him.

Home Bible Readings

Monday, February 2	Matthew 19:16-22	*If You Wish to Be Perfect*
Tuesday, February 3	James 2:8-13	*Mercy Triumphs over Judgment*
Wednesday, February 4	Joshua 22:1-6	*Keep the Instruction of Moses*
Thursday, February 5	Philippians 2:1-5	*Look to the Interests of Others*
Friday, February 6	Matthew 22:34-40	*The Foremost Commandment*
Saturday, February 7	Galatians 5:10-17	*Live by the Spirit*
Sunday, February 8	Luke 10:25-34	*Who Is My Neighbor?*

Background

Luke 10:25 states that one day a Jewish legal expert (that is, a scribe) asked Jesus a question to test Him. In Jesus' day, scribes were members of a learned class who studied the Mosaic law and served as copyists, scholars, and teachers. At first all the priests in Israel were responsible for the study and communication of this legal code. But this function eventually passed to the scribes.

The scribes' official interpretation of the meaning of the law gradually became more important than the law itself. Before A.D. 70, large numbers of priests in Jerusalem served as scribes. Because they were not paid for their services, they had to earn a livelihood in another way. Though some of the scribes were Sadducees, the bulk of them came from the ordinary priestly ranks (such as merchants, carpenters, flax combers, and tentmakers).

Notes on the Printed Text

The scribe who questioned Jesus asked, "What shall I do to inherit eternal life?" (Luke 10:25). According to John 17:3, eternal life is not mere endless existence, but a personal relationship with the Father based on knowing Him as the one true God (see Deut. 6:4; Mark 12:29; 1 Cor. 8:6; 1 Thess. 1:9; 1 Tim. 1:17). Furthermore, we can know the Father only through faith in the Son, Jesus the Messiah (see John 1:14, 18; 14:9; 20:31), whom the Father sent as His emissary (see 3:34; 4:34; 13:20). The legal expert's question in Luke 10:25 reflected the popular Jewish approach to finding favor with God. Most Jews thought one had to earn God's favor by doing good works. They couldn't fathom that eternal life is God's free and immediate gift to those who come to Him in repentance and faith (see Rom. 6:23; Eph. 2:8-9).

No doubt the scribe wanted to discredit Jesus by outwitting Him in public debate. But Jesus reversed the situation for the legalist. Instead of saying something that might sound like a contradiction of the law, Jesus asked the scribe to use the law to answer his own question (Luke 10:26). We can imagine Jesus pointing to the phylactery (a small square leather box or case) on the scribe's forearm or forehead, in which was written the compendium of the law.

In response, the scribe quoted Deuteronomy 6:5, which emphasizes love for God

(Luke 10:27). Together "heart," "soul," "strength," and "mind" are a way of saying "entire being." Every part of us should be involved in our devotion to God. The basis for doing so is found in Deuteronomy 6:4. Moses told the Israelites to "hear," or listen carefully to, a divinely revealed insight: "THE LORD OUR GOD IS ONE LORD."

In Jewish tradition, Deuteronomy 6:4-9 has been known as the *Shema'*. These verses contain the fundamental truth of Israel's religion and are the creed of Judaism. The name *Shema'* was given to these verses because the word "Hear" at the beginning of the passage is translated from the Hebrew word *shema'*. Pious Jews today recite the *Shema'* several times a day. In fact, early rabbis called for Jews to recite these verses once in the morning and once in the evening. Jesus called the instruction given in the *Shema'* the greatest commandment (Matt. 22:37-38) and the most important (Mark 12:29-30). Deuteronomy 6:4-9 may be the most often quoted verses from the Bible.

The scribe next quoted Leviticus 19:18, which says we are to love our neighbors as ourselves. The idea is that we need to work out our love for God in daily life. A supreme love for God will always find expression in unselfish love for others. The importance of doing the latter is seen in Jesus' statement recorded in Matthew 22:40, namely, that the entire Old Testament depends on loving God and others. Expressed differently, the Mosaic legal code is illumined and deepened by the presence of Christlike love (see Matt. 5:17; 7:12; Rom. 8:4; 13:8-10). Furthermore, just as the Savior loved us and gave His life for our eternal benefit, we also should reach out to others in a caring manner (see 1 John 4:9-12).

Jesus approved of the scribe's response and urged him to put his insight into action (Luke 10:28). Then Jesus said, "This do, and thou shalt live." This is the exhortation of the law (see Lev. 18:5). But since no sinner can obey it perfectly (see Jas. 2:10), the impossible demands of the law are meant to drive us to seek divine mercy (see Gal. 3:23-24). The scribe should have responded with a confession of his own guilt. Instead, he arrogantly tried to vindicate himself. The problem, then, was not with the law's commands. Rather, it was with the scribe's inability to keep them.

The scribe felt uncomfortable with his own answer. Perhaps he knew that his behavior didn't measure up to the standard he had quoted. So, he raised a technicality, hoping to account for and vindicate his failure. He would be glad to love his neighbor, he implied, if only Jesus would tell him who his neighbor was (Luke 10:29). In Jesus' day, the widespread opinion among scribes and Pharisees was that one's neighbors only included the upright. Supposedly, the wicked were to be hated because they were enemies of God. The religious leaders defined the wicked as sinners (such as tax collectors and prostitutes), Gentiles, and especially Samaritans. Psalm 139:21-22 was used to legitimatize this view.

It's true that a love for righteousness will lead to a hatred of evil. However, this does not excuse being hostile and malicious toward sinners. The upright should abhor the corrupt lifestyle of the lost, but never harbor a vindictive loathing of them as human beings. Instead, the godly should display a brokenhearted grieving over the sinful condition of the lost. Such is undergirded by a genuine concern for the eternal condition of the unsaved (see Matt. 5:44-48; Luke 6:27-36). Tragically, the scribes and Pharisees had made a virtue out of being antagonistic toward the sinful. The result was a renunciation of Leviticus 19:18, the command to love one's neighbor. The parable Jesus told shattered the legalistic notion of hating one's enemies.

Luke 10:30-35 is known as the parable of the good Samaritan. It concerned a man who traveled from Jerusalem to Jericho. Jesus' listeners would immediately recall that notorious stretch of road. In less than 20 miles it descended nearly 3,600 feet. It had plenty of hazardous twists and turns and steep inclines, with rocks and caves lining the way. The road's conditions gave robbers ample opportunity to prey upon travelers. That's what happened to the traveler in Jesus' story. Some men beat him, robbed him, and left him lying by the side of the road (vs. 30). But the wounded man was not alone for long. Three travelers passed by in turn: a priest, a Levite, and a Samaritan.

Many priests and Levites lived in Jericho. So perhaps we should imagine the priest returning home to Jericho after serving at the temple in Jerusalem. When he came along, he saw the victim, beaten and bloody. Now the priest was faced with a decision: to help or refuse to do so. Sadly, he chose not to help (vs. 31). Whatever reasoning he used in making his decision was inadequate to justify shirking his duty to show mercy to a hurting person (see Mic. 6:8). Next, a Levite came along. He was a member of a group that was responsible for maintaining the temple and its furniture and utensils. Like the priest, he too may have been coming from (or going to) the temple on religious business. And he, too, chose not to help the injured traveler (Luke 10:32). Likewise, the Levite was guilty of being unmerciful. The priest and the Levite saw no connection between their temple worship and the needs of the beaten traveler. Though the religious leaders affirmed their love for God, they denied by their actions the importance of loving their fellow human beings. Such hypocrisy was abhorrent to God.

A Samaritan was the third person to come upon the injured man. Samaritans were Jews who had intermarried with people from other nations following the deportation of much of the Israelite population by the Assyrians 750 years before Jesus (see 2 Kings 17:24-41). Over the following centuries, racial prejudice and a history of animosity fueled an intense rivalry between Jews and Samaritans. The Jews bitterly hated the Samaritans, for the Jews prided themselves on their supposedly "pure" ancestry. Additionally, Jews despised Samaritans for their hybrid religion. Samaritans accepted the Torah (the five books of Moses), but inserted some of their own interpretations. Also, they worshiped on Mount Gerizim rather than on Mount Zion in Jerusalem (see John 4:20).

Given this climate of animosity, the Samaritan in Jesus' parable could have rationalized failing to assist the injured man more easily than the priest and Levite did. But the Samaritan did not do that. Instead, feeling deep pity, he decided to help the stranger

(Luke 10:33). The Samaritan was thorough in the assistance he gave. He began by administering first aid. He bandaged the man's wounds, pouring on oil (which acted as a salve) and wine (which acted as an antiseptic). Then the Samaritan turned his donkey into a makeshift ambulance. He transported the man to an inn (vs. 34). Finally, the Samaritan arranged to pay the man's expenses. Since one denarius was equal to a laborer's daily pay, the two silver coins (denarii) that the Samaritan paid would probably have lodged the wounded man for several days (vs. 35).

At the end of the parable, Jesus asked the scribe which of the three passersby—the priest, the Levite, or the Samaritan—was a neighbor to the robbed man (vs. 36). The scribe correctly answered, the one who had assisted the man in distress. Jesus told the scribe to act the same way (vs. 37). The scribe had asked how far he had to go to love others. But Jesus turned the question around. Instead of "Who is my neighbour?" (vs. 29), the question became, in effect, "How can I be a good neighbor?" (vs. 36). The lesson Jesus taught, and the lesson we must live, is that we become good neighbors by showing mercy to everyone we encounter (vs. 37).

Though Jesus' parable takes place in a rural setting, it speaks to a number of urban issues: racial and ethnic divisions, violent crime, and even the struggle of small businesses to remain solvent. The Samaritan—the good neighbor—does not eliminate these problems, but he does act as an agent of mercy to overcome them in small but effective ways. The Samaritan's example challenges us to consider how we can be good neighbors to others, regardless of their racial, economic, social, political, or ethnic background. Ultimately, God is interested in mercy, not maintaining prejudice.

SUGGESTIONS TO TEACHERS

As the parable of the good Samaritan emphasizes, Jesus wants us to apply the principle of love to our lives—both for God and for our fellow human beings. To be a good neighbor, we should look for opportunities to do the following.

1. GET LOVE. Love is both a choice and an attitude. Without it, selfishness takes control of our hearts, and we become more concerned about what might happen to us than about helping those who are in need. God's love is the driving force that gets a good neighbor to take action.

2. GET INVOLVED. Our society is plagued with a lack of involvement. Like the priest and the temple assistant in Jesus' parable, there is a growing tendency to go out of our way to avoid getting involved. A good neighbor cannot cross to the other side of the road and leave a truly needy person without help. A good neighbor gets involved. A good neighbor stoops to help. A good neighbor sacrifices. And a good neighbor eases the pain.

3. GET MERCIFUL. There's never been, nor will there ever be, a human being for whom God did not show extraordinary mercy. We're all the recipients of His kindness, so let's pass a little of it on! May we strive to offer compassionate treatment to those around us. And may God grant us and develop within us a disposition to be kind.

4. GET HELP. None of us can do all that needs to be done alone. So, when the task seems overbearing or too much to accomplish on our own, we should enlist the help of other good neighbors who, out of the love of their hearts, are more than willing to get involved and to show mercy.

FOR ADULTS

■ **TOPIC:** Do We Know Our Neighbor?

■ **QUESTIONS:** 1. Why do you think the legal expert sought to put Jesus to the test? 2. Why did the scribe try to justify his actions? 3. What did the Samaritan sacrifice to get involved with the wounded traveler? 4. What rationalizations might busy Christians make to avoid assisting others? 5. How do you feel after you've stopped to help someone in need?

■ **ILLUSTRATIONS:**

Stretching Our Love. Booker T. Washington, the noted African-American educator, was taking a walk with a Caucasian friend when a pedestrian roughly elbowed Washington into the gutter. His friend was furious and asked him, "How can you tolerate such an insult?" Washington replied, "I defy any man to make me hate him."

This is what true Christian love does—it defies all the bitterness and hatred in the world. It also sweeps aside all the barriers that separate people. Because Jesus makes a difference in our social relationships, Christians can extend the love of God to others.

Jesus' parable of the good Samaritan forces us to look deep inside ourselves. How easy it is for us to say we love God, but then do nothing for our neighbors. Also, how hard it is for us to cast aside our own desires for the sake of helping those in great need.

Trashing Overlooked Human Beings. In an Indianapolis newspaper was this headline: "Homeless Woman Crushed with Trash." It seems that a homeless woman crawled into a dumpster to sleep, was loaded into a truck, compressed with the trash, and arrived at the incinerator, dead. They found her by her white tennis shoes and red windbreaker. Nearby residents had seen her climb into the dumpster, but when they heard the truck begin to grind, they did not warn the driver in time.

Accounts of the homeless being crushed—even crushed to death in trash bins—have actually become commonplace. In recent years, it happened in Denver at least twice, in Washington once, in Los Angeles once, and in Atlanta once (just to name some incidents). How tragic it is that overlooked human beings are being gathered up with the trash!

Jesus' parable of the good Samaritan might be one way to prevent such tragedies. A combination of love, involvement, mercy, and help makes a good neighbor. And that's what Jesus has called us to be. We cannot become hermits and adequately love our neighbors. We have to get to know them. The lesson that Jesus taught—and the lesson that we must live—is that we become good neighbors by showing compassion and kindness to everyone we encounter, including the homeless.

Do Something. Theodore Roosevelt, the twenty-sixth president of the United States, seemed to always display a vigorous determination to get involved. He was Assistant Secretary of the Navy in 1898 when the Spanish-American War broke out, and he resigned that post to form the Rough Riders, a volunteer cavalry group that was to become famous for its charge up San Juan Hill in Cuba. An advocate of a venturesome foreign policy, Roosevelt effected the construction of the Panama Canal, won the Nobel Peace Prize for his successful intervention in the Russo-Japanese War, and dispatched the U.S. Fleet on a round-the-world tour.

Roosevelt's famous motto was "Speak softly and carry a big stick." But he had another motto that he wrote as advice to himself and others that sounds as if it could have come from the mouth of the good Samaritan: "In a moment of decision, the best thing you can do is the right thing to do. The worst thing you can do is nothing."

FOR YOUTH

■ **TOPIC:** May I Help You?
■ **QUESTIONS:** 1. How did Jesus respond to the scribe's challenge? 2. Why do you think the priest and Levite refused to help the injured man in Jesus' parable? 3. How might Jesus' listeners have reacted when they learned that a Samaritan was the hero of the story, rather than the priest or the Levite? 4. Who are the people that might classify as your "neighbors"? 5. In what tangible ways can you show mercy to your fellow human beings?

■ **ILLUSTRATIONS:**

The Merciful Enemy. The expert in the Mosaic law who questioned Jesus was experienced in creating diversion, and, sadly, many people today follow his tactics. They find it relatively easy to talk about spirituality. But they find it difficult to stick to the main point, namely, their need for Jesus to save them from their hypocrisy and self-righteousness.

It's a huge step for us to confess that we aren't good enough to merit eternal life. Perhaps that's why some people talk about the sins of others without ever facing the reality of their own transgressions. They have no desire to repent of their misdeeds and be saved. And they have no interest in being kindhearted to their enemies.

From the parable of the good Samaritan we learn three principles about loving our neighbor. First, lack of love is often easy to justify, even though it is never right. Second, our neighbor is anyone of any race, creed, or social background who is in need. Third, love means acting to meet the person's need.

Stranger in Need. In his book, *The Samaritan's Imperative*, Michael J. Christensen cites a story about two monks walking back to their monastery in the freezing cold. As they cross a bridge, the monks hear a man calling for help in the ravine below. They want to stop, but they know they must reach the monastery before sunset or they will freeze to death.

The first monk chooses to risk the danger of the cold in order to help another to safety. He climbs down into the ravine, gathers the wounded man into his arms, and slowly makes his way back to the monastery. The second monk has already gone on ahead, determined to get back safely before sunset.

Night comes, and with it, the bitter cold. As the first monk nears the monastery, he stumbles over something in the middle of the road. To his sorrow, it is the body of his spiritual brother who had gone on alone and had frozen to death. In seeking to save his life, he had lost it. But the compassionate monk, willing to lose his life, was kept warm by the heat exchanged from carrying the stranger in need.

Modeling the Love of Jesus. In 1970, Samaritan's Purse was established. From the outset, the Christian organization has sought to provide spiritual and physical assistance to hurting people around the globe. Their teams find motivation for doing so in Jesus' parable of the good Samaritan. After Jesus described how a Samaritan showed kindness to a hurting fellow traveler, the Savior told His listeners, "Go, and do thou likewise" (Luke 10:37).

One of the organization's endeavors is called "Children's Heart Project" (CHP), which began in 1997. For the past 18 years, CHP has arranged life-saving operations for hundreds of children living in countries around the world, including Bosnia, Honduras, Mongolia, and Bolivia (to name a few places). CHP partners with reputable hospitals to provide surgery for children for whom the needed medical specialists and equipment are otherwise nonexistent.

To make this happen, the staff of Samaritan's Purse arranges airfare for a parent, the child, and a translator. Also, the organization locates a Christian church that agrees to sponsor the group. Members of the congregation pledge to pray for the endeavor and identify a host family. In turn, the host family provides housing, local transportation, food, and toiletries. Just as important, a host family offers emotional support and spiritual guidance for an average of five weeks.

What a wonderful example this is of God's people reaching out to others in need! Through the combined efforts of believers here and abroad, Jesus' followers can be proactive in showing compassion to the disadvantaged.

LESSON 11 — FEBRUARY 15

SERVING THE LEAST

BACKGROUND SCRIPTURE: Matthew 25:31-46
DEVOTIONAL READING: Psalm 10:12-18

Key Verse: Verily I say unto you, Inasmuch as ye have done it unto one of the least of these my brethren, ye have done it unto me. Matthew 25:40.

KING JAMES VERSION

MATTHEW 25:31 When the Son of man shall come in his glory, and all the holy angels with him, then shall he sit upon the throne of his glory: 32 And before him shall be gathered all nations: and he shall separate them one from another, as a shepherd divideth his sheep from the goats: 33 And he shall set the sheep on his right hand, but the goats on the left. 34 Then shall the King say unto them on his right hand, Come, ye blessed of my Father, inherit the kingdom prepared for you from the foundation of the world: 35 For I was an hungred, and ye gave me meat: I was thirsty, and ye gave me drink: I was a stranger, and ye took me in: 36 Naked, and ye clothed me: I was sick, and ye visited me: I was in prison, and ye came unto me. 37 Then shall the righteous answer him, saying, Lord, when saw we thee an hungred, and fed thee? or thirsty, and gave thee drink? 38 When saw we thee a stranger, and took thee in? or naked, and clothed thee? 39 Or when saw we thee sick, or in prison, and came unto thee? 40 And the King shall answer and say unto them, Verily I say unto you, Inasmuch as ye have done it unto one of the least of these my brethren, ye have done it unto me. 41 Then shall he say also unto them on the left hand, Depart from me, ye cursed, into everlasting fire, prepared for the devil and his angels: 42 For I was an hungred, and ye gave me no meat: I was thirsty, and ye gave me no drink: 43 I was a stranger, and ye took me not in: naked, and ye clothed me not: sick, and in prison, and ye visited me not. 44 Then shall they also answer him, saying, Lord, when saw we thee an hungred, or athirst, or a stranger, or naked, or sick, or in prison, and did not minister unto thee? 45 Then shall he answer them, saying, Verily I say unto you, Inasmuch as ye did it not to one of the least of these, ye did it not to me. 46 And these shall go away into everlasting punishment: but the righteous into life eternal.

NEW REVISED STANDARD VERSION

MATTHEW 25:31 "When the Son of Man comes in his glory, and all the angels with him, then he will sit on the throne of his glory. 32 All the nations will be gathered before him, and he will separate people one from another as a shepherd separates the sheep from the goats, 33 and he will put the sheep at his right hand and the goats at the left. 34 Then the king will say to those at his right hand, 'Come, you that are blessed by my Father, inherit the kingdom prepared for you from the foundation of the world; 35 for I was hungry and you gave me food, I was thirsty and you gave me something to drink, I was a stranger and you welcomed me, 36 I was naked and you gave me clothing, I was sick and you took care of me, I was in prison and you visited me.' 37 Then the righteous will answer him, 'Lord, when was it that we saw you hungry and gave you food, or thirsty and gave you something to drink? 38 And when was it that we saw you a stranger and welcomed you, or naked and gave you clothing? 39 And when was it that we saw you sick or in prison and visited you?' 40 And the king will answer them, 'Truly I tell you, just as you did it to one of the least of these who are members of my family, you did it to me.' 41 Then he will say to those at his left hand, 'You that are accursed, depart from me into the eternal fire prepared for the devil and his angels; 42 for I was hungry and you gave me no food, I was thirsty and you gave me nothing to drink, 43 I was a stranger and you did not welcome me, naked and you did not give me clothing, sick and in prison and you did not visit me.' 44 Then they also will answer, 'Lord, when was it that we saw you hungry or thirsty or a stranger or naked or sick or in prison, and did not take care of you?' 45 Then he will answer them, 'Truly I tell you, just as you did not do it to one of the least of these, you did not do it to me.' 46 And these will go away into eternal punishment, but the righteous into eternal life."

Home Bible Readings

Monday, February 9	Matthew 24:37-44	*You Must Be Ready*
Tuesday, February 10	Leviticus 19:9-15	*Compassion for the Poor*
Wednesday, February 11	Deuteronomy 15:7-11	*Open Your Hand to the Poor*
Thursday, February 12	Esther 9:19-23	*Presents for the Poor*
Friday, February 13	Psalm 10:12-18	*Do Not Forget the Oppressed*
Saturday, February 14	Romans 15:22-28	*Share Resources with the Poor*
Sunday, February 15	Matthew 25:31-46	*Minister to the Least*

Background

Matthew's Gospel includes five major discourses or lengthy sections that end with a specific formula. The first is usually called the Sermon on the Mount (chaps. 5–7; see lesson 5 for more information). The others are chapters 10, 13, 18, 24, and 25. (Matthew 23 is a long speech without the usual ending.) Because Jesus was sitting on the Mount of Olives when He taught the material in chapters 24 and 25 to His disciples, it has been called the Olivet Discourse. It contains some of the most noteworthy prophetic passages in all of Scripture.

Here we find the expression "Son of man" (25:31), which occurs over 80 times in the Gospels and spotlights both Jesus' lowly humanity and heavenly origin (see Ps. 8:4; Ezek. 2:1; Dan. 7:13). On the one hand, "Son of man" is associated with the glory and triumph of the Messiah at His second coming (see Matt. 16:27-28; 25:31; Mark 14:62; Luke 22:69; Acts 7:56). On the other hand, the title is connected with the suffering of God's Servant on the cross (see Matt. 17:22-23; Mark 8:31; Luke 9:22; John 3:13-15). In a similar vein, Paul referred to Jesus as the "last Adam" (1 Cor. 15:45) and the "second man" (vs. 47) to draw attention to His representative role over the human race as its Lord, Judge, and Savior (see Matt. 13:41-42; 19:28; Acts 17:31; Rom. 2:16).

Notes on the Printed Text

In the parable of the sheep and the goats, Jesus revealed that the righteous would be rewarded for their concern and hospitality, while the wicked would be punished for their indifference. In the final parable that Jesus delivered on the Mount of Olives, He provided a few details about what His return would be like. First, Jesus would come in "glory" (Matt. 25:31), or divine splendor, no longer simply appearing as an ordinary human being. Second, He would bring with Him "all the holy angels," who would no doubt serve as His assistants (see 2 Thess. 1:7). Third, Jesus would "sit upon the throne of his glory" (Matt. 25:31), meaning He would rule in splendor.

Once Jesus was seated on His glorious throne, all the nations would be gathered in His presence. Then He would segregate them into two groups (vs. 32). Expressed differently, the purpose of the judgment would be to set apart the righteous from the wicked. Only God can do that with perfect justice. We know from the parable of the wheat and the tares that during the church age, there would be a commingling of true and false disciples (see 13:30). Even until the end time of judgment, the good would coexist alongside the bad. Nonetheless, when the Messiah gathered together all humanity, then the separation would come.

Jesus compared the setting apart of humans to the way a shepherd would separate sheep from goats. In ancient Palestine, sheep and goats often grazed together during the day. When night came, however, they were herded into separate folds. That was because the goats, unlike the sheep, could not easily endure the cooler night air and thus had to be grouped to keep warm. The point of the comparison lies in the fact that sheep and goats were separated at the end of the day. As the Shepherd of judgment, Jesus would put the "sheep" on His right and the "goats" on His left (vs. 33).

There are two primary ways of understanding Jesus' parable. Some say the "nations" (vs. 32) refer to all peoples, while others claim they refer to Gentiles only. One group thinks the judgment occurs at the conclusion of history. In contrast, the second group says it takes place when Jesus comes to set up a kingdom on earth. For those in the first group, the judgment determines who goes to heaven and who goes to hell. Oppositely, those in the second group say the judgment concerns who enters Jesus' earthly kingdom and who does not.

The remainder of Jesus' parable describes what He would do with the sheep (or the righteous) and the goats (or the wicked) once He has them separated. First, He commented on the sheep (vss. 34-40) and then the goats (vss. 41-45). While seated on His throne, Jesus would reign and judge as King. He would address those on His right side as "blessed of my Father" (vs. 34). God would favor them in the blessing they received as an inheritance from Him, namely, the kingdom of heaven. Jesus described this kingdom as having been "prepared for you from the foundation of the world." All along it has been a part of God's plan to bless the righteous with His kingdom. Upon Jesus' return, it would be time for the plan's fulfillment.

Jesus said the righteous would inherit the kingdom because of how they have treated Him. They would have met His needs for food, drink, shelter, clothing, nursing, and visitation (vss. 35-36). These are emphases that anyone at any time in any society can understand, for they are the common concerns of life everywhere. So, the test of faith that stands up under Jesus' inspection would be how we performed deeds of mercy, love, and kindness. After all, this is what Jesus did for people while He was here on earth. Also, His righteous sheep follow His example. They show that their faith is practical and touches the lives of hurting people. Clearly, then, valid Christian faith is more than saying the right prayers or singing approved hymns. It includes standing alongside people in the harshest circumstances.

Jesus called His sheep "the righteous" (vs. 37). They were upright because of their faith in the Messiah, and godly living marked their lives because they cared for people in need. The righteous asked a series of good questions in verses 37-39. In their place, we might also wonder when we ever had an opportunity to do such charitable deeds for Jesus. Here we see that Jesus wants us to show His love to others. Even the simplest act of kindness to the seemingly most insignificant person meets with God's approval and will be eternally rewarded.

Jesus said that the deeds the righteous had done for "one of the least of these my brethren" (vs. 40) were performed for Him. Put another way, service carried out for Jesus' needy brothers and sisters is the same as service done for Him. This is an astounding truth, for it radically transforms our motivation for performing deeds of mercy. Because elsewhere Scripture clearly teaches that good works do not earn salvation (see Eph. 2:8-10; Titus 3:5), we know that the assessment of lifestyle in Matthew 25:40 refers to the results of salvation, not the cause of it. Once we are saved, we should expect to see the fruit of God's grace at work in our lives (see Eph. 3:10; Jas. 2:26).

There has been much discussion about the identity of the "brethren" (Matt. 25:40). Some have said they are the Jews; others say they are all Christians; still others say they are suffering people everywhere. Such a debate is much like the lawyer's earlier question to Jesus, "And who is my neighbour?" (Luke 10:29; also, see the corresponding commentary in lesson 10). The point of Jesus' parable is not the *who*, but rather the *what*; in other words, the importance of serving where ministry is needed. The focus of this story about the sheep and the goats is that we should love every person and reach out to anyone we can. Such compassion and kindness glorifies God by reflecting our love for Him.

Jesus next focused on the goats. Unlike the ones on the right, the ones on the left would be told to depart. Also, rather than being blessed by the Father, these people would be cursed. Moreover, instead of inheriting the kingdom prepared for the righteous, these people would be consigned to the eternal fire (Matt. 25:41). God did not prepare hell for people, but for the devil and his angels. God's plan was to redeem and restore human beings, not condemn and destroy them. This was His reason for the Cross. From the foundation of the world, He prepared an inheritance for His people (vs. 34). However, people sentenced to the place prepared for the devil go there because they chose to reject the Father's gracious offer of eternal life through faith in His Son—as evidenced by the lack of compassion in their lives (see Rom. 9:22; 1 Pet. 2:7-8).

Just as the righteous would inherit the kingdom for meeting Jesus' needs, the wicked would be consigned to hell for not meeting His needs. They would have been presented with the same opportunities to give Him food and drink and the rest, but they would have chosen not to do so (Matt. 25:42-43). Notice that even though the goats mingled with the sheep, that alone did not make them sheep. To be a sheep, we must be born a sheep. Spiritually speaking, we need a new birth from above (see John 3:3). For those who spurn the Messiah, all that remains is for Him to condemn them. It would be a terrifying scene as He issues a verdict of guilty against the unsaved (see John 5:22; 9:39; Acts 10:42).

The wicked would be just as mystified as the righteous about when they had the opportunities that Jesus mentioned. They would ask when they chose not to help the Lord (Matt. 25:44). They failed to realize that the basis for judgment would be whether they showed love to others, whom God has created in His image (see Jas. 2:15-16; 1 John 3:14-18). Jesus' solemn reply would be that refusing to help others in need is the same as refusing to help Him (Matt. 25:45). Verse 46 concludes both the story of the sheep and the goats. The wicked and righteous have radically different futures. The first group is eternally condemned, while the second group is eternally blessed. Jesus' judgments would be beyond appeal.

SUGGESTIONS TO TEACHERS

Though we may be unaware of it at the time, when we minister to the deprived and dispossessed, we are, indeed, ministering to Jesus. Still, even ministering to the Lord does not earn us our salvation. Instead, if our commitment to God is real, it will show in our actions. Clearly, then, serving and meeting the needs of others is not a substitute for our faith in Christ, but rather an affirmation of our trust in Him.

1. ACTS OF MERCY. Jesus' parable of the sheep and the goats describes acts of mercy we all can do every day—feeding the hungry, giving drinks to the thirsty, welcoming strangers, clothing the naked, taking care of the sick, and visiting the imprisoned. None of these deeds of kindness depend on our being wealthy, skillful, or intelligent. They are simple acts of mercy and compassion that are freely received just as much as they are freely given.

2. ACTS OF BELIEF. The most genuine evidence of our belief in Christ is in the way we act, especially toward those who need our help. Jesus calls us to treat others as if they were Him. Of course, carrying out this mandate is no easy task. But what we do for others demonstrates what we really think about Jesus' words: "Verily I say unto you, Inasmuch as ye have done [it] unto one of the least of these my brethren, ye have done [it] unto me." (Matt. 25:40).

3. ACTS OF CONCERN. God wants us to have sincere, heartfelt concern for our fellow human beings, and especially for our fellow believers in Christ. Because of the command to "love thy neighbor as thyself" (22:39), we have no excuse to neglect those around us who have deep needs. And we cannot hand the responsibility of caring and helping over to the government or even to our church. Jesus demands our personal involvement in caring for others' needs.

FOR ADULTS
■ **TOPIC:** Meeting Others' Needs
■ **QUESTIONS:** 1. What would be the first act Jesus performs after sitting on His glorious throne? 2. What would be the destiny of those on Jesus' right? Why would this be so? 3. What would be the destiny of those on Jesus'

left? Why would this be so? 4. How does Jesus say we can know that our good works are done for the right reason? 5. Who among our family, friends, and coworkers needs the touch of God's love from us?

■ ILLUSTRATIONS:

Reaching Out to Others. Several years ago, when King Abdullah succeeded his father, King Hussein, on the throne of Jordan, he decided to discover the needs of his people. The monarch assumed several roles in disguise, such as taxi driver, moneychanger, and so on. The people he worked with had no idea they were serving their king.

We recognize something similar taking place in Jesus' parable of the sheep and the goats. The sheep had no idea they helped Jesus, and the goats had no idea they refused to come to His aid. How many times do we make the same mistake? We simply do not recognize that by helping needy people, we are ministering to our Lord and King.

I Was Thirsty, and You Gave Me Milk. Jesus' parable of the sheep and the goats reminds us that we must take care of those who need our help. Indeed, Jesus will regard how we treat them as if our actions are meant for Him.

Dan West, a Christian relief worker in Spain during the Spanish Civil War, was handing out cups of powdered milk to a long line of hungry children on both sides of the conflict. All too often, the milk ran out before the line ended. As a farmer, Dan's response was practical. "Wouldn't it be better," he reasoned, "to supply families with an ongoing source of nutritious milk so that parents could feed their children themselves without having to depend on powdered milk from abroad?"

When Dan shared his idea back home in Indiana, his friends agreed. "I'll give a calf, if someone else will raise her," one person said. Soon afterward, the first boatload of heifers sailed in 1944, not to Spain, because the war there was soon over, but rather to Puerto Rico. And right from the start, families who received the heifers made a commitment to pass on their gift animal's first female offspring to another family in need.

In the decades since then, a parade of animals—some familiar (like goats, cows, chickens, sheep, and rabbits) and some exotic (like camels, water buffalo, llamas, and guinea pigs)—has circled the world. The oldest U.S. hunger organization, Heifer Project International, has helped millions of people in countries around the globe move toward self-reliance.

Showing That We Care. Jesus told His disciples that in the judgment, He would divide all people like a shepherd separates his sheep from the goats. The pivotal factor He would look at is how people treated those who are the "least of these my brethren" (Matt. 25:40).

One bitter winter morning in 1985, Flo Wheatley of Hop Bottom, Pennsylvania, took her son to Manhattan for a medical checkup. As they hurried through the cold, she noticed many homeless people huddled in doorways. One stood out because he was wrapped in a bright pink, hand-knit afghan.

Most of us have had similar encounters and felt helpless to do anything. But not Flo Wheatley. Back home that night, she took a pile of her children's castoff clothing and some old bedspreads and quickly assembled them into a simple sleeping bag. That first year she and her husband, Jim, distributed eight bags. Soon neighbors began to enthusiastically join in.

The project grew and acquired a name: My Brother's Keeper Quilt Group. In the years that followed, tens of thousands of "Ugly Quilts" (as these bags are sometimes called) have passed through Flo and Jim's own garage distribution center. And many thousands more are still being made and given away by church groups, youth groups, and individuals.

For Youth

■ **Topic:** Talking to Strangers

■ **Questions:** 1. Why do you think the King waited until the scene of the judgment to separate the sheep from the goats? 2. In what ways are those who carry out acts of mercy similar to those who don't? In what ways are they different? 3. Who do you think are "the least of these" (Matt. 25:40) mentioned in Jesus' parable? 4. What does Jesus' parable teach about our Christian responsibility to others in need? 5. What are some specific ways you can reach out to others in Jesus' name?

■ **Illustrations:**

Final Accounting. A group of Christian college students decided to find out what it was like to be homeless. They spent several weekends living among the homeless in Chicago by sleeping outside at night on cardboard pallets and scrounging for their food. This incident reminds us that young people generally have a keen sense of helping others. They organize food drives, and walk, run, and swim for charity. They go overseas to build houses, drill wells, and teach people to read.

In the parable of the sheep and the goats, Jesus said these sorts of activities really count with Him. The idea is that by investing our lives by helping others, we serve Him. Conversely, by refusing to help others in need, we also refuse to minister to our Savior.

Showing That We Care. Jesus' parable of the sheep and the goats teaches us that we should treat others as if they were Jesus. In one of the uplifting stories in *Chicken Soup for the Soul at Work*, Rick Phillips, a management trainer for the Circle K Corporation, tells about how hard it is to retain quality employees. During the management seminars that he leads, he asks the participants, "What has caused you to stay long enough to become a manager?" At one of his seminars, Cynthia, a new manager, slowly answered with her voice almost breaking, "It was a $19 baseball glove."

Cynthia told the group that she originally took a Circle K clerk job as an interim position while she looked for something better. On her second or third day behind the counter, she received a phone call from her nine-year-old son, Jessie. He needed a baseball glove for Little League. She explained that as a single mother, money was very tight, and her first check would have to go for paying bills. Perhaps she could buy his baseball glove with her second or third check.

When Cynthia arrived for work the next morning, Patricia, the store manager, asked her to come to the small room in back of the store that served as an office. Cynthia wondered if she had done something wrong or left some part of her job incomplete from the day before. She was concerned and confused.

Patricia handed her a box. "I overheard you talking to your son yesterday," she said, "and I know that it's hard to explain things to kids. This is a baseball glove for Jessie because he may not understand how important he is, since you have to pay bills before you can buy gloves. You know we can't pay good people like you as much as we would like to; but we do care, and I want you to know you are important to us."

The thoughtfulness, empathy, and love of this convenience store manager demonstrates vividly that people remember more how much an employer cares than how much the employer pays. And what an important lesson to be learned for the price of a Little League baseball glove!

Seeing the Face of Jesus. We learn from Jesus' parable of the sheep and the goats that if we do good works in order to gain credit with God, then our deeds will be worthless. But if our love for God prompts us to perform charitable acts for others, then we can know that God is pleased with our deeds, since those actions reflect our heart attitude.

In a 1997 *Sojourners* article, Jim Forest writes how for six years an American journalist named Dorothy Day looked for a way to connect her social conscience with her faith. Finally, her search gave birth to a relief movement in May 1933. Originally it was just a newspaper, but within weeks of the paper's publication, the first house of hospitality—her apartment—came into being simply because Dorothy couldn't turn away a homeless woman who had seen the paper and came asking for help.

Today, there are hundreds houses of hospitality, not to mention the many more places of welcome that wouldn't exist had it not been for Dorothy Day's struggle to live her faith with directness and simplicity. At the core of Dorothy's life was her experience of ultimate beauty—Jesus' face hidden in the faces of America's human castoffs. "Those who cannot see the face of Christ in the poor," Dorothy used to say, "are atheists indeed."

LESSON 12 — FEBRUARY 22

SERVING IN GOD'S STRENGTH

BACKGROUND SCRIPTURE: Ephesians 6:10-20
DEVOTIONAL READING: Colossians 3:12-17

Key Verse: Put on the whole armour of God, that ye may be able to stand against the wiles of the devil. Ephesians 6:11.

KING JAMES VERSION

EPHESIANS 6:10 Finally, my brethren, be strong in the Lord, and in the power of his might. 11 Put on the whole armour of God, that ye may be able to stand against the wiles of the devil. 12 For we wrestle not against flesh and blood, but against principalities, against powers, against the rulers of the darkness of this world, against spiritual wickedness in high places. 13 Wherefore take unto you the whole armour of God, that ye may be able to withstand in the evil day, and having done all, to stand. 14 Stand therefore, having your loins girt about with truth, and having on the breastplate of righteousness; 15 And your feet shod with the preparation of the gospel of peace; 16 Above all, taking the shield of faith, wherewith ye shall be able to quench all the fiery darts of the wicked. 17 And take the helmet of salvation, and the sword of the Spirit, which is the word of God: 18 Praying always with all prayer and supplication in the Spirit, and watching thereunto with all perseverance and supplication for all saints;

19 And for me, that utterance may be given unto me, that I may open my mouth boldly, to make known the mystery of the gospel, 20 For which I am an ambassador in bonds: that therein I may speak boldly, as I ought to speak.

NEW REVISED STANDARD VERSION

EPHESIANS 6:10 Finally, be strong in the Lord and in the strength of his power. 11 Put on the whole armor of God, so that you may be able to stand against the wiles of the devil. 12 For our struggle is not against enemies of blood and flesh, but against the rulers, against the authorities, against the cosmic powers of this present darkness, against the spiritual forces of evil in the heavenly places. 13 Therefore take up the whole armor of God, so that you may be able to withstand on that evil day, and having done everything, to stand firm. 14 Stand therefore, and fasten the belt of truth around your waist, and put on the breastplate of righteousness. 15 As shoes for your feet put on whatever will make you ready to proclaim the gospel of peace. 16 With all of these, take the shield of faith, with which you will be able to quench all the flaming arrows of the evil one. 17 Take the helmet of salvation, and the sword of the Spirit, which is the word of God.

18 Pray in the Spirit at all times in every prayer and supplication. To that end keep alert and always persevere in supplication for all the saints. 19 Pray also for me, so that when I speak, a message may be given to me to make known with boldness the mystery of the gospel, 20 for which I am an ambassador in chains. Pray that I may declare it boldly, as I must speak.

Home Bible Readings

Monday, February 16	Luke 4:1-12	*Ready with the Word*
Tuesday, February 17	1 Samuel 17:19-30	*The Battle Lines Drawn*
Wednesday, February 18	1 Samuel 17:31-39	*Choosing the Right Equipment*
Thursday, February 19	1 Samuel 17:40-50	*The Battle Is the Lord's*
Friday, February 20	Romans 13:8-14	*Put on the Lord Jesus Christ*
Saturday, February 21	Colossians 3:12-17	*The Dress for God's Chosen Ones*
Sunday, February 22	Ephesians 6:10-20	*The Whole Armor of God*

Background

As a prisoner in Rome, Paul was chained to a Roman soldier at all times. So, it was natural for him to see his guard as a model and to think of the spiritual struggle in military terms. Undoubtedly, the Old Testament influenced the apostle too, since the Hebrew Scriptures frequently use military images for spiritual realities (see Isa. 11:5 and 59:17).

Paul's guards probably did not wear full battle dress. But they could easily bring to Paul's mind the times he had seen Roman soldiers fully armed. As every Roman soldier knew, the occasion to dress himself in his protective covering was not when hostilities erupted. Before the battle, he prepared himself by taking up armor and weapons. In Paul's discussion, we are not told to take the offensive against Satan. But he is attacking us. Therefore, we need to look to our defenses and make sure we do not lose any ground to him. Our spiritual successes have been hard-won, and so we should stand firm and fight to hold onto them.

Notes on the Printed Text

As Paul and others ministered at Ephesus, they encountered the spiritual forces of darkness arrayed against the proclamation of the gospel. The apostle understood the power of evil as much as anyone. He had often been the object of satanic efforts to hurt him and hinder his work. Also, he knew the Ephesian Christians were on Satan's list of targets too. So, in bringing his letter to a close, the apostle focused on the spiritual struggle that they faced. Some people say that Satan and demons are a myth invented by primitive, ignorant people. In contrast, the Bible indicates that the devil and his fallen angels are real and pose a threat to the Christian way of life. Paul said that to withstand their attacks, believers must depend on God's strength and use every item that He makes available (Eph. 6:10).

In verse 11, the apostle exhorted his readers to "put on the whole armour of God" so that they could stand firm against all the strategies and tricks of the devil. In other places besides Ephesians, the Bible describes cosmic forces that are at work against God in the world (see Rom. 8:38; 1 Cor. 15:24; Col. 2:15; 1 Pet. 3:22). Moreover, Satan is called the "prince of the power of the air" (Eph. 2:2), and he has this world in his power (see 1 John 5:19). Believers fight against evil spiritual beings who are part of a hierarchy of power in heavenly and earthly places. The ultimate goal of these evil forces is to destroy the relationship between God and humanity. But one of the major themes of Ephesians is that Jesus is the supreme Lord of the universe. Once we believe in Him, we can escape defeat by the ruler of this world (see 1:21; 2:2).

The battle Paul described is not a human one, but rather a supernatural one. It involves a hierarchy of evil rulers and authorities in the unseen world, and wicked spirits in the heavenly realms (Eph. 6:12). The Greek nouns translated "principalites" and "powers" indicate that demons have a certain amount of control and influence at the present stage of history. But of course this power is far less than what belongs to Jesus. The Greek noun rendered "rulers" once indicated those who aspire to world control. In pagan religions, it was often used of idols and especially of the sun, which was considered a deity. So, Paul's use of the term in connection with the phrase "darkness of this world" might have been meant to suggest that while the demons masquerade as ambassadors of light (good), they are in fact agents of darkness (evil; see 2 Cor. 11:4).

The phrase translated the "spiritual wickedness in high places" (Eph. 6:12) reflects the language of astrology in Paul's day. Astrologers taught that demons live in the heavenly bodies, and from there control the destiny of people. The apostle's use of the phrase in this context indicates that believers need not be dominated by demons, but are able to fight against them. It is important for us to recognize that Satan rules a powerful demonic army whose prime objective is to defeat Jesus' followers. In this battle, the devil and his subordinates use whatever devices they have to turn us away from the Lord and back to sin. Christians today are engaged in a spiritual struggle no less fierce than the one that raged in the early years of the church. In fact, our battles are really the continuation of a war begun long ago.

Paul told the Ephesians not to delay preparing for spiritual battle. They should put on the "whole armour of God" (vs. 13) right away. Then they would be ready in the time of evil, that is, when Satan launches his attack (which is certain to come). Paul was convinced that with the right preparation (and of course courageous fighting), his readers would still be standing and retain their ground when the battle was over. According to traditional military doctrine, the army in possession of the field after a battle is the victor.

Having made his plea for preparedness, Paul began describing the six pieces of equipment that the Christian should take into spiritual battle (vss. 14-17). The apostle listed them in the order in which a soldier getting ready for a battle would put them on. The first piece of equipment is the belt of "truth" (vs. 14). A Roman soldier's belt held in his tunic and breastplate and became a place to hang his sword. For Christians, our belt is "truth." This general term might refer to the truth of the gospel and to our truthfulness in everyday life. Conversely, Satan is a liar and hates the truth (see John 8:44; Rev. 12:9).

The second piece of equipment Paul describes is the "breastplate of righteousness" (Eph. 6:14). Roman soldiers wore over the entire front of their torso a large protective plate made of bronze, or, if they were wealthy, of chain mail. The Christian's breastplate is "righteousness." As we draw on the Savior's righteousness, we are able to live devout and holy lives. Also, an upright life is an effective defense against Satan's attacks. Paul didn't specify what the third piece of equipment is, but he was obviously referring to footgear. Roman soldiers wore strong sandals or boots studded with nails for traction while marching. Similarly, Christians are to be shod with the "preparation of the gospel of peace" (vs. 15). This phrase was probably meant to suggest that our peace with the Father, won by the Son, gives us sure footing in our spiritual battle with Satan and His demonic cohorts.

The fourth piece of equipment is the "shield of faith" (vs. 16). Roman soldiers carried large shields made of wood covered with hide and bound with iron. These shields provided effective protection from blows and even from the burning darts fired at them by their enemies. Flaming arrows were often used in sieges of cities. Bows and arrows would effectively hit targets from long range (300–400 yards). If a soldier became terrified of burning darts stuck in his shield, he might throw down his shield and be more vulnerable to attack. Therefore, shields were sometimes dipped in water to extinguish flaming arrows. Faith is more effective than a Roman shield in defending us against Satan's attack, especially as we steadfastly anchor our trust in the Savior (see Heb. 6:19-20).

The fifth piece of equipment is the "helmet of salvation" (Eph. 6:17). Roman soldiers wore helmets of bronze and leather to protect their heads. Also, just as Roman soldiers received their helmets from their armor-bearers to put on, so Christians receive salvation from the Lord to use in their conflict with Satan. We look forward to a time when our salvation is complete and Satan is utterly defeated. The last piece of equipment in the Christian's armory is the "sword of the Spirit." For some reason Paul did not mention the long spear that was the Roman soldier's chief offensive weapon. Instead, the apostle referred to the short two-edged sword Roman legionaries carried. Paul compared this weapon to "the word of God." When Jesus was tempted in the wilderness, He used Scripture as a weapon against Satan. The Spirit can also help us use God's Word against the same foe.

Prayer is not a piece of spiritual armor for believers. We are not to use prayer just when under attack, but rather we are always to keep in touch with God through prayer and receive power and strength from Him. Accordingly, Paul urged his readers to pray "in the Spirit" (vs. 18). This probably means either to pray in communion with the Spirit or to pray in the power of the Spirit (or both). Paul described some qualities associated with prayer in the Spirit. First, it is frequent. We are to pray on all occasions and always keep on "praying." Second, prayer in the Spirit has room for variety. We are to pray "with all prayers and supplications." Third, prayer in the Spirit is well informed.

We are to be watchful, that is, on the lookout for needs. Fourth, prayer in the Spirit is unselfish. We are to pray not only for ourselves, but for all the "saints," meaning for all God's holy people (that is, Christians).

As an example of a saint for whom the Ephesians could pray, Paul offered himself (vss. 19-20). He did not ask his readers to pray for his release from prison. Instead, he requested prayer for a courageous spirit in proclaiming the Gospel while imprisoned (vs. 19). When Paul arrived in Rome as an inmate about A.D. 60, he was not kept in one of the civil or military prisons. He was permitted to rent his own home, to receive visitors, and to preach the Gospel (see Acts 28:30-31). Soldiers of the Praetorian Guard, the emperor's bodyguard unit, took turns watching the apostle while chained to him. Paul was able to share the Good News about Jesus with these soldiers as well as others associated with the apostle's case (see Phil. 1:12-14). The imprisonment lasted about two years. During this period, the apostle wrote Philemon, Colossians, Philippians, and Ephesians.

Ambassadors are usually afforded the privilege of diplomatic immunity from arrest. Even though Paul was "in bonds" (Eph. 6:20), he saw himself as an ambassador for the Messiah. There was no doubt in the apostle's mind that his imprisonment was a God-given opportunity. It would enable Paul to convey the Gospel to officials high in the Roman government—people he would not otherwise have had an opportunity to meet. The emperor might even have heard his case personally. Since the government officials had the power of life and death over the apostle, he naturally felt some anxiety. But he didn't want unease to prevent him from preaching the Good News clearly and powerfully. So his primary prayer request was for fearlessness and reliance upon God when it came time for Paul to witness at the risk of his life.

SUGGESTIONS TO TEACHERS

Paul said that the believers' strength was not found in themselves, for they are not fighting against "flesh and blood" (Eph. 6:12). Rather, the Lord is their source of spiritual strength (vs. 10). When God's people fight the enemy in His strength and not their own, they can be victorious.

1. HOLDING OUR GROUND. In Paul's mind, retreat was not an option. Instead, when faced with an attack from the enemy, believers are to stand fast, wearing the "whole armour of God" (vs. 11). The idea is that Christians should look to their God-given defenses and make sure that they do not lose any ground to Satan.

2. BEING PREPARED. The time to put on God's spiritual armor is not when Satan's arrows begin to fly. Rather, before the battle starts, Christians are to get themselves ready by donning the Lord's protective spiritual gear.

3. MAINTAINING PRAYERFULNESS. Paul couldn't have stressed more strongly the need to put on spiritual armor. However, because it is a largely invisible battle we are in, we might forget at times that we are in a fight at all. Paul's answer for this was prayerfulness, a constant communication between believers and God. Only by remaining in touch with the Father through the Spirit are we kept aware that we have an unseen enemy against whom we must rise up.

4. MAKING PRAYER AN ABSOLUTE PRIORITY. In prayer, we put on the armor God provides. In prayer, we remain aware of our need to keep the armor on. In prayer, we remain ready to do battle in the strength provided by the Spirit. In a war, if communication is cut off for one side, it is doomed to fail in its mission. Similarly, prayer for the believer isn't a badge of piety—it is an absolute priority.

FOR ADULTS

■ **TOPIC:** Always Be Prepared
■ **QUESTIONS:** 1. What should believers do when the devil and his subordinates attack? 2. When is the best time to put on God's spiritual armor? 3. What good is truthfulness when fighting against Satan? 4. Of what value is God's Word in the midst of the battle? 5. When did Paul envision believers praying?

■ **ILLUSTRATIONS:**

The Real Source of Power. In the movies, fighting evil is simply a matter of having the right equipment. But in real life, spiritual warfare involves a far more powerful weapon—faith in God. Anything less, and it is like waving a plastic wand over an empty top hat and expecting "magic" to happen. There's no power in the plastic. It's merely a prop. Only the trained illusionist can take that empty hat and fill it with a live rabbit.

When it comes to combating evil and sin in our world, the real source of power is the sovereign Lord of all creation. So, to be victorious, we must put ourselves in God's hand. When we do, He promises to give us the spiritual tools we need to stand our ground when the day of evil comes.

The Book of Acts tells us that's what happened in ancient Ephesus (19:11-20), especially as "the name of the Lord Jesus" (vs. 17) triumphed over evil. We can witness those same results today.

A Roaring Lion. Paul urged us to "put on the whole armour of God" (Eph. 6:11) so that we would be prepared to "stand against the wiles of the devil." We must not underestimate our foe, who rules over the "darkness of this world" (vs. 12) and oversees "spiritual wickedness in high places."

Similarly, Peter urged us to "be sober" (1 Pet. 5:8) and "vigilant" against our "adversary the devil." The apostle compared Satan to a "roaring lion" who prowls around looking for someone to "devour." The reference is to believers who leave themselves open to the devil's attacks.

In Bible times, the lion roamed in great numbers throughout Palestine, from the

Jordan Valley to the mountains of Judea and Samaria. Therefore, the roar of the lion was a relatively common—and frightening—sound, often mentioned in Scripture (see Job 4:10; Ps. 22:13; Prov. 20:2). Amos probably often heard lions roaring as he guarded his flocks. In his prophecy, he compared the Lord's voice of judgment on Israel and its neighbors to the "roar" (Amos 1:2) of a lion from "Zion."

Because of its ferociousness, speed, and power, the Asiatic lion was also used in Scripture to symbolize might. Judah was compared to a lion by his father, Jacob (see Gen. 49:9). Also, Jesus Himself is referred to as the "Lion of the tribe of Judah" (Rev. 5:5). He enables us to take our "stand" (Eph. 6:11) against Satan's schemes. When we submit ourselves to the Lord, He gives us the ability to "resist the devil" (Jas. 4:7) and experience him fleeing from us.

Finding True Meaning. When Randy and his young wife, Sally, learned they were expecting their first child, the couple knew they had to make significant life changes. Though they won't say specifically what their circumstances were, Randy admits, "We were not living for anyone but ourselves."

Neither Randy nor Sally wanted to raise a child that way, so they began pray "in the Spirit" (Eph. 6:18). They didn't just do this once. Instead, they committed themselves to do so with "all perseverance." The Lord, in His grace, gave the couple discernment in their search for something more than their current situation.

Because Randy had been raised in a churchgoing home, the couple visited a local congregation. The words sounded familiar, but the other attendees didn't seem to believe them. They weren't affected by truths of God's "word" (vs. 17).

So, the couple began visiting other churches, both large and small. After a while, the Spirit led Randy and Sally to what they needed most. The meaning the couple had sought for so long reentered their lives, not through a particular church, but by them renewing and strengthening their personal relationship with the Savior.

Today, Randy and Sally are strong leaders in their church. Also, their now grown children continue to follow Christ. For this couple, and for millions of other believers like them, living for Jesus is what gives existence its true meaning.

For Youth

■ **Topic:** Armed for Battle

■ **Questions:** 1. What does it mean to be strong in the Lord? 2. What are believers supposed to do with the full armor of God? 3. How is it possible for believers to stand firm against the attacks of the evil one? 4. What place does faith have in the midst of spiritual warfare? 5. Why is it important for believers to pray in the Spirit?

ILLUSTRATIONS:

Stand Firm in God's Armor. In Ephesians 6:13, Paul urged us to put on every piece of God's armor so that in the time of evil we will be able to resist our enemy, the devil. As believers, if we don't keep in mind who the real enemy is, we may sometimes begin to wage war on one another, rather than on the true enemy, as the following story shows.

When World War I broke out, the war ministry in London sent a coded message to one of the British outposts in the inaccessible areas of Africa. The message read: "War declared. Arrest all enemy aliens in your district."

The War Ministry received this prompt reply: "Have arrested ten Germans, six Belgians, four Frenchmen, two Italians, three Austrians, and one American. Please advise immediately with whom we're at war."

Hope from Above. Jill was 15 when she got into her parents' liquor cabinet and drank a lot of alcohol. She wound up vomiting, then blacking out. She continued to drink as an escape from what she saw as a miserable daily life. Her life in an upper-middle-class neighborhood in New England hit bottom when she was arrested for drunk driving. She suffered the humiliation of being handcuffed, put into the back of a police cruiser, and taken to jail.

Jill went into an alcoholics' treatment program at her local hospital. From there she began to attend Alcoholics Anonymous (AA) meetings. As she attended the AA meetings, her hope for the future grew. Jill found that hope came from above, not from within a bottle. She followed a course of life outlined by Paul, renounced her destructive behavior, and began to live a more godly life. Now she has a more confident hope for the future.

Help from Their Friends. Four hundred Pittsburgh teenagers sat and interacted with the speakers. A teenager with AIDS, a 15-year-old rape victim, and a pregnant 17-year-old spoke, but this was no talk show. They were part of a large gathering of teens brought together by a non-denominational evangelical organization. The adolescents shared information and workshops on sex, drugs, alcohol, gang violence, eating disorders, and other teen-relevant topics.

Church programs such as this are organized to speak with young people about problems, solutions, bad decisions, and alternatives to destructive behavior. Youth ministers and lay leaders are trained to engage teens in an effective way. Doing so empowers adolescents to talk to other youth and urges them to take responsibility for their lives.

Long before the emergence of such programs, Paul exhorted both young and old to live honorably and responsibly. He urged them to put on the whole armor of God, rather than revel in sin and gratify fleshly desires. The apostle wanted believers to be clothed with divine power, especially as they stood firm against the attacks of the devil and his evil cohorts.

LESSON 1 — MARCH 1

THE LAMB OF GOD

BACKGROUND SCRIPTURE: John 1:29-34
DEVOTIONAL READING: Joel 2:23-27

Key Verse: I saw, and bare record that this is the Son of God. John 1:34.

KING JAMES VERSION

JOHN 1:29 The next day John seeth Jesus coming unto him, and saith, Behold the Lamb of God, which taketh away the sin of the world. 30 This is he of whom I said, After me cometh a man which is preferred before me: for he was before me. 31 And I knew him not: but that he should be made manifest to Israel, therefore am I come baptizing with water. 32 And John bare record, saying, I saw the Spirit descending from heaven like a dove, and it abode upon him. 33 And I knew him not: but he that sent me to baptize with water, the same said unto me, Upon whom thou shalt see the Spirit descending, and remaining on him, the same is he which baptizeth with the Holy Ghost. 34 And I saw, and bare record that this is the Son of God.

NEW REVISED STANDARD VERSION

JOHN 1:29 The next day he saw Jesus coming toward him and declared, "Here is the Lamb of God who takes away the sin of the world! 30 This is he of whom I said, 'After me comes a man who ranks ahead of me because he was before me.' 31 I myself did not know him; but I came baptizing with water for this reason, that he might be revealed to Israel." 32 And John testified, "I saw the Spirit descending from heaven like a dove, and it remained on him. 33 I myself did not know him, but the one who sent me to baptize with water said to me, 'He on whom you see the Spirit descend and remain is the one who baptizes with the Holy Spirit.' 34 And I myself have seen and have testified that this is the Son of God."

Home Bible Readings

Monday, February 23	Genesis 41:38-43	*The Spirit and Joseph*
Tuesday, February 24	Exodus 31:1-6	*The Spirit and Bezalel*
Wednesday, February 25	Numbers 11:11-25	*The Spirit and the Elders*
Thursday, February 26	Numbers 11:26-30	*Would That All Had the Spirit!*
Friday, February 27	John 1:19-23	*Make the Way Straight*
Saturday, February 28	John 1:24-28	*Why Are You Baptizing?*
Sunday, March 1	John 1:29-34	*I Saw the Spirit Descending*

Background

John's Gospel has been described as a drama. In particular, the opening portion is considered the prologue (see 1:1-18). Subsequently, the apostle's account introduced a series of characters, including John the Baptizer (the subject of this week's lesson), Nicodemus, and the Samaritan woman at the well. John skillfully wove Jesus' encounters with these and other individuals into the narrative of the fourth Gospel to show Jesus as the pivotal figure of the universe. For instance, we learn in verses 1 and 2 that Jesus eternally existed before the dawn of Creation and that He, the Father, and the Spirit were inseparable. The text does not say that Jesus, the "Word," is "a god." Instead, we learn that the Son is in every way equal to the other members of the Godhead.

"Word" is *logos* in the Greek. The Greek philosophers used *logos* in various ways, usually to refer to a prevailing rational principle or force that guided the universe. But to John, the *logos* was not an impersonal rational force that remained detached from humanity. John used *logos* to refer to that supreme being who, although equal to the Father and the Spirit, became human and shared in the struggles and hardships of the human race. The person we know as Jesus of Nazareth is the eternal, living Word who spoke all things into existence (see Gen. 1). While John 1:3-4 are clear that we owe our physical existence to the Son, the meaning goes beyond that to include spiritual life. Jesus shines as our ultimate hope (vs. 5). He alone can offer eternal life in a world filled with depravity and death.

The fourth Gospel, in 1:6-8, explains that John the Baptizer was the key person who testified concerning the Messiah as the light of the world. In doing so, John prepared the hearts of people to accept Jesus as the unique Son of God. The primary purpose of the Baptizer's ministry was to point the lost to Jesus for salvation. By the time the fourth Gospel was written (around A.D. 85), some individuals held exaggerated views of Jesus' forerunner. While not directly confronting these people, the apostle made it clear that the Baptizer was simply a witness to the light. As verse 9 declares, Jesus is the genuine light who came to shine God's truth in a world bound in the darkness of sin and superstition.

Because John the Baptizer was slightly older than Jesus and began his ministry earlier, many naturally assumed that John was the greater of the two individuals. People in ancient times gave the older person more respect and honor than the younger one. But the Baptizer reversed that custom by proclaiming that Jesus was far greater than him, since Jesus existed as God the Son for all eternity before He was ever born (vs. 15). In verse 14, the apostle said that Jesus was "full of grace." Then, in verse 16, the apostle expanded on that theme, describing the Messiah as the source of all eternal blessings. God's grace to His people is never depleted. So, while Moses revealed God's justice through the law, Jesus showed us the "grace and truth" (vs. 17) of God Himself.

Notes on the Printed Text

John 1:19-23 indicates that because the Baptizer's preaching attracted so much attention, the Jewish authorities in Jerusalem sent a delegation to Bethany, beyond the Jordan River, where John was ministering (see vs. 28). Their job was to investigate and interrogate this unauthorized and unusual teacher, whom they thought posed a threat to their established traditions. John probably addressed the question of whether he was the Messiah many times without even being asked. Since he clearly and emphatically denied being Israel's Savior, the delegation wondered whether John was Elijah, the renowned Old Testament prophet.

In that day, the Jews believed Elijah would appear in Israel before the coming of the Messiah (see Mal. 4:5-6). After all, Elijah had not died, but had been taken up by a chariot into heaven (see 2 Kings 2:11). The Baptizer's rugged characteristics, ascetic behavior, and fiery temperament probably reminded people of the Elijah they knew from Scripture (see 2 Kings 1:8; Matt. 3:4; Mark 1:6). Based on Deuteronomy 18:15, the Jews also expected a great prophet to appear in connection with the Messiah. Although the Jews of that time were unclear as to whom this spokesperson might be, from the earliest days of the church, Christian scholars have identified Him as the Messiah.

Next, the delegation asked the Baptizer for an answer concerning his identity so they had something specific to report to the authorities in Jerusalem. In response, John applied the words of Isaiah 40:3 to his ministry. That passage pictures someone preparing a road through open and rugged territory so a monarch could travel on a smooth highway. The Baptizer claimed to be nothing more than a voice preparing people for someone who would be much greater than himself. The Pharisees, who were probably part of the original delegation, were unsatisfied with the progress of the interrogation and probed further into the nature of John's ministry. They questioned his authority to baptize, especially since it did not fit with their understanding of the Mosaic law, and no one else had acted in such a dramatic way (John 1:24-25).

John responded to the Pharisees' challenge in a manner that exalted Jesus and diminished John's own importance as the messenger. The other Gospels record that John mentioned the baptism of the Holy Spirit (see Matt. 3:11; Mark 1:8; Luke 3:16), but in John 1:26, the Savior's forerunner moved right into the importance of Jesus after briefly mentioning John's baptism with water. John's words seem to indicate that Jesus was in the crowd that day and listening to all that transpired. While the disciples of a rabbi would perform several menial tasks for their teacher, loosening a sandal was forbidden. The task was reserved for the lowest of slaves, who took off a person's sandals to wash that person's soiled feet (see 13:5). It is significant that the Baptizer's comment—that he was unworthy to be Jesus' slave—is recorded not only in 1:27, but also in the other three Gospels.

The entire Old Testament sacrificial code looked forward to the day when God would provide a "Lamb" (vs. 29) that would atone for the transgressions committed by people. The day after the Jewish delegation's visit, the Baptizer identified Jesus as that Lamb. Some think this refers to the idea of the Passover sacrifice (see Exod. 12:21; 1 Cor. 5:7). Others note that the title also fits the imagery of the suffering Servant described in Isaiah 53, who was to be led like a "lamb" (vs. 7) to the slaughtering block. Jesus, the ultimate suffering Servant, was sacrificed as a lamb at Passover (1 Pet. 1:19). In this way, the Father provided the "once" (Heb. 7:27) for all sacrifice of His Son to expiate the "sins of the whole world" (1 John 2:2).

God had earlier revealed to John that the Lord would identify the Messiah through John's baptizing ministry. Because they were related (possibly cousins; see Luke 1:36), John was most likely already acquainted with Jesus. But it wasn't until John baptized Jesus that John knew for certain that Jesus was the Messiah. In declaring Jesus to be the "Lamb of God" (John 1:29), John was fulfilling his role as the one who heralded the Redeemer. Because He eternally preexisted before His messenger was ever born, Jesus exceeded John in greatness (vs. 30). The Baptizer recognized the amazing privilege that God had given him to make the Messiah known to the people of Israel (vs. 31). Throughout the opening section of the fourth Gospel, the Baptizer was presented as a great prophet. Yet as God's spokesperson, John bore witness to the fact that Jesus would usher in the reign of the Lord (see Matt. 11:9-10; 14:5; 21:26; Luke 1:76; 7:26).

At the Savior's baptism, John saw the Holy Spirit appear in bodily form as a "dove" (John 1:32), descend from the sky, and settle on Jesus (see Matt. 3:16; Mark 1:10; Luke 3:22). In that culture, the dove was considered a symbol of reconciliation with God (see Gen. 8:8,10). Accordingly, the bird became an emblem of peace. The dove also represented tender affection (see Song of Songs 1:15; 2:14). Most likely, the Spirit's presence in the form of a dove signaled that Jesus was inaugurating the promised age of renewal for the people of God (John 1:33). This includes the Messiah's baptism of believers with the Holy Spirit (see Jer. 31:31-34; Joel 2:28-32; Acts 2:16-21). The New Testament reveals that the permanent, indwelling presence of the Spirit in believers started on the day of Pentecost (see Acts 1:5; 2:1-4; 11:15-16 and the Bible commentary in lesson 13) and is now the common experience of all who have repented of their sins and experienced the new birth (see Acts 2:38; 1 Cor. 12:13; Gal. 3:2).

The Spirit's presence as a dove and the Father's pronouncement concerning Jesus (see Matt. 3:16-17; Mark 1:11; Luke 3:22) confirmed His status as the divine, anointed Son (John 1:34).

Accordingly, the Baptizer testified publicly to the people and privately to his disciples that Jesus was the person whom God had chosen to be the Redeemer (see Isa. 42:1). Also, with John's blessing, some of his followers eventually became Jesus' disciples (see vss. 35-39). That said, the Baptizer made such a profound impression on his generation that a group of his followers formed a sect or community that continued long after his death (see Acts 19:1-4). As noted earlier, John was a prophet in the great tradition of Amos and Isaiah. Indeed, John's message echoed the inspired preaching of the greatest of the Lord's spokespersons in Israel and Judah. Furthermore, as the son of Zechariah and Elizabeth, John's priestly family meant that he was related to the aristocracy of Jerusalem. Most importantly, John shouldered his responsibility as Jesus' forerunner with integrity, earnestness, and humility.

SUGGESTIONS TO TEACHERS

Most cult leaders pose as authoritarian figures, who claim to be the only source of truth. In contrast, John the Baptizer's words remind us that any genuine spokesperson for the Father should point others to His Son, the Messiah.

1. BEING A WITNESS FOR JESUS. The testimony of John the Baptizer—undoubtedly one of the greatest religious personalities in history—helps us understand Jesus better. Use the verses in the fourth Gospel referring to the Baptizer's ministry to illustrate what being a witness for Jesus is all about.

2. PREPARING OTHERS TO RECEIVE JESUS. John refused to pose as the Messiah. Instead, the Baptizer simply called himself a road builder for the coming Messiah. Isn't this what it means to prepare others to receive Jesus? Sometimes, we imagine we must argue others into accepting the Messiah. Actually, Jesus expects us to smooth the path for Him to be known through our consistent demonstration of His ways. For instance, being forgiving, acting gently, and promoting justice are among a few virtues worth mentioning to the students.

3. POINTING OTHERS TO JESUS. Rather than call attention to himself, John pointed others to Jesus. Such humility is the road to true greatness. The questions before everyone, including the members of your class, boil down to this: To whom or to what is each person pointing? To himself or herself? To an ideology or a good cause? When others know us as Jesus' followers, do they sense we are pointing to Jesus?

4. PROCLAIMING THAT JESUS COMES FIRST. John was willing to work in the shadow of one greater than himself. Yet, in our "Me first!" culture, few of us are able to take second place cheerfully to anyone, including Jesus. The Baptizer serves as a role model for all of us by insisting that Jesus comes first. John's firm remarks about Jesus as the revealer of God give us the proper perspective for ourselves and our Savior.

For Adults

■ **Topic:** A Reliable Testimony

■ **Questions:** 1. What did John mean when he called Jesus the "Lamb of God" (John 1:29)? 2. In what sense was Jesus, who was born after John, before him in time (vs. 30)? 3. What was the significance of the Spirit's descent in the form of a dove on Jesus (vs. 32)? 4. Why is the baptism of the Holy Spirit an important truth to emphasize? 5. Why is pointing others to Jesus a privilege rather than an obligation?

■ **Illustrations:**

In Second Place. Derrick stood center stage in his royal finery as King Lear and read loudly from his well-thumbed script, "If your diligence be not speedy, I shall be there afore you." Then Jack suddenly stepped in front of Derrick, faced the darkened auditorium, and exclaimed, "I will not sleep, my lord, till I have delivered your letter."

"No, no, no," the director called out from the front row. "Jack, you're playing the Earl of Kent, not King Lear." "So?" asked Jack. "So, don't step in front of the king to deliver your line," responded the director. "Otherwise, you're upstaging the play's central figure."

In theater, it is crucial that minor characters not outshine the more important people on stage. It misleads the audience and can potentially damage the scene. A similar principle applies with believers pointing others to Jesus. Our role is to direct the lost to the Savior and not risk drawing attention to ourselves. As we learn in this week's lesson, John the Baptizer gladly took on that role.

Look to the Living Word. Workers renovating St. Makarios Monastery, a Coptic Christian Church 60 miles north of Cario, Egypt, discovered a coffin. It was buried 18 feet from the altar. A reference in an ancient fifth-century church manuscript noted that these remains were believed to be those of John the Baptizer.

Manuscripts claimed that John's remains were spirited out of Palestine in the fourth century by Christians fleeing Roman persecution. They allegedly brought the body to Alexandria. Investigators, archaeologists, and other experts spent a considerable amount of time, energy, and money studying the perceived treasure trove of the famed biblical figure.

Yet, during his lifetime, the Baptizer humbly and courageously directed the attention of his peers to the Word, who lives and reigns in our midst to this day. In fact, John only claimed to be a voice preparing the way for the suffering Servant. The Baptizer applied the words of Isaiah 40:3 to his ministry to validate his prophetic calling.

Acquiring and Sharing Knowledge. Today's society puts a premium on knowledge. Indeed, futurists state that over the last decade, we have made great strides in moving from an industrial society to post-industrial, cashless society in which information is prized above everything else. The image of this age is no longer the foundry or the assembly line, but digital technology. Cutting-edge mobile devices, not obsolete machinery and steel, are believed to rule the day.

From a theological perspective, the pressing question for the present and the future is not necessarily, "How do we process information?" Instead, it is "How do we acquire knowledge?" and "How do we learn?" Is the focus entirely on high-tech gadgets, or do people still have an important role to play?

Christians have always affirmed the value of sharing knowledge. From the vantage point of Scripture, though, this activity is most poignantly embodied in witnessing. For instance, John the Baptizer shared his knowledge of Jesus through personal testimony. Even today, we have the wonderful privilege of sharing our knowledge of Jesus with others by proclaiming to them the gospel.

FOR YOUTH

■ **TOPIC:** Let Me Point the Way

■ **QUESTIONS:** 1. If you were John, how do you think you would have felt as you saw Jesus coming toward you? 2. What did Jesus do to atone for the world's sins (John 1:29)? 3. How did John's baptism with water help reveal Jesus to the people of Israel (vs. 31)? 4. Why is it difficult to work in the shadow of someone greater than ourselves? 5. In what ways can pointing others to Jesus be a rewarding experience?

■ **ILLUSTRATIONS:**

Whose Way? At a University of Chicago religion class, a student declared, "I want to be like John: a voice in the desert, crying for the outcasts, unmasking the hypocrites, and showing sinners the way to righteousness!" Another student echoed the sentiment: "Please, not Jesus! John is my man!"

These remarks represent a desire for a revolutionary leader. But was the Baptizer really such a revolutionary? Or was John the one who humbly pointed to a far more effective leader: Jesus, who is an avenue beyond mere social change? Scripture reveals that John directed the attention of others away from himself to the "Lamb of God" (John 1:29). The Baptizer also spotlighted Jesus' messiahship.

John submitted to Jesus' lordship and His loving way. Jesus' way is based on love, not rebellion. Here we discover that both John and Jesus were far more than social activists.

Achieving a Smooth Transition. In a baton race, the winning team is comprised of several people, but only one athlete crosses the finish line with baton in hand. The win is a team effort, but the crowd's focus is on the last runner.

The spread of Christianity is similar. The race is not dependent on one luminary, such as John the Baptizer. Each "runner," giving his or her best, hands off the spiritual "baton" (the gospel) to the next person. The handoff is crucial. If any believer is not ready for the exchange, the "baton" drops. But if each participant runs well, remains alert, and stays ready, the transition is smooth.

John the Baptizer was a great example of someone who had an accurate perspective of the purpose of his life and ministry. He understood that his role was important, not in and of itself, but because it pointed to Jesus. And John faithfully fulfilled his purpose as one who humbly prepared the way for the Lord Jesus.

Bearing Witness. John the Baptizer's mission was to direct the attention of his peers to the Savior. Even though John played a crucial part in preparing the world for Jesus' coming, John was able to recognize when it was time to pull back so that Jesus' glory could be seen in all its fullness.

In March 1997, acclaimed actor Desi Arnaz Giles was hired to play the role of Jesus in a Passion play in Union City, New Jersey. The theater received cancellations and Giles received death threats from people who were incensed that he would play the role of Jesus. The reason: Giles is African American.

At the Park Performing Arts Center, Giles and a white actor alternated in the play depicting Jesus' final days. According to the *Associated Press*, word spread that an African-American actor was one of the two taking the part of Jesus. Two groups cancelled tickets for a performance featuring Giles. And another rescheduled for a day when the white actor was set to perform. Later, Giles received additional threats on his life for assuming the role.

Giles, however, calmly and courageously went on with the part, calling it the "most important role in my life . . . I will never do anything more important than this." When asked about the possibility of being murdered by racists who were opposed to his playing the role of Jesus, Giles showed that he was prepared to bear witness to his faith as a devout Christian: "Should someone clip me during a performance, don't cry for me. Just rejoice, because I'm ready to go home."

LESSON 2 — MARCH 8

THE PROMISED ADVOCATE

BACKGROUND SCRIPTURE: John 14:15-26
DEVOTIONAL READING: Psalm 23

Key Verse: The Comforter, which is the Holy Ghost, whom the Father will send in my name, he shall teach you all things, and bring all things to your remembrance, whatsoever I have said unto you. John 14:26.

KING JAMES VERSION

JOHN 14:15 If ye love me, keep my commandments. 16 And I will pray the Father, and he shall give you another Comforter, that he may abide with you for ever; 17 Even the Spirit of truth; whom the world cannot receive, because it seeth him not, neither knoweth him: but ye know him; for he dwelleth with you, and shall be in you.

18 I will not leave you comfortless: I will come to you. 19 Yet a little while, and the world seeth me no more; but ye see me: because I live, ye shall live also. 20 At that day ye shall know that I am in my Father, and ye in me, and I in you. 21 He that hath my commandments, and keepeth them, he it is that loveth me: and he that loveth me shall be loved of my Father, and I will love him, and will manifest myself to him. 22 Judas saith unto him, not Iscariot, Lord, how is it that thou wilt manifest thyself unto us, and not unto the world? 23 Jesus answered and said unto him, If a man love me, he will keep my words: and my Father will love him, and we will come unto him, and make our abode with him. 24 He that loveth me not keepeth not my sayings: and the word which ye hear is not mine, but the Father's which sent me.

25 These things have I spoken unto you, being yet present with you. 26 But the Comforter, which is the Holy Ghost, whom the Father will send in my name, he shall teach you all things, and bring all things to your remembrance, whatsoever I have said unto you.

NEW REVISED STANDARD VERSION

JOHN 14:15 "If you love me, you will keep my commandments. 16 And I will ask the Father, and he will give you another Advocate, to be with you forever. 17 This is the Spirit of truth, whom the world cannot receive, because it neither sees him nor knows him. You know him, because he abides with you, and he will be in you.

18 "I will not leave you orphaned; I am coming to you. 19 In a little while the world will no longer see me, but you will see me; because I live, you also will live. 20 On that day you will know that I am in my Father, and you in me, and I in you. 21 They who have my commandments and keep them are those who love me; and those who love me will be loved by my Father, and I will love them and reveal myself to them." 22 Judas (not Iscariot) said to him, "Lord, how is it that you will reveal yourself to us, and not to the world?" 23 Jesus answered him, "Those who love me will keep my word, and my Father will love them, and we will come to them and make our home with them. 24 Whoever does not love me does not keep my words; and the word that you hear is not mine, but is from the Father who sent me.

25 "I have said these things to you while I am still with you. 26 But the Advocate, the Holy Spirit, whom the Father will send in my name, will teach you everything, and remind you of all that I have said to you."

Home Bible Readings

Monday, March 2	Jeremiah 8:18-22	Is There No Balm in Gilead?
Tuesday, March 3	Lamentations 1:17-21	No One to Comfort Me
Wednesday, March 4	Isaiah 40:1-10	Here Is Your God!
Thursday, March 5	Psalm 119:49-64	This Is My Comfort
Friday, March 6	Psalm 23	The Shepherd's Comfort
Saturday, March 7	John 15:18-26	When the Advocate Comes
Sunday, March 8	John 14:15-26	An Advocate with You Forever

Background

During the Last Supper, Jesus encouraged His followers to calm their troubled hearts. The way to do this was to put their trust in the Father as well as in the Son (John 14:1). It is remarkable that Jesus focused on comforting His followers rather than dealing with His own needs. The treachery of Judas and the fickleness of the rest of the disciples did not prevent the Savior from remaining a calming presence among them. Jesus next spoke about heaven, perhaps to further ease the minds of His followers. He referred to heaven as a large house—belonging to His Father—that has plenty of room. Though Jesus was leaving the disciples, He was going there to prepare a place for them. Jesus told the disciples that if this were not so, He would not have made this promise to them (vs. 2). The pledge, however, was true, and so the disciples could count on Jesus one day returning to bring them back with Him to heaven (vs. 3).

Throughout Jesus' public ministry He had been teaching these men what it meant to be His followers. Now He told them that they should know the way to the place where He was going. As they followed that way, they would end up there with Him (vs. 4). Thomas openly expressed his confusion, and he was probably speaking for the other 10 as well. They did not know where Jesus was going, and they did not know the way (vs. 5). How could they? Had not Jesus already said that where He was going, they could not come (13:33)? They were dumbfounded. Jesus' reply to Thomas is the most profound "I am" declaration in the fourth Gospel. The Savior not only identified who He was, but also made it clear that He is the only possible path to God (14:6). When Thomas asked Jesus the way, Jesus did not hand him a road map and give him directions. Jesus told all of them that He Himself is the way to God. In a few hours some of His followers would see Jesus hanging on a cross and would wonder how this could be true. After His resurrection, they would understand that as the one who died for their sins, He is the only link between God and repentant sinners.

Furthermore, Jesus reminded His disciples that He is in the Father and the Father is in Him. After living with Jesus and experiencing the life He lived, the Eleven should have taken Him at His word. But even if they could not at this point, they could at least base their belief on the miraculous signs they had witnessed (vs. 11). Jesus was presenting faith based on miracles as second best. The supreme foundation of faith is

Jesus' proven character, especially when a wished-for miracle did not appear. Jesus told the disciples that those who believed in Him would do even greater things than what He had been doing (vs. 12). Jesus was not saying that they would possess greater powers than Him or that they would perform greater miracles. Evidently Jesus was talking about the mighty works of conversion. Whereas Jesus' ministry was primarily confined to Galilee and Judea, they would take the gospel to distant lands. Yet they could do none of this unless Jesus first returned to the Father.

According to verse 13, when we make our request known to God through Jesus' name, the Savior Himself would do it. Of course, Jesus was not providing a magical formula to be used as though one were bidding a genie to grant a wish. Nor did it mean that Jesus would always fulfill the request in the way His followers desired. Moreover, Jesus was referring to requests whose primary purpose is to glorify God, and so are in line with God's will. Jesus' statements do not limit the power of prayer. Instead, they require the petitioner to make his or her request consistent with the character of the Son and in accordance with the will of the Father (vs. 14). Since we pray in Jesus' name, He promised that He would do it. Accordingly, Jesus would be the one who is glorifying His heavenly Father. The two not only are one, but they also bring glory to each other. Jesus continually stressed that love was integral to the disciples' relationships with each other, with Him, and with the Father.

NOTES ON THE PRINTED TEXT

In the final hours before Jesus died on the cross, He said that if His disciples truly loved Him, they would obey His teachings (John 14:15). He did not demand obedience to prove our love for Him. Rather, obedience would be a natural result of loving Him. Morality for the ancient Hebrews was not an abstract concept disconnected from the present. Rather, it signified ethical imperatives concerning how people of faith should live. As an encouragement to those who would love and obey Jesus, He promised that His disciples would have the indwelling of the Holy Spirit. The third person of the Trinity would come and make His home in believers so that their love could be clearly defined and their obedience could be carefully directed. The Greek noun rendered "Comforter" (vs. 16) literally means "a person summoned to one's aid" and originally referred to a legal advocate. Since Jesus did not want to leave His followers alone in this world, He would ask His Father to give them another Helper.

The Spirit would serve as the believers' adviser, advocate, mediator, and intercessor. Expressed differently, the Spirit comes to the believers' aid to enable them to meet every challenge to their faith. As the Spirit of truth, He reveals the truth about God, shows what is true, and leads believers into all truth (vs. 17). In these ways, the Spirit remains ever present to help believers understand, accept, and apply what the Redeemer commanded. Jesus was confident that the Father would grant His request and send the Holy Spirit. Though nonbelievers would reject the Spirit, Jesus' disciples would know the Spirit intimately. At Pentecost, Jesus' prayer request was answered. Today, the Spirit takes up permanent residence in believers, and is always available to instruct, convict, and lead.

Jesus assured His disciples that He would not forsake them as helpless as orphans (vs. 18). In fact, after His death and resurrection, He would appear to them several times before His ascension into heaven. These appearances would be only for believers, in order to strengthen their faith and persuade them that He would never leave them alone in this world (vs. 19). After seeing the resurrected Lord, they would learn that the power that raised Him from the dead would be living in them. Since the ever-living Messiah conquered death, they too would be victorious over death through faith in Him. At that time, they would realize that the Son is indeed in the Father and that there is a mutual indwelling of the Son and believers (vs. 20).

Sixty years after John saw Jesus crucified, buried, and ascended into heaven, the Roman authorities exiled the apostle to the island of Patmos (see Rev. 1:9). John suddenly saw the Lord again. This time, however, Jesus did not look the same as He did when John leaned against Him at the Last Supper. Once again, here was his closest friend—but now exalted and honored as the glorified Son of God. The Messiah encouraged John not to be afraid, for He is "the first and the last" (vs. 17). This is a divine title that appears elsewhere in Scripture in reference to the Lord (see Isa. 41:4; 44:6; 48:12). It means essentially the same thing as the title the "Alpha and Omega" (Rev. 1:8).

In John 14:21, Jesus emphasized that it is not enough for believers simply to have affection for Him in their hearts. True love for Him is demonstrated when they keep His commandments in their daily lives. When believers demonstrate this kind of love for Jesus, they enjoy three specific blessings: the love of the Father, the love of the Son, and a deeper knowledge of Jesus. The Redeemer's statements puzzled one of His disciples. His first name was "Judas" (vs. 22), though he was not "Iscariot," that is the disciple who earlier had left to betray the Savior (see 13:30). The faithful disciple named Judas asked Jesus why He would show Himself to the Eleven but not to everyone (14:22). Judas probably voiced the confusion of all the disciples, who expected Jesus to reveal Himself before the entire world as the messianic King of the Jews. How, then, could Jesus claim such glory by revealing Himself to only a select few?

Very little is known about the other disciple named Judas. The Gospel writers listed him as one of Jesus' 12 apostles. He was probably the one whom Matthew and Mark called "Thaddaeus" (Matt. 10:3; Mark 3:18). Luke twice mentioned him literally as "Judas of James" (Luke 6:16; Acts 1:13), which could mean that he was the brother of James (as the KJV translates it) or perhaps a close relative of James the Less. John is the only Gospel writer who made Judas' presence known through a specific action or dialogue (John 14:22). Early church tradition simply notes that he founded a congregation at Edessa in Syria.

Jesus did not answer Judas' question directly, for the disciples would learn the ultimate purpose of Jesus' earthly ministry soon enough. He was more concerned about their relationship with Him. For a third time He stated that if they loved Him, they would obey His teachings. And once again the Son said that the Father loves those who truly love Him. In addition, both the Father and the Son would come to believers and make their home with them (vs. 23). In contrast, those who did not obey Jesus' teaching showed that they really did not love Him. The words the Son spoke came directly from the Father. So, to accept the Son is to accept the Father, and to reject the Son is to reject the Father (vs. 24). There was no middle ground.

Within a few hours Jesus was about to leave His close friends and begin His agonizing journey to the cross. But first He wanted to encourage the Eleven while He still had time to be alone with them. Much of "these things" (vs. 25) we would not know without John's record. Just as the Father had sent His Son into the world, He would also send the Spirit to this world to dwell within Jesus' followers. This Advocate would instruct believers by helping them recall all that Jesus taught. Having been sent in Jesus' name, the Spirit would officially represent Jesus in His behalf (vs. 26).

SUGGESTIONS TO TEACHERS

According to a survey done by a Christian research company called the Barna Group, a majority of adults do not believe the Holy Spirit exists. Six out of ten agreed that the "Spirit is a symbol of God's presence or power, but is not a living entity." Possibly this is the view that some in your class hold. So, your task this Sunday is a long-overdue study of the Spirit!

1. OBEYING JESUS' COMMANDS. Loyalty to Jesus means doing what He wants. He declared that if we truly love Him, we would heed His "commandments" (John 14:15). This verse impels us to put Jesus' concerns first. Beloved friends are those we think so highly of that we always want to remember their interests. This is what Jesus expects of us.

2. EXPERIENCING THE SPIRIT'S PRESENCE. Believers who live in daily obedience to Jesus' teachings will find that the Spirit blesses them with His abiding presence. In contrast, those who claim that they never realize the strengthening nearness of the Spirit usually have refused to abide by the "truth" (vs. 17) He upholds.

3. REMAINING CONCEALED TO THE WORLD. Unsaved humanity fails to appreciate the Spirit's presence and power. Those centered on themselves, rather than the Lord, will never know the goodness or recognize the nearness of the Spirit. But the community of faith is assured that the Spirit abides with them. Put differently, we in the body of Christ are blessed with an awareness of the Spirit's power that will always seem incomprehensible to outsiders.

4. RECEIVING THE SPIRIT'S COMFORT. Jesus assured His disciples that He would not leave them "comfortless" (vs. 18). As members of Jesus' own beloved family, we are assured that we will never be abandoned. The Father and the Son have sent us the Spirit to provide His caring, supportive presence. Consider taking some class time to discuss a few life situations in which the students might be inclined to think that they are helpless and alone. Also, be sure to remind them that the Spirit will never abandon them as "orphans" (so to speak) in the world.

FOR ADULTS

■ **TOPIC:** A Comforter and Much More
■ **QUESTIONS:** 1. Why did Jesus connect love for Him with obedience to Him? 2. In what sense is the Spirit the believer's Helper? 3. How is the Spirit the source of truth? 4. Why is it important for believers to affirm Jesus as the source of their eternal life? 5. What are some ways believers can share Jesus' compassion with the lost?

■ **ILLUSTRATIONS:**

A Comforting Advocate. The *Alliance Weekly* recounts the efforts of a missionary in Africa to translate the local dialect into a written form in order to produce the New Testament in that tribe's language. He was frustrated at times, especially when he couldn't find a tribal word to express the consoling ministry of the Holy Spirit.

One day, after three years of searching for just the right phrase, the missionary heard an elderly chief refer several times to a man as "Nsenga-Mukwashi" during a village proceeding. So, after the court closed, the missionary asked the chieftain what that term meant. The aging leader smiled and explained that "Nsenga-Mukwashi" was the title given to the one whose duty it was to represent all the people of the village and to stand up for them when they were in any trouble.

On that particular day, the "Nsenga-Mukwashi" had eloquently pleaded the cause of an old woman who had been unjustly treated. "My people see him as a comforting advocate," said the chief. Immediately, the missionary recognized that here was the term he could use to describe the Holy Spirit's work in the lives of believers. It beautifully expressed the truth that God's Spirit is both the Advocate and Comforter for Jesus' followers.

Stoking the Flames. It seems that every year, there's some prediction that the world is going to end. For example, in 2013, the *Punjab Newswire* reported that a prominent Indian scientist named Vasudev Moolrajani forecasted "mass destruction on the earth." The litany of catastrophic events included an "earthquake," a "typhoon," a "volcano burst," and a "strong solar storm." Yet, despite Moolrajani's assertions, the world did not come to an end.

Those who claim that the world is going to be destroyed by either natural or human forces make their assertions without the Spirit of God. In John Bunyan's *Pilgrim's Progress*, Christian once saw a fire burning brightly despite the water being thrown on it by a man who stood nearby. When Christian wondered why the fire was not extinguished, he was shown a man behind the wall who cast oil upon the fire.

Sometimes, it seems, the forces of evil will put out the fires of righteousness on this earth. But it is reassuring to know that the Holy Spirit continually pours everlasting "oil" upon the fires of God to keep them burning.

The Wind of the Spirit Blowing. In the Greek New Testament, as well as the Hebrew Old Testament, the word for *Spirit* is also translated in other contexts as *wind*. Some people in Washington, D.C., once discovered that the Spirit seemed to blow a surprising message in the form of a high wind.

Shortly after the Civil War, some women in America's capital decided to decorate the graves in Arlington Cemetery on the occasion of the first Memorial Day. They asked the War Department for permission. Consent was given, but they were told there were 300 graves of Confederate soldiers in the cemetery, and no flowers must be put on them.

That night there was a great windstorm, and the wind blew the flowers from the Union graves into the Confederate section of the cemetery and decorated the forbidden graves. Ever since that night, the graves in Arlington Cemetery have been decorated, regardless of what soldier lay beneath the headstone.

FOR YOUTH

■ **TOPIC:** Help Is on the Way

■ **QUESTIONS:** 1. What is the evidence that a believer truly loves Jesus? 2. How does the truth of the Spirit's abiding presence encourage you? 3. Why would Jesus not leave His followers helpless as orphans? 4. What are some ways you have recently experienced Jesus' love? 5. Why is it important for believers to know they belong to the Father and the Son?

■ **ILLUSTRATIONS:**

An Ever-Present Comforter. Students at a large city high school were upset because the adviser for their student council was always a student teacher who took the job for extra pay. The adolescents argued that there was never any continuity. Each year brought new leadership, which lasted only nine months and then changed. All programs halted. The students wondered why they couldn't have a staff member who would not leave them.

Like these students, many youth want an advocate who will not leave them in the lurch. Many want someone who will be with them for a long period so that there will not be changes or problems. Jesus promised the Spirit—the "Comforter" (John 14:16)—would always be present with His disciples. Since Pentecost, that promise has been fulfilled!

The Voice of God's Spirit. She was a 12-year-old at Franklin Graham's crusade in Cape Town, South Africa. She listened intently to every word the son of Billy Graham spoke. When Franklin asked those in the crowd who wished to commit themselves to Christ to come forward, the girl left her seat. She had heard the voice of God's Spirit calling her.

Are you sensitive to the voice of God's Spirit summoning you? Jesus described Him as the "Spirit of truth" (John 14:17), who would testify to each of us. Are you receptive to the comforting, supportive presence of the Spirit in your life? If not, be tuned in as that 12-year-old girl in Cape Town.

The Spirit's Sustaining Presence. Logan (not his real name) was an honor student at a high school on the east coast of America. He was captain of the forensics team, founder of the history and philosophy club, a National Merit Scholar, and was identified by the local newspaper as an All-Star Achiever. He had received a scholarship to attend a prestigious university, where he hoped to study politics, graduate, and become a speechwriter and a campaign organizer.

However, in Logan's senior year of high school, he was forced out of sports when a cancerous tumor was removed from his nasal passage. For seven years after he graduated, he underwent chemotherapy and radiation therapy. Also, during this time, Logan won numerous speaking awards. Sadly, though, the cancer could not be arrested. His friends, former high school principal, family, and others gathered for a special commencement ceremony in the hospital. Four weeks later, Logan died.

At the memorial service, some adults spoke about the joy that was to be remembered as Logan entered eternal life. However, most of the young people sat with tears on their cheeks, aware only that a friend had died. His death seemed to bring only separation and pain, not joy as the religious leaders stated.

Can you identify with those students? Jesus' disciples could. They had heard Jesus speak about His death and how His departure would usher in the presence of the Holy Spirit. Still, the news was initially disquieting. After a while, though, the disciples realized the value of having the sustaining presence of their "Comforter" (John 14:16), the "Spirit of truth" (vs. 17).

LESSON 3 — MARCH 15

THE SPIRIT OF TRUTH

BACKGROUND SCRIPTURE: John 16:4b-15
DEVOTIONAL READING: 1 Samuel 3:1-10

Key Verse: I tell you the truth; It is expedient for you that I go away: for if I go not away, the Comforter will not come unto you; but if I depart, I will send him unto you. John 16:7.

KING JAMES VERSION

JOHN 16:4 But these things have I told you, that when the time shall come, ye may remember that I told you of them. And these things I said not unto you at the beginning, because I was with you. 5 But now I go my way to him that sent me; and none of you asketh me, Whither goest thou? 6 But because I have said these things unto you, sorrow hath filled your heart.

7 Nevertheless I tell you the truth; It is expedient for you that I go away: for if I go not away, the Comforter will not come unto you; but if I depart, I will send him unto you. 8 And when he is come, he will reprove the world of sin, and of righteousness, and of judgment: 9 Of sin, because they believe not on me; 10 Of righteousness, because I go to my Father, and ye see me no more; 11 Of judgment, because the prince of this world is judged. 12 I have yet many things to say unto you, but ye cannot bear them now. 13 Howbeit when he, the Spirit of truth, is come, he will guide you into all truth: for he shall not speak of himself; but whatsoever he shall hear, that shall he speak: and he will shew you things to come. 14 He shall glorify me: for he shall receive of mine, and shall shew it unto you. 15 All things that the Father hath are mine: therefore said I, that he shall take of mine, and shall shew it unto you.

NEW REVISED STANDARD VERSION

JOHN 16:4 But I have said these things to you so that when their hour comes you may remember that I told you about them.

"I did not say these things to you from the beginning, because I was with you. 5 But now I am going to him who sent me; yet none of you asks me, 'Where are you going?' 6 But because I have said these things to you, sorrow has filled your hearts. 7 Nevertheless I tell you the truth: it is to your advantage that I go away, for if I do not go away, the Advocate will not come to you; but if I go, I will send him to you. 8 And when he comes, he will prove the world wrong about sin and righteousness and judgment: 9 about sin, because they do not believe in me; 10 about righteousness, because I am going to the Father and you will see me no longer; 11 about judgment, because the ruler of this world has been condemned.

12 "I still have many things to say to you, but you cannot bear them now. 13 When the Spirit of truth comes, he will guide you into all the truth; for he will not speak on his own, but will speak whatever he hears, and he will declare to you the things that are to come. 14 He will glorify me, because he will take what is mine and declare it to you. 15 All that the Father has is mine. For this reason I said that he will take what is mine and declare it to you.

Home Bible Readings

Monday, March 9	Proverbs 29:12-18	Where There Is No Prophecy
Tuesday, March 10	Isaiah 29:8-14	The Lord Has Closed Your Eyes
Wednesday, March 11	1 Samuel 3:1-10	Your Servant Is Listening
Thursday, March 12	1 Samuel 3:11-21	A Trustworthy Prophet
Friday, March 13	Psalm 31:1-8	I Commit My Spirit
Saturday, March 14	John 4:21-26	Worship in Spirit and Truth
Sunday, March 15	John 16:4b-15	The Spirit of Truth

Background

John 15 and 16 record additional farewell statements Jesus made to the Eleven in the upper room (see 13:1; 14:31). In 15:1-17, we find Jesus' well-known discourse about being the true vine. He stressed the importance of His disciples living in vital union with Him, obeying His commands, bearing abundant spiritual fruit, and loving one another. This kind of love was demonstrated by a willingness to lay down one's life for a friend (vs. 13). Indeed, Jesus did this very thing for humankind when He freely subjected Himself to death on the cross. Jesus knew His disciples needed each other's love because of the intense suffering that lay ahead for them (vs. 17).

There was a striking contrast between the love of believers and the hatred of non-believers (vs. 18). The world loved those who either renounced the Messiah or were indifferent to His commands. Resistance to the Son or apathy toward Him was an indication of allegiance to the world. Those who followed the Savior did not belong to the world, for Jesus had chosen them and set them apart from the world. The world hated those whom the Messiah had chosen because the world had lost its power over them and could no longer control them (vs. 19). Jesus told His disciples that allegiance to Him brought persecution and peace—never just one or the other. He further explained that those who identified with Him would suffer because their persecutors did not know God (vs. 21).

Notes on the Printed Text

Jesus knew that after His ascension, the Eleven would undergo terrible persecution. He also knew they would be expelled from the synagogues and branded as traitors to the Jewish faith (see John 9:22; 12:42). In fact, some would even die at the hands of those who, in their misguided zeal, thought they were serving God (16:1-2). So that Jesus' disciples would not falter in their commitment to Him, He revealed these truths to them the day before His arrest, trial, and execution. When Jesus spoke about the ignorance of His enemies, He was not referring to intellectual knowledge. His adversaries had seen His miracles and listened to His teachings. Jesus had in mind knowledge that comes from being in an intimate relationship with Him and the Father. This type of knowledge was profoundly absent in the hearts of Jesus' detractors (vs. 3).

On the eve of Jesus' crucifixion, He now shared these important truths with the Eleven so that when the events He foretold occurred, they would recall His warning and be prepared to act in a godly manner (vs. 4).

Jesus had not previously shared with His disciples important truths about the world's hatred, since His presence was sufficient to strengthen their faith. While He was with the Eleven, His enemies had primarily attacked Him. However, when Jesus left, the situation would change dramatically. His foes would direct their enmity toward His followers. When that time came, the disciples would be able to recall Jesus' warning and remain unwavering in their devotion to Him.

Jesus had mentioned several times that He was returning to His Father. For instance, earlier during Jesus' farewell discourse, Peter had asked, "Lord, whither goest thou?" (13:36). Then, not long after, Thomas stated, "Lord, we know not whither thou goest" (14:5). Even though the Eleven had been distressed about their Lord's leaving them, on the eve of His crucifixion, they were not really concerned about His destination (16:5). Otherwise, they would have pressed the issue to determine the reasons for His departure, which they did not. Instead, they were worried about what would become of themselves without Him. Here we see that when Christians become too focused on their own fates, they can lose sight of Jesus' ultimate purpose.

The thought of being separated from their Lord deeply saddened the disciples (vs. 6). Jesus said, however, that His leaving was in their best interest. Unless He returned to the Father, He could not send the "Comforter" (vs. 7) to be with them. As was noted in last week's lesson, the Greek noun rendered "Comforter" literally means "a person summoned to one's aid" and originally referred to a legal advocate. Only the Holy Spirit, through His abiding presence, could transform the disciples into the image of Christ. In addition, the Spirit would provide them with the guidance and power to proclaim the gospel throughout the world. Even today, it is only by the Spirit that believers can accomplish all the ministry that Jesus has prepared for them to undertake.

The Holy Spirit does not limit His involvement to believers. According to John 16:8, the Spirit also acts as a prosecutor to bring about the world's conviction. The verb the apostle used to describe the convicting work of the Spirit can be translated "to prove wrong." The Greeks used this term to describe the cross-examination of a person who either acknowledged personal guilt or was convinced of the weakness of his or her defense. Both meanings seem to apply in John's text. The Spirit does not merely accuse the world of transgression, but also presents indisputable proof of the world's sinfulness. He establishes the Father's case against unbelievers by putting forward evidence in three different areas: sin, righteousness, and judgment.

In verse 9, Jesus clarified that the reason the Spirit convicts the world about sin is because humanity refuses to trust in the Son. This implies that the central sin of pagan humanity is unbelief, a truth that is stressed time and again in the Gospels. Furthermore, in verse 10, Jesus explained that the Spirit convicted the world about

God's righteousness because the latter was manifested in the Son. His return to the Father vindicated His character and established Him as the standard of all integrity (see Rom. 1:4; 1 Tim. 3:16). When the Son returned to the Father, He was no longer physically visible to the disciples and the world. It was now the Spirit's responsibility to prove that the unsaved were wrong about the nature and source of divine righteousness.

In John 16:11, Jesus revealed that the Spirit convicted the world of the coming judgment because God has already condemned Satan, the prince of this world. In fact, Jesus' death on the cross and resurrection from the tomb sealed Satan's defeat. Since unsaved humanity has followed the "prince of this world" (see Luke 10:18; 2 Cor. 4:4; Eph. 2:2), the unsaved stood condemned with him. Jesus revealed in John 12:31 that Satan and his demonic cohorts cannot escape divine judgment. Likewise, Colossians 2:15 discloses that the Father, through the crucifixion of His Son, publicly declared the divine intent of judging sinners and their iniquity. According to 1 Corinthians 15:54-57 and Hebrews 2:14-15, even death itself stands condemned as a result of the atoning sacrifice of the Son at Calvary.

The purpose for the coming of the Holy Spirit was not only to convict the world of its guilt, but also to guide Jesus' disciples into a comprehensive understanding of "all truth" (John 16:13) concerning salvation. Jesus wanted to share these truths with His friends, but He knew that what the Spirit would later convey to them would be too much for them presently to "bear" (vs. 12). Jesus might have meant that this knowledge was too difficult for them to understand, or too difficult to emotionally absorb, or perhaps both. Following Pentecost, the Spirit—who is the source of "truth" (vs. 13) and bears witness to it—would help Jesus' disciples understand the significance of His ministry, death, resurrection, and exaltation (see 1:14, 18; 14:6). The Spirit never worked independently from the Father and the Son. The Spirit would pass along to Jesus' followers whatever He gave to the Spirit.

Just as Jesus glorified His heavenly Father during His earthly ministry, the primary function of the Holy Spirit's ministry was to glorify the Son (16:14). He did this by taking Jesus' teachings and making them known to His followers. Anything the Son conveyed to the Spirit was given to the Son by His Father (vs. 15). This should not be surprising, for there is unhindered communion, concert, and cooperation among the three Persons of the Godhead. Finally, Jesus told His disciples that soon He would be leaving them, but a little later they would see Him again (vs. 16). Jesus was alluding to His imminent arrest, trial, execution, and burial. During that time of adversity, they would abandon Him and not see Him. Then, after Jesus' resurrection, He would appear to them several times before His ascension into heaven.

Admittedly, some think the phrase "[in] a little while" refers either to the coming of the Spirit following the ascension of the Son or to the Messiah's second advent. But, as 14:19 and 16:22 suggest (see also 7:33; 12:35; 13:33), it is more likely that 16:16 is referring to Jesus' post-resurrection appearances to His disciples. Indeed,

Scripture reveals that He manifested Himself to them several times before His ascension into heaven (see Matt. 28; Mark 16; Luke 24; John 20–21; Acts 1:3-8; 9:1-19; 1 Cor. 9:1; 15:5-7). Jesus' statement about departing, returning, and going to the Father perplexed His disciples (John 16:17). They especially struggled to make sense of His words recorded in verses 10 and 16, which refer to His ascension and crucifixion, respectively. While Jesus had not connected these two events, His followers nonetheless considered them to be linked. Their desire to understand the Savior prompted them to keep on repeating fragmentary portions of His statements (vs. 18). Jesus, of course, was receptive to their desire to grasp the significance of His words.

SUGGESTIONS TO TEACHERS

For many Christians, the Holy Spirit is the least understood of the three Persons of the Trinity. Yet the Spirit is the one who dwells within believers and wants to teach and guide them. Through Him, your students can understand Scripture more clearly and be strengthened in their spiritual growth and service.

1. SENDING THE SPIRIT. Jesus' disciples were filled with "sorrow" (John 16:6) over His upcoming departure. Yet He said it was to their advantage that He return to heaven (by way of the cross). After His ascension, He would send the Spirit to the disciples, who would be with them wherever they went. Even today, the Spirit is able to be with your class members anywhere.

2. CONVICTING UNBELIEVERS. The Spirit would work not only in believers, but also in the world. He would convict people of their sin, of God's righteous standard (as seen in Jesus), and of a future time of judgment (vs. 8). This conviction would cause unbelievers to be so aware of their sin that they could no longer ignore it or dismiss it as just part of their human nature. The Spirit can use believers today to help their lost peers learn that they have rejected the Savior, that faith in Him is the only way to be right with the Father, and that Satan (along with all the wicked) is condemned by God (vss. 9-11).

3. LEADING JESUS' DISCIPLES. Jesus had many more truths to tell His disciples, but they were not ready to understand and apply these truths (vs. 12). So, He promised that the Spirit, who is the source of all truth, would lead the disciples into a fuller comprehension of truth (vs. 13). Similarly, today the Spirit is the believers' faithful and trustworthy guide in clarifying for them the truths of the gospel.

4. TEACHING JESUS' DISCIPLES. Jesus declared that the Spirit would not present His own ideas. Instead, He would disclose what He had received from the Son (vs. 14). The Spirit would tell the disciples only what He had heard, much as Jesus had told them only what He had heard from the Father (see 7:16). Emphasize that the Spirit remains present to translate the truths of the Father and the Son to the lives and circumstances of your students.

For Adults

■ **Topic:** Sorrow Turns to Joy

■ **Questions:** 1. What was the nature of the warning Jesus gave to the Eleven? 2. What are some ways you have seen the convicting ministry of the Spirit at work in the lives of unbelievers? 3. Why do you think unbelievers refuse to trust in Jesus for salvation? 4. In what ways does the Spirit guide believers into "all truth" (John 16:13) concerning the Son? 5. Why does the Spirit seek to bring glory to the Son?

■ **Illustrations:**

Pain and Joy! Jesus' disciples were filled with grief over the news that He was returning to heaven to be with the Father (John 16:5-6). Jesus also explained that after His departure, He would send the Holy Spirit (vs. 7). In turn, Jesus' followers would be filled with joy as the Spirit helped them better understand Jesus' teachings and overcome their selfish impulses.

Every adult knows about pain and joy in their lives. And while some have little hope for the future, apparently many more are optimistic. When polled by *TIME/CNN* and asked what happens after death, 61 percent of Americans felt that they would go to heaven. Joni Eareckson Tada, a quadriplegic since she was 17, trusts in full-body resurrection and the glorification of the body in heaven.

In Paul's letters, he talked about the indwelling presence of the Spirit. For instance, he taught in Ephesians 1:13-14 that the Spirit is given to every follower of Jesus as a pledge of their future inheritance in God's kingdom. Encourage the class members that with the Spirit in their lives, they have the assurance of salvation and the confident hope of one day being resurrected.

A Traveling Companion. David and Christine had never traveled overseas before. Now they were actually making plans for 10 days in Western Europe, with stops in France, Belgium, Luxembourg, Switzerland, and Germany.

David was earnestly listening online to some interactive, self-marking language exercises in French. One day, he was frantically trying to memorize key phrases in French (like "Help! We're lost!"), when he received an email notification on his computer. It was a high priority message from his Uncle Gabe, a missionary stationed just outside Paris.

"Instead of just stopping by on your way through," Gabe wrote, "why don't you and Christine stay with us? We can give you the grand tour, help with the language—you don't speak French or German, do you?—and make sure nobody takes advantage of you." In response, David said he and Christine would accept Gabe's offer.

David smiled in relief as he left his computer and went to share the news with his wife. Suddenly, David knew the entire trip was going to be better than the couple had thought. With Gabe and his family as their traveling companions, David and Christine were certain to have a great time. And even though David thought he might still try out some of his French, Gabe would be there to make sure David didn't get snails when he wanted to eat steak!

As this week's lesson points out, Jesus knew how beneficial it can be to have a traveling companion. This is someone who helps us make sense of what we're experiencing, empower us to try new things, and lead us on the most productive path. Also, because Jesus knew that companion would not be Him, He promised His followers the Holy Spirit—the same Person at work in the lives of believers today.

A Truly Suitable Companion. "Maybe all dogs do go to heaven," *Newsweek* reported. But first, they might want to drop by the Episcopal Church of the Holy Trinity on Manhattan's Upper East Side, where parishioners and their pooches are regulars at Sunday morning services. As long as they behave, dogs and their masters are welcome to sit side by side and even accompany each other to the altar during Communion.

"It's like being with a family member," says Judith Gwyn Brown, who attended the early Sunday morning service with her puli sheepdog, Cordelia. "We both get a lot out of it." But can a pet really be a fitting spiritual friend? Church spokesman Fred Burrell wouldn't touch the question, saying, "I don't think I'll go there."

During Jesus' farewell discourse, He promised not to leave His disciples alone and helpless, for He would He would send a truly suitable companion, the Holy Spirit. Jesus referred to the Spirit as the "Comforter" (John 16:7) and the "Spirit of truth" (vs. 13) who would accompany believers throughout their life journey.

For Youth

■ **Topic:** Never Alone

■ **Questions:** 1. Why were the Eleven filled with grief upon learning that Jesus would be returning to the Father? 2. In what ways has the Spirit recently been a "Comforter" (John 16:7) for you? 3. Why is it important for Jesus' followers to operate in the Spirit's power? 4. In what sense has the "prince" (vs. 11) of this "world" been "judged"? 5. What are some ways the Spirit seeks to "glorify" (vs. 14) the Son?

■ **Illustrations:**

The Spirit as Our Teacher. Long before we had mobile devices with applications for updating calendars, organizing tasks, and receiving notifications of pending appointments, my mother had a simple time management system. Because she disliked excess paper, she wasn't one to use notes or wall calendars. Instead, she would tell one of her children about an upcoming event and kindly say, "Please remember that for me."

At one point in my young life, I traveled the most with my mother and so became her appointment book. Upon request, I regurgitated upcoming schedules with speed and accuracy. But I seldom recalled everything.

Our heavenly Father knows the limitations of our minds and our tendency for distraction. So, He graciously provides the Holy Spirit. Along with teaching us "all things" (John 14:26) connected with our salvation, the Spirit's job is to remind us of important truths Jesus has taught us. What a relief! With the Spirit in our lives, we can remember what Jesus wants us to know.

God Is in Control. Jesus' followers were filled with "sorrow" (John 16:6) when He told them He would be returning to the Father. Jesus also wanted the Eleven to know that despite their fears, the situation was under control. They learned that through the abiding presence of the Holy Spirit, their hearts would be calmed and assured.

Gladys Aylward, a missionary to China during the 1930s, was forced to flee when the Japanese invaded Yangcheng. But she could not leave her work behind. With only one assistant, she led more than 100 orphans over the mountains toward Free China.

During Aylward's harrowing journey out of the war-torn city, she grappled with despair as never before. After passing a sleepless night, she faced the morning with no hope of reaching safety. Then a 13-year-old girl in the group reminded Aylward of their much-loved story of Moses and the Israelites crossing the Red Sea.

"But I am not Moses!" Aylward cried in desperation. "Of course you aren't," the girl said, "but the Lord is still God." When Gladys and the orphans made it through, they proved once again that no matter how inadequate we feel, the Lord is still God, and we can trust in His Spirit's guiding, sustaining presence.

Unconditional Acceptance. Before Jesus' crucifixion, He talked with His disciples about the persecution they would experience for being His followers (John 16:1-4). Despite the world's rejection of them, Jesus' disciples would experience the unconditional acceptance of the Holy Spirit, whom Jesus referred to as the "Comforter" (vs. 7).

Similarly, children with severe skin diseases continue to find unconditional acceptance at a Christian summer camp. These children, who are socially excluded because of their deformities, are accepted and make lifelong friends at Camp Knutson, near Cross Lake, Minnesota, run by Lutheran Social Services.

Most of the children have never been able to go to the beach or for a walk without getting stares or rude comments, *The Lutheran* magazine reported. Some are covered head-to-toe with bandages or use a wheelchair, and others require as much as five hours of medical treatment a day.

The campers get absorbed without self-consciousness in activities such as swimming, waterskiing, tubing, and horseback riding, or sitting around a campfire. These are big steps for the young people, who have been closely monitored since birth by parents and schools. "All we believe in at Camp Knutson are compliments," camper and junior counselor Shauna Egesdal said. "No putdowns are allowed."

LESSON 4 — MARCH 22

THE SPIRIT'S PRESENCE

BACKGROUND SCRIPTURE: John 20:19-23; Acts 1:4-8; 2:1-4
DEVOTIONAL READING: Romans 14:13-19

Key Verse: When [Jesus] had said this, he breathed on [the disciples], and saith unto them, Receive ye the Holy Ghost. John 20:22.

KING JAMES VERSION

JOHN 20:19 Then the same day at evening, being the first day of the week, when the doors were shut where the disciples were assembled for fear of the Jews, came Jesus and stood in the midst, and saith unto them, Peace be unto you. 20 And when he had so said, he shewed unto them his hands and his side. Then were the disciples glad, when they saw the Lord. 21 Then said Jesus to them again, Peace be unto you: as my Father hath sent me, even so send I you. 22 And when he had said this, he breathed on them, and saith unto them, Receive ye the Holy Ghost: 23 Whose soever sins ye remit, they are remitted unto them; and whose soever sins ye retain, they are retained.

NEW REVISED STANDARD VERSION

JOHN 20:19 When it was evening on that day, the first day of the week, and the doors of the house where the disciples had met were locked for fear of the Jews, Jesus came and stood among them and said, "Peace be with you." 20 After he said this, he showed them his hands and his side. Then the disciples rejoiced when they saw the Lord. 21 Jesus said to them again, "Peace be with you. As the Father has sent me, so I send you." 22 When he had said this, he breathed on them and said to them, "Receive the Holy Spirit. 23 If you forgive the sins of any, they are forgiven them; if you retain the sins of any, they are retained."

Home Bible Readings

Monday, March 16	Mark 13:5-11	*The Holy Spirit Speaks*
Tuesday, March 17	Acts 10:39-48	*Gentiles Receive the Holy Spirit*
Wednesday, March 18	Acts 11:19-26	*Full of the Spirit and Faith*
Thursday, March 19	Romans 14:13-19	*Joy in the Holy Spirit*
Friday, March 20	Acts 1:4-8	*Power from the Holy Spirit*
Saturday, March 21	Ephesians 5:15-21	*Be Filled with the Spirit*
Sunday, March 22	John 20:19-23	*Receive the Holy Spirit*

Background

The account of Jesus' appearance to His disciples is preceded by the discovery of the empty tomb and Jesus' appearance to Mary Magdalene. Once the Passover Sabbath had ended, Mary hurried to Jesus' tomb early Sunday morning apparently to complete the burial anointing of His body (John 20:1). She—and the other women with her—wondered how they would be able to move the massive stone away from the entrance. Their concern vanished when they discovered that the rock had already been removed. Mary dashed to Peter and John, the disciple whom Jesus "loved" (vs. 2). Mary frantically stated that people had transferred Jesus' body to a place Mary and the other women did not know. Mary had not considered the possibility that God had raised Jesus from the dead. Mary assumed that Jesus' enemies had stolen His body.

Being alarmed by Mary's news, Peter and John ran to Jesus' tomb to see for themselves whether the body was missing (vs. 3). John arrived at the tomb first, where he peered in and saw Jesus' burial clothes (vss. 4-5). Though John was hesitant to enter, Peter rushed by him. Once Peter reached the tomb, he stepped right in and saw the strips of linen that had wrapped Jesus' corpse. Peter also noticed that Jesus' head cloth was neatly folded and separate from the linen strips (vss. 6-7). Robbers would not have removed the burial clothes or left them in such order. John followed Peter into the tomb, and when he saw the graveclothes, he "believed" (vs. 8). Yet neither Peter nor John had a full understanding of Scripture's teaching about Jesus' resurrection (vs. 9).

Next, Peter and John left the tomb and returned to Jerusalem (vs. 10). Meanwhile, Mary remained near the empty tomb and wept because she assumed that Jesus' enemies had taken His body (vs. 11). At this point, Mary leaned forward to gaze into the tomb, perhaps to see for herself that the body was missing, or to confirm in her mind what she had seen before. What Mary saw amazed her. Two angels, robed in white, were in the tomb. One was sitting where Jesus' head had been, and the other where His feet had been (vs. 12). The angels asked Mary why she was weeping. Mary said Jesus' enemies had removed His body to an unknown location (vs. 13). The fact that Mary couldn't attend to Jesus' body and give Him a decent burial added to Mary's distress.

At that moment Mary sensed the presence of another person. She turned and saw someone standing outside the tomb with her, but she did not realize it was Jesus (vs. 14).

Either there was something different about Him that prevented not only Mary but also others of Jesus' friends from recognizing Him (see Luke 24:13-31; John 21:4), or they were supernaturally prevented from recognizing Him until the time was right. Initially, Mary thought Jesus was the gardener (John 20:15). In turn, Jesus first addressed Mary as "Woman" as the angels had done. Also, like the angels, Jesus asked Mary why she was weeping. Moreover, Jesus inquired as to whom Mary was seeking.

Previously, Mary had thought that Jesus' enemies might have stolen His body, but now she hoped that this person, whom Mary assumed was responsible for the upkeep of the private cemetery, might have moved Jesus' body. Mary did not answer Jesus' questions but implored Him to reveal the whereabouts of the Savior's body—if the "gardener" had carried it away. Mary promised to return the body to the tomb herself (which would have required considerable strength). Just then, Mary recognized the Lord when she heard Him say her name (vs. 16). Mary's immediate reaction was to turn toward Jesus again, but this time to exclaim, "Rabboni!" John translated this Aramaic word to mean "Master," but it can also carry overtones of "my dear Lord."

According to Matthew 28:9, when Mary Magdalene and another Mary encountered the risen Lord, they fell to the ground, clasped His feet, and worshiped Him. John 20:17 reports Jesus' instruction to Mary not to cling to Him. Jesus told Mary to get up and convey a message to Jesus' friends. Although He had not yet ascended into heaven, He wanted to assure His disciples that shortly He would be returning to His heavenly Father. The Son spoke about His Father and His God as the disciples' Father and God. Now that Jesus' redemptive work was fully accomplished, the reconciliation between God and His spiritual children was complete. Mary obeyed by rushing to the rest of the disciples and telling them that she had seen the risen Lord. Mary also related the message Jesus had entrusted to her (vs. 18).

Notes on the Printed Text

After Jesus first appeared to Mary of Magdala, other people encountered Jesus (see Luke 24:13-49). John, however, skipped these incidents and went to the evening's events of which he was an eyewitness. Many of Jesus' disciples, which included most of the apostles, had secretly convened to discuss the reports that their Lord had risen from the dead. Nevertheless, since they still feared the religious leaders, they bolted the doors (John 20:19). In light of how the civil and religious authorities had treated Jesus, the fears of His closest disciples were well founded.

In addition to fear, Jesus' disciples suffered horrendous grief. After all, when the authorities arrested Jesus in the garden of Gethsemane, all His followers deserted Him and ran away (see Mark 14:27, 50). Understandably, on the Sunday following Jesus' crucifixion, His disciples were still in the shock of mourning. Also, the Feast of Unleavened Bread was still going on, so they would not have left Jerusalem for Galilee. Most likely, they were in the upper room where they had previously met with

Jesus. As the disciples talked, Jesus suddenly stood among them (John 20:19). The verse does not explain how Jesus could have entered the house when the doors were locked. Clearly, Jesus' resurrected body had extraordinary powers and capabilities. In 1 Corinthians 15:35-44, Paul explained that the resurrection body is heavenly in origin and glorified in nature.

Jesus greeted His friends by exclaiming, "Peace be unto you" (John 20:19). Although this phrase was a common Hebrew salutation, Jesus probably said it to relieve the disciples' fears at His sudden and unexpected appearance. Luke 24:37-38 mentioned that Jesus' appearance had frightened His followers. To demonstrate that His resurrected body had substance, Jesus showed His disciples His nail-pierced hands and His spear-pierced side (John 20:20). Luke 24:39 adds that Jesus told His disciples to touch Him to see that He had flesh and bones and was not a spirit or a ghost.

Perhaps the disciples should have believed the reports about Jesus' resurrection, but because of the depth of their sorrow, they needed to see actual evidence for themselves. Their shock was so great that they also needed strong assurance. They could not deny Jesus' scars when they saw them. Once the disciples were convinced of Jesus' identity and presence, His friends were overcome with joy (John 20:20). Like Mary, they traveled from the depths of despair to the pinnacle of happiness in a matter of seconds. Even today, the presence of the risen Lord can do that in the life of believers.

Once again Jesus greeted His disciples with a greeting of "peace" (vs. 21), that is, an impartation of calmness, self-composure, and freedom from terror. This time, however, the Savior wanted to strengthen the resolve of His disciples to obey His commission and proclaim the message of redemption. In the same way the Father had sent the Son to earth to fulfill His redemptive mission, Jesus was sending His disciples into the world to continue His ministry. This commission and the peace He provided are also given to us as believers today.

For instance, in 14:27 we learn that Jesus would not only leave us the Holy Spirit and His teachings (see vss. 25-26, which were studied in lesson 2), but also the Savior's peace. His peace is not like the world's artificial sense of well-being. Jesus' peace does not guarantee the absence of war or difficult circumstances. Jesus' peace is the assurance of God's favor regardless of our circumstances. Since Jesus had repeatedly warned His disciples of His impending departure and the peril ahead for them, He knew they'd be upset. So He urged them not to nurture their feelings of distress and fear, but to allow His peace to calm their spirits and be a source of courage (vs. 27).

Jesus not only charged His disciples with the momentous commission to proclaim the gospel, but also empowered them with the Holy Spirit to do it. This was necessary, for the disciples could not possibly carry out Jesus' work without the Spirit's wisdom, protection, and power. In short, there could be no evangelistic mission without the Spirit. Accordingly, Jesus told His friends to wait in Jerusalem until the Spirit fell upon them (see Acts 1:4-8). The Greek word for "spirit" is *pneuma*, which literally means "breath." So, in anticipation of the day of Pentecost, it was fitting that Jesus breathed on the disciples to give them the Spirit (John 20:22). Apparently, at Jesus' post-resurrection appearance, He gave them a foretaste of what was to come on Pentecost (see Acts 2:1-4, to be studied in lesson 13). The Savior's followers had to be prepared for that momentous occasion, which motivated and made them courageous witnesses, instead of fearful cowards.

SUGGESTIONS TO TEACHERS

The Sunday Jesus rose from the dead, He did not reject His disciples because they were hiding in fear behind locked doors. He also did not spurn them because they needed their faith in Him strengthened. Instead, He reassured them about the truth of His resurrection.

1. SURPRISED BY THE RISEN LORD. Relate in your own words the disciples' encounters with the risen Lord as recorded in John 20:19-23. Let your imagination help make the account more vivid as you tell it. Fill in details such as a small dimly lit room with a door securely barred and a gathering of despondent disciples.

2. REASSURED BY THE RISEN LORD. Take time to bring out what significance John's account attaches to Jesus' appearing. Emphasize that the resurrection was not a mass hallucination. Nor was it merely a spiritually present Jesus, alive only in the disciples' memories. Likewise, note that the resurrection was not a tale concocted by Jesus' followers, but an unexpected experience of the risen Lord in their presence.

3. COMMISSIONED AS THE RISEN LORD'S FOLLOWERS. Stress that the risen Lord commissions His followers to continue His ministry of bringing God's saving mercy to a hurting, fractured world. Discuss areas where reconciliation is most needed in your community. Talk about interpersonal relationships in your congregation and the need for mutual acceptance.

4. SUSTAINED BY THE HOLY SPIRIT. Jesus does not expect us to carry out His work by relying on our own strength and intellects. When we received the promised Spirit, we were automatically empowered to do Jesus' work. Be sure you discuss the gift of the Spirit in this lesson.

FOR ADULTS

■ **TOPIC:** An Opportunity to Serve

■ **QUESTIONS:** 1. Why were Jesus' disciples hiding behind locked doors? 2. How would you write the script for the disciples' conversation in their hiding place? 3. Why do you think the disciples were unprepared for Jesus' post-resurrection appearance to them? 4. Why is being commissioned by Jesus something not just reserved for full-time Christian workers, pastors, and missionaries? 5. What fears do people today have about the future, and how can Christians help them with the good news of the Lord?

Illustrations:

Being Fully Committed to Serve. If there was no resurrection, the church would have no mission. The church's world mission explodes from the dramatic news that Jesus lives. The church advances on His resurrection power. Paul began the church's great missionary movement convinced that the risen Lord lived in the apostle and energized him.

That's why it is so important to settle the issue of who Jesus is in the way His closest disciples settled it. Unless a person is really convinced that Jesus has risen from the dead, no congregation can inspire obedience to Jesus' Great Commission.

Every believer, having met the risen Lord through faith, must ask the next question: "What do You want me to do, Jesus?" This is the product of genuine conversion. This week's lesson shows that ultimately we offer Jesus all we have and are, or we give Him nothing.

Enough Convincing Evidence? Sidney Hook was one of the 20th century's foremost intellectuals. His lectures and writings attracted widespread attention during his long career.

A year before Hook's death in 1990 at the age of 87, he appeared on a talk show. He had always described himself as an atheist. As an old-fashioned rationalist who demanded proof for everything, Hook was asked what he would say when the risen Lord asked the skeptic why he had not believed in Jesus. Hook gave one of his typical replies: "Lord, You didn't give me enough evidence!"

After the show, one of the panelists asked Hook what he would say if the risen Lord answered, "Sidney, there was evidence enough to convince a lot of people whom I did not make as smart as you, and quite a few whom I made considerably smarter." Hook allowed a faint smile, and finally stammered that he guessed he would probably say, "I was wrong, Lord. Please forgive me."

In this week's lesson, we read about Jesus' friends, who were filled with fear and doubt when He suddenly appeared to them on the first Easter Sunday. We learn that the risen Lord can take the uncertainties that people have about Him and use those doubts as starting points on the road to belief.

From Doubt to Trust. Many years ago, a young Scotsman studied for the ministry. He had charm, intelligence, and attractiveness. Suddenly, he seemed to be struck by a pair of circumstances. First, he learned he was going to be permanently blind. He had tried every specialist in Edinburgh, but to no avail. Slowly, the darkness began to close in.

The Scotsman rationed his precious hours of reading time each day to cram for his studies. The hours gradually dwindled as his eyesight grew dimmer and dimmer. Light gave way to grayness and shadow. Friends tried to help him by reading to him. He finally managed to graduate.

Then the second blow fell. The Scotsman's fiancée had conflicting thoughts about spending her life with a young blind minister. She sent his ring back. Now disillusioned and alone, this young Scot sank into deep skepticism. Days, weeks, and months of confusion and doubt passed. All the loneliness and anxiety of a man who tasted nothing but disappointment left him helpless.

This would-be minister wondered, *If Jesus is really alive from the dead, why doesn't He make me well? Why can't Jesus heal me—especially since I wanted to be a minister?* Friends for a time even worried about this young man's sanity. His experience is recorded best in the words of a hymn he wrote. The blind Scottish minister's name was George Matheson, and we sing the words often in worship:

O Love that will not let us go,
I rest my weary soul in Thee
I give Thee back the life I owe
That in Thine ocean depths its flow
May richer, fuller be.

For Youth

■ **Topic:** Peace, Power, and Presence

■ **Questions:** 1. What was the basis for Jesus' disciples fearing the religious leaders? 2. Why were Jesus' disciples initially hesitant to accept the fact that He had risen from the dead? 3. How did Jesus convince the disciples of His resurrection? 4. Have you ever been skeptical of Jesus? Why? 5. How can the church you attend enable others to accept the reality of Jesus' resurrection?

■ **Illustrations:**

Our Caring, Risen Lord. Growing up is often a time filled with doubt. We doubt our parents' rules and wisdom. We doubt what older people tell us. *What do they know?* We doubt the basic maxims of life—for example, that it's better to tell the truth and work hard.

But then one day we have to make some big decisions for ourselves. Where do we find the rules that guided our parents and our elders? Are we left to shift for ourselves?

Doubts can be beneficial if they lead us to look for the truth. If we do not investigate the claims of Jesus to be God when we are young, probabilities are good that we will never get around to it later. The fourth Gospel's account of Jesus' friends cowering behind locked doors and being filled with doubt shows us how much the risen Lord cares, wants to answer our questions, and meet our needs.

Genuine Proof of Existence. Five-month-old Dorothy Gage had been a sickly child. The infant died in 1898. As the little girl was buried, her aunt Maud, who had desperately wanted a daughter of her own, was so distraught that she required medical attention before traveling back to Chicago.

Maud's husband decided to give a gift to his wife. He wrote a book dedicated to her in an effort to make little Dorothy immortal. He wrote about Dorothy as he imagined what her life would have been like, had she lived. His book has become a children's classic describing Dorothy as a brave little farm girl in Kansas. The book is L. Frank Baum's *The Wonderful Wizard of Oz.*

Historian Sally Roesch Wagner was in Illinois as a scholar-in-residence at Lincoln's New Salem State historical site. She was writing a book on the mother of Maud Gage Brown, who was an early women's rights activist. Wagner had interviewed various family members. She had heard about little Dorothy, but Wagner did not know where Dorothy was buried.

Wagner researched her topic for years. Her efforts led her to Evergreen Cemetery in Bloomington, Illinois. She stood before a tiny gravestone, the letters of which had been reduced to illegible grooves. She spread some shaving cream on the stone and used a squeegee to remove the excess. The name Dorothy stood out. Wagner said that the little girl took on a life of her own there. Now she knew that there really had been a Dorothy.

For some, Easter requires the same proof. There are those who would like to go and find the grave of Jesus and make sure the body is not there. However, almost 2,000 years ago others with the same tests of truthfulness went and found the tomb empty. They concluded that Jesus had risen. They later met the risen Lord and shared that testimony with us.

No Hoax. Numerianus became emperor of the Roman Empire at the death of his father in A.D. 283. While leading the army in a campaign against Persia, he began a 1,500-mile retreat.

During the eight months of the long journey, Numerianus was not seen by his men. The aides announced that his absence was due to an eye ailment. Finally, suspicious army officers forced their way into the emperor's tent. They discovered that their leader had died months earlier and had been reduced to a skeleton by the desert heat.

Maybe some of you feel that Jesus' friends only announced that He was alive in an effort to perpetuate His memory, life, and teachings. Perhaps you feel that the resurrection announcement is one big hoax or a last effort by the disciples to keep Jesus' persona alive. Maybe you think they conned others into believing that Jesus was alive. Better check it out.

The resurrection was no hoax pulled off by loyal aides. Even a disbelieving look at the Gospels should make this clear. Jesus' followers never expected to see Him alive. Yet He appeared to them while they were cowering in fear and doubt behind locked doors. They truly encountered the risen Lord!

LESSON 5 — MARCH 29

THE SAVIOR'S ARRIVAL

BACKGROUND SCRIPTURE: Mark 11:1-11
DEVOTIONAL READING: Isaiah 45:20-25

Key Verse: [The people] that went before, and they that followed, cried, saying, Hosanna; Blessed is he that cometh in the name of the Lord. Mark 11:9.

KING JAMES VERSION

MARK 11:1 And when they came nigh to Jerusalem, unto Bethphage and Bethany, at the mount of Olives, he sendeth forth two of his disciples, 2 And saith unto them, Go your way into the village over against you: and as soon as ye be entered into it, ye shall find a colt tied, whereon never man sat; loose him, and bring him. 3 And if any man say unto you, Why do ye this? say ye that the Lord hath need of him; and straightway he will send him hither. 4 And they went their way, and found the colt tied by the door without in a place where two ways met; and they loose him. 5 And certain of them that stood there said unto them, What do ye, loosing the colt? 6 And they said unto them even as Jesus had commanded: and they let them go. 7 And they brought the colt to Jesus, and cast their garments on him; and he sat upon him. 8 And many spread their garments in the way: and others cut down branches off the trees, and strawed them in the way. 9 And they that went before, and they that followed, cried, saying, Hosanna; Blessed is he that cometh in the name of the Lord: 10 Blessed be the kingdom of our father David, that cometh in the name of the Lord: Hosanna in the highest. 11 And Jesus entered into Jerusalem, and into the temple: and when he had looked round about upon all things, and now the eventide was come, he went out unto Bethany with the twelve.

NEW REVISED STANDARD VERSION

MARK 11:1 When they were approaching Jerusalem, at Bethphage and Bethany, near the Mount of Olives, he sent two of his disciples 2 and said to them, "Go into the village ahead of you, and immediately as you enter it, you will find tied there a colt that has never been ridden; untie it and bring it. 3 If anyone says to you, 'Why are you doing this?' just say this, 'The Lord needs it and will send it back here immediately.' " 4 They went away and found a colt tied near a door, outside in the street. As they were untying it, 5 some of the bystanders said to them, "What are you doing, untying the colt?" 6 They told them what Jesus had said; and they allowed them to take it. 7 Then they brought the colt to Jesus and threw their cloaks on it; and he sat on it. 8 Many people spread their cloaks on the road, and others spread leafy branches that they had cut in the fields. 9 Then those who went ahead and those who followed were shouting,
"Hosanna!
   Blessed is the one who comes in the name of the Lord!
10   Blessed is the coming kingdom of our ancestor David!
Hosanna in the highest heaven!"
11 Then he entered Jerusalem and went into the temple; and when he had looked around at everything, as it was already late, he went out to Bethany with the twelve.

Home Bible Readings

Monday, March 23	Psalm 67	God Judges with Equity
Tuesday, March 24	Isaiah 45:20-25	A Righteous God and a Savior
Wednesday, March 25	Philippians 2:9-16	God Highly Exalted Jesus
Thursday, March 26	Mark 13:30-37	Beware, Keep Alert
Friday, March 27	Mark 14:55-62	The Coming Son of Man
Saturday, March 28	John 12:14-19	The World Has Gone after Jesus
Sunday, March 29	Mark 11:1-11	Blessed Is the Coming Kingdom

Background

In this week's lesson, we jump ahead in Mark's Gospel to what has commonly been called Jesus' "Passion Week." This refers to the final days of His earthly life. It began with a joyous event—Jesus' triumphal entry into Jerusalem as King. Set on a hill some 2,500 feet above sea level, Jerusalem is 33 miles east of the Mediterranean Sea and 14 miles west of the Dead Sea. Because access was difficult and the city lacked natural resources, it at one time enjoyed a relatively protected location. But when a major regional trade route developed through the city, Jerusalem became commercially and strategically desirable to every subsequent political force that came to power.

The following are some key facts about the holy city: it appears in the Bible as early as Abraham (Gen. 14:18), though the site had probably been inhabited for centuries before; it was captured by David and made the capital of Israel; Jerusalem was the site of Solomon's temple and, in the first century, Herod's temple; the city's estimated population in Jesus' day was probably 50,000 (though during Passover, it possibly grew to 120,000); Jerusalem was besieged and destroyed by the Romans in A.D. 70; and the city was relatively small geographically but had a sizable metropolitan area with numerous suburban towns.

Notes on the Printed Text

Jesus, having ministered in Perea and the Jordan River area, now headed westward with His disciples by the steep road leading uphill to Jerusalem. On Sunday, the first day of the week preceding Passover, they came to the towns of Bethphage and Bethany. Bethphage was near Bethany, which in turn was located on the southeastern slopes of the "mount of Olives" (Mark 11:1). Bethany was also about two miles east of Jerusalem near the road to Jericho. Because the Mount of Olives is approximately 2,700 feet in elevation and thus about 200 feet higher than the city of Jerusalem itself, it commanded a superb view of the city and its temple.

With Passover only a few days away, Jerusalem was already filling up with pilgrims from all over. Jesus, too, was expected to be there. On every hand there were high expectations and high tensions. Undoubtedly, some of Jesus' followers were hoping He would use the great national celebration to claim His place as king of the Jews.

The religious leaders were hoping to find an opportunity to arrest and execute Him. Knowing the danger, Jesus could have stayed away. Yet He chose otherwise. He decided to enter Jerusalem—but on His own terms.

Jesus instructed two of His followers to go into Bethphage. As soon as they entered the village, perhaps just inside the gate, they would find a mother donkey and her colt tethered there. The disciples were to untie the animals and bring them to Jesus (Matt. 21:2). The colt had never been ridden (Mark 11:2). Jesus would ride the colt, but the colt's mother could also have been taken along as a steadying influence, leading the way as the colt followed (Matt. 21:7). If the disciples were questioned by anyone (for instance, the animals' owner or onlookers), they were to explain that Jesus needed the donkeys (Mark 11:3).

We learn in Matthew 21:4-5 that Jesus' entry into Jerusalem on the back of a colt would fulfill Zechariah 9:9. Jerusalem, personified as the "daughter of Zion," was about to see its long-awaited King—the Messiah—humbly ride into the holy city. In Bible times, unused animals were often taken for religious purposes (see Num. 19:2; 1 Sam. 6:7-8). Also, while donkeys were commonly used for transportation, they had come to be associated with royalty and with peace (see 2 Sam. 16:2; 1 Kings 1:33-34). The Son was unmistakably different from human conquerors. His claim to sovereignty did not rest on political and military subjugation, but on the strength of His character and His obedience to His Father's will. Nowhere did the Son's distinctiveness become more apparent than when He rode into Jerusalem with much acclaim.

The two disciples left and found the animals standing in a street and tied outside a house (Mark 11:4). As Jesus' followers were untying the animals, some bystanders questioned what they were planning to do (vs. 5). When the disciples repeated what Jesus had said, they were permitted to take the animals (vs. 6). It may be that the donkeys' owner was a follower of Jesus and by prearrangement had agreed to provide the animals to the Lord. The two disciples successfully carried out Jesus' instructions by bringing the donkeys to Him (Matt. 21:6). To show Jesus honor and make Him more comfortable, they placed their cloaks on the animals as a makeshift saddle before Jesus took His seat (Mark 11:7). Presumably, while Jesus sat on the colt, the mother donkey walked beside to calm her offspring (Matt. 21:7).

Next, the Messiah started the steep ascent into the valley, a route that for years was jammed with thousands of pilgrims coming to Jerusalem for the Passover. The climb from the valley into the city was more gradual. Jesus' ride was a living parable that set forth His claim to be the Messiah. His kingdom was at hand, a rule characterized by peace, love, humility, and gentleness. This monarch was gentle and compassionate, even to the extent of doing good to His enemies. For instance, He bore their persecutions with a gentle, forbearing spirit, even on the cross.

As Jesus rode the donkey, a large crowd of people gathered at the Mount of Olives. Apparently, they sensed that something dramatic was about to happen. Admittedly, the throng included critics (see Luke 19:39-40). Even so, the majority of the group was full of high hopes, especially as they came from all over Israel and various parts of the Roman Empire to celebrate the Passover. According to a census taken by Emperor Nero, nearly three million Jews came to Jerusalem for the event. A spontaneous outburst of adulation, welcome, and praise filled the air. People removed their cloaks and spread them on the road (Mark 11:8).

As the triumphal procession made its way, other people cut branches off the trees and spread them on the road (Matt. 21:8). This action was a demonstration of respect such as might have been shown to royalty. From ancient times, people in the Middle East have valued the palm tree for its usefulness and beauty. Its branches and leaves are used as ornaments, while its sap is made into sugar, wax, oil, tannin, and dye. People in the Middle East eat its fruit and grind its seed for their camels. They use its branches in the production of mats, roofs, baskets, and fences. To desert travelers, the shade of a palm tree is a welcome sight.

Furthermore, in Bible times, the Jews applied religious symbolism to the palm tree. For example, the psalmist described the righteous as flourishing like the palm tree (Ps. 92:12). Also, in accordance with the Mosaic law, they celebrated the feast of tabernacles with palm branches (Lev. 23:40). In the time preceding the New Testament era, the Jews used palm branches in their observance of other feasts as symbols of national triumph and victory. Early Christians adopted this appreciation of the palm tree. John himself noted that people in heaven would pay homage to the Messiah with palm branches (see Rev. 7:9), which became a symbol of His victory over death. In fact, the emblem of the palm leaf frequently accompanied the monogram of the Savior on Christian tombs.

The people demonstrated their respect for Jesus by word as well as deed. As they accompanied Jesus on His journey, they hailed Him with such acclamations as "Hosanna!" (Mark 11:9) and "Blessed is he who comes in the name of the Lord!" These praises all come from Psalm 118:25-26. (Psalms 113—118 were usually sung at Passover.) Most likely, the crowds were thinking Jesus would liberate them from Rome. The interjection "Hosanna" (Mark 11:9) literally means "Save now!" or "Save, we pray!" The use of the expression "son of David" (Matt. 21:9) was a recognition of Jesus' royal lineage. The statement appearing in Mark 11:10 was a recognition that Jesus came with the authority and approval of God. "Hosanna in the highest" implied that the angels of heaven were to praise Jesus. In short, the crowd's words proclaimed Jesus to be the Messiah. The irony is that within a week nearly all support for Jesus would melt away. These truths mirror what the shepherds heard on the night of the Savior's birth. They were greeted by a chorus of angels who gave glory to God and announced peace for all who received the Lord's favor (see Luke 2:14).

By the time Jesus crossed from the Mount of Olives to Jerusalem, it was late in the afternoon (Mark 11:11). With darkness coming on, most of the people were beginning to leave the temple, the shops, and the gates, and were heading for their homes or inns. So all Jesus did in Jerusalem on this day was to stop briefly in the temple area. The phrase "he looked round about upon all things" in the courts of the sacred complex holds more significance than might at first appear. As the Son of God, Jesus was examining His property to see how it was being used. He said nothing, but from the events of the next day we know He had an opinion (see vss. 15-17). For the time being, Jesus left Jerusalem and spent the night in Bethany, perhaps at the home of Mary, Martha, and Lazarus (see John 12:1-2). This withdrawal from the city might have been for safety's sake, since Jesus knew it was not yet time for Him to fall into His opponents' hands. It might also have been to dramatize His unwillingness to be a part of what was going on in the temple.

SUGGESTIONS TO TEACHERS

Up to this point in Jesus' public ministry, He had tried to keep His identity veiled. But during the final week of His time on earth, and knowing that this was the divinely appointed moment for His crucifixion, Jesus openly proclaimed His identity as the promised Messiah. As He did so, others around Him chose how they would respond. Still today, all people must choose how they view Jesus, who is the unique Son of God.

1. JESUS REVEALED WHO HE WAS. By fulfilling the specific prophecy of Zechariah and then by taking authority over the temple, Jesus announced His identity to the city and all its guests. Through His Word and power, Jesus still reveals Himself to our world today.

2. JESUS' FOLLOWERS ASSISTED THE ANNOUNCEMENT. One group, represented by two disciples who brought the donkey, and another group represented by its owner who released the animal, actively helped Jesus reveal Himself to the people of Jerusalem. How do we, as twenty-first century disciples, assist Jesus, especially as He offers Himself to our world? When our character shows that we love Jesus, other people will notice that we are different. Also, how we live should be consistent with the faith we profess. When we walk our talk (so to speak), the Father will give us many opportunities to tell others about the Son.

3. SOME REJECTED JESUS IN ANGER. Those who saw Jesus as a threat to their security and to their control of the circumstances wanted to push Him away. Later in this same week, they would succeed in murdering Jesus. But even that strategy could not defeat Him. Are there those in your circle of acquaintances who are resisting Jesus?

4. OTHERS RECEIVED JESUS GLADLY. The enthusiasm of Jesus' followers attracted others who joined in worshiping Him. Perhaps there are members of your class who have been quietly hanging off to the side. This Sunday might be their day for joining the crowd of disciples.

FOR ADULTS

■ **TOPIC:** Hail to the Chief

■ **QUESTIONS:** 1. How do you think the disciples felt about Jesus' plan to enter Jerusalem? 2. Why is it sometimes hard to understand and obey the Lord's instructions? 3. Why did Jesus choose this time to enter Jerusalem in a royal way and accept the praises of the crowds? 4. How can believers show their exuberant, uninhibited praise to the Savior? 5. What impresses you most about this occasion?

■ **ILLUSTRATIONS:**

Purifying the Worshiping Community. An old saying warns us, "If you find the perfect church, don't join it, because you'll wreck it." Due to our sinful natures, this is always a possibility. Nonetheless, God calls His purified people to worship in a holy way. After all, there's no room for ungodliness in Christ's Body.

When Jesus accepted praise from the crowd, He could have felt good about the situation. But then He witnessed the wretched conditions around the temple, and He decided to risk the crowd's fury. Yes, there was a time to challenge worship that had been corrupted by commercialism. Pure worship was a worthwhile goal that required drastic action.

How easy it is to slip over the line and make worship into a business. This danger lurks everywhere. Therefore, we need constant reminders to purify our hearts before we lavish our praise in worship to the Lord.

Worthy of True Worship. On Palm Sunday, many churches hand out palm branches as a symbol of the praise Jesus received as He triumphantly entered Jerusalem the week of His crucifixion. The Gospels say palm branches and cloaks were spread out on the ground, covering Jesus' path like a red carpet for a monarch. The symbolism was perfect. Jesus did not want a potentate's crown. He wanted people's humble hearts. Palms worked just fine to show the world what kind of ruler Jesus was.

Our palms work fine today, too. The palms of our hands can symbolize Jesus' kingship and authority to our world. Held out open, our palms can offer our possessions and hearts to His service. Clasped together, they show how we come into His presence in prayer, seeking forgiveness and strength and sharing our needs. Clapping together, our palms applaud Jesus' power. Placed over our hearts, our palms show allegiance to the only Ruler worthy of worship.

This week's lesson explores people's responses to Jesus' kingship and authority in the first century A.D. Consider using the teaching time to suggest ways you can encourage your students to truly worship the Savior in the days ahead.

Overturned Expectations. Lorraine wondered why she hadn't heard from her mother since Christmas. She had made her mother's favorite candy—divinity fudge with walnuts—and shipped it to arrive just in time for the holidays. But except for a curt

"Thank you for the box" postscript on a letter back in January, her mother hadn't mentioned it. It was now spring. That wasn't like her mom.

Lorraine decided to call. After catching up on the latest family news, she asked her mother how she liked the Christmas candy. Her mom said, "I didn't get any, honey. I'd remember if you sent me fudge." Lorraine replied, "But you wrote back and said 'Thank you for the box,' so I know it arrived."

After a long pause, her mother said, "What did you send it in?" Lorraine responded, "An old fruitcake tin we had in the cupboard." Upon hearing this her mom exclaimed, "Oh honey, I'm so sorry!" She explained that she hadn't even bothered to open the tin. When she assumed it contained fruitcake—which she didn't like—she threw the tin in the trash. By not even looking inside, she missed her daughter's wonderful surprise.

When Jesus arrived on the scene, many rejected Him because He didn't look like a "savior" or "king" to them. They expected trumpets, finery, riches, and other symbols of power. Instead, He came on a donkey. That was only one way that Jesus overturned people's ideas of what religion and true power should look like. His whole life and ministry was a series of surprises from God.

FOR YOUTH

■ **TOPIC:** A Star Is Born

■ **QUESTIONS:** 1. What instructions did Jesus give to two of His disciples? 2. What was the significance of Jesus' riding into Jerusalem on a colt? 3. Why were the crowds excited to see Jesus? 4. What would you have done, had you been among the throngs of pilgrims that day? 5. What is something Jesus has done for you that you want to praise Him for?

■ **ILLUSTRATIONS:**

A Time for Personal Examination. Pageantry excites young people, whether it's a sports event, a political rally, an art or music fair, or even a religious gathering. In Christendom, Christmas, Easter, and Palm Sunday call for pageantry, including processions, music, and colorful banners. For many years, until politics intervened, the Palm Sunday procession leading from the Mount of Olives into Jerusalem was one of the most exciting religious ceremonies anywhere.

Jesus did not avoid a wild public demonstration when the time was right according to His purposes. His triumphal entry in Jerusalem—what we now call Palm Sunday—signified that He threw down the gauntlet to the nation of Israel. Would the people accept His coming as from heaven, from God above, or would they see Jesus simply as another impostor, a false messiah?

This week's lesson prompts your students to examine their motives in coming to Jesus. If they join the crowd in hailing Him, they must accept all He has to offer and the changes He wants to make in their lives.

Missing the Real Event. The story is told of a boy from the country who came to town many years ago to see the circus. He had never seen one before, and was excited at the prospect of watching the clowns, elephants, lions, and tigers. The boy got up early and drove his horse and wagon to town in time for the big parade. Standing at the curb, he clapped enthusiastically as the steam calliope tooted and the stream of gaudily painted circus wagons rumbled by.

The boy shrieked with delight at the clowns and acrobats, and he grew wide-eyed with wonder at the sight of the wild animals in their cages. He laughed at the shuffling lines of elephants and watched the jugglers with wonder. When the parade reached its end, the boy rushed up to the last man in the procession and handed him his money, and then the boy went back home. The lad didn't discover until later that he hadn't seen the circus but had merely watched the parade. He missed the acts under the big top and merely caught sight of the procession leading to the performance.

Some church members are a bit like that boy. They watch the Palm Sunday procession, but they never go any farther. They enjoy a brief emotional experience, but miss the real action of the cross and the empty tomb. They enjoy the pageantry and watch the parade briefly, but they never participate in the meaning of the resurrection. Sadly, they never get beyond Palm Sunday's events.

The Cheering Stopped. When World War I ended, American President Woodrow Wilson was a hero across Western Europe. The American forces had swung the battle to the Allies. Everyone felt optimistic. Maybe the nations had truly fought their last war and the world had been made safe for democracy. Everyone loved Wilson for his part in the flow of events.

After the war, when Wilson first visited Paris, London, and Rome, cheering crowds greeted him everywhere. Their enthusiasm lasted about a year. Then it gradually stopped. Europeans forgot what Wilson had done and focused their attention on resuming all facets of normal life. Back in Washington, D.C., the U.S. Senate vetoed Wilson's plan for an international peace organization, the League of Nations.

During the last days of his presidency, Wilson's health began to fail. His party lost the next national election. Within a short time, Wilson went from world hero to a broken man. How quickly the crowds turned on him! Jesus did not break under the strain, but He faced the same pattern. Crowds that welcomed Him as He entered Jerusalem on Palm Sunday deserted Him as He moved toward the end.

LESSON 6 — APRIL 5

AFFIRMING JESUS' RESURRECTION

BACKGROUND SCRIPTURE: 1 Corinthians 15:1-22
DEVOTIONAL READING: John 11:20-27

Key Verse: For as in Adam all die, even so in Christ shall all be made alive. 1 Corintthians 15:22.

KING JAMES VERSION

1 CORINTHIANS 15:1 Moreover, brethren, I declare unto you the gospel which I preached unto you, which also ye have received, and wherein ye stand; 2 By which also ye are saved, if ye keep in memory what I preached unto you, unless ye have believed in vain.
3 For I delivered unto you first of all that which I also received, how that Christ died for our sins according to the scriptures; 4 And that he was buried, and that he rose again the third day according to the scriptures:
5 And that he was seen of Cephas, then of the twelve:
6 After that, he was seen of above five hundred brethren at once; of whom the greater part remain unto this present, but some are fallen asleep. 7 After that, he was seen of James; then of all the apostles. 8 And last of all he was seen of me also, as of one born out of due time.
9 For I am the least of the apostles, that am not meet to be called an apostle, because I persecuted the church of God. 10 But by the grace of God I am what I am: and his grace which was bestowed upon me was not in vain; but I laboured more abundantly than they all: yet not I, but the grace of God which was with me. 11 Therefore whether it were I or they, so we preach, and so ye believed. . . .

20 But now is Christ risen from the dead, and become the firstfruits of them that slept. 21 For since by man came death, by man came also the resurrection of the dead. 22 For as in Adam all die, even so in Christ shall all be made alive.

NEW REVISED STANDARD VERSION

1 CORINTHIANS 15:1 Now I would remind you, brothers and sisters, of the good news that I proclaimed to you, which you in turn received, in which also you stand, 2 through which also you are being saved, if you hold firmly to the message that I proclaimed to you—unless you have come to believe in vain.
3 For I handed on to you as of first importance what I in turn had received: that Christ died for our sins in accordance with the scriptures, 4 and that he was buried, and that he was raised on the third day in accordance with the scriptures, 5 and that he appeared to Cephas, then to the twelve. 6 Then he appeared to more than five hundred brothers and sisters at one time, most of whom are still alive, though some have died. 7 Then he appeared to James, then to all the apostles. 8 Last of all, as to one untimely born, he appeared also to me.
9 For I am the least of the apostles, unfit to be called an apostle, because I persecuted the church of God.
10 But by the grace of God I am what I am, and his grace toward me has not been in vain. On the contrary, I worked harder than any of them—though it was not I, but the grace of God that is with me. 11 Whether then it was I or they, so we proclaim and so you have come to believe. . . .

20 But in fact Christ has been raised from the dead, the first fruits of those who have died. 21 For since death came through a human being, the resurrection of the dead has also come through a human being; 22 for as all die in Adam, so all will be made alive in Christ.

Home Bible Readings

Monday, March 30	Matthew 27:45-50	*Jesus Has Died*
Tuesday, March 31	Matthew 28:1-8	*Jesus Has Risen*
Wednesday, April 1	1 Thessalonians 4:13-18	*Jesus Will Come Again*
Thursday, April 2	John 11:20-27	*The Resurrection and the Life*
Friday, April 3	Titus 3:1-7	*The Hope of Eternal Life*
Saturday, April 4	1 Corinthians 15:12-19	*If Jesus Has Not Been Raised*
Sunday, April 5	1 Corinthians 15:1-11, 20-22	*In Fact, Jesus Has Been Raised*

Background

The first-century A.D. church at Corinth struggled with a number of problems that required Paul's attention. Among these were a growing laxity for discipline, a surge of lawsuits being brought before non-Christian judges, and a spreading propensity for sexual immorality. Also, there was probably some opposition to Paul in the church. Perhaps while the apostle was in the process of writing this epistle, the Corinthian believers sent him a letter in which they asked his advice on a variety of moral and social matters (1 Cor. 7:1). This gave rise to Paul's instruction about maintaining stable marriages, about discontinuing less than ethical actions, about what to do and what not to do in public worship, and about the reality of Jesus' resurrection. It may have taken the apostle days or weeks to write this letter.

After Paul concluded his lengthy section in 1 Corinthians on spiritual gifts (a topic discussed in lesson 11), he turned a corner and began talking about another major subject: the resurrection. Probably because of their faulty understanding about what it meant to be "spiritual," some of the Corinthians did not believe in the bodily resurrection of the dead. They might have believed that Christians, after death, live on forever in heaven as spirits. But to them the idea of one's soul being rejoined with one's body was distasteful. The apostle determined he had to correct their theological error.

To fully appreciate Paul's teaching in chapter 15 on the resurrection, it is necessary to have some knowledge of the Greek view of life and death. Generally speaking, the Greeks believed the soul was immortal, but the body would not be raised from the dead. In Greek thought, the body was the source of all human sin and weakness. So, death brought release of the soul from its fleshly prison. It was inconceivable, therefore, to accept a process by which the soul would be re-imprisoned.

The problem in the Corinthian church was that some could accept the teaching that Jesus had been raised from the dead, but they were reluctant to affirm the bodily resurrection of Christians in general. Paul corrected this theological error by first establishing the certainty of the resurrection and by making the connection between the resurrection of Jesus and that of believers (vss. 1-34). Next, the apostle explored key issues surrounding the idea of a bodily resurrection and Jesus' return (vss. 35-37). Finally, Paul made an appeal to his readers to stand firm in their labor for the Lord (vs. 58).

NOTES ON THE PRINTED TEXT

Paul began his argument by establishing common ground with his readers: they all believed that the Lord Jesus had been raised from the dead. When Paul had arrived in Corinth, he had proclaimed the gospel—the body of teachings about Jesus and salvation that had been handed down from the first Christians. Paul's readers had not only accepted the gospel, but also had based their faith squarely upon it (1 Cor. 15:1). Furthermore, it was by this gospel that they would reach final salvation (vs. 2). But now some of them had begun to believe that there is no future resurrection of the dead—an idea contradictory to the gospel. Paul warned his readers that if they held to that idea, then their Christian faith was made pointless. A little later in the chapter (vss. 12-19), the apostle would explain what he meant.

The Greek noun rendered "gospel" (see 1 Cor. 15:1) translates *euangelion* [you-ahn-GELL-ee-ahn], from which we get such words as *evangelism* and *evangelical*. The Greek noun literally means "good news." In the New Testament, the gospel is not merely historical facts about someone who lived long ago. Its message focuses on certain saving acts that were believed and proclaimed by the early church. Specifically, the term is used to refer to the message concerning the life, death, and resurrection of the Lord Jesus. It was also used to refer to the kingdom of God and salvation. The truths contained in the gospel are not optional to the believer's faith. Rather, they are central to it. What the gospel teaches is absolutely accurate and true, and thus to be readily accepted by all Christians.

In verse 3, Paul repeated a portion of the gospel he had preached in Corinth—the part that related to Jesus' death and resurrection. Also, this aspect was of foremost importance. Because of the structure, wording, and content of verses 3-5, many New Testament scholars believe that Paul was quoting an early Christian creed. The first statement in the creed is that the Messiah "died for our sins according to the scriptures" (vs. 3). Jesus' death was not a tragic accident; it had a purpose, namely, to rescue sinners. Passages in the Hebrew Bible, such as Isaiah 52:13–53:12, foretold Jesus' sacrificial death. Second, Jesus "was buried" (1 Cor. 15:4). Burial in a tomb certified the reality of the Messiah's death. Third, He was raised from death on the third day, just as the Scriptures had foretold. After being buried on Friday afternoon, Jesus was resurrected on early Sunday morning. As for the biblical prediction of this amazing event, such passages as Psalm 16:8-11 and Jonah 1:17 might be in view.

In the fourth part in the early Christian creed quoted by Paul, we learn that Jesus, after rising from the dead, appeared to "Cephas" (1 Cor. 15:5), and after that to the "twelve." These appearances proved the reality of the Lord's resurrection (see Luke 24:34; John 20:19). Paul expanded the creed he had been quoting by citing additional postresurrection appearances that he had learned about. To begin with, the apostle reported that the Lord had appeared to a group of Christians numbering more than 500. (This appearance is mentioned nowhere else in Scripture.) Since many of these people were still living at the time the apostle wrote, the Corinthians could have had plenty of eyewitness testimonies to the resurrection, if they wanted them (1 Cor. 15:6). Jesus also appeared to His half-brother James (vs. 7), who by this time was leader of the Jerusalem church. (Here, again, we know nothing more about this appearance.) In addition, Jesus appeared to "all the apostles"—perhaps meaning a larger group than just the Twelve. This might refer to the appearance described in Acts 1:6-11.

Finally, the Lord Jesus appeared to Paul (1 Cor. 15:8). Clearly, the apostle was referring to his meeting with the risen Savior on the Damascus road (see Acts 9:3-6). To Paul, this was more than just a vision. He had seen the Lord as surely as had all the other disciples. Many people today doubt or deny Jesus' resurrection. Yet while all the eyewitnesses have now died, there is still abundant biblical and circumstantial evidence that Jesus rose from the dead. In short, it is a historical fact.

As Paul described his own sighting of the resurrected Lord, the apostle called himself "one born out of due time" (1 Cor. 15:8). This translates a Greek noun that literally referred to a miscarriage or a stillbirth. The other apostles had all achieved their status through following Jesus in His earthly ministry. But Paul's entrance into apostleship was unusual, as someone who survived a freakish birth. Some in Corinth might have come to undervalue Paul in comparison to other apostles. Paul agreed that he was the "least" (vs. 9) important of all the apostles. Here Paul was probably making a pun on his Roman name, Paulus, which means "the little one." Indeed, Paul said he didn't deserve to be called an apostle. After all, before getting saved, he had acted like a predator who pursued and tyrannized God's "church" (see Acts 8:1; 9:1-2; 22:4; 26:9-11; Phil. 3:6; 1 Tim. 1:12-13).

Yet, despite all that, Paul was an apostle solely by God's grace. The Lord could have punished Paul for persecuting Jesus' followers, but instead He forgave the misguided Pharisee and called him to service. In turn, Paul responded by working harder than any other apostle in spreading the Good News. Again, he was quick to add that this, too, was by God's grace (1 Cor. 15:10). Since Paul was an apostle, he was preaching the same gospel that all the other apostles were proclaiming. Moreover, it was this Good News through which the Corinthians had come to faith (vs. 11; compare vs. 1). Clearly, Paul meant that if the Corinthians were disbelieving a part of the gospel—the part about the bodily resurrection of the dead—then they were going against not only him, but also all the rest of the apostles.

In 1 Corinthians 15:12-18, Paul told his readers that if Jesus had not been raised from the dead, their faith would be useless. The apostle argued that all the logical conclusions he had drawn from the Corinthians' implicit denial of Jesus' resurrection were meaningless, since He had been resurrected. Paul firmly asserted that Jesus is the "firstfruits" (vs. 20) of those who would be resurrected. By this the apostle meant Jesus' rising from the dead was the down payment or guarantee that believers who die would also be raised from the dead (see Rom. 8:23). In a manner of speaking, Jesus' resurrection was the prototype for the future resurrection of believers.

At harvest time, Israelite farmers took the first and finest portions of their crops and offered them to the Lord (see Exod. 23:16, 19; Lev. 23:9-14). The whole nation initially celebrated the offering of the "firstfruits" in the late spring, 50 days after Passover, at the beginning of harvest season. At first, this celebration was known as the Festival of Weeks. Later it became known as Pentecost, the Greek word meaning "fiftieth." The celebration was repeated throughout summer as other crops were brought in. The whole purpose of the festival was to give thanks to God for His bounty. It was a time of great rejoicing throughout Israel. In the same way, Paul pictured Jesus' resurrection as just the beginning, the "firstfruits" of the resurrection harvest yet to come. Indeed, Jesus was not only the first to rise from the dead, but He also serves as a pledge that more resurrections would one day follow. His resurrection guarantees that all the deceased who placed their trust in Him while alive would someday be resurrected (1 Cor. 15:20).

Paul's theological point is that the resurrection of the dead is one of the things that would inevitably happen because Jesus was raised. His resurrection set in motion an unstoppable chain of events. As an explanation of this inevitability, Paul set up a comparison between Adam and Christ. The apostle reminded his readers that because Adam sinned, death entered the world. And since the human race is related to Adam through natural birth, sin and death spread to all humanity (see Rom. 5:12-21). Even though one man's disobedience brought death to all, in the same way, another man's obedience would result in resurrection to eternal life for all who are spiritually related to Him (1 Cor. 15:21-22).

SUGGESTIONS TO TEACHERS

Is the Bible reliable? Are the writings in the New Testament merely "pious legends" as some critics allege? Some people have even dismissed the scriptural reports about Jesus, declaring them to be stories of a "fictitious" character. This week's lesson is a good opportunity to review the way the good news about Jesus was revealed, and to reflect on the trustworthiness of the information in 1 Corinthians 15.

1. EYEWITNESS REPORTS. Have the class look at the opening verses of this chapter. Impress on the students that many eyewitnesses saw Jesus risen from the dead. Based on their collective testimony, the historical accounts of Jesus' resurrection should never be classified as fiction.

2. ESSENTIAL RELIANCE. The account of Jesus' resurrection was not put together merely as a report, as a biographer might collect material on an interesting subject. Paul put it plainly: everything he told his readers about the risen Lord was meant for them to hold firmly. The purpose of the gospel is to bring into being a faith community that will rely on the Savior and strive to practice the reality of His resurrection in every area of life.

3. EFFECTIVE RELEASE. The good news of Christ to earlier believers and to us remains the same: Jesus' death and resurrection bring liberation from the bonds of guilt, anxiety, and futility. Emphasize that the Messiah died for our sins. Suggest to the class that a list be made of what that death on the cross might signify for people today. Note how pivotal the experience of the risen Lord was to Paul.

4. ETERNAL RELATIONSHIP. Finally, remind the class that Jesus' resurrection from the dead is truly good news they should share with their family, friends, neighbors, and coworkers. In the face of all the bad news found in various media outlets, which threaten to make us despair, the good news of the Father's gift of His risen Son brings new life.

FOR ADULTS

■ **TOPIC:** Fully Alive

■ **QUESTIONS:** 1. Why did Paul think it was important to remind his readers about the gospel? 2. In what way is our salvation tied to the gospel? 3. Why is it important for us to hold to the historical resurrection of Jesus? 4. How did Paul experience the mercy and grace of God? 5. How can believers use the truths Paul taught about the resurrection to encourage someone with a terminal illness?

■ **ILLUSTRATIONS:**

New Life in a New Body. Every Easter we celebrate the resurrection of our Lord Jesus Christ. His resurrection also guarantees the resurrection of our bodies. The two cannot be separated. Yet many adults are resigned to the mistaken idea that when they die, they will cease to exist.

Even brilliant, well-educated people assume that one day they will "die like a dog" (that is, as miserably and shamefully as a dog). They cannot conceive of life beyond the grave. They assume that we are no different than the animals, and to claim immortality is foolishness. They cannot see beyond the physical realm of existence.

But the Christian hope of the resurrection—of new life in a new body—gives meaning to every aspect of daily existence. Because Jesus lives, we will also live. More than ever, saved adults need to share the certainty of eternal life in Jesus with hopeless people.

The Death and New Life of Marigolds. Marigolds had adorned the landscape around our house beautifully all summer. Their gold, orange, and yellow blooms flourished through the sporadically rainy then hot and humid summer. Each plant seemed to yield scores of beautiful flowers that persevered through the seasons.

Yet, along with the onslaught of autumn's colors, the marigolds began to show their age. Flowers wilted and dried up. Stems stooped and succumbed to the inevitable end.

The marigolds were dying. But as the flower of this plant shriveled and curled with the passing of life, long, narrow, black and beige seeds formed at the center of its petals. Also, within every one of those seeds was contained the prospect for new life. It was the promise that a new plant would grow again come spring, that new and gloriously lovely flowers would bloom again next year.

And so it is with our lives. We live, we wilt, we droop, we succumb to the inevitable, we die. But within our natural bodies is a seed from which, the Bible promises, will grow a spiritual body, that is, one made for heaven with God. Moreover, this resurrection body will have no ending. Because of our faith in the Lord Jesus, we, too, will live again!

Triumph of the Risen Lord. For over 75 years during the twentieth century, the Soviet Union had repressed the church by closing congregations, shooting or imprisoning religious leaders, seizing Bibles and other religious literature, and forbidding any public proclamation of the good news of Jesus' resurrection. The powerful government promoted atheism. In fact, religion was said to be "the opium of the people" (a statement originally made by Karl Marx).

In a prominent location in Moscow, a poster had printed on it, "Glory to the Communist Party!" A number of years ago, a visitor was walking through that city with a Russian acquaintance when they came to the place where the poster had hung. "Look at that!" the Russian said, pointing to a large banner fluttering in the chill breeze of a Russian spring. "KHRISTOS VOSKRESE!" the banner proclaimed in swooping old Cyrillic letters. In other words, CHRIST IS RISEN!

The wonderful news of the resurrection has outlasted all revolutions, all ideologies, and all empires. The risen, living Savior triumphs over all forever!

FOR YOUTH

■ **TOPIC:** True Eyewitnesses
■ **QUESTIONS:** 1. How would you summarize the gospel message? 2. Why was it necessary for the Lord Jesus to die on the cross? 3. What are some ways you can affirm the truth of Jesus' resurrection to your peers? 4. What caused Paul to change from being a persecutor of the church to a believer? 5. In what way is Jesus the "firstfruits" (1 Cor. 15:20) of all who believe in Him?

■ **ILLUSTRATIONS:**

Counting on Resurrection. The hope of the resurrection of believers is not wishful thinking. As Paul declared in 1 Corinthians 15, it is the truth we can count on.

Jesus' resurrection was the foundation of early Christian preaching. The gospel spread and the church was established because Jesus is alive. Of all religions, Christianity alone claims that its founder was raised from the dead. This claim has been disputed, but never successfully refuted.

Here we discover that faith in Christ is not a close-your-eyes-and-take-the-plunge-and-hope-you're-not-wrong kind of thing. We did not see everything happen with our own eyes. But the facts are recorded for us in Scripture to examine and accept. And even though we have not physically seen Jesus as many did, we can still believe in Him and receive eternal life.

Death, Where Is Your Sting? A small boy was allergic to bee stings. The allergy was so severe that physicians warned the family that a single bee sting could produce anaphylactic shock. This is a severe medical emergency that could kill the child by preventing him from breathing.

One day, a bee landed on the boy's cheek. The child was almost paralyzed with fright. Calmly the father allowed the bee to walk onto his own finger. The father agitated the bee and then allowed it to attack him, thus causing it to lose its stinger. The bee flew back to the boy, but this time the child was unafraid. Death had been robbed of its power!

This story illustrates Paul's point to the Corinthian believers. They did not need to fear death, for Jesus had removed its sting through His resurrection. And through faith in the Messiah, they could conquer death.

The Evidence. A mother was explaining to her five-year-old daughter how Jesus died and then revisited His followers after rising from the dead. "That's what we believe," the mother said. "That's how we know Jesus is the Son of God, because He came back from the dead just as He said He would." "Do you mean like Elvis?" the daughter observed.

We have no evidence that Elvis ever came back from the dead, but there is a great deal of evidence for Jesus' resurrection. Perhaps some of the greatest evidence is the fact that Jesus lives in the hearts of believers today. For Christians, the resurrection of Jesus is at the core of their faith.

Without the resurrection, every word of Jesus is transformed into a lie, every belief we hold is undermined, and everything the church has accomplished for almost 2,000 years is pointless. But of course Jesus did rise from the dead. Our preaching, believing, and hoping have not been in vain. That's why on Easter, throngs of people crowd the church. They know that Easter is the most glorious day of the year, and they know why that is true. It's Resurrection Day!

LESSON 7 — APRIL 12

LOVING ONE ANOTHER

BACKGROUND SCRIPTURE: 1 John 3:11-24
DEVOTIONAL READING: John 11:20-27

Key Verse: For this is the message that ye heard from the beginning, that we should love one another. 1 John 3:11.

KING JAMES VERSION

1 JOHN 3:11 For this is the message that ye heard from the beginning, that we should love one another. 12 Not as Cain, who was of that wicked one, and slew his brother. And wherefore slew he him? Because his own works were evil, and his brother's righteous. 13 Marvel not, my brethren, if the world hate you.

14 We know that we have passed from death unto life, because we love the brethren. He that loveth not his brother abideth in death. 15 Whosoever hateth his brother is a murderer: and ye know that no murderer hath eternal life abiding in him. 16 Hereby perceive we the love of God, because he laid down his life for us: and we ought to lay down our lives for the brethren. 17 But whoso hath this world's good, and seeth his brother have need, and shutteth up his bowels of compassion from him, how dwelleth the love of God in him? 18 My little children, let us not love in word, neither in tongue; but in deed and in truth. 19 And hereby we know that we are of the truth, and shall assure our hearts before him.

20 For if our heart condemn us, God is greater than our heart, and knoweth all things. 21 Beloved, if our heart condemn us not, then have we confidence toward God. 22 And whatsoever we ask, we receive of him, because we keep his commandments, and do those things that are pleasing in his sight.

23 And this is his commandment, That we should believe on the name of his Son Jesus Christ, and love one another, as he gave us commandment. 24 And he that keepeth his commandments dwelleth in him, and he in him. And hereby we know that he abideth in us, by the Spirit which he hath given us.

NEW REVISED STANDARD VERSION

1 JOHN 3:11 For this is the message you have heard from the beginning, that we should love one another. 12 We must not be like Cain who was from the evil one and murdered his brother. And why did he murder him? Because his own deeds were evil and his brother's righteous. 13 Do not be astonished, brothers and sisters, that the world hates you. 14 We know that we have passed from death to life because we love one another. Whoever does not love abides in death. 15 All who hate a brother or sister are murderers, and you know that murderers do not have eternal life abiding in them. 16 We know love by this, that he laid down his life for us—and we ought to lay down our lives for one another. 17 How does God's love abide in anyone who has the world's goods and sees a brother or sister in need and yet refuses help?

18 Little children, let us love, not in word or speech, but in truth and action. 19 And by this we will know that we are from the truth and will reassure our hearts before him 20 whenever our hearts condemn us; for God is greater than our hearts, and he knows everything. 21 Beloved, if our hearts do not condemn us, we have boldness before God; 22 and we receive from him whatever we ask, because we obey his commandments and do what pleases him.

23 And this is his commandment, that we should believe in the name of his Son Jesus Christ and love one another, just as he has commanded us. 24 All who obey his commandments abide in him, and he abides in them. And by this we know that he abides in us, by the Spirit that he has given us.

Home Bible Readings

Monday, April 6	John 3:16-21	God So Loved the World
Tuesday, April 7	1 John 3:1-5	Love Given Us by God
Wednesday, April 8	John 13:1-15	Loved to the End
Thursday, April 9	Luke 7:44-48	Great Love Shown
Friday, April 10	1 John 3:6-10	Those Who Do Not Love
Saturday, April 11	John 13:31-35	A New Commandment
Sunday, April 12	1 John 3:11-24	Love Empowered by the Spirit

Background

First John was authored primarily to combat the emerging heresy of Gnosticism, which was influencing the churches in the apostle's day. Key Gnostic teachings included these beliefs: (1) virtue is inferior to knowledge; (2) only a few chosen people can understand the true meaning of Scripture; (3) to explain the existence of evil, God must have had a cocreator; (4) the Incarnation must be rejected because a spiritual deity would not unite with a material body; and (5) there can be no bodily resurrection since the body is evil and the spirit is good (see also the comments on Greek thought appearing in last week's lesson).

John's pre-Gnostic opponents might have been led by a man named Cerinthus. They denied that Jesus was the Son of God who had come in the flesh. To an extent, they denied their own sinfulness and that righteous conduct was necessary to remain in good standing within the church. Apparently, the proponents of these views had once been a part of the established church in Asia Minor, but at some time made a distinct break from this fellowship. It seems members of this subversive group were attempting to lure the faithful away from the apostles' authoritative teachings. For this reason, John wanted to make it clear that these people were false teachers. In fact, he considered them archenemies of the Messiah.

Notes on the Printed Text

In 1 John 3:11-24, the apostle wrote about the impact of Christian love. He began by stressing that what people believed was validated by the presence of compassion and kindness in their lives. John's message to his readers was not something new, but what they had heard from the beginning of their Christian experience, namely, that God's children were to "love one another" (vs. 11). In fact, the practice of love toward fellow believers was profoundly related to the reality of salvation in a person's life.

Before John told his audience exactly what Christlike love was, first he revealed what it was not (see also the Bible commentary in lesson 13 dealing with 1 Corinthians 13). The apostle used an illustration from the dawn of human existence. It is the account of the first murder in history (see Gen. 4:2-8). The point of the illustration is that Cain's murder of his brother, Abel, is the exact opposite of genuine love and certainly not the kind of behavior to be found among Jesus' followers. John pointed out that by murdering his brother, Cain proved he was a child of Satan, the "wicked one" (1 John 3:12). The reason for Cain's homicidal act was his jealousy and resentment toward Abel's virtuous character as compared with Cain's own ungodliness.

Numerous conjectures have been recorded as to why Abel's sacrifice was superior to Cain's. Some think God accepted Abel's sacrifice because, as an animal offering, it involved blood, whereas Cain's, as a type of grain offering, did not. However, we don't have clearly recorded specifications for blood sacrifices until the Book of Leviticus. Others note that Abel's sacrifice was living and Cain's was lifeless, or that Abel's grew spontaneously and Cain's grew by human ingenuity. Perhaps the strongest reason Abel's offering was accepted and Cain's was rejected lies in the attitude of both brothers. Abel offered his sacrifice willingly, and so his was a demonstration of faith (see Heb. 11:4). Because of the reference to Cain belonging to the "wicked one" (1 John 3:12), Cain's name became associated with the devil and wicked deeds in general. At first, the carrying out of such deeds was referred to as "raising the devil." But some, preferring not to mention Satan's name, substituted "raising Cain."

In general, Cain was an illustration of the world. This is the realm of evil, which one day would pass away (see 2:15-17). Since unsaved humanity displayed the heinous qualities Cain possessed and acted upon, Christians should not be astonished that unbelievers hated them (3:13). Moreover, Christians should expect the wicked to treat Jesus' followers just as wicked Cain treated his godly brother. Jesus warned His disciples that they should anticipate the world would hate them because it hated Him first (see John 15:18-19, 25). While the world's hatred of believers was commonplace, the hatred of one Christian for another was inexcusable. Indeed, it was out of sync with the eternal life that came through faith in the Messiah.

In 1 John 3:14, the apostle connected love to life and hatred to death. The test that one had truly experienced new life in Christ was an ever-deepening love for other believers. God's children naturally had a desire to meet together for prayer and fellowship. In contrast, an unbelieving world wanted no part of such activity. So, to harbor hatred for believers suggested a closer intimacy with the world than with the Savior. Verse 15 is even more blunt in equating hatred with murder and declaring that "eternal life" could not flourish in the toxic soil of a homicidal disposition. Likewise, in the Sermon on the Mount, Jesus equated the hatred of one person for another with spiritual or moral murder, just as He equated lust with adultery (see Matt. 5:21-22, 28).

In 1 John 3:16, the apostle pointed his readers to the Lord Jesus as the most sterling example of unconditional love. The Savior gave His life so that believing sinners might have new life in Him. John 3:16 teaches a similar truth. The Father, being motivated by His infinite love for lost humanity, sent His uniquely precious Son to die for the sins of the world. God summons all people to put their faith in Messiah—not only assenting to what He said as true, but also entrusting their lives to Him. Those who believe in the Savior do not suffer eternal separation from God, but enjoy a reconciled, deeply satisfying relationship with the Son and His heavenly Father.

The apostle declared that because the Lord Jesus gave His life on the cross to redeem the lost, His disciples should be ready and willing to demonstrate self-sacrificing love for their fellow Christians (1 John 3:16). Admittedly, not many believers will be called to literally sacrifice their lives for another believer. Nonetheless, as verse 17 reveals, Jesus' followers can show their unconditional love by meeting the needs of others. This includes believers giving sacrificially of their material resources. Christlike love should prompt God's children to display empathy and concern for others in need of the basic necessities of life—such as food, clothing, and shelter. God's love demands nothing less. Christians who refuse to be moved by the need of others reveal an absence of divine love in their hearts. Today it is often said that talk is cheap. Apparently, it was no different in John's time. For that reason, the apostle warned his readers that mere verbal expressions of love with no actions were useless in the face of dire need (vs. 18).

A great sense of failure or inadequacy might result when believers compare their faith in action to the high standard set by the Lord Jesus. In this regard, the hearts of His followers might condemn them, even though they have been performing the practical acts of love referred to in verses 16-18. The apostle reminded his readers that, as practicing Christians, they were not only abiding in the truth of the gospel, but also dwelling in the comforting presence of God (vs. 19). Even when His children felt a false sense of guilt, they could draw consolation from the truth that their heavenly Father knew everything about them. In fact, His knowledge exceeded that of their troubled hearts (vs. 20). Jesus' followers might have an oversensitive spirit to their own inadequacies, when they should be resting in the sufficiency of God's grace. In this instance, anxious believers ought to find repose in the knowledge that an all-compassionate God is aware of their genuine acts of faith.

John associated the serenity that comes from being in God's loving hands with confidence in prayer. As a result of performing deeds of mercy and kindness, believers could find peace for their troubled consciences and approach God's throne with confidence in prayer (vs. 21). As they did so, they could rest assured that God would hear and respond to their requests (vs. 22). In order for their petitions to be answered, the habitual conduct of their lives had to be characterized by submission and obedience to God. John was by no means suggesting that occasionally keeping God's commands and sporadically doing His will were sufficient grounds upon which to expect answers to prayer. Those who played fast and loose with God's boundaries for living and displayed little regard for His will had no claim upon Him. God was not a genie who existed to grant the selfish desires of humankind. Instead, He was the moral Governor of the universe who deserved unquestioned obedience from those He created.

Verse 23 draws attention to the Creator's supreme two-part command. God's children were directed to trust in His Son, the Lord Jesus, for eternal life and be unconditionally loving to one another. This is the first explicit reference to faith in John's epistle. Evidently, the false teachers of John's time insisted that "Jesus" and "the Messiah" were separate individuals. In contrast, the apostle taught that the historic person, Jesus of Nazareth, is identical with the Messiah, God's Son (see John 20:31; 1 John 4:15; 5:5). To put one's trust in Jesus' name meant to believe in everything that it represented. This included affirming Jesus as being fully human and fully divine. Faith in the Son's name also involved appropriating His redemptive work on the cross for oneself and depending upon the Spirit to help God's children mature.

In 1 John 3:24, the apostle discussed the concept of mutual abiding—the believer in the Son and He in the believer. This truth is evident in the parable of the vine and branches (see John 15:1-17). The apostle revealed that obedience is the basis for living in vital union with the Messiah. Furthermore, in 1 John 3:24, the apostle stated that the claim to abide in the Son was validated by a believer's fidelity to three foundational commands: (1) believing in the Savior; (2) loving one another (vs. 23); and (3) living in a godly manner (see vss. 7-10). Abiding in Jesus was not an assertion that could be successfully made without convincing evidence. For instance, such a claim must be accompanied by a confession that Jesus is the Son of God and Savior of the world, as well as by a life characterized by unconditional love for other believers and the practice of personal holiness.

SUGGESTIONS TO TEACHERS

We learn from 1 John 3 that a genuine relationship with God will make a difference in how a person lives. In fact, the apostle outlined for his readers what a person with a genuine relationship would be like. These identifying markers include living uprightly, obeying the Lord, and loving other believers. Plan to take a few moments to consider each of these with your students.

1. WALKING IN RIGHTEOUSNESS. This is the first of several marks of a genuine relationship with God. Broadly speaking, to walk in righteousness means to live uprightly. If we want to be followers of the Lord Jesus, we must be willing to conduct ourselves in a virtuous manner. That implies changing any attitude or action not in keeping with the example Jesus set for us.

2. OBEYING THE LORD. Another mark of believers should be their obedience to God. If you became aware that someone had been pretending to be your friend because that person felt obligated to or was just trying to look good in front of others, the "friendship" would be meaningless. We must not have that kind of relationship with God, one propped up by legalistically obeying His commands. Our obedience, like the Savior's, should come from our love for God, not from just doing what He says we should do. Then others will notice the joy we have in our relationship with Him.

3. LOVING OTHER BELIEVERS. This is a third identifying mark. Jesus stressed it in John 13:35, and showing love is a corresponding emphasis throughout 1 John.

When believers demonstrate sacrificial, not self-seeking, love toward each other, they stand out in our "me-first" world. Their priority becomes giving instead of taking. They are encouraging to each other rather than berating. That kind of love should show others the depth of our relationship with God.

4. ASSESSING OURSELVES. We should ask ourselves if areas of our lives need to change to better reflect a genuine, vibrant relationship with the Lord. How is our love for fellow believers? Are we living uprightly? Do we heed the teachings of Scripture? The answers to these questions aren't meant to condemn us, but to encourage us to press on in truth, obedience, and love.

For Adults

■ **Topic:** We Need Love

■ **Questions:** 1. Why is it important for believers to love one another? 2. Why does unsaved humanity tend to hate God's children? 3. When believers demonstrate Christlike love to others, how does it impact their witness? 4. How can believers obtain divine consolation when they feel a sense of false guilt? 5. Why did John place a strong emphasis on believing in the name of the Son?

■ **Illustrations:**

Love: The Bottom Line. In 1 John 3, the apostle used the word "love" multiple times. First, he described Jesus' great love for us. Then, the apostle emphasized that Jesus' followers would act like Him. Finally, John stressed the importance of believers demonstrating the Savior's love toward others, especially fellow believers.

In 1965, Jackie DeShannon wrote and performed the top ten single "What the World Needs Now Is Love." The chorus for this popular song stated that love is "the only thing that there's just too little of" and that "sweet love" is "not just for some but for everyone."

Few people would claim that DeShannon's sentiments don't apply today. In an era in which people tend to live for themselves and take advantage of others to satisfy their own desires, the world needs a special kind of love. It's not the sort, though, that we hoard for ourselves. We need the love of the Savior, a practical love that seeks the benefit of others, a caring love that is active and sincere.

Living in the Light of Jesus' Love. Depending on where we live, we are required to take our automobiles for periodic inspections, either for mechanical worthiness or for emission controls. When our vehicles pass the inspection, we are free to enjoy all the privileges of driving these marvels of technology.

John's letter is like that. In chapter 3, he writes so that his readers can pass the test and enjoy the blessings of eternal life in Christ. That's why John's epistle is so practical. He gives clear pass-fail grades. "If you do this, you pass. If not, you fail."

All of us need John's reminders about letting the light of Jesus' love shine in every aspect of our lives. After all, professing faith in the Son is supposed to make a difference. The changes include loving Jesus rather than the pagan ways of the world and displaying compassion instead of hatred toward our fellow human beings.

The Way of Love. Tax changes, human rights, welfare reform, food-safety regulations, healthcare legislation—numerous programs and laws have been developed to make life easier for various groups of people in the United States. In most cases, the intent is good. Some programs are successful in reaching individuals with needed services.

Then there is a new election, a new party in power, or a new social agenda. And the old programs are dismantled or put on hold, in favor of others that are more politically appropriate. The reason such changes happen is simple: the real heart behind the programs and laws is mere paper. Though they were good for a time, they lacked the one ingredient that could invest them with permanent value.

The apostle John knew what that ingredient was when he wrote to believers in Asia Minor. He called it *love*. We can spend all of our free time working in homeless shelters or volunteering at a nursing home. But John knew that such actions could have no eternal value unless they were the result of Christ-centered love.

For Youth

■ **Topic:** Show Me Love

■ **Questions:** 1. How is the proclamation of the gospel adversely affected when believers fail to love one another? 2. How can believers know for sure that they have passed out of spiritual death into eternal life? 3. Why did Jesus sacrifice His life on the cross for us? 4. What precondition did John place on believers receiving answers to their prayers? 5. What does it mean to live in vital union with the Messiah?

■ **Illustrations:**

Love Rules! What is it like to live in the light of Jesus' love, as 1 John 3:16 emphasizes? Have you ever entered a dark room or an abandoned apartment, turned on the light, and watched the cockroaches scurry away? Living in the light means we do not have to run away when Jesus shines the truth of His Word on our lives. It means we welcome His inspections. According to the apostle John, it means letting the Savior's love guide our conduct.

That's a tough assignment and sometimes we fail to make the grade. But Jesus forgives us when we confess our sins. He pardons our transgressions. That's why it's so important to stay close to Him, whatever our circumstances. Jesus not only tells us how to be compassionate, but also helps us to display kindness when we rely on Him.

Love Comes First. American pastor, author, and sociologist, Tony Campolo, tells the story of a 13-year-old hydrocephalic girl living in a Haitian missionary hospital. The girl, brain-damaged and deformed from an accumulation of fluid in her head, rocked nervously on her bed, day after day, year after year. The Haitian nurses, though very busy with more hopeful cases, lovingly tended this girl, feeding her, changing her diapers, and tending to her safety needs.

One day the girl accidentally rocked herself off her bed and onto the cement floor, seriously injuring herself. The nurses could have dismissed the fall as being "God's will" and cut down on her care. Instead, they chose to increase her care and to spend long hours in prayer for her.

We learn from 1 John 3 that loving the unlovely is a Christian's mandate and challenge. Will we love those we find physically and mentally repulsive? And will we care about and care for society's "hopeless"?

It is through our meaningful relationships—those based on love, full of grace and truth—that we best reflect Jesus' love and draw others to faith in Him. Love for others is the foremost commandment when it comes to practicing our profession of faith in the Savior.

Called to Love. Pastor Jeff Wallace recalls a time when his young daughter, Gracie, was holding his hand as they walked out of a convention hall where they had heard a gifted preacher convey afresh the love and mercy of the Lord Jesus. Jeff noticed Gracie's rapt attention as the preacher spoke. And Jeff, too, was greatly moved and impressed by the minister's sermon.

Jeff relates that he was not surprised when Gracie looked up at him and asked, "Daddy, did you think that was a good preacher?" "Oh, yes, sweetheart, he is a great preacher," Jeff responded. "Do you think he's a better preacher than you are?" Gracie continued. "Oh, yes, sweetheart, he's a much better preacher than I am," Jeff admitted. "Not really, Daddy," Gracie concluded. "The only preacher better than you is Jesus!"

Jeff made the following observation: "Of course, my confidence in my preaching ability has little affected my daughter's opinion. But my heart was overjoyed by her expression of pure love and devotion. Love does that. It always affects. It always brings joy. It always builds up. Love is the only service that power cannot command and money cannot buy. Love is the key to the universe that unlocks all doors. Love is more than a characteristic of God. It is His character."

LESSON 8 — APRIL 19

RECOGNIZING GOD'S LOVE

BACKGROUND SCRIPTURE: 1 John 4–5
DEVOTIONAL READING: Romans 8:31-39

Key Verse: Whosoever believeth that Jesus is the Christ is born of God: and every one that loveth him that begat loveth him also that is begotten of him. 1 John 5:1.

KING JAMES VERSION

1 JOHN 4:13 Hereby know we that we dwell in him, and he in us, because he hath given us of his Spirit.
14 And we have seen and do testify that the Father sent the Son to be the Saviour of the world.
15 Whosoever shall confess that Jesus is the Son of God, God dwelleth in him, and he in God. 16 And we have known and believed the love that God hath to us. God is love; and he that dwelleth in love dwelleth in God, and God in him.
17 Herein is our love made perfect, that we may have boldness in the day of judgment: because as he is, so are we in this world. 18 There is no fear in love; but perfect love casteth out fear: because fear hath torment. He that feareth is not made perfect in love. 19 We love him, because he first loved us. 20 If a man say, I love God, and hateth his brother, he is a liar: for he that loveth not his brother whom he hath seen, how can he love God whom he hath not seen? 21 And this commandment have we from him, That he who loveth God love his brother also.
5:1 Whosoever believeth that Jesus is the Christ is born of God: and every one that loveth him that begat loveth him also that is begotten of him. 2 By this we know that we love the children of God, when we love God, and keep his commandments. 3 For this is the love of God, that we keep his commandments: and his commandments are not grievous. 4 For whatsoever is born of God overcometh the world: and this is the victory that overcometh the world, even our faith. 5 Who is he that overcometh the world, but he that believeth that Jesus is the Son of God?

NEW REVISED STANDARD VERSION

1 JOHN 4:13 By this we know that we abide in him and he in us, because he has given us of his Spirit. 14 And we have seen and do testify that the Father has sent his Son as the Savior of the world. 15 God abides in those who confess that Jesus is the Son of God, and they abide in God. 16 So we have known and believe the love that God has for us.
God is love, and those who abide in love abide in God, and God abides in them. 17 Love has been perfected among us in this: that we may have boldness on the day of judgment, because as he is, so are we in this world. 18 There is no fear in love, but perfect love casts out fear; for fear has to do with punishment, and whoever fears has not reached perfection in love. 19 We love because he first loved us. 20 Those who say, "I love God," and hate their brothers or sisters, are liars; for those who do not love a brother or sister whom they have seen, cannot love God whom they have not seen. 21 The commandment we have from him is this: those who love God must love their brothers and sisters also.
5:1 Everyone who believes that Jesus is the Christ has been born of God, and everyone who loves the parent loves the child. 2 By this we know that we love the children of God, when we love God and obey his commandments. 3 For the love of God is this, that we obey his commandments. And his commandments are not burdensome, 4 for whatever is born of God conquers the world. And this is the victory that conquers the world, our faith. 5 Who is it that conquers the world but the one who believes that Jesus is the Son of God?

Home Bible Readings

Monday, April 13	1 Peter 1:8-12	*Obtaining Spiritual Discernment*
Tuesday, April 14	1 Peter 3:8-12	*Seeking Unity of Spirit*
Wednesday, April 15	Romans 12:9-18	*Be Steadfast in the Spirit*
Thursday, April 16	Romans 8:31-39	*Nothing Can Separate Us*
Friday, April 17	1 John 4:1-6	*Scrutinize What People Claim*
Saturday, April 18	1 John 4:7-12	*God's Incredible Love for Us*
Sunday, April 19	1 John 4:13—5:5	*Love God, Love Others*

Background

In John 4:13, the apostle discussed the mutual abiding of a believer and the Lord Jesus. *Meno* (MEE-know) was one of John's favorite Greek words to describe the nature of the believer's relationship with God. Most often translated as "remain," "abide," "live," or "continue," this term occurs 112 times in the New Testament. Of these occurrences, 66 are found in the writings of John (40 in the Gospel of John, 23 in 1 John, and 3 in 2 John). Some scholars have suggested that *meno* actually signifies something beyond simple fellowship with God. The progression is given as (1) knowledge of God, (2) fellowship with God, and finally, (3) abiding in God. Clearly, John desired the deepest possible relationship between God and His children.

For proof that this mutual abiding is in effect, one has to look for the work of the Holy Spirit in that believer's life. Obedience to the two-part command to believe in the Messiah and love one another is a direct result of the Spirit's work within a believer's heart (see Rom. 5:5; 1 John 3:24; 4:2). So, a Christian's Spirit-prompted obedience is the real evidence that a believer and the triune God abide in one another. The apostle had just told his readers that if we are characterized by Christlike compassion, then the invisible God lives in us and His love for us is brought to full expression in our love for others (1 John 4:12).

Notes on the Printed Text

First John 4:7-12 begins the apostle's third significant discourse on the subject of Christlike love. (The first was given in 2:7-11 and the second in 3:11-18.) This is also the third time in his letter that the apostle employed love as the supreme test of Christian commitment and character. Furthermore, in 4:7-12, John gave three significant statements about the essence and nature of God. The apostle had previously revealed that "God is a Spirit" (John 4:24) and "God is light" (1 John 1:5). In 4:7-12, he described what is perhaps the supreme quality of the Lord's character, "God is love" (vs. 8). While false teachers believed that God is a spirit being and that He is light, they also taught that God is passionless and so incapable of love.

John stated that if Christlike love is not present in an individual, then that person cannot possibly have an intimate knowledge of God. Though the phrase "born of God" is not present in verse 8 as it is in its counterpart in verse 7, John was likely talking about someone who had no faith in Jesus, and is incapable of showing divine, unconditional love. Believers should love one another because God is the source of love and because He is in fact the essence of love. In verse 8, John was referring to an aspect of God's character. It would be theologically incorrect, however, to declare "love is God," for love is not the sole quality that absolutely defines the nature of the Lord.

We learn in verse 13 that the Holy Spirit residing within believers is the way they can rest assured that they remain in God and that He dwells in them. Indeed, the preceding experience validates our testimony that the Father sent His Son to be the Savior of the world (vs. 14). In practical terms, while God is invisible to the eye, He becomes visible in a spiritual sense when His indwelling presence is evident in the mutual love between believers. In light of what the apostle just said, he told his readers that anyone who acknowledged that Jesus is the Son of God was indwelled by God and in turn dwells in God (vs. 15). Here is another test or evidence of mutual indwelling. Life-changing belief in the deity of the Savior suggests obedience to Him and surrender to His will.

John rounded out his discussion by declaring that believers know how much God loves them, and they have put their trust in the God of love. As Christians live in a community of mutual love with other believers, it results in an intimate experience of God's love and a renewed faith in that love. As before, John reaffirmed the truth that everyone who abides in love experiences intimate fellowship with the Lord (vs. 16). According to the apostle, abiding in love would also produce boldness in the day of judgment (vs. 17). Paul similarly described a time of evaluation in which the works of all believers would be judged. This is commonly known as the judgment seat or *bema* (bei-MAH). In ancient Greek literature, the judgment seat usually referred to a chair or throne set up in a public place. From this spot, judicial decisions and other official business were conducted.

At the judgment seat of Christ (see 1 Cor. 3:10-15), those spiritual buildings of believers that are constructed with imperishable materials will be left standing and their builders will be given a reward. Those buildings constructed of consumable materials will be reduced to ashes and their owners will suffer loss—while still being saved. Bible scholars differ on the nature of this "loss." Some claim it is regret when they have no works of any quality to present to Christ. Others say this loss will involve diminished responsibility in the kingdom of God and withholding of reward that might have been theirs if they had acted more faithfully.

Paul said the fires of God's omniscience and justice would test the believer's works. The apostle used the metaphor of an ongoing construction project to illustrate the materials with which Christians could build their lives. The indisputable foundation was faith in the Lord Jesus. Those who demonstrated a life of obedience were like contractors who selected the best stones available to construct their building. Those who compromised the commandments of God and wavered in their commitment were like laborers who used easily consumed materials such as wood, hay, and straw to shore up their structures.

As we live in God, our love for one another grows more perfect and is made complete among us (1 John 4:17). This unselfish kindness is the same compassion that God, who is love, reproduces in His children by placing His Spirit in them. If this love is perfected in the believer's life on earth, it will produce a confidence to approach the judgment seat of Christ without shame or regret. The basis for this confidence is the believer's present likeness to the Son, and in this particular case, a likeness in His love. As was John's habit, he followed the positive aspect of this spiritual truth with its negative counterpart. The apostle noted that fear is the opposite of confidence before the Savior at His coming (vs. 18). If a believer anticipates the judgment seat of Christ with fear of some impending punishment, love has not been made complete in that believer's heart. The full flowering of God's love is incompatible with fear. Perfected love expels anxiety from the heart.

The catalyst for loving other believers (and likewise for having confidence at Christ's return) is the love God first showed for us (vs. 19). Christians who love other believers also love God. The real proof that a Christian loves God, in John's estimation, is the love he or she demonstrates to fellow believers (vs. 20). A Christian's love for other believers (who are visible) proves his or her love for God (who is invisible). While it is easy to proclaim, "I love God," John pointed out that genuine piety is demonstrated by Christian love. The one who claims to love God while hating other believers, said John (in his typical bluntness), is a liar. These people are also commandment breakers, because God had established that we must love not only Him, but also our Christian brothers and sisters (vs. 21). Here the two objects of Christian love are joined together. Love for God cannot be separated from love for our fellow believers in Christ.

Throughout his first letter, John offered his readers three tests designed to gauge their relationship with God. These were (1) belief; (2) love for God and fellow believers; and (3) obedience to God's commands. The apostle's three tests are vitally connected. The genuine Christian believes in God's Son, loves God and His children, and obeys God's commands. All three, according to John, are hallmarks of the new birth. Of course, the ground of our fellowship with the Father and other believers is belief in the Son (1 John 5:1). This common belief in the Messiah unites God's children to Him and to each other in love.

John told his readers that the new birth brings us into a parent-child relationship with the all-powerful Creator of the universe. This naturally involves love for Him who reached out to us and saved us, even though we were undeserving. Next, the apostle went on to suggest that what is true in a human family is also true in the spiritual family. Love for the Father naturally leads to love for the Father's children. Like the people in our biological families, we love other Christians just because they are "family." From John's perspective, it is as impossible to love the children of God without loving Him as it is to love God without loving His children (vs. 2).

Besides love for believers, John identified one other inescapable result of loving God: obedience to His commands (vs. 3). As the Bible commentary in lesson 13 explains, love for God has less to do with emotions than with an unconditional obedience to His will. Just as love for other Christians is expressed, not in rhetorical statements, but by one's actions (3:18), so real love for God is actively demonstrated by keeping His commands. James, in his letter, wrestled with spurious claims to faith. For instance, 2:18 anticipates an imaginary objector declaring, "Thou hast faith, and I have works." The idea is that there are two equally-valid types of faith—one that simply believes and another that acts on that belief. James challenged the idea that genuine, saving faith has no effect on the way a person acts. In short, trusting in the Messiah is authenticated by doing kind deeds to others. Just as James taught, John insisted that genuine faith and good works go hand in hand. Moreover, God's commandments do not weigh down believers because the Spirit gives them the ability to obey the Lord (1 John 5:3).

Unsaved humanity views God's commandments as an unbearable drag. In contrast, those experiencing the new birth triumph over the world (vs. 4). This includes overcoming the false beliefs and practices of those opposed to the gospel. Indeed, this conquest has already been accomplished through the faith Christians have in Jesus as the "Son of God" (vs. 5). Put another way, faith in the full divinity and humanity of the Savior is the Christians' best defense against a dark world system controlled by Satan. Indeed, this truth is their greatest weapon and strongest shield (see Eph. 6:16).

SUGGESTIONS TO TEACHERS

We have an eternity to revel in the glory of the Father's gift of love through His Son. Even so, we can begin now to praise God for His goodness to us. Furthermore, we can honor His display of love by our acts of unselfish kindness and sacrificial compassion toward others.

1. GOD ACTED FIRST. God initiated the love He expressed toward us. Even though at first we did not love Him, He voluntarily chose to love us. In fact, while we were still rebellious and separated from the Father, He sent His Son to secure our redemption at Calvary (see Rom. 5:6-8).

2. GOD GAVE US HIS SPIRIT. Because we cannot see God, He has given us the Holy Spirit as evidence of His presence within us. God's Spirit enables us to acknowledge that Jesus is the Son of God. The Spirit also empowers us to live in a way that is characterized by patience, empathy, and sensitivity to others.

3. GOD ENABLES US TO APPROACH HIM WITH CONFIDENCE. God's love is made complete in believers as they show faith in Him and love to others. Moreover, God's children receive confidence regarding the future time of judgment. Living in union with the triune God enables them to someday confidently approach the judgment seat of Christ.

4. GOD CALLS US TO BELIEVE AND OBEY. John spoke of a decisive public confession of believers that the Son of God came in the flesh. This is not an academic exercise, but a realization of who Jesus is and the necessary response of His disciples: submission and obedience. Moreover, both correct belief and love are genuine evidences of God's presence in the lives of His spiritual children.

FOR ADULTS

■ **TOPIC:** Beloved Child

■ **QUESTIONS:** 1. What role does the Spirit play in our lives as Christians? 2. How much do you depend on the Spirit to show God's love to others? 3. Why is it important for us to rely on God's love as we live for Him? 4. Why is it impossible for love and hatred to coexist in our lives as God's children? 5. What is the connection between faith in the Son and overcoming the world?

■ **ILLUSTRATIONS:**

Love of the Highest Quality. An older carpenter prepared to retire. He told the contractor for whom he worked about his plans to stop building and to enjoy a more leisurely life with his wife and extended family. He would miss the paycheck, but he needed to retire. They could get by.

The contractor was sorry to see his good worker go and asked whether he would build just one more house as a personal favor. The carpenter agreed, but in time it was easy to see that his heart wasn't in his work. He grew careless and took shortcuts on quality. It was an unfortunate way to end his career. When the carpenter finished the house, the contractor handed him the front-door key. "This is your house," the contractor said. "It's my gift to you in appreciation for all your dedicated work."

If the carpenter had known he was building his own house, he would have done it all so differently! We build our lives every day by the way we express God's love to those around us (see 1 John 4:20-21). Our love should be like the love of Jesus—only the highest quality—so that our lives will be like His, too.

A Picture of Love. In 1997, the Tamagotchi first began to interest American children. It's a pocket-sized Japanese toy whose name literally means "crude little egg." For nearly three decades, American toy companies have met the challenge by designing their own versions.

For instance, in 2013, a mobile application of the toy was introduced as an egg-shaped virtual "pet" that needs to be fed, vaccinated, played with, disciplined, cleaned up after, and loved. If the owner forgets to love it or fails to meet its demands, the little figure on the screen "dies" and disappears into cyberspace.

Real love is always ready to make sacrifices. Consider our heavenly Father, who gave us the perfect picture of love by sending to earth His one and only Son, the Lord

Jesus (see 1 John 2:14). In John 3:16, we learn that the Father made salvation available to the lost through the advent of His Son. In turn, all who put their faith in the Redeemer have eternal life (see 1 John 2:25).

God's Incomparable Love. In the 1979 American drama film *Kramer vs. Kramer*, there is a heart-wrenching incident when a father momentarily turns his eyes away from his son playing on a jungle gym. In that instant, the boy slips and falls to the ground. The child's father rushes to his side, sees blood running from his son's head, and panics.

Next, as the father carries his son, he races for the nearest emergency room. Once there, the father holds the boy's head as the physician makes the necessary stitches. With every tug of the thread, the child whimpers in pain. And so does his loving father.

No parent wants to see his or her child experience pain. Our heavenly Father is no different. Nonetheless, He sent His Son, Jesus Christ, to die for our sake (see 1 John 4:14, 19). This week's lesson takes a close look at God's incredible love for human beings and the extraordinary price He was willing to pay to save us from our sin. It was a gift He gave to us that we can never repay.

For Youth

■ **Topic:** Loving My Brothers and Sisters

■ **Questions:** 1. Why did the Father send His Son into the world? 2. With whom can you share the good news of the Father sending His Son? 3. What are some ways we can demonstrate to others that we truly love God? 4. Why does the presence of fear prevent us from being made spiritually complete by God's love? 5. Why is it sometimes hard for us to love our fellow Christians?

■ **Illustrations:**

Blessed by Love. We like to sing, "They'll know we are Christians by our love," which is straight from the teaching of Jesus. But how much harder it is to practice the words. Any group of Christian teens is bound to include some who are not especially lovable. In fact, they may turn others off by their rude behavior.

Yet we cannot dodge the tough commands of Jesus and John. To love is our inescapable imperative and the source of one of God's greatest blessings. Failure to do so negates our Christian profession. Perhaps we need to confess our bad attitudes and listless behavior. Out of our weakness we must ask Jesus to make us more loving toward others, including those who may turn us off.

Who Loves You? An old man died, leaving one child—a son—as his sole survivor. The father had been hard to know. The son remembered a respectful but formal relationship. Suddenly he was alone in his father's house looking through all the items kept in all the places a child never looks when his or her parents are alive.

The big stuff was easy to deal with—property, life insurance, and bank accounts. It was the personal stuff that was difficult to handle. Finally the son came to the bureau drawers in the bedroom. Here were carefully sorted socks. There were several small boxes and a cigar tin. One box held military insignia, another tie tacks and foreign coins. This one had miscellaneous keys. That one held his mother's wedding ring and a lock of her hair.

In the cigar tin was a yellowed index card wrapped in tissue paper. Tiny teeth were glued to the card. A date was jotted under each tooth in his father's neat handwriting. His father had been the tooth fairy. The son always assumed it was his mother.

As 1 John 4:14 and 19 reveal, God first loved us in ways we've never imagined. He isn't distant and uncaring, either. He has been looking out for us since the day we were born. We can depend on Him to keep doing so forever. He isn't going to leave us as orphans, like the son in the story. Be sure your relationship with your heavenly Father is closer than the relationship in the story. God wants it that way!

Genuine Faith in the Son. The story is told of a man who wanted to learn everything about jade. He went to an old Chinese master who was reputed to be one of the world's experts in jade. The elderly Chinese authority told the man that he would teach him, but the lessons would require ten days of complete attention. The man agreed to give full attention to the master.

On the first day, the master brought out an exquisite piece of green jade. He instructed the man to examine it closely for ten hours. The next day, the aged Chinese expert handed the man another beautiful jade, and gave him the same instruction to study the piece for ten hours. No other word was spoken. That evening, as before, the master collected the jade piece he had handed the learner in the morning. The same procedure was followed the third day, the fourth, and so on.

At the end of the tenth day, the master informed the learner he had nothing more to teach him. The man was perplexed. He complained, "The expert never said a word about jade to me during any of those ten days. On the last day, he wasted my time by handing me a fake piece of jade."

When you learn the difference between the false ways and the real God, you will move from a fake faith to one that is centered in the Son and overcomes the world (see 1 John 5:1, 4-5). Moreover, when you know Jesus so well, your life will proclaim the truth of God's love (see 4:16). You will have a fresh message that those around you desperately need to hear.

LESSON 9 — APRIL 26

REMAINING VIGILANT

BACKGROUND SCRIPTURE: 1 John 5:6-12, 18-20; 2 John
DEVOTIONAL READING: Galatians 6:6-10

Key Verse: Look to yourselves, that we lose not those things which we have wrought, but that we receive a full reward. 2 John 8.

KING JAMES VERSION

2 JOHN 1 The elder unto the elect lady and her children, whom I love in the truth; and not I only, but also all they that have known the truth; 2 For the truth's sake, which dwelleth in us, and shall be with us for ever. 3 Grace be with you, mercy, and peace, from God the Father, and from the Lord Jesus Christ, the Son of the Father, in truth and love. 4 I rejoiced greatly that I found of thy children walking in truth, as we have received a commandment from the Father.

5 And now I beseech thee, lady, not as though I wrote a new commandment unto thee, but that which we had from the beginning, that we love one another. 6 And this is love, that we walk after his commandments. This is the commandment, That, as ye have heard from the beginning, ye should walk in it.

7 For many deceivers are entered into the world, who confess not that Jesus Christ is come in the flesh. This is a deceiver and an antichrist. 8 Look to yourselves, that we lose not those things which we have wrought, but that we receive a full reward. 9 Whosoever transgresseth, and abideth not in the doctrine of Christ, hath not God. He that abideth in the doctrine of Christ, he hath both the Father and the Son.

10 If there come any unto you, and bring not this doctrine, receive him not into your house, neither bid him God speed: 11 For he that biddeth him God speed is partaker of his evil deeds.

12 Having many things to write unto you, I would not write with paper and ink: but I trust to come unto you, and speak face to face, that our joy may be full. 13 The children of thy elect sister greet thee. Amen.

NEW REVISED STANDARD VERSION

2 JOHN 1 The elder to the elect lady and her children, whom I love in the truth, and not only I but also all who know the truth, 2 because of the truth that abides in us and will be with us forever:

3 Grace, mercy, and peace will be with us from God the Father and from Jesus Christ, the Father's Son, in truth and love.

4 I was overjoyed to find some of your children walking in the truth, just as we have been commanded by the Father. 5 But now, dear lady, I ask you, not as though I were writing you a new commandment, but one we have had from the beginning, let us love one another. 6 And this is love, that we walk according to his commandments; this is the commandment just as you have heard it from the beginning—you must walk in it.

7 Many deceivers have gone out into the world, those who do not confess that Jesus Christ has come in the flesh; any such person is the deceiver and the antichrist! 8 Be on your guard, so that you do not lose what we have worked for, but may receive a full reward.
9 Everyone who does not abide in the teaching of Christ, but goes beyond it, does not have God; whoever abides in the teaching has both the Father and the Son.
10 Do not receive into the house or welcome anyone who comes to you and does not bring this teaching;
11 for to welcome is to participate in the evil deeds of such a person.

12 Although I have much to write to you, I would rather not use paper and ink; instead I hope to come to you and talk with you face to face, so that our joy may be complete.

13 The children of your elect sister send you their greetings. [Amen.]

Home Bible Readings

Monday, April 20	Jeremiah 9:1-7	*Deceivers Do Not Know the Lord*
Tuesday, April 21	Acts 15:22-35	*Don't Listen to Impostors*
Wednesday, April 22	Matthew 24:3-14	*False Prophets Lead Many Astray*
Thursday, April 23	Romans 16:16-20	*Avoid Those Who Cause Strife*
Friday, April 24	1 John 5:6-15	*The Boldness We Have in Jesus*
Saturday, April 25	1 John 5:16-21	*God Watches Over His Children*
Sunday, April 26	2 John 1-13	*Be on Your Guard*

Background

The letters of 1 John and 2 John are similar in style and content. This also suggests that the same person wrote the two letters. Furthermore, no compelling reason has ever been given for rejecting the tradition of the early church that the writer of this letter was John the apostle. The identity of the intended readers of the Second Letter of John has posed more difficulty for interpreters of Scripture than the identity of the author. Who were the "elect lady and her children" (vs. 1)? No personal names are given in the correspondence. In contrast, three specific individuals are named in 3 John (to be studied in next week's lesson).

There are two possibilities worth considering. Either the designation "elect lady and her children" (2 John 1) was a literal reference to specific individuals known by the apostle, or else it was a figurative representation of a church in Asia Minor. If the terms are taken literally, the interpretation is clear. The chosen lady was an unidentified individual Christian woman. The children were her natural offspring and the chosen sister mentioned in verse 13 was her natural sibling. If the expression is understood figuratively, then the "elect lady" was a particular church. In the latter case, the "elect sister" of verse 13 was a different body of believers, perhaps John's church at Ephesus. Also, in a figurative understanding of the verse, the chosen lady's children would represent the members of the congregation.

Notes on the Printed Text

The apostle began his second letter with an affirmation of his love for the church and its members. This love was shared by "all they that have known the truth" (2 John 1). This seems to imply that this particular congregation was well known to other churches. The truth about the Savior compelled John and others to love this body of believers (vs. 2). Furthermore, the truth, as revealed in the Son, is the basis of all Christian love. For John, truth is more than objective facts (or "secret knowledge" as taught by a group of religious frauds). Truth indwells believers and enables them to be compassionate to others in an unconditional, unselfish manner.

The apostle, in wishing his readers "grace" (vs. 3), "mercy," and peace," used a greeting common in the New Testament. "Grace" speaks of God's unmerited favor toward sinners and the bestowing of blessings we do not deserve. "Mercy" has to do with divine compassion and the withholding of judgment that we do deserve. "Peace" speaks of the inner serenity that comes from being in a reconciled and growing relationship with God. What is interesting in the apostle's greeting is his declaration that grace, mercy, and peace would be with them in "truth and love" (vs. 3). Here and elsewhere, the apostle emphasized the spiritual qualities he desired for his readers. If they experienced the heavenly virtues of truth and love, they could anticipate the grace, mercy, and peace that come from knowing the Father through faith in the Son.

John wasted no time getting to the two concerns that prompted him to write this second letter. His first concern was for the inner spiritual life of this church, specifically that they continue to walk in obedience to God (vss. 4-6). The apostle's second concern had to do with the external doctrinal danger posed by false teachers and that John's readers staunchly resist their heresies (vss. 7-11). The apostle's two concerns were closely intertwined. A vibrant inner spiritual life is always the best defense against doctrinal error. A believer who is not walking closely with the Lord is vulnerable not only to temptation, but also to wandering from the path of divine truth.

John began the main body of his letter by stating that he was overjoyed to know that some of the members of this church were "walking in truth" (vs. 4). This, plus the apostle's expression of love for the congregation (see vs. 1), suggests that John had either interacted personally with these Christians on another occasion or that he had received some detailed report about their spiritual progress. Like Paul, who began many of his letters with expressions of thanksgiving and joy, John launched the heart of his epistle on a positive note of affirmation.

The apostle's expression of joy, however, was qualified. Only some of the believers to whom he wrote were living according to God's truth. Perhaps some of the people in this congregation had already been swayed by the spiritual charlatans and had left the fellowship—or worse, had remained and were influencing others. The expression "walking in truth" includes believing all that God has revealed in His Word, especially in regard to the Incarnation. In a practical sense, living according to the truth involves conforming one's life to apostolic teaching. Walking in the truth is an act of obedience, because God commands it.

John continued with the subject of God's precepts by using the word "commandment" three more times in verses 5 and 6. First, the apostle pointed out that what he wrote to this church was not some new expectation of believers, but one that was known to his readers from the earliest days of their Christian experience (compare 1 John 2:7, 8; 3:11). In fact, this message was as old as the gospel itself. In this regard, John encouraged his readers to follow Jesus' teaching as first delivered by the apostles, and reject the newly arrived heresies of the false teachers. Here again John addressed the question about the nature of Christian love. The apostle's definition of love is once more stated in terms of obedience to God (2 John 6). Believers who sincerely desire

God's best for their fellow Christians must act in accordance with God's revealed will. At its heart, Christlike love is not just a matter of feeling, but also of doing. It is not a result of warm sentiment, but of unselfish service. This is what it means to fulfill God's command to live in obedience to His will.

John had just admonished his readers to dwell in truth and love. He next addressed one of the key reasons why this was so important. Many false teachers, who denied the incarnation of the Son, were living among the people. These "deceivers" (2 John 7; which could also be translated "ones who lead astray") were a clear and present danger to early Christians such as the apostle's readers. The charlatans were numerous and their doctrine was deadly. The false teachers' rejection of the Messiah's coming in the flesh and taking on a human nature was tantamount to driving a stake into the heart of God's plan of salvation. After all, if Jesus were not truly human, then there could be no sacrificial death and no atonement for sin. Anyone who denied the doctrine of the Incarnation was "a deceiver and an antichrist."

The prefix "anti" means "opposed to." The antichrists opposed the Messiah and His teaching. The false teachers present in John's day were an indicator that human history had passed into the "last time" (or "last hour"; 1 John 2:18). The phrases "last hour" or "last days" in the New Testament usually refer to the historical time period following Jesus' earthly ministry. The coming of many religious frauds heralded the final stage of humanity's experience on earth. The charlatans John referred to in his letters were a group of individuals who had sold out to the ungodly world system (see 4:5). While the apostle's original readers were aware of prophecies concerning the Antichrist, who would appear at the end of time (see 1 John 2:18; Rev. 13:1-10), they needed to be aware that before then many others would come who shared that evil one's enmity for the Savior.

The apostle warned his readers to be on the lookout for spiritual frauds and to be aware of the danger of their teaching (2 John 8). The consequence of compromise with their malignant doctrine was the potential loss of eternal reward. The apostle also warned about those who turned aside from the truth and failed to remain in agreement with what the Messiah taught about Himself. In rejecting the Son, they also spurned the Father (vs. 9). Perhaps there was an imminent danger of defection among the congregation's members.

John contrasted those who depart from the truth with those who continue in it. The faithful have "both the Father and the Son." God remains in close fellowship with those who remain faithful to the truth about Jesus' incarnation. In John's view, the believer who "abideth in the doctrine" is linked in vibrant fellowship with the Father and the Son. Clinging to God's truth is an essential ingredient for the maintenance of one's spiritual life and for progress in growth and maturity. John insisted that it was necessary for believers to have nothing to do with spiritual charlatans (vs. 10). Traveling preachers, teachers, and philosophers were common in New Testament times. In the Christian community, itinerant believers routinely sought and usually found hospitality in the homes of fellow Christians (see 3 John 5-8). It was regarded as an important Christian duty to take them in when they came to town.

These observations notwithstanding, John warned his readers about people who came to them for hospitality but did not bring God's truth with them. The Greek verb rendered "bring" (2 John 10) can also be translated "carry." The picture is of someone who shows up at the door seeking hospitality, but whose luggage does not include God's truth. These religious frauds hauled around lies with them wherever they traveled. Christians, who were faithful to God's truth, were forbidden to show hospitality to anyone who denied what Jesus taught about Himself. The apostle told his readers not only to refuse hospitality to false teachers, but also to refuse to even wish them "God speed." The latter is more literally translated "speak a greeting." To extend a welcome was to have a part in the charlatans' "evil deeds" (vs. 11).

The apostle closed his letter by telling his readers that while there was much he could write to them, he preferred a face-to-face meeting over paper and ink correspondence (vs. 12). The apostle's paper was probably made from the papyrus reed. The pith was cut into strips and laid at right angles. Next, it was pressed and pasted together to make sheets of writing material. The Greek adjective translated "ink" literally means "black." The apostle's "ink" was a compound made of charcoal, gum, and water. John was confident that by personally meeting with his fellow believers, their mutual joy would be made "full" or "complete." The apostle signed off with greetings from members of a "sister" (vs. 13) church who, like the members of the congregation to whom he was writing, were chosen by God's sovereign grace.

SUGGESTIONS TO TEACHERS

Even within the first-century church there were those who promoted distorted teachings. John, in his second epistle, warned his readers to beware of these spiritual deceivers. The apostle also censured them as evil people, particularly for denying the truth Jesus taught about Himself.

1. REMAINING ALERT. We are not immune to the evil schemes and work of false teachers who can creep into our churches. So, we must always be on the lookout for them. We must know what we believe about the Lord Jesus and why.

2. WHEN TO AVOID CULTISTS. Believers who are not deeply rooted in the faith should avoid interacting with cultists. By cleverly twisting the Scriptures, members of these heretical groups have led many new church people astray. Christians who are emotionally vulnerable or not closely tied to a local body should also avoid talking with cultists.

3. WHEN TO CONFRONT CULTISTS. Believers who are firmly grounded in the Word of God should prayerfully consider interacting with members of cults when they come knocking on the door. It is possible to plant seeds of God's truth in the minds of cultists without supporting or enabling them in their efforts.

4. SPOTTING AREAS OF THEOLOGICAL WEAKNESS. If any of the members of your class do engage these cultists, the students' theological weaknesses will probably come to the surface. Encourage them to resolve their vulnerabilities as they appear. By doing so, they will be better able to refute any teaching that falsifies the person and work of the Messiah.

For Adults

■ **Topic:** Fraud Alert

■ **Questions:** 1. What is God's truth and why is it so important to uphold? 2. How have you recently lived out the truth that abides within you? 3. What is the link between believing the truth and being compassionate to others? 4. What was the nature of the false teaching being promoted by religious frauds? 5. What can believers do to remain anchored to the truth Jesus taught about Himself?

■ **Illustrations:**

Recognizing a Fake. The young professional made fun of the owl in the taxidermist's window. "Oh, even I could stuff one better than that," he bragged to his buddies. "That bird hardly looks real at all!" Then the live bird turned to him—and blinked.

Sometimes things are not as they appear. Would you be able to tell a decorative bird from the real one? How about a false teacher from a true one? As 2 John emphasizes, believers have to keep on the lookout for spiritual impostors. One way to recognize them is their denial of the truth Jesus taught about Himself.

From the apostle's letter we discover that even the early church faced the threat of religious frauds. They claimed to speak for the Savior, but denied He had come in the flesh (see vs. 7). It's no wonder John warned his readers not to share in the evil work of these heretics (vs. 11).

A Brightly Shining Truth. Robert P. Dugan, in *Winning the New Civil War*, describes an eerie incident that occurred one day in 1789. The sky over Hartford, Connecticut, had darkened ominously. In the Connecticut House of Representatives, some of the state legislators gathered at windows and began to talk about the end of the world.

Quelling a clamor for immediate adjournment, the Speaker of the House rose and said, "The Day of Judgment is either approaching or it is not. If it is not, there is no cause for adjournment. If it is, I choose to be found doing my duty. Therefore, I wish that candles be brought."

John taught that the best defense against false teaching in these last days is the brightly shining truth Jesus taught about Himself. This includes refusing to support those spiritual frauds who spread falsehoods about the person and work of the Son (see 2 John 10-11).

Do Not Be Deceived. At first, Julie was thrilled about her church's new pastor. Four months later, Julie was searching for a new church secretary's job. The reason? Falsehood.

When the new pastor began, he told the staff they were trusted, talented, and valued employees. Within months, however, he wanted nothing to do with those who had served his predecessor. For instance, the choir, he initially claimed, was known far and wide for helping visitors feel welcomed. Allegedly, it would be supported. Yet, within months, the group was dissolved.

While Julie searched for a new job, she demurred, "For all I know, the new pastor thought those were good decisions. But I resent the fact that we were lied to at the outset." As Julie discovered, the church, like anyplace else, is no stranger to falsehood.

Whether the reason is financial debt, power, or notoriety, lying leaders are a constant threat to the integrity of the gospel and the believers' own spiritual health. This week's lesson from 2 John helps believers remain on the lookout for those who would undermine their commitment to the truth Jesus taught about Himself.

For Youth

■ **Topic:** Beware of Deceivers
■ **Questions:** 1. What are some wholesome ways to express Christian love to others? 2. How well do you know the basic doctrines of the Christian faith? 3. Why is it sometimes challenging to live according to God's truth? 4. Who were the deceivers John referred to in his letter? 5. Why is it tempting for some in the church to wander away from God's truth?

■ **Illustrations:**

Walking in the Truth. When Mason graduated from college, one of his professors expressed disappointment that he had not been able to shake what he called Mason's "Sunday school" faith. The academic had assumed that when Mason got a college education, he would outgrow his childhood beliefs.

Mason, however, learned how to grow in and defend his faith, because in college he joined a Christian group and studied the Bible, prayed, and told other students about the truth Jesus taught concerning Himself. When Mason's faith was attacked in class, he consulted the library shelf where Christians had placed a number of scholarly books that held the Bible to be true and trustworthy.

Keeping the faith required commitment, perseverance, knowledge, and Christian fellowship. Mason knew he could not go through college in neutral as far as his faith was concerned. If he did not spiritually grow, he would coast into indifference and unbelief. So, he shifted into first gear by "walking in truth" (2 John 4) and finished the race.

Being Able to Spot Counterfeits. As a young man, Walter P. Chrysler worked as a master mechanic on a railroad. When Chrysler was 35 years old, he borrowed $5,000 and purchased his first automobile. It was a four-door Locomobile. The car was delivered to his hometown in Iowa and towed—not driven—to a barn at the Chrysler home.

For three months, Walter Chrysler studied that car without ever attempting to drive it. He took his $5,000 Locomobile apart, spread the pieces on newspapers, and made sketches of them. Then Chrysler put the car back together. His theory was that he had to understand that car before he could drive it.

Most of us would benefit from a similar study of the basics of our Christian faith. The apostle John knew that the best way to recognize a counterfeit is to become very familiar with the genuine article. So, he appealed to his readers to walk in the "truth" (2 John 4) and abide in the "doctrine of Christ" (vs. 9). The apostle maintained that if his readers recognized and remained committed to the truth Jesus taught about Himself, they could spot frauds immediately.

A Disconnect between Life and Faith. A youth worker boarded an airplane in Sacramento, California, for a flight to San Diego to attend a national youth ministry conference. He had fastened his seat belt, made sure his chair was in the full upright position, locked his tray table, and properly stowed his luggage when two well-dressed Taylor Swift look-alikes took the seats between him and the aisle.

The youth worker really did try to read his magazine, but it was rather tame compared to the young women's conversation. They talked about the club scene and what they enjoyed drinking. They moved on to discuss their intimate relationships with men, both single and married.

Then it turned into a gripe session. "Why do guys have such a hard time committing?" one asked. "And why don't they ever leave their wives like they promise to?" the other complained. The young women talked about work for a while, and about the time the youth worker thought he could focus on his reading, one of them said, "But you know, if it wasn't for church, my life would fall apart." The women had the youth worker's full attention.

"Wow, you go to church too?" the second girl asked. "I know exactly how you feel. If it wasn't for church, I don't know where I'd be." "Yeah," the first girl said, "if I miss more than two weeks of church everything in my life goes nuts." The plane started its descent into San Diego and everything got quiet as the girls gathered their belongings.

Someone doesn't have to be a false teacher to disconnect faith and life. Too often, our relationship with Jesus and our attendance in church is a religious "fix" that soothes our conscience for the sinful things we did the week before. Perhaps this is one reason why 2 John reminds us to know God's truth and walk in it (see vss. 1, 4).

LESSON 10 — MAY 3

PROMOTING THE TRUTH

BACKGROUND SCRIPTURE: 3 John
DEVOTIONAL READING: 2 Timothy 2:14-19

Key Verse: We therefore ought to receive such, that we might be fellowhelpers to the truth. 3 John 8.

KING JAMES VERSION

3 JOHN 1 The elder unto the wellbeloved Gaius, whom I love in the truth. 2 Beloved, I wish above all things that thou mayest prosper and be in health, even as thy soul prospereth.

3 For I rejoiced greatly, when the brethren came and testified of the truth that is in thee, even as thou walkest in the truth. 4 I have no greater joy than to hear that my children walk in truth. 5 Beloved, thou doest faithfully whatsoever thou doest to the brethren, and to strangers; 6 Which have borne witness of thy charity before the church: whom if thou bring forward on their journey after a godly sort, thou shalt do well: 7 Because that for his name's sake they went forth, taking nothing of the Gentiles. 8 We therefore ought to receive such, that we might be fellowhelpers to the truth.

9 I wrote unto the church: but Diotrephes, who loveth to have the preeminence among them, receiveth us not. 10 Wherefore, if I come, I will remember his deeds which he doeth, prating against us with malicious words: and not content therewith, neither doth he himself receive the brethren, and forbiddeth them that would, and casteth them out of the church. 11 Beloved, follow not that which is evil, but that which is good. He that doeth good is of God: but he that doeth evil hath not seen God.

12 Demetrius hath good report of all men, and of the truth itself: yea, and we also bear record; and ye know that our record is true. 13 I had many things to write, but I will not with ink and pen write unto thee: 14 But I trust I shall shortly see thee, and we shall speak face to face. Peace be to thee. Our friends salute thee. Greet the friends by name.

NEW REVISED STANDARD VERSION

3 JOHN 1 The elder to the beloved Gaius, whom I love in truth.

2 Beloved, I pray that all may go well with you and that you may be in good health, just as it is well with your soul. 3 I was overjoyed when some of the friends arrived and testified to your faithfulness to the truth, namely how you walk in the truth. 4 I have no greater joy than this, to hear that my children are walking in the truth.

5 Beloved, you do faithfully whatever you do for the friends, even though they are strangers to you; 6 they have testified to your love before the church. You will do well to send them on in a manner worthy of God; 7 for they began their journey for the sake of Christ, accepting no support from non-believers. 8 Therefore we ought to support such people, so that we may become co-workers with the truth.

9 I have written something to the church; but Diotrephes, who likes to put himself first, does not acknowledge our authority. 10 So if I come, I will call attention to what he is doing in spreading false charges against us. And not content with those charges, he refuses to welcome the friends, and even prevents those who want to do so and expels them from the church.

11 Beloved, do not imitate what is evil but imitate what is good. Whoever does good is from God; whoever does evil has not seen God. 12 Everyone has testified favorably about Demetrius, and so has the truth itself. We also testify for him, and you know that our testimony is true.

13 I have much to write to you, but I would rather not write with pen and ink; 14 instead I hope to see you soon, and we will talk together face to face.

15 Peace to you. The friends send you their greetings. Greet the friends there, each by name.

Home Bible Readings

Monday, April 27	Daniel 4:34-37	*All God's Works Are Truth*
Tuesday, April 28	1 Kings 2:1-4	*Walk before God in Faithfulness*
Wednesday, April 29	Ephesians 4:17-25	*Truth Is in Jesus*
Thursday, April 30	Hebrews 10:23-27	*Knowledge of the Truth*
Friday, May 1	2 Timothy 2:14-19	*Explaining the Word of Truth*
Saturday, May 2	1 Timothy 2:1-7	*A Teacher in Faith and Truth*
Sunday, May 3	3 John	*Coworkers with the Truth*

Background

John's third letter paints a picture of what church life was like in the first century A.D. We read about three individuals—Gaius, Diotrephes, and Demetrius—who collectively exhibit strong spiritual qualities and serious character defects. In many respects, it is a portrait of the church today. Contrary to what many believe, life in the decades after Jesus' resurrection was not some kind of spiritual ideal, free from posturing and strife. Rather, the church was like a growing adolescent who has to deal with the trials and challenges that maturity inevitably brings.

This epistle, like the apostle's second one, is brief and deals with the issue of itinerant ministers and how they should be received. The key concepts of Christian truth and love as they relate to hospitality are also addressed in both letters. There are, however, significant differences between 2 John and 3 John. While 3 John opens with the writer's self-description as "the elder" (vs. 1; compare 2 John 1), the recipient in this case was not a church personified as a woman and her children, but a specific individual named Gaius. Furthermore, the messages of the two letters present opposite sides of the same subject—Christian hospitality. In John's second letter (which was studied in lesson 9), the apostle instructed the church to refuse hospitality to false teachers who denied Jesus' incarnation. But in the apostle's third epistle, he commended Gaius for showing hospitality to teachers of God's truth. Together, the two letters present a balanced view of Christian hospitality.

Notes on the Printed Text

Third John opens in a distinctive way. Absent is the customary wish for grace and peace found in other New Testament correspondence. Even so, at the conclusion of the epistle, the apostle did wish "peace" (vs. 14) to Gaius. All that is known for sure about Gaius is his name. But it is probable that he was a leader in the church to which he belonged, since John candidly discussed the matter of Diotrephes with Gaius (see vss. 9-10). It is clear that the aged apostle felt genuine affection for Gaius. This is revealed by the apostle's reference to Gaius as the "wellbeloved" (vs. 1). John was especially pleased with the unwavering commitment Gaius demonstrated to the truth Jesus taught about Himself. John's inclusion of Gaius among the apostle's spiritual "children" (vs. 4) could mean that Gaius was one of the apostle's converts.

In any case, John was pleased with the spiritual health he found in Gaius, as seen in his devotion to theological orthodoxy (vs. 2). John also cared about the state of physical health Gaius experienced. Here we learn that the apostle not only cared about the spiritual well-being of his fellow Christians, but also about their physical condition. From traveling missionaries (vs. 3), whom John had sent (see vs. 5), he learned about the fidelity Gaius maintained for God's truth. This delegation of itinerant ministers (perhaps led by Demetrius; see vs. 12) had visited Gaius and had witnessed the depth of his spiritual character. Perhaps Gaius provided lodging for them in his home. If so, this gave the evangelists an even more personal look at his godly demeanor and lifestyle.

The character of Gaius included two notable traits as reported by the missionaries. First, Gaius had been faithfully living according to God's truth (vs. 3). Second, Gaius was well-known for his practice of Christian love (see vs. 6). His piety and integrity were so obvious that even strangers quickly recognized these virtues (see vs. 5). The apostle was overjoyed to learn how his child in the faith was grounded in God's truth. John's parental affection and concern for the spiritual development of his children extended to all of his readers (vs. 4). As a pastoral leader in the early church, nothing brought the apostle greater joy than to know that his children were adhering to the truth first delivered by the Lord Jesus.

The apostle again addressed Gaius as his friend as "beloved" (vs. 5). Also, the apostle once more commended Gaius for his cordial reception of itinerant ministers who came to his faith community. He had welcomed into his home fellow Christians, whom he did not know, and provided for their physical needs at his own expense. Verse 6 indicates that this display of hospitality was not a onetime occurrence. It was something Gaius did faithfully as a regular ministry. His generosity to traveling missionaries showed his devotion to God's truth.

The itinerant ministers returning to John reported to his community of believers in Ephesus about the hospitality Gaius had shown (vs. 6). Possibly during one or more church services, the traveling missionaries spoke openly about both the faithfulness of Gaius to God's truth and the generous way in which Gaius had welcomed the evangelists (see vs. 3). The apostle encouraged his child in the faith to continue providing for these believers in a way that honored and pleased God. This included supplying the missionaries with adequate provisions for their journey ahead. John explained that this should be done because the ministers had traveled on behalf of the Lord Jesus (vs. 7). It would have been inappropriate for these itinerant ministers, as Jesus' representatives, to seek the support of unbelievers. So, as a matter of policy and practice, the evangelists neither sought nor received help from pagans. Since traveling teachers did not seek support from unbelievers, it was all the more necessary for Christians to provide these ministers with assistance (vs. 8).

In verses 9-10, the apostle commented on the thorny problems caused by Diotrephes. Here was a leader whose character was the exact opposite of Gaius. John's beloved child in the faith lived according to God's truth, loved his fellow Christians, and was hospitable even toward strangers. In contrast, Diotrephes was arrogant, verbally attacked others with evil accusations, spurned itinerant ministers, and punished those in his church who tried to be hospitable to Jesus' ambassadors. The apostle stated that he had written to the congregation in which Diotrephes was a leader. But because the upstart insisted on being preeminent in his faith community, he rejected John's pastoral authority and refused to pay attention to the apostle (vs. 9).

Apparently, even though John's letter had been addressed to the entire congregation, Diotrephes kept it from being read during any corporate gatherings. This inference is supported by the fact that John had to inform Gaius that the apostle had written the letter. Perhaps Diotrephes simply read the letter and then destroyed it without letting anyone else know about it. John's representatives (the persons mentioned in vs. 5) delivered the letter in question, but were denied hospitality by Diotrephes. A rejection of these Christians would have amounted to a repudiation of the apostle and the truth about Jesus he taught. John knew that in light of Diotrephes' blatant disregard for the apostle's authority, he should probably deal with this matter in person. John's statement in verse 10 that he intended to report some of the abuses committed by Diotrephes suggests a public rather than private rebuke of his practices. John might have confronted Diotrephes privately in a previous letter. If so, it was a reproof Diotrephes had spurned. For this reason, the apostle intended to subject Diotrephes to disciplinary action.

The slanderous allegations Diotrephes made were not only wicked, but also they were contradicted by an objective analysis of the facts. It seems that Diotrephes hoped to elevate his own authority in the church by defaming John's integrity. Furthermore, Diotrephes brazenly rejected the apostle's instruction to welcome visiting missionaries, probably because those in question were the apostle's representatives. Diotrephes' abuse of power contrasted sharply with the humble and generous actions of Gaius. Diotrephes went even further in his defiance of John's apostolic authority by penalizing believers who dared to show hospitality to traveling evangelists. The renegade leader did this by casting them out of the church. The power Diotrephes held was such that he could get away with excommunicating Christians who went against his will.

It is unclear what relationship Gaius had with this faith community. One possibility is that he belonged to another local congregation several miles away from Diotrephes' church. It's also possible Gaius was a member of the same faith community Diotrephes tried to control. If so, it is difficult to know whether or how Gaius might have dealt with Diotrephes' abuse of power. Gaius appears to have held a position of rank in his church. Also, the fact that he could afford to routinely entertain visiting Christians suggests he possessed some wealth. Whatever the situation, Gaius was in a position to stand up to Diotrephes. So, John wrote to Gaius to explain what was occurring and how he should deal with the problem in an effective manner.

The apostle exhorted Gaius not to copy the "evil" (vs. 11) deeds of individuals such as Diotrephes. Instead, Gaius was to follow the example of those who did what was "good." While the apostle censured Diotrephes for his abuse of power, John commended Demetrius for adhering to God's truth. Most of what we know about this believer is found in verse 12. In keeping with the Old Testament directive about witnesses (see Deut. 19:15), John offered a threefold testimonial to the high character of Demetrius. The first witness consisted of all who personally knew Demetrius. They uniformly spoke well of him (3 John 12). The second witness was the truth of the gospel. So conformed was Demetrius' life to what Jesus taught that in a personified way it testified in support of Demetrius' godly demeanor. Third, John himself could vouch for the integrity of Demetrius. With this threefold commendation, Gaius was encouraged to receive Demetrius (perhaps the bearer of 3 John) without reservation.

With much still on the apostle's mind to share with Gaius, the aging church leader declined further written correspondence in favor of a face-to-face meeting in the near future (vs. 13; compare 2 John 12). The apostle wished Gaius "peace" (3 John 14) and passed on greetings from friends in the Ephesian congregation. In turn, the apostle asked Gaius to "greet the friends by name." Here we discover that a shared faith within the worldwide network of believers creates a bond of friendship that accompanies Christians wherever they go.

SUGGESTIONS TO TEACHERS

John, now an aged apostle, appealed as an elder to Gaius (3 John 1). The apostle commended Gaius for his integrity. John also encouraged Gaius to remain devoted to truth, love, and obedience where he found it.

1. BE LOVING. The first article of the truth of the gospel, as far as John was concerned, is that we should love one another (vs. 6). In John 15:13 and 1 John 3:16, love is defined as sacrificing one's self for the welfare of a fellow human being. John reminded Gaius to remain on that spiritual path.

2. BE HOSPITABLE. John commended Gaius for hosting the evangelists the apostle had sent to proclaim the gospel (3 John 5-8). John reported that Gaius' reputation was sterling and appealed to him to treat the next group of missionaries in the same way. The apostle reminded his child in the faith that all who support itinerant ministers share in the blessings of their spiritual harvest.

3. BE ON GUARD. If the command to love was the positive note in all of John's letters, the negative note in them was a warning against church leaders such as Diotrephes, who abused their pastoral authority (vss. 9-10). John feared that Jesus' followers would be undermined in their faith by dictatorial individuals who sought to browbeat Christians in an overbearing, manipulative way.

4. BE HUMBLE. The apostle urged Gaius to follow the humble example of Christians such as Demetrius who were submissive to the authority of God's Word (vs. 12). The apostle also directed Gaius to stand up against those like Diotrephes who would abuse their position and other believers in order to stay in control (vs. 11).

FOR ADULTS

■ **TOPIC:** Let's Work Together

■ **QUESTIONS:** 1. What is God's truth and why is it so important to uphold? 2. How have you recently lived out the truth that abides within you? 3. What is the link between believing the truth and being compassionate to others? 4. What was the nature of the false teaching being promoted by religious frauds? 5. What can believers do to remain anchored to the truth Jesus taught about Himself?

■ **ILLUSTRATIONS:**

Remain Loyal. Some of history's great battles were lost because troops deserted, in some cases to the enemy. For instance, the first American president, General George Washington, was plagued by deserters. Some of his soldiers got tired of the bitter struggle, left camp, and went home. The fight for independence evidently wasn't worth it to them.

Churches have also suffered losses from deserters and deceivers. These are individuals who abandoned their commitment to God's truth and mistreated believers. In John's day, this was a life and death issue. The tiny congregations had no resources other than the faithfulness of their members. Many wavered and reverted to paganism.

Perhaps today it's too easy to drop out. We think we won't be missed. We think there are others to take our place and do our work. But when that attitude takes over, our churches suffer and the individuals who leave often weaken spiritually or turn away. We must remain loyal because we need each other.

Don't Abuse Power. In 3 John, the apostle wrote to his beloved friend, Gaius, about a person named Diotrephes who abused his power as a church leader (vss. 9-10). The apostle urged Gaius not to imitate what is "evil" (vs. 11) but what is "good."

One day, in 1888, Alfred Nobel picked up the morning newspaper and read his own obituary. His brother had passed away, but an over-zealous reporter had failed to check the facts. The obituary presented Alfred Nobel as the inventor of dynamite, an armaments manufacturer, and a merchant of death.

Because Nobel received this unusual opportunity to see his life as others did, he resolved to use his influence to accentuate his desire for peace. He arranged that the income from all of his fortune would fund an award for those persons who did the most for the cause of peace. Today we remember Alfred Nobel, not as an arms merchant, but as the founder of the Nobel Peace Prize.

Real Leaders Aren't Proud. Third John draws attention to an arrogant character named Diotrephes (vs. 9). He loved to be the number-one leader in his church. So, in his quest for power, he treated others in a despicable manner (vs. 11).

Now let's shift our attention to an American folk hero named Daniel Boone. He explored the great wilderness of Kentucky and Tennessee. And it was Boone who marked the Wilderness Road that brought settlers into the new land west of the Appalachians.

Boone often wandered over vast areas of forest, living off the land and dodging arrows. Once he was asked if he had ever been lost. Boone replied, "No." He claimed he had never been lost, but he did admit that he was "a mite confused once for three or four days."

Boone was gently joking, but he showed a common trait of tough guys and gals. We don't like to be wrong. It's hard to admit personal errors, but godly leaders will. They aren't leading for praise on earth. They are leading for a heavenly "Well done" that is based on faithfulness, rather than performance.

FOR YOUTH

■ **TOPIC:** Live According to the Truth

■ **QUESTIONS:** 1. What are some wholesome ways to express Christian love to others? 2. How well do you know the basic doctrines of the Christian faith? 3. Why is it sometimes challenging to live according to God's truth? 4. Who were the deceivers John referred to in his letter? 5. Why is it tempting for some in the church to wander away from God's truth?

■ **ILLUSTRATIONS:**

Walk this Way. Third John reveals that the Christian life (or walk) can be reduced to simple principles—obedience and love. As we grow in our intellectual understanding of our faith, we also grow in how to live our faith.

Sometimes, though, the situation works the other way around. When we dare to live our faith in front of others, we find that our understanding grows as well. It turns out that we believe what we do as well as do what we believe.

A young man entered a university terrified that he would lose his faith. He was determined to follow Jesus. After his first year, he told his Christian friend, "You know what? They threw me to the lions and I survived. Now I'm really convinced that my Christian faith is true!"

Love Builds Up. This week's lesson from 3 John focuses on the divine summons for us to live in a way that clearly reflects our commitment to God's Word and His children. This includes being persons of integrity who show unconditional kindness and compassion to those around us.

Edward Steichen (1879–1973), who eventually became one of the world's most renowned photographers, almost gave up on the day he shot his first pictures. At age 16, young Steichen bought a camera and took 50 photos. Only one turned out—a portrait of his sister at the piano.

Edward's father thought that was a poor showing. But Edward's mother insisted that the photograph of his sister was so beautiful that it more than compensated for 49 failures. The encouragement Edward received from his mother convinced the youngster to stick with his new hobby. He stayed with it for the rest of his life, but it had been a close call.

What tipped the scales? Love spotted excellence in the midst of a lot of failure.

Focus on What Is Good. An ambitious young woman came to a minister to be counseled. The woman had lost money and lamented, "I've lost everything!"

Minister: "Oh I'm sorry to hear you have lost your faith."

Woman: "No, I've not lost my faith."

Minister: "Well then I'm sorry to hear you have lost your character."

Woman: "I didn't say that. I still have my character."

Minister: "I'm sorry to hear you have lost your assurance of salvation."

Woman: "I didn't say that either. I haven't lost my assurance of salvation."

Minister: "You have your faith, your character, and your assurance of salvation. It seems to me that you've lost none of the things that really matter."

Do not spend your energies on what is evil. Instead, spend your energies on what is good (see 3 John 11).

LESSON 11 — MAY 10

THE GIFTS OF THE SPIRIT

BACKGROUND SCRIPTURE: 1 Corinthians 12:1-11
DEVOTIONAL READING: Romans 12:1-8

Key Verse: The manifestation of the Spirit is given to every man to profit withal. 1 Corinthians 12:7.

KING JAMES VERSION

1 CORINTHIANS 12:1 Now concerning spiritual gifts, brethren, I would not have you ignorant. 2 Ye know that ye were Gentiles, carried away unto these dumb idols, even as ye were led. 3 Wherefore I give you to understand, that no man speaking by the Spirit of God calleth Jesus accursed: and that no man can say that Jesus is the Lord, but by the Holy Ghost. 4 Now there are diversities of gifts, but the same Spirit. 5 And there are differences of administrations, but the same Lord. 6 And there are diversities of operations, but it is the same God which worketh all in all. 7 But the manifestation of the Spirit is given to every man to profit withal. 8 For to one is given by the Spirit the word of wisdom; to another the word of knowledge by the same Spirit; 9 To another faith by the same Spirit; to another the gifts of healing by the same Spirit; 10 To another the working of miracles; to another prophecy; to another discerning of spirits; to another divers kinds of tongues; to another the interpretation of tongues: 11 But all these worketh that one and the selfsame Spirit, dividing to every man severally as he will.

NEW REVISED STANDARD VERSION

1 CORINTHIANS 12:1 Now concerning spiritual gifts, brothers and sisters, I do not want you to be uninformed. 2 You know that when you were pagans, you were enticed and led astray to idols that could not speak. 3 Therefore I want you to understand that no one speaking by the Spirit of God ever says "Let Jesus be cursed!" and no one can say "Jesus is Lord" except by the Holy Spirit.

4 Now there are varieties of gifts, but the same Spirit; 5 and there are varieties of services, but the same Lord; 6 and there are varieties of activities, but it is the same God who activates all of them in everyone. 7 To each is given the manifestation of the Spirit for the common good. 8 To one is given through the Spirit the utterance of wisdom, and to another the utterance of knowledge according to the same Spirit, 9 to another faith by the same Spirit, to another gifts of healing by the one Spirit, 10 to another the working of miracles, to another prophecy, to another the discernment of spirits, to another various kinds of tongues, to another the interpretation of tongues. 11 All these are activated by one and the same Spirit, who allots to each one individually just as the Spirit chooses.

Home Bible Readings

Monday, May 4	Deuteronomy 17:14-20	*Not Exalted over Other Members*
Tuesday, May 5	Romans 11:25-32	*God's Gifts Are Irrevocable*
Wednesday, May 6	Hebrews 2:1-9	*God Distributed Gifts of the Spirit*
Thursday, May 7	Romans 12:1-8	*Grace Gifts Given to Us*
Friday, May 8	1 Corinthians 2:11-16	*Understanding the God's Gifts*
Saturday, May 9	1 Corinthians 14:1-5	*Gifts That Build Up the Church*
Sunday, May 10	1 Corinthians 12:1-11	*One Spirit, a Variety of Gifts*

Background

Paul was at Ephesus when he received the news about what was happening in Corinth. According to 1 Corinthians 5:9, the apostle had sent a previous letter to the congregation, a letter that apparently was not preserved by the early church. Sometime after sending this epistle, Paul received either a personal or a written report from members of Chloe's household about several problems that were threatening the church and its ministry. That's when Paul began composing this letter that would be a vital resource for sustaining the ongoing work of the Corinthian church. A key purpose of the apostle was to explain that Jesus Christ crucified—who embodies the gospel—creates the church's unity, service, and hope.

Part of that unity is maintained through the presence of "spiritual gifts" (12:1) in the body of Christ. The Greek text is more literally rendered "spiritual things" and can either refer to persons filled with the Holy Spirit or the special abilities He bestows on them to serve others. In verses 8-10, Paul supplied a representative list of spiritual gifts. In this letter, the Greek noun rendered "gifts" is *charismata* (car-ISS-mah-tah). The singular form of this word is *charisma*. Both terms relate to the word *charis* (CAR-iss), which means "favor" or "grace." While *charisma* denotes a personal endowment of grace, *charismata* refers to a concrete expression of grace. The main idea is that the Spirit bestows His gifts of grace on Christians to accomplish God's will (see vss. 4-6 and the lesson commentary to follow).

Notes on the Printed Text

Paul was aware of the spiritual gifts that the Corinthian Christians were diligently exercising. The apostle admonished them for misusing their gifts, which was due in part to their being theologically uninformed (1 Cor. 12:1). In 1:5-7, Paul expressed gratitude for the spiritual enrichment his readers enjoyed in union with the Savior. The apostle said that in every way they had been blessed with a multitude of gifts. For example, God had given the Corinthians the ability to speak in tongues, to prophesy, to interpret tongues, and to discern spirits. No spiritual gift was lacking in the congregation.

What Paul and his coworkers had declared about the Messiah had been confirmed in the lives of the believers at Corinth. Their behavior was transformed in measurable ways and their service for the Lord was dynamic and effective as they waited for the Second Coming. Yet, from what is said in chapter 14 (see also the Bible commentary in lesson 13), it seems the Corinthian Christians were emphasizing the gift of speaking in tongues almost to the exclusion of all other gifts.

Next, Paul reminded his readers of how they had once lived as "Gentiles" (vs. 2). The apostle meant they were pagans who needed to be saved. He noted that they had by some means been drawn into idol worship, which was prevalent in their city, even though none of the idols could speak a word. Scripture reveals that idols are powerless, lifeless objects (see Ps. 115:4-8; Hab. 2:18-19). In contrast to the idols, the Spirit of God was not mute and was the only true source of divinely-inspired speech. He spoke through Jesus' followers, never directing them to curse the Savior but rather prompting them to confess Jesus as Lord (1 Cor. 12:3). Put another way, the speech empowered by the Spirit was always edifying, never blasphemous.

Admittedly, anyone could say either "Jesus [is] accursed" or "Jesus is the Lord." Be that as it may, no one who slandered the Lord ever was enabled by the Spirit to do so. Oppositely, no one who ever affirmed Jesus' divine lordship—and genuinely meant it—did so apart from the Spirit of God (see John 20:28; Rom. 10:9; Rev. 19:16). Paul's point seemed to be that having an inspired utterance was, in itself, not most important. Instead, the content of that utterance was what mattered most.

In 1 Corinthians 12:4-6, Paul focused on the sovereignty of the triune God in the distribution and exercise of spiritual gifts among believers. For instance, while there are varieties of "gifts," they have their source in the "same Spirit." Also, there are varieties of ministries, yet believers serve the "same Lord." Moreover, even though there are varieties of activities, it is the "same God" who produces all of them in everyone. In these verses, Paul linked each of three synonyms for endeavors of the Spirit—"gifts," "ministrations," and "operations"—with different names for God. In this way, the apostle showed that the variety of spiritual gifts within the unity of the church mirrors the diversity of the Persons within the one divine Trinity.

Paul stated that to each believer was given a "manifestation of the Spirit" (vs. 7) for use in serving the whole congregation of believers. Peter likewise taught that the Lord had given believers spiritual gifts (such as teaching and preaching) and that they were to use these to serve others (1 Pet. 4:10-11). As previously noted, the Holy Spirit bestows on Christians special abilities to accomplish the will of God. They do not own the gifts. Instead, they are stewards of what God has graciously provided for them. These gifts of grace take various forms, and they are to be faithfully used wherever and whenever possible.

In 1 Corinthians 12:8-10, Paul listed nine special abilities, which represent only a few of the many gifts the Spirit has entrusted to Jesus' followers. "Word of wisdom" denotes the ability to deliver profound truths consistent with biblical teaching. Some think "word of knowledge" refers to information received through supernatural means. Others believe it points to the effective application of Bible teaching to people's lives. While all Christians have saving "faith," the reference here is to the display of amazing trust in God regardless of circumstances.

"Gifts of healing" denotes a believer's ability to restore someone else to health through supernatural means. "Working of miracles" spotlights the ability to perform supernatural acts, that is, signs and wonders. "Prophecy" refers to the proclamation of revelations from God, including predictions of future events. "Discerning of spirits" highlights the ability to distinguish which messages and acts come from the Spirit of God and which come from evil spirits.

Speaking in different "kinds of tongues" could be human languages or dialects unknown to the person speaking them (see Acts 2:1-12). Others think they are heavenly languages (see 1 Cor 13:1). Either way, it seems these languages are unintelligible to both the speaker and the hearers (unless they had the gift of interpretation), and are directed to God as prayer or praise (see 14:2, 14-16). Finally, "interpretation of tongues" (12:10) refers to the ability to translate what was being spoken and clearly explain what it meant to listeners.

In Romans 12:6-8, Paul put forward another shorter representative list of seven spiritual gifts. In line with what was said earlier, those with the gift of prophesying are to communicate God's revealed truth to believers for their edification. Also, this and the other special abilities mentioned by Paul are to be exercised in accordance with the measure of faith the Lord provides. "Ministry" denotes meeting the needs of others in unique ways. "Teaching" points to the communication of biblical truth in a clear and relevant manner.

"Exhortation" spotlights the provision of reassurance or admonition as needed. "Giveth" has in mind believers whom the Spirit enables to contribute significantly to those in need, and they do so generously. "Ruleth" refers to a special ability to shepherd and govern the body of Christ, and it is to be done with devotion and enthusiasm. Lastly, showing "mercy" points to the exceptional aptitude some believers have to be warmhearted and considerate, especially as they show the kindness of the Spirit to the disheartened.

Believers often disagree about which gifts are still given by God's Spirit to Christians to use in ministry today. Some argue that all of the gifts described in Scripture are still given to the church because its needs are still the same and because there is evidence of these gifts operating in Christians today. Others maintain that one or more of the gifts ended with the early church, while most of the gifts still exist. For example, some hold that the gift of apostleship died out with the original apostles, but the other gifts are still in operation. Still others think that all of the so-called spectacular gifts—such as miracles, speaking in tongues, and healings—were only given to the early church and not to the church today.

Regardless of which of these views is favored, 1 Peter 4:11 reminds us that as believers diligently help one another and rely on the Father for enabling, they bring Him honor through His Son, the Lord Jesus. For instance, others will see believers ministering in the name of the Son and praise the Father for it. Indeed, the thought of God being honored moved Peter to write a doxology of praise at the end of the verse. Glory and power belonged to the Lord for ever and ever. Peter then affirmed this truth with an "Amen," which might be paraphrased "So be it!"

Paul reminded his readers that they had done nothing to receive the gifts of the Spirit, for He gives them openly and unsparingly according to His sovereign will (1 Cor. 12:11). This meant believers were not to become conceited or divisive because of their gifts. Rather, they were to use their special endowments to help others become better Christians.

SUGGESTIONS TO TEACHERS

This week's lesson encourages the members of your class to ponder the importance of the gifts of the Spirit to everyone in the congregation. The lesson should also remind them that every ability given by the Spirit is equally valued and important to the proper functioning of the church.

1. VALIDITY OF SPIRITUAL GIFTS. First Corinthians 12:1-11 presumes that every believer has at least one spiritual gift, if not more than one. In brief, the presence and practicality of spiritual gifts is a theologically valid truth to affirm to the students.

2. VARIETIES OF THE SPIRIT'S GIFTS. Examine with your class the different kinds of gifts bestowed by the Spirit to a congregation. Work to understand what each of these may mean for your church today. Consider who in your church seems to be blessed with what gifts. Are these persons encouraged to minister their gifts to others? How can the congregation give equal emphasis to all the gifts of the Spirit present within the church?

3. VALUE OF INDIVIDUAL GIFTS. Invite the students to share how they might be a blessing to others through the exercise of their spiritual gifts. To get the discussion started, you might consider sharing a few personal thoughts about how the Spirit has equipped you to serve the church.

4. A VITAL PART OF THE CHURCH. It is important for us to get in touch with our mission in life. What has God called and appointed your students to do in the body of Christ? Whatever their specific gift might be, assure them that it is a vital part of the total ministry of the church. Remind the class members that they are one of the many individual links that keep the chain strong. God has blessed them with special endowments so that they may be a blessing to others. Therefore, they should be eager to use their gifts!

FOR ADULTS

TOPIC: Unity in Diversity

QUESTIONS: 1. What incentive do believers have to learn more about spiritual gifts? 2. How does coming to faith in Christ free us from idolatry? 3. What are some ways the variety of spiritual gifts in your church have been used for the benefit of everyone? 4. Why is it important to affirm the sovereignty of God in the distribution of spiritual gifts? 5. What are some creative ways you could use your spiritual gifts to minister to others?

ILLUSTRATIONS:

An Unopened Gift? How would you feel if you discovered that the gift you gave someone you love had never been unwrapped and opened? The hurt and anger that you would feel might be similar to how God feels when we fail to unwrap the spiritual gifts He has given to each of us.

Regrettably, some adult believers have not unwrapped their spiritual gifts. They don't know what the Spirit has given them, much less have they used these special abilities. They need to understand that God will not shrug off the fact that they have disregarded the spiritual gifts with which He has blessed them.

This week's lesson encourages your students to discover and use their various God-given abilities to minister to others around them. Each spiritual gift brings unique care to meet the needs of other Christians. And each of your class members has one or more of these spiritual gifts.

The Need for Diversity. Imagine that the main hospital in your community is staffed only by heart specialists. They are all world famous experts who can deal with the unique needs of heart patients. In fact, these physicians can utilize the best and latest medical technology in their field. But how effective is the hospital in meeting the diverse medical needs of your community?

In this fictional situation, there is no one to suture lacerations and set broken bones. There's also no one to care for the trauma victims and cancer patients. Furthermore, no one has any desire to treat patients who have problems of the stomach, liver, gall bladder, intestines, brain, or urinary tract.

A hospital cannot survive long with just heart specialists. Similarly, a church is ineffective if it only has believers with one spiritual gift. The congregation needs a whole spectrum of believers with a wide variety of special abilities to meet the needs of their fellow Christians (see 1 Cor. 12:1-11).

Uniquely Gifted for God's Work. Jennie was delighted when she found them. They were the right style, color, and size. Her husband's shoes-to-be called Jennie from the store's clearance rack. She responded by scooping them up and taking them to the register.

At home, Jennie triumphantly handed the prize to Colin. Jennie was ecstatic that she did not have to hunt the shoes down, store by store. It seemed so simple. In fact, it was too simple. After Colin tried on the shoes, it became apparent that these size 10 shoes were actually size 13.

Unfortunately, sometimes people and ministries are matched in the same hasty way Jennie bought those shoes. The people and ministries seem to go together. But when they're connected, it becomes obvious they were not meant for one another.

God has given us spiritual gifts that are suited to particular ministries (see 1 Cor. 12:1-11). To insist that believers stay in positions that are "bad fits" not only places them in ministries in which they don't really belong, but also prevents other Christians who do belong in those ministries from exercising their spiritual gifts. Ultimately, "good fits" are what God wants most for those who serve Him, and that should be all of us.

FOR YOUTH

■ **TOPIC:** What's My Spiritual Gift?

■ **QUESTIONS:** 1. What is your definition of "spiritual gifts" (1 Cor. 12:1)? 2. Before the believers in Corinth became Christians, how were they led astray by idols? 3. Why is it important for us to affirm to others that "Jesus is the Lord" (vs. 3)? 4. What are some of the different kinds of spiritual gifts in your church? 5. What are some spiritual gifts the Lord has given you to use for the benefit of others?

■ **ILLUSTRATIONS:**

Mitten Theology. In *The Secret Place*, Charlotte Burkholder tells us that fingers in a mitten are in contact with one another, and that each contributes body heat. Therefore, these fingers keep warmer than those in a glove where each finger is wrapped separately.

The preceding observations are a reminder that believers must remain together spiritually and allow each other to contribute to the common good of the church. This is done when every believer uses his or her God-given spiritual gifts without hesitation (see 1 Cor. 12:1-11). In short, we are most useful to the Lord and to one another in the body of Christ when we are practicing a "mitten" faith together instead of "glove" living.

Members of the Same Team. Youth today are introduced early to the values of working together. They work on class projects, participate in musical groups and plays, and join athletic teams. They all know that if any member slacks off, the team suffers. They also realize that if any player tries to steal the whole show, the team is weakened.

These are the kinds of illustrations adolescents can understand when applied to the church, which is Christ's spiritually-gifted team (see 1 Cor. 12:1-11). When teens put their faith in Him, He brings about a profound change in their lives. They now have the

Spirit empowering them to serve one another in a loving and sacrificial manner. The beauty of the church is that faith in Jesus is the only requirement to be on His team. It doesn't depend on skill or experience.

Faith in Jesus is also required to accept the contributions of all other team members. Perhaps the final production will not be as stellar as we would prefer it to be. But we have to remember that the church is not just for professionals. It is also for life-long learners and followers of the Savior. In this regard, we need to coach each other, so that our team can become as strong as possible.

Code Talkers. In early February, 1998, Carl Gorman died. The ninety-year-old was a Navajo artist who taught at the University of California. He was also the father of celebrated artist R.C. Gorman.

Carl, though, gained fame as the original and oldest of 400 Navajo Code Talkers. During World War II, the Japanese broke the Army, Navy, and Air Corps codes. However, the Marines used the native Navajo tongue and turned the language into a secret weapon. Navajo is a language with an irregular syntax and without an alphabet. In 1942, only about 50,000 Navajos actually spoke the language, having resisted all the efforts by the U.S. government to Americanize them. (Gorman's teachers at a mission school had chained him one whole week to an iron pipe in an effort to force him not to use his native tongue!)

Gorman and his colleagues worked out words for military terms and used a two-tier code where English terms were represented by Navajo words. (For instance, a hummingbird was a fighter, and a swallow became a torpedo plane.) The code was so secure that it was never broken by the Japanese. And the code was so valuable that it remained top secret until it was finally declassified in 1968, when secure high-speed electronic coding was developed. Thirty-four years later, in 2002, the Code Talkers were awarded the Congressional Medal of Honor.

Gorman's gift was simple and plain. However, without his gift and those few others that also had that this special ability, the war effort in the Pacific might have gone differently. From this we can see that every believer's spiritual gifts, no matter how seemingly insignificant, are important to the body of Christ (see 1 Cor. 12:1-11).

Sadly, many believers tend to dismiss their God-given talents, skills, and aptitudes—even their spiritual gifts—as trivial or unimportant in the ongoing life of the church. Nothing could be further from the truth! Every spiritual gift is important and needed. It is vital that these gifts be put into practice so that the church's ministry is complete and God is praised through them.

LESSON 12 — MAY 17

THE UNITY OF THE BODY

BACKGROUND SCRIPTURE: 1 Corinthians 12:12-31
DEVOTIONAL READING: Galatians 3:23-29

Key Verse: For by one Spirit are we all baptized into one body, whether we be Jews or Gentiles, whether we be bond or free; and have been all made to drink into one Spirit. 1 Corinthians 12:13.

KING JAMES VERSION

1 CORINTHIANS 12:14 For the body is not one member, but many. 15 If the foot shall say, Because I am not the hand, I am not of the body; is it therefore not of the body? 16 And if the ear shall say, Because I am not the eye, I am not of the body; is it therefore not of the body? 17 If the whole body were an eye, where were the hearing? If the whole were hearing, where were the smelling? 18 But now hath God set the members every one of them in the body, as it hath pleased him. 19 And if they were all one member, where were the body? 20 But now are they many members, yet but one body. 21 And the eye cannot say unto the hand, I have no need of thee: nor again the head to the feet, I have no need of you. 22 Nay, much more those members of the body, which seem to be more feeble, are necessary: 23 And those members of the body, which we think to be less honourable, upon these we bestow more abundant honour; and our uncomely parts have more abundant comeliness. 24 For our comely parts have no need: but God hath tempered the body together, having given more abundant honour to that part which lacked: 25 That there should be no schism in the body; but that the members should have the same care one for another. 26 And whether one member suffer, all the members suffer with it; or one member be honoured, all the members rejoice with it.

27 Now ye are the body of Christ, and members in particular. 28 And God hath set some in the church, first apostles, secondarily prophets, thirdly teachers, after that miracles, then gifts of healings, helps, governments, diversities of tongues. 29 Are all apostles? are all prophets? are all teachers? are all workers of miracles? 30 Have all the gifts of healing? do all speak with tongues? do all interpret? 31 But covet earnestly the best gifts: and yet shew I unto you a more excellent way.

NEW REVISED STANDARD VERSION

1 CORINTHIANS 12:14 Indeed, the body does not consist of one member but of many. 15 If the foot would say, "Because I am not a hand, I do not belong to the body," that would not make it any less a part of the body. 16 And if the ear would say, "Because I am not an eye, I do not belong to the body," that would not make it any less a part of the body. 17 If the whole body were an eye, where would the hearing be? If the whole body were hearing, where would the sense of smell be? 18 But as it is, God arranged the members in the body, each one of them, as he chose. 19 If all were a single member, where would the body be? 20 As it is, there are many members, yet one body. 21 The eye cannot say to the hand, "I have no need of you," nor again the head to the feet, "I have no need of you." 22 On the contrary, the members of the body that seem to be weaker are indispensable, 23 and those members of the body that we think less honorable we clothe with greater honor, and our less respectable members are treated with greater respect; 24 whereas our more respectable members do not need this. But God has so arranged the body, giving the greater honor to the inferior member, 25 that there may be no dissension within the body, but the members may have the same care for one another. 26 If one member suffers, all suffer together with it; if one member is honored, all rejoice together with it.

27 Now you are the body of Christ and individually members of it. 28 And God has appointed in the church first apostles, second prophets, third teachers; then deeds of power, then gifts of healing, forms of assistance, forms of leadership, various kinds of tongues. 29 Are all apostles? Are all prophets? Are all teachers? Do all work miracles? 30 Do all possess gifts of healing? Do all speak in tongues? Do all interpret? 31 But strive for the greater gifts. And I will show you a still more excellent way.

Home Bible Readings

Monday, May 11	Exodus 19:1-8	*Speaking with One Voice*
Tuesday, May 12	Exodus 24:1-7	*We Will Be Obedient*
Wednesday, May 13	2 Corinthians 11:1-5	*Sincere and Pure Devotion*
Thursday, May 14	Romans 15:1-7	*Living in Harmony*
Friday, May 15	Philippians 1:21-30	*One Spirit, One Mind*
Saturday, May 16	Galatians 3:23-29	*One in the Lord Jesus*
Sunday, May 17	1 Corinthians 12:14-31	*Many Members, One Body*

Background

To a church that was emphasizing the gift of speaking in tongues almost to the exclusion of all other spiritual gifts, Paul began a new section of his letter. As we learned in lesson 11 dealing with 1 Corinthians 12:1-11, the apostle reminded his readers that they possessed a diversity of special endowments given to them by the Holy Spirit. In turn, these were to be used for the edification of Christ's spiritual body.

Paul not only listed some of these gifts, but also told his readers that the Spirit granted them unique abilities according to His will and for the benefit of everyone. Next, in verses 12-20, the apostle compared the church to the human body to stress that there is unity and diversity within the faith community. While Christ's body has numerous members, it remains spiritually one (vs. 14; see also Rom. 12:4-8).

Notes on the Printed Text

Paul's list of spiritual gifts was representative, not exhaustive, in nature. His intent was to stress that each special endowment is important to the church. To further emphasize this truth, the apostle drew an analogy between the faith community and a human body. In particular, a human body has many different parts, and yet it is a single entity. Expressed differently, it is a unity made up of diversity. Paul declared that the same situation holds true for the body of Christ (1 Cor. 12:12).

In verse 13, Paul explained that what unites diverse believers in the faith community is their common experience of being indwelt by the Holy Spirit. The apostle described this experience as everyone being "baptized" into a single "body" by "one Spirit." Some think this verse refers to water baptism. However, that would seem to teach that this religious ritual is necessary for salvation—something that is not taught in other passages of Scripture (see Acts 10:44-48; 16:29-33). Salvation hinges solely on believing in the Savior (see Rom. 9:30; Eph. 2:8-9). Water baptism dramatizes the work of salvation in a person's heart. For this reason, others maintain that Spirit baptism is in view in 1 Corinthians 12:13. In accomplishing this work of grace, God's Spirit places believers into the body of Christ and unites them with the Savior (see Rom. 6:3-5).

In the Roman world (as often in ours) ethnic, religious, and cultural distinctions were clearly drawn, thus setting up barriers between people. Paul took note of this situation by mentioning "Jews" (1 Cor. 12:13) and "Gentiles," as well as "bond" (or "slave") and "free." Regardless of one's social status in life, all Christians were part of the same spiritual body (vs. 14).

In verses 15-16, Paul described two hypothetical situations in which a part of the human body declared itself independent from the other members on the grounds that it was not like any of them. For example, the foot might say that it did not belong to the body because it was not a hand. In the same way, the ear might declare that it was not connected to the body because it was not an eye. Even if body parts could make such assertions, they would be incorrect. Just putting forward a statement would not automatically make it true.

Of course, Paul wasn't really talking about human body parts. The apostle had in mind believers and their spiritual gifts. He was afraid that someone might think, for example, *I have only the gift of distinguishing between spirits, not the gift of speaking in tongues. So, I must not really be a significant part of the faith community.* Paul taught that even if some Christians reasoned in this way, they would still be a part of the church. Having one spiritual gift rather than another did not disqualify anyone from usefulness in the body of Christ.

A body that is nothing but an eye might see fine, but it is deaf. Similarly, a body that is limited to an ear can certainly hear, but it is incapable of smelling. We might paraphrase Paul's questions in verse 17 according to the subject he had in mind: If everyone in a congregation has the gift of speaking in tongues, how will the members of the church be taught? How will believers receive prophecies from the Lord? How will they even interpret what's spoken in tongues? While the Corinthians might have been emphasizing just one spiritual gift, God was not so foolish as to give them only one. It is similar to the way in which He arranged the human body.

Far from being made up of just an eye or just an ear, the body has every part it needs. That's the judicious way God designed it (vs. 18). With this truth in mind, Paul repeated what he had said before when he explained that the human body has many parts and yet is a unity (vss. 19-20). The Spirit has prudently distributed special endowments among Christians so that the faith community can have a complete and well-rounded ministry. He has given to every believer specific gifts, and they can be certain that He has a good reason for doing so. Somewhere in the overall activity of the church there's a place where each of our God-given abilities—whether it's administration, mercy, or whatever else—fits perfectly into the Lord's will.

In verses 21-26, Paul used the body-church analogy in a slightly different way. It appears that here the issue is not the relationship between different spiritual gifts in the body of Christ, but the relationship between different people in the faith community. The apostle started off by saying that one member of the human body cannot declare that it alone is sufficient apart from another member. Verse 21 personifies the eye asserting this to the hand, and the head to the feet. Of course, what Paul meant was that one member of Christ's body could not say he or she did not need another member.

Evidently, the apostle was thinking about the division between rich and poor, which had caused enormous problems at the Lord's Supper in the church at Corinth (see 11:17-34). The "haves" in the congregation possibly thought they could get along fine without the "have-nots." In no uncertain terms, Paul told the believers who considered themselves to be self-sufficient that they were wrong. By way of analogy, the apostle explained that those members of the human body that appear to be the weakest are essential (12:22). Here he was probably referring to the internal organs. These seem to be weak, since they are protected inside the body. Yet without them and the crucial tasks they performed, the body would die.

Furthermore, a notable effort is made to clothe with great care those parts of the body that are considered "less honourable" (vs. 23). Likewise, those members that should not be seen are afforded more decorum. In contrast, the more "comely" (vs. 24) members do not require this level of dignity. Here Paul meant that the sexual organs are treated with greater propriety by being clothed. More presentable parts of the body, such as the face, are not covered with garments. Regardless of which portion of the body is considered, Paul was really referring to believers in the faith community. Members who were too little appreciated by others were as important, if not more so, than the others. Perhaps the apostle believed that God is especially gracious to the have-nots of this world.

In keeping with what Paul stated in verse 18, he noted in verse 24 that God arranged the human body in just the right way. For instance, He gave "more abundant honour" to the members that lacked it. God also made the body in such a way that it harmoniously works together and each part matters equally to every other part (vs. 25). To draw further attention to this mutual concern, the apostle noted that when one member of the body is hurting, all the other members suffer along with it. Likewise, if one member flourishes, the rest of the members are filled with joy (vs. 26). That's because the human body is a unit.

In verse 27, Paul reminded his readers that he was really talking about each and every one of them as a member of the "body of Christ." Then, in verse 28, the apostle provided a list of eight items (compare vss. 8-10 and the comments appearing in last week's lesson). The first three items on the list are believers who had certain spiritual gifts, while the last five are special endowments that believers had. Since Paul used the words translated "first . . . secondarily . . . thirdly" (vs. 28), some see in this list a ranking of gifts from most important to least important. But the apostle did not carry the numbering pattern through to the end. Also, miracles and healings are mentioned in the reverse of their previous order (compare vss. 9-10). Perhaps, then, it is better to see the list as being random, not ranked, or possibly Paul meant to rank just the first three items.

"Apostles" (vs. 28) is the category to which Paul himself primarily belonged. Apostles were people who helped lay the foundation for Christian churches. "Prophets" refers to those who proclaimed divine revelations, including (though not limited to) predictions about the future. "Teachers" were believers who, with their learning and maturity, instructed others in biblical truth. Workers of "miracles" refers to those who performed signs and wonders. This spiritual gift is followed by believers who healed (or supernaturally restored others to health), Christians who ministered to the spiritual and physical needs of others (those able to help), believers who were gifted with the ability to lead and guide the church ("governments"), and Christians endowed with the ability to communicate in various "diversities of tongues." Some think Paul placed this gift last because he considered it the least important. Others, however, maintain the apostle placed it last because it was the gift over which he and his readers were having a disagreement.

In verses 29-30, Paul asked some rhetorical questions. In doing so, he highlighted several of the items he had just mentioned and expanded on the meaning and significance of spiritual gifts. Repeatedly, he asked whether all Christians had the same special endowment, and each time the appropriate answer was no. By emphasizing speaking in tongues, the Corinthians forgot about the diversity of gifts. Each believer had his or her own God-given abilities—all of which were important, for that's how the Spirit wanted it.

Paul concluded this part of his argument with a brief statement in verse 31 that has led to some disagreement among interpreters. Here are three of the most common interpretations. (1) Paul exhorted his readers to earnestly strive for the "best gifts" appearing at the beginning of his list in verse 28, rather than the lesser ones at the end. (2) Verse 31 should be translated, "but you are eager for the greater gifts" (in which the apostle was making a simple statement of fact, rather than issuing a command). (3) Paul was introducing the teachings he would convey in 14:1-25, after the digression of chapter 13 about the "more excellent way" (12:31) of Christlike love.

SUGGESTIONS TO TEACHERS

As noted in last week's lesson, it's clear that Paul's readers were emphasizing the gift of speaking in tongues almost to the exclusion of all other special abilities. Probably they thought this gift confirmed their mistaken view about their "spiritual" nature. Paul, hearing about the overemphasis on tongues, taught that a diversity of gifts was needed in the church.

1. ALL OF US ARE SPECIAL. Every believer is special in the eyes of God. Each one is important and valuable to the ministry of the church as a whole. We do not have to be like or compare ourselves to others.

2. ALL OF US ARE VALUED. The value of each of us is attested throughout Scripture. God made human beings in His image and after His likeness as the crowning act of creation (see Gen. 1:26-27). Our belief in the incarnate Messiah, who takes away the sins of the world, makes us God's children (see John 1:12) and laborers with Him (see 1 Cor. 3:9).

3. WE HAVE WHAT WE NEED. God has given us exactly what we need to complete the task He has called us to do. Our importance in the kingdom of God comes from the fact that we are His unique and wondrous handiwork through which His love is manifested (see Eph. 2:10). Therefore, all believers should prayerfully seek to discover God's purpose and plan for them.

4. WE ARE A BODY OF BELIEVERS. End the class session by discussing the ways in which the church is similar to a human body. Be sure to stress that every member of the congregation—even believers who seem least significant—are needed to help the church remain healthy, growing, and productive.

FOR ADULTS

■ **TOPIC:** The Sum Is Greater than Its Parts

■ **QUESTIONS:** 1. How does the human body represent the diversity and unity within the church? 2. Why would it be wrong for a believer to think he or she is the most important part of Christ's body? 3. Why is it important for all believers to have an opportunity to grow, develop, and use their gifts? 4. What are some ways believers can carry out the ministries of mutual support and caring? 5. How can Christians better accept, love, and learn from other members of Christ's body?

■ **ILLUSTRATIONS:**

Every Believer Valued. In the 1938 movie *The Citadel*, Robert Donat plays a talented, idealistic young Scottish physician named Andrew Manson. He is committed to provide medical care to Welsh miners who have tuberculosis. Yet, by the film's conclusion, he is on trial for assisting an unlicensed medical practitioner during an operation.

Manson's accusers claim that the physician forsook his oath in order to help a "quack." They don't seem to care that the operation was a success or that the so-called quack clearly had a gift for medicine. For the critics, medical talents must fit their specific image to be valid. Otherwise, they are disregarded.

Thankfully, God does not operate that way. As Paul stated in 1 Corinthians 12:18, God has placed together all the members of Christ's body in a way that He decided is best. God accepts and works through every believer's unique and valued spiritual gifts.

Work Together. Too often today a discussion about spiritual gifts ends up in arguments and division, not in spiritual unity. We don't have to agree on the precise meaning of the special endowments mentioned in 1 Corinthians 12:1-11 to find common ground in a larger purpose. But many times, our larger purpose and our common bond in Christ get lost in our heated debates.

Meanwhile, some churches are weakened because of a false dichotomy between so-called gifted believers and the rest of ordinary Christians. We have to make room for all believers to exercise their gifts for the common good. We cannot afford to let some Christians think they are second-class just because they might not have some of the more publicly recognized gifts.

Thankfully, Paul emphasized oneness, unity, and harmony. He did not glorify the gifts. He would not tolerate fighting over any special endowment, all of which are intended to build Jesus' spiritual body. The whole point of Paul's teaching was to produce a vital, loving, growing, and unified fellowship, not one shattered by arguments and bickering.

Shared Grief and Pain. In 1 Corinthians 12:25-26, Paul stated that God does not want the body of Christ divided. Instead, His will is for every member of the faith community to display an equal concern for one another. In this approach to ministry, shared joys are doubled and shared sorrows are halved (see Rom. 12:15).

The rescue of Jessica McClure was a local event that gained national sympathy and concern. One Wednesday in October 1987, while playing with four other children, this 18-month-old toddler accidentally slipped into an abandoned well shaft. When Jessica's babysitter finally discovered her whereabouts, the child's family, along with the community of Midland, Texas, came to the rescue of this little girl.

Jessica's 58-hour dramatic ordeal ended with a sigh of relief from thousands of people who watched the rescue by television. Much of the strength for the family of Jessica came from the public sentiment of the individuals who "shared" their grief and pain through letters, telephone calls, and other gestures of kindness.

For Youth

■ **Topic:** Many Members Equal One Body

■ **Questions:** 1. Why is it necessary for churches to have a variety of spiritual gifts among its members? 2. How can church leaders signal that all Christians are important and valuable to the congregation? 3. At Corinth, how did some Christians act like the foot or the ear in Paul's hypothetical illustration? 4. Why is it important for believers to endure hardship and joy together? 5. How can believers help one another appreciate their need for each other?

■ **Illustrations:**

Called to Share Our Gifts. In this week's lesson, we examine the source and purpose of the spiritual gifts. We also learn how God grants special endowments to believers so that they can serve the church and glorify the Lord.

As a young woman, Senia Taipale knew that God had given her a gift for comforting others. She felt called to a life of ministry, but she did not believe that God wanted her to be a church leader. Others questioned whether she understood God's calling at all. But, in time, God made clear His plans for her gifts.

From 1992 to 2010, Senia oversaw the chaplaincy program at a large Midwestern hospital. She saw it as a perfect fit. "When people are in the hospital, they're worried, stressed," Senia points out. "Patients don't usually have folks who can take the time to come in and just listen to them. A hospital chaplain's job is to get to the patients and listen to their stories. I try simply to be a listener and a companion on the patient's spiritual journey." For that, Senia was uniquely gifted.

Lesson from the Hive. Tommy decided that he would capture a honey bee, care for it, and eventually collect some honey. He cautiously lowered a large jar over a flower on which a bee had settled to gather nectar. He snipped off the stem, capped the jar, and jubilantly carried the trapped bee to the little one-bee hive that he had painstakingly prepared.

The new home for Tommy's lone bee had plenty of water, plenty of clover for food, plenty of warmth, and plenty of fresh air. Tommy was certain that he had provided all the necessary ingredients to care for his bee. But to his dismay, the bee was dead three days later. Only when he talked to an experienced beekeeper did Tommy learn that a bee cannot survive in isolation. Individual bees are kept alive by living in community with one another.

The same lesson might be applied to us as a community of faith. We need each other to survive as Christians. In isolation, we would find it impossible to remain faithful. But as we work together through the ongoing exercise of our spiritual gifts, we can encourage one another (see 1 Cor. 12:14-31). Clearly, our unity as fellow believers is a great source of spiritual strength!

Building a Solid Team. Michael Jordan is often considered one of the best basketball players ever. Yet when he first joined the NBA's Chicago Bulls out of the University of North Carolina, the Bulls failed to have a winning season for years.

Jordan told the management that to win championships, the Bulls would have to build a strong and solid team. He could not win championships on his own. Only when the management listened to Jordan's advice and brought in other multi-talented players like Scottie Pippen and Horace Grant did the Bulls begin winning back-to-back championships.

God, too, is interested in building a strong and solid team called the church. To do so, the Lord grants a perfect mix of talents, skills, and gifts. Yes, some players on His team may have more talents than others, but only when the players work together as a team—or as Paul called it, a body—is the Lord glorified.

LESSON 13 — MAY 24

THE GIFT OF LANGUAGES

BACKGROUND SCRIPTURE: Acts 2:1-21; 1 Corinthians 14:1-25
DEVOTIONAL READING: Deuteronomy 4:32-40

Key Verse: What is it then? I will pray with the spirit, and I will pray with the understanding also: I will sing with the spirit, and I will sing with the understanding also. 1 Corinthians 14:15.

KING JAMES VERSION

ACTS 2:1 And when the day of Pentecost was fully come, they were all with one accord in one place. 2 And suddenly there came a sound from heaven as of a rushing mighty wind, and it filled all the house where they were sitting. 3 And there appeared unto them cloven tongues like as of fire, and it sat upon each of them.
4 And they were all filled with the Holy Ghost, and began to speak with other tongues, as the Spirit gave them utterance.
5 And there were dwelling at Jerusalem Jews, devout men, out of every nation under heaven. 6 Now when this was noised abroad, the multitude came together, and were confounded, because that every man heard them speak in his own language. 7 And they were all amazed and marvelled, saying one to another, Behold, are not all these which speak Galilaeans? . . . 12 And they were all amazed, and were in doubt, saying one to another, What meaneth this? . . .

1 Corinthians 14:13 Wherefore let him that speaketh in an unknown tongue pray that he may interpret.
14 For if I pray in an unknown tongue, my spirit prayeth, but my understanding is unfruitful.
15 What is it then? I will pray with the spirit, and I will pray with the understanding also: I will sing with the spirit, and I will sing with the understanding also.
16 Else when thou shalt bless with the spirit, how shall he that occupieth the room of the unlearned say Amen at thy giving of thanks, seeing he understandeth not what thou sayest? 17 For thou verily givest thanks well, but the other is not edified. 18 I thank my God, I speak with tongues more than ye all: 19 Yet in the church I had rather speak five words with my understanding, that by my voice I might teach others also, than ten thousand words in an unknown tongue.

NEW REVISED STANDARD VERSION

ACTS 2:1 When the day of Pentecost had come, they were all together in one place. 2 And suddenly from heaven there came a sound like the rush of a violent wind, and it filled the entire house where they were sitting. 3 Divided tongues, as of fire, appeared among them, and a tongue rested on each of them. 4 All of them were filled with the Holy Spirit and began to speak in other languages, as the Spirit gave them ability.
5 Now there were devout Jews from every nation under heaven living in Jerusalem. 6 And at this sound the crowd gathered and was bewildered, because each one heard them speaking in the native language of each. 7 Amazed and astonished, they asked, "Are not all these who are speaking Galileans? . . . 12 All were amazed and perplexed, saying to one another, "What does this mean?" . . .

1 Corinthians 14:13 Therefore, one who speaks in a tongue should pray for the power to interpret. 14 For if I pray in a tongue, my spirit prays but my mind is unproductive. 15 What should I do then? I will pray with the spirit, but I will pray with the mind also; I will sing praise with the spirit, but I will sing praise with the mind also. 16 Otherwise, if you say a blessing with the spirit, how can anyone in the position of an outsider say the "Amen" to your thanksgiving, since the outsider does not know what you are saying? 17 For you may give thanks well enough, but the other person is not built up. 18 I thank God that I speak in tongues more than all of you; 19 nevertheless, in church I would rather speak five words with my mind, in order to instruct others also, than ten thousand words in a tongue.

Home Bible Readings

Monday, May 18	Deuteronomy 4:32-40	*Made You Hear God's Voice*
Tuesday, May 19	James 3:1-5	*A Small Member, Great Boasting*
Wednesday, May 20	Revelation 7:9-12	*All Languages, One Loud Voice*
Thursday, May 21	Acts 2:8-13	*We Hear in Our Own Languages*
Friday, May 22	Acts 2:14-21	*People Will Prophesy*
Saturday, May 23	1 Corinthians 14:6-12	*Excel in Your Gifts*
Sunday, May 24	Acts 2:1-7, 12; 1 Corinthians 14:13-19	*Building Up Others*

Background

Luke began his historical account of the Christian church with a description of Jesus' ascension to heaven. His last words to His disciples were His promise to send them the Holy Spirit, who would fill them with power to be Jesus' witnesses in Jerusalem, in Judea, and throughout the globe (Acts 1:1-11). The disciples were obedient to the Lord's command. They returned to Jerusalem to wait until the Spirit came as promised. About 120 followers of the Savior spent 10 days together, praying and encouraging each other. During this time, Matthias was selected to replace Judas Iscariot, who had committed suicide after betraying Jesus (vss. 12-26).

From Acts 2:1-4 we learn that that the Holy Spirit came upon Jesus' followers on the "day of Pentecost." Pentecost was a celebration of the grain harvest, a period that lasted about seven weeks. Barley and wheat were the primary harvest foods. The poor and strangers were especially welcome during this festival. During Pentecost, the people would bring their offerings of first fruits to the Lord. A special sacrifice was presented in the temple during this time. A wave offering of new bread made from the recently harvested wheat was presented before the Lord, along with sin and peace offerings. No celebrating was to occur until after this ceremony. Every male Israelite was to appear in the sanctuary. Jews from all over the known world would come to Jerusalem to celebrate this feast of thanksgiving.

Notes on the Printed Text

Acts 2:1 reveals that the Spirit came upon Jesus' disciples while they were assembled in one place. In addition to the fact that they gathered together in a single location, this verse implies that the disciples were in agreement in their thinking and purpose on Pentecost. All at once and unexpectedly, the disciples heard a sound from heaven that was similar to that of a turbulent "wind" (Acts 2:2). The noise filled the entire house where they were meeting. In the context of this incident, the wind was a physical indication of the presence of the Spirit. In Scripture, wind and breath are common symbols of God's Spirit (see Ezek. 37:9, 14; John 3:8). The sight of "tongues . . . of fire" (Acts 2:3) was even more unusual than the sound of the wind, perhaps being reminiscent of the thunder and lighting that accompanied God's giving of the law to Moses on Mount Sinai (see Exod. 19:16-19).

The tongue-shaped flames appeared to stand over each disciple's head (Acts 2:3). This incident was significant, for it indicated that God's presence was among Jesus' followers in a more powerful and personal way than they had ever experienced before. The disciples could sense the Spirit's coming audibly (through wind) and visibly (through fire). Moreover, they were filled with the Spirit (vs. 4). As evidence of His presence, the Spirit enabled them to speak in other tongues. Apparently these were actual languages or dialects being voiced by the disciples to the visitors from many countries in Jerusalem. The Spirit had come to empower Jesus' followers to reach out to the lost with the saving message of the gospel.

Jesus' disciples, being enthusiastic in their baptism of power, spilled out into the streets of Jerusalem. At this time, the population of Jerusalem swelled with pilgrims attending the festival of Pentecost (vs. 5). This event proved to be a strategic occasion for the Father and Son to send the Spirit. Visitors who heard God being miraculously praised in their own languages—and were perhaps among that day's 3,000 converts (see vs. 41)—could take the good news of salvation in the Messiah back with them to their homelands.

While the Spirit operates quietly, God sometimes sends visible and audible signs of His work. The wind, fire, and inspired speech all have their roots in Jewish tradition as indicators of God's presence. This did not escape the notice of the foreign Jews who heard the sound of tongues-speaking. They were amazed that locals could fluently speak languages from around the Roman Empire (vs. 6). With their curiosity aroused, crowds of people quickly gathered together to discuss what could be behind all the commotion. They could tell by the distinctive accent of Jesus' followers that they were mainly from Galilee (vs. 7). In general, the Jews living in Jerusalem looked down upon those from Galilee because it was so far away from the religious center of the nation (see John 7:52).

Evidently, the throng operated under the assumption that the disciples spoke only one or two languages. Consequently, they were perplexed that these seemingly uneducated Galileans could speak fluently in so many different native dialects, which in turn could be understood by the diverse group of pilgrims (Acts 2:8). In this amazing turn of events, the Lord began to reverse the confusion that occurred at the tower of Babel thousands of years earlier (see Gen. 11:1-9). Whereas then God scattered the human race over all the earth, on the day of Pentecost He brought all sorts of different people back together to hear the message of salvation.

Both ethnic Jews and converts to Judaism heard Jesus' disciples using the crowds' own languages to declare to them the wonderful things God had done. These visitors came from all across the Roman Empire (Acts 2:9-11). At the time when the New Testament was written, the entire civilized world (with the exception of the little known kingdoms of the Far East) was under the domination of Rome. From the Atlantic Ocean on the west to the Euphrates River and the Red Sea on the east, from the Rhone, the Danube, the Black Sea, and the Caucus mountains on the north, and to the Sahara on the south, stretched one vast empire under the headship and virtual dictatorship of the emperor.

The pilgrims were excited but confused by the tongues-speaking episode unfolding before them. The crowds kept asking one another what its significance might be (vs. 12). Regrettably, some in the throng took a less charitable view. They crassly joked that Jesus' disciples were drunk from having ingested too much wine (vs. 13). The Savior would use the bewilderment of the pilgrims as an opportunity to shine the light of the gospel into their sin-filled lives. Moreover, the Spirit empowered Peter to stand before a crowd to explain what they were seeing. He was "with the eleven" (vs. 14), suggesting that while Peter was the primary speaker, the others all affirmed what he said (vss. 15-36). Jesus' resurrection was the central message of Peter's sermon. His listeners were so moved that 3,000 converts were added to the church (vss. 37-41).

In 1 Corinthians 14:1-12, Paul taught that one of the main purposes of spiritual gifts—including the speaking in tongues that occurred at Pentecost—was to build up the body of Christ. With that truth in mind, the apostle said the gift of tongues occurring during a worship service, if uninterpreted, did nothing to edify the attendees. This is due to the fact that no one in the congregation could understand what was being said. For this reason, Paul said it was better for believers to proclaim God's truth in a language everyone could understand. Accordingly, the apostle directed tongues-speakers to pray that the Spirit would give them the ability to explain the meaning of what they said (vs. 13). The ability to interpret tongues was, in itself, a spiritual gift (see 12:10). So, if believers had both gifts, they could speak in tongues and then interpret what had been said for the edification of others.

Paul explained that when people spoke in tongues, they prayed with their spirit but not with their mind (14:14). While the tongues-speaking was no doubt a spiritually uplifting experience, it did not directly involve the intellect. More specifically, it did not contribute to the tongues-speakers' knowledge of the things of God. Given that situation, what was Paul's advice? It was not to neglect either one's mind or one's spirit (vs. 15). Through their tongues gift, the believers in Corinth could pray and sing. (Evidently, some worshipers would offer spontaneous hymns of praise to God, with lyrics in an unknown language.) They could do the same apart from that gift. Undoubtedly, Paul was thinking that the praying and singing in the Spirit were to be done in private. During church worship services, these activities were to be done only in limited amounts and when accompanied by interpretation.

Paul proposed a situation in which a believer in a worship service praised God with his or her spirit through speaking in tongues. The Greek noun rendered "understandeth not" (vs. 16) refers to inquirers who were uninitiated in the Christian faith (see vss.

23-24). In the absence of interpretation, these outsiders would not know what was being said and so would not know when to affirm the praise with an "Amen" (vs. 16). That would show that others were not being edified, even though the tongues-speaker was praising God (vs. 17).

It would be incorrect to conclude from Paul's previous statements that the tongues gift was unimportant. In fact, the apostle was grateful to God for being personally blessed with this gift. Those in Corinth who were overemphasizing tongues-speaking could not truthfully claim to have experienced it more than Paul himself had (vs. 18). However, when it came to a corporate worship service, the apostle would have preferred to speak a brief message that could be understood by others than prattle on for hours making utterances in a tongue that made no sense to his listeners (vs. 19). In church, intelligibility is essential because edification is the goal.

SUGGESTIONS TO TEACHERS

According to Paul, one of the main purposes of spiritual gifts is to build up the church, the body of Christ. For that reason, special endowments such as tongues, prophecy, and knowledge are useless if they are not expressed in love and used to edify others.

1. ENCOUNTERING THE SPIRIT. The disciples on the day of Pentecost vividly remembered the Spirit's presence and power in their midst. He was among them like wind and fire. The Spirit's presence came upon them in such force that they were changed forever. The Spirit kindled a burning awareness of Jesus' nearness and love. Be sure to discuss how the promise of the Spirit applies to Jesus' followers today. Are the members of your class fervent in their devotion to the Savior?

2. BEING ATTENTIVE TO UNBELIEVERS. We should give some thought to how unbelievers view our church. If we care about the lost, as Paul did, then we will want to make our church attractive to spiritual seekers. Such concern is a part of mature Christian thinking.

3. STRIKING A BALANCE IN GROUP WORSHIP. Paul's ideal for a church service was that it would make room for spontaneity without letting it get out of control. Spontaneity would be open to the Spirit without degenerating into disorder. That ideal presents Christians today with two questions: (1) Is our worship so filled with the exercise of people's gifts that it is chaotic and unedifying? (2) Is our worship so routine and controlled that we are not prepared for God to touch us in a fresh way? Spend some time with your students exploring the issues raised by these questions.

4. SEEKING TO EDIFY OTHERS. As we use our spiritual gifts, we should want others to be strengthened and encouraged in their faith. Also, we should want to be as useful as we can, praying for the gifts that will enable us to contribute more to building up Jesus' followers.

FOR ADULTS

■ **TOPIC:** Seeking to Be Understood

■ **QUESTIONS:** 1. Why were the disciples gathered together on the day of Pentecost? 2. What did Jesus' followers do when they became filled with the Holy Spirit? 3. What are some ways that tongues-speaking can be used to edify believers? 4. What is the God-given purpose of prophesying? 5. If you were an unbeliever, would you find your church attractive and welcoming? Explain.

■ **ILLUSTRATIONS:**

United by the Spirit. People are usually skeptical if they cannot see evidence of a claim. The motto of the state of Missouri (the "Show Me State") reflects the attitude of many adults. If we claim that God's Spirit is dwelling in us, then we need to give evidence of His presence. One way to show we have had a genuine and lasting encounter with the Spirit is by the powerful changes in behavior He has made in us (for example, by our trusting in the Savior, shunning sin, and remaining united in love with our fellow believers).

This was the central thrust of Peter's message on the day of Pentecost. Adults need to know that the promise of forgiveness and the indwelling Holy Spirit extended beyond his current audience to future generations and to those living in other lands. Although Peter may not have realized it at the time, his words included the Gentiles as well.

Difficulty of Waiting. Retired television host Hugh Downs and his wife were once in Washington, D.C., preparing to return to New York. A call came telling them that their flight had been canceled. Downs quickly checked on train schedules and discovered a train that was leaving for New York in 45 minutes.

Mrs. Downs was in the shower, so Hugh decided to speed up their departure by packing their bags. He hurriedly threw their clothing and belongings into suitcases, called the bellhop, and had their luggage sent to Union Station. A few minutes later, Mrs. Downs emerged from the bathroom, wrapped in a towel. Calling to her husband, she asked if he would bring her green dress.

Sometimes, as Hugh Downs discovered, we take matters into our own hands too hastily. Jesus' disciples may have wanted to do that before the day of Pentecost by doing the Lord's will impulsively in their own strength. But Jesus told them to wait patiently until they were "baptized with the Holy Ghost" (Acts 1:5). Being willing to wait for the Lord is not easy, but absolutely necessary!

Contributions to Worship Services. Based on 1 Corinthians 14, we discover that group worship in the early church had a variety of believers participating in the corporate event. If a poll were taken today, how many believers could immediately identify the ways in which they contribute to their worship services? Too often, they would not be able to do so. But the truth is that all believers can contribute.

And the church can help us find ways we can participate in worship, which will edify others.

Case in point, for some time at the Palo Alto Peninsula Bible Church, a Sunday evening Body Life gathering was held. Here someone could voice a prayer need for a neighbor who had cancer. Another person could take time to exhort from verses he found meaningful that week. Still another Christian might feel free to share the joy she felt when her cherry pie met an emotional need in a neighbor's life.

The sky's the limit if churches remain open to maximum participation. A congregation in Geneva, Illinois, included a five-to-ten minute section during the Sunday morning worship called "A Window into My Life." Each week one person would share his or her personality, background, testimony, and something significant he or she had learned. Gradually, many more people in attendance got to know numerous others because this format lent itself to increased congregational awareness. By this means, an entire church can be exposed to one more person they might not have met yet. Furthermore, this is one way the church can communicate, "We value people."

The formats of these congregations allowed Christians to participate during worship. There are many other ways churches can arrange for believers to use their gifts while God is being worshiped. Small prayer groups, men's and women's breakfasts, services at convalescent homes, and other such meetings provide more opportunities for the use of spiritual gifts. So what might benefit more members in your congregation?

For Youth

■ **Topic:** Communicating in a Different Language

■ **Questions:** 1. What was significant about the visible ways in which the Spirit of God manifested His presence to the disciples? 2. What sorts of people heard Jesus' disciples proclaim the wonderful things God was doing? 3. In what ways can prophesying be used to spiritually build up Jesus' followers? 4. What is the God-given purpose of the gift of tongues? 5. How can believers ensure they are helping others by the exercising of their gifts?

■ **Illustrations:**

The Power of the Faithful. Some of the most interesting conversion stories I have heard involve people studying to be ministers. The standard assumption is that these people are already saved. Occasionally, this isn't the case.

There are many reasons why individuals want to train for church leadership. Even teens are known to wrestle with this issue. Often, though, the desire—whether it is to help others, exercise abilities in teaching and counseling, enjoy a position of respect and influence, and so on—is void of God's presence and power.

As we learn in this week's lesson, an individual claiming to be a Christian, regardless of his or her age, is spiritually powerless when not connected with the Savior and operating in the Spirit. What a dynamic change occurs when a young person stops trying to live for God in his or her own strength and starts faithfully serving Him with the limitless resources the Spirit made available on the day of Pentecost.

A Lesson in Importance. In 1 Corinthians 14, we learn that Paul's readers overvalued some spiritual gifts to the exclusion of others. At the top of the list was tongues-speaking. But the apostle explained that other special abilities, including prophesying, were just as important. Indeed, all the gifts bestowed on believers by the Spirit were vital to building up Christ's body.

When I was a child, I had a clear notion of who was most important in my home church. At the top of the pecking order was the minister. Then came the head usher. Next stood the superintendent of the Sunday school, who could offer the kind of elaborate prayers that are usually voiced only by the clergy.

Following these people was the lead soprano in the choir, who commanded immense respect and whose word was law in the music department. At the foot of this flow chart was a moon-faced widow who sang off-key, could barely read or write, dressed poorly, and never held any church offices. I dismissed her as someone without any spiritual gifts and therefore of minimal importance.

Years later I remember (in retrospect) the countless acts of kindness that this woman performed with her mason jars of homemade soup and sincere prayers while visiting the sick and elderly. Her gift was more important to the life of my home congregation than I realized. This elderly, nearly-illiterate widow taught me that the spiritual gifts of every church member are important, and that God has blessed every believer with some special ability that is indispensable for the ministry of the church!

Exposed. In 1 Corinthians 14, Paul explained that unbelievers, after hearing prophecy, were more likely to grasp God's judgment against sins, acknowledge their own iniquity, repent, and then worship God. In addition, they would affirm that the truth was present among Jesus' followers.

The acclaimed radio preacher Donald Grey Barnhouse (1895–1960) once spoke on a college campus in the 1950s. Afterward, a student told him that she didn't see how the Bible could be true. Immediately, Barnhouse had the audacity to say to her, "You're living in sin, aren't you?" It was true. Her inner condition had been exposed. Her intellectual arguments were only a cover-up for her transgressions.

Similarly, popular author and pastor Gene Getz told about an open sharing session held in his church. A young man had come in who had not been present there for a while. Getz knew the man was undergoing a moral problem, but Getz was one of only a few who was aware of it. Nevertheless, during this session, several Christians amazingly shared Scripture verses that had a direct bearing on that particular man's problem. It was as if he could not escape the scrutiny and exposure from an all-seeing God.

LESSON 14 — MAY 31

THE GREAT GIFT OF LOVE

BACKGROUND SCRIPTURE: 1 Corinthians 13
DEVOTIONAL READING: Ephesians 3:14-21

Key Verse: Now abideth faith, hope, charity, these three; but the greatest of these is charity. 1 Corinthians 13:13.

KING JAMES VERSION

1 Corinthians 13:1 Though I speak with the tongues of men and of angels, and have not charity, I am become as sounding brass, or a tinkling cymbal. 2 And though I have the gift of prophecy, and understand all mysteries, and all knowledge; and though I have all faith, so that I could remove mountains, and have not charity, I am nothing. 3 And though I bestow all my goods to feed the poor, and though I give my body to be burned, and have not charity, it profiteth me nothing.

4 Charity suffereth long, and is kind; charity envieth not; charity vaunteth not itself, is not puffed up, 5 Doth not behave itself unseemly, seeketh not her own, is not easily provoked, thinketh no evil; 6 Rejoiceth not in iniquity, but rejoiceth in the truth; 7 Beareth all things, believeth all things, hopeth all things, endureth all things.

8 Charity never faileth: but whether there be prophecies, they shall fail; whether there be tongues, they shall cease; whether there be knowledge, it shall vanish away. 9 For we know in part, and we prophesy in part. 10 But when that which is perfect is come, then that which is in part shall be done away. 11 When I was a child, I spake as a child, I understood as a child, I thought as a child: but when I became a man, I put away childish things. 12 For now we see through a glass, darkly; but then face to face: now I know in part; but then shall I know even as also I am known. 13 And now abideth faith, hope, charity, these three; but the greatest of these is charity.

NEW REVISED STANDARD VERSION

1 Corinthians 13:1 If I speak in the tongues of mortals and of angels, but do not have love, I am a noisy gong or a clanging cymbal. 2 And if I have prophetic powers, and understand all mysteries and all knowledge, and if I have all faith, so as to remove mountains, but do not have love, I am nothing. 3 If I give away all my possessions, and if I hand over my body so that I may boast, but do not have love, I gain nothing.

4 Love is patient; love is kind; love is not envious or boastful or arrogant 5 or rude. It does not insist on its own way; it is not irritable or resentful; 6 it does not rejoice in wrongdoing, but rejoices in the truth. 7 It bears all things, believes all things, hopes all things, endures all things.

8 Love never ends. But as for prophecies, they will come to an end; as for tongues, they will cease; as for knowledge, it will come to an end. 9 For we know only in part, and we prophesy only in part; 10 but when the complete comes, the partial will come to an end. 11 When I was a child, I spoke like a child, I thought like a child, I reasoned like a child; when I became an adult, I put an end to childish ways. 12 For now we see in a mirror, dimly, but then we will see face to face. Now I know only in part; then I will know fully, even as I have been fully known. 13 And now faith, hope, and love abide, these three; and the greatest of these is love.

Home Bible Readings

Monday, May 25	Hosea 6:1-6	*Love and the Knowledge of God*
Tuesday, May 26	Jonah 3:10–4:11	*Abounding in Steadfast Love*
Wednesday, May 27	Galatians 5:19-26	*Guided by the Spirit*
Thursday, May 28	2 Thessalonians 1:1-5	*Increasing Love for One Another*
Friday, May 29	2 Thessalonians 3:1-5	*Love and Steadfastness*
Saturday, May 30	Ephesians 3:14-21	*Filled with New Life from God*
Sunday, May 31	1 Corinthians 13	*Love Endures Forever*

Background

In lessons 12 and 13, we studied Paul's teaching to the Corinthians on the purpose and use of spiritual gifts. In this week's lesson, we look at a digression in the apostle's argument. He stepped aside from the subject of spiritual gifts to discuss Christlike love. As 12:31 reveals, love is not a spiritual gift. Instead, it is the way in which all spiritual gifts should be used. Paul's purpose in chapter 13 was to set the issue of spiritual gifts within an ethical framework. Evidently, he thought the Corinthians were too fascinated with the spiritual gifts (particularly speaking in tongues) and had lost sight of a more basic concern, namely, demonstrating Christlike love.

With respect to the Greek language spoken by Paul and his contemporaries, there were three terms used to refer to love. In verse 3, the noun rendered "charity" translates *agape* (ah-GAH-pay). The apostle used this term to indicate unselfish compassion and unconditional kindness. Such love is prompted as much by will as by emotion. Also, it seeks to reach out to others in need, even if the object seems unworthy of being loved. *Philia* (fih-LEE-ah) is a second Greek term for love that is used in the New Testament. It primarily indicates the fondness, affection, or affinity that exists between family members or close friends. *Eros* (ERR-os) is a third Greek term for love that was frequently used in secular literature but does not appear in the New Testament. This word indicates passionate love of a sensual nature.

Notes on the Printed Text

In 1 Corinthians 13:1, Paul named certain representative gifts and actions and then indicated how they are worthless unless done in love. As the apostle explained, if he did not have Christlike love, then his speech would have been useless noise, like that produced in a pagan ritual from a deafening gong or a rattling cymbal. Paul next referred to three other spiritual gifts: "prophecy" (vs. 2), "knowledge," and "faith." For instance, the apostle might be able to deliver spectacular messages from God. Also, Paul might have insight into all sorts of divine secrets and enigmatic truths. Furthermore, he might have such strong belief that he could dislodge mountains from their foundations. Yet, if no compassion and kindness were present, there would be no redeeming value to the gifted one's endeavors.

In verse 3, Paul referred to two pious actions he might perform. The first of these would be parceling out all his possessions to the poor. The second was sacrificing his body to the flames. In either scenario, the apostle's undertakings were spiritually bankrupt in the absence of Christlike love. Next, Paul personified "charity" (vs. 4) for his readers. The apostle did so by using both positive and negative terms to describe godly compassion. The Greek verb rendered "suffereth long" denotes a forbearing spirit, whereas the verb translated "kind" points to acts of benevolence. As Christians, we are to have a long fuse to our temper. We must not retaliate when wronged. Instead, we are to remain steadfast in spirit, consistently responding to others in a gracious and considerate manner.

After describing Christlike love using two positive terms, Paul next used a series of expressions to indicate what love is not and does not do. For example, the Greek verb rendered "envieth" signifies the presence of intense jealousy. We are not to resent what others are or have, nor wish to take those things for ourselves. The verb translated "vaunteth" refers to those who brag about themselves, especially by using flashy rhetorical skills. We should never gloat over our own achievements. The verb rendered "puffed up" means we should not be inflated with arrogance.

The Greek verb translated "unseemly" (vs. 5) means to act in an indecent or rude way. We should not behave in a disgraceful or dishonorable manner. The reference to "seeketh . . . her own" points to an egotistical mindset that borders on narcissism. We are not to be primarily concerned with getting our own way or obtaining what's best for us. The verb rendered "not easily provoked" denotes an irritable disposition that becomes annoyed at the slightest inconvenience. We should not become enraged by what others do. The verb translated "thinketh no evil" brings to mind individuals who maintain an inventory of how others allegedly have shortchanged them. We should not brood over offenses or keep a scorecard of how many times we have been hurt. "Rejoiceth . . . in iniquity" (vs. 6) could also be rendered "be glad about injustice." We should never encourage wrongdoing by obtaining pleasure in misdeeds. Instead, Christlike love takes delight in God's "truth," especially as it is revealed in the gospel.

In verse 7, Paul closed this paragraph with four examples of what Christlike love always does. Together, these illustrations show us that, through godly kindness and compassion, believers have the inner strength to face whatever trials come their way. "[Love] beareth all things" refers to believers enduring troubles or persecution. Or, if the original phrase is translated "[love] always protects," then it means Christians should strive to keep others from evil. Love "believeth all things" indicates that Jesus' followers should have such faith that they search for what is finest in people and commend what is best about them. Love "hopeth all things" indicates there should be no limit to the believers' confidence in the promises of God or in His ability to fulfill them. "Endureth all things" conveys the idea is that when tragedy strikes, Christlike love refuses to collapse or quit. Instead, it has the God-given fortitude to persist through whatever hardships it encounters in life. Put differently, the Spirit enables believers to remain strong to the end of the ordeal.

Paul revealed that unlike spiritual gifts, Christlike "charity" (vs. 8) endures forever. While one day even the most spectacular abilities would no longer be needed, this would never be true of love. Expressed differently, even though special endowments would pass from the scene, love would never become invalid or obsolete. For example, "prophecies" would be discontinued. Similarly, "tongues" would come to an end. Moreover, "knowledge" would be set aside. Paul was contrasting two periods—an earlier one in which the spiritual gifts were needed and a later one when the need for them would expire. That said, interpreters differ over the time scheme the apostle had in mind. One view is that the first period extended between Pentecost and the completion of the New Testament (or the close of the apostolic age), with the second period coming after. Another view is that the first period is the time between Jesus' first and second comings (or the interval between when individual believers live and die), with the second period following that.

Paul explained that the difference between the first and second periods is like the distinction between the partial and the complete, or between the imperfect and the perfect (vss. 9-10). For instance, the spiritual gifts of knowledge and prophecy put believers in touch with God only in a partial way. But in the later period, Christians would be in full and perfect fellowship with Him. Next, Paul illustrated his meaning by drawing an analogy involving childhood and adulthood (vs. 11). He said that when he was a child, he talked, thought, and reasoned as a child. But now that the apostle had become an adult, he had put those "childish" ways behind him. Childhood is like the first period, and childish ways are comparable to spiritual gifts. Just as childish ways are appropriate for a child, so spiritual gifts are appropriate for believers in the first period. But then (to follow the analogy further), adulthood is like the second period. At that time, Jesus' followers would set aside their spiritual gifts, for these would no longer be appropriate.

In verse 12, Paul used an analogy involving a "glass" or "mirror." In his day, this would have been a flat piece of highly polished silver or bronze attached to a handle. The image this metal disc reflected would be quite inferior to the mirrors in use today. In a spiritual sense, the glimpse of God that we get in the first period, as He is made known through our spiritual gifts, is like the imprecise and obscure image produced by a mirror. However, in the second period, our vision of God would not be mediated by our spiritual gifts, for our encounter with Him would be "face to face." This means it would be direct and personal in nature. Interpreters disagree over Paul's exact meaning here. Was he saying that the vision obtained using a mirror is either blurry or reflected? In other words, do our spiritual gifts give us a flawed sense of who God is or do they give us an indirect sense? Either way, the contrast between our vision of God (involving our spiritual gifts) in the first period and our vision of Him (apart from our spiritual gifts) in the later period still stands and deserves thoughtful consideration.

Next, Paul switched from the language of sight to that of knowledge. He explained that he (like all believers in the first period) knew God only partially. Even so, the apostle looked forward to a time when he would know God fully. Of course, Paul was not suggesting that human beings would ever have knowledge equaling that of God. The Lord is not limited, as believers are, by conditions of the first period. God already knew Paul (and all other believers) fully. In verse 13, Paul revealed that the trio of "faith, hope, and charity" abide for the benefit of God's children. Indeed, these three virtues sum up the Christian life. "Faith" denotes trust in the Savior and commitment to His teachings. "Hope" signifies an unshakable confidence that the Son would ultimately fulfill the Father's promises. And thanks to Paul's explanation, we have a full description of what "charity" or "love" means.

Some think that faith and hope, like love, are eternal, for they are manifestations of love. Others maintain that Paul included faith and hope in verse 13 to remind his readers that Christlike love is for now, just as are faith and hope. Yet, when the apostle went on to say that the "greatest of these is charity," he signaled that the latter is superior to faith and hope because love lasts forever. In contrast, faith and hope (like the spiritual gifts) are for this age only. According to this view, faith is superfluous in eternity because then believers would be in God's presence. Likewise, hope is unnecessary in the age to come, for then the divine promises would be fulfilled.

Suggestions to Teachers

Ask the class to tally some uses of the word "love" that they've heard recently. Use these examples to emphasize how overworked is our English word "love." Next mention that "charity" in 1 Corinthians 13 translates *agape*, which refers to unselfish, unconditional compassion, not sentimental feelings or erotic stirrings. Then note the following points.

1. SUPREMACY OF LOVE. Paul mentioned several gifts of the Spirit, such as speaking in tongues, profound thinking, and acts of philanthropy. Yet love surpasses them all!

2. SHAPE OF LOVE. Note the various qualities of Christian love. Then have the class members discuss times when either they or some other believers they know demonstrated the love of Christ. Remind the students that Jesus is the best example of love. Point out how consistently He exhibited a patient, unselfish compassion for others.

3. STAMINA OF LOVE. In an era of road rage and "in your face" confrontations, we might be persuaded that Christlike love is wimpish and futile. But love outlasts everything. In fact, love triumphs! The cross and resurrection pronounce God's verdict on violence and retaliation. Love proves to be more powerful than anything!

4. SUPERIORITY OF LOVE. Paul listed the top three virtues: faith, hope, and love. Each is great and each is needed. But love is the greatest!

For Adults

■ **Topic:** Love Never Ends

■ **Questions:** 1. Why are the gifts of prophecy, knowledge, and faith pointless in the absence of love? 2. How is it possible for Christians to be patient and kind when others are rude to them? 3. What enables a believer characterized by love to bear, believe, hope, and endure all things? 4. What was Paul's main purpose in stressing that spiritual gifts are temporary but love is permanent? 5. In what sense will love last forever?

■ **Illustrations:**

Never Obsolete. In the mid-1980s, I bought my first computer, monitor, and printer. Though certain minor problems arose with the equipment, these were repairable. And I chose to ignore such inconveniences as an aging ribbon. But a few years later when the computer broke down again, the technician said that he could not repair the equipment, for it had become obsolete. In fact, I learned that it was cheaper simply to scrap the computer and buy a new one than to continue having the old one repaired.

Unlike aging electronic equipment, Christlike love never grows obsolete. While even the most spectacular spiritual gifts will outlive their usefulness, this will never be true of love.

What Is Love? In 1967, the BBC broadcast a song titled "All You Need Is Love," which was written by John Lennon of Beatles fame. Then, in the 1970 film *Love Story*, viewers twice heard the statement that "love means never having to say you're sorry." A decade later, the 1980 theme song for the television series, *The Mary Tyler Moore Show*, declared to viewers that "love is all around." More recently, a 2008 music video produced by entertainer Armin van Buuren refers to people falling "in and out of love." There are also clichés about love, such as "all's fair in love and war" and "I love you more than life itself."

The Bible, especially 1 Corinthians 13, presents us with a vastly different view of love than the preceding casual and simplistic notions. We learn that serious relationships last because both parties are genuinely committed to each other, even when they might not feel like it. Regardless of whether it is a marriage or a church relationship, mutual devotion and loyalty undergird the love that each party has for the other.

Moreover, Jesus' love for us was not based on a fleeting emotion or sappy feeling. He loved us to the highest degree and fullest extent. His commitment to us was so strong that He was willing to be crucified for us. His devotion to us was so great that He paid the price for our sin, enabling us to enjoy a relationship of peace with God.

If genuine commitment is undergirding our love for one another, then inconveniences and disagreements will not be devastating. Our unwavering pledge to display Christlike love—regardless of the situation and how we feel—will bring glory to God and enable our relationships to endure.

Love Enacted. Early on a misty Saturday morning, Roy stood alone in the front yard of Mrs. Balthrop's dilapidated old house. She would be returning to her house Monday from the hospital, and Roy wanted the saintly old lady to return to a home in good repair. But now, as he realized how much work was needed, Roy's mind flashed back to his heated words of the previous Sunday night.

At the church meeting, one man after another had announced that he had other obligations Saturday. Roy was fed up when he blurted out, "Well, if nobody else is out there Saturday morning to fix her house, I guess I'll do it all by myself." Now he would have to do just that. But as Roy grabbed his toolbox, he looked up to see a caravan of headlights—maybe half a dozen trucks—heading for Mrs. Balthrop's driveway.

Jon hopped out first and walked over to Roy. "Hey, Roy!" he shouted. "Thought you could use a hand." "Man, am I glad to see you guys!" Roy admitted. "But I didn't think anybody else could make it." "Well," Jon answered, "we couldn't stand to think of you doing all this work alone. At first we just saw this as another job on our to-do list. But when Gene called around and asked us how we could best express our love for Mrs. Balthrop—and for you—we decided to rearrange plans. Besides, what are friends for?"

Day in and day out, acts of kindness, generosity, and compassion are being rendered. Paul pointed out, however, that for any action to have lasting value and meaning, Christlike love must be added.

For Youth

■ **Topic:** Love Is Forever

■ **Questions:** 1. Why is it important for Christlike love to be present when believers exercise their spiritual gifts? 2. In what way is the love of Christ enduring? 3. How might you show the love of Christ to your family and friends? 4. How might you encourage your fellow believers to let the love of Christ permeate their attitudes and actions? 5. Why should we long for the day when we will see the Savior face-to-face?

■ **Illustrations:**

What Needs Love. Nobel Peace Prize winner Mother Teresa died in the fall of 1997, but her example, words, and works continue to have a lasting influence. The woman who headed a religious community that cared for the victims of disease and starvation and demonstrated unconditional and enduring love for all, declared that the greatest illness in the world was not cancer or leprosy, but a lack of love. She further said that the greatest evil was indifference and intolerance.

Paul declared that the love of Christ is the greatest gift that a believer can pass on to others. In light of Mother Teresa's words and Paul's teaching, how are you going to act?

How Jesus' Love Conquers. Five missionaries—Nate Saint, Jim Elliot, T. Edward McCully, Peter Fleming, and Roger Youderian—were brutally slain while trying to share the gospel to members of a wild tribe, the Huaorani people, in a remote part of Ecuador. Later, the Huaorani realized that the five men they had murdered were armed and could have defended themselves. To the amazement of the people in the tribe, the Christian missionaries had not tried to fight back, despite having rifles, ammunition, and time to prepare to open fire against their attackers. This realization ultimately opened the way for the Huaorani to listen to the truth about Jesus' love.

The martyrdom of these five young men in 1956 moved many, including Rachel Saint, Nate's sister, and Elizabeth Elliot, Jim's widow, who went to Ecuador to minister to the people who had murdered their loved ones. Young Steve Saint, Nate Saint's small son, moved to Ecuador with his Aunt Rachel, and was raised among the Huaorani people, and continued to witness as a Christian with them. Most of the Huaorani tribe are now faithful followers of Christ. The love of Christ, as exhibited through the sacrifice and witness of Jesus' valiant servants, has brought love to a once wild tribe in the remote vastness of South America.

The Way of Love. In 1 Corinthians 13:5, Paul noted that Christlike love does not keep a tally of wrongs done against a believer. A converted drunkard of South India named Abraham had settled down to do honest work. But during the harvest season, some bullies attacked him, cut off his fingers with an ax, and stole his crops. The public conscience of the village was so roused that they gathered subscriptions to help the victim prosecute his attackers in court. The Indian Y.M.C.A. Secretary, whom God used to convert Abraham, urged him to go to court, for he could identify the bullies.

After Abraham spent several minutes considering the possibility, he said, "Sir, just two things would I say to you. You are an educated man; I am an illiterate man. You have been a Christian all your life, and I trusted in Jesus not long ago. But when I became believer, I promised to follow in His footsteps. You told me how He was crucified. The nails were driven through His hands and feet. The crown of thorns was placed on His head; but He never said: 'O God, punish My enemies.' Rather, His last words were, 'Father, forgive them, for they know not what they do.' So, just as my Master forgave His enemies and prayed for them, so must I pray for mine and forgive them, for they have done this in the ignorance of their hearts. They did not know anything better."

LESSON 1 — JUNE 7

Pronouncing God's Judgment

Background Scripture: Amos 2:4-16
Devotional Reading: Psalm 75

Key Verse: Thus saith the Lord; For three transgressions of Judah [and Israel], and for four, I will not turn away the punishment thereof. Amos 2:4.

KING JAMES VERSION

AMOS 2:4 Thus saith the Lord; For three transgressions of Judah, and for four, I will not turn away the punishment thereof; because they have despised the law of the Lord, and have not kept his commandments, and their lies caused them to err, after the which their fathers have walked: 5 But I will send a fire upon Judah, and it shall devour the palaces of Jerusalem. 6 Thus saith the Lord; For three transgressions of Israel, and for four, I will not turn away the punishment thereof; because they sold the righteous for silver, and the poor for a pair of shoes; 7 That pant after the dust of the earth on the head of the poor, and turn aside the way of the meek: and a man and his father will go in unto the same maid, to profane my holy name: 8 And they lay themselves down upon clothes laid to pledge by every altar, and they drink the wine of the condemned in the house of their god.

9 Yet destroyed I the Amorite before them, whose height was like the height of the cedars, and he was strong as the oaks; yet I destroyed his fruit from above, and his roots from beneath. 10 Also I brought you up from the land of Egypt, and led you forty years through the wilderness, to possess the land of the Amorite. 11 And I raised up of your sons for prophets, and of your young men for Nazarites. Is it not even thus, O ye children of Israel? saith the Lord. 12 But ye gave the Nazarites wine to drink; and commanded the prophets, saying, Prophesy not. 13 Behold, I am pressed under you, as a cart is pressed that is full of sheaves. 14 Therefore the flight shall perish from the swift, and the strong shall not strengthen his force, neither shall the mighty deliver himself: 15 Neither shall he stand that handleth the bow; and he that is swift of foot shall not deliver himself: neither shall he that rideth the horse deliver himself. 16 And he that is courageous among the mighty shall flee away naked in that day, saith the Lord.

NEW REVISED STANDARD VERSION

AMOS 2:4 Thus says the Lord:
For three transgressions of Judah,
  and for four, I will not revoke the punishment;
because they have rejected the law of the Lord,
  and have not kept his statutes,
but they have been led astray by the same lies
  after which their ancestors walked.
5 So I will send a fire on Judah,
  and it shall devour the strongholds of Jerusalem.
6 Thus says the Lord:
For three transgressions of Israel,
  and for four, I will not revoke the punishment;
because they sell the righteous for silver,
  and the needy for a pair of sandals—
7 they who trample the head of the poor into the dust of the earth,
  and push the afflicted out of the way;
father and son go in to the same girl,
  so that my holy name is profaned;
8 they lay themselves down beside every altar
  on garments taken in pledge;
and in the house of their God they drink
  wine bought with fines they imposed.
9 Yet I destroyed the Amorite before them,
  whose height was like the height of cedars,
  and who was as strong as oaks;
I destroyed his fruit above,
  and his roots beneath.
10 Also I brought you up out of the land of Egypt,
  and led you forty years in the wilderness,
  to possess the land of the Amorite.
11 And I raised up some of your children to be prophets
  and some of your youths to be nazirites.
Is it not indeed so, O people of Israel?
  says the Lord.
12 But you made the nazirites drink wine,
  and commanded the prophets,
  saying, "You shall not prophesy."
13 So, I will press you down in your place,
  just as a cart presses down
  when it is full of sheaves.
14 Flight shall perish from the swift,
  and the strong shall not retain their strength,
  nor shall the mighty save their lives;
15 those who handle the bow shall not stand,
  and those who are swift of foot shall not save themselves,
  nor shall those who ride horses save their lives;
16 and those who are stout of heart among the mighty
  shall flee away naked in that day, says the Lord.

321

Home Bible Readings

Monday, June 1	Psalm 75	*I Will Judge with Equity*
Tuesday, June 2	Amos 2:9-16	*I Will Press You Down*
Wednesday, June 3	Amos 3:1-8	*I Will Punish Your Iniquities*
Thursday, June 4	Amos 3:9-15	*I Will Punish Your Transgressions*
Friday, June 5	Amos 4:1-6	*Judgment Is Surely Coming*
Saturday, June 6	Amos 4:7-13	*You Did Not Return to Me*
Sunday, June 7	Amos 2:4-8	*I Will Not Revoke Punishment*

Background

Amos was a Hebrew prophet from the southern kingdom of Judah whose ministry was directed mainly toward the northern kingdom of Israel (see Amos 1:1). The prophecies of Amos were most likely delivered between 760 and 750 B.C. Israel and Judah were politically at the height of their power and enjoying a prosperous economy. Sadly, however, both nations were corrupt. For instance, idols were worshiped throughout the land and especially at Bethel, which was supposed to be a national religious center.

Moreover, Amos was a shepherd and fig grower, not a prophet by vocation (see 1:1; 7:14). Even though he may not have had the formal religious training of his professional counterparts, he nevertheless was inspired by the Lord. God called Amos while he was still living in Tekoa, his hometown. This village was located in the rugged sheep country of Judah about 10 miles south of Jerusalem. Undoubtedly, while there, he meditated on God's Word, formed clear judgments, and learned how to be God's spokesperson to His people in the northern kingdom.

Amos began each of his oracles with a stock phrase: "For three transgressions . . . for four" (2:4). This refrain didn't mean these nations were guilty of only four crimes. It was simply an expression that indicated a large number. The offenses Amos mentioned were specific—but not all-inclusive—examples of unethical behavior. "Damascus" (1:3) refers to the capital of Aram or Syria, which was northeast of Israel. "Gaza" (vs. 6) was the southernmost of the five major cities in southwest Canaan belonging to the Philistines. "Tyrus" (vs. 9) was a prominent seaport in Phoenicia north of Israel. "Ammon" (vs. 13) was a nation located east of Israel in the Transjordan. "Moab" (2:1) was another Transjordan state situated east of the Dead Sea.

"Judah" (vs. 4) was the last of Israel's neighbors to receive a pronouncement of judgment. The two nations' inhabitants had once been joined. The Israelites and Judahites shared the same ethnic origin, history, and religion. This included the special revelation the Lord gave to His chosen people through Moses at Mount Sinai (see Exod. 19–20; Deut. 5; Rom. 3:1-2; 9:4-5). So perhaps a few (though undoubtedly not all) of Amos' Israelite listeners might have become uncomfortable to learn that God refused to rescind His decree of judgment against Judah.

Notes on the Printed Text

Amos 2:4 reveals that Judah's inhabitants had treated the teachings of the Mosaic law with contempt and flaunted His ordinances. They were guilty of turning their backs on God and acting in sinful, destructive ways. The Hebrew noun that is rendered "lies" possibly denotes the deceptions spread by counterfeit prophets, especially to worship pagan deities. For centuries, idolatry plagued God's chosen people. Even in Amos' day, the inhabitants of Judah (along with Israel) venerated and served false gods and goddesses.

In short, Judah was guilty of violating the Mosaic covenant. Not surprisingly, God's oracle of judgment delivered through Amos was conveyed in language reminiscent of Leviticus 26:14-15, Deuteronomy 5:1, 28:15, and 2 Kings 17:15. Judah's sins were worse than those of other nations because Judah should have known better. After all, others did not know God as the people of Judah did. He manifested His presence among them in the temple at Jerusalem. Since they possessed God's law and had enjoyed His material and spiritual blessings, He held them more responsible for their actions. A "fire upon Judah" (Amos 2:5) is a reference to the terrible devastation and destruction that the nation, like its pagan neighbors, eventually would experience.

The prophecy of Amos was fulfilled when the Babylonians overran Jerusalem, tore down the city's walls, leveled the temple, and took the people into captivity in 586 B.C. (see 2 Kings 25:1-25). The Judahites should have understood from the sobering declarations of Amos that God takes obedience to His ethical standards seriously. They also should have realized that God would not overlook transgressions committed by His own people, any more than He would overlook the misdeeds of other peoples. One day He would punish all who rebelled against Him.

Many in the northern kingdom undoubtedly would have been glad to hear about the troubles in store for their enemies, and perhaps even their longtime rivals, the people of Judah. The Israelites may have thought that such judgment would mean things would go better for them. But Amos also had a sobering message for the proud Israelites. Judgment would visit them as surely as it would other nations.

After years of financial setbacks and foreign intrusions, the Israelites finally were experiencing an economic rebound. Unstable international conditions enabled the nation to recover lands lost earlier and to gain control of some major trade routes. Consequently, many people became prosperous and enjoyed lives of luxury. Even though the Israelites thrived outwardly, inwardly their souls had become impoverished. Sin, corruption, and idolatry entangled their lives. The wealthy had gained their riches at the expense of the poor, leaving them even more destitute. The rich mistakenly thought their prosperity was a sign of God's favor.

Amos declared that the wealthy had not used their material resources to honor God by showing compassion to the poor. For example, the rich had sold the innocent into slavery, including those who couldn't afford to pay their negligible debts—even for an amount worth no more than a "pair of shoes" (Amos 2:6). The wealthy craved what little the innocent had and treated them shamefully to get it. This included stepping on the dirt-covered heads of the "poor" (vs. 7). The next phrase is literally rendered "they turn aside the way of the impoverished." Most likely, this refers to the wicked rich shoving the rights of the afflicted out of the way so that the oppressors could gain some sadistic pleasure from seeing the defenseless suffer.

Amos denounced the sexual sin of a father and son both having intimate relations with a young woman. Amos also declared that at religious festivals, wealthy Israelites reclined at pagan altars while wearing the attire they seized as collateral from those unable to pay their paltry debts (vs. 8). The Hebrew noun rendered "clothes" literally means a "covering" and refers to large, square cloaks. During the day, these items were worn as garments, and during the night, they functioned as blankets to keep their owners warm. The greed displayed by the wicked rich dishonored the name of God and violated His law. The latter said no one was permitted to keep a person's cloak overnight as a pledge for a debt (see Exod. 22:26-27; Deut. 24:12-13).

Amos 2:8 makes reference to righteous people who were being punished by fines. If the sanction could not be paid, the wine of the indigent was taken and consumed by the greedy extortionists in the shrine of their pagan deity. In their greed, these Israelites ignored the law and took even the basic staples of life—food and clothing—from those in desperate straits. The poor and oppressed no doubt would have welcomed the message proclaimed by Amos. They would see that they had not done anything to warrant the abuse they received from their oppressors. The destitute would also have been encouraged to know that the Lord had neither forgotten them nor their terrible plight.

Amos gave the people a history lesson. First, he reminded them of what God had done to the Amorites (or Canaanites; see Gen. 15:19-21; Josh. 24:11, 15). Their inhabitants once seemed to be as lofty as massive "cedars" (Amos 2:9) and powerful as huge "oaks." In fact, they had occupied Canaan before the Israelites arrived. Even though the Amorites appeared to be invincible giants (see Num. 13:26-33; Deut. 1:26-28), God had totally wiped out the "fruit" (Amos 2:9) of their branches and completely uprooted their trunk from the ground (see Job 18:16; Ezek. 17:9; Hos. 9:16).

Amos next reminded the Israelites of God's past mercies in bringing them out of slavery in "Egypt" (Amos 2:10), leading them for 40 years through the wilderness, and giving them the territory inhabited by the "Amorite" (see Exod. 12:17; Num. 21:25; Deut. 8:2). Amos used this information to show far how God's people had fallen from His mercy. Even though the Israelites had sinned, God's grace had opened the way for them to conquer and occupy Canaan. The Lord had given them a verdant land in which to develop a new society based on His laws.

Deliverance from Egypt was for the sake of God's name and so that the Israelites could be His holy people. Yet the Israelites repaid God's goodness by committing further sins, such as coercing the Nazirites to break their vow not to drink wine and gagging the prophets when they tried to declare God's truth (Amos 2:11-12; see Num. 6:3; Judg. 13:7; Isa. 30:10). The judgments Amos announced were intensified by his referring to God in the first person: "destroyed I the Amorite" (Amos 2:9); "I brought [Israel] up from the land of Egypt" (vs. 10); "I raised up of your sons for prophets" (vs. 11); and "I am pressed under you" (vs. 13).

The result of Israel's disobedience would be devastating judgment. Just as a utility "cart" groaned when bogged down with heavy, mature "sheaves" of grain, so too the Lord would press down on the Israelites by allowing them to be thoroughly defeated in battle. No footsoldier, archer, or cavalryman (including chariot riders) in Israel—not even the fastest, strongest, and bravest among their heroes—would be able to escape or withstand that punishment (vss. 14-16). If the nation's mightiest warriors could not deliver themselves from the impending calamity, what fate awaited the rest of the people? The oracle Amos foretold was the solemn declaration of the Lord.

The pronouncement of divine judgment was fulfilled about four decades later. Around 722 B.C., the Assyrians conquered all of Israel, killing thousands and deporting more. That was the end of the northern kingdom. God's promises of judgment for Israel and for the surrounding nations might seem harsh to us. In reality, however, they are evidence of God's love. His objective was to move sinners to repent so that they could receive His mercy. When people ignore God, they do so at their own risk. Also, when the lost reject the Savior, they must fall into His hands as their enemy. While God is not afraid to judge, He prefers to show mercy (see 1 Tim. 2:4; 2 Pet. 3:9).

SUGGESTIONS TO TEACHERS

Amos was a layperson, not a professional prophet. That didn't matter, however, for the Lord had commissioned him to prophesy (Amos 7:14-15). So, despite Amos' humble background, God used him mightily. Here is an opportunity for you to remind your students that committed lay people are just as essential as paid clergy in speaking for the Lord.

1. CONDEMNATION. Amos' contemporaries felt God would approve of them, regardless of how much they ignored their basic responsibilities before Him. According to Amos, such an attitude of disobedience would inevitably cause moral collapse, and eventually personal and national disaster.

2. CRIMES LISTED. Amos' list of the Israelites' ways of disobeying the Lord deserves a careful look. Have your students examine and comment on what the prophet said. Some of the iniquities he mentioned are forms of social injustice, such as ignoring the poor. Other transgressions he noted are forms of sexual immorality. All of them led to God's judgment of His people.

3. CONSEQUENCES OF SIN. Amos reminded his listeners about the doom the wicked Amorites experienced. The prophet then warned that the same grim day of reckoning would come for Judah and Israel. From this we see that all human actions have consequences and that God holds us accountable for what we think, say, and do.

4. COMING CALAMITY. Amos bluntly told his audience that Judah and Israel would suffer calamity as a result of their sins. Unpleasant though it may be, sometimes we have to face up to the sins of our own culture. Is the nation we live in exempt from God's judgment?

FOR ADULTS

■ **TOPIC:** Injustice Is Intolerable!

■ **QUESTIONS:** 1. Why did God want the people of Judah to obey the teachings of the Mosaic law? 2. In what ways did powerful Israelites deny justice to the destitute? 3. How had the Lord been gracious in the past to His chosen people? 4. Why does God want us to be loving and kind to others in need? 5. What benefits do you see in being ethical with others?

■ **ILLUSTRATIONS:**

Consequences of Disobedience. Sometimes we are prone to jump to indefensible conclusions. For instance, we see others overcome by difficulties and we incorrectly assume that God is judging them for their sins. It's important to remember that God alone knows the reasons why people suffer. We, however, rarely know all the facts.

This doesn't mean, though, that God has left us in the dark about the importance of righteousness and justice. Consequently, we have no excuse for tolerating the kinds of sins against which Amos preached. We know that such vices as idolatry, sexual immorality, bribery, and exploiting the poor (to name a few iniquities) are always wrong.

We also know that a holy God judges sin, and that we suffer personally and our society suffers as a whole when we flout God's teachings in Scripture. That's why we need the sermons that Amos preached to remind us of the kind of behavior God expects from us as His children. We also need these ancient messages because we are prone to stray from God like lost sheep.

Tuning Fork Truth. An elderly music teacher once showed his minister a tuning fork hanging on a cord. Striking the tuning fork and listening to the hum for a moment, the teacher said, "That is the good word. That is G, and no matter how the weather may change or what may happen in human affairs, it remains G."

Continuing, the instructor pointed out that refusing to listen to the correct note and trying to do the performance in another key would result in discordant music. As a musician, he knew the consequences of not obeying the basic tenets of harmony.

The same is true with God's spiritual and moral requirements. The inhabitants of Israel were guilty of selling the poor into slavery, consorting with shrine prostitutes, and misappropriating items given in pledge for the repayment of debts. For these and other transgressions God would bring judgment on His people.

Bad Decision's Consequences. The battle of Midway abruptly changed the course of World War II in the Pacific. Up to that point, the Japanese had experienced nothing but victory. Yet, on the morning of June 3, 1942, the situation dramatically changed. The Americans followed up a Japanese air attack on Midway Island with one of their own from the island and from aircraft carriers.

Admiral Nagumo had four aircraft carriers (the Akagi, Kaga, Soryu, and Hiryu, which were all Pearl Harbor veterans), two battleships, two cruisers, several destroyers, and a few support craft. Nagumo used his fleet to beat back every American plane. The admiral then received word that another attack would be necessary to invade Midway. However, Nagumo also received surprising information about the presence of additional American ships, including an aircraft carrier.

This news caught the admiral by surprise and prompted him to hesitate in making a decision. His own airborne planes needed to land and refuel. Others sat ready on the aircraft carrier decks. A colleague named Admiral Yamaguchi advised that an immediate air attack be launched on the American fleet, and other officers agreed with this advice.

But Nagumo ignored the counsel of the other admirals and ordered that the flight decks be cleared of all aircraft. So, fully loaded planes, laden with bombs and torpedoes, were moved below in the hangar bay as the returning planes were landed and readied for a second attack.

Meanwhile planes from the American aircraft carrier, Yorktown, flew over the Japanese armada and found the flight decks of the four enemy aircraft carriers crowded with planes that were ready to be launched and loaded with fuel and explosives. The American pilots immediately decided to attack. By day's end, all four of the Japanese carriers and a heavy cruiser lay at the bottom of the Pacific Ocean.

The American victory occurred because a Japanese admiral ignored the prudent advice of his subordinates. Similarly, the failure of Judah and Israel to heed the wise council of prophets such as Amos, led to the downfall of these two nations at the hands of their foes.

FOR YOUTH

■ **TOPIC:** Are We Responsible?

■ **QUESTIONS:** 1. In what ways had the people of Judah rejected the Mosaic law? 2. How had the wicked rich in Israel mistreated their impoverished neighbors? 3. Why would God allow Israel's inhabitants to be overrun by invaders? 4. Why is it important for believers to treat other people fairly? 5. Why should Christians obey a higher ethical standard (namely, one from the Lord) than nonbelievers?

ILLUSTRATIONS:

The Lord Has Spoken! A young, successful businesswoman stated, "Most of my friends aren't at all religious, and if they are, they fall into a feel-good spirituality." Her colleague nodded in agreement and then added, "People we work and party with frankly don't feel it's anybody's business how we live or what we do. The main thing is to be happy."

With slight variations, these words express the outlook and values not only of young adults (commonly referred to as Generation Z or the iGeneration), but also of most Americans today. Likewise, these words sum up the attitude of Amos' hearers in Israel in the eighth century B.C. This outspoken prophet's stern warnings were not well received then and may not be welcomed today. But God's message must be heard!

Can We Pay the Price? Social problems can erupt over seemingly insignificant matters. One person is offended by a remark and the next thing we know shots are fired and someone is killed. The influential leaders in Israel probably thought nothing about a little cheating here and there. But before long many people were dispossessed and found no recourse in the legal system.

Even a seemingly slight departure from God's rules can lead to serious trouble. In fact, the patterns of behavior we adopt when we are young carry over into later life. We can pretend to be Christians by going to church even while our hearts are elsewhere. But eventually our hypocrisy will catch up with us, and our lives will become sterile and meaningless.

Amos warned God's people about their refusal to obey His teachings. Wealth, power, and prestige had become more important to them than following the Lord. So, He judged them by sending calamity upon them.

Costly Consequences. Amos declared that God's people had rebelled against His covenant with Moses. They had rejected the teachings found in the Mosaic law and did not keep God's decrees. Because they chose to venerate idols, rather than worship the one true God, they would suffer the costly consequences of their actions.

An east coast high school soccer team recently had an outstanding season. With exceptionally talented players, it moved to the state playoffs. The team won their first two tournament games and were poised to move on to the championship. Then two star starting players, a goalie and a halfback, were arrested and charged with having alcohol in their possession and drinking in a car on the Saturday night before the semifinals.

Both players, who had known the rules about not using alcohol, were immediately suspended from the team. Hampered by not having these two key players, the soccer team lost 3-1, despite good performances by substitute players. The team coach voiced the feelings of disappointment that everyone else felt: "Some kids made the team their priority, and some didn't. And it's obvious who the ones are who didn't."

LESSON 2 — JUNE 14

DOING WHAT IS RIGHT

BACKGROUND SCRIPTURE: Amos 5
DEVOTIONAL READING: Psalm 14

Key Verse: Let judgment run down as waters, and righteousness as a mighty stream. Amos 5:24.

KING JAMES VERSION

AMOS 5:14 Seek good, and not evil, that ye may live: and so the LORD, the God of hosts, shall be with you, as ye have spoken. 15 Hate the evil, and love the good, and establish judgment in the gate: it may be that the LORD God of hosts will be gracious unto the remnant of Joseph. . . .

18 Woe unto you that desire the day of the LORD! to what end is it for you? the day of the LORD is darkness, and not light. 19 As if a man did flee from a lion, and a bear met him; or went into the house, and leaned his hand on the wall, and a serpent bit him. 20 Shall not the day of the LORD be darkness, and not light? even very dark, and no brightness in it?

21 I hate, I despise your feast days, and I will not smell in your solemn assemblies. 22 Though ye offer me burnt offerings and your meat offerings, I will not accept them: neither will I regard the peace offerings of your fat beasts. 23 Take thou away from me the noise of thy songs; for I will not hear the melody of thy viols. 24 But let judgment run down as waters, and righteousness as a mighty stream. 25 Have ye offered unto me sacrifices and offerings in the wilderness forty years, O house of Israel? 26 But ye have borne the tabernacle of your Moloch and Chiun your images, the star of your god, which ye made to yourselves. 27 Therefore will I cause you to go into captivity beyond Damascus, saith the LORD, whose name is The God of hosts.

NEW REVISED STANDARD VERSION

AMOS 5:14 Seek good and not evil,
  that you may live;
and so the LORD, the God of hosts, will be with you,
  just as you have said.
15 Hate evil and love good,
  and establish justice in the gate;
it may be that the LORD, the God of hosts,
  will be gracious to the remnant of Joseph. . . .
18 Alas for you who desire the day of the LORD!
Why do you want the day of the LORD?
It is darkness, not light;
19 as if someone fled from a lion,
  and was met by a bear;
or went into the house and rested a hand against the
    wall,
  and was bitten by a snake.
20 Is not the day of the LORD darkness, not light,
  and gloom with no brightness in it?
21 I hate, I despise your festivals,
  and I take no delight in your solemn assemblies.
22 Even though you offer me your burnt offerings and
    grain offerings,
  I will not accept them;
and the offerings of well-being of your fatted animals
  I will not look upon.
23 Take away from me the noise of your songs;
  I will not listen to the melody of your harps.
24 But let justice roll down like waters,
  and righteousness like an ever-flowing stream.
25 Did you bring to me sacrifices and offerings the forty years in the wilderness, O house of Israel? 26 You shall take up Sakkuth your king, and Kaiwan your star-god, your images, which you made for yourselves; 27 therefore I will take you into exile beyond Damascus, says the LORD, whose name is the God of hosts.

Home Bible Readings

Monday, June 8	Psalm 14	Fools Say, "There Is No God"
Tuesday, June 9	Job 13:7-12	Can You Deceive God?
Wednesday, June 10	Matthew 23:23-28	Full of Hypocrisy and Lawlessness
Thursday, June 11	1 Samuel 15:17-23	To Obey Is Better than Sacrifice
Friday, June 12	Amos 5:7-13	I Know Your Transgressions
Saturday, June 13	Amos 5:1-6	Seek the Lord and Live
Sunday, June 14	Amos 5:14-15, 18-27	Love Good and Establish Justice

Background

In Amos 4, the Lord declared that He would overthrow the Israelites because they persisted in sinning and refused to take advantage of opportunities to repent. God offered a lament for Israel (5:1-3) and called on the nation's inhabitants to change their ways (vss. 4-9). If the people refused to do so, there was coming a time of sadness in the northern kingdom (vss. 16-17). The Lord's judgment of His people was warranted. Consider the fact that injustice prevailed in Israel's court system. When Amos lived, town elders would meet in the city gate (a large passage with adjacent rooms) to resolve legal disputes. God noted that His people hated those who arbitrated in law courts. The Israelites even despised those who spoke truthfully in such settings (vs. 10). In this case, both honest judges and witnesses were detested.

Other examples of the northern kingdom's unjust ways existed. One was the government's insistence on trampling the poor by levying an excessive agricultural tax on their scant crops (vs. 11). Amos is not the only prophet who condemned such injustices. In fact, the exploitation of the poor and needy—a clear violation of the law of Moses (see Exod. 23:6-8)—is condemned in several prophetic books (see Isa. 1:17; 32:7; Jer. 5:26-29; Mic. 7:3). Meanwhile, the wicked rich built mansions for themselves out of chiseled stone. These expensive structures contrasted with the mud-brick houses of the common people. The wealthy also planted lush vineyards in the countryside (Amos 5:11). Yet the Lord would prevent them from enjoying these symbols of affluence.

Notes on the Printed Text

Israel's leaders were self-deceived if they thought the Lord was unaware of their rebellious acts. No transgression was too slight and no sin was too minimal. Whether it was tormenting the innocent, taking bribes, or denying the poor of justice in the city gates, God knew everything that occurred, and He refused to look in the other direction (Amos 5:12).

One way of understanding verse 13 is that, because the time was characterized by evil leaders and oppressive practices, the wise kept silent. Such seemed to be the only sensible course of action. Another possibility is that the verse is referring to those who used shrewd tactics to achieve success. In turn, they would lament under the weight of the Lord's judgment. For them, such a time to come would be filled with disaster, not prosperity.

Regardless of how verse 13 is understood, the thrust of verse 14 remains clear. God wanted to avert bringing judgment on His chosen people. And this was possible if they despised evil (including pagan religious practices) and longed for what is right. Promoting justice and shunning lawlessness would lead to life, both temporal and eternal. Undoubtedly, the Israelites wanted the Lord, the Commander of heaven's vast armies, to be with them. Yet this would only be true if they radically amended their ways.

Verse 15 builds on the emphasis found in verse 14 of seeking what is good by stressing the importance of promoting what is right. For instance, God's spokesperson emphasized the necessity of hating what is vile and loving what is virtuous. The Hebrew verb rendered "hate" denotes a strong abhorrence, in this case for what is morally reprehensible. In contrast, "love" refers to an intense affection, especially for what is upright in character. The point is that "judgment" (or "justice"), not injustice, was to prevail. This would occur when impartial verdicts in legal disputes were rendered in the city gates. Only then would the all-powerful Creator of heaven and earth be gracious to the upright remnant of Joseph (see Isa. 1:9; Joel 2:12-14). Here we see that Joseph, as the most prominent of the 10 northern tribes, represented the entire northern kingdom of Israel.

God's spokesperson challenged the Israelites' glibness and smugness about the "day of the LORD" (Amos 5:18). The latter concept runs throughout the prophetic writings. For instance, in the Book of Joel, the day of the Lord is the time of Israel's final redemption, when God would "pour out [His] Spirit upon all flesh" (2:28) and "bring again the captivity of Judah and Jerusalem" (3:1). Here we see that the Israelites saw this time as something like the Exodus, when God destroyed His enemies and brought His people to safety.

Evidently, then, the people expected that God would punish other nations but deliver Israel on the day of the Lord. So, the Israelites were looking forward to that time. But Amos explained that what they longed for would not be a bright episode of deliverance for them. Instead, it would be an ominous occasion of judgment for them. As Christians, we should remember that the New Testament "day of the Lord"—which refers to the second coming of the Savior—would also bring judgment and destruction upon the earth, as well as the glory of Jesus' eternal kingdom.

God's spokesperson used two vivid metaphors to illustrate the intensity of the day of the Lord. First, that time of judgment would be comparable to people running away in terror from a "lion" (Amos 5:19), but encountering a "bear." Falling prey to either animal would be equally life threatening. Second, the period of distress was like individuals escaping to their home. But just when they thought they could safely rest one of their hands on a "wall," a snake would unexpectedly appear from a crevice and bite them. In short, the episode would be characterized by gloomy "darkness" (vs. 20), not a bright ray of "light."

Beginning in verse 21, we read the Lord's own declaration that He loathed the Israelites' religious practices. The Hebrew verb rendered "hate" is the same one used in verse 15. Added to this is the verb translated "despise" (vs. 21), which can also be rendered "spurn" or "abhor." Together, these terms indicate that God absolutely rejected His people's idolatrous festivals (see Isa. 1:11-14). Even their religious "assemblies" (Amos 5:21) brought Him no pleasure, being more like a putrid stench than a sweet-smelling aroma. So, whether it was informal times of celebration or formal gatherings for corporate worship, the Lord equally detested the way in which the Israelites observed them (see Jer. 6:20).

Amos 5:22 singles out three of the five major kinds of offerings prescribed in the Mosaic law. The "burnt" offering could be a bull, ram, or bird that was wholly consumed by the fire. It was used to show worship, to atone for unintentional sins, and to express commitment to God (see Lev. 1; 6:8-13). The "meat" (Amos 5:22; or "grain") offering consisted of cereal grasses, flour, oil, incense, bread, and salt. It was offered to show worship, to recognize God's goodness, and to express commitment to God (see Lev. 2; 6:14-23). The "peace" (Amos 5:22; or "fellowship") offering could be bread or an animal. It was given to show worship, express thanks, and promote mutual well-being (see Lev. 3; 7:11-34).

The Lord declared that when the corrupt and hypocritical Israelites brought to Him various kinds of sacrificial offerings, He would neither accept nor look upon them with favor (Amos 5:22). Even the performance of sacred music had become odious to God. Whether songs delivered by a choir or music played on stringed instruments (such as viols, lyres, or lutes), He refused to listen (vs. 23). Of course, God had ordained the rituals of worship. Nonetheless, they were supposed to support personal righteousness, not replace it. The people were acting as though they worshiped the Lord, but in fact their human relationships indicated otherwise. For this reason, their external signs of worship, far from pleasing God, infuriated Him.

The Lord desired real signs of faith and obedience. Also, that is why He wanted "judgment" (vs. 24; or "justice") to flow like a river and upright acts like a "stream" that never ran dry. The arid Middle East has many riverbeds called wadis, where water flows only after a rain. Unlike these wadis, Israelite society was to flow continually with equity for people and rectitude toward God. In the Bible, the concept of "righteousness" is essentially the same as holiness. Central to the meaning of both words is the idea of acting in harmony with God's character. When this is done by faith, one enjoys a right relationship both with God and with other believers. Accordingly, if justice and uprightness did not prevail in the religious life of Israel (see Matt. 25:31-46; Jas. 1:27; 1 John 3:17-18), not even the remnant could hope to survive the coming time of divine judgment.

Amos 5:25-27 records God's condemnation of Israel's idolatry. Admittedly, some of the details in these verses are debatable, but the basic sense is discernable. The Israelites did not truly worship the Lord. So, He was going to send them into exile far from their homeland. The Hebrew construction of verse 25 indicates that the question God posed demanded a negative response. Specifically, the Israelites of the wilderness generation (more than 600 years before Amos) did not offer sacrifices to the Lord.

Yet Scripture indicates that sacrifices were actually offered on at least two occasions during the wilderness wandering (see Exod. 24:4, 5; Num. 7). Bible scholars resolve this apparent discrepancy by suggesting that sacrifices were not offered on a regular basis until the nation settled in Canaan. More than one explanation has been given for the reason God posed this question. According to one view, the point is that Israelite disobedience toward God began as early as the wilderness generation. According to another view, the point is that the wilderness generation demonstrated that a relationship between the people and their God was not dependent on the sacrificial system.

Amos 5:26 confirms other Old Testament passages showing that Israelites were involved with false worship. However, it's debated whether the false worship condemned in this verse occurred in the wilderness or in Israel during Amos' time. Some scholars suggest that the Hebrew noun rendered "tabernacle" refers to Sakkuth, the Assyrian god of war who brought either defeat or victory in battle. Others think the noun rendered "Chi'un" is associated with Kaiwan, the Mesopotamian deity for the planet Saturn. In any case, the text indicates that the Israelites performed pagan religious ceremonies, probably parading detestable images fixed to the tops of poles (see Jer. 8:2; Acts 7:43).

Amos 5:26 also implies that it was foolish of the Israelites to worship idols they had made with their own hands. After all, these objects were powerless and lifeless. Moreover, Israel's idols could not rescue them from God's judgment. For the people's sins, the Commander-in-Chief of the heavenly host would exile the Israelites "beyond Damascus" (vs. 27). This refers to their deportation to Assyria. From the northern kingdom's perspective, Assyria was located east of Damascus (Syria's capital) on the trade routes of the Fertile Crescent.

Suggestions to Teachers

When is worship a sham? When is it real? What should we look for when we worship? Is worship mostly well-rehearsed choral music, beautiful liturgies, and eloquent speakers? These are the kinds of questions raised by the material you will cover in this week's lesson.

1. DELUDING HUMAN ATTAINMENTS. Form and rituals without repentance and concern for the hurting count for nothing with God. Amos warned that worship in Israel was spiritually empty because the people failed to back their elaborate words to God with acts that promoted peace and justice. From this we see that social concerns go hand-in-hand with prayer and personal piety among believers.

2. DECLARING GOD'S INTENTION. Next, focus the attention of your students on 5:14-15, "Seek good, and not evil, that ye may live . . . Hate the evil, and love the good, and establish judgment" (or "justice"). Why are these virtues lacking among believers today, and how can the church reemphasize them? Be sure to give specifics.

3. DENOUNCING VAIN WORSHIP. Amos dealt sternly with those blithely longing for the day of the Lord because they thought God would rescue them and make everything pleasant. Instead, Amos stated that it would be a time of reckoning for Israel. Have your students consider the implications of 1 Peter 4:17, which says, "For the time is come that judgment must begin at the house of God: and if it first begin at us, what shall the end be of them that obey not the gospel of God?"

4. DEMANDING JUSTICE AND RIGHTEOUSNESS. End the lesson time by discussing Amos 5:21-24. Be sure to stress that worship without justice and righteousness is empty.

FOR ADULTS

■ **TOPIC:** Justice Is Not "Just Us"

■ **QUESTIONS:** 1. How could the Israelites foster the practice of fairness within their society? 2. Why should believers detest what is evil? 3. Why would God bring anguish on the inhabitants of Israel? 4. Why did God despise Israel's religious festivals? 5. How can believers ensure that their times of worship are pleasing to the Lord?

■ **ILLUSTRATIONS:**

Committed to Doing Right. A wealthy church member offered his congregation a quarter of a million dollars to build a huge steeple. His offer was declined because such a steeple did not fit the message his church was trying to convey to unbelievers. His was an empty gesture because he had missed the point of his congregation's ministry—that doing what is right for the good of the people comes before building imposing structures.

Amos preached that the spiritual condition of our hearts is more important than how much we put in the offering plate (see Amos 5:24). Similarly, Paul taught that even if we give away everything to the poor, but lack love, our offering is meaningless (see 1 Cor. 13:3).

This is a hard concept to accept, because religious duty is so deeply ingrained in us. That's why Amos is good medicine for our souls. We need to understand what God looks for and what's most important to Him. He wants our love, trust, and obedience, not just our offering of money. The foremost command is to love Him with the totality of our being (see Deut. 6:5; Matt. 22:37). When we make that our aim, we will be doing what is right in His eyes.

Holy, Not Hollow, Worship. In this week's lesson, we learn that God despised the Israelites' hollow acts of worship, and He rejected their pretentious offerings. Instead, the Lord desired that there would be justice in Israel and that His righteousness would be the law of the land.

Connor is a songwriter who performs at Christian churches. He tells a funny story about himself that illustrates the misguided role we sometimes take in our worship of God. Connor and his wife, Avery, were on their way to a local ministry engagement when they began to have a "heated" discussion over some normal issues of family life. As they arrived at the church, Connor began to feel the pressure of having to minister with an unresolved conflict staring at him from the first row.

In an act of humble submission, Connor decided that he had better ask Avery's forgiveness. As Connor turned to Avery to seek her favor, she looked at him and said, "I don't know whether I'm ready to forgive you, especially when your main motivation is so you won't have to feel convicted by the Holy Spirit the whole time you're preaching."

Connor was shocked and humbled, especially because he knew Avery was correct. Connor had sought the peace of his marital relationship for motives that were less than pure.

What Would Amos Say Today? This week's lesson is an opportunity for your students to compare their own worship to the worship God despised from the ancient Israelites. He declared through His spokesperson that Israel's religious rituals had become empty and godless.

So, is our worship today different from that of the ancient Israelites? Arthur W. Pink (1886–1952), author of *The Sovereignty of God*, critiqued modern worship in a way that echoes Amos. Pink drew attention to the following attitudes as producing empty acts of praise: a self-serving spirit; love of money; love of material possessions; a pompous attitude; a critical spirit; disrespect; obstinacy; unfaithfulness; and disobedience.

As Amos reminds us, our style of worship is not God's main concern. What's most important to Him is our hearts. Are we listening to Him, willing to obey His instructions, and ready to repent? If not, any of our attempts at worship are displeasing to the Lord.

For Youth
■ **Topic:** Words Are Cheap
■ **Questions:** 1. In what ways can Jesus' followers seek what is good? 2. Why did God want His people to maintain justice in the law courts? 3. Under what condition could the Israelites anticipate God's mercy? 4. Why did God send Israel into exile? 5. What are some ways believers can replace injustice with justice?

■ **ILLUSTRATIONS:**

God Has High Expectations. In Amos' day, it was relatively easy for the Israelites to play the religious game. What they said sounded good, but the way they lived was characterized by evil.

It's also easy for us to pretend we're Christians when we really haven't trusted in Jesus. We want to please our parents, our friends, and our church leaders, so we go along with the game. Perhaps this is one reason why Christian apologist Josh McDowell has asked, *if we were put on trial as a follower of Jesus, would there be enough evidence to convict us?*

At some point, our facade crashes. Sometimes we can put the pieces together. But on other occasions that's not possible. It's better to confess our lack of genuine faith now than to keep pretending otherwise. Besides, God knows us as we truly are, and we cannot fool Him.

Only a Show. Melvin Adams, who retired from the Harlem Globetrotters in 2000, described his mother waking him each Sunday to go to church. He went with his mother, but sat in the back of the church in the last pew.

Instead of an open Bible on Melvin's lap, he held an open copy of *Sports Illustrated*, which he read. Outwardly, he looked religious and committed, but his worship participation was only a show. Not until much later in his life did he finally make a commitment to Christ.

Like Melvin, many youth are mechanical in their worship participation. They may sit in church, but their minds are somewhere else. Their worship is phony, for they make empty offerings of praise to God. Amos called his listeners to make their offerings to the Lord genuine and wholehearted.

End of Time. A *Peanuts* cartoon strip pictured a frightened Peppermint Patty. She had heard that the end of the world was near. Trembling, she asked her friend, Marcie, "What if the world ends tonight?" Marcie responded, "I promise there'll be a tomorrow, sir. In fact, it is already tomorrow in Australia."

Many youth now, as well as in Amos' time, reflect Marcie's belief. They assume that the end will be a wonderful time when God will bless His people. Yes, this is true for believers. But the prophet also said that the end would be a time of judgment for those who have not committed themselves to the Lord in faith. All lives would undergo scrutiny.

LESSON 3 — JUNE 21

ENDING COMPLACENCY

BACKGROUND SCRIPTURE: Amos 6
DEVOTIONAL READING: Psalm 119:31-38

Key Verse: Ye have turned judgment into gall, and the fruit of righteousness into hemlock. Amos 6:12.

KING JAMES VERSION

AMOS 6:4 That lie upon beds of ivory, and stretch themselves upon their couches, and eat the lambs out of the flock, and the calves out of the midst of the stall; 5 That chant to the sound of the viol, and invent to themselves instruments of musick, like David; 6 That drink wine in bowls, and anoint themselves with the chief ointments: but they are not grieved for the affliction of Joseph. 7 Therefore now shall they go captive with the first that go captive, and the banquet of them that stretched themselves shall be removed.

8 The Lord God hath sworn by himself, saith the Lord the God of hosts, I abhor the excellency of Jacob, and hate his palaces: therefore will I deliver up the city with all that is therein. . . . 11 For, behold, the Lord commandeth, and he will smite the great house with breaches, and the little house with clefts. 12 Shall horses run upon the rock? will one plow there with oxen? for ye have turned judgment into gall, and the fruit of righteousness into hemlock: 13 Ye which rejoice in a thing of nought, which say, Have we not taken to us horns by our own strength? 14 But, behold, I will raise up against you a nation, O house of Israel, saith the Lord the God of hosts; and they shall afflict you from the entering in of Hemath unto the river of the wilderness.

NEW REVISED STANDARD VERSION

AMOS 6:4 Alas for those who lie on beds of ivory,
and lounge on their couches,
and eat lambs from the flock,
and calves from the stall;
5 who sing idle songs to the sound of the harp,
and like David improvise on instruments of music;
6 who drink wine from bowls,
and anoint themselves with the finest oils,
but are not grieved over the ruin of Joseph!
7 Therefore they shall now be the first to go into exile,
and the revelry of the loungers shall pass away.
8 The Lord God has sworn by himself
(says the Lord, the God of hosts):
I abhor the pride of Jacob
and hate his strongholds;
and I will deliver up the city and all that is in it. . . .
11 See, the Lord commands,
and the great house shall be shattered to bits,
and the little house to pieces.
12 Do horses run on rocks?
Does one plow the sea with oxen?
But you have turned justice into poison
and the fruit of righteousness into wormwood—
13 you who rejoice in Lo-debar,
who say, "Have we not by our own strength
taken Karnaim for ourselves?"
14 Indeed, I am raising up against you a nation,
O house of Israel, says the Lord, the God of hosts,
and they shall oppress you from Lebo-hamath
to the Wadi Arabah.

Home Bible Readings

Monday, June 15	Luke 11:37-42	Full of Greed Inside
Tuesday, June 16	Proverbs 16:1-11	A Large Income with Injustice
Wednesday, June 17	Philippians 1:12-20	Selfish Ambition
Thursday, June 18	Luke 12:15-21	Guard against Greed
Friday, June 19	Psalm 119:31-38	Turn from Selfish Gain
Saturday, June 20	Psalm 37:14-22	The Righteous Are Generous
Sunday, June 21	Amos 6:4-8, 11-14	The Idle Rich

Background

The first half of Amos 6:1 censured those in Judah who felt at ease and rebuked Israel for their false sense of security. Then, in the second half of the verse, the focus shifts entirely to the northern kingdom. The passage refers to Israel's overly confident leaders, who thought of themselves as an elite group of princes to whom the nation's inhabitants turned for insight and guidance. Such an arrogant view is reinforced by the reference to Israel as the "chief of the nations." The ruling class in Samaria refused to consider that other stronger, nearby countries would fall to the onslaught of the Assyrian juggernaut.

Verse 2 draws attention to several "kingdoms" north and south of Israel. Calneh was in south-central Mesopotamia, Hamath was located in northern Syria, and Gath was one of the five cities belonging to Philistines near the coast of southern Canaan. The territory belonging to these cities was not larger than that of Samaria. Likewise, Israel and Judah were no better off than their neighbors. All of them would be subject to the conquest of foreign invaders. Despite this harsh reality, the leaders of the northern and southern kingdoms deluded themselves into thinking the prophesied time of calamity either would not occur or would happen in the far distant future (see Ezek. 12:27).

This false hope bolstered Israel to establish a "seat of violence" (Amos 6:3), which included the abuse of the poor. The Lord condemned Samaria's haughty and wicked rulers. While many in the northern kingdom were destitute and suffered mistreatment, their leaders indulged themselves with wealth they had stolen from the poor. According to 3:15, the wicked rich owned summer and winter homes filled with panels and furniture adorned with expensive "ivory." Even the "beds" (6:4) on which they reclined were decorated with "ivory." Moreover, they pampered themselves by loafing on "couches." Even worse, they satiated their cravings by feasting on tender "lambs" from the flock and the finest "calves" from the middle of the stall.

Notes on the Printed Text

The individuals of privilege and rank in Israel congratulated themselves for being as musically gifted as King David (see 1 Sam. 16:15-23; 2 Sam. 23:1). For instance, Samaria's leaders chanted frivolous songs as they played music on their lyres and lutes. They even thought of themselves as artistic geniuses who created original tunes and strummed them on musical "instruments" (Amos 6:5) they allegedly invented. All the while, they ingested "wine" (vs. 6) from large, costly, sacrificial basins and anointed their bodies with the finest scented, perfumed "ointments." Tragically, these same decadent princes were neither saddened by the moral decay of their nation nor lamented the impending judgment that was about to fall on the northern kingdom. "Joseph" refers to the two of the tribes of Israel, Manasseh and Ephraim (see 5:6). They were descended from Jacob's son, Joseph.

The first part of 6:7 is literally translated, "they will go into exile at the head of the exiles." Put differently, among a large number of peoples whom the Assyrians conquered and uprooted from their homelands, the invaders would first lead away the inhabitants of the northern kingdom as their captives. Indeed, the wicked rich in Samaria would be at the front of the long caravans of shackled refugees whom the Assyrians deported. This gloomy outcome would abruptly end the Israelite nobles' pagan religious banquets. Ironically, the upper class—who prided themselves on being first among the nations—would soon be banned from their estates. Also, existence as the slaves of the brutal Assyrians would not be nearly as pleasant as the life the princes of Samaria had taken for granted.

In verse 8, the Hebrew phrases rendered the "Lord GOD" and the "LORD the God of hosts" depicted the Creator as the invincible, divine Warrior and uncontested moral Governor of the universe. Through His spokesperson, God let the Israelites know more about the destruction He would soon be sending their way. It would be a complete defeat for the inhabitants of Samaria. They thought they were safe. Yet, before long, the Assyrians would be beating down Samaria's gates.

To strengthen the credibility and finality of what the Lord had to say, Amos explained that God had sworn an oath on His own authority. First, He announced that He loathed Jacob's arrogance, as seen in the complacency of the northern kingdom's leaders. Second, God declared that He despised the nobility's fortress-like citadels, which they trusted for safety. So, on the one hand, the Israelites were confident their military readiness would be enough to protect them. On the other hand, God would allow foreigners to thoroughly destroy "the city" (probably the capital, Samaria). This meant that all of Israel would be vulnerable to the invaders.

After the lines of poetry in verse 8 comes their prose amplification in verses 9 and 10. In a general sense, this passage describes a hypothetical situation in which at first only a small number of people evaded an onslaught, but afterward the enemy killed the rest of the survivors. In a specific sense, verse 9 is understood in at least three different ways: (1) only ten persons remained in a large, wealthy home; (2) only ten members of a household were left alive; or (3) only ten soldiers of an army unit found refuge in a solitary house not destroyed by the invaders.

The exact meaning of verse 10 is also debated. The first part is literally rendered "a man's kinsmen and his burner." Most likely, the same person is being referred to, namely, a relative who is responsible for removing the corpses of the deceased from the house. In turn, this individual would either cremate the dead or burn a memorial fire to honor them before burying the bodies (see Jer. 34:5). The second part of Amos 6:10 pictures a lone survivor who is trembling in fear within an inner room of a house and being asked whether there are any other persons alive with him. At first, he answers "No." But then, he urges those who are outside to remain quiet and not call upon the "name of the LORD" (either to ask for a divine blessing on the dead or to request additional help from God). Evidently, the situation would be so traumatic that it would feel too risky to invoke God's name and bring down further judgment on the group (see Isa. 48:1).

In Amos 6:11, the poetry resumes with a vivid statement that the sovereign Commander of heaven's armies had issued the decree for the adversary to invade and destroy Samaria. In turn, the Assyrians would pulverize the "great" houses of the rich (undoubtedly financed with stolen wealth) and the "little" homes of the poor. Put differently, the destruction would be so thorough that no household in the northern kingdom would be spared by God's hand of judgment rendered through His instrument, the Assyrians.

The next stanza begins with two ludicrous questions, both of which demanded a negative answer. First, it was preposterous for "horses" (vs. 12) to gallop over jagged, vertical rocks, for either the animals would be severely injured or killed. Also, it was absurd for a farmer to use "oxen" to cultivate boulders. After all, doing so would maim the animals. Despite that, Israel's leaders were guilty of perverting the moral order the Creator intended for the world. For instance, by denying "judgment" (or "justice") to the innocent, the wicked rich subverted the restorative potential of the law courts and made it into a poisonous plant. Also, the corrupt rulers so misused the judicial system that what should have been the sweet "fruit" of upright actions literally turned out to be "hemlock" (or "wormwood"), that is, a bitter herb (see 5:7).

Centuries earlier at Mount Sinai, God had made a covenant with the Israelites. Also, He had given them the Mosaic law so that they would know what He expected from them. Moreover, He had shown them mercy after mercy. Yet, despite all this, the upper class of Israel were leading the way in unrighteous behavior. Mixed up with the Israelites' injustice was their pride. Amos 6:13 describes them as rejoicing in their overthrow of two places, which are referred to as a "thing of nought" (literally, "Lo Debar") and "horns" (literally, "Karnaim"). The first town was located in Gilead near where the Yarmuk River joined the Jordan River, while the second town was situated about 23 miles east of the Sea of Galilee. Evidently, both of these cities were captured or recaptured from the Syrians by the Israelite king, Jeroboam II, during his campaigns of expansion (see 2 Kings 14:25-28).

Most likely, Amos 6:13 mentions the two preceding towns because of the meanings of their names. The prophet deliberately misspelled the name of "Lo Debar," or Debir, so that it literally meant "no word," that is, "not a thing." The implication is that the Lord regarded as nothing the minor victory over which Israel rejoiced. Also, the name literally translated as "Karnaim" comes from a Hebrew noun meaning "horns." Since horns were a symbol of strength in the ancient Near East (see 1 Kings 22:11), "Karnaim" probably appears in Amos 6:13 because the Israelites assumed their victories were achieved by their own military might. Pride in accomplishments becomes sin when it is divorced from recognizing one's dependence upon God. The Israelites were not wrong to celebrate their successes. Their failure lay in taking credit for achievements that God had accomplished through them.

Before long, the Israelites' pride in their conquests would be obliterated. This is due to the fact that the all-powerful Commander of the heavenly host would bring an adversary, the Assyrian Empire, against the entire northern kingdom. The invaders would completely defeat the "house of Israel" (vs. 14) from one end of its border to the next. In particular, the advancing armies would overrun the Israelites from the northernmost extent of their control, represented by "Hemath" (on the Orontes River in the valley between the Lebanon and anti-Lebanon mountains), to the southernmost extent of their control, represented by the "river of the wilderness" (or the "Wadi Arabah"; in the far south between the Dead Sea and the Gulf of Aqabah).

SUGGESTIONS TO TEACHERS

Most likely, everyone in your class would admit that money and possessions are very important in American culture. For instance, success is measured by the size of one's salary. Even in Amos' day, one's importance was linked to one's material wealth. Then, as now, people were caught up in a greedy lifestyle.

1. AN ADDICTION TO AFFLUENCE. Amos 6 warns us against greed. The danger of thinking that life's true meaning comes from getting and hoarding is vividly portrayed in verses 4-7. Even though the ruling class in Israel wallowed in self-indulgent pleasures, these would not shield them from God's judgment.

2. AN ANSWER TO SMUGNESS. Verses 8-14 reveal that the Lord abhors all forms of smugness. Encourage the members of your class to wrestle with the unvarnished implications of the somber oracle found here. How might they recast the imagery by using illustrations from contemporary life?

3. FALSE VERSUS TRUE SECURITY. The Israelites incorrectly assumed that true security came from their military conquests. It's not difficult to find examples of such skewed thinking today. Have the students deliberate why it's foolish to depend on success for happiness and wealth for security.

4. WHERE REAL TREASURE IS FOUND. The oracle of judgment Amos declared teaches us that our real treasure is found in living as Jesus' kingdom citizens, not in piling up investments or amassing ever-increasing bank accounts. Encourage the class members to discuss ways they can withstand the pressures to keep up with the lifestyles of others. Also, have the students consider how they can keep from trusting too much in their possessions.

For Adults

■ **Topic:** A Deadly Trio: Selfishness, Greed, and Pride
■ **Questions:** 1. In what ways were the upper class of Israel acting self-indulgently? 2. Why did the Lord detest Israel's fortified citadels? 3. Why would God allow all the homes of the rich and poor in Israel to be destroyed? 4. How are Christian standards of success different from those of the world? 5. How might believers use their wealth or influence responsibly?

■ **Illustrations:**

Putting the Lord First. Amos 6 reveals that human relationships change when hoarding wealth becomes more important than anything else in life. For instance, friends are looked upon as business contacts. A spouse is regarded as an additional source of income to maintain an elevated standard of living.

Even children are affected by a greed culture, and look upon parents as sources for handouts. Instead of young children learning to help spontaneously or to show kindness without being rewarded, they are often programmed to expect or demand payment for any good deed they might perform. Ultimately, their behavior becomes based on the money that's given to them.

The greed and money lust in our society affects other relationships besides in families. A preoccupation with amassing possessions makes us prone to bargaining rather than sharing. We learn to calculate what we will do in terms of what it will cost us and what the payoff will be. As we discover from this week's lesson, the best way to break this insidious cycle is to put the Lord first in our lives.

The Focus of Our Heart. The leaders of Israel during the lifetime of Amos had skewed priorities. They were plagued by a deadly trio of selfishness, greed, and pride. From a New Testament perspective, the upper class was guilty of loving the world. This included the cravings of sinful people, the yearning for everything the eyes see, and the arrogance produced by material possessions. They failed to realize that all these sorts of evil desires were fading away (see 1 John 2:14-16).

In the financial world, investors use money to make more money. In a sense the Spirit is like a broker who is continually reinvesting God's resources in His children's lives. The Father first invested in us when He sent His Son to buy us back from Satan's kingdom. Now the resulting "dividends" include the fruit of the Spirit (Gal. 5:22-23).

Since everything we have belongs to God, we are stewards, obligated to use our possessions, time, and energy as investments for our Master. Every act of faithful stewardship adds to our spiritual treasure. Where, then, is our heart focused? Do our spiritual lenses need cleaning? Are we using our resources to invest in God's kingdom? Where have we stockpiled our treasures? The answers to these questions indicate that the contents of our character matter more to God than the size of our stock portfolio.

Coming Up Empty. Magazine editor Lewis Lapham, in his book, *Money and Class in America*, tells the story of a chance encounter with a Yale University classmate who had become a New York businessman. The two ran into each other about 30 years after their college graduation, and the businessman immediately began to cry on Lapham's shoulder.

"I'm nothing," the man said. "You understand that, nothing. I earn $250,000 a year, but it's nothing, and I'm nobody."

The businessman's despair struck Lapham as being rather grotesque. After all, if the average American family of four earns an annual income in the tens of thousands of dollars, how could this person possibly feel deprived? But when the businessman listed his expenses—a Park Avenue apartment, private school tuitions, taxes, salaries for a maid and a part-time laundress—the total came to $300,400. He was clearly going broke on an income of $250,000 a year!

"As it is," said the businessman, "I live like an animal. I eat tuna fish out of cans and hope that when the phone rings it isn't somebody harassing me for a bill." He might have been pulling down a quarter of a million dollars a year, but according to Lapham, he "had the look of a man who was being followed by the police." Like the upper class in Israel during Amos' lifetime, this businessman had put his treasures where his heart was and had come up empty.

FOR YOUTH
■ **TOPIC:** Greed Won't Win
■ **QUESTIONS:** 1. How did the ruling elite in Israel squander their time? 2. What would bring Israel's feasting and lounging to an abrupt end? 3. In what ways had the leaders of Israel perverted justice? 4. How do you think people today would regard the actions of the upper class of Amos' day? 5. Why is it foolish to depend on success and wealth for happiness and security?

■ **ILLUSTRATIONS:**

Where Our Priorities Lie. In Amos' day, Israel was divided into two classes: the haves and the have-nots. Those in the first group thought only about themselves and were indifferent to the struggles faced by the second group. God used Amos to censure the ruling elite in Samaria for their smug, indulgent ways.

In his book, *Come Before Winter*, Charles R. Swindoll writes, "I don't have many temptations to worship evil things. It's the good things that plague me. It isn't as difficult for me to reject something that is innately bad or wrong as it is to keep those good and wholesome things off the throne."

Although many teens try to meet the demands of living, they seem to pile up like unfolded laundry. Since each day has only 24 hours, Christian young people need to be selective. Meanwhile, their use of the time and energy that God gives them indicates where their priorities lie. This week's Scripture passage will help young people to understand how they can spend their time and energy in ways that have eternal value.

Redirecting Our Gaze. Amos 6 reveals that because the rich and powerful in Israel were acting complacently, God would send them into exile. In fact, He so abhorred their pride that He would allow Assyria to overthrow the northern kingdom. From this we see that no form of smugness has any place in the lives of believers.

What turns your head? Lots of money? A stockpile of material possessions? An impressive physique? Whatever it is, we all share a love of "things." Advertisers depend on this love to get us to buy their products, and we all get sucked in to buy, buy, buy. But things can't give us the contentment that our hearts desire. Only God can.

The next time you see that commercial or that brochure, redirect your spiritual gaze to the Lord. Ask Him to fill the place that is in need of being filled. Then, like Paul, we will be able to say that regardless of our material wealth, we "can do all things through Christ which strengtheneth [us]" (Phil. 4:13).

Greed Never Pays. Marguerite Jackson of Spring Mills Estates—an affluent suburb of Indianapolis—was known to be rich. People spoke of her wealth. The plump, white-haired, 66-year-old widow seldom left her home or the three acres of weed-choked property enclosed by a chain-link fence. Couriers honked, then passed their parcels over the fence. She tipped the people and neighborhood children who performed odd jobs or errands with 20-dollar bills.

Over a stretch of several weeks, neighbors grew increasingly alarmed when Jackson failed to respond when they tried contacting her. Firefighters finally forced their way into Jackson's home and found her dead on the floor. When police searched her house, they discovered just how much wealth she acquired. Because Jackson distrusted banks, she hoarded her money. Stashed in toolboxes, drawers, vacuum-cleaner bags, garbage cans, and a shopping cart were *five million dollars in crisp, 100-dollar bills!* After a thorough investigation, police soon discovered that over three million dollars were missing due to burglars, who had looted the house and murdered Jackson.

Jackson's death was a genuine tragedy. Even more distressing is the fact that even though she devotedly read her Bible, she apparently never understood the lesson on life's priorities found in Amos 6. There we discover that being greedy never pays.

LESSON 4 — JUNE 28

ANSWERING TO GOD

BACKGROUND SCRIPTURE: Amos 8
DEVOTIONAL READING: Hosea 11:1-7

Key Verse: [God] said, Amos, what seest thou? And I said, A basket of summer fruit. Then said the LORD unto me, The end is come upon my people of Israel; I will not again pass by them any more. Amos 8:2.

KING JAMES VERSION

AMOS 8:1 Thus hath the Lord GOD shewed unto me: and behold a basket of summer fruit. 2 And he said, Amos, what seest thou? And I said, A basket of summer fruit. Then said the LORD unto me, The end is come upon my people of Israel; I will not again pass by them any more. 3 And the songs of the temple shall be howlings in that day, saith the Lord GOD: there shall be many dead bodies in every place; they shall cast them forth with silence.

4 Hear this, O ye that swallow up the needy, even to make the poor of the land to fail, 5 Saying, When will the new moon be gone, that we may sell corn? and the sabbath, that we may set forth wheat, making the ephah small, and the shekel great, and falsifying the balances by deceit? 6 That we may buy the poor for silver, and the needy for a pair of shoes; yea, and sell the refuse of the wheat? . . . 9 And it shall come to pass in that day, saith the Lord GOD, that I will cause the sun to go down at noon, and I will darken the earth in the clear day: 10 And I will turn your feasts into mourning, and all your songs into lamentation; and I will bring up sackcloth upon all loins, and baldness upon every head; and I will make it as the mourning of an only son, and the end thereof as a bitter day.

NEW REVISED STANDARD VERSION

AMOS 8:1 This is what the Lord GOD showed me—a basket of summer fruit. 2 He said, "Amos, what do you see?" And I said, "A basket of summer fruit." Then the LORD said to me,

"The end has come upon my people Israel;
I will never again pass them by.
3 The songs of the temple shall become wailings in that day,"
    says the Lord GOD;
"the dead bodies shall be many,
cast out in every place. Be silent!"
4 Hear this, you that trample on the needy,
and bring to ruin the poor of the land,
5 saying, "When will the new moon be over
so that we may sell grain;
and the sabbath,
so that we may offer wheat for sale?
We will make the ephah small and the shekel great,
and practice deceit with false balances,
6 buying the poor for silver
and the needy for a pair of sandals,
and selling the sweepings of the wheat." . . .
9 On that day, says the Lord GOD,
I will make the sun go down at noon,
and darken the earth in broad daylight.
10 I will turn your feasts into mourning,
and all your songs into lamentation;
I will bring sackcloth on all loins,
and baldness on every head;
I will make it like the mourning for an only son,
and the end of it like a bitter day.

Home Bible Readings

Monday, June 22	Amos 8:11-14	A Famine of Hearing God's Word
Tuesday, June 23	Hosea 8:7-14	Reaping the Whirlwind
Wednesday, June 24	Hosea 9:5-9	Days of Punishment Have Come
Thursday, June 25	Hosea 10:1-8	Israel's Sin Shall Be Destroyed
Friday, June 26	Hosea 11:1-7	Israel Refused to Return to Me
Saturday, June 27	Jeremiah 14:1-10	God Will Remember Iniquity
Sunday, June 28	Amos 8:1-6, 9-10	A Day of Mourning

Background

Amos continued to warn the Israelites about the judgment God would soon be sending their way. Specifically, the prophet related to them four visions he had received from the Lord. The first two visions—locusts (7:1-3) and fire (vss. 4-6)—both present judgments God agreed to withhold. The third and fourth visions—a plumb line (vss. 7-9) and ripe fruit (8:1-3)—both present judgments God would send.

Since Amos' four visions are closely related, one might expect them to follow one right after another. But that's not the case. Instead, between the third and fourth visions comes a historical passage (7:10-17). God's spokesperson had been delivering most, if not all, his prophecies in Bethel, one of Israel's two main religious centers (the other one was Dan). At that time, the head of Bethel's priestly establishment was Amaziah. Not surprisingly, he did not like what the foreigner from the south was declaring. Perhaps Amaziah was most upset at the statements about Bethel that Amos had communicated for God (see 3:14; 4:4; 5:4-6).

When Amaziah heard Amos' vision of the plumb line, he thought he had a way to dislodge the prophet from Bethel. Amaziah wrote to King Jeroboam II, accusing Amos of plotting against the monarch at the religious epicenter of the northern kingdom (7:10). The provocative wording of the charge was intended to grab the attention of the king. If he was like most rulers, he was constantly on the alert to learn about attempts at rebellion. In his communication to Jeroboam, Amaziah quoted Amos as predicting the monarch's death and the Israelites' exile (vs. 11). For the first part, Amaziah probably went beyond Amos' actual words. The prophet had declared that God would raise a sword against Jeroboam's house (see vs. 9), whereas Amaziah quoted Amos as saying Jeroboam himself would die by the sword (vs. 11). For the second part, however, Amaziah accurately communicated the prophet's warning of exile for the nation (see 5:5, 27).

We don't know what reply, if any, the priest received from Jeroboam. Probably if the king was convinced that Amos posed a threat to his reign, Jeroboam would have ordered the prophet killed. Yet, we have no historical evidence that Amos was murdered. On his own initiative, Amaziah derogatorily referred to Amos as a "seer" (7:12) or "visionary" and ordered him to leave Bethel. The priest also ordered Amos to go back home to

Judah and earn his living there as a prophet. Evidently, Amaziah suspected that Amos came to Bethel to make money. In that day, prophets sometimes received support by donations from those who heard their pronouncements. Amaziah asserted that one of Israel's major shrines, along with the king's palace, were in Bethel (vs. 13). While true, this description contained a veiled threat that royal power might be used to cleanse the city of the offending prophet.

Amos responded by defending his own prophetic ministry (vss. 14-15) and then prophesying against Amaziah (vss. 16-17). Amos said he was a layperson, not a professional prophet. He had a thriving agricultural business (herding flocks and tending sycamore fig trees) when God had called him to prophesy to Israel. So Amos did not need money from that activity. Also, since God had appointed Amos as His spokesperson, Amos would not dodge his responsibility. Moreover, even though Amaziah tried to silence Amos, the prophet would not be deterred from his God-given task.

NOTES ON THE PRINTED TEXT

Amos' fourth vision concerned a "basket" (Amos 8:1) of ripe "summer fruit." The basket probably looked like an ordinary harvesting container made out of woven wicker. The produce in the basket may have been any kind of fruit—such as grapes, olives, pomegranates, and figs—that ripened in August-September and was harvested in the autumn. When the Lord asked Amos what he saw, Amos stated that he saw a container filled with fresh, ripe "fruit" (vs. 2).

The prophet's answer opened the way for God to make the play on words that is the point of this vision. Specifically, the Hebrew noun translated "summer fruit" (*kayitz*; literally "end-of-the-year fruit") sounds like the noun that is translated "the end" (*ketz*). God used this coincidence to make His oracle memorable. Just as the summer fruit was ready to be harvested at the end of the summer growing season, so too the national existence of Israel had come to end. The all-powerful Lord declared that He would no longer overlook their transgressions. Moreover, this prophecy, like the vision of a plumb line, shows that there was no stopping the divine judgment. The Israelites' wickedness had gotten to a point where God had to punish it.

As with the oracle about a plumb line, the vision of the ripe summer fruit contains a description of what would happen when the prophecy was fulfilled (7:9; 8:3). Whereas the Israelites had been singing joyful religious songs (even though hypocritically) in their pagan shrine at Bethel, they would one day wail in sorrow over the horrible circumstance that was about to overtake their nation. A large number of Israelite corpses would be scattered all about by the violence of their attackers. (The prediction came to pass at the time of the Assyrian invasion in 732 B.C.) Due to the dreadfulness of this scene, the all-powerful Lord commanded there be a moment of respectful "silence" (8:3) among those who heard Amos' prophecy.

In verses 4-6, several acts of injustice are detailed, especially against the destitute.

For instance, the wicked rich were guilty of treating the indigent with contempt and seeking to eliminate from the northern kingdom those who were impoverished (see 2:7; 5:11). The godless even disdained such religious festivals as the "new moon" (8:5; observed at the beginning of every month with various offerings) and the "sabbath" (observed at the end of every week). These were supposed to be sacred occasions when any form of work was discontinued. Yet Israel's greedy merchants were eager for these holy days to pass by so that they could reopen their bins and resume selling their grain (including barley and "wheat").

The last part of verse 5 is literally rendered "to make small the ephah and to make great the shekel." The ephah was a unit of dry measure used to determine the volume of grain, flour, or meal being sold and bartered. The shekel of silver was the standard unit used to measure weight in the ancient Semitic cultures. Merchants could increase their profits by using an undersized ephah (that is, selling less) and a heavier shekel (that is, to obtain a higher price). Also, by utilizing out-of-balance scales, corrupt vendors could swindle even more money from their customers (see Lev. 19:35-36; Deut. 25:14; Prov. 11:1; Hos. 12:7).

As noted in lesson 1 concerning Amos 2:6, the wealthy misused their material resources by exploiting the poor. The wicked rich also dishonored God by enslaving the innocent. This included trading the poverty-stricken with "silver" (8:6) and the penniless for a "pair of shoes." The dishonest merchants even mixed worthless chaff and other refuse they swept from the ground with "wheat" so they could get more money when they sold the grain to unsuspecting customers.

Previously, in 6:8, the Lord declared how much He loathed Jacob's arrogance, as evidenced by the complacency of the northern kingdom's leaders (see the Bible commentary appearing in lesson 3). Now, in 8:7, God used sarcasm to confirm His oath by the "excellency of Jacob" that He would always remember the wicked deeds the rich and powerful in Israel were guilty of committing. Verse 8 draws attention to the inevitability of the coming flood of judgment, in which God would bring upheaval on the nation and its inhabitants.

The convulsions to be felt throughout the land (perhaps produced by an earthquake; see 1:1) were as certain to occur as the yearly flooding (in September) and receding (in October) of the Nile River in Egypt (see 9:5). As Israel was tossed about and sank after each jarring episode (especially at the hands of the Assyrians; see Isa. 8:6-8), the northern kingdom would "tremble" (Amos 8:8) and its residents would "mourn." In that time of reckoning, the supreme Creator would upturn the natural order by causing the "sun" (vs. 9; which some of the Israelites venerated) to set at midday and the land to "darken" when it should have been bright (perhaps produced by either a solar or lunar eclipse; see also the Bible commentary in lesson 2 on 5:18-20).

As previously noted, Israel's times of celebration were characterized by idolatry and immorality. Furthermore, during the reign of Jeroboam II, the northern kingdom reveled in a season of seemingly endless prosperity. But in Amos 8:10, the Lord declared through His spokesperson that "mourning" would soon replace their festivals and dirges would supplant their "songs." Moreover, the carnival atmosphere would give way to the wearing of "sackcloth" and the shaving of heads.

Sackcloth was a rough fabric woven from the long, dark hair of camels and goats. The color and coarseness of the material made it appropriate for wearing during times of national calamity. On such occasions, it was also customary for people to demonstrate grief and signal humiliation by shaving their heads. Centuries earlier, Egypt lamented the death of their firstborn sons during the tenth plague God brought upon the nation (see Exod. 11:1-10; 12:29-30). So too in Israel's day of judgment, they would express a similar level of grief. Indeed, everyone in the nation would be overcome by the bitterness of the occasion (see Jer. 6:26; Zech. 12:10).

SUGGESTIONS TO TEACHERS

Most of us have heard dramatic accounts of past heroes who have courageously demonstrated their faith in the face of great peril. We rightly express appreciation for them and are inspired by their example. But we sometimes think that ordinary persons today could never stand up for God in such ways. This week's lesson can be a call to us to prepare ourselves to show courageous faith, no matter our roles as "ordinary" citizens, workers, or students.

1. A STARK VISION BY A STERN SPOKESPERSON. Amos was not a member of the guild of professional religious speakers. Nonetheless, he courageously proclaimed God's warning. Amos foretold the devastation of the pagan shrines and the ruin of the royal dynasty, all due to the widespread corruption in Israel. Sometimes God uses seemingly unsophisticated persons like your students to get His message across.

2. A FALSE ACCUSATION MADE BY A SELF-SERVING PRIEST. Briefly note the trumped up charges Amaziah, the priest, made against Amos. Also point out that the phony religious leaders of the world can seem terrifying and their accusations intimidating. Remind the class members that anytime they stand for truth and justice, they can expect opposition.

3. A BOLD TESTIMONY BY A BRAVE PROPHET. Even though Amos carried no prophetic credentials, he didn't let that stop him. Even today, others might belittle your students for not having the proper training or pedigree. Encourage them with the truth that God genuinely knows them and has called them to witness for Him. Remind them that such an awareness and respect for God's intentions are all the credentials they need to serve Him effectively.

4. AN OPPORTUNITY TO MAKE A REAL DIFFERENCE. Let the class members know that God has summoned them to confront sin. Clarify that it should not be done self-righteously but humbly. Also explain that the risks they take could change a person or situation for the better.

FOR ADULTS

■ **TOPIC:** Sin Has Its Consequences
■ **QUESTIONS:** 1. Why had the time of judgment come for Israel? 2. Why would God allow death and destruction to fall on Israel? 3. Why did God refuse to overlook the exploitation of the needy by Israel's ruling class? 4. In confronting society's problems, what approaches might be most effective? 5. What are some of the consequences (whether positive or negative) of confronting sinful behavior?

■ **ILLUSTRATIONS:**

Paralyzing Fear or Virtuous Faith. The people of Amos' day faced a real dilemma. On the one hand, a small group within society enjoyed considerable wealth and privilege. On the other hand, a much larger group struggled to survive the daily grind of impoverishment. Amos called on the ruling class to abandon their worldly ways, beginning with their neglect and abuse of the poor.

Evidently, an intense fear of giving up power and influence prevented the elitists from doing what was right. We sometimes hear the expression "scared stiff." This is an insight about the nature of fear. It wants to paralyze us and take all the action right out of us. If we allow it, it will keep us from taking any risks at all. This especially includes setting aside our wealth and influence for the betterment of the disadvantaged living around us.

Paralyzing fear, worry, and any other self-imposed limitations must be faced for what they are—the opposite of virtuous faith. John knew what it was like for believers to see only their limitations. That is why the apostle encouraged us by saying that "whatsoever is born of God overcometh the world; and this is the victory that overcometh the world, even our faith" (1 John 5:4).

Caring Enough to Confront. Ben and Traci appeared to be the perfect Christian couple—talented, committed to God, and heavily involved in their church. But things were not what they seemed.

Ben hadn't really wanted to marry Traci when he did. He went along with the marriage because friends convinced him it was the right thing to do. Traci entered the marriage expecting it to be like her parents' marriage—apparently effortless and altogether loving. Little premarital counseling and her own naiveté meant that issues such as leadership and communication styles—not to mention Ben's apprehension—were not discussed.

Five years into the marriage, Ben had an affair. Even though he agreed to end it, he remained unhappy. Two difficult years later, Traci felt herself giving up. When a male friend convinced her that "you shouldn't have to work so hard to have a good relationship," Traci believed him. Soon Traci was having an affair of her own.

Traci now says, "Satan hit me where I thought I was absolutely untouchable. I became someone I hated." The couple points to a mutual friend who dared to confront

Traci as the catalyst for their turnaround. "Todd just got in my face one Sunday and said, 'Traci, you know this isn't right.'" That confrontation motivated her to change.

It wasn't easy. But now, five years later, the couple have recommitted themselves to one another and to God. Also, both Ben and Traci agree that a good Christian friend, who cared enough to confront them, helped make God's miracle possible.

About 2,700 years ago, God called a shepherd and farmer to proclaim His message of judgment to the people of Israel. His outspoken speech was offensive to the religious and political leaders of the northern kingdom. Yet, Amos refused to be silenced and continued to preach against hypocrisy and corruption.

A Brave Stand for Justice. Amos had no religious credentials, military might, or political clout behind him. And since Israel was prospering at the time Amos prophesied, it was doubtful that his warnings of impending doom would be taken seriously. Yet he spoke boldly because God had called Amos to do so.

Before being assassinated on March 24, 1980, Oscar Romero was a leading religious figure in San Salvador. At one point, he mentioned that when he fed the hungry, he was called a pious individual. But when he criticized a governmental system that brought about hunger, he was denounced as a traitor.

Romero's brave stand for justice in his country ignited the fury of the ruling class. And even though powerful interests eventually silenced him, his courageous example continues to inspire Christians 35 years later, not only his own country, but also throughout the world.

FOR YOUTH

■ **TOPIC:** God's Unchanging Standard

■ **QUESTIONS:** 1. What did the basket of ripe summer fruit symbolize? 2. Why would God no longer spare the people of Israel? 3. How had the wicked rich cheated the poor? 4. Why should believers risk confronting sinful behavior? 5. Do you sense a call to witness for the Lord? What would that mean in practical terms?

■ **ILLUSTRATIONS:**

Only One Permanent Standard. For many years, running the four-minute mile was long held as the ultimate in human athletic performance. Then, on May 6, 1954, Roger Bannister, a 25-year-old British medical student, made history.

While Bannister was running at Iffley Road near Oxford, he broke the standard. As about 3,000 enthusiastic spectators watched, he set a record with 3 minutes 59.4 seconds. The fans went wild when his time was announced. However, the new standard didn't last long. Only 46 days later, an Australian named John Landy knocked 1.5 seconds off the time and established a new world record.

Human standards rapidly change (especially in the arena of sports). Amos reminded his readers that only one standard was permanent—God's. All of us must look to His standard and, with His help, seek to live by it every day.

Courage in China. Amos could see the selfish living and hypocritical attitude of the Israelites. Of course, the easy way out would have been to ignore what he saw. But God had called Amos to prophesy against the sins being committed in the northern kingdom.

In 2013, a Chinese pastor was detained by security agents and told that he had to be an informer for the state on the whereabouts of his church members. The pastor was warned that he was under surveillance and considered a threat to the state. He was pressured to cooperate or suffer severe consequences.

The minister knew the high personal price he would pay for refusing to do what the authorities demanded. He asked for a few days to consider the threats and promises. Then, with some of his trusted laypersons, he announced that if the government took him away from his congregation in his city, the Lord Jesus would give him another in a detention camp!

Sometimes all a person needs is to be shown the right way—the way to live. God calls us to show the way to those around us. What persons or situations do you think He might be calling you to confront?

Heartbroken but Determined. Joy was 14 when she volunteered to sing in the choir for the Billy Graham crusade being held in her city. Each evening, the teenager listened to the evangelist's message, and on the last evening, Joy decided to answer Jesus' call.

That night, however, Joy found the door locked due to an overflow crowd. Security guards would not let her enter the crusade, even when she told them that she was in the choir. There were simply too many people. Heartbroken but determined, Joy tried the other doors, yet all were locked. In a back alley, she saw a fire escape. She built a tower out of trashcans, but was still too short to reach the ladder.

Then, a homeless man helped Joy get up the fire escape, which she climbed to the open skylight. Carefully, the teenager lowered herself down and landed right next to a security guard! Thinking she would be arrested, Joy explained that she had to give herself to Christ and answer His call. The guard believed her and let her pass. That evening, Joy put her faith in the Savior.

Early in life, Joy understood God's call and courageously planned her future around His will. Like Amos, the teenager sensed the Lord's claim on her life and boldly accepted His leadership, regardless of the personal cost. Have you done the same?

LESSON 5 — JULY 5

CENSURING FALSE PROPHETS

BACKGROUND SCRIPTURE: Micah 2
DEVOTIONAL READING: Proverbs 11:1-10

Key Verse: O thou that art named the house of Jacob, is the spirit of the LORD straitened? are these his doings? do not my words do good to him that walketh uprightly? Micah 2:7.

KING JAMES VERSION

MICAH 2:4 In that day shall one take up a parable against you, and lament with a doleful lamentation, and say, We be utterly spoiled: he hath changed the portion of my people: how hath he removed it from me! turning away he hath divided our fields. 5 Therefore thou shalt have none that shall cast a cord by lot in the congregation of the LORD.

6 Prophesy ye not, say they to them that prophesy: they shall not prophesy to them, that they shall not take shame. 7 O thou that art named the house of Jacob, is the spirit of the LORD straitened? are these his doings? do not my words do good to him that walketh uprightly? 8 Even of late my people is risen up as an enemy: ye pull off the robe with the garment from them that pass by securely as men averse from war. 9 The women of my people have ye cast out from their pleasant houses; from their children have ye taken away my glory for ever. 10 Arise ye, and depart; for this is not your rest: because it is polluted, it shall destroy you, even with a sore destruction. 11 If a man walking in the spirit and falsehood do lie, saying, I will prophesy unto thee of wine and of strong drink; he shall even be the prophet of this people.

NEW REVISED STANDARD VERSION

MICAH 2:4 On that day they shall take up a taunt song against you,
  and wail with bitter lamentation,
and say, "We are utterly ruined;
  the LORD alters the inheritance of my people;
  how he removes it from me!
  Among our captors he parcels out our fields."
5 Therefore you will have no one to cast the line by lot
  in the assembly of the LORD.
6 "Do not preach"—thus they preach—
  "one should not preach of such things;
  disgrace will not overtake us."
7 Should this be said, O house of Jacob?
  Is the LORD's patience exhausted?
  Are these his doings?
Do not my words do good
  to one who walks uprightly?
8 But you rise up against my people as an enemy;
  you strip the robe from the peaceful,
from those who pass by trustingly
  with no thought of war.
9 The women of my people you drive out
  from their pleasant houses;
from their young children you take away
  my glory forever.
10 Arise and go;
  for this is no place to rest,
because of uncleanness that destroys
  with a grievous destruction.
11 If someone were to go about uttering empty falsehoods,
  saying, "I will preach to you of wine and strong drink,"
  such a one would be the preacher for this people!

HOME BIBLE READINGS

Monday, June 29	Job 29:7-17	*Good Deeds for the Oppressed*
Tuesday, June 30	Job 31:13-22	*Attention to the Needs of Others*
Wednesday, July 1	Psalm 7:1-8	*Judge Me, O Lord*
Thursday, July 2	Psalm 7:9-17	*Test My Mind and Heart*
Friday, July 3	Psalm 9:15-20	*The Lord Executes Judgment*
Saturday, July 4	Proverbs 11:1-10	*The Righteous and the Wicked*
Sunday, July 5	Micah 2:4-11	*A Day of Bitter Lamentation*

BACKGROUND

We know little about Micah, the prophet, apart from his hometown and his time period (Mic. 1:1; compare Jer. 26:18). Micah hailed from Moresheth Gath, a frontier outpost that lay about 25 miles southwest of Jerusalem (see Josh. 15:44; 2 Chron. 11:8; 14:9-10; 20:37). Some scholars, however, theorize that Micah spent much of his adult life in the capital. He prophesied during the reigns of three kings of Judah: Jotham (about 750–732 B.C.), Ahaz (about 735–715 B.C.), and Hezekiah (about 715–686 B.C.). This means Micah's career lasted from about 750 B.C. at the earliest to about 686 B.C. at the latest. So, Micah was a contemporary of Isaiah (see Isa. 1:1) and Hosea (see Hos. 1:1).

After the opening title (Mic. 1:1), the book's content can be divided into three major sections: the Lord's judgment of Israel and Judah (chaps. 1–3); the vision of future restoration (chaps. 4–5); and the promise of kingdom blessings (chaps. 6–7). As a courageous spokesperson for God, Micah condemned such sins as idolatry, false prophecy, and oppression of the poor. He also predicted judgment from God, including the downfall of Samaria and Jerusalem (see Mich. 1:1, 5-7, 9-16; 3:12). Even though the Creator would punish the northern and southern kingdoms for violating the Mosaic law, He would preserve a remnant of His chosen people and one day restore them to Judah, with Jerusalem as their capital. Micah even foretold the birth of the Messiah (see 6:8, which is covered in lesson 7).

Micah 1:2 constitutes an introduction to the prophecy that follows. God summoned everyone to pay attention to the way He would judge His own people—the Israelites and Judahites—because of their disobedience. In turn, earth's inhabitants would recognize the way God would treat them unless they turned to Him. Verses 3 and 4 draw attention to a visitation of the Lord, in which He descends from heaven and uses the high places as His stepping-stones. Under His feet the mountains melt and the valleys split apart. All this is symbolism for the way God would send judgment on His rebellious people. The leaders and inhabitants of Israel ("Jacob"; vs. 5) and Judah had violated God's covenant by worshiping pagan deities. The mention of the two capitals may mean either (1) that false worship was going on in both cities or (2) that the political leadership of both nations was involved in the sin of idolatry. Perhaps both were true.

NOTES ON THE PRINTED TEXT

In Micah 2, God's spokesperson turned his attention to rich landowners in Judah. God had an appropriate punishment in mind for these sinners. When a prophet pronounced woe upon somebody, it was a warning about impending destruction and death against them. Micah declared that sorrow awaited those who fabricated wicked schemes. They lay awake at night, hatched "evil" (2:1) plans, and then arose at the first light of dawn to enact their offenses. Evidently, no one could stop the scoundrels, since they controlled the levers of power in society. Specifically, Micah had in mind influential leaders in Israel who committed the crime of land grabbing (vs. 2). The Hebrew verb rendered "covet" is the same term used in the Ten Commandments (see Exod. 20:17; Deut. 5:21) and indicates that the greed of the unscrupulous individuals trampled on the essence of God's covenant with His people. The criminals used fraud (perhaps by manipulating the court system) to seize real estate (including "fields," "houses," and inherited assets) belonging to others.

God was aware of the unlawful acts occurring in Judah. The Hebrew verb translated "devise" in Micah 2:1 is the same term rendered "devise" in verse 3. Because the wicked were guilty of planning corrupt schemes, the Lord would bring adversity upon them. Also note that the same Hebrew adjective is translated "evil" in verses 1 and 3 (two times in the latter). Previously, the wicked rich got away with abusing others. Yet, a time of captivity was coming when the reprobates literally would not be able to "remove [their] necks." They would be like an animal shackled to a yoke that others forcibly placed on its shoulders (see Isa. 9:4; 10:27; 47:6; Jer. 27:8; 28:14; Ezek. 34:27). In days gone by, the villains were arrogant and overbearing in depriving people of their property (which God regarded as a permanent, sacred trust; see Lev. 25:10, 13). But in the future day of reckoning, God would see to it that the lawbreakers could no longer act "haughtily" (Mic. 2:3). That outcome was just and suitable, for the divine punishment fit the nature of the human crime.

The Hebrew noun translated "parable" (vs. 4) denotes a brief, memorable saying that was filled with disdain and intended to serve as an object lesson for all who heard the maxim. In this case, Micah foretold a time when bystanders would scorn Judah's greedy elite. Also, spectators literally would "wail a bitter wailing," which refers to mocking the land barons with a chant filled with despair. The lament song would proclaim that the oppressors were completely destroyed, for they were guilty of confiscating what belonged to others (see vs. 2). In turn, God would use invaders to seize the evildoers' property (including their orchards, vineyards, and grain fields) and allow the conquerors to divide the spoil among themselves (vs. 4). Micah literally referred to the victors as the "rebellious" or "apostates" (namely, those who did not worship the Lord), due to the fact that they would act in a defiant and treacherous manner against the people of Judah. This suggests that Micah was looking ahead to the time of the Babylonian captivity.

Micah's prophecy not only anticipated the Babylonian captivity, but also the restoration of God's people from exile to their homeland in Judah. It would be a time of rejoicing in which tribal allotments within the Promised Land would be redistributed to the returnees. There is one group, however, who would not participate in joyous occasion—the former land barons who treated the innocent unfairly. That said, scholars are divided over what the prediction in verse 5 specifically denotes. Some say it means that the villains would have no descendants among those who would later return from exile and occupy land in Judah. Other specialists think this verse means the reprobates would have no descendants among those who received allotments of God's benefits in the end times.

Micah was not the only spokesperson in Judah. Some of his peers, such as Isaiah and Hosea, were true prophets, while others were false ones. The religious frauds spurned Micah's message, because it contradicted their own. For this reason, they tried to shut him up. The last part of verse 6 can be rendered "humiliation will not befall us." In this case, the false prophets meant that the disgrace Micah had foretold for Judah would not occur. The phrase can also be translated, "humiliation will not be turned back." The latter rendering indicates that the false prophets felt personally reproached as long as Micah predicted judgment.

In verse 7, Micah's opponents accused him of being too negative in his theology. They felt that the kind of wrath Micah predicted was inconsistent with God's benevolent nature. Allegedly, the Lord was too patient and loving ever to judge His covenant people (see Gen. 19:16; Exod. 34:6; Num. 14:18; Pss. 78:38; 86:15; 108:4; 115:1; 138:2; Lam. 3:23; Rom. 2:4). The second half of Micah 2:7 can be interpreted in two different ways, depending on whether one takes it as being spoken by the false prophets or by God. If the self-serving charlatans made this assertion, they were claiming to be virtuous people, whom God would bless, not judge. In contrast, if God made the statement, He was correcting the religious frauds' one-sided view by declaring that He does good only for the upright, not the wicked.

Verses 8 and 9 describe predatory acts the upper class committed against the impoverished people of Judah. Micah accused the rich and powerful of behaving like a foreign adversary toward the poor and powerless of their nation. One minute a group of the destitute would be feeling as safe as soldiers who returned home from war. Then, the next minute, the ruling elite would assault the unwary travelers and steal the cloaks (or outer garments) off their backs, leaving them with only their tunics. One minute a defenseless widow and her fatherless, young children would be enjoying their comfortable home. Then, the next minute, land barons would be ejecting the family from their dwelling and onto the street and keeping the seized property for themselves. "Glory" renders a Hebrew noun that also means "blessing," "splendor," or "honor" and refers to the highly-prized inheritance children were to receive, by law, from their parents. The denial of this right produced untold hardship and anguish for the innocent.

Once again, God promised an appropriate punishment for Judah's tyrants. Those who had stolen homes would be cast out from their homeland (referred to as their place of "rest"; vs. 10) and permanently banned from the covenantal community (see Deut. 12:10; Ps. 95:11). This is another prediction of captivity. The sins of the despots had "polluted" (Mic. 2:10) the land. Their transgressions had made Judah so unclean that it was as if the land could never be purified. For this reason, God considered Judah to be uninhabitable. Likewise, He would not permit His chosen people to have contact with the land, like any unclean thing. The threats in this verse remind us that the nature of our behavior often determines the consequences of that behavior (see Gal. 6:8).

Micah 2:11 contains the prophet's sarcastic description of the kind of seer or visionary the people of Judah really wanted. Those who foretold only times of increased prosperity and affluence (represented by an abundance of "wine" and "strong drink") were just the type of spokespersons the inhabitants craved. They did not want to hear the stark truths that a prophet like Micah declared. This goes to show that our evaluation of those who preach God's Word should not be based on whether we like their message. Our assessment must be determined by the message's accuracy with Scripture.

SUGGESTIONS TO TEACHERS

When Judah's upper class focused on satiating their covetous desires, they abandoned the ethical demands of their covenant with God. For instance, corrupt land barons seized the fields, houses, and other assets belonging to the poor. In turn, the Lord used Micah to declare that these practices were unjust and deserved to be judged.

1. GOD CONDEMNS INJUSTICE. The wicked rich in Judah thought they were getting ahead by fabricating evil schemes to exploit the impoverished in society. But Micah proclaimed that anyone who attempts to gain power, wealth, or position by unrighteous and unjust means also faces divine condemnation.

2. GOD COMMANDS JUSTICE. Greedy land grabbers were guilty of ejecting defenseless widows and their young, fatherless children from their homes. Micah was correct to censure such abusive practices. The way a nation or a person treats poor and needy people is still a good gauge of the righteousness and justice of that nation or person.

3. JUDAH DISPLAYS INJUSTICE. The upper class in Judah knew that the Lord condemned injustice. Yet the priorities and actions of these despots were characterized by self-centeredness and violence. The greatest problem, however, was that when God demanded a just society, no one seemed to heed Him. It's deplorable when Christians cheat their employees and favor policies that hurt the poor. But the same behavior is worse when believers ignore God's summons to treat the poor and needy in a humane and equitable manner.

4. GOD DESCRIBES JUDGMENT. God had given Judah's materialistic elite repeated opportunities to repent of their crimes. Prophets such as Micah warned that God would judge the tyrants for their misdeeds. In particular, the Lord would allow outside foes to act in a defiant and treacherous manner against the people of Judah. Shame and disgrace are often the outcome for those who choose to spurn the Creator and the teachings of His Word.

For Adults

■ **Topic:** Justice, Not Injustice
■ **Questions:** 1. What crimes were the land barons in Judah guilty of committing? 2. Why would God allow calamity to overtake Judah and its people? 3. Why did Micah, despite peer pressure, refuse to stop speaking for the Lord? 4. How should believers respond to the presence of injustice in society? 5. How can Christians encourage the unrighteous to trust in the Savior?

■ **Illustrations:**

Justice Demanded. Justice is much more than meting punishment to criminals. In God's view of things, justice requires that we use what we have to help meet the needs of others. Justice also demands that we do not exploit other people to get what we want. Moreover, justice demands that we set aside our materialistic ambitions so that we can address suffering and hardships.

Injustice, then, is more than the absence of justice. It is also the failure to do the right things when we can. In Micah's day, the rich landowners in Judah were guilty of this. They could have helped the impoverished, but the tyrants refused to do so. Instead, they chose to gratify their own selfish desires. Micah's pronouncement of judgment against them shouts to us a powerful message about how easy it is not only to fail the Lord, but also to ignore His warnings.

The Old Man's Folly. Micah lived in a time when rich landowners in Judah exploited people on the lower rungs of society. Elite rulers did whatever they could to amass wealth and clutch tightly onto it for as long as possible.

In the Mount Hope Cemetery in Hiawatha, Kansas, there is a strange memorial to a farmer and his wife. An orphan named John M. Davis married a young woman whose family he disliked intensely. Davis decided early on that he would leave nothing of his growing fortune to his wife's family.

In 1930, when Mrs. Davis died, John began commissioning the work of stonemasons to construct a giant mausoleum with statuary commemorating different periods of their life together. The lifelike poses of Mr. and Mrs. Davis were hewn out of Kansas granite and were extraordinarily expensive.

However, after his death in 1974 at the age of 92, John Davis left no money for the upkeep of the expansive work. Because of the weight of this huge monolith, today the tomb is sinking into the earth and becoming an eyesore. Local residents refer to it as "the old man's folly."

What's a Person Worth? In the 1950s, Buddhist monks in Bangkok, Thailand, tried to move a massive clay statue of the Buddha because a modern highway was being planned through their temple grounds. As the crane began to hoist the statue, the clay cracked to reveal a solid gold Buddha under a thin layer of clay. Historians think monks covered the gold Buddha with clay centuries earlier just before a Burmese army invaded and killed everyone who knew what was under the clay.

In Micah's day, the ruling class in Judah thought their acquisition of power and wealth were important and the needs of the impoverished were irrelevant. In other words, the despots valued material objects and exploited the destitute. The land barons were wrong. People bear the image of God, no matter how encrusted with poverty or illness that image may be. This truth reminds us that it's vital for us to value people and use things. When we treat people humanely and justly, we show evidence that we truly are God's spiritual children.

For Youth

■ **Topic:** Serving Self or Others?

■ **Questions:** 1. How did the upper class abuse the lower class in Judah? 2. In what way would God judge the wicked rich in Judah? 3. Why did the false prophets in Judah try to stop Micah from speaking for the Lord? 4. How should believers respond to those who reject God? 5. How might the truth of God's Word be used to encourage the humane treatment of people in society?

■ **Illustrations:**

Gotta Have It! Retailers face huge obstacles trying to keep up with the fast-changing tastes of teenagers. One year's fashions are next year's disappointments. The teen market in the West is driven by the impulse to have everything new right away. How hard it is for adolescents to resist this consuming urge. If they are aware of what is happening, they struggle not to be swept along with the idea that we obtain happiness with a brilliant array of designer clothes, fast muscle cars, and high-tech gadgetry.

The greedy land barons in Judah tried to obtain security and happiness by exploiting others, but they utterly failed in their attempt. We cannot afford to follow the foolish example of the wicked rich who were contemporaries of Micah, the prophet. If we put our trust in the Lord Jesus, we are guaranteed eternal joy and peace with Him in heaven. What more could we possibly want?

A God-Focused Life. Judah's wealthy landowners did whatever they could to exploit the lower classes. In turn, the wicked rich tried to consolidate power into their own hands. Micah rightly condemned such a self-focused life. He also advocated a life that is God-focused, namely, one that is committed to helping others.

Since she was a child, Barb had wanted to be a missionary nurse. She attended a Christian college to prepare for the work to which she believed she was called. Yet, as a student, it was difficult for Barb to get good grades. Even though her heart was in her studies, it seemed her mind just couldn't remember all the details.

After completing her degree, Barb applied to a mission board and was accepted. But it was contingent on her receiving a registered nurse (R.N.) license. Barb thanked the Lord and studied hard. On testing day, everyone from the college passed, that is, except her.

Barb learned that she needed to wait a year before she could retake the test. During that time, when licensed friends went to missionary hospitals, began work in the states, or used their skills in other capacities, Barb got a job as a nursing assistant and studied diligently.

When Barb finally passed her licensing exam, she had a deeper appreciation for her calling, and for God's graciousness in allowing her to fulfill it. Twenty years later, she is still on the mission field and being a witness for Christ by helping others in need.

Obedience Takes More Than Words. Zoë went home after school with her best friend in the first grade. She had never eaten at another house without her mother present, so her mother carefully coached Zoë in etiquette.

The vegetable at dinner was buttered broccoli, and the lady of the house asked Zoë if she liked broccoli. Zoë remembered her mother's directions and said politely, "Oh, yes, I love buttered broccoli." When the dish was passed, Zoë declined to take any vegetable. The hostess was confused. "I thought you said you loved buttered broccoli?" The little girl smiled sweetly and said, "Oh, yes, Mrs. Johnson, I do, but not enough to eat any!"

Sometimes we talk about justice for the poor and needy more readily than we do anything about it. However, as we learn from Micah's prophecy against the wicked rich of his day, God will not be pleased until our actions match our speech.

LESSON 6 — JULY 12

Rebuking Corrupt Leaders

Background Scripture: Micah 3
Devotional Reading: Matthew 7:15-20

Key Verse: Truly I am full of power by the spirit of the Lord, and of judgment, and of might, to declare unto Jacob his transgression, and to Israel his sin. Micah 3:8.

KING JAMES VERSION

MICAH 3:5 Thus saith the Lord concerning the prophets that make my people err, that bite with their teeth, and cry, Peace; and he that putteth not into their mouths, they even prepare war against him. 6 Therefore night shall be unto you, that ye shall not have a vision; and it shall be dark unto you, that ye shall not divine; and the sun shall go down over the prophets, and the day shall be dark over them. 7 Then shall the seers be ashamed, and the diviners confounded: yea, they shall all cover their lips; for there is no answer of God.

8 But truly I am full of power by the spirit of the Lord, and of judgment, and of might, to declare unto Jacob his transgression, and to Israel his sin. 9 Hear this, I pray you, ye heads of the house of Jacob, and princes of the house of Israel, that abhor judgment, and pervert all equity. 10 They build up Zion with blood, and Jerusalem with iniquity. 11 The heads thereof judge for reward, and the priests thereof teach for hire, and the prophets thereof divine for money: yet will they lean upon the Lord, and say, Is not the Lord among us? none evil can come upon us. 12 Therefore shall Zion for your sake be plowed as a field, and Jerusalem shall become heaps, and the mountain of the house as the high places of the forest.

NEW REVISED STANDARD VERSION

MICAH 3:5 Thus says the Lord concerning the prophets
who lead my people astray,
who cry "Peace"
when they have something to eat,
but declare war against those
who put nothing into their mouths.
6 Therefore it shall be night to you, without vision,
and darkness to you, without revelation.
The sun shall go down upon the prophets,
and the day shall be black over them;
7 the seers shall be disgraced,
and the diviners put to shame;
they shall all cover their lips,
for there is no answer from God.
8 But as for me, I am filled with power,
with the spirit of the Lord,
and with justice and might,
to declare to Jacob his transgression
and to Israel his sin.
9 Hear this, you rulers of the house of Jacob
and chiefs of the house of Israel,
who abhor justice
and pervert all equity,
10 who build Zion with blood
and Jerusalem with wrong!
11 Its rulers give judgment for a bribe,
its priests teach for a price,
its prophets give oracles for money;
yet they lean upon the Lord and say,
"Surely the Lord is with us!
No harm shall come upon us."
12 Therefore because of you
Zion shall be plowed as a field;
Jerusalem shall become a heap of ruins,
and the mountain of the house a wooded height.

Home Bible Readings

Monday, July 6	Exodus 23:1-8	*Do Not Pervert Justice*
Tuesday, July 7	Ezekiel 13:15-20	*False Prophecies of Peace*
Wednesday, July 8	2 Chronicles 19:4-10	*Act in the Fear of the Lord*
Thursday, July 9	Psalm 15	*Walk Blamelessly*
Friday, July 10	Matthew 7:15-20	*Known by Their Fruits*
Saturday, July 11	Isaiah 45:5-13	*Woe to Transgressors*
Sunday, July 12	Micah 3:5-12	*Sold Out Religion*

Background

The third chapter of Micah contains three judgment oracles that share several common literary features. For instance, these prophecies concern the same group of individuals who controlled the southern and northern kingdoms. Verse 1 refers to them as the "heads of Judah" and the "princes" over the "house of Israel." Each oracle is four verses in length, and each contains the same elements: an opening address (vss. 1, 5, 9); an indictment preceded by the term "who" (vss. 2, 5, 9); and a verdict introduced by the word "then" (vs. 4) or "therefore" (vss. 6, 12).

Moreover, the three judgment oracles emphasize the travesty of justice occurring in Israel and Judah at the hands of its dishonest and inept leaders. In the first oracle (vss. 1-4), God accused the political and judicial authorities of the southern and northern kingdoms of exploiting and abusing the people. God vowed not to hear the prayers of those wicked tyrants. In the second oracle (vss. 5-8), God accused the false prophets of leading the people astray and of modifying their messages, depending on their fee. In the third oracle (vss. 9-12), God again accused all the rulers, priests, and prophets of injustice and cruelty. So, God declared that Jerusalem would be destroyed at the hands of merciless invaders.

Notes on the Printed Text

In Micah 3:1, God's spokesperson rhetorically asked whether it was the responsibility of the ruling elite of the entire nation to "know judgment." "Know" renders a Hebrew verb that denotes the ability to recognize, understand, and teach. "Judgment" translates a noun that refers to civil and religious decisions made by magistrates in courts of law. God expected the leaders of the southern and northern kingdoms to comprehend His statutes and discern how to administrate His ordinances equitably. The latter activity included the officials rendering objective, impartial verdicts when they decided cases. The intended outcome would be to punish evildoers and vindicate the oppressed.

Verses 2-4 indicate that the situation in Judah and Israel deviated greatly from God's holy moral standard, as revealed in the Mosaic law. Instead of dealing with the poor, the widowed, and the orphaned in a humane and just manner, the despots of the southern and northern kingdom maltreated the lower classes. Specifically, the upper echelons of society perverted the legal system by continuously despising what God considered to be "good" (vs. 2) and savoring what He regarded to be "evil." Indeed, the lives of the oppressed were so imperiled that Micah portrayed the magistrates as cannibals who butchered, cooked, and devoured their victims (see Pss. 14:4; 27:2; Prov. 30:14; Isa. 9:19-21).

It was as if the wicked skinned alive God's chosen people and ripped their "flesh" (Mic. 3:2) off their bodies. The tyrants were so bloodthirsty that they devoured the innocent. The grisly imagery included the oppressors flaying the "skin" from the defenseless and crushing their "bones" (vs. 3). Even more ghastly is the idea of the tormentors hacking off portions of the cadavers like meat to be tossed into a kettle to make cannibal stew. One can only imagine how calloused the magistrates became as they committed their atrocities against vulnerable groups of people. For this reason, when the reprobates cried out to God for help in the day of their calamity, He would refuse to pay attention to their pleas. In a metaphorical sense, the Lord would not even look at them, so appalling were the crimes they committed (vs. 4; see Deut. 31:17; Isa. 1:15).

The civil rulers were not the only group in Judah and Israel guilty of violating the Mosaic law. Similarly, there were also false "prophets" (Mic. 3:5) who misled the Lord's chosen people. The image here is that of sheep who follow their shepherd. The seers not only claimed to receive messages from God, but also enjoyed the support of the wicked rulers in Judah and Israel. While Micah and his peers (such as Isaiah and Hosea) announced that captivity awaited evildoers, the spiritual impostors assured their benefactors that they were safe. Also, as long as the clients fed and clothed the religious mercenaries, they were eager to preach a message of "peace," health, and prosperity (see Jer. 6:13-14; 8:10-11; Ezek. 13:10). Oppositely, the profit-seeking hucksters launched a crusade against those who refused to pay a cent for the pabulum being offered.

The Lord announced through Micah that unlike God's true prophets, the religious impostors would not experience the Spirit's illuminating presence. For example, instead of a revelatory "vision" (Mic. 3:6), night would close in on the frauds. Likewise, darkness would put an end to their attempts to make predictions by reading various omens (involving astrology, arrows, sticks, the livers of animals, and so on). Evidently, the soothsayers forgot that sorcery and divination were strictly forbidden in Israel (see Deut. 18:14). The blackout of God's favor was comparable to the "sun" (Mic. 3:6) going down on the hucksters and the daytime of their spurious activities ending. Those who falsely claimed to be "seers" (vs. 7) would be humiliated. Similarly, others who alleged to be "diviners" would feel reproach. All of them would cover their lips because God refused to give them a favorable reply.

Unlike the profit-seekers, who spouted religious platitudes, Micah declared that he was "full of power" (vs. 8). He clarified that the divine Spirit was the source of a genuine prophet's strength, especially in vigorously promoting the cause of "judgment" in Judah and Israel. The Spirit enabled Micah to boldly announce to the southern and northern kingdoms their "transgression" (or rebellious acts) and "sin" (or offensive crimes). Zechariah 4:6 contains a helpful reminder that whatever God calls His servants to perform are not accomplished by brute force. Instead, it can only take place through the Holy Spirit. With His abiding presence and help, even obstacles that seemed like insurmountable mountains would be plains to God's true spokespersons.

The oracle in Micah 3:9-12 reiterates the indictment God brought against the feckless leaders of Judah and Israel. The magistrates in the southern and northern kingdoms were guilty of abhorring "judgment" (or "justice") and perverting what should have been morally upright. Archaeological evidence indicates that a considerable amount of building took place in Micah's day. The Lord declared through His spokesperson that innocent blood was shed in the process and violent acts of injustice were committed against the defenseless.

In particular, Judah and Israel's magistrates issued wrongful verdicts in exchange for bribes. Also, the priests offered religious instruction only when paid handsomely to do so. Even the covenant community's visionaries read omens as a result of being given silver (the standard of currency for economic activity in the ancient Near East). Amid all this fraudulent activity, the wicked had the audacity to claim that they were trusting in God. For instance, they asserted that the Lord manifested His presence in their shrines. So, they assumed that no calamity (such as invasions and exile) would overtake them.

These corrupt leaders were counting on Judah and Israel's historic relationship with the Lord to protect them. They thought to themselves, *How can we be conquered if God is in our midst?* This is an Old Testament example of grace turned into a license to sin. The false messages of these princes and seers created a sense of optimism among the people that was unfounded. Fittingly, since Jerusalem was established and prospered through violence, the city would also be demolished by violence.

Because of the transgressions of the corrupt magistrates, greedy priests, and mercenary prophets, the same disaster that loomed on the horizon for Samaria (see 1:6) also awaited Jerusalem (3:12). Foreign invaders would overrun the city, raze its buildings, and demolish its wall. Consequently, Judah's capital would become a rubble pile and its environs would be cleared like an open field.

Moreover, before judgment struck, God's glory would abandon the mount where the temple sat (see Ezek. 10), leaving it to be covered with thick brush (in turn, providing habitat for wild animals). When Micah's prophecy reached King Hezekiah's ear, the monarch initiated reforms. As a result, Judah procured a temporary reprieve from God's judgment (see 2 Kings 18:1-6; 2 Chron. 29–32; Jer. 26:17-19). But Hezekiah's moral reformation only forestalled certain military defeat and captivity. Micah's oracle of judgment was fulfilled in 586 B.C. at the hands of the Babylonians (see 2 Kings 25:1-21; 2 Chron. 36:17-20; Jer. 39:1-10; 52:4-27).

About a century after Micah first gave his prophecy of Zion's destruction, Jeremiah 26:18 quoted Micah 3:12. This is the only biblical incident in which one Old Testament prophet quoted another prophet and cited the source of the quote. When Jeremiah first predicted that Jerusalem would be demolished, he was imprisoned. Some even sought his execution. Calmer heads pointed out that Micah had made similar predictions without King Hezekiah ordering his death. Tragically, another prophet named Uriah was martyred for preaching the same message (see vss. 19-23).

As Jeremiah's prophetic ministry progressed, he lived an increasingly lonely life. He consistently proclaimed an oracle of judgment that would come at the hands of Babylon. Jeremiah advocated submission to Babylon, for he knew that Jehoiakim and Zedekiah were pursuing a pro-Egyptian policy. The prophet was branded as a traitor and accused of treason. He was imprisoned for a time, first in a dungeon cell and then in a muddy cistern (Jer. 37–38). After that, he remained a prisoner in the courtyard of the guard until Babylon captured Jerusalem (38:28). After the destruction of the city, Jeremiah was forced to go to Egypt with a group of survivors who had rebelled against Babylon (43:4-7). Through it all, the prophet remained true to the Lord and the message of judgment He wanted him to deliver.

SUGGESTIONS TO TEACHERS

The future of Judah and Israel hung in the balance. Micah urged the civil and religious leaders of both nations to return to the Lord. Regrettably, the magistrates, prophets, and priests were entrenched in their rebellious ways. This week's lesson gives your students an opportunity to consider the consequences of habitually turning away from God and resisting His appeals to return to Him.

1. A FIRM WARNING. The southern and northern kingdoms stood at a spiritual crossroads and rejected Micah's oracle of judgment. In particular, the upper echelons of society spurned his exhortation to treat the poor, the widowed, and the orphaned in a humane and just manner. The leadership of both nations would pay a heavy price for disdaining God's final warning.

2. A FAIR VERDICT. On the one hand, Micah repeatedly declared that dark days of judgment awaited Judah and Israel for their violations of the Mosaic covenant. This was an entirely fair verdict. Yet, false prophets continued to proclaim a message of peace and prosperity. Also, few, if any, in the southern and northern kingdoms believed the day of reckoning had arrived, but it had. From this we see that it is important to remain sensitive to God's warnings against sin.

3. A FINAL REJECTION. The Lord announced that just as Judah and Israel had rejected His decrees, so too He would reject them. They had a covenant relationship with God, but they had violated it over and over until their being exiled from the promised land was the only recourse God had left. Christians who consistently resist the Spirit of God and live sinful lives also face God's hand of discipline (see Heb. 12:8-11).

4. A FITTING EMPHASIS. Let the class members know that God urges His spiritual children to flee from sin. Also, explain that He condemns religious activity apart from just behavior. Finally, point out that those who pervert justice will eventually meet with God's disapproval.

FOR ADULTS

■ **TOPIC:** Public Trust Betrayed

■ **QUESTIONS:** 1. What crimes were the land barons in Judah guilty of committing? 2. Why would God allow calamity to overtake Judah and its people? 3. Why did Micah, despite peer pressure, refuse to stop speaking for the Lord? 4. How should believers respond to the presence of injustice in society? 5. How can Christians encourage the unrighteous to trust in the Savior?

■ **ILLUSTRATIONS:**

Which Way to Go? According to statistics issued by the U.S. Department of Transportation's Inspector General, on average about 500 people each year are killed at railroad crossings. Some communities require people to pay steep fines for crossing the tracks when the gates are down. But in many rural areas the only warnings are old, battered "Stop, Look, and Listen" signs.

When Micah began ministering in Judah and Israel, he resembled those warning signs. God had sent him to preach against the transgressions the leaders committed in the southern and northern kingdoms. After hearing him, the civil and religious authorities of both nations had to make a choice.

We can imagine Micah saying that judgment and disaster would come like a roaring freight train. In a sense, he urged God's people not to "cross the tracks." Micah also exhorted them to turn back to the Lord. That same message of repentance and faith runs throughout the Bible and is worthy of our consideration.

Living with the Consequences. The Yankees let Babe Ruth go in 1934. Ruth accepted that his playing days were over. He wanted to manage. Then something awful happened. No one took him seriously. Manage? How could Babe Ruth manage a baseball team when he'd never even been able to manage himself?

The Babe had jumped straight from an orphanage to the big leagues. He had scoffed at discipline, eaten hotdogs by the dozen, drank alcohol like a fish, and womanized without restraint. Everybody looked the other way while he was the Sultan of Swat, but when he wanted to be taken seriously as a leader of others, they just looked away. It broke the Babe's heart to live with the consequences of his self-indulgence.

As we learn from the third chapter of Micah, sin gives with one hand and takes away with ten others. It gives false promises of satisfaction and takes away integrity, peace, reputation, and the trust of those closest to us. The consequences of sin never seem like much until they burst on us and overwhelm us.

Habits Are Hard to Break. A successful businessman escaped to his lake house every weekend like clockwork. To save time, he flew to a small airport near his retreat. It dawned on him he could save even more time by fitting his plane with pontoons and landing on his lake. That Friday he and his wife headed for the lake. Mentally he was already fishing as he made his approach to the airport. His wife's scream brought him to reality. "You can't land here! You've got the pontoons on!"

The man jerked his plane out of its approach. With trembling hands, he flew to the lake, touched down, and taxied right to his dock. He looked at his wife, laughed sheepishly, and said, "Old habits die hard." Then he opened his door and hopped out into five feet of water.

This man's wife must have felt like Micah warning Judah and Israel. The woman's husband was so habituated to one way of doing things that he had a hard time acting differently, even when he wanted to. We have to beware of letting any sin become a part of our way of living. It may become hard to disengage from the habit.

For Youth

■ **Topic:** Crime and Punishment

■ **Questions:** 1. How did the upper class abuse the lower class in Judah? 2. In what way would God judge the wicked rich in Judah? 3. Why did the false prophets in Judah try to stop Micah from speaking for the Lord? 4. How should believers respond to those who reject God? 5. How might the truth of God's Word be used to encourage the humane treatment of people in society?

■ **Illustrations:**

Facing Consequences. The tired mother asked her pastor for advice concerning her son, who repeatedly got into trouble. Time after time the son came to his mother for help, telling her that he loved her. And repeatedly she went to his aid by bailing him out of trouble.

In this case, the young man had lost his car and had no way to get to work. What should his mother do? The pastor thought it was time for the young man to face the consequences of his misbehaviors. If his mother kept "rescuing" him from taking responsibility, most likely he would not change his ways. How hard this truth was for his mother to accept!

This scenario illustrates the way it is for many of us. Perhaps we like to drift through life, thinking we can do what we want and get away with it. However, a prophet named

Micah would remind us that God cares about how we live. In His love for us, He will not allow us to continue down a sinful path. He makes us face the consequences of our actions.

Choosing the Right Path. When the Germans started bombing London in 1940, Elizabeth was a teen-aged girl from a wealthy family. She could have moved to one of their country homes and waited out the war riding horses and visiting her rich friends. But Elizabeth had seen Winston Churchill with his cigar clamped in his mouth striding through London in defiance of danger from the air.

Elizabeth made a choice. She pulled on dungarees, rolled up the bottoms, and drove a truck through debris-littered streets—one more teenager supporting the war effort. Only Elizabeth wasn't just one more teenager. Her father was George VI, king of England. Elizabeth's choice marked her. She earned the respect of the British people. And she's never lost it since becoming the queen of England in 1952.

The choices you make now will shape your life for decades to come, even as Elizabeth's did. Choose the ancient paths—especially the humane and just way—that Micah proclaimed to the people of his day. Be sure to heed the warnings of God's Word and walk in His ways.

Unwelcome Consequences. The young man had grown up in a Bible-believing church but wanted some "freedom." Soon he found himself experimenting with drugs and alcohol with his new "friends." He knew it was wrong, and he expected God to strike him down with a lightning bolt. But nothing dramatic happened. He dropped most contact with his parents and took a cheap apartment in a rundown part of town.

Then the young man moved in with a girl. She was pretty and willing and made him feel important. But he didn't love her and resented her hints that they should marry. Now the young man really thought God was going to get him. He interpreted most comments from his family as criticisms. He grew increasingly angry and suspicious.

Then the girl got pregnant, and the young man wondered whether she did it on purpose to trap him. He married her for the baby's sake, but now he hated her. They moved to a bigger apartment and started going into debt. The young man drank more, missed work more, and eventually got fired. The only good thing he could see in it all was that God hadn't struck him down. But then one day it occurred to him that his judgment was the result of his sin. He was living the consequences of his disobedience.

Micah 3 reveals that spiritual blindness can grip individuals, as well as groups and nations, when they forget God's ways. Even Christians must be on guard to identify sin in their lives, appreciate its gravity, and turn away from it. If we do not, unwelcome consequences will result.

LESSON 7 — JULY 19

FOSTERING GODLY VIRTUES

BACKGROUND SCRIPTURE: Micah 6
DEVOTIONAL READING: Deuteronomy 10:12-22

Key Verse: [God] hath shewed thee, O man, what is good; and what doth the LORD require of thee, but to do justly, and to love mercy, and to walk humbly with thy God? Micah 6:8.

KING JAMES VERSION

MICAH 6:3 O my people, what have I done unto thee? and wherein have I wearied thee? testify against me. 4 For I brought thee up out of the land of Egypt, and redeemed thee out of the house of servants; and I sent before thee Moses, Aaron, and Miriam. 5 O my people, remember now what Balak king of Moab consulted, and what Balaam the son of Beor answered him from Shittim unto Gilgal; that ye may know the righteousness of the LORD.

6 Wherewith shall I come before the LORD, and bow myself before the high God? shall I come before him with burnt offerings, with calves of a year old? 7 Will the LORD be pleased with thousands of rams, or with ten thousands of rivers of oil? shall I give my firstborn for my transgression, the fruit of my body for the sin of my soul? 8 He hath shewed thee, O man, what is good; and what doth the LORD require of thee, but to do justly, and to love mercy, and to walk humbly with thy God?

NEW REVISED STANDARD VERSION

MICAH 6:3 "O my people, what have I done to you? In what have I wearied you? Answer me!
4 For I brought you up from the land of Egypt,
and redeemed you from the house of slavery;
and I sent before you Moses,
Aaron, and Miriam.
5 O my people, remember now what King Balak of Moab devised,
what Balaam son of Beor answered him,
and what happened from Shittim to Gilgal,
that you may know the saving acts of the LORD."
6 "With what shall I come before the LORD,
and bow myself before God on high?
Shall I come before him with burnt offerings,
with calves a year old?
7 Will the LORD be pleased with thousands of rams,
with ten thousands of rivers of oil?
Shall I give my firstborn for my transgression,
the fruit of my body for the sin of my soul?"
8 He has told you, O mortal, what is good;
and what does the LORD require of you
but to do justice, and to love kindness,
and to walk humbly with your God?

Home Bible Readings

Monday, July 13	Deuteronomy 10:12-22	*What Does the Lord Require?*
Tuesday, July 14	Exodus 4:10-17	*Who Gives Speech to Mortals?*
Wednesday, July 15	Numbers 22:1-14	*The Word the Lord Speaks*
Thursday, July 16	Numbers 22:15-21	*Do Only What I Tell You*
Friday, July 17	Numbers 22:31-38	*Speak Only What I Tell You*
Saturday, July 18	Numbers 23:1-12	*You Have Blessed My Enemies*
Sunday, July 19	Micah 6:3-8	*Justice, Kindness, and Humility*

Background

The politics of Micah's day shaped his prophetic message. Both the southern kingdom of Judah and the northern kingdom of Israel had previously been enjoying a time of peace and prosperity. Yet, rather than growing closer to God out of gratitude for this wealth, Judah and Israel had slipped into moral bankruptcy. Those who became prosperous during this time ruthlessly exploited the poor. Consequently, Micah foretold the fall of both Samaria and Jerusalem.

Of all people, the civil and religious leaders of Judah and Israel should have understood how important justice was to the social fabric of their respective nations. The magistrates often heard and settled disputes among the people, and the decisions made by the leaders were final. The people living in Judah and Israel looked to these rulers for justice. Regrettably, though, the princes of the southern and northern kingdoms perverted the administration of the Mosaic law for their personal gain. The scales of justice especially favored the wicked rich. Indeed, if the price was right, the courts would issue verdicts benefitting those offering the bribes.

Notes on the Printed Text

The Hebrew verb rendered "hear" (Mic. 6:1) marks off the three major divisions of the book (see 1:2; 3:1) and signals the Lord's judgment oracle, as delivered by His spokesperson, Micah. The verb rendered "contend thou" (6:1) can also be translated "defend yourself." It indicates that what follows in this chapter is a lawsuit speech in which the Lord presents the evidence and renders the verdict against His chosen people for violating the Mosaic covenant. The literary form mirrors that found in international treaties used throughout the ancient Near East. In this imaginary courtroom scene, God is depicted as the plaintiff and prosecuting attorney, Micah is His emissary, the mountains are the jury, and the covenant community is the accused.

It might seem odd to us that the Creator would call upon the "mountains" (vs. 1) and the "hills" to testify on His behalf in a cosmic court of law. A clue to the meaning of this poetic passage might lie in the phrase "strong [or enduring] foundations of the earth" (vs. 2). The mountains were ancient. They had been around throughout the history of Judah and Israel and were silent observers of what God's people had done.

So, these inanimate objects were personified as legal witnesses who could agree with the Lord that His people had broken the covenant (see Deut. 4:26; 30:19; 31:28; 32:1).

The reference in Micah 6:3 to "my people" served as a reminder of the covenant relationship between the Lord and the inhabitants of Judah and Israel. The two questions that follow suggest the southern and northern kingdoms believed God had neglected and abused them. This mistaken notion is especially evident in the Hebrew verb rendered "wearied." The idea is that the Lord had burdened and exhausted His people with His unreasonable demands. Understandably, God did not want to leave room for either nation to claim that He—rather than they—were at fault. Judah and Israel could not legitimately argue that the Creator had been unfaithful to the promises of the Mosaic covenant. Neither could the southern and northern kingdoms rightfully claim that the stipulations of the law were either excessive or perverse. So, with the statement "testify against me," God directed His people to confirm their grievances against Him (that is, if they really could; see Jer. 2:5).

In Micah 6:3, God gave His people an opportunity to explain how He had wronged them. The truth is that God had never been unreasonable or burdensome to Judah and Israel. In fact, He had lavished His love on both the southern and northern kingdoms. To prove this, God recounted four areas of His mercy toward the twelve tribes in their infancy (vss. 4-5). First, God mentioned how He had rescued His people from slavery in Egypt. Between the time of Joseph and Moses, the Israelites spent 430 years in Egypt. The Hebrew verb translated "redeemed" can also mean "to ransom" and calls attention to all that God did on behalf of the Israelites to deliver them from servitude in Egypt. The Egyptians had forced the Israelites to do construction projects, but God used miracles to convince Pharaoh to let the Israelites go (see Exod. 1:1–15:21).

Second, God mentioned the leaders He had given the nation. These individuals included Moses, the deliverer (Exod. 3:10), lawgiver (Deut. 4:45), and prophet (18:15); Moses' brother, Aaron, the high priest (Lev. 8); and Miriam, their sister, a prophetess (Exod. 15:20). With such noteworthy servants of the Lord, the Israelites had exceptional guidance. Third, God recalled the incident in which He preserved the early Israelites from a threat presented by the Moabites. Balak, the king of Moab, had wanted the soothsayer, Balaam, to curse Israel, but instead God caused Balaam to bless the Israelites (Num. 22–24). Fourth, God cited the young nation's final journey into the Promised Land, from Shittim (a plain in Moab on the east side of the Jordan River) to Gilgal (on the west side). During that journey, God parted the Jordan River just as earlier He had parted the Red Sea (Josh. 3–4). By rehearsing these historic episodes, the Lord wanted His people to be certain of His upright acts, including how He had always treated them faithfully and fairly.

Previously, the Lord asked His people what fault they found in Him (Mic. 6:3). Now, a new voice speaks in 6:6 and 7. God's envoy poses as an inquiring worshiper (possibly a priest or other religious official) at the entrance to the Jerusalem temple (see Ps. 15:1;

24:3; Isa. 33:14). As a representative of the entire covenant community, he responded to God's accusation in a way that reflected the pathetic spiritual state of His chosen people. The speaker wanted to know what sacrifices the transcendent Lord required to appease His anger for Judah's rebellious acts and Israel's offenses. The petitioner's suggestions begin with the typical and quickly go to the extreme. Did almighty God want His people to bow before Him with offerings and yearling calves? Or should they offer Him thousands of rams and tens of thousands of rivers of olive oil? Or should they sacrifice their firstborn children to pay for the trespasses they had committed?

Child sacrifice, while probably never common, was known in both Judah and Israel. The pagan inhabitants of the surrounding nations carried out child sacrifices (see 2 Kings 3:26-27) and this practice crept into the southern and northern kingdoms with the veneration of foreign gods and goddesses. For instance, the pagan deity, Molech, was especially associated with child sacrifice. Idolaters built a sanctuary to Molech called Topheth (which means "burning place") south of Jerusalem, and there sometimes burnt children (see 23:10). Undoubtedly, it was to Molech that the Judahite kings Ahaz and Manasseh sacrificed their sons (see 16:3; 21:6).

Micah 6:6-7 indicate that God's people were quite mistaken in thinking that He would take delight in their innumerable and extreme sacrifices (see 1 Sam. 15:22; Ps. 51:17; Isa. 1:11-15). Admittedly, the Lord had ordained the sacrificial system for the Israelite people (even though He never approved of child sacrifice). But in this case, the people were clearly using the system to try to buy His favor. They were willing to carry out rituals, but were not truly obedient when it came to dealing with others.

What can mere mortals do to please their Creator? That is the burning question in the heart of every person who approaches the Lord in heartfelt worship. The responses recorded in Micah 6:6-7 were theologically way off the mark, even though they reflected the thinking of unsaved humanity. Against the backdrop of God's redemptive acts, He clarified what He really wanted (vs. 8; see Ps. 15:2-5; 24:4-5; Isa. 33:15-16). The eternal Creator did not desire to receive meaningless religious acts from His chosen people. Instead, He wanted their thoughts, words, and actions to be characterized by equity and compassion.

God decreed that the covenant community make the following three principles a priority: (1) to promote justice (that is, honesty and fairness); (2) to let persistent acts of kindness undergird their dealings with one another; and (3) to ensure that reverence, prudence, and obedience were the foundation of their relationship with the Lord (see Isa. 29:19; Jer. 22:16; Hos. 6:6; Amos 5:24; Jas. 1:27). These requirements progress from what is external to what is internal and from one's relationship to other people to one's relationship with God. Specifically, in order to be just toward other people, one must display loyal love. Also, such compassion demands a circumspect walk before the Lord. These virtues are ones that believers today ought to strive to fulfill. God still expects His people to treat others with Christlike love and to live in devotion to Him.

The importance of these three characteristics is seen in Jesus' repeating their essence to the religious leaders of His day (see Matt. 23:23). Acting in a just manner means we are determined to do God's will, that is, to love Him with all our heart, soul, mind, and strength, and to love our neighbors as ourselves. Also, our resolving with God's help to carry out justice includes revering Him, honoring our commitments to Him and others, and defending the rights of the innocent. To prize mercy involves more than treating others fairly. It signifies unfailing compassion, which is a key attribute of God Himself, who abounds in love (see Exod. 34:6; Neh. 9:17; Ps. 103:8). Moreover, God's type of mercy shows empathy to the undeserving, offers spiritual resources to those who are less fortunate, donates to charitable causes, and actively shares with others in need. To relate to God in a humble manner means understanding that we have sinned and are saved by His grace. Furthermore, submission to the Creator involves fellowship, namely, spending time with Him and devoting our motives, goals, and integrity to Him.

SUGGESTIONS TO TEACHERS

Many persons are cynical about their leaders. The scandalous behavior and the unscrupulous practices of certain government and religious officials have caused confusion and disillusionment, especially among the younger generation. Some media personalities' lack of values has also had a corrupting effect. Some of your students might be wondering what is right and what is wrong, and also how God wants them to act. Use Micah 6 to address these important issues.

1. CONDEMNATION OF RELIGIOUS LEADERS. Micah referred to corrupt civil and religious leaders, and his words remind us as God's children that we carry a heavy burden of duty to the impoverished living around us. Your congregation might already be doing noble service through a food pantry or participation in housing programs for the poor. Are there other areas that should be addressed? Also, how do you overcome "compassion fatigue"?

2. CONSEQUENCES OF DISOBEDIENCE. Like all prophets, Micah warned his hearers that their heartless lack of concern for those suffering in society would result in the destruction and end of their comfortable way of life. How do Micah's pronouncements apply to our society?

3. CONTROVERSY WITH THE COVENANT COMMUNITY. Micah, like Hosea, told how deeply disappointed God was with His faithless people. The disobedient had deliberately broken the sacred relationship between God and His people, and this in turn immensely grieved the Lord. How do your students think God feels toward the church in general and toward their congregation in particular?

4. CONCENTRATION ON GOD'S REQUIREMENT. Be sure to focus at length on verse 8, especially discussing what it means to "do justly, and to love mercy, and to walk humbly" before God. You might even want to save the largest part of the lesson time to discuss this key verse.

For Adults

■ **Topic:** Knowing How to Please God

■ **Questions:** 1. In what ways did the people of Judah and Israel believe God had neglected and abused them? 2. What was the nature of the case God brought against His chosen people? 3. Why did God refuse to delight in countless and extreme sacrifices? 4. What does it mean to be fair, merciful, and humble to others? 5. When do you most remember seeing justice, kindness, and modesty being shown by other Christians?

■ **Illustrations:**

Doing the Right Thing. A father regularly taught his son to do what is right. One day, while they worked together with some other men, the language became increasingly profane. When the youngster joined in the talk, his father reminded him that such language was inappropriate.

Through His spokesperson, Micah, God revealed that He expected Israel and Judah to live up to His high moral standards. Instead, people throughout society wallowed in the ways of their corrupt neighbors, allowed immorality and injustice to prevail, and worshiped the Lord hypocritically.

It's perilously easy for those who have been Christians for a long time to go through the motions of worship, prayer, and other religious activities. We forget that God wants us to grow in our love for Him, to mature in our spiritual wisdom and understanding, and to become more like Jesus in our thoughts and actions. This week's Scripture passage helps us to see how dangerous it is to pretend we're walking with God when we're not.

Divine Expectations. It was on the night of his 40th birthday that Randy stole away from the festivities for some private time with the Lord. As was Randy's custom when he turned 20, and again when he turned 30, he prayed and read his Bible and asked the Holy Spirit to give him illumination for the next decade. Each time God brought a Scripture verse to Randy's attention that would be a special guide for the next 10 years.

For Randy's 40th birthday, the verse was Micah 6:8. Randy found it to be a simple declaration of what God was asking him to work on in his next decade. Randy hadn't been overtly guilty of transgressing this verse in the past, but he knew that God was leading him to follow more closely what this Scripture admonished.

Halfway through his 40s now, the following is what Randy has learned. First, to act justly means that we will never knowingly or purposefully allow any advantage to come to us through manipulation or deceit. Every benefit and opportunity that Randy now receives, he makes sure it comes as a result of the service he renders to others, and never at their expense.

Second, Randy discovered that to be a lover of mercy, one must first be the recipient of mercy. He found himself in experiences where God's mercy was freely given to him on a personal level. Showing mercy to others seemed much easier now. Third, humility seems to be the natural by-product of choosing to obey this life calling of justice and mercy. Randy often finds himself overwhelmed by the grace of God.

Showing Mercy. On May 20, 2013, a severe tornado struck Moore, Oklahoma. The twister had estimated wind speeds of 200–210 miles per hour, a width of up to 1.3 miles, and a path length of 17 miles. In its wake, two elementary schools, a medical center, and several subdivisions were destroyed. The storm also took the lives of 23 persons, as well as injured 377 others.

In the aftermath of the natural disaster, *NPR* correspondent Kirk Siegler reported that "hundreds of volunteers" came to the region to "help the community." Some pitched in to "clear debris," while others brought out "water and supplies" to local residents whose lives had been thrown in "disarray."

Siegler drew attention to one particular group, Oklahoma Baptist Relief Organization. The correspondent found some of its volunteers stacking "25-pound containers of meals" and "bottled water." Others were busy "cooking more than 10,000 meals a day." Siegler also spotted "mobile kitchens, trucks, and handymen crews" hard at work. One volunteer named Jack White recalled people asking him, "You're not getting paid for this?" According to Siegler, White's typical response was, "I get paid nothing. It's for the glory of God."

This relief group is a striking example of the emphasis Micah placed on God's children showing mercy to others in tangible ways. The heroic effort of the organization's volunteers reminds us that meaningful displays of mercy bring about a healthy relationship between God and one another that makes for a blessed community.

FOR YOUTH

■ **TOPIC:** Doing What Is Right
■ **QUESTIONS:** 1. Why were the people of Israel and Judah wrong to claim that what God commanded in the Mosaic law was unfair? 2. In what ways had God acted redemptively toward His chosen people? 3. What mistaken notions about the covenant community's relationship with God are revealed in Micah 6:6-7? 4. What steps can believers take to be more fair and honest in all their dealings? 5. Why should the three requirements found in verse 8 be the hallmark of every believer's life?

■ **ILLUSTRATIONS:**

What Does God Want, Anyway? High school students who know early on that they are headed for college get a clear picture of what the universities expect of all applicants. They take various tests to be sure they can compete. They work hard, and it pays off, often with valuable scholarships.

The main reason Christians highly recommend studying the Bible is not to pass an exam, but to learn what kind of behavior God desires of them. Unless we saturate ourselves in Scripture, we will fall prey to various popular ideas that are contrary to God's Word and will. Everything we do must be evaluated by what God has revealed in the Bible.

Micah preached against phony religion as well as against other kinds of sins. The prophet declared that God's basic command was to love Him. Micah also noted that God has revealed righteous principles of conduct for our good. When we love God, we can trust Him to take care of us and lead us in the best way, regardless if the ways of the ungodly sound better.

The Weed of Envy. "Envy is wanting what another person has and feeling badly that I don't have it. Envy is disliking God's goodness to someone else and dismissing God's goodness to me. Envy is desire plus resentment. Envy is anti-community," asserts John Ortberg in *Love Beyond Reason: Moving God's Love from Your Head to Your Heart*.

An envious heart is incapable of showing the justice, mercy, and humility called for in Micah 6:8. It is too preoccupied. Have you witnessed the results of envy? Envy frequently makes its way into criminal acts. But on a private level, envy is damaging too. Its seed of discontentment quickly grows into the weed of resentment. This weed can choke relationships—even among Christians.

So how does a young believer eradicate this weed? Extermination begins with developing a right attitude toward the Father and the blessings He, in His wisdom, bestows through faith in His Son.

Modeling Care. South Bend's Center for the Homeless helps dozens of people each day. What is surprising is that young alumni and students run it from the University of Notre Dame's Center for Social Concerns.

Consider Shannon Cullinan. She developed a landscaping business that employs homeless people for eight months of training and then places them in other landscaping companies, especially as it cares for the properties in the City of South Bend, Memorial Hospital, WNDU Broadcasting, and the university properties. Then there's Drew Buscarieno. He developed a medical clinic, early childhood center, and drug and alcohol treatment center. He also developed educational facilities, job training, and care for the mentally ill.

The executive director of the National Coalition praised the Center for the Homeless as a model of collaboration between university students and the local community. The center seeks to find solutions to the problems of the homeless. Here is a group of young people working to implement the sorts of godly qualities appearing in Micah 6:8 that God requires in their lives.

LESSON 8 — JULY 26

Experiencing God's Pardon

Background Scripture: Micah 7:14-20
Devotional Reading: Psalm 13

Key Verse: Who is a God like unto thee, that pardoneth iniquity, and passeth by the transgression of the remnant of his heritage? he retaineth not his anger for ever, because he delighteth in mercy. Micah 7:18.

KING JAMES VERSION

MICAH 7:14 Feed thy people with thy rod, the flock of thine heritage, which dwell solitarily in the wood, in the midst of Carmel: let them feed in Bashan and Gilead, as in the days of old. 15 According to the days of thy coming out of the land of Egypt will I shew unto him marvellous things. 16 The nations shall see and be confounded at all their might: they shall lay their hand upon their mouth, their ears shall be deaf. 17 They shall lick the dust like a serpent, they shall move out of their holes like worms of the earth: they shall be afraid of the LORD our God, and shall fear because of thee.
18 Who is a God like unto thee, that pardoneth iniquity, and passeth by the transgression of the remnant of his heritage? he retaineth not his anger for ever, because he delighteth in mercy. 19 He will turn again, he will have compassion upon us; he will subdue our iniquities; and thou wilt cast all their sins into the depths of the sea.
20 Thou wilt perform the truth to Jacob, and the mercy to Abraham, which thou hast sworn unto our fathers from the days of old.

NEW REVISED STANDARD VERSION

MICAH 7:14 Shepherd your people with your staff,
   the flock that belongs to you,
which lives alone in a forest
   in the midst of a garden land;
let them feed in Bashan and Gilead
   as in the days of old.
15 As in the days when you came out of the land of Egypt,
   show us marvelous things.
16 The nations shall see and be ashamed
   of all their might;
they shall lay their hands on their mouths;
   their ears shall be deaf;
17 they shall lick dust like a snake,
   like the crawling things of the earth;
they shall come trembling out of their fortresses;
   they shall turn in dread to the LORD our God,
   and they shall stand in fear of you.
18 Who is a God like you, pardoning iniquity
   and passing over the transgression
   of the remnant of your possession?
He does not retain his anger forever,
   because he delights in showing clemency.
19 He will again have compassion upon us;
   he will tread our iniquities under foot.
You will cast all our sins
   into the depths of the sea.
20 You will show faithfulness to Jacob
   and unswerving loyalty to Abraham,
as you have sworn to our ancestors
   from the days of old.

HOME BIBLE READINGS

Monday, July 20	Psalm 13	*I Trusted in Your Steadfast Love*
Tuesday, July 21	Ezekiel 34:1-6	*My Sheep Were Scattered*
Wednesday, July 22	Ezekiel 34:7-16	*The Lord Shepherds His Sheep*
Thursday, July 23	Ezekiel 34:23-31	*You Are My Sheep*
Friday, July 24	Micah 7:1-6	*Troubling Times of Woe*
Saturday, July 25	Micah 7:7-11	*I Will Look to the Lord*
Sunday, July 26	Micah 7:14-20	*God Shows Clemency*

BACKGROUND

In lesson 5, we noted that Micah 6 and 7 form a literary unit that focuses on the Lord's indictment and restoration of His chosen people. We also learned in lesson 7 that the charges against the covenant community are detailed in 6:1-8, while the guilt and punishment the people received for their transgressions are described in verses 9-16. The first seven verses of chapter 7 are presented as an agonizing lament that details the crimes Judah and Israel committed and how that decadence led to the disintegration of society. Micah, as the speaker, voiced his thoughts as though he were the only righteous person left within the covenant community. Of course, he was exaggerating. Nonetheless, verses 1-7 indicate that wickedness had become widespread.

Verses 8-20 contain a liturgical hymn of praise for God's deliverance of His chosen people from the oppression of their enemies. In verses 8-10, the prophet spoke on behalf of Lady Jerusalem, in which the holy city (personified as an individual) confessed her faith in the Lord. Next, verses 11-13 present a divine pledge of blessing on the upright remnant. Most likely, the plight experienced by Zion was due either to the Assyrian siege of 701 B.C. or to the Babylonian victory in 586 B.C. The promises applied in part to the rebuilding of Jerusalem after the Babylonian captivity, but also apply in part to the messianic age.

NOTES ON THE PRINTED TEXT

The final section of Micah contains several different literary elements. First, God's spokesperson prayed on behalf of the chosen people (vs. 14). Next, the Lord responded with an assurance (vs. 15). Then, Micah stated confidently that the nations would submit to God (vss. 16-17) and that He would show mercy to His people (vss. 18-20). In the opening prayer (vs. 14), Micah depicted the Lord as a shepherd and the faithful remnant as His prized "flock" (see Gen. 48:15; Pss. 23:1; 28:9; John 10:11).

The King made it possible for His "heritage" (Mic. 7:14) to dwell safely in the woodland far from any predators (see Ps. 94:14). The Hebrew text of Micah 7:14 more literally says that the covenant community was living "in the middle of Carmel." Carmel is a mountain range famous for its garden-like forests covered with vegetation.

Micah also asked for God to let His people feed in Bashan and Gilead. These were lush grasslands on the eastern side of the Jordan River. In certain periods, Israel possessed those territories, but it probably did not control them at the time Micah wrote. So, this request might be a petition for the Lord one day to return those areas to the covenant community.

Verse 15 appears to be God's response to the prayer recorded in verse 14. The Shepherd-King promised to perform miraculous deeds as in the time of the Exodus. The "marvellous things" during that earlier time included the ten successive plagues on Egypt, the parting of the Red Sea, the provision of manna and water in the wilderness, and the appearance of God on Mount Sinai. Concerning the ten plagues, these were blood (Exod. 7:17-24), frogs (7:25–8:15), gnats (8:16-19), flies (vss. 20-32), livestock disease (9:1-7), boils (vss. 8-12), hail (vss. 13-35), locusts (10:3-20), darkness (vss. 21-23), and the death of the firstborn (11:1-8; 12:21-30).

Some Bible scholars think the first nine plagues were natural phenomena in Egypt that were miraculous in nature in their intensity and the time of their occurrence. In this case, God used natural means to achieve divine objectives. In contrast, others see these calamities as being more directly supernatural (for example, blood being taken literally). The final plague—the death of the firstborn in Egypt—was unquestionably different. It was clearly outside the realm of the natural and normal experience of the Egyptians. Yet, like the other plagues, it fell upon prince and peasant alike. This most devastating of the afflictions reached even the family of Pharaoh himself.

After the tenth plagued occurred, Egypt's ruler, under cover of darkness, called Moses and Aaron and virtually ordered them to take the Hebrews and their animals and go out to the desert to worship God. The once-arrogant pharaoh was even reduced to asking Moses and Aaron to "bless" (12:32) him. In effect, the Egyptian monarch was requesting prayer for himself and his devastated nation. After nine burdensome plagues capped by a horrific tenth, Pharaoh no doubt had a much-changed opinion of the God he had earlier defied.

Amazingly, after the Hebrews left, Pharaoh's heart was hardened again. So, his army headed across the desert in pursuit of the former slaves. But God delivered the Hebrews once more from their oppressors as the Egyptian army followed them into the Red Sea. The antagonists eventually drowned when the waters closed in behind the Hebrews (see 14:29-31). After witnessing the Lord's awesome power, His chosen people sang a song of adoration (see 15:1). They extolled the great strength and majestic power of the Creator that resulted in the destruction of the horses and riders of the Egyptian army. God alone was given credit for the deliverance of the Hebrews. Also, for this He was extremely worthy of their praise and exaltation (see vss. 2-16).

While God's people could expect to benefit from His power, other peoples would not fare so well. The divine Warrior would judge the pagan "nations" (Mic. 7:16) for their iniquities. These transgressions included taunting and tormenting the upright remnant. Appropriately, God would humiliate the tyrants. Specifically, the might of their armies would be ineffective in resisting the Lord of heaven's vast legions. Indeed, His awesome might so astounded them that they would lose all ability to speak or hear.

Genesis 3 reveals that at the dawn of humanity, a serpent tricked the first woman and man to disobey their Creator (see 1 Tim. 2:13-14). Part of God's curse on the tempter included experiencing the humiliation of slithering on the ground and being forced to ingest dirt as it moved along (Gen. 3:14). In a future day, when the Lord rescued His chosen people from their foes, He would shame the oppressors by consigning them to "lick dust like a serpent" (Mich. 7:17). The Hebrew phrase translated "lick dust" might reflect the ancient practice in which defeated kings were made to kiss the feet of their victorious enemies as a sign of subjugation. Micah foretold that in abject disgrace, the vanquished tormentors would crawl out of their fortresses like reptiles and approach the sovereign Ruler of the universe with "fear" and trembling.

The prophet's declaration parallels the truths recorded in Philippians 2:9-11. Paul, after discussing the Son's sacrificial death on the cross (see vss. 6-8), shifted the focus to His exaltation. The place of honor that Jesus willingly forsook was given back to Him with the added glory of His triumph over sin and death. In response to the Son's humility and obedience, the Father supremely exalted Jesus to a place where His triumph will eventually be recognized by all living creatures (vs. 9). The apostle emphatically tells us that every person who has ever lived will someday recognize the Son for who He is, namely, the supreme Lord revealed in the Old Testament as Yahweh (see Acts 2:33-36).

The "name of Jesus" (Phil. 2:10) signifies the majestic office or position the Father bestowed on the Son, not His proper name. By bowing their knees, every human being and angel will acknowledge Jesus' deity and sovereignty. Also, everyone will confess that Jesus is Lord—some with joyful faith, others with hopeless regret and anguish (vs. 11). Centuries earlier, Isaiah the prophet had announced the words of the Messiah: "unto me every knee shall bow, every tongue shall swear" (Isa. 45:23; see Rom. 14:11; Rev. 5:13). Philippians 2:6-11 affirms that this universal acknowledgment of Jesus' lordship will ultimately come to pass.

Micah closed his book with an expression of wonder at God's mercy and confidence in His faithfulness. The prophet's name means "Who is like Yahweh?" and at Micah 7:18 he apparently wove this name into the fabric of his praise to the Lord. This verse and the next one convey the idea that God is gracious toward His chosen people. For instance, He lifts away the guilt and punishment of their iniquity (see Exod. 34:6-7; Ps. 30:5). He also passes over the rebellious acts committed by the upright "remnant" (Mic. 7:18), who are His heritage (see Pss. 28:9; 33:12; Isa. 19:25; Joel 2:17). Unlike petulant human rulers, the Creator does not hold onto His anger indefinitely. Rather, He is pleased to lavish His "heritage" (Mic. 7:18) with His steadfast love.

Micah was confident that even though the Lord brought a season of affliction on

His people for their violations of the Mosaic covenant, He would once more shower them with His unfailing kindness. Micah revealed that due to God's clemency, He would subdue their misdeeds like a warrior tramples his defeated foes. The prophet also declared that the Shepherd-King would toss their trespasses into the "depths of the sea" (vs. 19). In ancient Near Eastern literature, the sea was a symbol of chaos. The idea is that the Creator would trounce such a despot. In doing so, God would fulfill the pledge He made centuries earlier to the patriarchs—Abraham, Isaac, and Jacob—to bless their descendants with complete and unconditional forgiveness (see Gen. 12:2-3; 13:15-16; 15:5, 18-21; 17:4-8; 21:12; 22:17; 28:13-15; 35:10-12).

New Testament believers have also experienced the kind of pardoning love Micah described (see Rom. 4:17; Gal. 3:6-29; Heb. 11:12). They know God's faithfulness in both discipline and forgiveness. The main message of the Bible is that we cannot help ourselves—not one bit. Much as we would like to have the key to our own salvation, so we could effect our own rescue, we need to admit to ourselves that we have lost the key and cannot be our deliverers. But the closing chapter of Micah's prophecy reminds us of some good news. The Creator has the ability to deliver us and become our salvation.

SUGGESTIONS TO TEACHERS

Micah's prophecies are not all gloom and doom. For instance, in 7:18-19, we read about God's unfailing love and forgiveness. Despite our rebellion, the Lord offers unconditional pardon. Also, His mercy toward us is so great that He does not hesitate to toss our misdeeds into the depths of the sea. In light of these truths, take some class time to emphasize the following points.

1. OUR SIN IS REAL. God does not minimize the heinousness of our transgressions. He also does not try to shift the blame to others. Instead, the Lord wants us to recognize our trespasses and in this way prepare ourselves to experience His forgiveness.

2. OUR SIN MUST BE ACKNOWLEDGED. God will not pardon anyone who remains firmly entrenched in rebellion. Because the Lord is holy and righteous, He cannot allow unrepentant sinners to go unpunished. So, by acknowledging our wrongdoing, we admit our need to be forgiven, renounce our evil actions, and indicate our desire to once again have fellowship with God.

3. OUR SIN CAN BE FORGIVEN. There is no sin of ours that is too great or terrible for God to pardon. Like the chosen people in Micah's day, we can confess our iniquity to the Lord and experience His clemency. He will not only remove our guilt, but also renew our joy and restore our fractured relationship with Him.

4. OUR SAVIOR IS THE REASON WE ARE PARDONED. The Father's provision of forgiveness and spiritual cleansing are made possible to us through His Son. Jesus is the perfect sacrifice God offered to take away the sins of the world (see John 1:29). The Son, by dying on the cross, accepted the wrath of the Father and paid the penalty associated with our rebellion against the Lord (see 1 John 2:2). This means that if we want to receive God's pardon, we must accept the salvation He freely offers through faith in the Messiah (see Acts 16:30-31).

FOR ADULTS

■ **TOPIC:** God Freely Pardons Us

■ **QUESTIONS:** 1. In what sense was the faithful remnant of Micah's day the flock of God's inheritance? 2. What miracles did the Lord perform to free the Hebrews from Egypt? 3. How will the pagan nations respond to God's vindication of His chosen people? 4. What is the basis for the Lord pardoning our transgressions? 5. What sins in your life has God completely and unconditionally forgiven?

■ **ILLUSTRATIONS:**

Learning the Hard Way. What are some lessons we have learned the hard way? What stories could we tell about how we suffered because we thought we knew better? It is humbling to admit that we failed because we were too proud and stubborn to listen to someone's advice or to the wisdom of God's Word.

Nevertheless, how thankful we are that God often delivers us from our follies. Also, how marvelous it is to tell others about His grace. We should mention not just our mistakes, but also God's mercy and goodness.

Imagine the prophet Micah assembling the people in Jerusalem so that they could acknowledge their wrongdoing to the Lord. In turn, consider the joy they would feel when God freely forgave them. This is exactly what the Father has done for us in His Son. When we accept the pardon God freely makes available in Jesus, we have the assurance that our misdeeds will not be held against us.

Being Freed from Sin's Burden. There are various "strongman" competitions that are staged each year around the world. One of the more interesting is usually held in the Scandinavian countries of Sweden, Norway, and Denmark. In those countries, contestants compete in a multitude of events for top time, weight, or distance. At the end of the competition, the judges total the individual feat scores together and announce a winner.

Some of the strength tests include holding sledgehammers away from one's body for as long as one's arms will endure. Another event involves lifting and placing a certain number of round, heavy "Atlas Stones" on five tall platforms spread out over a long course. Still, another feat entails pulling buses, trains, or planes by hand for a fixed distance as quickly as possible.

In many ways, life is a parallel to this strongman competition. However, for believers the goal is not how far they can travel with the weight of their sin. Instead, it is how many of these burdens they can be free of so that they might be assured of finishing their course. Micah 7:18-19 reveals that God is the One who makes this possible. He does so by forgiving our transgressions. Likewise, Hebrews 12:1 encourages us through faith in Christ to lay aside the load of our iniquities so that we might "run with patience the race that is set before us."

Forgiveness Restores Relationships. It had been a long evening at the Johnson house. The three kids—ages six, seven, and ten—had been fighting with each other since supper. Bedtime stopped the shouting, but tension hung in the air.

At two in the morning, a clap of thunder right overhead woke everybody in the house to lashing wind and rain and flashing lightning. In the parents' bedroom, the father heard strange noises from the kids' wing. He shuffled down the hall to find everyone's room empty. "Where are you," he called. A little voice whimpered, "We're in the closet forgiving each other."

Think how many relationships needed to be healed in Micah's day after he announced God's promise to cast the transgressions of His people into the deepest part of the sea (Mic. 7:19). Also, consider how the reality of God's pardon to us can restore our relationships with one another (vs. 18).

This week's lesson speaks of the Lord's willingness to extend clemency to those who confess their sin and repent of it. Certainly, we who are given the ministry of teaching God's Word have a critical part in bringing class members to an understanding of sin as well as the Lord's offer of forgiveness and salvation.

For Youth

■ **Topic:** God Is Merciful to Us

■ **Questions:** 1. Why did Micah ask the Lord to shepherd His chosen people? 2. In what way would God shame the pagan nations? 3. Why was it important for all of earth's inhabitants to revere the Lord? 4. How is it possible for God to show us mercy, even when we've sinned? 5. What are some ways you have recently experienced God's compassion?

■ **Illustrations:**

God's Unfailing Compassion. Early in 1993, British police accused two ten-year-old boys of the brutal murder of two-year-old James Bulger. The two boys initially claimed they were innocent. Nevertheless, the young defendants responded to police questioning with noticeable inconsistency.

The climax came when the parents of one of the boys assured him that they would always love him. As a result of being confronted with irrefutable evidence linking him with the crime and the assurance of his parents' love, the boy confessed in a soft voice, "I killed James."

Through Micah the prophet, God declared that He knew the sins His people had committed. The Lord also knows about our misdeeds. Yet, He still loves us. The presence of His unfailing compassion encourages us, as it did the people of Micah's day, to confess our sins and experience the Lord's abundant forgiveness.

Experiencing God's Grace. He'd been sneaking money out of the register at the fast-food restaurant—five dollars here, ten dollars there, never much at a time, and not very often. Now he was caught, and it added up to more than three hundred dollars. He and his manager were in a booth in the back corner. Would the teenager go to jail? What would his parents say?

The manager asked questions and the adolescent answered them. He forgot the excuses he'd cooked up and just told what he'd done. It took a long time, and when it was over, the manager stared at the tabletop. He finally looked up and said, "If I don't press charges and if I don't fire you, can I trust you in the future?"

"What?" was all the young man could stammer. "You'll have to pay the money back, and you'll have to tell your parents and bring me a note from them that says you did," the manager went on. "You see, you're not the first to pull a stunt like this. I did pretty much the same thing, and my manager said he thought I was truly sorry and ready for some grace of God. I think you are too. What about it?"

Micah 7:18-19 encourages us to confess our sin and experience God's grace. Part of the process includes admitting our guilt and being honest about our shortcomings. Admittedly, this is difficult to do, because we are by nature prone to pride. Only the grace of God offered in Christ can enable us to humbly admit our wrongs and receive His unconditional pardon.

Forgiveness All the Way. The pastor's little boy had spent the whole afternoon at the mall with his mom. As time passed, the bored boy got in more and more trouble—wanting this, running off, and trying to get coins out of the fountain in front of a store.

In the car on the way home, the child could tell he was in for it. He thought he'd try theology. "When we ask God to forgive us when we're bad, He does, doesn't He?" "Yes, He does," replied the boy's mother. "And when He forgives us, He buries our sins in the deepest seas, doesn't He?" the child pressed on. "Yes, that's what Micah 6:19 says," his mother snapped with evident impatience. She knew her son was hoping to avoid discipline. "Well," the boy added, "I've asked God to forgive me, but I bet when we get home, you're going fishing for those old sins. Aren't you?"

Sin does have its unavoidable consequences in our lives, but when God forgives, He forgives all the way.

LESSON 9 — AUGUST 2

THE REDEEMER'S PRESENCE

BACKGROUND SCRIPTURE: Isaiah 59; Psalm 89:11-18
DEVOTIONAL READING: Exodus 6:2-8

Key Verse: The Redeemer shall come to Zion, and unto them that turn from transgression in Jacob, saith the LORD. Isaiah 59:20.

KING JAMES VERSION

ISAIAH 59:15 Yea, truth faileth; and he that departeth from evil maketh himself a prey: and the LORD saw it, and it displeased him that there was no judgment.

16 And he saw that there was no man, and wondered that there was no intercessor: therefore his arm brought salvation unto him; and his righteousness, it sustained him. 17 For he put on righteousness as a breastplate, and a helmet of salvation upon his head; and he put on the garments of vengeance for clothing, and was clad with zeal as a cloke. 18 According to their deeds, accordingly he will repay, fury to his adversaries, recompence to his enemies; to the islands he will repay recompence. 19 So shall they fear the name of the LORD from the west, and his glory from the rising of the sun. When the enemy shall come in like a flood, the Spirit of the LORD shall lift up a standard against him. 20 And the Redeemer shall come to Zion, and unto them that turn from transgression in Jacob, saith the LORD. 21 As for me, this is my covenant with them, saith the LORD; My spirit that is upon thee, and my words which I have put in thy mouth, shall not depart out of thy mouth, nor out of the mouth of thy seed, nor out of the mouth of thy seed's seed, saith the LORD, from henceforth and for ever.

NEW REVISED STANDARD VERSION

ISAIAH 59:15 Truth is lacking,
and whoever turns from evil is despoiled.
The LORD saw it, and it displeased him
that there was no justice.
16 He saw that there was no one,
and was appalled that there was no one to intervene;
so his own arm brought him victory,
and his righteousness upheld him.
17 He put on righteousness like a breastplate,
and a helmet of salvation on his head;
he put on garments of vengeance for clothing,
and wrapped himself in fury as in a mantle.
18 According to their deeds, so will he repay;
wrath to his adversaries, requital to his enemies;
to the coastlands he will render requital.
19 So those in the west shall fear the name of the LORD,
and those in the east, his glory;
for he will come like a pent-up stream
that the wind of the LORD drives on.
20 And he will come to Zion as Redeemer,
to those in Jacob who turn from transgression, says the LORD.
21 And as for me, this is my covenant with them, says the LORD: my spirit that is upon you, and my words that I have put in your mouth, shall not depart out of your mouth, or out of the mouths of your children, or out of the mouths of your children's children, says the LORD, from now on and forever.

Home Bible Readings

Monday, July 27	Isaiah 59:1-14	*Our Sins Testify against Us*
Tuesday, July 28	Isaiah 48:12-19	*Taught for Our Own Good*
Wednesday, July 29	Isaiah 54:1-8	*God's Everlasting Love*
Thursday, July 30	Jeremiah 50:28-34	*Our Redeemer Is Strong*
Friday, July 31	Psalm 89:11-18	*Walking in the Light*
Saturday, August 1	Exodus 6:2-8	*Redeemed by God*
Sunday, August 2	Isaiah 59:15-21	*The Lord Our Redeemer*

Background

In keeping with what was noted in lesson 13 from the September quarter, Isaiah is one of the richest and most rewarding prophetic books in the Old Testament. Its inspired texts are a compilation of history, predictions, warnings, and promises relayed through the prophet to the people of Judah. At this time, they approached a great turning point in their history. Eighteen years after Isaiah began his ministry in 740 B.C., Assyria would conquer and exile the northern kingdom of Israel (722 B.C.). Then, 136 years later, Babylon would defeat and deport the southern kingdom of Judah (586 B.C.). Isaiah explained the reason for these tragic turns in history. His words burn with God's denunciation of the sins into which His people had fallen.

Even so, Isaiah's messages of doom are lined with a shining hope. The prophet not only graphically pictured the chastisements God's people would experience, but also glowingly depicted the blessings of a future kingdom age. In that light alone, the Book of Isaiah has a clear message for believers today. The sins that are prevalent in our time are strikingly similar to those of which Judah was guilty of committing. And equally so, the prospect for humanity now is the same divine judgment. Yet, beyond the horizon of judgment, there also lies a far greater hope: the return of the Lord Jesus and the establishment of His universal peace and righteousness on earth. Isaiah's portrayal of this unfathomable glory that awaits God's children is enough to leave one gaping in awe.

Notes on the Printed Text

Previously, in Isaiah 51:4-6, the Lord's justice and righteousness symbolized the salvation He graciously provided. If His people waited expectantly for the promised deliverance, it would come. Yet, their lack of faith in God prevented the people from experiencing the full extent of the blessing He pledged to give them. In particular, "judgment" (59:14) was beaten back and "justice" (or "righteousness") was nowhere to be found. Similarly, "truth" staggered in the city squares and "equity" (that is, integrity and rectitude) was shoved aside. Moreover, "truth" (vs. 15) had vanished from the courts, being replaced by lies. Also, the wicked rich plundered those who renounced "evil." Not surprisingly, the all-knowing God was fully aware of the corruption and cruelty taking place among His people, and He found the circumstance to be abhorrent.

As the Lord looked upon Judah, He not only witnessed the rampant injustice going on, but also noticed that there was no one to intercede on behalf of the innocent in the courts of law. Similarly, God was disgusted to learn that the defenseless were without an advocate to assist them (vs. 16). A parallel thought is recorded in 63:5. In both passages, we discover that the covenant-keeping God of Israel would come to the aid of the oppressed and rectify the injustices they experienced. The Lord would do so by drawing on His all-sufficient resources. With His own powerful "arm" (59:16) He would win "salvation" for His people, and His commitment to promote justice upheld Him in His righteous cause.

In 53:12, we learn that God would use His Servant to intercede on behalf of the "transgressors." He is none other than the Messiah, the One who would bring true deliverance, not from national slavery, but from humanity's more horrible and eternal slavery to sin (see 42:1, 7). The typical first-century expectations of the Messiah included political agendas, military campaigns, and great fanfare (John 6:14-15). Matthew 12:18-21 quotes Isaiah 42:1-4 to stress that the Messiah was not this type of king. Instead, He would be a quiet, gentle ruler who would bring justice to the nations. Also, as God's chosen Servant, the Messiah would be noted for His encouragement and truth, not violence and trickery (John 18:33-37). As God's Servant, the Lord Jesus brought justice by dying on the cross for sinners. Without His sacrifice, no one could be saved since justice demands that all sinners be punished. When the Messiah returned, He would also bring justice by rewarding good and defeating evil.

In Isaiah 53:5, we discover that God's Servant was wounded because of our "transgressions." The latter renders a Hebrew noun that can also be translated "rebellious deeds" or "acts of insurrection." Moreover, the Servant was "bruised" because of our "iniquities." The reference here includes the guilt and punishment connected with our trespasses. In short, the holy one of God allowed Himself to be profaned and brutalized to bring us "peace" with God. The noun rendered "peace" comes from a term that means health, wholeness, and well-being in every area of life, including people's relationship with God. Moreover, the "stripes" inflicted on the Servant from being beaten would bring spiritual healing to people's sin-sick souls (see Ps. 22:16; Zech. 12:10; John 19:34).

In Isaiah 59:17-19, God is portrayed as an ancient warrior who gets ready to enter battle on behalf of his nation and people. The Lord wears His commitment to justice as a coat of chainmail (a type of armor comprised of small metal rings linked together to create a mesh). Likewise, the "helmet" on God's "head" is His intent to deliver the faithful remnant. This includes vindicating their cause and punishing their oppressors. For this reason, the Commander of heaven's armies clothes Himself with an overcoat of "vengeance" (or retribution) and clads Himself with a mantle of "zeal" for upholding

His people's cause. In short, the divine Warrior trounces His enemies and restores the covenant community to its rightful place of honor (see Exod. 15:3; Isa. 42:13; 49:25; 52:10). In Ephesians 6:13-17, Paul used the imagery of God's armor to describe the nature of the spiritual battle Jesus' followers wage against the forces of darkness. (See the exposition of this passage in lesson 12 of the December quarter.)

Not everyone would experience God's blessing. In the coming day of judgment, the Lord would punish ungodly Israelites and wicked nations (see Isa. 65:6-7; 66:6; Jer. 25:29). As Isaiah 59:18 reveals, God would deal with His foes in an objective and equitable manner. Based on the way in which His "enemies" abused His people, the divine Warrior would dispense His fury. He would even pay back His adversaries to the coastlands, regardless of whether they were near or far away.

Verse 19 states that people all over the world—from west to east—would see God's saving work on behalf of His faithful remnant. Also, these witnesses to the Lord's redemptive acts would "fear" His "name" and revere His "glory." God's name signifies His holy and righteous reputation. Also, His glory denotes His majesty and splendor. Nations from all over the globe would honor and praise the Creator because of His awesome power. The coming of the Lord in judgment would seem like a rushing stream or torrent, and God's "Spirit" would move it forward like a violent windstorm. Some think that while the initial fulfillment of this prophecy occurred when the Babylonians were destroyed, the ultimate fulfillment awaits the end times.

God would come to the members of the covenant community, not as their Judge, but as their "Redeemer" (vs. 20). These are individuals who had turned away from their transgressions. This verse probably refers initially to God's protection of the returned exiles from Babylon, but ultimately to the Messiah. As was noted in lesson 6 of the September quarter, the underlying Hebrew verb translated "Redeemer" refers to a protector and vindicator. This term is always used for a next of kin who endeavors to safeguard the family interests. For example, if a man was sold into slavery, it was the duty of a blood relative to act as that man's family guardian and buy him out of slavery (see Lev. 25:47-49). Jesus is the Kinsman-Redeemer for sin-enslaved humanity. In order for Jesus to become our Savior, He had to become related to the human race by blood. This theological truth indicates the necessity of the Incarnation. Put differently, Jesus became human in order to redeem us (see Heb. 2:14-15).

Isaiah 59:21 might be considered a brief appendix to the preceding verses. God promised to establish an everlasting "covenant" with those whom He redeemed. His "spirit" and His "words" would remain with them and their "seed" from that moment onward. This promise seems to refer to the new covenant Jesus established through His atoning sacrifice at Calvary (see Jer. 31:31-34; Luke 22:20; and the Bible exposition appearing in lesson 2 of the September quarter).

In Romans 11:25-26, Paul identified the Redeemer with the Lord Jesus. The apostle revealed that Israel's spiritual stumbling was a "mystery." In Scripture, a mystery is not an enigmatic saying that is difficult to comprehend, but rather is a truth that was previously unknown but had now been revealed and publicly proclaimed. Paul wanted the mystery of Israel's spiritual darkness to be clearly understood by his Gentile readers. By comprehending God's sovereign dealings with Israel, the Gentiles could avoid arrogance over their inclusion in the people of God. In the Lord's sovereign plan, He desired for people of all nations to become a part of His eternal family. In achieving this goal, Israel for a time was set aside and experienced a hardening of the heart until the "fulness of the Gentiles" came in. God has a certain complement of Gentiles and Jews among the redeemed.

It is important to understand two facts about Israel's "blindness." First, it is only partial. This means there has always been a remnant of Jews whose hearts have not become hard. Second, this callousness is temporary. It would end when God's sovereignly chosen number of Gentiles have been saved and brought into God's family. Following this time, Paul said, "all Israel shall be saved" (vs. 26). What did Paul mean by "all Israel"? Scholars have suggested three possible views: (1) It could be referring to the majority of Jews living in the final generation. (2) "All Israel" could be referring to the total number of God's elect Jews from every generation. (3) It could be referring to the total number of God's elect—both Jew and Gentile—from all generations. (Regardless of which view is correct, "all Israel" would be saved by personal faith in Christ.) To confirm his assertion, Paul blended passages from Isaiah (under the inspiration of the Holy Spirit) to state that Israel would return to God after the Messiah appeared (see Isa. 59:20-21; 27:9).

SUGGESTIONS TO TEACHERS

As God looked on His chosen people, He saw their many problems. He also saw that no one else could solve those problems. So, as Isaiah 59:16-17 reveals, the Lord took it upon Himself to judge the wicked and redeem the righteous.

1. A SPIRITUAL MALAISE. Isaiah ministered both in times of calamity and prosperity. For instance, under the rule of Uzziah, Judah prospered economically, politically, and militarily. However, as verses 14-15 reveal, this state of prosperity ended up producing a spiritual malaise, paving the way for greed, injustice, religious insensitivity, and dead formalism in worship.

2. NO HELP FOR THE OPPRESSED. Through Isaiah, the Lord declared that He was astonished to see that there was no one within Judah to help the oppressed. That is why, according to verses 16-17, God would use His own power to rescue them from their plight and avenge the wrongs that the dispossessed suffered. Isaiah had to declare these truths with unwavering conviction, for there were others who claimed to be prophets of God but who were in effect spreading disinformation from the enemy—Satan.

3. PUNISHMENT ON EVILDOERS. Isaiah encouraged the faithful, beleaguered remnant in Judah that the Lord was on their side. We learn in verses 18-19 that God, like a valiant warrior, would punish His enemies according to the evil deeds they committed. Even those in distant lands were not out of reach from just judgment.

4. VINDICATION FOR THE UPRIGHT. God's spokesperson reminded his upright peers that God would defend their cause. As verses 20-21 indicate, they could remain committed to Him, for He would uphold and fulfill the covenant He made with their descendants. The Lord would intercede on their behalf through His Servant (see 53:12) and through Him bring justice to the nations (see 42:1).

For Adults

■ **TOPIC:** The Rescuer Comes!

■ **QUESTIONS:** 1. Why was truth so difficult to find in Judah's law courts? 2. Why did the Lord decide to intervene on behalf of the innocent in Judah? 3. In the coming day of judgment, how would God deal with His foes? 4. What does it mean for believers to "fear the name of the LORD" (Isa. 59:19)? 5. Why is it important for God's spiritual children to "turn from [their] transgression" (vs. 20)?

■ **ILLUSTRATIONS:**

Divine Intervention. It appalled the Lord that all traces of justice and truth had vanished from Judah (Isa. 59:14-15). That is why God would intervene on behalf of the innocent (vs. 16). Indeed, He would do so through His Suffering Servant (see 53:12).

We cannot read Isaiah's description of the Suffering Servant without sensing that a great miscarriage of justice occurred. We know from the Gospels that the compelling reasons for Jesus' affliction were entrenched religious hatred and the ruling elite's fear of losing their power. They condemned Jesus to die for having exposed their heartless, rigid hypocrisy.

Adults need to know that Jesus allowed Himself to be sentenced to death at the hands of hypocritical authorities so that His saving grace might be made known through the proclamation of the gospel (see Rom. 1:16). Adults also need to understand that it's only through faith in the crucified, risen Savior that they can be forgiven and receive eternal life (see Acts 4:12).

The Offer of a Pardon. The Constitution of the United States grants the nation's president the authority to issue pardons: "The President . . . shall have power to grant reprieves and pardons for offenses against the United States, except in cases of impeachment."

Perhaps one of the most controversial pardons was made by President Gerald Ford on behalf of his predecessor, Richard Nixon, who resigned in disgrace in the wake of the Watergate scandal. When Ford announced the pardon on live television on September 8, 1974 (a little over a year after Nixon left the White House), he explained that it was to end "an American tragedy in which we all have played a part."

Isaiah 59:20 declares that the Redeemer has come to rescue us from our sins. We also learn from Luke 2:11 that God makes our salvation possible through Jesus, the Messiah. John Bunyan, author of *Pilgrim's Progress*, imagined Jesus coming after him "with a pardon in His hand." When Jesus' pardon comes to us, how will you or others you know respond? All people need to seek God's forgiveness for their sins by receiving the awesome pardon the Father offers through the Son's atoning sacrifice. This is the message we need to embrace by faith and declare to the lost around us.

Take It to the Lord in Prayer. When the Baker Street Church felt the time was right to move ahead on a building project, congregational leaders made plans to develop a monthly prayer calendar for the parishioners. It was God's faithful answers to prayer that had made the project possible. The church had no desire to move forward without making prayer a reality.

Sometimes it may seem that our prayers reach no higher than the ceiling. And sometimes we may fear that there is really no one on the other end. But Isaiah 59:16 reveals that God cares about us enough to intervene on our behalf. We need not feel dismayed, for He hears our prayers. In fact, He understands our deepest needs—even those we can't bring ourselves to voice.

God's commitment to respond to our petitions is why Baker Street lists prayer concerns in the weekly bulletin. It is also why every meeting begins and ends with prayer. And it is why some of the church members believe there is no sweeter sound than someone saying, "I'll remember you in my prayers."

For Youth

■ **Topic:** Our Redeemer Cares!

■ **Questions:** 1. Why did the wicked rich maltreat those in Judah who renounced evil? 2. How did the Lord respond to the lack of justice in Judah? 3. In what sense did God enter battle on behalf of His people? 4. How can the truth of God as our "Redeemer" (Isa. 59:20) encourage us to live for Him? 5. Why is it important for believers to testify to others about the grace and goodness of God?

■ **Illustrations:**

Vindication for the Upright. The Lord was astonished that there seemed to be no one in Judah either willing or able to rescue the oppressed from their terrible situation. So, the all-powerful God decided He would bring about their deliverance (Isa. 59:16). He would use His faithful Servant to vindicate the cause of the defenseless (53:5, 11).

Jesus' willingness to suffer in order to make salvation available to the lost shows young people that obedience to God is costly. This should come as no surprise, for Jesus said that no one can follow Him without taking the path of self-denial (Luke

9:23). Whenever Christian youth think they can't endure a severe test of their faith, they should recall how Jesus suffered for them (Heb. 12:2-3).

Jesus was far more than a martyr. He was God's sacrificial Lamb (1 Pet. 1:18-19). The one who atoned for our sins was genuinely humble and gracious, even to His enemies (2:23). No one else can enable young people to go through trials with a peace that "transcends all understanding" (Phil. 4:7). And He alone can keep them from spiritually stumbling (Jude 24).

A New Remedy. In *The Healing of Persons*, Paul Tournier describes an incident involving a Christian physician who had heard from an old friend suffering from Parkinson's disease. The man wrote a note in which he told the physician, "Come only if you have some new remedy. I've had enough of doctors who say they cannot cure me."

The physician decided to accept the challenge. After arriving at his friend's home and greeting him, the physician said, "I brought you a new remedy—Jesus Christ!" As the physician talked, his friend gradually started to soften in his attitude. It took several more visits before the man began to show a remarkable change in the way he thought and spoke. Because of his decision to trust in the Lord's Suffering Servant for salvation, he became less irritable and more pleasant.

Isaiah 59:15 reveals that all of us are characterized by rebellion, self-centeredness, bitterness, and self-pity—just as the afflicted man who is mentioned above (see also Rom. 3:9-18). And like him, we all have an incurable disease called sin. We learn that only Jesus' atoning sacrifice can enable us to win the battle against this ailment.

Timely Support. In 2010, *The Karate Kid* was released in the United States. This remake of the 1984 original is about a lonely, fatherless, 12-year-old boy named Dre. He moves with his mother, Sherry, from their hometown, Detroit, to Beijing.

Not long after arriving in China, Dre finds himself bullied several times in the area near his apartment complex by a martial arts wunderkind named Cheng. A little later, Dre is aided by Mr. Han, who teaches him a Chinese fighting style called kung fu. Through this benevolent but firm instructor, Dre gets a new outlook on life.

In the climax, Dre is involved in a martial arts tournament. At first, because the odds of winning seem too great, Dre feels like giving up. However, Mr. Han offers him encouragement and support. Through Mr. Han's reassuring presence and gentle direction, Dre finds hope and perseveres. And this enables him to prevail against his archrival, Cheng, in a concluding match.

Perhaps there are youth in your class who are struggling with loneliness and dejection. They can benefit from the reminder in Isaiah 59:16 and 21 that God has not forsaken them, just as He did not abandon the innocent living in Judah. The Redeemer's supporting, guiding presence can give saved teens the strength they need to serve Him with renewed hope and vigor.

LESSON 10 — AUGUST 9

A CALL TO REFORM

BACKGROUND SCRIPTURE: Ezra 7:1, 6, 21-28; Jeremiah 7:1-15
DEVOTIONAL READING: Jeremiah 26:8-15

Key Verse: Thus saith the Lord of hosts, the God of Israel, Amend your ways and your doings, and I will cause you to dwell in this place. Jeremiah 7:3.

KING JAMES VERSION

JEREMIAH 7:1 The word that came to Jeremiah from the LORD, saying, 2 Stand in the gate of the LORD'S house, and proclaim there this word, and say, Hear the word of the LORD, all ye of Judah, that enter in at these gates to worship the LORD. 3 Thus saith the LORD of hosts, the God of Israel, Amend your ways and your doings, and I will cause you to dwell in this place. 4 Trust ye not in lying words, saying, The temple of the LORD, The temple of the LORD, The temple of the LORD, are these. 5 For if ye throughly amend your ways and your doings; if ye throughly execute judgment between a man and his neighbour; 6 If ye oppress not the stranger, the fatherless, and the widow, and shed not innocent blood in this place, neither walk after other gods to your hurt: 7 Then will I cause you to dwell in this place, in the land that I gave to your fathers, for ever and ever. 8 Behold, ye trust in lying words, that cannot profit. 9 Will ye steal, murder, and commit adultery, and swear falsely, and burn incense unto Baal, and walk after other gods whom ye know not; 10 And come and stand before me in this house, which is called by my name, and say, We are delivered to do all these abominations? 11 Is this house, which is called by my name, become a den of robbers in your eyes? Behold, even I have seen it, saith the LORD. 12 But go ye now unto my place which was in Shiloh, where I set my name at the first, and see what I did to it for the wickedness of my people Israel. 13 And now, because ye have done all these works, saith the LORD, and I spake unto you, rising up early and speaking, but ye heard not; and I called you, but ye answered not; 14 Therefore will I do unto this house, which is called by my name, wherein ye trust, and unto the place which I gave to you and to your fathers, as I have done to Shiloh. 15 And I will cast you out of my sight, as I have cast out all your brethren, even the whole seed of Ephraim.

NEW REVISED STANDARD VERSION

JEREMIAH 7:1 The word that came to Jeremiah from the LORD: 2 Stand in the gate of the LORD's house, and proclaim there this word, and say, Hear the word of the LORD, all you people of Judah, you that enter these gates to worship the LORD. 3 Thus says the LORD of hosts, the God of Israel: Amend your ways and your doings, and let me dwell with you in this place. 4 Do not trust in these deceptive words: "This is the temple of the LORD, the temple of the LORD, the temple of the LORD."

5 For if you truly amend your ways and your doings, if you truly act justly one with another, 6 if you do not oppress the alien, the orphan, and the widow, or shed innocent blood in this place, and if you do not go after other gods to your own hurt, 7 then I will dwell with you in this place, in the land that I gave of old to your ancestors forever and ever.

8 Here you are, trusting in deceptive words to no avail. 9 Will you steal, murder, commit adultery, swear falsely, make offerings to Baal, and go after other gods that you have not known, 10 and then come and stand before me in this house, which is called by my name, and say, "We are safe!"—only to go on doing all these abominations? 11 Has this house, which is called by my name, become a den of robbers in your sight? You know, I too am watching, says the LORD. 12 Go now to my place that was in Shiloh, where I made my name dwell at first, and see what I did to it for the wickedness of my people Israel. 13 And now, because you have done all these things, says the LORD, and when I spoke to you persistently, you did not listen, and when I called you, you did not answer, 14 therefore I will do to the house that is called by my name, in which you trust, and to the place that I gave to you and to your ancestors, just what I did to Shiloh. 15 And I will cast you out of my sight, just as I cast out all your kinsfolk, all the offspring of Ephraim.

Home Bible Readings

Monday, August 3	Psalm 140:6-13	*Justice for the Poor*
Tuesday, August 4	Jeremiah 18:11-17	*My People Have Forgotten Me*
Wednesday, August 5	Ezra 7:21-28	*Judgment for the Disobedient*
Thursday, August 6	Jeremiah 26:1-7	*If You Will Not Listen*
Friday, August 7	Jeremiah 26:8-15	*Amend Your Ways and Your Doings*
Saturday, August 8	Psalm 78:56-62	*God Abandoned Shiloh*
Sunday, August 9	Jeremiah 7:1-15	*Let Me Dwell with You*

Background

The name of the principal deity of Canaan was "Baal" (Jer. 7:9). It devotees regarded Baal to be the supreme, cosmic god who controlled the amount of fertility that people, animals, and the land experienced. Israel's pagan neighbors also venerated "other gods."

The foremost idols of Aram (or Syria) included Hadad (a storm-god), Mot (the god of death), Anath (a fierce goddess of war and love), and Rimmon (a god of thunder). Eshmun (a fertility god) was the chief deity of Sidon. Chemosh (a savage war-god) was the principal idol of Moab. Molech (or Milcom, an astral deity) was the chief god of the Ammonites. Dagon (a grain deity) and Baal-Zebub (a god of health and divination) were the foremost idols of the Philistines.

Notes on the Printed Text

Jeremiah 7 through 10 contain a series of oracles from the Lord to Jeremiah that focus on the Jerusalem temple (7:1). As noted in lesson 4 of the September quarter, the people of Judah incorrectly assumed that because of the presence of this sanctuary, God would always lavish His approval on the nation. They also mistakenly concluded that the Babylonians would fail in their attempts to overrun Jerusalem. The Lord used Jeremiah to challenge and discredit the Judahites' false confidence in the temple of God. Scholars have noted the strong overlap in content appearing in chapters 7 and 26. Based on this observation, they conclude that the oracle recorded in chapter 7 might have been delivered during Jehoiakim's reign (609–598 B.C.; see 1:3; 26:1).

Regrettably, King Josiah's extensive reforms died when he did, and the idolatry of the Canaanites rapidly reemerged in Judah during the early reign of Josiah's son, Jehoiakim. So, late in 609 or early in 608 B.C., the Lord instructed Jeremiah to deliver a warning to the worshipers at the temple. Following God's directions, Jeremiah positioned himself by the gate of the sanctuary, namely, the entrance located in the wall that separated the inner and outer courts (perhaps the New Gate; see 26:10). From there, he could address all those who entered the temple complex to venerate God and acknowledge His lordship (7:2).

Even though the Judahites attended temple activities, their religion was nothing but insincere ritual. The Lord of heaven's armies was not fooled by such disingenuous behavior. As the sovereign King of the universe (see 2:19; 5:14; 6:6, 9), God not only charged His people with hypocrisy, but also threatened to judge them for violating the stipulations of the Mosaic covenant. In 7:3, the Lord exhorted His people to "amend" their lives. The verse is more literally translated, "make good your ways and your deeds" and indicates that the entire pattern of their attitude and conduct needed to be consistent with their apparent worship. If the Judahites changed how they behaved, especially in doing what was right, God said He would allow them to continue to live in the promised land. Otherwise, He would expel them from it (see Lev. 26; Deut. 28).

In defiance of God's judgment oracle delivered through Jeremiah, the false prophets repeated the slogan, "The temple of the LORD" (Jer. 7:4). They deluded themselves and their patrons into thinking that endlessly chanting this incantation would ward off any disastrous outcome. Surely God would not allow His own home to be destroyed—or so they believed. But the Lord's true spokesperson warned the leaders and people of Judah that trusting in the Jerusalem temple would not keep their city and nation safe from destruction. Furthermore, the would-be seers who declared otherwise had uttered fraudulent, useless statements and were not to be trusted.

A century earlier (701 B.C.), the Lord had delivered Jerusalem from the invading armies of Assyria, commanded by Sennacherib (see Isa. 37:36-37). Later, King Josiah refurbished the rundown temple as a major part of his reform (see 2 Chron. 34:8-13). In Jeremiah's time, the "temple theology" of the false prophets concluded that none of Judah's enemies could touch the sanctuary—or, for that matter, the people who worshiped there. In contrast, the Lord revealed that the temple was not some sort of magical charm that would turn away evil. The only thing that would protect Jerusalem was the people's obedience to their covenant with God.

Accordingly, the Lord exhorted His wayward people to honor Him with correct beliefs and righteous actions. For instance, they were to deal fairly and humanely with the most vulnerable groups in society (Jer. 7:5). This included ending all forms of exploitation of foreigners, orphans, and widows. God's decree also involved eliminating all aspects of bloodshed, idolatry, and oppression of the powerless (vs. 6). When the leaders and people of Judah honored God by their actions, they would enjoy the only security they needed to continue living in the promised land (vs. 7). But if the rich and powerful tyrannized the defenseless, murdered the innocent, and venerated pagan deities, God would judge them for their crimes. Moreover, no amount of confidence in the erroneous beliefs uttered by religious charlatans would deliver the nation from ruin (vs. 8).

There are several reasons why the Jerusalem temple was so important to the people living in Judah. The ornate sanctuary was a symbol of God's holiness, His covenant with Israel, and His willingness to forgive their sins. The Lord used the temple to centralize worship at Jerusalem. In the sanctuary, God's people could spend time in prayer.

Finally, its design, furniture, and customs were object lessons that prepared the people for the advent of the Messiah. The goodness and grace of God, as represented by the Jerusalem temple, should have prompted the leaders and inhabitants of Judah to revere the Lord exclusively and treat the defenseless in a compassionate and caring manner. Instead, the nation brazenly violated at least five of the Ten Commandments (see Exod. 20:1-17; Deut. 5:6-21). Specifically, they were guilty of theft, murder, adultery, lying, and idolatry (Jer. 7:9; see Hos. 4:2).

After wantonly disregarding the Mosaic covenant, the people of Judah had the audacity to trot off to the Jerusalem temple to offer sacrifices. The fact that the sanctuary bore the Lord's holy "name" (Jer. 7:10) meant He had claimed it as His own and exercised complete authority over it (see 1 Kings 8:41-43; 2 Chron. 6:33). Yet, the nation's leaders and inhabitants desecrated the temple by using it as a pretext for iniquity. Supposedly, the people could breathe a sigh of relief as they asserted, "We are delivered" (Jer. 7:10). In response, the Lord wanted to know whether they really were safe. After all, they mistakenly assumed they could persist in committing one abhorrent crime after another without experiencing the Creator's wrath.

God declared that He would not overlook the crimes the people of Judah committed. The seriousness of their iniquities is emphasized in the Hebrew text by the placement of the phrase rendered "den of robbers" at the very beginning of verse 11. In short, the Lord announced His house of worship had been defiled by it being turned into a hideout for thieves. This was not an unfounded charge. It was backed by God's personal knowledge of the situation. Bible students note that Jesus quoted part of this verse (along with Isa. 56:7; see Matt. 21:13; Mark 11:17; Luke 19:46). In Jesus' day, money-hungry vendors and bankers had made the Jerusalem temple a haven for their wicked practices. In a display of righteous indignation, He emptied the sanctuary of these despicable people (vs. 12).

Babylon's deportation of Judah from the land was the catastrophe looming on the horizon. As Jeremiah 7:7 revealed, if God's people abandoned their evil ways and lived uprightly, He would allow them to remain in Judah. This was the land of promise He had given to their ancestors as a perpetual inheritance. To impress upon the Judahites the certainty of the judgment that awaited them, God noted what had happened to Shiloh many years earlier (vs. 12). This town was located in the hill country of Ephraim, about 20 miles north of Jerusalem. Shiloh was once the center of worship for the 12 tribes of Israel, from the time of Joshua until the end of the period of the judges (see Josh. 18:1; Judg. 18:31; 1 Sam. 1:3; 4:3-4). Because the people living there were wicked, God allowed the city to be overthrown.

The Hebrew text of Jeremiah 7:13 literally says that God's spokespersons were "rising up early [in the morning] and speaking." The idea behind this idiom is that the prophets whom the Lord sent had called on His people over and over again to repent. But the inhabitants of Judah had refused to listen to God's messengers, and the people continued to offend Him with their idolatry. They seemed to have heard the message so often that they just tuned it out. The people of Judah had not entirely stopped worshiping God. In fact, archaeological evidence dating to this time period from the area of Judah confirms that the inhabitants still venerated the Lord, but often as just another god alongside the old Canaanite and foreign deities.

The preceding practice is called syncretism. Pottery inscriptions have been found addressed "To Yahweh and his Asherah," showing that people believed the Lord had a female consort, just like the other pagan gods. Carved goddess figurines also have been unearthed, many from the area of Jerusalem near the site of the temple. Interestingly, almost no figurines have been found dating to the period after the Babylonian exile. Captivity seems to have burned out the corruption from God's people.

In Jeremiah's day, despite the importance of the Jerusalem temple, it would not shield God's people from His hand of discipline. The Lord knew the crimes the inhabitants of Judah had committed, and He would deal firmly with them for their wicked ways. The Lord declared that He would allow the promised land and the sanctuary in the holy city to be devastated, just as He permitted Shiloh to be destroyed (7:14). The residents of Judah knew that God had allowed the 10 northern tribes—their relatives, the descendants of Ephraim—to be conquered by the Assyrians and deported from their land (see 2 Kings 17:6, 20). The Lord promised that He would also thrust the people of Judah from His presence (Jer. 7:15; see Deut. 28:64-68; 29:28).

SUGGESTIONS TO TEACHERS

Jeremiah 7:14 reveals that the leaders and people of Judah placed their trust in the Jerusalem temple to shield them from divine judgment. Even today believers can misplace their trust. The three primary ways are undue confidence in circumstances, other people, or ourselves.

1. THE PROBLEM OF EVIL. With so much evil and injustice in the world, it is sometimes difficult to discern how God is working through various circumstances. Like people in ancient times, we might feel upset or discouraged by the crime and hatred all around us. God's answer to us is the same as He would have given back then. He wants us to be patient and place our confidence exclusively in Him. We can trust Him to bring about His perfect justice in His time.

2. THE WISE PLANS OF GOD. All of us go through times when life seems bleak and hopeless. If we had to rely solely on ourselves, our circumstances, or others, we would surely lose hope. The way to prevent this from happening is to continue to rely on the Lord. We can rest assured that He is directing all things according to His wise plans. We also know that He will never let us down, regardless of how difficult our times might be.

3. THE SUPREME POWER OF GOD. It is not always easy for us to be patient when we see a multitude of wrongs taking place all around us. We should remember that God is in full control and that His timing, not ours, is perfect. If we find the sinful activities of the world abhorrent, He does even more. As the sovereign and just Lord, He cannot allow iniquity to go unpunished forever. At the right moment, He will deal with all who have rebelled. Until then, we need to continue to trust Him fully, even when we cannot figure out why He has allowed certain events to take place.

4. THE FOCAL POINT OF FAITH. The world is filled with egotistical, self-satisfied people who place all their confidence in themselves. We know from this week's lesson that ultimately such individuals will fail. This reminds us that we must trust in God for temporal and eternal matters. We are saved through faith in Jesus, and we live each day by continuing to trust in Him.

FOR ADULTS

■ **TOPIC:** Doing Justice

■ **QUESTIONS:** 1. Why did the Lord direct Jeremiah to position himself at the gate of the temple? 2. In what ways had the people of Judah acted unjustly? 3. What precondition did God make for His people remaining in Judah? 4. Why is it pernicious when Christians trust in anyone or anything other than the Lord? 5. Why can't the rituals of worship compensate for the lack of a growing relationship with God?

■ **ILLUSTRATIONS:**

Spiritual Blindness. The kicking in of their gate awakened an elderly Jewish couple living in Cottbus, Germany. Neo-Nazis shouted, "Come out! We'll beat you all to death!" After the thugs moved on, the emotional fright lingered. What if they returned?

German police offered the couple *Schutzhaft* (a word meaning "protective custody"). In another culture, the couple might have welcomed the offer. But the term *Schutzhaft* is an affront to German Jews. In Hitler's era, the Gestapo used it to round up and jail Jews. "Imagine what memories this triggered for me," the elderly man said. "I couldn't believe my ears."

As Jeremiah 7:1-15 reveals, spiritual blindness can grip individuals, groups, and even nations, especially as they forget God's ways. Today, Christians must be on guard to identify injustice, appreciate its gravity, and root it out. If not, spiritual blindness will inevitably result.

Impostors and Real Friends. How do you get a great parking space at a New York Yankees baseball game? One man thought he had a way. According to the Fresno, California *Bee*, this man pulled his car into the VIP parking lot and casually told the attendant that he was a friend of George Steinbrenner. Until his death in 2010, Steinbrenner was the principal owner and managing partner of the Yankees.

Unfortunately for the impostor, the person attending the parking lot that day was

George Steinbrenner himself, doing some personal investigation of traffic problems at the stadium. When he heard this, the surprised impostor looked at Steinbrenner and said, "Guess I've got the wrong lot." You can be sure that he did not park in the VIP lot that day or ever!

The owner knows his friends. The owner determines who gets in the VIP lot. According to Jeremiah 7:1-3, the Creator also knows who His friends are and who the impostors are. He determines the result of our actions and our lives.

Tune in to the Truth. A hundred years ago in Chicago, Montgomery Ward pioneered the mail-order catalog and the money-back guarantee. It built a department store empire of green-awninged buildings on Main Streets across the country.

After World War II, cross-town rival Sears Roebuck gambled everything it had on stores in suburban shopping centers. Montgomery Ward sneered at Sears and promised to buy up failed stores at pennies on the dollar. Sears Roebuck had seen the future of retail shopping. Meanwhile, Montgomery Ward began a 60-year slide into bankruptcy.

The people of Judah got fat and comfortable doing what they wanted. When God sent prophets such as Jeremiah to call them to live lives committed to Him, they laughed and listened to false prophets, who told them what they wanted to hear. We need to be bold enough to stay tuned to God's truth, even when others around us ignore it.

For Youth

■ **Topic:** Hope or Doom

■ **Questions:** 1. Why did the Lord exhort His people to reform their ways? 2. What distorted beliefs did the Judahites have about the temple? 3. Why did the Lord, through Jeremiah, mention the town of Shiloh? 4. What can Christians do to ensure that the Lord is the center of their trust? 5. What is the connection between a life of integrity and worshiping God?

■ **Illustrations:**

A Safe Place. The people in Jeremiah's day incorrectly believed the Jerusalem temple would keep them safe from all harm. The Lord's spokesperson declared that this sanctuary would not shield the nation's inhabitants from God's judgment on their sins.

In the days of the pioneers, prairie fires posed a life-threatening problem. Even horses could not outrun the spread of wildfire in open land. So what did the pioneers do when they saw that a prairie fire was on its way? They took a match and burned the grass in a designated area around them. Then they took their stand in the burned area. As the roar of the flames approached, they didn't need to be afraid. Even as the ocean of fire surged around them, they had no fear because fire had already passed over the place where they stood.

When the judgment of God comes to sweep people into hell for eternity, there is one spot that is safe. Two thousand years ago the wrath of God was poured out on Calvary. There the Son of God took the wrath that should have fallen on us. Now, if we take our stand by the cross, we are safe for time and eternity. We do not need to fear, because hell's fires can no longer reach us.

They Won't Listen. Talking to a friend who's made up his or her mind to disobey God can be a lot like the guy who called Information to get the telephone number for *Theatre Arts* magazine. "I'm sorry," the operator drawled after a long pause. "There's no one listed by the name of Theodore Hartz."

"It's not a person," the caller explained. "It's a publication. I want *Theatre Arts*." The operator's voice grew cold, and she spoke in clear, loud tones: "I told you, we have no listing for Theodore Hartz." The caller's temper flared and he shouted, "Listen, you ninny. The word is Theatre: T-H-E-A-T-R-E." The operator's training helped her control herself, and she replied sweetly, "Sir, that is not the way to spell Theodore," and disconnected from the call.

When you're thinking along the lines of God's Word and your friend is thinking along the lines of selfishness or rebellion, it takes a long time to connect. Anger never helps. Patience and love are keys to keep communication going. Remember, there are no guarantees that you will succeed any better than Jeremiah did with the leaders and people of Judah in his day.

Hidden Treasure. In the motion picture *Charade*, Cary Grant and Audrey Hepburn search for a treasure hidden in plain view by Hepburn's mysterious husband, who is thrown from a train as the opening credits roll. Everyone—good guys and bad guys—combs through the handful of personal effects Charles left on the train.

A child innocently pursuing his hobby discovers that the three stamps on Charles's unmailed letter to his wife are the most rare specimens in the world. Every villain and hero in the movie had handled that letter. They all had looked at the stamps, but no one really "saw" them. They couldn't break the habit of ignoring the envelope while focusing on the letter inside it.

The people of Judah had become habitual idolaters. Jeremiah's messages from the Lord made no sense to them. So, the people made the same spiritually disastrous errors over and over because they were ingrained in the way they lived every day. When we let sinful thinking or behaving become our normal way of responding in an area of life, we will have trouble recognizing the true value of God's Word. It will seem irrelevant.

LESSON 11 — AUGUST 16

A CALL TO OBEY

BACKGROUND SCRIPTURE: Ezekiel 18; Proverbs 21:2-15
DEVOTIONAL READING: Hosea 14

Key Verse: Cast away from you all your transgressions, whereby ye have transgressed; and make you a new heart and a new spirit: for why will ye die, O house of Israel? Ezekiel 18:31.

KING JAMES VERSION

EZEKIEL 18:1 The word of the LORD came unto me again, saying, 2 What mean ye, that ye use this proverb concerning the land of Israel, saying, The fathers have eaten sour grapes, and the children's teeth are set on edge? 3 As I live, saith the Lord GOD, ye shall not have occasion any more to use this proverb in Israel. 4 Behold, all souls are mine; as the soul of the father, so also the soul of the son is mine: the soul that sinneth, it shall die. 5 But if a man be just, and do that which is lawful and right, 6 And hath not eaten upon the mountains, neither hath lifted up his eyes to the idols of the house of Israel, neither hath defiled his neighbour's wife, neither hath come near to a menstruous woman, 7 And hath not oppressed any, but hath restored to the debtor his pledge, hath spoiled none by violence, hath given his bread to the hungry, and hath covered the naked with a garment; 8 He that hath not given forth upon usury, neither hath taken any increase, that hath withdrawn his hand from iniquity, hath executed true judgment between man and man, 9 Hath walked in my statutes, and hath kept my judgments, to deal truly; he is just, he shall surely live, saith the Lord GOD.

10 If he beget a son that is a robber, a shedder of blood, and that doeth the like to any one of these things, 11 And that doeth not any of those duties, but even hath eaten upon the mountains, and defiled his neighbour's wife, 12 Hath oppressed the poor and needy, hath spoiled by violence, hath not restored the pledge, and hath lifted up his eyes to the idols, hath committed abomination, 13 Hath given forth upon usury, and hath taken increase: shall he then live? he shall not live: he hath done all these abominations; he shall surely die; his blood shall be upon him. . . .

31 Cast away from you all your transgressions, whereby ye have transgressed; and make you a new heart and a new spirit: for why will ye die, O house of Israel? 32 For I have no pleasure in the death of him that dieth, saith the Lord GOD: wherefore turn yourselves, and live ye.

NEW REVISED STANDARD VERSION

EZEKIEL 18:1 The word of the LORD came to me: 2 What do you mean by repeating this proverb concerning the land of Israel, "The parents have eaten sour grapes, and the children's teeth are set on edge"? 3 As I live, says the Lord GOD, this proverb shall no more be used by you in Israel. 4 Know that all lives are mine; the life of the parent as well as the life of the child is mine: it is only the person who sins that shall die.

5 If a man is righteous and does what is lawful and right— 6 if he does not eat upon the mountains or lift up his eyes to the idols of the house of Israel, does not defile his neighbor's wife or approach a woman during her menstrual period, 7 does not oppress anyone, but restores to the debtor his pledge, commits no robbery, gives his bread to the hungry and covers the naked with a garment, 8 does not take advance or accrued interest, withholds his hand from iniquity, executes true justice between contending parties, 9 follows my statutes, and is careful to observe my ordinances, acting faithfully—such a one is righteous; he shall surely live, says the Lord GOD.

10 If he has a son who is violent, a shedder of blood, 11 who does any of these things (though his father does none of them), who eats upon the mountains, defiles his neighbor's wife, 12 oppresses the poor and needy, commits robbery, does not restore the pledge, lifts up his eyes to the idols, commits abomination, 13 takes advance or accrued interest; shall he then live? He shall not. He has done all these abominable things; he shall surely die; his blood shall be upon himself. . . .

31 Cast away from you all the transgressions that you have committed against me, and get yourselves a new heart and a new spirit! Why will you die, O house of Israel? 32 For I have no pleasure in the death of anyone, says the Lord GOD. Turn, then, and live.

401

Home Bible Readings

Monday, August 10	Isaiah 1:24-28	*Justice and Repentance*
Tuesday, August 11	Proverbs 21:10-15	*Justice: A Joy to the Righteous*
Wednesday, August 12	Ezekiel 18:14-19	*A Parent's Negative Example*
Thursday, August 13	Ezekiel 18:21-28	*Changing Behaviors*
Friday, August 14	Proverbs 21:2-8	*The Lord Weighs the Heart*
Saturday, August 15	Hosea 14	*Walking in the Lord's Ways*
Sunday, August 16	Ezekiel 18:1-13, 31-32	*The Person Who Sins Shall Die*

Background

Together, the Greek and Hebrew words for "heart" are used over 900 times in Scripture. In all these references, few are referring to the heart as a literal, physical organ. A rare example of the literal use is found in Exodus 28:29-30, where Aaron was instructed to wear the breastpiece of decision over his heart whenever he entered the Lord's presence in the Holy Place. Almost always, the heart is presented in the Bible as the symbolic seat of human intellect, emotions, or will.

For example, the intellectual concept is in view in Genesis 6:5, where it is recorded that God "saw that the wickedness of man was great in the earth, and that every imagination of the thoughts of his heart was only evil continually." This verse is immediately followed by one in which the heart is seen as the center of emotion, for humankind's wickedness "grieved [God] at his heart" (vs. 6). The psalmist described the heart as the wellspring of the will when he declared, "Blessed are they that keep his testimonies, and that seek him with the whole heart" (Ps. 119:2).

Notes on the Printed Text

In Ezekiel 18:1-2, we learn about a popular proverb that was circulating among the Jews in Jerusalem and Babylon. The Hebrew noun rendered "proverb" signified a comparison of some sort, but it came to mean any wise or moralistic saying. Proverbs are usually thought of as short, pithy sayings, while parables are extended stories. But the distinction is not hard and fast among biblical writers. In this case, when the parents ate "sour grapes," allegedly the mouths of their children became numb from the bitter taste of the unripe fruit (see Jer. 31:29). Behind this adage was the recognition that normally one person's unpleasant experience could not be transferred to someone else.

Granted, the moral and spiritual decay of one generation might have profound, long-lasting effects upon those who follow (see Matt. 23:35-36). But Ezekiel's peers quoted the popular maxim so they could excuse themselves of responsibility. The proverb, which seems to be based on a misunderstanding of Exodus 20:5 and Numbers 14:18, meant that because of the sins of previous generations, the present one was suffering. According to this logic, one generation could blame their troubles on the misdeeds of previous generations. Even more distressing was the fact that the adage, as it was improperly applied by the exiles, asserted that God was punishing their generation for the transgressions their ancestors had committed. Expressed differently, in a miscarriage of justice, God was unfair in the way He treated His people.

The phrase "as I live" (Ezek. 18:3) indicates that the Lord was making a solemn oath (see 5:11; 14:16; 20:3). As noted in lesson 3, since there was no one greater than Him, He swore by His own life when He revealed His will. It was His desire that the Jews no longer use the proverb about intergenerational responsibility, for it represented a warped view of how He executed justice. Since God does not punish the innocent for the sins of the guilty, He rejected outright the Israelites' attempt to avoid guilt for their own idolatry and disobedience.

Furthermore, God was offended by His peoples' audacity in hiding behind this patently untrue notion. So, the supreme Lord declared that this widespread adage of the exiles would be repeated in Israel no more. In verse 4, God announced that every living entity belonged to Him, including the parent and the child. As the Creator of life, He had the right to execute judgment as He desired. It was His unchanging will that guilt would not be transferred from one generation to the next. Only the person who sinned would die for his or her sins (see also the similar point made in Jer. 31:30).

The overriding truth in Ezekiel 18 is that people are held responsible for their own sin, and that guilt is not transferred across generations. To illustrate this fact, God presented three hypothetical situations. He talked about a man (vss. 5-9), his son (vss. 10-13), and his grandson (vss. 14-18). The first example concerned a person of integrity who lived justly and righteously and was fully obedient to God's law (vs. 5). The individual of moral rectitude did not practice idolatry or pagan practices of any kind. Furthermore, he was faithful to laws governing relationships with other Israelites (vs. 6). For example, he maintained sexual purity. This is probably a reference to the Mosaic law's prohibitions against adultery and having intercourse with a woman during her period of menstruation (see Exod. 20:14; Lev. 18:19).

Ezekiel described the righteous man as a person who refused to oppress anyone. For instance, he would not keep as collateral for a loan any item the borrower might require, such as a cloak needed for warmth at night (see Exod. 22:26). He would never steal from anyone (see Exod. 20:15). On the contrary, he gave food and clothing to the needy. This Israelite of exemplary character cared more about giving to others than receiving anything for himself (Ezek. 18:7). In financial matters, if the upright person made a loan to anyone, his dealings were fair (vs. 8). "Given forth upon usury" meant to charge an exorbitant amount of interest. The phrase "taken any increase" refers to exploiting the destitute to amass a fortune.

The Mosaic law allowed interest on loans to Gentiles, but not on those made to fellow Israelites (see Deut. 23:19-20). Whether the hypothetical loan here was to a Gentile or an Israelite, in either case, the virtuous person's conduct was praiseworthy.

It was divine law that guided him in all his financial dealings, not the profit motive. The devout Israelite tried to do what was right and fair in every situation by carefully observing God's statutes and regulations (Ezek. 18:9). This person's outward actions revealed an inner moral character that was firmly based on obedience to the covenant. In keeping with a life based on God's grace, the upright would not suffer judgment for the misdeeds committed by others. We learn from the New Testament that righteousness is not simply a matter of adhering to a checklist of rules. Instead, the believers' life of virtue results from their restored relationship with the Father through faith in His Son (see Rom. 3:21-31; Eph. 3:8-10; Titus 2:11-14).

After Ezekiel discussed the case of the righteous person, he set forth two more hypothetical cases to confirm the principle of individual responsibility. The second illustration supposes that the virtuous father had a cutthroat son (Ezek. 18:10). Unlike his father, the son ate pagan sacrifices on the hilltops and was physically intimate with someone else's wife (vs. 11). The abhorrent crimes this reprobate committed also included murdering the innocent, cheating the impoverished, extorting the defenseless, and venerating idols (vs. 12). God's judgment upon the wicked son was clear and decisive. He would surely be punished for his atrocious behavior. Indeed, death would be the penalty this tyrant experienced for the guilt of his iniquities (vs. 13; see Lev. 20:9, 11-12, 16, 27). Moreover, the son would derive no benefit from his father's upright character and conduct.

The final hypothetical case presented by Ezekiel involved a third generation. The righteous father's wicked son now had a son of his own. This individual witnessed all the iniquities his father had committed (Ezek. 18:14). But instead of following in his father's evil footsteps, the son followed the example of his upright grandfather (compare vss. 15-17 with vss. 6-8 and 11-13). The conclusion, based on God's principle of individual responsibility, is inescapable. The last son would not die because of his father's wrongdoing. Instead, the virtuous son would live due to his own integrity, not that of his grandfather. Also, the father would receive the just consequences of his evil deeds (vs. 18).

Moreover, the current generation of idolatrous, disobedient Israelites would be responsible for the fall of the nation—not generations past. So, the only hope of avoiding calamity was for the people to repent of their sin (vs. 30). By casting away all of their past transgressions, they would not be dragged down and ruined by their iniquity. The Lord questioned whether His people really wanted to be put to death for their sins. Accordingly, He urged them to allow the Holy Spirit to bring spiritual revival among them. Indeed, only He could give each of them a "new heart and a new spirit" (vs. 31; see 11:19; 36:26; see also the commentary in lesson 2 of the September quarter on Jeremiah 31:33).

Abandoning their sinful ways and embracing the will of the Lord would enable the exiles of Ezekiel's day to think pure thoughts and remain faithful to God. It would also prevent the all-powerful Creator from putting people to death because of their sins. After all, He did not delight in condemning a person. He wanted all people to turn away from the precipice of destruction and live by trusting in and obeying Him (Ezek. 18:23, 32). God longed to give His people a new heart and spirit that would result in renewed hope, purpose, and power in Israel. Only this would bring pleasure to the Lord. But God's offer of grace was refused. So, from the rulers of Israel to the beggar on the street, God's people were destined to feel His wrath.

SUGGESTIONS TO TEACHERS

Even today God calls us to live according to His values. We need to place our lifestyles and priorities under the focus of His Word and see what is reflected before Him and the world. If we are true to His teachings, then we will please our Lord and draw others to Him. If we are not true, then we need to change our lifestyles, or like the people of Ezekiel's day, we will incur His displeasure.

1. A NEW HONESTY. God does not accept blame-shifting for anyone's sin. He would not let the exiles in Babylon blame their ancestors for the judgment they were facing. He wanted them to know that He responds to individuals on the basis of their own behavior, not that of their parents or children. Urge your students to examine their lives to see whether they tend to blame their past or their situation for their mistakes or sin. God understands the influences that affect people, but He doesn't accept excuses for sin.

2. A NEW ACCOUNTABILITY. Ezekiel taught that even in a family—the most closely-knit human social unit—each individual must account for his or her actions before God. Ezekiel was not downplaying the importance of family relationships. Instead, he was emphasizing personal accountability. Help your students explore the significance of that truth for themselves. Adults are not responsible before God for the mistakes of their children. Also, young people are not limited in God's eyes by the failures of their parents.

3. A NEW START. Ezekiel taught that a person's spiritual condition could change. One's parents don't determine it, and it isn't locked in by one's past or present behavior. A habitual sinner can turn from his or her sin, commit to obeying God, and enjoy the eternal life that God gives. Ezekiel viewed repentance primarily from this perspective. You can expand on the idea of repentance from sins by relating the concept to faith in the sacrificial death of Jesus as the payment for those transgressions.

4. A NEW EQUITY. The exiles from Judah who were living in Babylon, accused God of unfairness for punishing them, for they believed their ancestors were the ones who had provoked Him to act. God asserted that they were the unfair ones for refusing to accept responsibility for their own wicked actions. In the case of those who were formerly wicked, it was only God's grace that prevented them from dying before they repented. And in the case of those who were formerly upright, it would only be God's mercy that would spare them. In either situation, the Lord's desire was for all people to abandon their rebellious acts and trust in His Son for eternal life.

5. A NEW HEART. Ezekiel 18:31 reveals that effective repentance and renewed living depends on a new heart and a new spirit. Both Ezekiel and Jeremiah anticipated a future era when God would relate to His people in a new way, one that would change people's motivation and ability to live by God's standards. We are living in that era now with the advent of the Messiah.

FOR ADULTS

■ **TOPIC:** The Error of Our Ways

■ **QUESTIONS:** 1. What was it about the false proverb that disturbed God? 2. How did God pledge to deal with righteous and wicked people? 3. Why were God's people wrong to accuse Him of unfairness? 4. Why does God want us to shun the wicked ways of the world? 5. How are others negatively affected when we refuse to accept personal responsibility for our misdeeds?

■ **ILLUSTRATIONS:**

Turn and Live! Ezekiel 18 reminds us that the effects of sin can be cumulative and impart moral and spiritual decay from one generation to the next. Yet, we also learn that each person in each generation will answer to God for his or her own moral choices.

In one of the favorite anecdotes from Clarence Day's *Life with Father*, his father tries to sew on a button, stabs himself with a needle, and then blames his wife for his bloody finger and shirt. After all, she was talking to him and spoiled his concentration!

We can all tell similar stories, but it's hard to admit how easily we slip into the blaming mode. That's why it is refreshing to hear someone say, "I'm sorry. It was my fault." We have to learn to say this to others and to God. When we acknowledge our wrongdoing, it brings healing and joy to our lives.

Why Would Anyone Argue with God? The people of Ezekiel's day accused God of being unfair when He held them accountable for their sins. They were like the naval officer who realized his lifelong ambition when he was given command of a battleship. One stormy night, as the powerful vessel sailed toward a harbor, the lookout spotted a strange light rapidly closing with them.

Immediately the captain ordered his signalman to flash the message, "Alter your course ten degrees to port." Almost instantly the reply came, "Alter your course ten degrees to port."

Determined to take a back seat to no one, the officer sent this message: "Alter course ten degrees. I am a highly decorated captain." Back came the reply: "Alter your course ten degrees. I am a third class seaman."

Infuriated, the captain grabbed the signal lamp and flashed, "Alter course. I'm a battleship." Back came: "Alter your course. I'm a lighthouse."

The moral of this story is that we shouldn't argue with God, for He knows where the "rocks" are (metaphorically speaking). He doesn't want anybody to end up spiritually shipwrecked. Also, He wants everyone to trust in the Messiah. Of course, they have to heed His warnings about death and life and do what He says.

A Parent's Discipline. Jake's dad occasionally took a standardized approach to discipline. It was a one-punishment-fits-all deal. There were times when, unable to sort through all the lies, blame shifting, and wheedling of his three children, the father just hushed them up and administered punishments to all of them. *Case closed.*

Usually, in these situations, Jake's dad realized that all three of his children shared at least a little of the blame for whatever had happened. So the siblings rarely got a punishment they flat-out didn't deserve. But from time to time, one of the children did get a punishment they didn't have coming. Of course, Jake's dad, in his limited ability to know what had really taken place, could only operate on his instincts and experience. While those were pretty good, there were certainly times when the parent got it wrong. In those instances, his children felt the sting of injustice.

Our heavenly Father has no such limitations. He doesn't need to take a one-discipline-fits-all approach in dealing with His children. He doesn't operate on mere instincts or experience. Ezekiel 18 reveals that we will never be blamed for someone else's sin, nor will they be blamed for ours. After all, nothing we do is hidden from God. Also, where our attitudes and actions are concerned, He will administer to us only what is fair and just. *Case closed.*

For Youth

■ **Topic:** A New Heart Builds a Just Community

■ **Questions:** 1. What was the nature of the proverb being quoted by the Jewish exiles in Babylon? 2. What could God's people do to avoid the downfall caused by their sin? 3. What awaited the wicked if they repented of their sin? 4. How can believers avoid playing the "blame game"? 5. What does a believer's life look like when he or she is taking accountability to God seriously?

■ **Illustrations:**

Personal Consequences of Sin. How and why adolescents change is the subject of much social research, both by producers of consumer goods and political leaders. The upshot is that it's very hard to change our ingrained ways and habits. Ezekiel found this was true among the Jewish exiles in Babylon. They resented their troubles and complained that God was being unfair to them.

Even saved teens find it hard to accept God's ways as loving, true, wise, and just.

When we rebel, we need to confess our sin and ask God to renew us spiritually. He promises to cleanse us of our sin and bring about the transformation needed for us to live uprightly.

As long as we hide behind our excuses and shift blame for our sinful behavior, we'll never be free from its consequences. We'll always be angrily pointing our fingers, hiding, and hurting. Ezekiel 18 reveals that God wants something better for us. He wants to bring us peace and freedom. Yet, we can only receive it when we humble ourselves and come clean in His presence.

A New Spirit. You might suppose that the most important day in renowned novelist John Grisham's life was when he sold his first book or graduated from law school. Instead, he says it was one Sunday when he was eight years old. The Grishams were in Arkansas where John's father worked construction seven days a week. His mother always scrubbed her kids and took them to the local church for Sunday school and worship.

Grisham told an interviewer, "I came under conviction when I was in the third grade, and I talked with my mother. I told her, 'I don't understand this, but I need to talk to you.' We talked and she led me to Jesus. The following Sunday I made a public confirmation of my faith. In one sense, it was not terribly eventful for an eight-year-old, but it was the most important event in my life."

With the Spirit of God abiding within us, we are able to live for the Lord (see Ezek. 18:31). Regardless of who we are or what we do (even writing award-winning novels), our lives can be transformed by the power of God through faith in the Messiah.

Who's to Blame? A 19-year-old boy from a small Midwest town wrote his parents a note that said, "I'm out of control." Then he killed himself because he couldn't pay his gambling debts. Three East coast high schoolers were arrested for running a $6500-a-week sports betting operation. A 16-year-old paid off his gambling debts by turning his girlfriend into a prostitute. The Director of the Harvard Medical School Center for Addiction Studies said, "We will face in the next decade more problems with youth gambling than we'll face with drug use."

All of these young people were manipulated by adults to start gambling. Maybe their parents gambled, too. But no matter how much one can explain their behavior and understand what influenced it, one can't remove the responsibility each person had for what he or she did. That's because God holds each individual accountable for his or her actions.

When this life is over, we'll stand before God as our Judge, with all our excuses stripped away and with no choice but to own up to the truth. However, it is far more desirable to "own up" to God now, confess our sinful behavior to Him, and ask Him to forgive us. Only through the Father's grace in the Son can we find true no-fault living.

LESSON 12 — AUGUST 23

ADMINISTER TRUE JUSTICE

BACKGROUND SCRIPTURE: Zechariah 7:8-14; Isaiah 30:18-26
DEVOTIONAL READING: Psalm 147:1-11

Key Verse: Oppress not the widow, nor the fatherless, the stranger, nor the poor; and let none of you imagine evil against his brother in your heart. Zechariah 7:10.

KING JAMES VERSION

ZECHARIAH 7:8 And the word of the LORD came unto Zechariah, saying, 9 Thus speaketh the LORD of hosts, saying, Execute true judgment, and shew mercy and compassions every man to his brother:
10 And oppress not the widow, nor the fatherless, the stranger, nor the poor; and let none of you imagine evil against his brother in your heart. 11 But they refused to hearken, and pulled away the shoulder, and stopped their ears, that they should not hear. 12 Yea, they made their hearts as an adamant stone, lest they should hear the law, and the words which the LORD of hosts hath sent in his spirit by the former prophets: therefore came a great wrath from the LORD of hosts. 13 Therefore it is come to pass, that as he cried, and they would not hear; so they cried, and I would not hear, saith the LORD of hosts: 14 But I scattered them with a whirlwind among all the nations whom they knew not. Thus the land was desolate after them, that no man passed through nor returned: for they laid the pleasant land desolate.

NEW REVISED STANDARD VERSION

ZECHARIAH 7:8 The word of the LORD came to Zechariah, saying: 9 Thus says the LORD of hosts: Render true judgments, show kindness and mercy to one another; 10 do not oppress the widow, the orphan, the alien, or the poor; and do not devise evil in your hearts against one another. 11 But they refused to listen, and turned a stubborn shoulder, and stopped their ears in order not to hear. 12 They made their hearts adamant in order not to hear the law and the words that the LORD of hosts had sent by his spirit through the former prophets. Therefore great wrath came from the LORD of hosts. 13 Just as, when I called, they would not hear, so, when they called, I would not hear, says the LORD of hosts, 14 and I scattered them with a whirlwind among all the nations that they had not known. Thus the land they left was desolate, so that no one went to and fro, and a pleasant land was made desolate.

Home Bible Readings

Monday, August 17	Jeremiah 16:9-13	Wicked Behavior
Tuesday, August 18	2 Samuel 22:1-7	I Call upon the Lord
Wednesday, August 19	Psalm 147:1-11	Hope in God's Steadfast Love
Thursday, August 20	Judges 2:16-23	Walking in the Way
Friday, August 21	Deuteronomy 16:16-20	Pursue Justice and Only Justice
Saturday, August 22	Isaiah 30:18-26	The Lord Waits to Be Gracious
Sunday, August 23	Zechariah 7:8-14	The Results of Not Listening

Background

In 538 B.C., when the exiles returned to Jerusalem under Zerubbabel, they eagerly began work on rebuilding the temple (see Ezra 3:7-13). However, after the foundation was finished, the joy turned to discouragement as the enemies of Judah succeeded in stopping the construction (chap. 4). After almost 18 years of inactivity, God called Haggai and Zechariah to encourage the people to finish the temple. Both prophets began their ministry during the second year of King Darius, that is, in 520 B.C. Haggai completed his work that same year with messages that outlined the consequences of disobedience as well the results of obedience. Specifically, obedience brought blessing, while disobedience resulted in discipline.

Like Jeremiah and Ezekiel, Zechariah was both a priest and prophet. He was born in Babylon and returned to Jerusalem under the leadership of Zerubbabel and Joshua. Nehemiah 12:16 records that Zechariah succeeded his grandfather, Iddo, as head of that priestly family. Apparently, Zechariah's father died early or for some reason was not able to carry on the leadership of the family. Like Haggai, Zechariah encouraged the people to finish building the temple. Even though Zechariah and Haggai were contemporaries, Zechariah's ministry continued on long after that of his counterpart. For instance, in 519 B.C., he experienced a series of eight visions in one night, which are recorded in 1:7–6:8. Then, in 518 B.C., he urged his fellow Jews to repent (chap. 7) and experience the blessings God promised (chap. 8).

Notes on the Printed Text

On December 7, 518 B.C. (Zech. 7:1), a delegation from Bethel (vs. 2) went to the prophets (including Zechariah) and priests serving at the Jerusalem temple (vs. 3). The inquirers asked whether their faith community should continue to weep and fast during the "fifth month" (namely, about mid-July to mid-August in the Jewish calendar) on the anniversary of the temple's destruction. They maintained these practices throughout the duration of the captivity. Yet, now that the temple was being rebuilt and Jerusalem was once again inhabited, the delegation wanted to know whether it was necessary to continue these rituals of humiliation and repentance.

The all-powerful Lord, through Zechariah, responded to the delegation's inquiry with a series of rhetorical questions meant for all the returnees, including their civil leaders and priests (vss. 4-5). The Creator asked whether His people's ritual mourning was truly done for Him (see Isa. 1:11; Amos 5:21). It seems that while in Babylon, the exiles had turned the fasting into a time of self-pity. So, instead of feeling sorrow for their sins, they had lamented for themselves and their deplorable circumstances. They had focused solely on their problems, rather than on God and His righteousness.

The Lord's second question brought out the underlying self-interest of the ceremonies observed by the returnees. Specifically, during their holy festivals, their joyful celebrations were motivated by a desire to satiate their bodily appetites (Zech. 7:6). Put differently, their commemorative observances signified legalistic posturing, not heartfelt repentance to God. Just as they feasted for their own enjoyment, they used fasting to indulge their desire for sympathy and comfort. The denial of food had become times of mourning for themselves, not of remorse for how they had sinned against the Lord. Also, when the remnant in Jerusalem and Judah ate and drank, they gave little or no thought to their Creator, who had showered them with material and spiritual abundance.

The problem of meaningless religious exercise was not unique to the returnees of Zechariah's generation. The third question recorded in verse 7 indicates that the former prophets—such as Isaiah, Jeremiah, and Ezekiel—proclaimed the same sort of message that Zechariah delivered (see 2 Chron. 36:15-16; Isa. 45:22; Jer. 18:11; Ezek. 33:11). Before the fall of the southern kingdom in 586 B.C., Jerusalem was peacefully inhabited. Also, the nearby cities, along with Negev (the desert area along the southern boundary of Judah) and the Shephelah (the lowlands in southwest Judah between the central plateau and the seacoast) were populated and flourishing. If the people living during the time of those earlier spokespersons had heeded God's oracles, the Captivity and subsequent need for fasting could have been avoided. Furthermore, if such disastrous consequences could come upon a previous generation for their disobedience, then it could certainly occur again to the current inhabitants of the promised land, who were experiencing far less favorable circumstances.

Zechariah proclaimed the essence of God's former message to His chosen people. What follows are four commands, two of which are positive and two of which are negative. With these declarations, the Lord's spokesperson summed up the teaching of the earlier prophets (Zech. 7:8). The supreme commander of heaven's armies directed the residents of Jerusalem and Judah to dispense equitable decisions in their courts of law. This included delivering the oppressed from their tormentors, along with showing steadfast love and kindness to one another (vs. 9). Here we see that "true judgment" included more than maintaining a minimal level of fairness in society. It also meant protecting all individuals from inequities and partiality. That is why Zechariah told the returnees to show tender love and loyalty in their relationships with each other.

As previous lessons this quarter have emphasized, the Lord's prophets denounced oppression (see Isa. 1:17; Jer. 5:28; 7:6; Ezek. 22:7; Amos 4:1). The Hebrew verb rendered "oppress" (Zech. 7:10) denotes abuses of power and authority, resulting in the maltreatment of the defenseless. Zechariah selected some of the common victims of persecution to illustrate his point: widows, orphans, foreigners, and the destitute. All of them could easily be exploited and abused by the wicked rich. However, God made it clear that any infringement upon the rights of the socially marginalized would bring His wrath. Not only did God's spokespersons prohibit the returnees from tyrannizing each other, but also the prophets warned against even contemplating the idea of harming someone else. True fasting could not even take place if the inhabitants of Jerusalem and Judah were treating the innocent unjustly. This included failing to show love to each other, taking advantage of the weak, or even just considering an action that would hurt someone else.

Even though God repeatedly commanded through His prophets the importance of showing justice, mercy, and compassion, the preexilic Israelites spurned the divine oracles. Rather than take God seriously, the people obstinately turned away (Zech. 7:11; see Deut. 9:6, 13, 27). It's as if they placed their fingers in their ears to prevent them from hearing what the divine spokespersons preached (see Ps. 58:4; Isa. 6:10; 33:15). Zechariah's message to the people of his generation was clear. They were not to imitate the behavior of their headstrong and disobedient ancestors, or the returnees might suffer a similar fate.

In keeping with what was said in lesson 11, the Hebrew term rendered "hearts" (Zech. 7:12) denotes the inner desires, attitudes, thoughts, and endeavors of people. Zechariah accused the former generations of making the center of their spiritual life as hard as diamonds. It seems as if nothing could penetrate their souls. Likewise, the preexilic Israelites grew so calloused that they refused to heed the teaching and directives found in the Mosaic law. They also became increasingly desensitized to the oracles the all-powerful Creator heralded by the Spirit through the former prophets. Understandably, this breach of the covenant infuriated the Lord and resulted in Him judging His people.

In the past, the people of Jerusalem and Judah had refused to pay attention to the Lord's summons to repentance. In turn, God refused to be attentive to them when they cried for help in the midst of their distress (vs. 13). His anger was like a typhoon that swept away the inhabitants of Judah. In turn, they were hurled to faraway locales, where they lived as strangers (vs. 14). Because of their transgressions, their once fruitful and populated land became barren. Invaders ravaged the land so extensively that virtually no one traveled through it (see Jer. 7:34; Ezek. 12:19).

The preceding dire outcome was one of the curses for breaking the Lord's covenant. For instance, Moses declared in Deuteronomy 28:64-68 that the exiled people would be forced to venerate pagan deities made out of wood and stone. The deportees would also long to return their homeland, but would have no way to do so. They would struggle with anxious hearts and be overwhelmed by the constant fear of death. Each day would feel so horrible that the refugees would wish it were night. But then, nighttime would seem so terrible that they would yearn for it to be day. Even when, out of desperation, they tried to sell themselves as male and female slaves, no would be interested in their offer.

Suggestions to Teachers

The example of the Judahites in Zechariah's day presents the real but terrifying possibility that people can be involved in religious activities and yet have no real concern for the things about which God is concerned. This happens when people become engrossed in their own interests and disregard how they are treating others.

1. A SUMMONS TO BE VIRTUOUS. Many of the conditions in postexilic Judah during Zechariah's time are also present in our world today. And this is why we need the message Zechariah preached to his generation. The words of God through this prophet call us back to moral values and ethical guidelines.

2. A SUMMONS TO BE UPRIGHT. God chose Zechariah to denounce sin, and the prophet did so with candor. He was not afraid to condemn the superficial religion and oppression of the poor prevalent in his day. God has also called us to advance the cause of truth and goodness as well as justice and righteousness in the world. Furthermore, He wants us to act compassionately to stop injustice and to help care for those in need.

3. A SUMMONS TO BE SOCIALLY CONSCIOUS. Instead of spending so much time on our wants and even our needs, we should evaluate our walk with Jesus and determine whether we are aware of God's concerns for social issues. If we do not, we may find ourselves in the same spiritual condition as Zechariah's listeners.

4. A SUMMONS TO RETURN TO GOD. The people of Zechariah's day related to God in a perfunctory manner. Our devotion to God becomes formal and lifeless when we merely go through the motions of worship. Rather than love God and the people He created, we busy ourselves in a flurry of religious activities. The solution is to unclutter our minds of everyday concerns and chores and refocus our attention on God's concerns for social issues.

FOR ADULTS

■ **TOPIC:** Making a Difference

■ **QUESTIONS:** 1. Why was it important for God's people to administer true justice? 2. In what ways had the socially marginalized in Judah been oppressed? 3. Why is it foolish for us to refuse to heed the admonitions recorded in Scripture? 4. Why did God refuse to listen to an earlier generation of His people? 5. Why did God allow the Promised Land to become desolate for an extended period of time?

■ ILLUSTRATIONS:

A Willingness to Change. Several years ago, a broadcasting company in Finland conducted a contest to find out how many synonyms people could call to mind. First place went to a contestant who came up with 747 synonyms for drunkenness. Someone in prison was awarded second place for sending in 678 words for the same thing. The inmate also won a prize for thinking of 170 synonyms for stealing. Another person knew 203 words for lying. It certainly was an interesting contest!

Now, there is nothing wrong with using synonyms. Writers have books of synonyms and refer to them all the time. But we run into a problem when we begin to call sin by other, more polite words. Believers sometimes do that by labeling it as a mistake, a blunder, a weakness, the result of conditioning or environment, or even a disease. However, transgressing God's holy Word is sin—no matter what we call it—and sin can destroy our walk with God.

This week's lesson from Zechariah 7 shows the consequences of compromising with what is contrary to God's will. As you study the Scripture passage with your class, it should renew their willingness to change those things in their lives that might be displeasing to God.

Called to Loving Commitment. On the night before Jesus was crucified, He said that everyone would know who were His true followers by the kindness and compassion they demonstrated for each other (see John 13:35). Just as in Zechariah's day, Jesus' desire was for loving commitment to characterize the community of believers.

The Calvary Chapel association has caught the essence of Jesus' call to His original disciples by training laypersons to live out their Christian commitment. Founded in 1965 by Chuck Smith, Calvary Chapel now claims over 1,500 congregations throughout the world.

Chuck Smith and his fellow pastors stress strong lay leadership, and they plant new churches by sending these lay people as a small core from parent churches. The leadership often quote the following slogan: *God does not call the qualified. He qualifies the called.* Are those in your class aware of the truth of this saying?

What Kind of Commitment? The Roper Center for Public Opinion Research at the University of Connecticut publishes a journal entitled *Public Perspective*. In it, the Center shows the results of careful polls carried out by George Gallup. A couple of years ago, one survey indicated what Gallup called "gaps" in the religious affairs of Americans. For instance, "the ethics gap" showed the disturbing difference between what people said and what they did.

Gallup also identified what he labeled "the knowledge gap." He pointed out the huge difference between what persons in the United States claim to believe and their appalling lack of the most basic knowledge about their faith.

The third was "the church gap." Gallup found that Americans tended to view their faith as a matter between themselves and the Lord, and not tied to or affected by any congregation or religious institution. Neither the church nor any form of organized religion influenced them, and they saw no need to be committed to any faith community.

Gallup summed up his report by suggesting that Americans want the fruits of faith but few of its obligations. Of the list of 19 social values tested in the polls, "following God's will" ranked low on the list, coming after "happiness, satisfaction, and a sense of accomplishment."

Zechariah 7 reveals that religious devotion can be devoid of meaning if we lose the proper purpose and motivation for it. Even Scripture reading and prayer can become outward rituals, rather than opportunities for genuinely desiring to know and commune with the Lord. Any time our worship loses its focus on the "grace" (2 Pet. 3:18) and "knowledge" of the Son, it ceases to please our heavenly Father.

For Youth

■ **Topic:** Becoming Responsible Persons

■ **Questions:** 1. Why did God want His people to demonstrate kindness and compassion to each other? 2. Why did God condemn those who secretly plotted evil against their fellow human beings? 3. Why did God sweep away His people into exile? 4. How are we spiritually benefited from paying attention to the teachings of God's Word? 5. Why is it important for believers to recognize that God sovereignly rules over all creation?

■ **Illustrations:**

Rules to Live By. We had lots of rules in college, but I didn't mind. The rules had drawn me to this small Christian school in the first place. I appreciated knowing that a stereo wouldn't be blasting next door while I was writing a term paper or trying to sleep.

A few students, however, had little respect for the restrictions. They stayed out well past curfew, neglected to clean their room before the weekly inspection, and routinely skipped chapel services. In time they became frustrated with the school and their classmates, and resented any school authorities.

The acerbic attitude of those students mirrors the rebellious spirit of the people of Judah living during the time of Zechariah. God had given them rules to live by, but they rejected these. Instead, they wallowed in sin and scorned His attempts to get them to repent. In this week's lesson, we learn about the personal anguish and loss they would experience for their disobedience.

Assured of God's Presence. In Zechariah 7, the Lord noted that His people had sinned in the same way their ancestors had done, by turning from Him to worship other gods.

Both the northern kingdom of Israel and the southern kingdom of Judah were guilty of breaking the covenant. Even today, when God saves us, He wants us to reject the ways of the world and live for Him. We are living in harmony with this noble calling by saying *no* to sin and *yes* to virtue and righteousness.

The movie *The Hiding Place* shows how Corrie ten Boom and her sister, Betsie, were sent by the Nazis to a women's work camp for their part in helping to hide Jews in their father's home. In one scene, after Corrie's sister had died, the women of the camp were all standing at roll call on a bitter cold December day. This particular morning, Corrie's name was called, and she was told to step forward, presumably to be taken away and put to death.

But before leaving her place in the lineup, Corrie handed her tiny New Testament to the woman next to her, encouraging her in her newfound faith. Then, as Corrie made her way forward, she turned to the rest of the women, and in a voice husky with emotion, declared, "God is with you!"

God, not the Nazis, would prevail in the prisoners' hearts and lives. God, not the Nazis, held their days, hours, and months in His hand. And God, not the Nazis, could give them eternal salvation.

Godly Leadership. There is an Aesop's fable about a pond full of frogs that badly wanted a leader. First, they turned to an immense log that was floating in the pond. They were happy for a while until they realized that even though it was an imposing log, they could jump on it and run all over it, and it offered no resistance. In fact, it offered no direction, either. It just floated around the pond without any purpose.

Soon the frogs were tired of the listless log. They wanted stronger oversight and direction. So, they turned to a stork that had come to the pond. The stork was tall and imposing. It looked like a leader. It stalked about the pond making loud noises and attracting attention. However, it was not long before the joy in the pond turned to sorrow, for the stork began to eat its subordinates!

One key principle from this fable is that God does not want leaders of His people who will do almost nothing. Neither does He want leaders who will lord it over others and take advantage of them (see Luke 22:25). Somewhere in between these two extremes are godly leaders who honor the Lord, humanely serve His people, and make justice the foundation of their government (see Zech. 7:9-10).

Perhaps in the not too distant future, God will bless you with the opportunity to serve as a leader in the church. This is a noble responsibility, one that should not be taken lightly. In the meantime, allow the Lord to shape and mold your character into the image of His Son, Jesus Christ. We can be of good character if we choose. And if we truly love the Lord, we will certainly seek to be like Him, whether as leaders or followers in the church.

LESSON 13 — AUGUST 30

FIDELITY TO THE LORD

BACKGROUND SCRIPTURE: Malachi 3:1-12; Matthew 7:12
DEVOTIONAL READING: Psalm 25:4-11

Key Verse: Therefore all things whatsoever ye would that men should do to you, do ye even so to them: for this is the law and the prophets. Matthew 7:12.

KING JAMES VERSION

MALACHI 3:1 Behold, I will send my messenger, and he shall prepare the way before me: and the Lord, whom ye seek, shall suddenly come to his temple, even the messenger of the covenant, whom ye delight in: behold, he shall come, saith the LORD of hosts. 2 But who may abide the day of his coming? and who shall stand when he appeareth? for he is like a refiner's fire, and like fullers' soap: 3 And he shall sit as a refiner and purifier of silver: and he shall purify the sons of Levi, and purge them as gold and silver, that they may offer unto the LORD an offering in righteousness. 4 Then shall the offering of Judah and Jerusalem be pleasant unto the LORD, as in the days of old, and as in former years. 5 And I will come near to you to judgment; and I will be a swift witness against the sorcerers, and against the adulterers, and against false swearers, and against those that oppress the hireling in his wages, the widow, and the fatherless, and that turn aside the stranger from his right, and fear not me, saith the LORD of hosts. 6 For I am the LORD, I change not; therefore ye sons of Jacob are not consumed.

7 Even from the days of your fathers ye are gone away from mine ordinances, and have not kept them. Return unto me, and I will return unto you, saith the LORD of hosts. But ye said, Wherein shall we return? 8 Will a man rob God? Yet ye have robbed me. But ye say, Wherein have we robbed thee? In tithes and offerings. 9 Ye are cursed with a curse: for ye have robbed me, even this whole nation. 10 Bring ye all the tithes into the storehouse, that there may be meat in mine house, and prove me now herewith, saith the LORD of hosts, if I will not open you the windows of heaven, and pour you out a blessing, that there shall not be room enough to receive it.

NEW REVISED STANDARD VERSION

MALACHI 3:1 See, I am sending my messenger to prepare the way before me, and the Lord whom you seek will suddenly come to his temple. The messenger of the covenant in whom you delight—indeed, he is coming, says the LORD of hosts. 2 But who can endure the day of his coming, and who can stand when he appears?

For he is like a refiner's fire and like fullers' soap; 3 he will sit as a refiner and purifier of silver, and he will purify the descendants of Levi and refine them like gold and silver, until they present offerings to the LORD in righteousness. 4 Then the offering of Judah and Jerusalem will be pleasing to the LORD as in the days of old and as in former years.

5 Then I will draw near to you for judgment; I will be swift to bear witness against the sorcerers, against the adulterers, against those who swear falsely, against those who oppress the hired workers in their wages, the widow and the orphan, against those who thrust aside the alien, and do not fear me, says the LORD of hosts.

6 For I the LORD do not change; therefore you, O children of Jacob, have not perished. 7 Ever since the days of your ancestors you have turned aside from my statutes and have not kept them. Return to me, and I will return to you, says the LORD of hosts. But you say, "How shall we return?"

8 Will anyone rob God? Yet you are robbing me! But you say, "How are we robbing you?" In your tithes and offerings! 9 You are cursed with a curse, for you are robbing me—the whole nation of you! 10 Bring the full tithe into the storehouse, so that there may be food in my house, and thus put me to the test, says the LORD of hosts; see if I will not open the windows of heaven for you and pour down for you an overflowing blessing.

Home Bible Readings

Monday, August 24	Psalm 25	Teach Me Your Paths, O Lord
Tuesday, August 25	Matthew 7:7-14	How Shall We Treat Others?
Wednesday, August 26	Malachi 3:11-18	How Have We Spoken Against You?
Thursday, August 27	Joel 3:9-16	How Shall We Be Judged?
Friday, August 28	Jeremiah 6:26-30	How Shall We Repent?
Saturday, August 29	Isaiah 57:10-21	The Contrite and Humble in Spirit
Sunday, August 30	Malachi 3:1-10	How Shall We Return?

Background

Malachi (whose name means "my messenger") arranged his book to reflect arguments between God and His people. Much of it has to do with temple personnel, priests, and Levites. Malachi's message was directed toward the second generation of those who returned from captivity. The message Malachi proclaimed was one of condemnation and judgment. God brought a number of charges against the priests and people of the restored community. Each time they questioned the veracity of an accusation He made, God responded by validating His point.

For instance, the Lord accused the Israelites of wearing Him out with their words (see Isa. 1:14; 43:24). The cynical had asserted that God was pleased with evil and did not care about justice (Mal. 2:17). Their suffering in the Exile caused them to think that God favored the cause of the wicked, who seemed to enjoy prosperity while breaking God's moral law. The despondent in postexilic Judah also reasoned that if God was holy, He would certainly have judged the unrighteous by now.

Notes on the Printed Text

In response to the questioning of God's justice, He promised to send His "messenger" (Mal. 3:1), who would prepare the way before Him. In Hebrew, the phrase rendered "my messenger" is *mal'aki*, which is the same form as the prophet's name. However, in this verse, the herald is an end-time figure who is about to come. According to 4:5, "Elijah the prophet" is the messenger. The New Testament identified this person as John the Baptizer (see Matt. 11:10; Mark 1:2), for he came in the power and authority of Elijah (see Matt. 11:14; 17:11-12; Luke 1:17). So, John could be a separate personality from Elijah and yet fulfill the Old Testament promise. John's work is described as clearing the way before the Lord (Mal. 3:1). In ancient times, Eastern kings sent emissaries before them in their travels to remove barriers from their path. John's purpose was to remove opposition to the Lord by proclaiming a message of repentance to sinners (see also the Bible commentary in lesson 1 of the March quarter).

A second view states that John did not completely fulfill the prophecy. For instance, when a delegation of priests and Levites from Jerusalem questioned the Baptizer, he denied that he was Elijah (see John 1:19-21). The mention of the day of the Lord in connection with Elijah in Malachi 4:5 also shows that an aspect of this prophecy remains to be fulfilled in the future, since that day has not yet come. Accordingly, some have identified the two witnesses in Revelation 11:1-14 as Moses and Elijah. A third view equates the "messenger of the covenant" (Mal. 3:1) with the Lord Himself. Along with the other cases, the heavenly agent enforces God's covenant with His people, who were guilty of violating that solemn agreement. Concerning the Messiah, He came to the Jerusalem temple as a baby and then most notably during the week before His crucifixion. Even in their sin, the people of the postexilic community desired deliverance through the Messiah. Yet, as Malachi proceeded to point out, the people were not ready for the Redeemer's coming.

Along with vindication for the righteous, the coming of the Lord ultimately meant judgment for the wicked. The covenant-breaking Judahites, as well as the wicked of all other nations, would find the day of the Lord to be a terrible time of punishment. Although the people of the postexilic community expressed a desire for it, none of them would be able to endure it in their present moral state. The Lord's judgment at His coming is compared with two purifying agents: fire for metals and soap for clothing (vs. 2). With respect to the "refiner's fire," people in ancient times used intense heat to melt metal. This allowed the dross, which floated to the top, to be scooped off. Concerning the strong "soap," a launderer would rub cloth with lye and trample the material to remove the loosened dirt. Both metaphors indicated that God's intention was not to destroy the nation, but to purify it spiritually. His purpose was to purge out the wickedness in Judah.

In verse 3, the Lord is represented as a smelter who watches both the intensity of the fire and the metal being purified of its dross. The Messiah would cleanse the entire nation, beginning with the Levites, due to their violation of God's covenant (see 2:7-9). Above all else, the Lord was concerned about the holiness of His people. Once the refining process was complete, God would have an acceptable priesthood to carry out the sacred temple ministry. Because the offerings and gifts would be given from hearts right in the sight of God, they would be acceptable before Him. As in the past (probably the days of Moses and Phinehas), the sacrificial worship of the priests would be pleasing to the Lord (3:4). For us, Jesus' future return would also result in purification and a time of examination before Him (see 1 John 3:3).

Besides purifying the Levites, God would judge sinful people when He came (Mal. 3:5). Sorcerers—namely, those practicing divination and witchcraft—are the first addressed in the list of wicked behavior. Magical arts prevailed in Judah in postcaptivity days, perhaps due to the influence of the foreign wives. Adulterers included those who divorced their Jewish wives so they could marry idolatrous women. Those who swore falsely were perjurers. For instance, while under oath in a court of law, they gave fraudulent testimony. They also broke vows. Malachi's concern for social justice comes out clearly in the last half of his list. Those who treated their servants unfairly in regard to wages are included along with the adulterers, those who oppressed the weak in society (such as widows and orphans), and those who deprived immigrants and resident foreigners of justice. All these examples of evil behavior are traced to one source: a lack of reverence and respect for the Lord.

Even though God must judge sinners, His unchanging nature kept the nation of Judah from perishing (see Num. 23:19; Deut. 4:31; Ps. 102:27; Jas. 1:17). Put differently, despite the Judahites' violation of the Mosaic covenant, the Lord remained faithful to it, including His preservation of His people. Malachi 3:6 specifically focuses on God's unfailing commitment to the "descendants of Jacob." The latter name was understood to mean "he takes by the heel," "he supplants," or "he deceives" (see Gen. 27:35-36). In a play on words, Malachi 3:6 indicates that the Judahites were even more deceitful and unfaithful than their ancestor, Jacob, had been in his youth. Yet, because God would keep the promises He made to His chosen people, the passing away of the current evil generation would not preclude another generation from fearing God and inheriting what He pledged to do long ago. In short, the refining fires would not completely consume the nation (see Exod. 34:6-7; Jer. 30:11).

The Creator called His chosen people to return to Him. One way to do so was in the area of giving, which was an indicator of the covenant community's spiritual condition. Indeed, this issue required immediate attention, for the Judahites were guilty of robbing God (vs. 8). According to the Mosaic law, the people were required to give a tenth of their accumulated wealth to the Lord (in which the word "tithe" means "tenth"; see Num. 18:21, 24). Without these tithes and additional offerings, the priests and Levites would have been required to turn to secular work to support themselves. The failure of the Judahites to give God what was His due amounted to defrauding Him. Otherwise stated, He equated the faulty stewardship of His people with theft.

The giving of a set portion to the Lord from one's herds, flocks, fruit, and grain was an ancient biblical custom. For instance, Abraham offered a tenth of the spoils to Melchizedek (see Gen. 14:20), and at Bethel, Jacob promised God a tenth (see Gen. 28:22). Moreover, the Old Testament describes several different tithes God required His people to give. One tithe went to the Levites for their inheritance (see Lev. 27:30-33; Deut. 14:22-27). From this tithe, the Levites gave a tenth (that is, a tithe of a tithe) to the priests for their livelihood (see Num. 18:21-32). A third special tithe was given every third year to destitute widows, orphans, and foreigners (see Deut. 14:28-29).

Nehemiah 13:10 confirms that the tithes were not properly given during the time in which Malachi ministered. It is possible that adverse economic conditions caused the Judahites to decrease their giving. But if that was the case, they only ended up hurting themselves, for their lack of giving led to widespread crop failures and famine. Because of their carelessness in giving, the Lord declared that the entire covenant community was "cursed with a curse" (Mal. 3:9). The combination of a verb and a noun in the Hebrew text intensified God's censure that the nation in its entirety was guilty of wrongdoing. Furthermore, they were enduring God's displeasure, as evidenced by their inability to flourish and experience wellness in their daily activities.

The solution to the preceding problem was for all the inhabitants of Judah and Jerusalem once again to give "all the tithes" (vs. 10). The reference to the "storehouse" was a treasury room in the temple that served as a depository for the produce brought by the people. The priests and Levites lived all year from the offerings and tithes that the covenant community brought to the sanctuary. The mention of "all the tithes" suggests that the people made a pretense of giving a tenth, but were actually giving far less than the minimum amount required of them.

The Lord gave His chosen people a challenge. He invited them to "prove" (vs. 10) His faithfulness, which means He wanted them to confirm what He pledged to do. If they began faithfully tithing again, He would open wide His heavenly storehouse of "blessing" (vs. 10). The wording of this verse brings to mind the description of the cataclysmic flood that occurred in the days of Noah (see Gen. 7:11; 8:2). The all-powerful Creator declared that as a result of the covenant community's action, they would run out of room to stockpile the overflow of His provision. God's amazing proposal ensured a positive outcome to the people's giving. The implication is that their situation was far from hopeless, assuming they accepted the Lord's offer. In turn, His blessing would enable them to continue being generous.

SUGGESTIONS TO TEACHERS

God knows everything. But have you ever argued with Him? Malachi 3 contains God's reply to complaints from the people of Judah that He was unjust. They thought He wasn't blessing them. In response, God declared the certainty of His judgment and the offer of His blessing.

1. SOME DON'T KNOW HOW MUCH DANGER THEY ARE IN. Many in Malachi's day looked forward to the Messiah's coming, little suspecting that His advent might mean judgment for them. Likewise, many of our peers take the possibility of judgment too lightly.

2. GOD WANTS TRUE WORSHIP. Some are "high church"; some are "low church." Some are "charismatic"; some are not. What matters more than these kinds of distinctions is that we worship God honestly and openly, with contrite hearts, purified through faith in the Messiah.

3. GOD IS AWARE OF EACH BELIEVER. None of us need ever think that God is so busy with great world events that He overlooks a single believing heart. Do we really trust in Jesus, God's Son? Are we trying to live a holy life? We can take comfort, for God knows everything.

4. THE DESTINIES OF THE WICKED AND OF THE RIGHTEOUS DRASTICALLY DIVERGE. Though many in our day refuse to accept it, there is a time of reckoning coming. Destruction awaits those who live for themselves instead of for God, while joy awaits the forgiven.

5. JESUS CHRIST IS AT THE CENTER OF JUDGMENT. For each person, Jesus is either their Savior or Judge. His coming forces each one to choose, and what we decide to do with Him determines what will occur when we stand before His throne.

FOR ADULTS

■ **TOPIC:** The Change Agent
■ **QUESTIONS:** 1. Why were God's people so eager for the "messenger of the covenant" (Mal. 3:1) to come? 2. What would happen to those who persisted in wickedness? 3. In what way is God merciful to us, even when we sin against Him? 4. How had the Judahites robbed God? 5. What are some ways God has recently proved His faithfulness to you?

■ **ILLUSTRATIONS:**

Fear the Lord? Along with Malachi 3:5, the rest of the Bible calls on us to fear God and love Him. Israel feared what they saw and heard at Mount Sinai. And they asked Moses to be their mediator. He agreed, but told them not to cringe in terror. God had come to test them so that their fear of Him would keep them from sin (see Exod. 20:18-20). They were to have confidence in God's goodness (do not be afraid) and to recognize His awesome holiness so they would not consider sin a minor matter.

So, in the Old Testament, to fear God could refer to having a right relationship with Him, one that seeks to honor and obey Him. This was the sort of relationship that led to wisdom (see Ps. 111:10). Malachi's hearers who feared the Lord, trusted in His character and made decisions in their lives on the basis of His revealed will. Even today, when we seek to revere and honor God in our thoughts, feelings, and actions, He spiritually blesses us in ways we cannot even begin to imagine.

The Road We Take. In Robert Frost's poem, "The Road Not Taken," a traveler coming to an intersection must choose between two roads. He selects the route that fewer people have traveled. As he reflects on the journey "somewhere ages and ages hence," the speaker says that this choice "has made all the difference."

We learn from Malachi 3 that walking with the Lord involves two types of decisions for us. First, we acknowledge our sins and trust in Jesus as our Savior. Our second kind of choice is made repeatedly as we learn to walk with our Redeemer. By studying the Scriptures, under the guidance of the Holy Spirit, we discern the Lord's will and receive wisdom from Him (see Jas. 1:5-6).

By rejecting Jesus, unbelievers have chosen the world's reward. In eternity, they will experience unending separation from the Savior. In contrast, those making godly choices should gradually mature from toddler steps to the mature stride of spiritual adulthood. As the Spirit guides believers, they take one step at a time.

From these truths we see that we need daily forgiveness and strength. We must practice the disciplines of prayer, Bible study, and godly living as if we are in a competition. Like Frost's traveler, our choices will "make all the difference" in eternity. Scripture reveals that the Lord treasures us and shows us compassion like a parent. So we know that one day He will bring us into intimate fellowship with Him forever.

Choosing to Live Responsibly. Tom lay seriously ill in the intensive care unit of the hospital after having major surgery. Although a good family man, he had not been a faithful, practicing Christian. Did he understand the different destinies that confronted him? He heard the pastor's words about the Father's love and forgiveness in the Son. How hard it was to be sure whether Tom understood his need to admit his sins and trust in Jesus.

Sadly, many people are like Tom. They do not reach out to God early in life, even though they have a religious upbringing. God is not a major factor in their lives. They do not realize that the choice they make in this life will determine their future in the next.

Malachi made different destinies clear in his powerful images of judgment and blessing. How much better it is to turn to God as our loving Father than to receive His just condemnation in the end. Our lives will be filled with His eternal blessings when we choose to live responsibly in the community of faith.

For Youth

■ **Topic:** Justice Is Coming

■ **Questions:** 1. What harsh things had some of God's people said about Him? 2. What would God's "messenger" (Mal. 3:1) do when he came? 3. What was the destiny of those who revered the Lord? 4. How can the truth that God does not "change" (vs. 6) encourage believers? 5. Why does God want us to be sacrificial in our giving?

■ **Illustrations:**

Eternity Begins Today—For Everyone. Malachi reminded the people of Judah that no one was exempt from God's objective evaluation. Those who rejected His Word and lived for themselves faced a bleak eternal future. In contrast, those who trusted in Him, obeyed His Word, and treated others humanely would experience God's abundant favor.

The story is told of a person who died and went to heaven. There Peter showed this individual the mansions of believers. Then the two came to a small shack that Peter said belonged to this person. The shocked individual asked why his reward was so small. In turn, Peter replied, "We did the best we could with what you sent us."

From the preceding observations, we learn that the decisions we make now have eternal consequences. For instance, even after we choose to trust in Jesus for our salvation, we continue to make decisions that either help or hinder our spiritual growth. And more than that, we make choices that can have unending ramifications for others, such as whether we invite our non-Christian classmate to church with us next week.

Decisions That Make a Difference. Once again, a legal technicality had rescued Cheryl—she was free to go. The prosecutor threw down his notepad in disgust as Cheryl smirked at him on her way out of the courtroom. It was another loss for justice and another step toward darkness for Cheryl.

The young woman had been in courtrooms since childhood, first for custody hearings, but soon for a variety of crimes. Cheryl was a "habitual offender" who knew how to play the system, and she was rarely convicted. Among the crowd of unsavory characters she ran with, she was affectionately known as "Cheryl: Princess of Thieves."

Three years later, the same prosecutor again had his grip on Cheryl. She was sentenced to two years in jail. While serving her time, Cheryl was gloriously saved. She said it was the persistent witness of a volunteer chaplain who had made the difference.

When Cheryl got out of jail, she went right back to her old crowd, but with a calling from God to win them for Jesus. Cheryl shared the Good News with them, and the results were extraordinary. Her unconditional love was her pulpit, and her changed life was her message.

Malachi 3 concerns the differences between believers and unbelievers. This includes what each group does in this life and where they will spend eternity. To blur those distinctions is to slash the heart of the gospel. All is not well with a person's soul until it is united with the Savior through faith.

The Difference Our Decisions Make. Mason's best friend and fellow athlete went for a drive one night. Logan seemed like a good guy who went to church. Despite the fact that they were both under the legal drinking age, Logan took a six-pack of beer in his car and urged Mason to drink a can with him. Mason refused. From then on they drifted apart, Logan into a rather typical pattern of short-term jobs and drinking, and Mason into the Christian service.

Of course, that one decision did not determine how Mason and Logan would live their lives. But it does illustrate the different choices young people have to make, not just about drinking but also about sexual practices, using drugs, cheating in class, and so on. That's why we should teach and demonstrate that Christian values differ sharply from the world's.

In Malachi's day, God's people thought the unbelievers were enjoying the good life while they suffered. Many of them decided to join the evildoers. Malachi told God's people to repent, especially if they wished to be spared divine judgment and receive the Lord's blessings when the Savior appeared.